PRAISE FOR

The Apache Wars

"Where *The Apache Wars* really shines is in the richness of its details, well researched and deeply understood. . . . In terms of colorful characters, there is an embarrassment of riches."

—*Wall Street Journal*

"[A] major work of history on a much-neglected subject . . . *The Apache Wars* is an epic tale filled with Homeric scenes and unforgettable characters. It's a quintessential American story that too few Americans know."

—*Chicago Tribune*

"Sharply and unflinchingly explores the many years of bloody, thunderous conflicts between soldiers based in camps and forts and elusive Apaches in New Mexico and Arizona."

—*Albuquerque Journal*

"Well researched . . . Engrossing . . . [H]utton's excellent book can help many readers get a much better understanding of a long, complicated, and still-disturbing chapter in American history."

—*Dallas Morning News*

"A comprehensive narrative, as encompassing as the American West itself."

—*Denver Post*

"An important contribution to boosting everyone's understanding about the consequences of the longest war in the nation's history . . . Hutton has written what will certainly be long regarded as a definitive history of the almost three-decades-long war between Apaches and white Americans."

—*New Mexico Magazine*

"Hutton . . . is an engaging storyteller who . . . puts a nice finishing touch on the fascinating saga."

—*Wild West*

"The long, often harsh story of the Apache wars in the hands of solid researcher and masterful storyteller Paul Andrew Hutton becomes fast-paced and more gripping than a Cochise and General O. O. Howard handshake."

—*Roundup*

"Vivid and dramatic prose . . . Hutton's masterful chronicle of *The Apache Wars* is both a homily and a eulogy: a homily about the scourge of Conquest, War, Famine, and Death, and a long-overdue eulogy for windswept spirits of the dead long forgotten in the dark, blood-stained canyons of Apacheria."

—*True West*

"[A] sprawling, fascinating tale of conflict in the late nineteenth-century American southwest . . . Hutton moves beyond standard descriptions of battles between Apache warriors and American troops (though there are plenty of those) to paint a larger, more detailed picture of Southwestern life: slavery, gold mining, territorial politics, and the creation of reservations. Fascinating people flit in and out of the story, including the Apache warriors Mangas Coloradas, Cochise, Lozen, Victorio, and Geronimo; and American scouts Kit Carson and Al Sieber. . . . Hutton provides an unexpected twist that keeps the story fresh until the end."

—*Publishers Weekly*

"The accounts of armed conflict are stirringly told and often read like a Western thriller. . . . [T]horoughly researched."

—*Kirkus Reviews*

"An outstanding, comprehensive overview of the Apache Wars of Arizona and New Mexico . . . This recounting of the Southwestern battles for Apacheria will be valued by general readers and researchers alike for its colorful personalities and strong representation of the cultural context of historical events."

—*Library Journal*

"Paul Hutton is one the great scholars of Western Americana, but he's also a natural-born storyteller, with a rare gift for locating the deep ironies that suffuse history. Hutton has brought this sere landscape—and this classic clash of the borderlands—to pungent life on the page."

—Hampton Sides, author of *Blood and Thunder* and *In the Kingdom of Ice*

"Humane, insightful, and vivid, *The Apache Wars* immerses readers in the rugged landscape of Apacheria, the meeting ground and battlefield of nations. In telling the gripping story of the Apaches' long fight against Mexico and the United States, Hutton proves once again why he is a great writer as well as a great historian."

—T. J. Stiles, Pulitzer Prize–winning author of *Custer's Trials: A Life on the Frontier of a New America*

"Hutton captures the intensity and drama of the history of both sides in this vibrant segment of Western history."

—Robert M. Utley, author of *Geronimo* and *The Lance and the Shield*

"A fast-paced, well-written page-turner. Hutton gives an excellent account of individuals, both Native American and white, who contested for control of the Southwest in the nineteenth century."

—R. David Edmunds, Watson Professor of American History, University of Texas at Dallas

"After reading this masterfully researched and written book, I thanked my lucky stars for Paul Hutton. It took an author and historian of his caliber to at long last deliver the definitive explanation of the longest war in the nation's history. The wait was worth it. By using the legendary Apache scout and manhunter Mickey Free as a vehicle to tell the story, Hutton cuts through layers of myth exposing one of the most exciting and pivotal episodes in the annals of the American West."

—Michael Wallis, author of *The Wild West: 365 Days*

THE

APACHE
WARS

The Hunt for GERONIMO,
the APACHE KID,
and the CAPTIVE BOY
Who Started the Longest
War in American History

PAUL ANDREW
HUTTON

B\D\W\Y
BROADWAY BOOKS
NEW YORK

Library of Congress Cataloging-in-Publication data is available upon request.

ISBN 978-0-7704-3583-7
Ebook ISBN 978-0-7704-3582-0

Printed in the United States of America

Book design by Lauren Dong
Maps by Jeffrey L. Ward
Title page art courtesy of the author
Cover design by Oliver Munday
Cover photograph: C. S. Fly/Corbis

10 9 8 7 6 5 4 3 2 1

First Paperback Edition

TO TRACY LEE

Let me not to the marriage of true minds
Admit impediments. Love is not love
Which alters when it alteration finds,
Or bends with the remover to remove:
O, no! it is an ever fixed mark
That looks on tempests and is never shaken;
It is the star to every wandering bark,
Whose worth's unknown, although his height be taken.
Love's not Time's fool, though rosy lips and cheeks
Within his bending sickle's compass come;
Love alters not with his brief hours and weeks,
But bears it out even to the edge of doom.
   If this be error and upon me proved,
   I never writ, nor no man ever loved.

—W.S., Sonnet CXVI

Contents

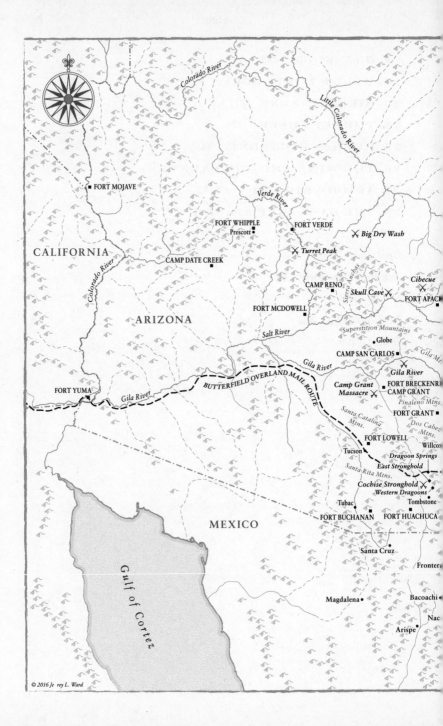

© 2016 Jeffrey L. Ward

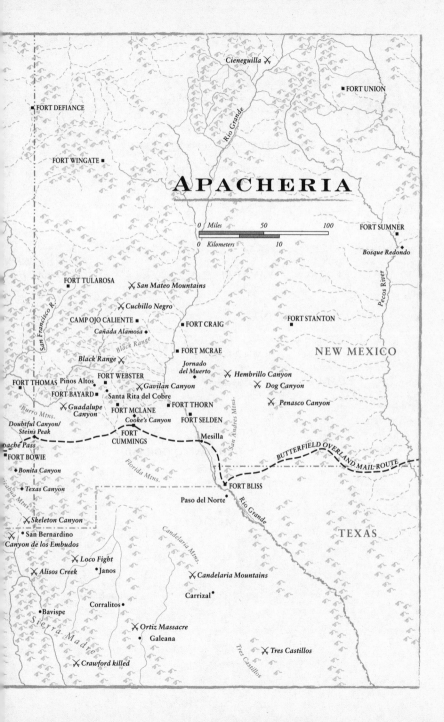

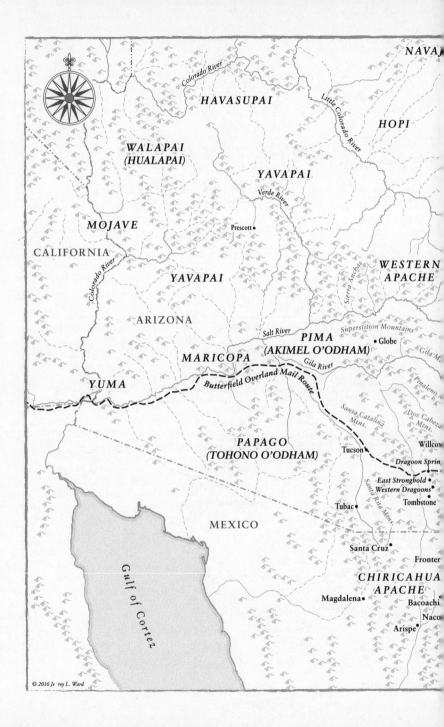

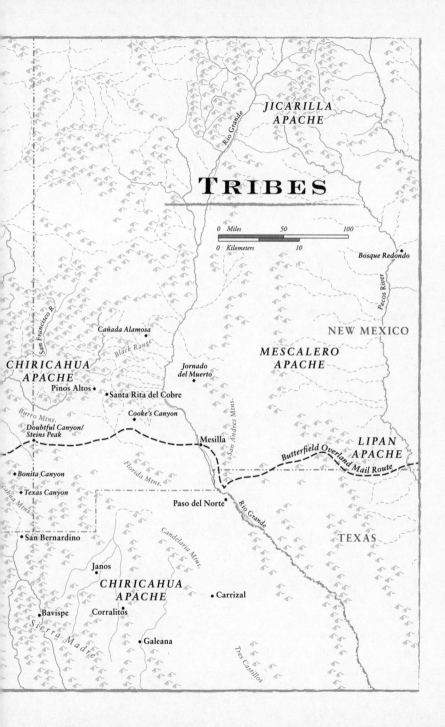

PROLOGUE

ON A CRISP MORNING IN LATE JANUARY, THE BOY tended his stock as he watched the dust cloud rising to the south, at the far end of the narrow timbered valley. Felix was almost twelve, but short and scrawny for his age, with a mop of red hair and fair skin. When the boy saw riders emerging one by one from the cloud of dust, their ponies splashing across the shallow creek, he ran to the little grove of peach trees some three hundred yards from the ranch buildings where his mother and sister were. He knew this area was contested ground, in the heart of what the Mexicans, and the Spanish before them, had named Apacheria. The Mexicans had failed to settle the valley, driven out by the fearsome Apaches who lived in the mountains to the east and north.

A dozen Apaches, wildly painted and heavily armed, galloped onto the ranch. They swept past the buildings to gather up all the horses and cattle. His heart pounding, Felix climbed a peach tree and hid himself as best he could. The Apache leader rode up to the tree as his men began herding the horses and cattle back down the valley and looked up at the terrified boy. Felix expected to be killed instantly, but instead the Apache laughed and motioned for him to climb down. Felix obliged. The Apache, who was called Beto, had a heavily scarred face that bore the imprint of some terrible battle in which he had lost an eye. Felix also had but one eye. The Apache pulled him onto the back of his pony, and off they galloped after the warriors.

These Apaches were of the Aravaipa band, who lived to the northeast of the Sonoita Valley. The Aravaipa would come to call the kidnapped boy Coyote, after their trickster god, because they could never decide if he was friend or foe. Years later, white men would name him Mickey Free. The boy's kidnapping started the final struggle for Apacheria—the longest war in the history of the United States. This conflict would leave a trail of blood from the Pecos River in Texas through New Mexico and Arizona and deep into Mexico from 1861 to 1886. All sides in that conflict blamed Mickey Free for starting it. In time, the boy would come to play a pivotal role in the war, moving back and forth between the harshly conflicted worlds of the Apache and the white invader, never really accepted by either but invaluable to both.

This is Mickey Free's story, but it is also the story of his contemporaries—both friend and foe, red and white—whose lives were shaped by the violent history of the deserts and mountains of the American Southwest and northern Mexico. It was a land where every plant bore a barb, every insect a stinger, every bird a talon, every reptile a fang—an inhospitable, deadly environment known to the outside world as Apacheria. In this bleak and unforgiving world, the one-eyed, deeply scarred Mickey Free was at home.

1

APACHERIA

JOHNNY WARD WAS NOT AFRAID OF HARD WORK. Born in Ireland in 1806, he had followed thousands of his brethren to America sometime in the 1840s. While many Irishmen took day labor jobs in the eastern cities, Ward pressed on to the far West in search of his fortune. The California gold fields proved barren of opportunity to him, so he drifted south to the Yuma Crossing and in 1857 appeared in Arizona's Santa Cruz Valley.

"He went on to the Sonoita and took up a ranch," Charles Poston, the self-styled father of Arizona, remembered, "forming a temporary partnership with a Mexican woman, according to the customs of the country at that time." Poston also noted that "she had a little boy who also appeared to be partly of Celtic descent, as he had a red head."

The 1848 discovery of gold in California, the subsequent population explosion, and the admission of California to statehood in 1850 had made it increasingly urgent to establish overland mail and protected transportation routes to the West Coast. Sectional rivalry over which route a future transcontinental railroad might take flared hot in Washington. Secretary of War Jefferson Davis was determined that the railroad route was to be a southern one, and he indeed had logic, climate, and geography on his side.

The problem for Davis and his political allies was that the controversial boundary established by the 1848 Treaty of Guadalupe Hidalgo, the agreement that ended the Mexican War, had failed to secure the land south of Arizona's Gila River—land that army explorers had reported as the most suitable route for a wagon road or a future railroad.

James Gadsden, the American minister to Mexico, solved the problem when he secured this new territory from the shaky and corrupt regime of President Antonio López de Santa Anna. The infamous Mexican general faced a soaring national debt and a weak army, which frustrated efforts to defend the northern states of Sonora and Chihuahua. At the time Tucson contained fewer than three hundred residents, and they were essentially besieged by the Apaches, while the natives also made exploration north of the Gila River nearly impossible. The Apache raiders had made the situation so untenable that it proved far more sensible for the Mexican president to sell the violence-racked land rather than continue to defend the indefensible.

On December 30, 1853, Gadsden signed an agreement for the $15 million purchase of New Mexico's Mesilla Valley and all of Arizona's land south of the Gila River from a point seventy miles below the Yuma Crossing of the Colorado River, then angling eastward to and then along the 31st degree of latitude. Article XI of the Treaty of Guadalupe Hidalgo, promising to halt Indian depredations originating in the United States, was also abrogated. It had proven impossible to enforce.

The United States Senate debated and tinkered with this proposed treaty, moving the new boundary line northward and ending hope for an Arizona port on the Gulf of California (a reduction of 9,000 square miles) and cutting the payment to Mexico by $5 million. The treaty was ratified by the Senate and then signed by President Franklin Pierce on June 29, 1854. The Gadsden Purchase added nearly 30,000 square miles of territory to the United States, which included the towns of Mesilla and Tucson, as well as all the mountains in between. Those mountains constituted the heart of Apacheria.

THIS NEW LAND offered the promise of grand opportunity to Charles Poston and his fellow adventurers like Johnny Ward. Poston had lobbied Secretary of War Davis to provide troops to protect any future mines and settlements. The Apaches had to be convinced to leave the Americans alone and Davis promised to station troops near Tucson as soon as possible. Poston's Sonora Exploring and Mining Company established its headquarters south of Tucson at the abandoned Spanish presidio of Tubac in 1856. Supplies and workers came north from Sonora so that by the end of the year nearly a thousand people settled around Tubac.

While Apache raiding parties continually traveled past Tubac on their way south to raid in Sonora, they did not molest the miners, ranchers, lumbermen, or farmers. Still, the land remained wild and dangerous, as American and Mexican outlaws were everywhere. Every man went about heavily armed. "Generally worthless, dissipated, dangerous low white trash" was how Poston characterized the few Americans in the area. Still, Poston felt as if he had founded a frontier Eden: "We had no law but love, and no occupation but labor. No government, no taxes, no public debt, no politics. It was a community in a perfect state of nature."

JOHNNY WARD CERTAINLY agreed with his new friend Poston. He soon found hard but profitable work cutting hay and hauling wood from the nearby Santa Rita Mountains to Fort Buchanan. This first American outpost in the Gadsden Purchase had been established by Captain Richard Ewell in 1857 on a little plateau above Sonoita Creek some twenty-five miles from Tubac. Secretary of War Davis kept his pledge to Poston and, in the fall of 1856, sent out four companies of the First Dragoons. These soldiers were followed by a great train of mule- and ox-drawn wagons and a herd of cattle, who had headed west from Fort Thorn on the Rio Grande. But the dragoons, camping just south of Tucson near the ancient (to the Americans) San Xavier del Bac Mission that November, could find no suitable site for a new post.

Captain Ewell established Camp Moore at the old Calabasas Ranch on the Santa Cruz River some sixty miles to the south. Jesuit missionaries had found a sizable Papago (Tohono O'odham) village here in 1699, and in 1732 silver was discovered on the ranch of a Basque settler to the southwest (his ranch was called Arizona, which roughly translates as "good oak tree" in Basque, and the name stuck). By 1777 the Spanish were working mines in most of the nearby foothills and mountains. It was certainly the most isolated outpost of the republic, with supply wagons taking nearly a hundred days to reach it from the Albuquerque depot. Ewell soon relocated the post to a plateau above Sonoita Creek, just to the east of Tubac. Fort Buchanan, much like Camp Moore, had no outer walls and was constructed of logs chinked together with adobe. While the soldiers offered little in the way of protection, their fort opened a new market for cattle and crops.

Ward profited from this new federal presence and quickly invested his wages in a ranch in the lush Sonoita Valley two miles south of where the little creek angled west toward the Santa Cruz River. He built a home out of stone and adobe and hastily constructed some outbuildings and corrals. The temperate climate and perennial flow of Sonoita Creek allowed Ward to put in two crops each season, one of barley and one of corn, and he even planted a little orchard of peach trees.

He often traveled south to Santa Cruz in Sonora to purchase cattle using the money he had made hauling lumber. This impoverished village had the misfortune of sitting astride a favorite Apache plunder trail into Sonora, but its grinding poverty spared it from further spoliation. The only tempting targets in Santa Cruz were the children and young women. "As soon as a town or rancho is built," noted a traveler on the Santa Cruz River, "the Apaches tear it down and kill all the males and carry off all the females."

On one of these trips Ward met Jesus Maria Martinez, a young woman of considerable beauty and passion. Although unmarried, she had borne a son, named Felix, at seventeen and a daughter, Teodora, two years later. The woman, called Modesto after her mother, somehow managed to scrape together enough to feed and clothe her babies, assisted no doubt by her extended family and the village church. In 1858, when Ward offered her and the children a new life on his 160-acre ranch thirty miles to the north on the Sonoita, she accepted. Her son, Felix, took his stepfather's name.

Ward's ranch house rested on a small bluff above the creek. The Sonoita Valley, some eleven miles in length, was narrow and heavily wooded with black walnut, velvet ash, and towering cottonwoods. Hemmed in by high bluffs on each side with the towering Santa Rita Mountains to the northwest, the valley occasionally widened out enough to allow for irrigation, and at one of these points, Ward had established his ranch.

Ward's house was impressive by frontier standards, with stone footings, a packed earth floor, and ten-foot-high, two-foot-thick adobe walls supporting its grass roof. A thick wall divided the main living area of the sixty-by-sixteen-foot adobe from a little bedroom for John and Modesto. There was no kitchen, since cooking was customarily done outdoors. With five large windows for light and three doors to the front, side, and rear, Ward's spacious home must have seemed like a mansion to Modesto and her two children.

The Sonoita settlement, as it was called, consisted of seven ranches along the dozen miles of the valley floor. The census of 1860 listed fifty-one citizens in the valley, identified as farmers, teamsters, laborers, a cook, a clerk, a shoemaker, a lawyer, a printer, and one simply as an "idiot." Fort Buchanan provided nominal protection, although the soldiers could barely guard their own horse herd, and Indians once made off with several of the officers' tents. Not far from the fort stood the local general store, and supplies could also be secured from the old presidio of Tubac or from Santa Cruz, both about thirty miles from Ward's ranch. Four miles south of the fort was James "Paddy" Graydon's United States Boundary Hotel, a rollicking establishment that everyone called the White House or Casa Blanca. The Sonoita Valley, proclaimed the *Tubac Weekly Arizonian,* was "a treasure beyond price to the farmers in the neighborhood."

THIS LAND WAS a new frontier full of promise to Ward and the other pioneers, but it was also an ancient place haunted by the ghosts of those who had vanished from here before. Primitive man had walked this ground for thousands of years before Johnny Ward built his adobe house. Ten thousand years ago, ancient hunters had felled great mammoths along the banks of the nearby San Pedro River. Two thousand years before Ward reached the Sonoita, the Hohokam (from the Pima word for "those who have gone") built extensive canals and planted maize, corn, beans, and squash along the Gila, Salt, and Verde rivers. They constructed housing projects four stories high at Casa Grande, and their irrigated fields sustained a population of perhaps fifty thousand. Then, around 1400, like the Anasazi of the Four Corners region to the north, they vanished. They left behind crumbling ruins and cliff dwellings, a mute testimony of their passing.

Captain Ewell, while exploring the Arizona mountains, mused over this mystery. "A great part of my scout has been in a country without inhabitants, but with the ruins of what must have been large towns abandoned centuries ago," he wrote home to Virginia in 1857 from his camp on the Gila River. "It would seem to be a semi-civilized people, migratory and followed by another race at war—as the schools of herring are followed by the dolphin and shark."

The "race at war" came from the northeast. These people, who shared the Athabaskan language spoken by the hunting peoples of Alaska and northern Canada, had migrated southward along the front range of the Rocky Mountains, following the great buffalo herds and battling anyone who dared dispute their passage. In time they were confronted by another tribe that was also expanding onto the western Great Plains—the Comanches, fierce fighters who forced them farther west to seek sanctuary and better hunting grounds in the mountain ranges of what would become New Mexico and Arizona.

They called themselves Dine, or Indeh, which means "the people," a name they shared with their linguistic relatives, the Navajos. It is likely that they migrated south as one people but then split apart from the Navajos as they moved to the south and west, preying on those unfortunate enough to be in their way. In time the Navajos became bitter enemies to their southern cousins. These southern people came to be known to all by the name given them by their Zuni victims—Apache, "the enemy."

They were a people of mysticism and magic. Nature dictated the rhythms of their lives, and almost everything in it held spiritual meaning. Usen, the life giver, was the God they worshipped. Ghosts and witches moved among them. Coyote, the eternal trickster, was central to their cosmology—his loyalty to the people often fluctuated in an origin myth of a great game between the animals to determine if the Apaches were to live in perpetual darkness or not. Coyote, although often evil, nevertheless secured fire for the people, giving them light.

They were all united as Apaches but divided into many tribal bands. To the east, in New Mexico's Sierra Blanca and on the buffalo grasslands of Texas, lived the Mescaleros. Their close cousins, the Chiricahuas, lived in the Gila and Dragoon mountains of western New Mexico and southeastern Arizona as well as the Sierra Madre of Sonora and Chihuahua. The Jicarilla lived far to the north, ranging from the mountains of northern New Mexico all the way eastward onto the plains. The more distant Lipans lived along the Pecos River in Texas.

The Western Apaches, divided into five bands, were scattered throughout the eastern and central mountains of Arizona. These Western Apache bands, unlike the eastern Apaches, separated into clans and, like the Navajo, practiced some agriculture. It is possible that these Apache migrants had divided in prehistoric times, with the ancestors of the Western Apache moving through the mountains while the ancestors of the Mescaleros, Jicarillas, Lipans, and Chiricahuas followed the front range south to New Mexico. The Mescaleros, Jicarillas, and Chiricahuas had considerable contact with the Pueblo tribes of the Rio Grande, even adopting several of their ceremonies and dances. The Western Apaches were far less influenced by the Pueblos and their Spanish overlords. Nevertheless, they also embraced, as did their eastern Apache cousins, a devotion to the cult of the warrior and an adherence to raiding as a primary source of economic sustenance.

Although they shared the same name and language, they lived

lives of isolation that kept them from developing any overall sense of tribal unity. Loyalty was given first to the family or the clan, rather than to the tribe. Personal and family honor were of the utmost importance. At its peak their population was between eight and ten thousand, and perhaps less.

WHEN FRANCISCO VÁSQUEZ de Coronado's *conquistadores* first entered Arizona and New Mexico in 1540, they encountered no Apaches, even though they made a systematic exploration as far north as the Grand Canyon and eastward onto the Great Plains. Indeed, it is no small irony of history that the Europeans may well have reached Arizona before the people who became the Apaches did. It would be forty years before the Spanish returned, but when they came back, they came to stay. In 1598, Juan de Onate began the colonization of northern New Mexico, and it was he who first identified the native peoples to the north and west of his Rio Grande settlements as Apaches. In time the Spanish came to know these people all too well, and they gave the name "Apachería" to all the country north of the Gila River in Arizona and in the mountains of western and southern New Mexico.

It was 1699 before the Spanish attempted to colonize southern Arizona. By then the Pueblo Revolt of 1680 had forced them out of their New Mexico settlements, so that the Spanish horse herds ran free, in time becoming the wild mustangs of the American West and reordering the lives of Indian people everywhere. These horses gave a new mobility to the Apaches, although as a mountain people they did not embrace the animal as did the Indians of the Great Plains. The horse became for them in equal parts a form of transportation, a valuable trade commodity, and a tasty food source. Horses allowed Apache raiders to conduct swift raids against their traditional prey—the various Pueblo tribes along the Rio Grande and the Papagos (Tohono O'odham) of Arizona's Santa Cruz River Valley and the Pimas (Akimel O'odham) along the Gila River—as well as seek plunder much deeper into Sonora and Chihuahua.

In the spring of 1699, Father Eusebio Francisco Kino, as bold and ambitious as he was compassionate and charismatic, brought his gospel to the O'odham people along the Santa Cruz and north to the Gila. The Italian Jesuit had much to offer these people besides his religion, for the wheat seed he brought allowed them to plant year-round and the iron plows he gave them made that planting more efficient. Kino's horses and mules, sheep, goats, and cattle all allowed the O'odham to settle in more permanent communities near the mission churches he founded. The missions and the O'odham villages became the first line of Spanish defense against the Apaches.

In 1767 Carlos III of Spain expelled the Jesuits from the New World, replacing them with the brown-robed Franciscans. Even more important for the Apaches, the monarch assumed control over the interior provinces of New Spain, appointing a *commandante general* to assume both civil and military authority on the frontier. The mission system was now to be subordinated to the military. While this had much to do with international colonial competition, it was manifested on Spain's far northern frontier by an effort to subdue the Apaches and extend Spanish control beyond the Gila River. The skirmishing and back-and-forth raiding now become an all-out war between Spain and the Apaches.

On August 20, 1775, just as a great revolution was sweeping the English colonies far to the east, the Spanish founded the *presidio* (fort) of Tucson. The leather-clad Spanish soldiers, armed with sword and lance, were brave and skilled fighters—heirs to the warrior tradition that had expelled the Moors from Spain and toppled the New World empires of the Aztecs and Incas. Their *compañías volantes* (flying companies) penetrated deep into Apacheria and soon decorated the Tucson battlement walls with the heads of fallen Apaches. It was to be a war of extermination.

THE APACHES, MUCH like the Vikings, lived by raiding. They made a clear distinction between raiding, an economic necessity, and warfare, which was almost always an act of revenge. Raids were conducted by small parties usually numbering under a dozen

warriors; the purpose was not to kill but to acquire plunder or prisoners to adopt or enslave. Raids were carefully planned by warriors; the fighters scattered if pursued, and plunder was quickly
discarded or destroyed if the pursuers came too close. After all,
there was always more to be taken later. Much of this booty was
traded away for weapons, food, and clothing. They did not want to
kill the people who tended to the fields and flocks, and haughtily
referred to the Spanish as their "shepherds."

War was for revenge and revenge only. It was a warrior's duty;
mercy was not viewed as a virtue. Torture had long been a common
practice among the Apaches, but they practiced it on the Spanish
with a vengeance. A chief of the Aravaipa Apaches once bragged of
how he had buried a captive alive up to his neck and then watched
the ants devour his head. Prisoners were often staked out on ant-
hills with their mouths propped open to allow ravenous insects easy
entry. Men were tied naked to cactus or thorn-laden trees and then
skewered with lance and arrow. Teamsters were tied upside down
to their wagon wheels with hot coals placed under their heads. Men
were flayed alive until they slowly bled to death. Female relations of
slain warriors were given captives to torture to help assuage their
grief. They proved particularly ingenious at this work, often orna-
menting the mouths of male victims with their own penises. "Every
expression of pain or agony is hailed with delight," noted a frontier
soldier, "and the one whose inventive genius can devise the most
excruciating kind of death is deemed worthy of honor." It was not
good to be taken captive by the Apaches.

The threat of mutilation only enhanced the spiritual power of
war, but it was not common among the various bands until their
Spanish enemies introduced the practice to them. Because Apaches
had an almost pathological fear of ghosts and the walking spirits of the dead, they did not care to touch those who had fallen,
even among their own people. Scalping was never an Apache custom, but once the Europeans had introduced the horrific act, it
was sometimes practiced. While the Mescaleros scalped more than
other Apaches, it was not uncommon by the nineteenth century for
even Western Apaches to take scalps, a practice they called *bitsa-*

ha-digihz, or "his head top cut off." Scalps were displayed during a victory dance but immediately discarded afterward, then those who had touched the scalp underwent a purification ceremony to ward off the spirits of the dead.

The land itself was the Apache warrior's greatest ally. He knew where the life-giving springs were and could find the many caves that might hide him. Often bleak, arid, and cut by innumerable ravines, canyons, and mountain outcroppings, this land offered sanctuary to the Apache. In the land he knew best, he could hide or wait in ambush for his enemies.

Mobility was always the key to Apache success. If pressed, warriors might make a stand on a rocky hillside, throwing up boulders to form rough defensive works. The Spanish called these spontaneous fortifications *refugios,* and they were extraordinarily difficult to assault. The Apache warrior did not throw his life away with careless bravado, but carefully sought just the right time to strike, flee, or make a stand.

The primitive firearms of the Spanish were cumbersome, inaccurate, and difficult to reload. The lance and bow and arrow were better weapons, especially with the iron tips acquired from the Europeans. An experienced Apache warrior could fire four to ten arrows in the time it took a Spanish soldier to load and fire his muzzle-loading musket once. "The bow is always ready for use," noted a Spanish officer. "The first arrows shot from it carry a powerful force, which many times neither the shield, nor the leather-jacket can withstand." The Apaches even used a form of chemical warfare, dipping their arrow points into poison collected from plants, venomous snakes, or the putrefied flesh of dead animals. The Spanish never had a chance.

Not only did the Apaches live off the land with ease, but they also made almost all of their own weapons. They had no supply lines, towns, or fortifications, and no centralized leadership to take hostage or kill. It was impossible for the Spanish to destroy so elusive an enemy, noted the viceroy, for "having no towns, castles, or temples to defend they may only be attacked in their dispersed and movable *rancherias.*"

Finally, in 1786, the Spanish government decided to buy peace and instructed field commanders to purchase Apache goodwill by offering those who would stop raiding "defective firearms, strong liquor, and such other commodities as would render them militarily and economically dependent on the Spaniards." Within twenty years this policy had been institutionalized into so-called peace camps or feeding stations, such as Tucson and Janos, where the Apaches could receive cattle, flour, sugar, and tobacco.

While Apache raids never completely stopped, this peace policy—essentially the payment of tribute by the Spanish to the Apaches—brought relative peace to Pimería Alta (the land from Sonora's Altar River north to the Gila River) for over a generation. More Spanish settlers now moved north, and by the dawn of the new century nearly a thousand lived along the Santa Cruz. Then it all collapsed.

One reason for the vulnerability of the Spanish settlers was that the royal government, fearful of rebellion, kept armaments from the people. This Spanish paranoia was well placed, for in 1821, a decade of rebellion resulted in independence for Mexico. Mexican independence did not mean peace with the Apaches, and in fact led to increased violence. The already beleaguered northern frontier was abandoned by Spanish soldiers and ignored by the new and ever-changing governments in Mexico City. Soldiers were needed in Mexico City to prop up tottering administrations and none could be spared for frontier defense. With the "feeding stations" closed, the Apaches resumed their raids, not only along the Santa Cruz but also against the Rio Grande settlements and deep into Sonora and Chihuahua as well. The tenuous peace crumbled and the warriors laid waste to the land.

AFTER THEIR SUCCESSFUL fight for independence, the Mexicans quickly descended into civil war and chaos. In the northern Mexican states alongside the US border, warlords soon rose to power. Often at odds with one another, these *caudillos* mounted independent expeditions against the Apaches. This lack of cooperation resulted in ineffective campaigns as well as separate peace agreements between some Mexican communities—most notably the Chihuahua village of Janos—and the Apaches. Janos became a center of trade with the Apache, with the residents trading for Apache plunder and slaves, then selling the goods and people south to Chihuahua City or east to El Paso. The war with the Apaches now became a local, rather than national, affair.

Sometimes bands of Mexican militia from Sonora or Chihuahua marched into the neighboring state in search of Apaches. Janos was a particular target for Sonoran patrols, who knew that Apaches often traded there. In 1851, during a trading parley in Janos, the Mexicans and their Apache guests got roaring drunk on mescal to celebrate their bargain. While the men were drinking, a force of Sonoran militia murdered most of the Apache women and children in the unprotected Apache village outside of the town.

A young warrior named Goyahkla (One Who Yawns) found his aged mother alongside his wife and three children, all scalped in pools of blood. "Whenever I saw anything to remind me of former happy days," he declared years later, "my heart would ache for revenge on Mexico." He had a vision while weeping over his loss, and from it came his mystical warrior power. "Goyahkla," said a voice four times—the Apache magical number, "no gun can ever kill you. I will take the bullets from the guns of Mexicans. And I will guide your arrows." He might be wounded but he could never be killed. From that day onward, vengeance became his driving passion. In time he exacted ghastly blood atonement from the Mexicans. His terrified enemies called out to Saint Jerome for deliverance and thus gave to him a new name—Geronimo.

As Apache raids intensified in the wake of all these conflicts, the increasingly desperate Mexican state governors hired foreign mercenaries, paying them bounties for Apache scalps—$100 for an adult male, $50 for a female, and $25 for a child. This ruthless policy achieved nothing save adding to the Apache vengeance tally against Mexico.

The most prominent of these mercenaries were the Kentuckian John J. Johnson, who worked for the governor of Sonora, and the

Irishman James Kirker, who was employed by the governor of Chihuahua. Johnson's massacre of the camp of Chief Juan José Compa in the Animas Mountains of southwestern New Mexico in April 1837 made him a hero to his Sonoran employers but inflamed the Chiricahuas against the Mexicans for two generations. More than twenty Apaches were slain, and Johnson presented the scalps of three Apache chiefs to the commander of the presidio at Janos. In a macabre change from the Spanish and Mexican practice of collecting pairs of ears as *piezas*, or evidence of death, Johnson collected the whole Apache scalp with the ears attached. This was the gruesome moment when scalping transitioned from the Spanish tradition of taking ears to the American custom of lifting hair.

One man who escaped the carnage was a prominent warrior named Fuerte, who now inherited the leadership of the eastern Chiricahuas after the death of Juan José. He swore vengeance and, after a mourning period, started to lead reprisal raids. The Apaches did not much care whom they killed—guilty and innocent alike—in order to avenge their dead.

In 1848, the conclusion of the Mexican War ended the brief, unhappy rule of Mexico over much of Apacheria. But the land south of the Gila River remained part of the Mexican Republic until it was opened to American settlement by the Gadsden Purchase. Those who wished to enter this new land first had to deal with the undisputed Lord of Apacheria—the great chief Fuerte, who now bore the new name Mangas Coloradas.

2

RED SLEEVES

THE MEXICANS CALLED HIM MANGAS COLORADAS—
Red Sleeves. He was born in 1790, during the time of
peace, and his Apache name was Kan-da-zis-tlishishen.
He was of the Bedonkohe (Bee-don-ko-hee) band of Chiricahuas,
who lived near Santa Lucia Springs on the headwaters of the Gila
River. His father was a prominent Bedonkohe warrior, and his
mother may well have been a Spanish captive. He grew to manhood
amid the grandeur of the Mogollon Mountains, where great stands
of Douglas fir, Ponderosa pine, and aspen sheltered wolves, bears,
panthers, and great herds of elk and deer that fed the people. These
high and rugged mountains, cut by innumerable canyons, afforded
relief from the searing summer heat of the piñon and juniper wood-
lands below. It was a natural Eden, replete with game as well as a
wide variety of edible nuts and berries. The mescal, or agave, plant,
a staple for all the Chiricahuas, grew abundantly in the foothills
above the desert to the east.

Mangas was well over six feet tall, not only much taller than
other Apaches, but also almost all Mexicans and Americans of
that time as well. His first Apache name, Fuerte, was reflective of
his people's awe over his physique. He married into the Chihenne
(Chee-hen-ee) band—the "Red Paint People"—whom the Americans came to call by various names depending on where they lived.
Although they made their home in the mountains of southwestern New Mexico, eastern Arizona, and northern Chihuahua, they
were often referred to by their favorite *rancheria* locations—the
Mimbres, Warm Springs, Copper Mines (after the Spanish mines

at Santa Rita del Cobre), and the Gilas. Mangas's first marriage led to his identification with the Chihenne, even more than his own Bedonkohe people. Chiricahua custom led a man to live with his wife's people, and their children were known as members of the mother's band.

In time, Mangas came to have influence over the other two Chiricahua bands as well. To the south in Chihuahua, Mexico, lived the Nednhis (Ned-nee), often called Janeros because they resided near the old Spanish presidio of Janos some seventy-five miles south of the New Mexico border. The final band, perhaps the most famous of all the Chiricahuas, lived in the mountains of southeastern Arizona as well as parts of northern Chihuahua and Sonora, and were called Chokonens (Cho-ko-nen), or "Ridge-of-the-Mountain People." Each band held the loyalty of individual Chiricahuas, but the whole tribe might sometimes unite under a strong leader for military action to avenge a great wrong. Mangas Coloradas was just such a leader.

Despite the peace with the Spanish, there were always Navajos, Pueblos, Pimas, and Papagos to raid, and in this work, Mangas rose to prominence. But it was John Johnson's 1837 massacre that truly elevated Mangas as a leader of his people. Although Johnson was a "White Eye," or American, Apache vengeance was directed at the Mexicans who had hired him. (The term *White Eye* was the Apache response to the perceived paleness of the eyes of the Americans.) Mangas, then still known as Fuerte, led his warriors out on revenge raids that left scores dead. In this war, Fuerte won the new name of Mangas Coloradas. Some said it was for the red shirt he wore, but others were emphatic that it described the blood that stained his sleeves as he waded in the gore of the Mexicans he had slain.

Throughout the summer of 1837, Mangas led retaliatory raids throughout Sonora and Chihuahua, so that within a year all roads were unsafe, the Santa Rita mines had been abandoned, the haciendas overrun, and towns such as Janos and Galeana put in constant danger. Few Mexican citizens had guns, and those who did could not procure any ammunition. The unstable Mexican state governments, like the Spanish before them, kept the people unarmed for fear of the same kind of rebellion that earned them their independence. The peasants fought back as best they could with improvised lances, bows and arrows, and clubs, and they wrapped their bodies in cowhides for protection, but it was all for naught. The Apaches, now often as not armed with guns and ammunition provided by American fur traders, killed them and left their bodies to rot in their fields and on the roads.

Unprotected by the army, the Mexican peasants were helpless to resist the Apache raiders, with scores carried off into captivity and hundreds more slaughtered. The desert now reclaimed the untilled fields. Cattle, sheep, mules, and goats wandered free only to fall prey to the great packs of wolves and coyotes that trailed the Apache raiding parties just as the raven shadows the predator on his rounds. Skeletons lined the roads, littered the burned haciendas, and were picked clean by scavengers in deserted villages. It was a perfect reign of terror.

IN CHIHUAHUA CITY, the desperate owners of the once highly profitable Santa Rita del Cobre copper mines sent a messenger to Bent's Fort, far to the north on the Arkansas River. They requested the unique services of James Kirker. The scalp hunter was in exile in United States territory, having feuded with Mexican officials who had placed a price on his head for selling guns to the Apaches. It was common knowledge among the American trappers headquartered at Taos, New Mexico, and at Bent's Fort in Colorado that the only way to trap in the profitable headwaters of the Gila River was to purchase safe passage from the Apaches with trade goods. Kirker had long ago learned that a liberal disbursement of powder, ball, and muskets purchased considerable goodwill. When he was not hunting Apaches, he was trading with them while trapping beaver, thereby profiting from the Mexicans and the Apaches simultaneously.

Santa Rita had long been a favorite camping spot for Kirker and other trappers. For several years he had provided security to the caravans of mule trains winding south from the mountains of southwestern New Mexico along the "Copper Road" to Janos and Chihuahua City. His old employers from the copper mines, in concert with the governor of Chihuahua, now made him an offer that would be difficult to refuse. They offered Kirker one hundred thousand pesos (at that time equal to the same in dollars) to return from exile to Santa Rita with a company of men to fight the Apaches.

Kirker must have smiled, not only at the princely sum, but also at the official redemption offered to him. He set about finding some fighters. His right hand was Spybuck, a mixed-blood Shawnee born in Ohio but removed by the government to a Moravian mission in Kansas. He was an imposing figure at more than six feet tall with a great Roman nose, black hair, and a light complexion courtesy of his French father. His muscular frame was covered with the scars of deadly encounters with both man and beast. He was Kirker's bloodhound, renowned across the frontier for his prowess with a rifle as well as his tracking skills. Spybuck and Kirker had no trouble recruiting fifty strong men from Bent's Fort. The beaver trade had played out and men were looking for both adventure and silver in their pockets. It was a formidable band of cutthroats.

In July 1846, Kirker achieved true infamy when he conspired with the leading citizens of Galeana, Chihuahua, to lure a mixed band of Chokonen and Nednhi Chiricahuas into town with promises of a peace treaty and rations. Negotiations were held between the Mexicans and the Apaches while Kirker and his men hid themselves. A pledge of eternal peace was secured and to cement the bargain a liberal disbursement of whiskey was provided. On the morning of July 7, while the Apache men lay in a drunken stupor after a nightlong fandango, Kirker and his land pirates slaughtered 130 Chiricahuas.

Spybuck supervised the scalping, for his Shawnees had perfected a rapid technique. A neat circle was cut at the crown of the victim's head. The scalper then grabbed hold of the Apache's long hair and pushed off with his feet against the victim's shoulders. A loud pop followed as the scalp came off. The scalps were taken to Spybuck, who treated them with some salt for preservation and attached them to long scalp poles. Each scalp was a debit against the treasury of the state of Chihuahua.

Kirker marched his men into Chihuahua City in a grand procession headed by the governor and several priests, with musicians escorting them into the town in triumph. They carried the Apache scalps before them on long poles. In the fiesta that followed, the priests ornamented the front of their church with the scalps. "Opposite the principal entrance, over the portals which form one side of the square, were dangling the grim scalps of one hundred and seventy Apaches," noted an English visitor, "who had been inhumanely butchered by the Indian hunters in pay of the state."

So enraged were all the Chiricahua bands over Kirker's Galeana massacre that retribution was planned at the tribal level. Almost every band had lost a friend or relative. The chief of the Warm Springs Apaches, Cuchillo Negro (Black Knife), called for a grand council of all the chiefs. Mangas Coloradas led his warriors to the council. Mangas's son-in-law Cochise, who would become the greatest chief of the Chokonen, also attended. It was decided to attack Galeana itself. That night a huge fire was built and the people all gathered in a great circle as the drums beat and the singers raised their high-pitched chant to the heavens.

The singers called out the names of the most prominent warriors. Among the first names to be called was a warrior named Goyahkla, a young Bedonkohe who had already distinguished himself in countless raids. He walked around the fire as the singers praised his deeds in battle. Those who wished to ride with him joined him in the parade.

Goyahkla was the grandson of the revered Bedonkohe chief Mahco, but the bloodline had not secured him a position as chief. He had grown to manhood in New Mexico's Mogollon Mountains and was held in awe by many Apaches for his spiritual power as well as his warrior skills. When he was about nine or ten, what the Apaches called "Night the Stars Fell" occurred. This majestic 1832 meteor shower terrified people all across North America. Three years later it was followed by the equally awesome appearance of Halley's Comet. Goyahkla understood that both of these cosmic events portended great changes to come. He sensed a call to glory and greatness while others shrank before a dark omen of calamity.

Once all the warrior leaders and their followers had been selected for the war party, the men formed a great line across from the drummers. They advanced toward the singers as the drums pounded, brandishing their weapons and leaping about as if in the heat of battle. In the flickering firelight, Goyahkla and his fearsome companions were preparing themselves for the grim business of revenge on the people of Galeana.

The various bands soon returned to their villages to prepare for the campaign. Lances and bows and arrows had to be shaped from the mulberry trees on the bottom slopes of the mountains. Turkey feathers would be mounted on the arrows to ensure that they would drive true to their marks. Despite the trade muskets they had acquired from the Americans, the bow and arrow remained their weapon of choice. "I knew men who could put seven arrows in the air before the first one that was fired fell to the earth," recalled an Apache warrior.

While these preparations were under way, an unexpected visitor arrived at the camp of Mangas Coloradas, some ten miles from the abandoned copper mines at Santa Rita. Kit Carson, the famed mountain man and scout for John Charles Frémont—inheritor of the buckskin mantle of Boone and Crockett—was traveling with a party of fifteen men en route to Washington, DC, in September 1846, with dispatches announcing the conquest of California by American troops. He found his trail blocked by the Apache village and decided to parley. He carefully approached the village and announced that he wished to trade. His mules were exhausted, and he was in desperate need of remounts.

Mangas visited Carson in his camp and was gratified to receive the welcome news that the Americans were at war with the Mexicans. Mangas had information to share, too. He informed Carson that a white man he called the "Horse Chief of the Long Knives" had taken New Mexico from the Mexicans. Mangas had always admired the Americans, often befriending trappers such as Carson who had visited the headwaters of the Gila. Borderlines changed, loyalties blurred, and racial identity became meaningless as men made their way as best they could in this wild country. Carson, who had married into a Mexican family, and Mangas Coloradas, who may well have had a Mexican mother, agreed to make common cause against Mexico that day.

Mounted on the fresh mules provided by Mangas, Carson pushed on to the Rio Grande. On October 6, 1846, he encountered General Stephen Watts Kearny with three hundred dragoons. Kearny, the "Horse Chief of the Long Knives" Mangas had alluded to, had indeed taken New Mexico and was now on his way to conquer California. Kearny sent two-thirds of his men back to Santa Fe, then ordered Carson to guide him back through Apache country and along the Gila River to the west. Based on Carson's news from California, that the state had already been conquered by the Americans, Kearny assumed that he needed but a two-company escort for the rest of his journey. He retained Lieutenant William H. Emory and his fourteen-man topographical unit to make maps of the conquered territory.

ON OCTOBER 18, General Kearny's soldiers set up camp two miles to the west of the deserted Santa Rita del Cobre presidio. Carson sent up smoke signals to invite Mangas to come to the American camp. The Apaches did not actually communicate with smoke signals; the smoke simply meant "Come and investigate." Mangas did just that, arriving that evening with a single companion to meet with the American general. This was the first recorded meeting of a representative of the United States government with a Chiricahua leader.

Mangas pledged "good faith and friendship to all Americans," pleased to have an ally in his tribe's war against the common enemy, Mexico. As Kearny presented Mangas with several presents, Carson turned to Kearny's companion, Lieutenant Emory, and winked. "I would not trust one of them," he said of Mangas's pledges with a wry smile.

The next day they met again at Santa Lucia Spring to trade.

Mangas brought in thirty of his people and a fine herd of mules, freshly stolen from Sonora. Lieutenant Emory was impressed by how shrewd the Apaches were at trade. He was also enthralled by the Apache braves, who reminded him "of pictures of antique Grecian warriors." He was most struck, however, by a scene that spoke eloquently to the humanity of these strange people. "There was amongst them a poor deformed woman, with legs and arms no longer than an infant's," he recorded in his diary. "She was well mounted, and the gallant manner in which some of the plumed Apaches waited on her, for she was perfectly helpless when dismounted, made it hard for me to believe the tales of blood and vice told of these people."

It proved to be a productive and happy meeting, made all the more memorable when, upon departure, one of Mangas's warriors approached the American general with some sage advice: "You have taken New Mexico, and will soon take California; go then and take Chihuahua, Durango, and Sonora. We will help you. The Mexicans are rascals; we hate and will kill them all." Kearny smiled, although it was still far too early to see the deep irony in the warrior's statement.

THE CHIRICAHUAS PROCEEDED to do their part in assisting the Americans in the war against Mexico. Soon after Kearny headed west to California, nearly two hundred Chiricahuas followed the Warm Springs Apache chief Cuchillo Negro to Galeana in the winter of 1846. Mangas Coloradas, Cochise, and Delgadito were the major war chiefs in this attack, and the campfire tales told of their great deeds at Galeana lived on for generations. Goyahkla's already impressive reputation as a warrior was enhanced on that fateful day as well. According to Goyahkla's young nephew, everyone agreed that "this was the greatest of Apache victories."

A New Orleans journalist who visited Galeana in 1849 described it as "once a flourishing spot but the Indians have been its ruin and impoverished its wealthiest citizens." The presidios at Fronteras and Tubac were also soon attacked by the Apache warriors, and as a result abandoned by their garrisons. Apache vengeance was complete.

Mangas Coloradas next met with John Russell Bartlett, the US boundary commissioner assigned to settle the new international line with Mexico. Bartlett treated Mangas with respect when they met at the old copper mines on June 23, 1851, and even bestowed a fine blue military frock coat on the chief. He also informed Mangas that under the provisions of the treaty ending the war with Mexico, the United States government was now obliged to protect Mexico from Indian raids originating within its boundaries. Mangas was perplexed by this, but agreed not to attack the Mexican boundary party operating on the border under General Garcia Conde. He agreed to nothing else.

As word spread about the arrival of the Americans at the border, more Indians arrived in the vicinity of the commissioner's encampment. They were curious and anxious to meet these new White Eyes. The war chief Delgadito and nearly three hundred Chihennes united with Mangas's band, which was of equal strength. Delgadito's people camped along the Mimbres River some twenty miles away. Even more surprising was the arrival of nearly four hundred Navajos who made camp along the Gila River some thirty miles from Santa Rita. Although Bartlett was delighted at the arrival of so many Indians, thinking that he would win their loyalty to the United States, the more experienced frontier hands became nervous.

John C. Cremony, a veteran of the Mexican War who now served as Bartlett's chief interpreter, was particularly puzzled as to why the Navajos, so often the bitter enemies of the Apaches, would dare venture so far south. His Apache friends explained that it was Mangas's astute diplomacy that had secured peace with their northern neighbors. According to Cremony's informants, on a raid in Sonora, Mangas had "carried off a handsome and intelligent Mexican girl, whom he made his wife, to the exclusion of his Apache squaws." This forced Mangas to fight duels with two of the outraged relatives of his Apache wives. This domestic turmoil yielded rich diplomatic dividends.

"By his Mexican wife Mangas had three really beautiful daughters," the Apaches explained, and through his diplomatic ability, he married one of them to a chief of the Navajos. The other two married important Apache chiefs and in this way, as Cremony put it, Mangas became "undoubtedly the most prominent and influential Apache who has existed for a century . . . and carried his influence from the Colorado River to the Guadalupe Mountains." Cremony was wise enough to realize that even though Mangas "was a power in the land," the Apaches remained "pure democrats, each warrior being his own master."

The question of the fate of Mexican captives quickly became crucial when Cremony liberated a young girl and two boys who had been captured by the Apaches. Mangas demanded the return of the captives or a liberal payment by Bartlett for them.

"Why did you take our captives from us?" Mangas demanded, no longer wearing his fine blue coat, for he had wagered it away.

Bartlett replied that the Americans had promised to protect all Mexican captives, but that the Mexicans might pay a reasonable ransom for them. "Let our Apache brother reflect and name his price," Bartlett concluded with perfect Yankee logic.

The Apaches departed in a foul mood. Three days later, a few returned to accept a payment of two hundred dollars in trade goods for the captives. Bartlett thought he had taught the Indians a valuable lesson, but Cremony realized that they had accepted payment only because they were realists. He knew full well that they would soon claim a greater recompense for their loss.

Two days later, the bad temper of the Apaches was intensified when a stock handler shot and mortally wounded an Apache during an argument. Mangas conferred with Bartlett on July 21, 1851, demanding that the murderer be turned over to the Apaches for justice. Bartlett refused but promised to send the man in chains to Santa Fe for trial. Mangas thought this a pretty good joke, for he well knew that no White Eye would be punished for killing an Apache. He promptly decamped with his people for the springs at Santa Lucia.

The following day Ponce, a Chihenne band leader, and Delgadito brought the mother of the murder victim to meet with Bartlett. The commissioner offered compensation to her, and when the Apaches angrily refused, he ended the conference with a prophetic warning of what would happen if they did not bend to American will: "War will then follow; thousands of soldiers will take possession of your lands, your grazing valleys, and your watering places. They will destroy every Apache warrior they find, and take your women and children captives."

Ponce and Delgadito led their people away from Santa Rita. Within days, horses and mules began to vanish from the American camp. The Navajos soon returned to their own country, trailing a large herd of Bartlett's animals with them. Cremony estimated the number of lost horses and mules at nearly three hundred. Bartlett decided to abandon Santa Rita in late August and move westward. His stay among the Apaches, which had begun in warm friendship, had ended in rancor and lingering bitterness that foreshadowed so many events to come.

THE BANDS OF Ponce, Delgadito, and Cuchillo Negro were soon at war with the Americans. In January 1852, a company of the Third Infantry established Fort Webster at the copper mines and quickly provoked a skirmish with the Apaches that left three soldiers dead. All along the Rio Grande, travelers were attacked, and when American dragoons from Laguna responded, the Apaches ambushed them, killing five and wounding three more.

Soon after, a supply train of eight wagons returning from Fort Webster had all its stock stolen. The teamsters abandoned their wagons and fled toward the Rio Grande. The army, unable to supply the post at Santa Rita, had to relocate Fort Webster farther east, to the west bank of the Mimbres River. The Apaches saw this as a victory of sorts, and now approached the Americans with an olive branch—but the Apache chief Cuchillo Negro informed the American commander at the new Fort Webster that he could agree to nothing until Mangas Coloradas returned from Sonora.

Meanwhile, as the Apaches' war with the Americans heated

up, so did their war against Mexico. In a surprising show of military efficiency, the Mexican commander in Sonora had simultaneously sent forth columns from Santa Cruz, Tucson, Bavispe, and the reoccupied Fronteras. By March 1852, more than five hundred Mexican soldiers were in the field. They kept up operations against the Chiricahuas throughout the spring and into the early summer months.

Mangas realized that he could not sustain a two-front war with the Americans and the Sonorans. On July 11, 1852, he met with Lieutenant Colonel Edwin Vose Sumner of the First Dragoons far to the north at the Pueblo of Acoma. Sumner was as tough a soldier as the American army ever produced. A musket ball had glanced off his skull at Cerro Gordo during the Mexican War, earning him the nickname "Bull" from his troops. He was also a complete martinet, for which his soldiers both loathed and admired him. But the Chiricahua leader could match Sumner in both arrogance and boldness. Wearing the uniform coat of a Mexican artillery officer whom he had recently slain, Mangas greeted the colonel and got right to business: "You are chief of the white men. I am chief of the red men. Now let us have a talk and treat."

The treaty that they jointly signed, the first by the Chiricahuas with the United States, recognized the jurisdiction of the Americans and allowed the government to establish military posts and Indian agencies in the lands of the Apaches. The tribe would liberate all Mexican captives and cease raids into Mexico. In exchange, the Americans promised to give goods to the Chiricahuas at a future unspecified time.

Mangas, although willing to sign the treaty on behalf of his people (at least the Bedonkohes and Chihennes), expressed his objection to the clause on raiding Mexico. He was prepared to pledge peace and friendship with the White Eyes, but not the hated Mexicans. "Are we to stand by with our arms folded while our women and children are being murdered?" he asked Sumner. The colonel, who viewed the citizens of Sonora with contempt, cared little if the Chiricahuas slaughtered them. Mangas and Sumner were kindred warrior spirits, and the chief later claimed that the colonel then gave him a wink and a nod in approval of his demand to continue the war against Mexico, despite the treaty forbidding it.

The festering problem of Apache raids into Mexico was soon partially rectified by diplomatic and political developments in the East. Bartlett's boundary line became controversial even before his survey with General Conde was completed. By accepting Conde's interpretation of where the boundary line would depart the Rio Grande and go due west, Bartlett ceded New Mexico's valuable Mesilla Valley to Mexico.

The boundary was soon caught up in presidential politics as Democrats accused Bartlett, a Whig, of giving up the valley in order to prevent construction of a southern transcontinental railroad. The new boundary line was put in place and new maps were drawn on parchment. The new international line made no sense to the Chiricahuas. It placed many of their relatives in Mexico while leaving others in the United States. The Apaches discovered that the Americans seemingly worshipped these lines that they drew on paper.

The lingering controversy over Bartlett's Boundary Commission soon contributed to the Gadsden Purchase, the diplomatic initiative that would have an enormous impact on the Apaches. This time, when the Americans drew even more lines, they divided off the western half of New Mexico into a new territory. This would further divide the Apaches and in fact make it more complicated for civilian and military authorities to deal with them. The paper lines meant more to the Americans than trade, efficiency, family, or justice. So important were these paper lines to the White Eyes that they were willing to write them in blood.

DESPITE THE CONTROVERSY over imaginary lines being drawn and redrawn, Mangas worked diligently to keep the peace with the Americans. He was aided in this by the new Indian agent for New Mexico. Dr. Michael Steck had come to New Mexico in 1849 as a military contract surgeon. He was appointed as Indian agent for New Mexico's Apaches in 1852. An intelligent man of compassion along with bedrock honesty, he was reappointed as agent by three other presidents: Pierce, Buchanan, and Lincoln. As agent for the Mescalero and Mimbres Apaches, he gained their confidence and then used them to make the first Indian Bureau contacts with the Chiricahuas, Pinals, and Coyoteros to the west. Steck successfully negotiated with the Mescaleros of southeastern New Mexico in 1855 and had even lured Cuchillo Negro and his Chihenne people to attempt farming near Fort Thorn. It was his job as agent to distribute annuity goods and also negotiate with local contractors as well as with the various Apache bands. He had to both protect his natives from the military while also cooperating with the army and local politicians. It was a difficult job and Steck accomplished it with skill and tact.

In July 1856, Steck invited Charles Poston to accompany him to Santa Rita del Cobre, where he could introduce him to the Apache leaders. Poston was on his way to Tucson with a wagon train and a party of skilled German miners guarded by what he labeled as Texas "buckskin boys." He readily accepted the invitation and selected five men to go with him. Steck had two wagons loaded with corn for Mangas Coloradas's Chihenne band. This corn, Poston observed, was promptly made into that favorite Apache brew *tiswin*.

On July 25, Poston and Steck camped at the old presidio. Mangas soon brought in 350 of his people and a grand party followed. Poston had his boys put on quite a show for the Apaches with their new revolvers and carbines. The Apaches joined in, and Poston was charmed that they carefully cut the bullets from the trees they used for targets "as they were economists in ammunition if nothing else." Poston and his men "exhibited our new firearms, which were then Sharp's rifles and Colt's revolvers, shot at marks, and drank *tiswin*, roasted venison, and made the Indians some presents." Poston was amused that the most valued gift he could give was matches, which the Apaches carefully wrapped in buckskin.

Steck introduced Mangas to Poston and asked him to protect the Americans as they journeyed to the Santa Cruz River. Mangas promised peace with his new American friend, but again warned Steck "that the Spanish and Mexicans had treated them badly and that they would kill them and rob them as long as they lived." Steck talked with Mangas about his desire to establish a reservation for the Chihennes and Bedonkohes on the Mimbres River at Santa Lucia Springs. Even in Steck's brief time in New Mexico, he had noticed a rather dramatic decline in the Apache population as a result of the long war with Mexico. Now was the time to increase rations and farming assistance to induce Mangas and his people to come in and settle down. Unfortunately his pleas would have more success with the Apaches than with his superiors in Santa Fe and Washington.

The visit was a grand success, at least from Poston's perspective. To cement his friendship with Mangas and the other chiefs, he distributed several little tintypes of himself that he had acquired back in New York. He wanted them to remember him as a friend. Years later he would learn from an Apache woman that a band of warriors lying in ambush had spared him because their leader carried his tintype. "I have generally found the Indians willing to keep faith with the whites," Poston wrote, "if the whites will keep faith with them."

AN EVENT FAR to the north suddenly shattered the peace Mangas and Steck had worked so hard to protect. In November 1856, Coyotero Apache raiders killed the Navajo agent Henry L. Dodge, the eldest son of Senator Henry Dodge of Wisconsin. The killing caused a national sensation. Steck, hoping the rumors were untrue, sent a message to Mangas Coloradas offering a large ransom for Dodge. But Mangas responded that he was certain that the Coyoteros had slain the popular Indian agent.

Colonel Benjamin Bonneville, in command of all troops in New Mexico, was determined to avenge Dodge. The colonel pulled in military units from all across the territory, and in May 1857, he led nearly six hundred men toward the Coyotero heartland north of the Gila River. As the column advanced, they were met by fire. Mangas Coloradas had set the forest ablaze as he took his people south to Mexico.

First blood was drawn by Colonel William Loring and his Mounted Riflemen. The one-armed hero of Chapultepec in the Mexican War led a large scouting party eastward from Bonneville's Gila River camp toward the Mimbres River. This was, of course, in the opposite direction from the homeland of the targeted Apaches. The march was difficult over rough country where the grass had all been burned off. On May 24, Loring's troops attacked an Apache *rancheria* hidden in a steep canyon. The camp belonged to Cuchillo Negro, one of Steck's prize converts, who had been drawing rations at Fort Thorn. He was returning from a raid into Mexico, driving hundreds of captured sheep. Loring's assault caught the Chihennes completely by surprise. Cuchillo Negro, along with five warriors and one woman, was killed, and nine women and children were captured.

Bonneville was delighted at Loring's victory, gleefully reporting to his superiors that "Loring has inflicted a blow upon this Mimbres band of Apaches which must have a salutary effect upon all others." This was but the beginning of a trend on the part of American military officers to slaughter innocent Apaches and convert it on paper into a major victory over notorious hostiles. While Cuchillo Negro was hardly an innocent, he was in no way involved in the Dodge murder; he and his people had simply provided a convenient target for the frustrated American soldiers.

Captain Richard Ewell, with three companies of dragoons from Fort Buchanan, stumbled upon a large Coyotero camp some thirty-five miles from Mount Graham on June 27 and attacked late in the afternoon. It was all over in less than an hour. The soldiers counted twenty-four dead warriors, including the man who had slain Dodge, with twenty-six women and children taken captive.

Colonel Bonneville, well satisfied with this victory, ordered his troops to return to their posts. While the campaign added to the martial reputations of Bonneville, Loring, and Ewell, the most important consequence was to enrage the Coyoteros. These White Mountain Apaches of the upper Gila were by far the most numerous of the various Apache bands, with some 2,500 people among them. They greatly outnumbered the 500 Pinals on the middle Gila above Tucson, the 200 Aravaipas to the south on the San Pedro, and the 600 or so Chiricahuas in the rugged mountains to the southeast. Isolated from the American settlements, they had, for the most part, left the White Eyes alone while continuing their traditional raids into Mexico. Now their quest for revenge—a primal cultural calling for all Apaches—would change everything.

3

THE LOST BOY

IT WAS EARLY IN JANUARY 1861 WHEN BETO LED HIS raiders south. The one-eyed Mexican captive of the Aravaipa wore a distinctive leather patch over his bad eye. The Mexicans called him Victor, and through warrior deeds he had risen to be a leader of one of the Aravaipa bands. For a captive to take such a position of leadership was rare. Captives, never entirely trusted, were called by the name *yodascin,* or "born outside." But Beto had proven himself. He possessed what the Western Apache knew as "enemies against power," a war power that made a warrior fast and lithe, like a cougar. "Such a man who knows this medicine," remarked a White Mountain Apache, "the rest would follow anywhere on the warpath." Beto, like the feared warrior Geronimo, was just such a man.

Beto had called together a dozen friends to join him in this raid because the people were in need. Some young men joined because they were bored or wished to escape for a time from their nagging wives. Others went for adventure or to enhance their warrior reputations. Novices, teenage boys not yet warriors, were always anxious for a chance to go even if they were merely allowed to tend to the horses.

Beto's men had painted themselves for the raid; some men put a white stripe across their face, across the nose, and under the eyes, while others chose red or black. They tied their hair up on top of their heads so it would not get into their eyes during battle. Some men painted two white bands across their chests; others wore a red cloth headband to identify themselves in combat. At least four extra pairs of moccasins hung on each pony. Dried mescal, buck-skin sacks filled with dried corn, and cakes made from the fruit of the prickly pear cactus were carried as rations.

They observed the language of war during the raid. The warriors had special words for horses, women, mules, Mexicans, white men, trails, grass, and water. A man had to be careful that his wife was not pregnant before he went out, for if a pregnant woman touched his weapons, his aim in battle would be bad. No one ever talked of fear or accused anyone of being afraid. If a man decided not to go on a raid, he was considered lazy, but never a coward. These and other taboos were central to the warrior ethos, and to break one invited catastrophe.

A novice warrior, or *dikohe,* was carefully instructed in the special language of war and in the taboos of the raid. The teenager would be used for camp work or to hold horses and was not expected to fight; he was there only to learn. For four days before the raiding party departed, the boy would receive instruction from an older man on the language to be used, the various taboos, and how to act around the other warriors. The novice observed special taboos: he was not to look back toward home for four days; he could never eat any meat from inside an animal; and he must always sleep with his head to the east. He was not instructed about "enemies against power," for that was too powerful a medicine for the novice. He must seek it on his own, in due time.

At the end of his instruction the boy received his water tube, for his lips must not touch the water; his scratcher, for it was taboo for a warrior to scratch himself with his fingers; and his novice cap. The cap was quite different from a warrior's cap, which was plainer and had eagle feathers on it. The novice cap had four different bird feathers: two hummingbird pinfeathers for speed; oriole breast feathers to keep the boy's mind clear; small quail breast feathers to scare the enemy; and downy eagle feathers for protection from harm.

"White men will be scared of that," the teacher said of the quail feathers. "You know how quail jump right out from under you and scare you."

The boy carried a bow and four wooden-pointed bird arrows. These arrows, meant just for hunting, not for war, were to remind the novice to forget war and keep his mind on the purpose of the raid.

When Beto led the party out of the village at dawn, the people lined the trail to put pollen over the novice and say prayers. They called out to him to say he would return in thirty days. When he replied that he would be back in that time, they knew it would come true. The novice made a gathering motion with his hands and declared: "These two things I must have in my mind—horses and cattle—so I would like to have those."

No one prayed for death to enemies, for this was a raid for booty; no one need die. The novice was never to think of such things. The people sang four happiness songs to him and called the young man "the Child of the Water." After four successful raids, he would be a warrior.

THE MOON WAS bright on the cold night Beto and his warriors came upon Johnny Ward's ranch in the narrow valley cut by Sonoita Creek. The ranch was rich in cattle and horses, so they watched and waited all night in the bluffs above the sprawling ranch house.

At dawn the raiders made their way down the rugged bluffs to the valley floor. Most of the men went on foot, but Beto and a few of his men followed on their ponies in order to round up the herd. They must have been puzzled but delighted over the lack of movement about the place. No men were visible, just a scrawny boy tending some sheep and goats across the creek to the west of the ranch house. The small herd of two dozen cattle grazed alongside the ditches Johnny Ward had dug to irrigate the little orchard of peach trees he had planted.

Nine warriors slowly approached the quiet ranch house while another group rounded up the cattle across the creek. Beto rode over to the little peach orchard near where the cattle grazed. A boy had climbed up into one of the small, bare trees in his fright. Usually the Apaches would kill a boy this age, either during a raid or later in the village. But Beto, for some reason, did not kill the boy. Instead he motioned for him to come down from the tree and climb up behind him on his horse. The one-eyed warrior could see that the boy also had but one eye. The boy's blind eye, recently hooked by a wounded deer, was not covered with a patch.

A sudden cry went up. Two riders were coming. The warriors charging the ranch house hurried back to their ponies while the others gathered in the cattle. Beto led the way north with the captive boy clinging to his back.

Two cowboys rode up to the ranch house to discover Modesto and the rest of the children unharmed. They then pursued the raiders in hopes of saving the boy. The Apaches quickly scattered, splitting into three groups. Beto instructed the novice to draw a line across their trail and say, "Let no one pass over this." A little farther on he was instructed to do this again and again, until he had done it four times. In this way they escaped the pursuing White Eyes.

Ward returned from Santa Cruz later that day to discover his stricken household. Modesto was inconsolable—her worst nightmare had come true. The Apaches who had preyed upon her ancestors, the Mexican people, for untold generations, who had made her once-thriving village into little more than a ghost town, who had slain her relatives and friends, had now taken her firstborn child. She pleaded with Ward to recover the lost boy.

LIEUTENANT COLONEL Pitcairn Morrison, at sixty-five, was far better suited to a rocking chair than a frontier command. But he had recently replaced Captain Ewell as commander of Fort Buchanan when he received word of the raid on Ward's ranch, just twelve miles south of his fort, on January 27, 1861. A boy and twenty head of cattle had been taken.

Morrison ordered Second Lieutenant George Nicholas Bascom, Seventh Infantry, with a small detachment of infantry and dragoons, to set out after the raiders the following morning. Bascom, a promising young officer from Kentucky who had graduated from West Point in 1858, followed an Apache trail headed northeast toward Apache Pass, but then lost it and returned to the fort. The trail, however, pointed toward the Chokonen village of Cochise near the narrow pass that separated the Chiricahua Mountains from the Dos Cabezas peaks. Bascom suspected Cochise's people of being the guilty raiders despite the fact that the great chief was, like his father-in-law, Mangas Coloradas, a peace advocate among the Apaches.

Johnny Ward arrived at Fort Buchanan the next day, demanding to know what Morrison planned to do to recover his boy and his cattle. Morrison's predecessor Ewell was long gone. Ewell's right-hand man, the able Lieutenant Isaiah Moore, along with two companies of the First Dragoons, had been ordered north to Fort Breckinridge, a new post on the San Pedro some sixty miles northeast of Tucson, in November. So it fell to the inexperienced Bascom to pursue the Apaches and rescue Felix Ward. Morrison's orders were quite clear. Bascom was to "pursue the Indians and recover a boy made captive by them" and was "authorized and instructed to use the force under his orders in recovering [him]." Bascom could use whatever force he deemed necessary to recover the lost boy.

APACHE PASS HAD the one thing all men sought in the desert—a dependable source of water. Apache Spring flowed into a small ravine that fed into Siphon Canyon, which in turn cut through the mountains to form a broad, sandy wash opening out to the wide San Simon Valley below. Some six miles from the valley, about halfway between the pass entrance and its exit into the Sulphur Springs Valley, was the Butterfield Overland Mail stagecoach station. This life-giving spring, about a quarter mile from the stage station, was quite an oasis along the barren overland trail. The road was steep and difficult, hemmed in by towering cliffs covered by piñon and juniper and bordered with oak, ash, hackberry, and willow. The rough road ascended from the station to Helen's Dome and the towering Dos Cabezas (two heads) peaks before descending fifteen miles out of the Chiricahua Mountains to the rolling tablelands below.

The Butterfield Overland Mail Company station was an integral part of the new mail system being built to provide a vital official link between the East and California. The first overland mail had been inaugurated on September 16, 1858, when an all-weather southern route had been selected by the US postmaster general. The federal mail contract, worth $600,000 a year plus some choice parcels of public land, had been awarded to John Butterfield, former stage driver, freight line operator, and cofounder of the American Express Company. Butterfield was required to carry passengers and deliver the mail semiweekly within a twenty-five-day one-way trip. Postage was ten cents per letter. Passenger fare from St. Louis to San Francisco was two hundred dollars one way. The total length of the contracted route was a bone-jarring 2,795 miles.

Butterfield's achievement was truly monumental. He carefully supervised the building of bridges, the grading of existing roads, and the digging of wells at the 141 stations that had to be established. Corrals, barns, and outbuildings were constructed, and then stocked with a thousand horses and five hundred mules. He employed eight hundred men in various capacities, from drivers to stock tenders to station managers. It was hard, dangerous work, but it provided the main artery of connection to "the states" of the far western settlements.

The stations were all built of local materials, which meant that the station at Apache Pass was built of adobe and stone. The corral was also made of stone, with portholes in each stall. An L-shaped building housed the kitchen and employee sleeping rooms. Two small rooms, a grain room and a storeroom, were located on the west end of the corral. It was built like a small fort, and sat in a precarious situation in the heart of Cochise's country. Its survival was dependent upon the goodwill of the mighty Chokonen chief.

Cochise, undoubtedly influenced by his father-in-law, Mangas Coloradas, was determined to keep peace with the Americans while actively pursuing raids into Mexico. He even assisted the Butterfield Overland Mail Company by supplying hay and wood to the Apache Pass station. On several occasions he returned stolen stock to the stage station and forbade his warriors to attack the mail coaches.

Stationmaster James Tevis knew Cochise well and had a rather jaded opinion of the chief. He admired Cochise's physical appearance: "Cochise was as fine a looking Indian as one ever saw. He was about six feet tall and as straight as an arrow, built from the ground up, as perfect as any man could be." But Tevis felt appearances to be deceptive. "At first appearance a man would think he was inclined to be peaceable to Americans but he is far from it," Tevis told the Tucson newspaper in 1859. "For eight months I have watched him, and have come to the conclusion that he is the biggest liar in the territory! And would kill an American for any trifle, provided he thought it wouldn't be found out."

Born in 1810 deep in the Chiricahua Mountains, Cochise, the son of the Chokonen band leader Relles, had grown up during a period of relative peace. His Apache name was Goci, which meant simply "his nose," because of his large Roman nose. He was often called Chees by both Apaches and Americans, but Cochise eventually became the name used by all. He married at least twice, and his second and principal wife was Dos-teh-seh, the daughter of Mangas Coloradas. Although by Chiricahua custom a man should live with his wife's people, Cochise was already too important a leader to leave his Chokonen band. Dos-teh-seh bore Cochise two sons—Taza and Naiche.

Relles, the father of Cochise, had been killed by James Kirker's scalp hunters in the 1846 Galeana Massacre. Cochise was part of the war party that slaughtered the people of Galeana in revenge, and from that day forth, he led countless raids against the hated Mexicans. By 1856 he had emerged as the leading Chokonen chief and second only to Mangas Coloradas as a leader of the Chiricahua people.

Cochise usually camped in Goodwin Canyon, about a mile north of the Apache Pass stage station, and often visited with the stationmaster Tevis. They kept up a cordial but sometimes testy relationship that mirrored Cochise's increasing frustration over the American invasion of his homeland. As tensions mounted throughout the spring of 1860, Tevis departed Apache Pass to follow the lure of gold to the old copper mines at Santa Rita del Cobre. A gold discovery in May 1860 had set off a stampede. The miners named their strike Pinos Altos for the tall ponderosa pines around it, and within weeks hundreds of men swarmed over the country of Mangas Coloradas. The old chief, determined to keep the peace with the Americans, visited Pinos Altos on occasion to trade and to reaffirm his friendship with all Americans. Other Apache leaders, including Cochise, were not so optimistic.

LIEUTENANT GEORGE BASCOM was a young man in a hurry. The abduction of the Ward boy presented Bascom with exactly the sort of opportunity for distinction he was hoping for. Major Morrison's orders had given Bascom wide latitude of action in recovering the boy and the cattle.

On Tuesday, January 29, 1861, Bascom rode out of Fort Buchanan at the head of fifty-four infantrymen, all mounted on mules. Antonio Bonillas, the post interpreter, accompanied the column, as did Johnny Ward. Bascom made directly for Apache Pass, crossing over the flat Sulphur Springs Valley along the Overland Mail road and up into the mountains. If one pressed his animals hard it was but a two- or three-day ride from Fort Buchanan to Apache Pass, but Bascom advanced with some caution, carefully scouting the country. The young officer and his soldiers reached the stage station early on Sunday afternoon, where they discovered a thirteen-man detachment camped just to the south of the stage station. Sergeant Daniel Robinson was returning with four empty wagons after delivering supplies to Fort McLane on the Mimbres River. Bascom, delighted to acquire these extra men along with the veteran sergeant, ordered Robinson to move his wagons down Siphon Canyon to join his camp just to the southeast of the stage station.

Charles Culver, who had recently replaced Tevis as station manager, had two additional Butterfield employees with him: his assistant Robert Welch and stage driver James Wallace. Bascom asked Wallace, who was quite friendly with Cochise, to take a message to the chief requesting a parley. Cochise was encamped only a mile away and soon sent word that he would meet with Bascom the following day.

The next day the soldiers were settling down for their dinner, as the noon meal was then called, when Cochise arrived. The chief, oblivious to any danger, had brought with him his wife Dos-teh-seh and six-year-old son, Naiche; brother Coyuntura; as well as three young warriors and another child. Bascom asked Cochise and Coyuntura to join him in his tent for dinner. The other Apaches were invited to eat in the Sibley tent of the soldiers.

As Cochise and Coyuntura entered his tent, Bascom called Sergeant Robinson over to him. He ordered him to bring in the military herd and secure the mules to the wagons. When Robinson departed, he heard Bascom order the sergeant of the guard to post sentinels around the tents. No Apaches were to leave without Bascom's consent.

Bascom offered the Apaches some coffee but wasted little time on other pleasantries. With Johnny Ward acting as interpreter, he demanded that Cochise release the captive boy and restore the stolen cattle. Cochise, in broken Spanish, truthfully replied that he did not have the boy but, if given time, would try to find where he was. He told Bascom he suspected the Coyoteros north of the Gila. Bascom then told Ward to tell Cochise that he and the rest of his people would be held as hostages until the boy was returned.

As Ward translated his words into Spanish, Cochise and Coyuntura acted as one. They sprang away from Bascom and Ward and turned toward the tent opening, only to find it blocked by the bayoneted muskets of the guards. Cochise pivoted to the back of the tent and cut it open with his knife.

"Shoot them down!" Bascom shouted as Cochise leapt from the tent.

Ward pulled his pistol and fired, wounding Cochise in the leg. The chief scrambled up the side of the canyon wall, trailing blood as he dodged back and forth from boulder to boulder. Siphon Canyon echoed with musket fire as several of the soldiers fired after him.

Sergeant Robinson was herding in the mules when he heard Ward's initial pistol shot. He stopped, confused, then was startled by a young Apache running past him with a soldier right behind him. Robinson watched as the warrior stopped, wheeled around, and threw stones at the soldier. The Apache disappeared behind some boulders as the soldier pursued, then suddenly appeared and hurled himself at the man. A musket blast stopped him in mid-stride.

Back at the camp, another warrior tried to escape but a bayonet thrust pinned him to the ground. Coyuntura and the other Apache prisoners were quickly herded into one of the tents at bayonet point. From the ridgetop Cochise looked down on the soldier camp. Only then did he realize that he had been wounded in the leg and that, inexplicably, he still carried a tin coffee cup in his hand.

AN HOUR LATER, Cochise appeared again on the ridgeline above the army camp. He called down to Bascom to bring out Coyuntura to prove he was still alive. He promised that if his people were released, no vengeance would be taken. But Bascom ordered the nearest soldiers to unleash a volley at the Apache chief, in response to which Cochise extended his hands to the heavens and swore revenge. "Indian blood was as good as white man's blood!" he roared. Then he vanished.

The young lieutenant suddenly seemed to realize just what he had done. Wallace, the stage driver, was enraged by Bascom's actions and berated the lieutenant in front of the men. Bascom, totally unnerved, ordered his men to break camp and move down to the stout stone walls of the stage station. Sergeant Robinson pointed out that they would need water from the spring farther up the canyon, but Bascom feared an ambush there.

"Lieutenant, one may better be shot than die of thirst," Robinson replied. "I will go to the spring."

Robinson brought back several canteens filled with water, then later returned to the spring with a burro to secure two kegs of water. At dusk, as the men settled in at the stage station, they saw the orange glow of Apache signal fires on every surrounding mountain peak. It would be a very long night.

The signal fires brought Geronimo and dozens of Bedonkohe warriors to the village of Cochise. Francisco, a White Mountain Apache leader who had often raided into Mexico with Cochise, came in with another large party of warriors. To them all, this day would forever be known as the time Cochise "cut the tent."

Mangas Coloradas soon arrived with a large following of warriors as well. Cochise must have been concerned over what his father-in-law would do, for Mangas had devoted fifteen years of his life to keeping the peace with the Americans. Cochise need not have worried. Mangas listened to Cochise, then turned his back and dropped his blanket to reveal a lacerated, deeply scarred back.

A month earlier he had gone alone to the gold camp at Santa Rita del Cobre to tell the miners, quite truthfully, that there were far richer veins to the west in the mountain homeland of the Yavapais and Tontos. Victorio, the Warm Springs leader, and Geronimo had both pleaded with him not to go. Old Nana, the wise Chihenne war leader, had held forth two coins, one of gold and the other of silver, and offered a solemn prophecy: "The Mexicans and the greedy White Eyes are superstitious about this stuff. The love of life is strong in all people, but to them it is not so strong as their greed for gold. For it, they risk their lives." Still, Mangas was determined to go alone to Pinos Altos.

The Warm Springs Apache Kaywaykla, a nephew of Nana, later described what happened on that fateful day at Pinos Altos:

The White Eyes bound him to a tree and lashed him with ox goads until his back was striped with deep cuts. He crept away like a wounded animal to let his wounds heal. He went to his favorite camping site—near the Ojo Caliente, and there he stayed until the wounds had healed. Victorio knew; he knew too that the chief must not know that he did lest his heart break with shame. Never before had anyone struck him, and there is no humiliation worse than that of a whip.

At Pinos Altos the white miners had laughed and whooped as the old chief staggered away into the trees beyond the camp. It would have been better for them to have killed him, for now Mangas Coloradas pledged to join with Cochise to fight the White Eyes in a war to the death.

THE SOLDIERS AT Apache Pass awoke to see the surrounding hills ringed with hundreds of warriors. A single Apache approached under a white flag to request a parley. Cochise wished to meet with Bascom on the stage road some hundred yards from the station. Bascom agreed, providing that no more than three warriors accompany Cochise and all be unarmed. The lieutenant then ordered his soldiers to man the station's stone wall and open fire at the first sign of treachery. Robinson had parked the wagons on the southwest side of the station, and the men had filled grain sacks for breastworks and dug trenches around the wagons and the station. Sacks of grain were also placed atop the station house to form a covering breastwork behind which the company's best shots were placed.

Bascom handed a white flag to Sergeant William Smith, and along with Johnny Ward and Sergeant Robinson, the three men sallied forth to meet Cochise. Four unarmed Apaches, led by Cochise, emerged from a deep ravine about a hundred yards distant and slowly walked toward the soldiers.

Erect and majestic in his fiftieth year, Cochise wasted few words on Bascom. The bearded but still baby-faced twenty-five-year-old soldier seemed insignificant to him. He demanded that Bascom immediately release the hostages. Bascom refused to do so unless the Ward boy was returned. With Johnny Ward again translating, Cochise reiterated that he did not have the boy, but promised to search for him as soon as his people were released.

While the two men talked, Robinson caught sight of considerable movement in the nearby ravine. Apaches, their heads and shoulders covered with cedar brush, were slowly making their way along the ravine as if to set up firing positions flanking Bascom's little group. Bascom also noticed but made no mention of it to Cochise.

Simultaneously, the stage driver Wallace, Cochise's friend, along with Culver and Welch, suddenly appeared above the parley group at the head of the ravine. They had walked a circuitous route to the southeast of the stage station to get a better view of the parley. Bascom saw them and ordered them back to the stage station, but almost at the same moment Apaches from the ravine rushed them. Wallace was carried away but Culver and Welch broke downhill for the station.

Cochise and his men rushed back to the ravine as the soldiers at the stage station opened fire. Bascom's party cut to the west at a dead run to escape the Apaches as well as dodge friendly fire from the station. Welch was not so lucky, taking a soldier's bullet through the head just before he reached the station. The Apaches in the ravine opened fire as well, wounding both Sergeant Smith and Culver. They both staggered behind the stone walls and collapsed. Ward was also wounded, either during the race for life or after he reached the station. The Apaches kept up sporadic sniping until dusk.

That night the fires once again glowed from the mountaintops. The besieged soldiers could hear the drums of a war dance mixed with the wails of the newly widowed Apache women. Robinson was certain that several warriors had been slain, but there were no celebrations at the stage station.

THE NEXT MORNING passed without any sign of the Apaches. At noon Sergeant Robinson and a handful of men led the thirsty mules up the six hundred potentially deadly yards to the spring. They arrived uneventfully, and hopes began to rise that the Apaches had withdrawn.

At noon, Cochise appeared on the high hill directly overlooking the stage station. Wallace was with him, a rope around his neck and his hands bound behind his back. When Bascom again demanded the return of Felix Ward, the chief dragged his prisoner away and vanished beyond the hill.

The next day, at about three o'clock, the overland stage from the east arrived at the Apache Pass station. The stage was, luckily for the occupants, several hours ahead of schedule. Driver A. B. Culver, the brother of the station manager, was oblivious to any danger but became perplexed by the great quantity of hay spread across the road not far from the station. Cochise had intended to set the hay on fire to block the road and capture the coach, but he and his warriors had then been distracted by an even more tempting prize.

A wagon train, loaded with flour intended for the miners at Pinos Altos, was laboring up the trail from the Sulphur Springs Valley to the summit of Apache Pass. Cochise's scouts had discovered a perfect mission for Geronimo. At dusk the wagons were corralled near the crest of the trail some two miles west of the stage station. Geronimo and his warriors attacked just at dark, quickly overwhelming the eleven men and capturing the five wagons. Six Hispanic teamsters were killed before Cochise halted the slaughter. Frank Brunner, a German immigrant; William Sanders, a mixed-blood Cherokee; Sam Whitfield; and two Hispanic teamsters were taken captive.

Cochise had the three white men bound so they could watch as their Hispanic companions were lashed to the wheels of the wagons. The chief had obviously decided that only the white men had bargaining value. Geronimo's men then set fire to the wagons. The reflective glow from the fire could be seen in the clouds above the stage station, but the distance was too great to be able to hear the screams of the roasting men.

Later that night, Cochise instructed Wallace to write a note to Bascom. It read: "Treat my people well and I will do the same by yours, of whom I have three." He then dispatched a warrior to tie the note to some brush where it could be seen from the stage station. Cochise was desperate: his wife and son, as well as his brother and two nephews, were in Bascom's hands. Family was central to everything important in Chiricahua life. It was the same for Mangas: his daughter and grandson were held captive at the stage station. But the soldiers did not see the note, and two critical days passed before they found it.

On Thursday morning, February 7, the eastbound stage departed from Tucson. Driver King Lyons was hauling a full load of eight passengers along with the US mail. It was a fairly distinguished group, including William Buckley, superintendent of the Overland Mail route; Nelson Davis, the stage conductor; W. S. Grant, the supply contractor for Fort Buchanan; and Lieutenant John Rogers Cooke, on furlough from the Eighth Infantry and returning home to Virginia to resign his commission in anticipation of civil war.

It was after midnight before Lyons urged his footsore mules over the crest of the mountain at the western entrance to Apache Pass. A sudden volley out of the darkness raked the stage. One of the mules was shot and fell in his tracks and the stage lurched to a sudden halt. Lyons jumped down to cut loose the stricken mule and immediately went down from a bullet that shattered his leg. Buckley staggered out of the stage to a scene of pure horror. The coach was in the middle of the wagon train massacre site, with mutilated bodies strewn about and the whole scene dimly illuminated by the embers of the burning wagons. Directly in front of Buckley were the charred bodies of the teamsters tied to the wagon wheels. He had no time to process it all, as the crack of gunfire and whizzing sound of incoming arrows spurred him to action. Spits of flame from the Apache guns came out of the darkness as several other passengers piled out of the coach. Lieutenant Cooke opened a covering fire as Buckley and Davis cut the traces on the dead mule. Others pulled the wounded driver into the coach as Buckley mounted the seat and lashed the team with his whip. As the stage jerked forward, the Apaches unleashed another volley.

The stage careened down the mountain road, swaying back and forth as it bounced over boulders placed in the roadway by the Apaches, hell-for-leather in a mad two-mile dash to the stage station. A mile down the road, they discovered that a small stone bridge erected by the stage company had been dismantled by the Apaches. The center board had been removed and only the stone abutments at each end and the underside support beams remained.

Cochise's warriors waited here, opening a desultory fire on the approaching stage. As Cooke and the other passengers blazed away from inside the coach into the darkness, Buckley cracked his whip at the struggling team of mules. He did not see the destroyed bridge in the darkness until it was too late. It was suicide to stop and insane to cross. Buckley lashed the mules as Apache gunfire echoed across the little arroyo. The terrified animals jumped the chasm as the axles of the stage slid across the outside bridge supports. They bounced across and back onto the road and pulled into the stage station at two that morning. One of the wheel mules died on the spot.

THE ARRIVAL OF the two stages had added considerably to the besieged population at the Apache Pass station. The next day Bascom reluctantly decided to send for help. It was an admission of failure, but he was in desperate need of medical assistance for his own men as well as the three wounded civilians. Stage driver A. B. Culver volunteered to ride to Tucson, while five soldiers stepped forward to volunteer for the dangerous journey west to Fort Buchanan. The soldiers wrapped the hooves of their mules with cloth to muffle the sound and departed after dark. They met with no resistance and so reached Fort Buchanan late the following evening. Culver reached Tucson at about the same time.

Culver reported to William Sanders Oury, agent for the Butterfield Overland Mail Company and one of the most notable citizens of Tucson. Born in Virginia in 1817, he had migrated to Texas in 1834 just in time to join the independence movement. He claimed to have been a messenger sent out just before the fall of the Alamo and to have fought alongside Sam Houston at San Jacinto on April 21, 1836, although the record on both stories is murky. He certainly served as a Texas Ranger in campaigns against the Comanches and as a scout during the Mexican War. With his brother Granville, he traveled by wagon train to Tucson in 1856. Three years later the *Tucson Weekly Arizonian* characterized him as a man "possessing a high tone of character, and unyielding will, with conservative principles." He was also a recklessly bold man of action who left a bloody handprint on the history of both Texas and Arizona.

Oury immediately sent a messenger off to Fort Breckinridge

requesting assistance. The next morning, Saturday, February 9, Oury headed out with a coach and four heavily armed companions. Oury caught up with Lieutenant Isaiah Moore and two companies of dragoons about six miles west of the pass.

Meanwhile, at Fort Buchanan, Lieutenant Colonel Morrison had few troops to spare. Assistant Surgeon Bernard J. D. Irwin, knowing that there were wounded men with Bascom, volunteered to go. Bascom's messengers all volunteered to go back with Irwin, as did eleven men from H Company. Morrison sent a messenger to Fort Breckinridge requesting assistance from the dragoons and sent another to nearby Casa Blanca to enlist Paddy Graydon. Graydon, a jovial but tough Irishman, had seen hard service with Ewell's dragoons before opening a saloon and was always anxious for adventure. As soon as the Irishman arrived, the detachment mounted their mules and departed for Apache Pass. Despite a fierce snowstorm, they covered sixty-five miles the first day, camping at Dragoon Springs that night. Irwin was delighted to have Graydon with his little command, later writing in his official report that "his character for daring and courage needs no commendation at my hands."

The messengers had been able to escape safely that night because the Apaches had been busy preparing to assault the stage station the next morning. Cochise sent the Apache families deeper into the mountains while he and his warriors danced and performed the necessary ceremonies in preparation for battle.

ALL WAS QUIET at the stage station on Friday morning, but Bascom began to wonder if the Apaches had not actually departed. He sent a small scouting party up to the hill above the station, and they soon gave the all-clear signal. It had snowed that night, so Bascom waited for the noon sun to dry the ground a bit before sending a party to the spring to water the stock. Since the spring could not be seen from the station, Bascom put a sentinel atop what he now called Overlook Ridge, above the main road. The snow had not been disturbed, so the soldiers moved out with a relaxed sense of confidence.

Cochise watched from the distant ridgeline and waited. His plan was simple. Once the soldiers reached the spring, his warriors would strike. When the men from the station rushed to their rescue, he would send a second group against the station and free his family. Mangas, Francisco, and Geronimo all led groups of carefully concealed warriors.

Sergeant Robinson, who was leading the party to water, suddenly noticed considerable movement in a ravine about three hundred yards from the spring. The warriors were crouched low and moving fast. The faint sound of their war song reached Robinson just as he yelled the alarm. Suddenly the ridge on the opposite side of the ravine was alive with another large band of Apaches. Robinson shouted for the men at the spring to fall back, and just then the warriors on the ridge opened fire. Robinson's greatcoat was riddled with bullets and one lodged just below his knee. The sergeant gritted his teeth against the pain and carefully reloaded his weapon. If he was going down, he planned on taking several Apaches with him.

At the stage station Bascom turned to Lieutenant John Rogers Cooke, future brigadier general in the army of the Confederate States of America. Although Cooke outranked Bascom, he had graciously placed himself under the young lieutenant's command upon reaching the stage station. Bascom asked Cooke to take a small relief party to the spring, while he retained most of the men in case of an attack on the station. Cooke hurried up the ravine to cover the retreat of the watering party and rescue Sergeant Robinson. All forty-two military mules along with fourteen Butterfield mules were scattered, soon to be corralled by Cochise's warriors.

As Cooke's men fought a short but hot skirmish at the spring, Cochise led his remaining men against the station. Bascom had not taken his bait. The bulk of the soldiers remained behind the station's stone walls and opened up a lively fire on the Apaches. Cochise could ill afford to throw away the lives of his warriors in a frontal assault and promptly pulled his men back. His plan had failed.

Irwin's Fort Buchanan relief party camped overnight at Dragoon Springs and then pressed on along the Overland Mail road on Sunday morning, February 10. Along the desolate Playa de los Pimos, on the eastern edge of the Sulphur Springs Valley, the soldiers saw a distant dust cloud. It turned out to be a raiding party of Coyotero Apaches heading north with stolen cattle and horses.

This was made to order for Paddy Graydon. The former dragoon led the mule-mounted infantry in a wild seven-mile chase that captured thirteen cattle, three horses, and most important, three of the Apache raiders. Graydon had the Coyotero warriors bound, then proceeded on with the cattle and horses toward Apache Pass. This strange caravan reached the stage station later that evening. Wild cheers erupted as the besieged men welcomed Irwin, the desperately needed doctor, who had brought not only medical care but also reinforcements and beef for dinner.

Four days later, Lieutenant Moore and his two dragoon companies, along with Oury and his men, reached the stage station. Bascom had remained immobile since Irwin's arrival, fearful to venture away from his fortified position. He did not know that Cochise and his warriors had scattered after the Friday battle.

MOORE WAS NOW the ranking officer at Apache Pass. He organized a reconnaissance-in-force on February 16 to explore the nearby mountains for Apaches. They found an abandoned Apache *rancheria* but otherwise saw no sign of Cochise. On the third day, Dr. Irwin and Oury noticed circling buzzards in the distance and rode over with a small party to investigate. Not far from the Overland Mail road, they discovered four butchered bodies. The corpses were so riddled with lance wounds that they had probably been unrecognizable even before the vultures had feasted on them. But Oury, who knew Wallace well, was able to identify the stage driver's body by the gold fillings in his teeth. Wallace, despite his friendship with Cochise, had been tortured to death along with the prisoners from the wagon train. Neither Irwin nor Oury had been present when Cochise had dragged Wallace away from the stage station after the failed parley with Bascom, and it was now impossible to tell just when he and the others had been killed. As several dragoons rode back to the stage station to get shovels, Oury and the officers searched for a suitable burial site. Not far from the stage road, near the charred vestiges of the wagon train, they selected a small hill studded with oak trees as a burial ground.

Lieutenant Moore went straight to Bascom to inform him that he had decided to hang the Apache prisoners. Bascom protested— the prisoners were his responsibility, and he was determined to deliver them to Fort Buchanan. The prisoners were the only tangible result of his failed mission to rescue the lost boy. Irwin now joined in the debate, stating that three of the prisoners were his and that he intended to hang them. Bascom pressed his argument, but Moore pulled rank on him. The Apaches were to hang and he would take full responsibility.

In a macabre twist, a pack of cards was produced and a game of seven-up proposed to settle this disagreement between officers and gentlemen. Dos-teh-seh watched this, confused by what the White Eyes were doing. Somehow she understood that the card game was to decide her fate, as well as that of Naiche and the other little boy. One of the infantrymen noted that the card game was over whether to hang the Apache men or not. The game was won by Lieutenant Moore. The Apache prisoners would hang.

The next morning, Bascom assigned a dozen men to remain behind and guard the stage station. Then the combined commands of Bascom and Moore, along with the civilians and the Apache prisoners, climbed westward up the stage road. When they came to the grove of oak trees near the summit of Apache Pass, Bascom told Ward to inform the Apaches of their fate.

Coyuntura asked that they be shot rather than hanged, but Bascom refused. The dragoons tossed six lariats over the sturdy limbs of the four big oaks as Coyuntura began to dance and sing his death song. The other warriors began to sing as well. The ropes were placed around the warriors' necks, and on Bascom's command, groups of soldiers pulled the men upward to strangle. "The Indians were hoisted so high by the infantry," Sergeant Robinson observed, "that even the wolves could not touch them." Dos-teh-seh and Naiche were forced to watch.

Robinson, along with the other wounded men in Oury's coach, had mixed feelings: "It was a sad spectacle to look upon. An illustration of the Indian's sense of Justice: 'That the innocent must suffer for the guilty.' And the white man's notion—'That the only good Indians are dead ones.'"

The group then parted ways. Bascom, Irwin, Graydon, and the infantrymen returned to Fort Buchanan, Moore's two dragoon companies went back to Fort Breckinridge, and Oury and the civilians returned to Tucson. Upon reaching the fort, Lieutenant Bascom filed a self-serving and duplicitous account of the affair, which was readily accepted by Morrison and passed up through military channels. Bascom and Irwin were both officially commended by the department commander for their "excellent conduct" at Apache Pass and for the hanging of the six prisoners. Bascom was promoted to captain and Irwin was later awarded the Medal of Honor for leading the rescue column.

Dos-teh-seh, Naiche, and the other boy were briefly held in the Fort Buchanan guardhouse. The soldiers, not realizing that they held the wife and son of Cochise, soon released the three captives. In early March 1861 the three made their way south to Mexico, where Cochise was encamped near Fronteras.

Charles Poston summed up the feelings of most Arizona residents concerning the debacle at Apache Pass when he wrote: "The cost of the war against Cochise would have purchased John Ward a string of yokes of oxen reaching from the Atlantic to the Pacific; and as for his woman's son, Mickey Free, he afterwards became an Indian scout and interpreter, and about as infamous a scoundrel as those who generally adorn that profession."

At Apache Pass, the bodies of the six warriors hung precariously from the four oak trees for days, then weeks, and then months. The Apaches, in fear of the spirits of the dead, avoided the place. They would not touch the bodies. The wolves and coyotes took turns engaging in a leaping dance beneath the bodies in hopes of pulling them down—but they had been hanged too high. The ravens plucked out their eyes, and the owls and vultures fed upon their flesh. As spring turned to summer the unrelenting sun scorched the ropes by which they hung until, finally, they snapped and the bodies tumbled to the ground. Then the ants marched forth to consume what was left. The rains of August swept away the bleached bones, and all that was left of the six Apaches vanished back into the desert sands over which they had once so freely roamed.

4

APACHE PASS

BETO TOOK THE CAPTIVE ONE-EYED BOY NORTH OF the Gila to Eskiminzin's village in Aravaipa Canyon, where the people would feast on Johnny Ward's cattle and celebrate the successful raid. Beto soon sold, traded, or gifted the boy to Eskiminzin, the stout principal chief of the Aravaipa Apaches, for it was the duty of the leader of a raid to be generous. Eskiminzin was a Pinal Apache who had married the daughter of Chief Santos of the Aravaipa. As Santos grew older, Eskiminzin had risen to be the band leader of around 150 Aravaipa people. His Apache name was Hashkibanzin, which translated as "Angry, Men Stand in Line for Him," and denoted his well-earned reputation as a warrior. There was something about the skinny, five-foot-tall, one-eyed boy that led Eskiminzin and the Aravaipa to enslave him instead of killing him outright.

Felix's new home, hemmed in by canyon walls and given life by running water, was not unlike the ranch on Sonoita Creek. Ash, cottonwood, willow, and towering sycamores shaded the creek banks, providing a rich habitat for every sort of native bird, from hummingbirds to desert wrens to hawks and eagles. Deer roamed throughout the canyon floor, while desert bighorn sheep climbed the steep canyon walls amid the saguaro cactus, cholla, and yucca. Cougars and wolves preyed on the deer, and coyotes cleaned up after them. This land provided the "black rocks people" almost everything they needed, and what it did not provide, they took from others.

The "black rocks people" of the Aravaipa were Western Apaches, often mistakenly called Pinals or Coyoteros by the whites. Although they were closely related to them and had strong family connections with the White Mountain people to the north, the Aravaipa had developed subtle differences in speech and cultural practices due to their geographic isolation from these other groups. This sense of place gave each band a particular identity, and it also meant that there was never any concept of the Apaches as one people, not even among the Western Apache bands, and certainly not with the Chiricahuas, Mescaleros, or Jicarillas.

Adahay, a White Mountain Apache married to an Aravaipa man, remembered when Felix first came to Eskiminzin's village in Aravaipa Canyon. "Only Apache know how to follow that canyon," Adahay's great-granddaughter Mary Velasques Riley remembered her saying. "She used to say 'that's a *Nakaiye,* a captured Mexican,' but by who or how she didn't say," Mary recalled. "My mother and dad used to talk about how Mickey was captured; Mickey say, 'When I was captured, I was on a peach tree.'"

Among Eskiminzin's people, the boy remained an outsider, a *Nakaiye,* and a slave. He did as he was told, learned their ways, their language, and how to stay alive. Although the captive boy never found acceptance among the Aravaipa, he was not despised by them, either. Among the Chiricahuas, however, an abiding hatred against him endured for generations. Kaywaykla, of the Warm Springs Apaches, spoke for all Chiricahuas when he declared that "though the trouble was precipitated by the ignorance and arrogance of a young officer, it was occasioned by the abduction of Mickey Free by other Apaches than Cochise's men, and indirectly the child was held to be responsible." To the Chiricahuas, the boy would always be "the coyote whose kidnapping had brought war to the Chiricahua."

Felix had not been with the Aravaipa for long when, only a few months after his capture, a child was born to one of the warriors there, Toga-de-chuz, and his wife. The baby boy became a member of Captain Chiquito's band and would grow up among the protective rocks of the canyon that gave the "black rocks" name to the Aravaipa. One day, this child, much like Felix, would influence the

destiny of all the Apache people. He came to be known by many
names. The Apaches called him both Has-kay-bay-nay-ntayl and
Ski-be-nan-ted. He seemed to them to live a charmed life from an
early age. The Americans came to know him first only as Kid, and
then as the last of the great lords of Apacheria—the Apache Kid.

WITHIN SIXTY DAYS of "cut the tent," the Apaches seemed to
strike everywhere. Cochise's warriors hit five stage stations, repeatedly attacked the mail coaches, and swept through the Santa
Cruz Valley killing 150 of the hated White Eyes, including Charles
Poston's brother. The Apaches ambushed an army patrol not far
from Fort Buchanan, killing one soldier and driving the others off.
In early June, Cochise's warriors rounded up the entire Fort Buchanan herd of ten mules and twenty-three cattle that were grazing
just south of the post near Casa Blanca.

Mangas Coloradas was equally busy in the Pinos Altos area and
along the Overland Mail road. Joined by Victorio's warriors, Mangas ran off with all the stock at Fort McLane, attacked a party of
Hispanic freighters near Pinos Altos and took all their mules, killed
an American at a hay camp near the mines, and drove the handful of farmers out of the Mimbres River Valley. Mangas still had a
score to settle with the miners at Pinos Altos, but that would have
to wait until after his warriors shut down the Overland Mail road.

By June 1861, the combined forces of Mangas and Cochise had
all but closed the road between Mesilla and Tucson. The demise
of John Butterfield's Overland Mail, however, came not as a result
of Apache raiders but because of secessionist politicians. With the
withdrawal of Texas from the Union on February 1, 1861, Butterfield's bold enterprise was doomed. Texans began to raid stations,
steal stock, and even destroy the bridges built by the company.
Unionists in Congress, never happy with the southern mail route,
voted in March 1861 to shift the Overland Mail to a central route
from St. Joseph, Missouri, to Sacramento, California. On March
6, 1861, two days after Abraham Lincoln's inauguration, the Butterfield Overland Mail came to a halt. As a temporary measure

to keep mail service open to California, a pony relay service was established between St. Joseph and Sacramento—they called it the Pony Express.

El Paso was the largest station on Butterfield's nearly defunct Overland Mail route. A station manager there named Freeman Thomas was determined to escape from the rebels and deliver all remaining Butterfield records, funds, and mail in the final coach to California. He recruited six companions for this dangerous journey. The men slipped out of El Paso, dodging rebel patrols, and reached Mesilla on July 19, 1861. They left the next morning and reached the Cooke's Canyon stage station just east of the Mimbres River at dusk.

Mangas and Cochise waited in the canyon west of the station with two hundred warriors. At dawn, the little party of frontiersmen had only traveled about a mile when the Apaches opened fire. The stage driver turned his team off the road and up a little hill, where the whites adopted Apache tactics by throwing up rocks to build a *refugio*. Thomas had the coach stripped of everything essential and then sent the mules galloping back down the hill. He hoped the Apaches might be satisfied with the mules and coach. He was wrong. This was not a raid. This was war.

The Apaches unleashed a torrent of arrows backed up with musket fire and the Americans responded with well-aimed fire from their new Sharps carbines and Colt revolvers. Well supplied with guns, ammunition, and courage, Thomas's handful fought off the Apaches for three long days.

The Butterfield men killed twenty warriors and wounded many more, including Cochise's son Taza. For the Chiricahuas to take such losses was unheard-of. Now they were compelled to keep fighting to avenge their dead. Finally the remaining Americans, by now out of water, made an attempt to break out. All were killed. The last man left a trail of blood and shell casings as he crawled from boulder to boulder firing his final rounds.

Both Mangas and Cochise later spoke of the bravery of the seven White Eyes in this battle. Mangas admitted to the deaths of more than twenty warriors. Cochise told an American official that "with twenty-five such men he would undertake to whip the whole United States."

James Tevis, on his way from Pinos Altos to Mesilla to enlist in the rebel army, found the bodies of these brave men a few days later. Tevis and his companions were amazed at the battle scene, for every rock was pocked with bullet marks. The seven white men had all been stripped and horribly mutilated. The nervous rebels buried the bodies and hurried onward to Mesilla.

The Chiricahuas headed south to Janos. There they traded the gold watches and other goods looted from the dead Americans for guns and ammunition and sought medical care for their wounded, but were soon on their way back to Cooke's Canyon.

ON JULY 9, 1861, an express rider reached Fort Buchanan with orders to abandon the post and retreat to Fort Fillmore on the Rio Grande. Lieutenant Moore soon arrived with his two dragoon companies from the abandoned and burned Fort Breckinridge to join the two companies of the Seventh Infantry on their eastward trek. After the April attack on Fort Sumter off the South Carolina coast the Lincoln administration had decided to recall all troops to the East to meet the rebel threat. While the Freeman Thomas party had been battling for their lives in Cooke's Canyon, the very soldiers who had started this war were preparing to abandon them and the people of Arizona.

As the troops departed on July 23, they torched Fort Buchanan and all the supplies they had left behind. Orders were orders. It was the desire of the government to destroy property rather than turn it over to the citizens of Arizona, for they feared the citizens and their rebel sympathies even more than they feared the Apaches. Moore's orders were to have his men march with weapons loaded and not allow any citizens to approach his column.

The game was up, and the now unprotected Americans along the Sonoita and the Santa Cruz quickly packed and left their fields. Johnny Ward took the remainder of his family into Tucson. Paddy Graydon abandoned Casa Blanca. Tubac, besieged by a large Coyotero war party, was soon abandoned as well. Most of the Mexican mine and ranch workers fled south to Sonora. The remaining settlers at Canoa were slaughtered by the Apaches in late July. To make matters worse, a large party of Mexican bandits came north to loot the abandoned mines and ranches.

Charles Poston also finally gave up on his Arizona dream and headed for Yuma. Poston was struck by the lonesome sound of cocks crowing on the deserted farms as smoke from the burning wheat fields filled the sky. "It was sad to leave the country that had cost so much money and blood in ruins, but it seemed to be inevitable," he lamented.

The exodus took on biblical proportions when, in mid-August, a large party of settlers from the Santa Cruz and Sonoita painfully lumbered eastward in their ox-drawn wagons herding their remaining stock. They avoided Apache Pass, for signal fires on the ridgelines lit the evening sky. A few young men were sent to the pass for water. They saw no sign of Apaches save for the rags still clinging to the skeletons of the six warriors hanging from the oaks near the summit of the trail.

By August fewer than sixty Americans were still in Tucson. The farms and ranches along the Sonoita and Santa Cruz were all abandoned, as were all the mines, save one near the border. The Apaches had successfully thrown back the advance of the American frontier.

Cochise and Mangas were certain that the retreat of the soldiers, miners, and settlers was because of the war they had unleashed on the White Eyes. "We were successful," Cochise later proclaimed to an American official, "and your soldiers were driven away and your people killed and we again possessed our land."

Not satisfied with their victory, Cochise and Mangas returned to Cooke's Canyon with their warriors to await the American wagon train that had departed Tucson on August 15, 1861. The party was large, with twenty-four men, sixteen women, and seven children, but still undermanned to protect the animal herd they were driving if the Apaches should attack.

On August 27, the Apaches sprang their ambush. Those defending the wagon train were just barely holding out when Captain

Thomas Mastin and Lieutenant Jack Swilling of the Arizona Guards led their thirty-five-man detachment to the rescue. Mastin, who had organized his men to defend Pinos Altos once the federal troops withdrew, had since attached his unit to the Confederate army. The rebels now galloped to the rescue of the besieged settlers in Cooke's Canyon, routed the Apaches, and inflicted severe casualties on them. Mastin's men delivered the remnants of the wagon train safely to the Rio Grande settlements and then hurried back to Pinos Altos. They returned there not a moment too soon.

AFTER THE BATTLE at Cooke's Canyon, Mangas was more determined than ever to destroy the miners at Pinos Altos who had whipped and shamed him. He called on his son-in-law to gather his warriors and Cochise brought both Chokonens and Nednhis north from Mexico to join with the Bedonkohes and Chihennes assembled by Mangas in the Mogollon Mountains.

On the morning of September 27, 1861, Cochise and Mangas unleashed more than two hundred warriors against Pinos Altos. The mining camp was spread out, with groups of cabins scattered about the pines. Mangas had divided his men into several bands under his most trusted war leaders. Geronimo was not with him. Just when they needed him most, he had gone off on a revenge raid against the Mexicans.

Captain Mastin, his men still exhausted from the battle at Cooke's Canyon, had reached Pinos Altos with fifteen of his Arizona Guards the night before. He had not expected any trouble, but as soon as he realized how many Apaches were on the attack, he sent an express rider off to Jack Swilling, still posted at the old Mimbres River stage station, to bring his men to Pinos Altos.

The Apaches, who had spent the night concealed in the heights surrounding the little community, took the miners completely by surprise. The warriors went from cabin to cabin kicking in doors and fighting the whites hand-to-hand. They attempted to set fire to the log cabins, but only a few flared up. By noon the combat had shifted to the main town, where Captain Mastin and his soldiers were busy defending the two main supply stores. An Apache volley struck down the captain and one of his men as the warriors surged toward the buildings. Mangas now had victory within his grasp.

Mastin had gathered all the women from Pinos Altos into Bean's Supply Store for protection, and they now retrieved a small cannon stored away in a back room. Six women hauled it to the front door, loaded it up with nails and scrap, threw open the door, and fired away. Several Apaches were killed by the blast and many more wounded. Just as the stunned warriors regrouped, Swilling and his fresh Arizona Guards galloped into town. The miners joined Swilling's men in a counterattack that drove the Apaches back into the hills.

Swilling's men found much of Pinos Altos in flames, with corrals pulled down and stock run off. Four men were dead and eight wounded. Captain Mastin lingered for a few days before succumbing to blood poisoning. Swilling found ten dead Apaches, but it was assumed that many more had been carried off.

Among the dead Apaches were Delgadito and two other prominent war leaders. These losses were devastating to the Chiricahuas, but they had also managed to deal the miners a deathblow. Within weeks, the mines were abandoned save for a handful of holdouts and a detachment of Swilling's Arizona Guards. Mangas had avenged his humiliation at the hands of these White Eyes.

WHILE THE AMERICAN SETTLERS—Yankee and rebel alike— were fighting for their lives against the Apaches, a bold lieutenant colonel named John Baylor, with 258 Confederate troops, had brushed aside token Union resistance and taken control of Mesilla, New Mexico, on July 25, 1861. He and his men soon advanced against Fort Fillmore to the north. The panicked Yankees had quickly abandoned the post and attempted to flee, only to be captured by the rebels. Baylor, who barely had enough men to guard his five hundred prisoners, had won a stunning victory.

Baylor now began to develop a grandiose scheme to occupy all of New Mexico and Arizona. On August 1, 1861, he issued a proclamation creating the Confederate Territory of Arizona with himself as governor and Mesilla as the territorial capital. The northern boundary of this new territory was to be the 34th parallel from Texas to the Colorado River. The Confederate Congress ratified Baylor's proclamation on February 14, 1862.

Baylor, determined to defeat the Apaches and reopen the road between Mesilla and Tucson, informed the new commander of the Arizona Guards that a "Black Flag" policy was now in place regarding the Apaches. He instructed the captain to lure the Chiricahuas into a parley: "When you get them together, kill all the grown Indians and take the children prisoners and sell them to defray the expense of killing the Indians."

On February 28, 1862, Captain Sherod Hunter led one hundred cold and weary Confederate soldiers into Tucson. Lieutenants James Tevis and Jack Swilling rode with the column, which consisted of several Arizona and New Mexico men along with Hunter's Company A, Second Texas Mounted Volunteers. Hunter's men immediately raised the rebel flag over Tucson. It was reported that old Bill Oury danced a jig.

Captain Hunter and his handful of men were to be the spear point of a grand vision expressed by the Confederate secretary of war to secure "a portion of the territory formally common to all the states but now forming a natural appendage to our Confederate States, opening a pathway to the Pacific." Once the rebel flag was raised over Tucson, Captain Hunter busied himself acquiring loyalty oaths of dubious sincerity from all the leading citizens. At the same time, he kept a wary eye to the west. Hunter was skeptical, but there was some hope among Confederate leaders that secessionists in California might yet pull the Golden State over to the rebel cause.

General George Wright, the Union commander in California, had other ideas. He selected an officer named James Henry Carleton to command the "California Column" that was to cross along the Gila River Trail to reoccupy Tucson and then on to defeat the rebels in New Mexico. The forty-seven-year-old Carleton, a major in the Second Dragoons, had seen twenty years of hard frontier service, much of it in New Mexico. Wright assured his superiors in Washington that Carleton was the perfect man for the job: "an officer of great experience, indefatigable and active." He was correct about Carleton's many positive attributes, but the dragoon major, while undeniably brilliant, was also a rigid, self-righteous tyrant.

Carleton commanded a 2,350-man force consisting of ten companies of his own First California Infantry, five companies of the First California Cavalry under Colonel Edward Eyre, and a light battery of four bronze field howitzers. General Wright also assigned Captain John Cremony's company of the Second California Cavalry to the column along with ten more infantry companies and two mountain-howitzer batteries under Colonel George Bowie. Cremony, with his experience on the Bartlett Boundary Survey, was a particularly important addition to the command.

Carleton's men faced a daunting, nearly six-hundred-mile march to Tucson. His plan was to send them forward in small units so as not to overtax the wells and springs on the route. They would march at night to avoid the desert heat, with a goal of making twenty miles a day.

Captain Hunter, aware that the Union soldiers were on the march to Tucson, called in his patrols and attempted to gather as many horses and cattle as possible to mount a defense. Despite a rebel victory at Picacho Peak to the northwest of Tucson on April 15, he knew that without reinforcements he must retreat to the Rio Grande. His small force could barely guard the town and fend off Apache attacks, much less face a formidable Union army. One of Hunter's patrols had already been ambushed by Cochise at Dragoon Springs, sixty-five miles east of Tucson. Four rebels died and the Apaches made off with thirty mules and twenty-five horses. Hunter was caught in a vise between the Apaches astride his line of supply and communication back to Mesilla, and Carleton's army advancing from the west. On May 14, 1862, Captain Hunter led his men out of Tucson and toward Apache Pass. He left James Tevis and a squad of men in the town as a rear guard, all of whom barely managed to escape when Union cavalry thundered into the old pueblo four days later.

⤜═◉═⤛

CARLETON, FRESHLY MINTED a brigadier general of volunteers by President Abraham Lincoln, reached Tucson on June 6, 1862, and promptly declared martial law over the five hundred inhabitants of the town. He sent three express riders with dispatches to General Edward Canby in New Mexico, but two were killed by Apaches and the third was captured by the rebels. With scant intelligence on the military situation on the Rio Grande front, Carleton next sent Colonel Eyre and two companies of cavalry on a reconnaissance in force to the east. Eyre and his soldiers camped at the old Apache Pass stage station on June 25. At noon that day, shots were heard in the nearby hills. Eyre, who had been ordered to avoid hostilities at all cost, raised a white flag. Carleton's sights were set on rebels, not Apaches.

After about an hour, Cochise and a dozen warriors appeared and signaled for a parley. On the ridgeline beyond the stage station, many more heavily armed Apaches watched and waited. Cochise rode forward to meet with Eyre.

"He carried a fine rifle and two six shooters," recalled one of the soldiers, "and rides as fine a horse as anybody." Eyre explained to Cochise that he was only traveling through Apache country and wished safe passage.

Cochise assured Eyre that he also desired peace. Eyre gave the Apaches tobacco and some pemmican from the Pacific Northwest, then they all shook hands and parted ways. Not long afterward, the bodies of three of Eyre's men were found, stripped and tortured to death, not far from the stage station. Eyre had made a grave error. He had not only parleyed while his men were being tortured, but he had also given Cochise presents and, more important, vital intelligence on the position of Carleton's army. Eyre hurriedly moved his men out of Apache Pass. On July 4, they reached the abandoned Fort Thorn on the Rio Grande.

Shortly after this incident, Cochise sent runners to all the Chiricahua bands. Mangas came, of course, with a large contingent of Bedonkohes, including Geronimo. Victorio and Nana led the Chihennes. Juh, the Nednhi leader and friend of Geronimo, led his people up from Mexico, and Francisco came over with his eastern White Mountain warriors. They all gathered at Apache Pass to contest the passage of this new American army.

Carleton, concerned that Eyre had not reported back and worried that his small force might have been attacked by the rebels, decided to send out a force to establish supply depots along the trail and be ready to support Eyre's command. The rest of the California column would follow in smaller contingents. The springs along the old Butterfield route were vital to this advance, and none more so than the one at Apache Pass.

On the morning of July 10, 1862, Captain Thomas L. Roberts departed Tucson with his company of the First California Infantry, Captain John Cremony's troop of the Second California Cavalry, and two mountain howitzers called the "Jackass Battery" under Lieutenant William Thompson. The column reached the San Pedro River two days later, where Roberts divided his command. He was worried about water ahead, for the season had been dry even by Arizona standards. Roberts advanced with sixty of his infantrymen, eight of Cremony's cavalrymen, the Jackass Battery, and two supply wagons. Cremony would follow with the rest of the men, the cattle herd, and a wagon train. The wagons were loaded with supplies to be deposited at various points along the march for the main column that was to follow.

No sooner had Roberts left the San Pedro crossing than a torrential rain fell. The soldiers now trudged through mud and, on the flats of the Sulphur Springs Valley, standing water above their ankles. Roberts, no longer worried about water, sent a courier back to hurry Cremony along. He rested his men at Dragoon Springs for a few hours before beginning the forty-five-mile march to Apache Pass.

Chiricahua scouts watched the advance of the White Eyes and reported back to Cochise on the slow progress of the soaked soldiers. Cochise and Mangas deployed their two hundred warriors under trusted war leaders along the road to the west of the stage station and in the hills surrounding the spring. They would conceal themselves until just the right moment to strike.

Captain Roberts and his infantry reached the old stage station at noon on July 15. As the exhausted men broke ranks to rest and eat, they heard firing in the hills to the west. Thompson, with his howitzers and two wagons, had been bogged down in the mud and had fallen about a half mile behind the infantry. As Thompson's men were descending the road to the stage station, the surrounding hills erupted with gunfire. One man was killed and two wounded in the initial ambush.

Roberts organized his men at the station and sent them back up the road to support Thompson. The fire from the infantry quickly halted the Apache advance. Thompson turned his guns and sent several rounds into the hills, which scattered the warriors and allowed all the soldiers to reach the station. Roberts now confronted the same problem that had bedeviled Bascom the year before—how to get to the spring six hundred yards away.

Roberts sent Sergeant Albert Fountain with twenty men to seize the spring while he led a second group in support. Thompson quickly deployed his howitzers as Fountain's men rushed the spring. At first they suffered no casualties because the Apaches above them were firing too high, but as they neared the spring, the Indians killed one soldier and pinned down the rest. Roberts ordered his bugler to sound recall.

The artillery lobbed several shells but was momentarily disabled because the wooden trails had broken on recoil as Thompson attempted to elevate his guns. Roberts called on the redoubtable Sergeant Fountain to seize the high ground on Overlook Ridge above the stage station and from there lay down a covering fire for men advancing toward the spring.

Fifty warriors had built a *refugio* atop the ridge, and Fountain led twenty volunteers in a bayonet charge up the steep hill. The Apaches again overshot their foe, and Fountain quickly gained the high ground. As the retreating Apaches scurried down the back side of the ridge, Fountain turned his musket fire toward the Apaches above the spring. Protected by this covering fire, Roberts led a charge that captured the spring. The Apaches carried off their wounded and pulled back to the distant hills. They later claimed that the cannons had made all the difference that day.

As his men filled camp kettles and canteens at the spring, Roberts moved the howitzers to higher ground and lobbed more shells into the Apache positions. As the Indians scattered, Roberts called over Sergeant Titus Mitchell and six of his cavalrymen. He instructed Mitchell to ride back to Captain Cremony and warn him to stay in the valley until Roberts could join him later that night. Roberts knew that Cremony's wagons would be vulnerable to ambush on the steep climb into Apache Pass.

Sergeant Fountain, from his perch atop Overlook Ridge, watched through his binoculars as Mitchell and his troopers headed west on the trail. No sooner had they exited from his view than a large band of mounted Apaches came into view and took up their trail. He hurried down the slope to report this to Roberts.

Mitchell's troopers just made it out of the pass before the Apaches struck. The first volley wounded one man and killed two horses. As Mitchell pulled the wounded man up behind him, he looked back to see Private John Teal in the distance. His horse had tired, and so Teal had dismounted to walk him. Mitchell and his men galloped away as twenty Apaches turned toward Teal.

The trooper quickly mounted but had not gone far before an Apache bullet brought down his horse. Determined to sell his life as dearly as possible, Teal crawled behind his dead horse and took careful aim at the leader of the warriors. The chief tumbled off his pony onto the ground. Teal watched in amazement as the other warriors dismounted and rushed to his side. They gingerly carried the fallen Apache off into the nearby hills.

Teal had shot Mangas Coloradas. The wound was serious, and so Geronimo and several other Bedonkohe warriors carried him off to Janos. There, at gunpoint, the village doctor operated on the revered chief with his life and all those in the town hanging in the balance.

It was midnight when Teal, having already been reported dead by his companions, staggered into Captain Cremony's camp. A few hours later, Roberts arrived with half of his infantrymen. At daybreak, they all headed back to Apache Pass. Roberts wisely deployed skirmishers to meet any Apache threat but they met no resistance.

Roberts, now with 150 men and supported by the howitzers, again assaulted the Apaches at the spring that afternoon. The fighting did not last long, as Cochise pulled back his remaining warriors. Most of the Bedonkohes and Chihennes had already departed for Janos.

The 1862 Battle of Apache Pass was a turning point in the long war for Apacheria. Although there were few casualties on either side—perhaps ten warriors were killed, and several more wounded, along with two dead and two wounded soldiers—the serious wound suffered by Mangas Coloradas had a profound effect upon the Chiricahua coalition. Never again would Cochise be able to command hundreds of warriors against the White Eyes. The war would go on, but it would now take on a very different form.

5

KIT CARSON'S WAY

O N SEPTEMBER 8, 1862, JAMES HENRY CARLETON officially assumed command of the Department of New Mexico. He was well acquainted with this beautiful yet harsh land, having served with the First Dragoons in New Mexico for five years, from 1851 to 1856. He had many old friends in the territory and none closer than the man he immediately sought out—Colonel Christopher "Kit" Carson. With the rebel threat neutralized by the Union victory at Glorieta Pass in March 1862, Carleton was determined to use his new command to settle the Apache and Navajo problem once and for all. He envisioned Kit Carson as the spearpoint of this forthcoming campaign.

Carleton and Carson had a shared history with New Mexico's Apaches—most notably with the Jicarillas of the northern mountains and eastern plains. By 1700 Spanish authorities had named the people living in the lands bordered by the Taos Valley on the west and the Raton Mountains on the east the "Apaches of la Xicarilla." The name, which means "Little Basket Maker" in Spanish, made reference to the beautiful baskets handcrafted by the Jicarilla women. This bucolic name seemed deeply ironic to Carleton and Carson, for baskets were the last thing that came to their minds when they thought of the Jicarillas.

By 1862, Kit Carson was one of the most celebrated Americans in the world—the nation's preeminent frontiersman. Taciturn and unassuming, slight of frame and well below average in height, Carson hardly met the blood-and-thunder image of the frontier demigod told and retold in the wild tales that exaggerated his very real adventures.

Born on Christmas Eve, 1809, in Madison County, Kentucky, Carson had been raised near Boone's Lick, Missouri, where his family had resettled in 1811. As a boy, Carson had been apprenticed to a saddler in Old Franklin in 1821, but in 1826 he had run away to join a caravan bound for Santa Fe. He fell in with the trappers at Taos and by 1831, he was a mountain man of the first rank. A chance encounter in 1842 with young Lieutenant John Charles Frémont led to a second career as a guide for that officer's two expeditions of western exploration. Frémont's reports of their adventures together made "the Pathfinder," as Frémont was then known, and his intrepid scout Kit Carson into national celebrities. In August 1845, Carson joined Frémont for a third "exploring expedition" westward. With sixty heavily armed men Frémont entered California, supposedly to explore mountain passes over the Sierras, but actually under secret orders from President James K. Polk to seize that most valuable of territorial prizes once an "expected" war erupted between Mexico and the United States. Carson emerged from that war as an even greater national hero.

Everyone now sought Carson out, but they were invariably surprised to meet the great man himself. "His fame was then at its height, from the publication of Fremont's book," noted Lieutenant William Tecumseh Sherman upon being introduced to Carson at Monterey, California, in the autumn of 1847. "I was very anxious to see a man who had achieved such feats of daring among the wild animals of the Rocky Mountains, and still wilder Indians of the Plains. I cannot express my surprise at beholding a small stoop-shouldered man, with reddish hair, freckled face, soft blue eyes, and nothing to indicate extraordinary courage or daring."

INDIAN AFFAIRS IN New Mexico had deteriorated rapidly following the 1846 American conquest of the Mexican province. The Llaneros (Plains Band) of the Jicarilla Apaches had reached a shaky balance of power with the New Mexicans over the previous generation, but it had quickly broken down once American troops arrived. Comanche hostility had long ago forced the Llaneros from the plains back onto the traditional mountain homeland they shared with their cousins the Olleros (Mountain Band). Isolated in these northern mountains or roaming eastward onto the plains, the Jicarillas had been far less influenced by the Spanish settlers than had other tribes. Their traditional economy of hunting and gathering continued to flourish, augmented by both trade with and plunder from the Hispanics to the south. By 1849 they numbered about a hundred lodges—a population of around five hundred.

The Jicarillas, roving east of the upper Rio Grande and southeast to the Canadian River, made life miserable for settler and traveler alike. "They are not considered a numerous band," declared New Mexico Indian superintendent James Calhoun from his Santa Fe office, "but they are bold, daring and adventurous spirits; and they say they have never encountered the face of a white foe, who did not quail, and attempt to fly from them." This hostility, ever increasing, was fueled by their northern friends the Utes, who provided a ready trade market for their plunder, and by the rivalry between two chiefs, old Chacon of the Olleros and young Lobo Blanco of the Llaneros, for tribal supremacy. Regular troops and New Mexico volunteers repeatedly clashed with Lobo's band, driving him southeast toward his favorite haunts along the Canadian River.

Superintendent Calhoun, who in January 1851 was appointed as the first governor for the newly organized Territory of New Mexico, found himself in a three-front diplomatic war. He had to keep the Hispanic New Mexicans from attacking the Apaches, he had to offer the Apaches some incentive to keep the peace, and he had to persuade reluctant military officers to cooperate with him. On more than one occasion, spiteful officers refused to provide military escorts for treaty councils, making it impossible for Calhoun to do his job. Calhoun found it difficult to deal effectively with the Jicarillas, and in fact literally wore himself out attempting to keep the peace, but not long after his untimely death the government made a surprisingly wise appointment as Indian agent.

On Christmas Day in 1853, Kit Carson learned that he had been appointed federal Indian agent for northern New Mexico (which then included southern Colorado) at a salary of one thousand dollars a year. This appointment was a rare flash of intelligence on the part of the Washington political class. These positions were usually doled out as patronage favors to politicos of varying degrees of competence and honesty. Even when honest men received such appointments, by the time they finally learned the customs, rituals, and politics of Indian Country, they were usually replaced as another administration took office. All could agree that Carson was a superb selection as agent, even if he was illiterate and had to hire a clerk to write his reports. The forty-four-year-old frontiersman would serve as Indian agent to this territory for the next seven years.

Carson now found himself in charge of the small tribe of the Jicarilla Apaches, who he felt to be "truly the most degraded and troublesome Indians we have in our department." Headquartered in Taos, his jurisdiction included not only the Jicarillas but also the Muache Utes and the Pueblo of Taos. Carson had a particularly warm relationship with the Utes, but the Jicarillas were another matter altogether. A day of reckoning was coming.

The government attempted to settle the Jicarilla problem by moving all of them west of the Rio Grande. This seemed an absurdity to Lobo Blanco and his Llaneros, for the plains east of the river were their homeland. But old Chacon and his Olleros, the mountain people, readily agreed and settled along the Rio Puerco some twenty miles west of Abiquiu. Chacon's people cleared fields and planted crops of corn, wheat, pumpkins, and melons and attempted to live in peace with their Hispanic neighbors.

Lobo Blanco scoffed at this. He led his Llaneros onto the plains, where they raided with impunity, even striking the cattle herd at Fort Union. But in February 1854, a detachment of the Second Dragoons from Fort Union pursued the Apaches along the Red River. In a running fight, they killed Lobo Blanco.

The death of the charismatic chief inflamed the passions of all the Jicarillas, including Chacon's mountain people. Carson attempted to cool their ardor, meeting with Chacon and several of his warriors in March. He urged them to remain at peace while he traveled south to Santa Fe to plead their case. While he was gone, a detachment of sixty dragoons from Cantonment Burgwin, in search of Chacon's Apaches, were ambushed on March 30 some twenty miles south of Taos in a canyon near the Embudo Mountains. The dragoons were taken completely by surprise and within a few minutes twenty-two of the soldiers were dead and nearly every other member of the command wounded. If the warriors had been better armed, all of the soldiers might well have been killed. The Indians, content to capture the remaining horses and loot the dead, let the survivors go.

The territorial governor promptly declared that "war existed between the United States and the Jicarilla band of the Apache tribe of Indians, and all their aiders and abetters," remarking that "the highest dictates of humanity demanded their extinction." To accomplish this task, the American military could muster but 1,600 troops, mostly of the First and Second Dragoons and Third Infantry, scattered about in several isolated outposts throughout the vast territory.

As soon as word of the battle reached Fort Union, Lieutenant Colonel Philip St. George Cooke took the field, stripping the fort of every available man. On April 4, 1854, Cooke marched westward toward the Rio Grande with nearly two hundred men of the First and Second Dragoons and a company of the Second Artillery serving as infantrymen. Carson was chief scout for the expedition. Carson led the troops to a steep canyon of the Rio Ojo Caliente, near hot springs that he knew to be a favorite Apache campsite. So prominent was Carson in this fight that the Jicarillas long remembered "Gidi," as they called him, as the leader of the white soldiers. Carson was anxious to capture the Apache women and children to be held as hostages to force the warriors to surrender. The last thing he wanted was for any of them to be killed, for that would leave the men with nothing to live for save vengeance. The soldiers quickly secured the camp, although all but five warriors escaped while seventeen women and children perished. Cooke, in his report, claimed a grand victory over 150 of Chacon's warriors, with but one soldier killed and another seriously wounded.

Carson was disgusted. Even with his prejudice against the Jicarillas, he had little stomach for this so-called victory. He feared that innocents had been slaughtered by Cooke's detachment while the warriors had fled east to the Canadian River or south to find sanctuary with the Mescaleros.

Cooke's attempt to pursue the fleeing Apaches was frustrated by terrain, weather, and the elusive nature of his foe. He returned to Fort Union in frustration, his claim of victory ringing hollower by the day. Jicarilla war parties struck all along the line of New Mexican settlements north of Santa Fe. Fearing an alliance of the Jicarillas and Utes with the Mescaleros to the south, Cooke ordered Captain James Carleton to take two companies of the First Dragoons north from Taos into Colorado's San Luis Valley to intercept Jicarilla raiders. Kit Carson was once again to be chief-of-scouts.

Carleton, the rigidly austere captain from Maine, did not immediately warm to the famed frontiersman, feeling Carson's reputation absurdly exaggerated. His opinion quickly changed as Carson led the soldiers out of the mountains and directly to the Jicarilla camp just to the north of Raton Pass. The Jicarilla, as usual, made their escape with but few casualties, although the soldiers recovered forty head of stolen horses and a considerable quantity of camp goods and plunder taken from the settlements. "Kit Carson," Carleton confessed in his after-action report, "is justly celebrated as being the best tracker among white men in the world."

At the end of Carleton's expedition, Carson returned to Taos and his agency duties. It was critical to keep the Utes from joining their Jicarilla friends, and it was equally important to keep the Hispanic settlers and military authorities from provoking the Indians. For most New Mexicans—Hispanic farmer, Pueblo tribesman, and white soldier alike—all of the northern tribes, the Jicarillas, Utes, and Navajos, were viewed simply as hostiles.

The weary Apaches and their Ute allies finally requested a peace parley in August 1855. The Jicarillas and Utes were promised thousands of acres of land that Carson knew were part of Hispanic claims based on Mexican land grants. The Indians agreed to a treaty with the territorial governor at Abiquiu in September despite Carson's sullen disapproval. The treaty, however, was never ratified by the US Senate, no reservation was ever created, and Carson and the Indians were left to pick up the pieces.

Within a few months Carson lamented to his superiors that "the Indians are the masters of the country." He condemned the practice of having "a grand talk," with the distribution of presents and sacred promises that would be broken whenever convenient. He knew the people of the West well—Indian, Hispanic, and Anglo—and spoke from a wealth of experience that no other Indian agent in Apacheria ever possessed. He felt that the Jicarillas and Utes had to be segregated away from the settlements and protected from the Hispanic and Anglo settlers.

With the treaty a dead issue, the Jicarillas continued to draw rations at Abiquiu and to visit with Carson at Taos. He grew increasingly pessimistic. In his final report as agent in September 1859, Carson warned that the Apaches would "continue to sink deeper into degradation" unless protected by the United States government.

ON MAY 18, 1860, Abraham Lincoln was nominated by the fledgling Republican Party as its candidate for president of the United States. Lincoln, like Carson, had been born in Kentucky in 1809 and bred on the frontier. Carson had followed the organization of the new political party and had avidly supported his old friend, the "Pathfinder" John Frémont, as its first candidate for president in 1856. Little did Carson know then how much Lincoln's nomination would change his life. For the Apaches that impact would be far more profound, and ultimately devastating.

Within a few weeks of the bombardment of Fort Sumter in April 1861, the opening salvo of the American Civil War, nearly half of all the US military officers stationed in New Mexico and Arizona had resigned to cast their fates with the rebelling Confederate States of America.

On May 24, 1861, Carson left his post as Indian agent to accept a commission as lieutenant colonel of the First Regiment of New Mexico Volunteers. The new Union commander, Colonel Edward R. S. Canby, a Kentuckian loyal to the Old Flag, had taken command by default when every officer senior to him had resigned to join the rebels. Canby had neither uniforms nor arms with which to equip the volunteers, nor coin to pay them. Carson, promoted to regimental colonel on October 4, 1861, led his raw recruits 150 miles down the Rio Grande to Fort Craig to meet the rebel invaders. His men, almost exclusively Hispanic, were mostly illiterate like their colonel, and totally ignorant of even the most rudimentary military drill. Canby had no faith in the volunteers, declaring them "worse than worthless," but Carson was proud of his regiment.

Brigadier General Henry Hopkins Sibley, who had until the previous May served as a dragoon officer in New Mexico, now commanded the Confederate invasion force. A West Point graduate of the class of 1838, he was notorious in military circles as a hard drinker—"a walking whiskey keg" according to one critic. It must have been whiskey that fueled his scheme of a Confederate empire stretching across the Southwest to California and north to the goldfields of Colorado.

In January, Sibley's Army of New Mexico—2,590 men who were mostly Texans—had united with John Baylor, the self-appointed governor whose rebel soldiers were still holding Mesilla and Tucson. The road to California looked open and inviting but Sibley's besotted gaze was fixed northward on Santa Fe and the Colorado goldfields beyond. Only Fort Craig, about 160 miles south of Santa Fe, stood in his way.

Canby, anticipating this showdown, hurried reinforcements to this last bastion of federal power. By February 1862, he had nearly 4,000 men under arms at Fort Craig, 1,200 of whom were regulars. Among these regulars were the Arizona troops from Forts Breckinridge and Buchanan, including young George Bascom, who had been promoted to captain in the Sixteenth Infantry in the wake of his supposed heroics against Cochise at Apache Pass.

Bascom's companion, the Irishman James "Paddy" Graydon,

was at the fort as well, also a captain and commanding a volunteer spy company. Graydon had joined the Union forces in New Mexico not long after departing the Sonoita in July. Few officers were as popular, or as notorious, as the thirty-year-old Graydon. The hard-drinking, colorful Irishman had made quite a reputation in the months between joining the Union army and his arrival at Fort Craig. He had recruited his "Independent Spy Company" quickly, aided by his Catholic faith, long experience in the Southwest, and fluency in Spanish. They were the "hardest cases he could find," one of Canby's officers recalled.

Graydon won even more plaudits at Fort Craig as he continually harassed the rebels. The rebel invaders, with no stomach for a frontal assault, attempted to bypass the post. Before dawn on the morning of February 21, 1862, Graydon's irregulars, along with a mounted company of Carson's regiment, splashed across the Valverde ford of the Rio Grande to discover the rebels arrayed in the barren cottonwoods on the eastern bank. A brisk volley of shots suddenly erupted from the trees and the Battle of Valverde was under way. Federal reinforcements soon arrived, including Captain Bascom's Arizona regulars, and they held the northern flank of a Union line strung out a considerable distance down the Rio Grande. Kit Carson's regiment was held in reserve on the west bank.

The befuddled Canby accidentally assisted the rebels by shifting Carson and the reserves over to the right flank just as the Texans counterattacked and crashed down on the federal artillery. It was hand-to-hand combat around the cannons, with federal bayonet against rebel bowie knife. The rebels swept over the battery and sent the supporting Union soldiers into a wild retreat.

Captain Bascom fell during this retreat as he attempted to cross the river. As the panicked soldiers splashed past him, the young officer slowly floated down the Rio Grande. His body was later recovered from a sandbar in the middle of the river and buried near Fort Craig.

Canby watched helplessly as his left flank collapsed and as darkness approached ordered a retreat back to Fort Craig. It had been a costly day. The butcher's bill for Canby was 111 dead and 160 wounded, while for Sibley and the rebels, it was 72 dead and 157 wounded.

Sibley marched north to occupy Albuquerque and settled into comfortable quarters in Santa Fe on March 10. Only Fort Union stood between him and the Colorado mines, but Colorado volunteers rushed south to reinforce the federals at the fort. On March 28, 1862, the Colorado volunteers delivered a devastating blow to the Confederate forces near Glorieta Pass, just to the east of Santa Fe. Sibley had no choice but to abandon Santa Fe and Albuquerque on April 12. The retreat south became a death march, with the rebels continually harassed by both Yankees and Apaches before they were able to reach Texas.

Canby now reorganized the New Mexico volunteer regiments into a single unit under Carson's command and then returned in triumph to Santa Fe on May 3, 1862. His reward was a brigadier general's star and a transfer to the East. He was replaced by Brigadier General Carleton.

IN SEPTEMBER, Colonel Kit Carson received Special Order 176 from his old friend and new commander Carleton. He was to take five companies of his command and reopen abandoned Fort Stanton, in the Mescalero country of the Sierra Blanca of southeastern New Mexico. Upon reaching Fort Stanton on October 26, Carson found most of the fort in shambles and everything of value already carried off.

Once there, he received detailed orders from Carleton: "As your scouts come near the mouth of the Penasco they will, doubtless, find a plenty of Mescaleros. All Indian men of the Mescalero tribe are to be killed whenever and wherever you can find them. The women and children will not be harmed, but you will take them prisoners and feed them at Fort Stanton until you receive other instructions about them."

The Mescaleros, like the Jicarillas to the north, were not a numerous people, but they had prospered in the Sierra Blanca. They made the mountains their home, moving in a pattern to favorite campsites in the Guadalupes, the Capitans, and the Sacramentos. They harvested the abundant mescal plant, which provided both a staple food and a beverage to them. The Spanish, whom they both preyed upon and traded with, named them Mescalero, or "mescal maker," because of their dependence on the huge desert plant. This agave, with its thick green leaves coming to cutting spikes at its ends, was harvested by Mescalero women in late spring when the red flower stalks began to emerge. The excavated root, or crown, was baked in large underground ovens, and the eating of the freshly cooked mescal was a favorite time of the year. The cooked mescal was then dried in the sun and stored or carried as an easily transportable food. Mescal as a fermented beverage, although popular in Mexico, was never favored by the Mescaleros. They preferred *tiswin* made from fermented corn sprouts. They also, like the Jicarillas, developed a taste for the rotgut whiskey peddled by the Comanchero traders who infested the region.

Almost every edible mountain plant, from piñon pine nuts to the fruit of the prickly-pear cactus, was put to good use. The Mescalero men hunted deer, elk, and antelope, and once the Spanish arrived, they developed a taste for cattle, horse, and mule meat as well. Spanish horses allowed Mescalero hunters to roam eastward onto the Great Plains in search of buffalo. Despite Comanche resistance, the Mescaleros hunted east into Texas to the headwaters of the Brazos and Colorado rivers and south to the Big Bend of the Rio Grande.

This expansion onto the plains led the Mescaleros to adopt Comanche-style teepees when buffalo hunting, although the brush wickiup was still favored in the mountains. Mescalero warriors also adopted the buckskin shirts of the plains tribes, and more so than other Apaches sometimes did scalp their enemies. Unlike plains warriors, however, Mescalero warriors always discarded the scalps, sharing the universal Apache fear of contact with the dead.

By the time of the 1846 American conquest, the Mescaleros held sway over a vast territory that included most of southeastern New Mexico and spilled east and south into Texas. Within a decade, however, the Americans had them hemmed in with five forts, the most important of which was Fort Stanton in the heart of their Sierra Blanca homeland. It was to this post, named for a dragoon captain killed by Mescaleros in 1855, that Carleton now sent Carson.

Carleton, nervous about his old friend's sympathy for the Indians, also ordered out four companies of California troops with instructions that "there is to be no council held with the Indians, nor any talks. The men are to be slain whenever and wherever they can be found." The California troops were soon hunting Mescaleros in the Sacramento and Guadalupe mountains.

First blood was drawn by Carson's New Mexican troops. In the May reorganization of the First New Mexico Volunteers, Paddy Graydon had been assigned to command Company H. On October 11, Captain Graydon led two companies and a supply train of wagons south from Anton Chico, on the Pecos River, toward Fort Stanton.

The Mescaleros had welcomed the August 2, 1861, abandonment of Fort Stanton, taking it as a sign of the withdrawal of the White Eyes from their country. Emboldened Mescalero raiding parties struck exposed Hispanic farms and ranches throughout southern New Mexico, and travel became a dangerous proposition even for military couriers. They had also attacked the retreating Confederates after the battle at Glorieta Pass. Graydon, still worried about the return of the rebels, hoped to enlist the Mescaleros as scouts. He wrote his superiors that they "could be put to good use as guides and spies down the Pecos."

A chance meeting with Chief Manuelito and a dozen Mescalero warriors at Gallinas Springs in early October 1862 offered the Irish captain the opportunity to stop a war before it started. Manuelito told Graydon that he wished to open peace talks with the White Eyes, and that his people were hungry and needed food. Graydon distributed what few rations he had to the Apaches, so that Manuelito and his people departed in a good humor.

When Graydon reported his meeting to Major Arthur Morrison, he was reprimanded for disobeying Carleton's orders. The thirty-five-year-old major, a German immigrant, had developed an intense contempt for the swashbuckling Graydon. Hardly a man to take criticism lightly, Graydon "in the most emphatic language, protested against such a course in attacking or butchering these Indians." Morrison replied that the captain had his orders to shoot Indians on sight. Morrison, a drunkard unworthy of the uniform he wore, who would later be forced to resign to avoid court-martial, had deeply wounded the proud Irishman, and this feud set up one of the greatest tragedies in the history of Apacheria.

The next morning Graydon led a scouting party back to Gallinas Springs. He was naturally anxious to get away from Morrison, but he also knew that Manuelito would be easy to find. Graydon intercepted Manuelito's band and made peace signs, and as the Mescaleros approached, he ordered his men to be ready to fire. Manuelito walked up to Graydon, saying he was on his way to Santa Fe to meet with Carleton, and asked for some tobacco. Graydon responded by sending a shotgun blast into his head at point-blank range. All the soldiers opened fire. Eleven warriors and an old woman were killed.

When Major Morrison learned of the fight, he promptly labeled it a massacre. He now changed course and loudly denounced Graydon for deceiving the Apaches with offers of liquor and then murdering them. Any sense of a search for truth was lost in the feud between the two soldiers, with the dead Apaches pawns in Morrison's personal vendetta. Graydon had further confused the issue by distributing seventeen captured horses and mules, as was the New Mexico custom, to his men. Morrison confiscated the animals as government property and ordered an official inquiry into the "Gallinas Massacre."

Carson reached Fort Stanton just as this feud unfolded. Although unwilling to take sides in the dispute, Carson was highly suspicious of Graydon's "victory" over the Mescaleros and reported his concerns to Carleton. But Carleton used the opportunity to brag to his Washington superiors about Graydon's triumph, then ordered Carson to return the captured horses and mules to the Mescaleros as a sign of goodwill. Either way, the issue was soon settled on the Fort Stanton parade ground in a duel between Paddy Graydon and one of his critics that left both men dead.

⊷⟝⟞⊶

Two weeks after Manuelito's death, a detachment of California troops surprised a large Mescalero village in Dog Canyon. This spot, where US dragoons had first battled the Apaches back in 1849, was a favored Sacramento Mountain campsite for the Mescaleros. The soldiers routed the Indians and captured their camp. The fight at Dog Canyon, along with the death of Manuelito, convinced the Mescaleros that further resistance was futile.

Several hundred Mescaleros now hurried to Fort Stanton to surrender to Carson. The colonel disobeyed Carleton's orders and accepted their surrender, distributing army rations to the Mescalero families. Indian agent Lorenzo Labadie had also just arrived at Fort Stanton. He and Carson were old friends, and they now devised a scheme to send a Mescalero delegation to Santa Fe to make peace with Carleton. Carson would remain at Fort Stanton to protect the Mescaleros who had come in, while Labadie, with a military escort, would accompany Chief Cadete and four other Mescalero leaders to Santa Fe.

Carleton met with the chiefs on November 24. Cadete spoke eloquently for the Mescaleros: "You have driven us from our last and best stronghold, and we have no more heart. Do with us as may seem good to you, but do not forget we are men and braves."

Carleton had decided that the Mescaleros would be the first to settle on his new Indian reservation on the plains of eastern New Mexico. He had already ordered the construction of a new post on the Pecos River at the Bosque Redondo (Round Forest), where his forty-square-mile reserve would be located. Fort Sumner, named for Carleton's hero, Bull Sumner, was to protect New Mexico from Comanche raiders to the east while overseeing the general's grand experiment in Indian removal. The Mescaleros and other hostile tribes were to be imprisoned there and kept from contact with the Rio Grande settlements. Carleton assured his superiors that he would transform these Apache warriors into productive farmers.

Labadie returned to Fort Stanton with the Mescalero chiefs to gather their people for the journey to Bosque Redondo. While the

Bosque had long been a favorite campsite for the Mescaleros, especially when trading with the Comancheros, it was still no place for a mountain people to live. But Cadete knew he had no option but to submit to Carleton's will. By the time the chiefs reached Fort Stanton, Carson had nearly 250 Mescaleros ready to be loaded onto government wagons and pointed north toward the Bosque Redondo. By March some 400 had made the sad journey northward, while Carson's patrols scoured the mountains for any holdouts.

Soon after New Year's Day, 1863, Carson reported the end of the Mescalero campaign to Carleton, assuring the general that "the Bonito and Pecos valleys might now be cultivated without danger of Indian depredations." Carson was being overly optimistic. At least a hundred Mescaleros were still at large, some hiding out in the Sacramentos, but most fleeing west to seek sanctuary with their cousins, the Gila Apaches of Mangas Coloradas.

Carson was back in Santa Fe by February, having resigned from his command. He had joined the army to fight rebels, not Indians, and now wanted to return home to his wife and children in Taos. But Carleton simply tore up the resignation. He had other plans for his favorite officer—a summer campaign against the Navajos.

While Carson reluctantly prepared his regiment for the Navajo campaign, Carleton turned his attention toward Mangas Coloradas. "I shall organize and send into the country around the headwaters of the Gila an expedition to punish, for their frequent and recent murders and depredations, the band of Apaches which infest that region," he informed Washington in January 1863. "The Pinos Altos gold mines can then be worked with security."

Carleton, determined to crush both the Navajos and Apaches, felt that they "must be whipped and fear us before they will cease killing and robbing the people." Carleton's Navajo campaign would prove to be a resounding—if controversial—success, as Carson captured nearly 9,000 Navajos and sent them to join the 400 Mescaleros he had already imprisoned at the Bosque Redondo. But the Apaches would soon frustrate the general's grand plan—and the plans of many more generals to come.

6

PEOPLE OF THE
WHITE MOUNTAINS

YOUNG FELIX WARD DID NOT REMAIN WITH ESKIM-
inzin's Aravaipas for long. Even while the White Eyes
battled each other to the east along the Rio Grande, the
rhythms of Apache life in the mountains of central Arizona went
on as usual. Nayundiie, a White Mountain Apache chief of the
"Cottonwoods Joining" band, who lived near the forks of Cedar
Creek, received the boy as a gift from a shaman. The shaman had
traded some special medicine to Eskiminzin for him. Although the
boy was traded as a slave, he was treated as an adopted son by Nayundiie.

Black Rope, later known to the White Eyes as John Rope, was
the son of Nayundiie and was raised alongside the captive boy. He
and other Apaches were fascinated by the boy's long red hair. "We
were brought up together, so we called each other brothers," he
explained. The lost boy now had a family.

There was much to learn. His new parents were his teachers, and
sometimes close relatives might help as well. This extended family was the center of Felix's new world. Five families made up this
group, and they all planted, gathered, hunted, and went on raids
together. This family organization, based around clans, meant that
the group was tied closely together by blood.

Felix's new father had two wives, both of the "Slender Peaks
Standing Up" clan. Their sister was Adahay, who had first met the
captive boy in Eskiminzin's village. Adahay left the Aravaipa and
her husband and returned to the White Mountain people about the
same time that Felix was traded to them. Both her sisters eventu-

ally died in childbirth and so she helped raise their children, including the adopted captive boy. She was astonished by the skinny redhead's appetite. "I was always afraid to feed him, he's gonna work for it," she joked. "I leave enough in the pot. I was so afraid he will dig down too fast and make a hole in my pottery." Her main memory of the boy was that he "sure could eat."

The hungry boy won a place in Adahay's heart by working harder than the other boys, bringing home birds, pack rats, and rabbits for the stewpot. "Soon she started to love him a little, so she didn't care anymore and she treated him just like her own," her great-granddaughter remembered. "She said pretty soon the boys used to go huntin' with their daddy."

It was an important day when Nayundiie took Felix along with Black Rope and his other boys on a hunt. Hunters sometimes went north of the Mogollon Rim and even as far as the San Francisco Mountains, but they had to be wary of the Navajo in that country. The White Mountain hunters usually stayed close to home and tried to return within a few days. It was a particularly grand day when Nayundiie and his boys, including Felix, returned to the village carrying a fat wild pig hung from a pole. A great feast followed, and even Felix got enough to eat for once.

Before being allowed to go on the hunt, Felix had undergone the rigorous strength training received by all the Western Apache boys: baths in icy creek water; rolling in the snow; wrestling matches; endless races up and down the steep mountain ridges. Arrow games were played constantly, using primitive bows and arrows made with bluebird or flicker feathers. In the games, the boy won the arrows of his competitors by placing his arrow right against the other arrow. Various target games were played, with everyone's carefully crafted arrows going to the winner. In such a way did Felix become strong in body and an expert with the bow and arrow.

Felix and Black Rope often hunted pack rats together. They started early in the morning and hunted until midday. One boy would poke the nest with a long stick while the other waited on the opposite side of the opening with his bow and arrow at the ready. When the rat stuck his head out to investigate, he was shot. If the arrow missed, then they had to dig the rat out. The boys took the rats home and put them in the fire to burn all their hair away. Only then did they skin them and give them to their mother or aunt to either boil or roast.

Felix had a lot of catching up to do with the other boys, for most of them were already skilled hunters of small game by the time they reached ten or eleven. An Apache boy learned to shoot with slings and miniature bows and arrows from a young age. By the age of twelve, he was going out alone or with other boys to hunt quail, rabbits, squirrels, small birds, and the elusive pack rats. They often raided bird's nests for eggs.

Boys did not hunt deer, antelope, elk, or mountain sheep, for that was work only for warriors, but they might go along on the hunt to observe and to learn the ritual songs, hunting methods, and how to skin the animal. True hunting power rarely came before the age of twenty. "Hunting power was dangerous and not a thing for a bungling youth to meddle with," declared a White Mountain elder. "His heart would not be strong enough to stand it; it could make him ill or even kill him."

Whites did not understand things like "hunting power." It was obvious to the Apaches that Felix had lost his eye because he had hunted when he was far too young. The wounded deer that hooked his left eye was but one example of the dangers of not possessing "hunting power." Such power, as with all powers, had to be gradually learned and carefully earned.

The hunting of bears was rare because all Apaches held them as an animal ancestor. If an Apache came upon a bear, he would say "Go away, Grandpa." The problem was that the bear often did not go away, and maulings of women gathering nuts and berries were common. Only shamans with "bear power" could hunt these dangerous animals. Four or five men might form a bear hunting party after a bad bear had attacked a White Mountain woman. They used lances and bows and arrows to try to kill the beast, but the hunter always hoped to kill the animal with one arrow so that it would not suffer.

When the bear was killed, a dance, not unlike a war dance, was held. The skin of the bear was donned by all the warriors as they danced throughout the night. Medicine men threw pollen into the air during this ceremony. A few people would eat bear meat, but most would not.

Every Apache band had stories of bear encounters. Chief Loco of the Warm Springs people had famously killed a bear with only a knife but it had scarred his face and lamed his leg. Kaywaykla's grandmother warned him, "Bear is very different from other animals. We do not eat its meat. We do not kill it except in self-defense. A bear is very much like a person." His grandmother feared bears as others feared owls, telling him "that when the wicked die, their spirits return to earth in the body of a bear. Others deny this but few of them will touch a bear."

The Chiricahuas believed in bear sickness, which led to lethargy, foaming at the mouth, sleepless nights from bear dreams, and in extreme cases deformity. Crossing the path of a bear or even touching where it had slept might cause this sickness and only the powerful song of a shaman could cure it. Some shamans talked with bears and afterward possessed "bear power," which helped them cure the sick.

SPRING AND LATE FALL were the principal hunting seasons. In the spring, food stores were low after the winter snows, and in the late fall, the animals were fat and their pelts prime. Hunting parties headed out in the spring before the snow melted so that the animals were easier to track. This was also an important time for raiding, and the cattle and horses taken in raids formed a vital part of the Apache food supply. Fish were never eaten. Meat from hunting formed a major part of the White Mountain Apache diet, with venison being the most important. The lowly but prolific pack rat, hunted by the boys, was also a dietary staple.

A great hunter became highly esteemed and was often elevated to a leadership position. It was assumed that such men had supernatural powers, and these often translated into the skills and special powers of a great warrior.

⊷≡ ⊜⊱

NAYUNDIIE'S BAND WAS often on the move, for while they practiced agriculture more than their Apache cousins to the east, they
still constantly migrated in a rotation to hunting and gathering
grounds. They would leave their cornfields unattended except for
planting, irrigating, and harvesting times, although the farm sites
were regarded as the band's home. In good years, surplus corn
would be cached in mountain caves or underground. The arrival
of American military forces disrupted planting and harvesting and
forced even more band movement.

Nayundiie's people left the "Cottonwoods Joining" clan when
the corn was about three feet high and went out in order to gather
wild plants. Since the natural foods grew at different mountain
elevations and ripened in different seasons, this dictated the people's migrations. After harvesting their corn in the fall as well as
gathering acorns, the people headed south to the Salt River to harvest mescal until April. Since they destroyed the mescal plants in
a season's harvest, they always had to move to a different location
the following year. In these long marches, the boys like Felix were
made to walk and carry heavy loads to strengthen their bodies.
The boys also carried the pitched torches for making fire. This was
a busy but relaxed time. These winter camps were primitive and
temporary, as the women and girls harvested the mescal while the
men and boys hunted. The camps moved every two weeks in search
of more mescal plants.

An important event was the cooking of the mescal, which was
always a delicate task. A summer-born person, assumed to be quite
lucky, had the honor of lighting the oak in the pit at sunrise. The
wood was ignited with a fire drill, never matches, and the man or
woman selected said a prayer as the wood was ignited at the east,
south, west, and north sides of the pit.

Despite the serious nature of this event, the old people often
seized the moment to have some fun and embarrass the young
married couples. It was taboo for anyone involved with the mescal
roasting to have sex during the forty-eight hours it was cooking.

To do so would spoil the mescal. A stern lecture to the obviously uncomfortable young people was a good joke.

Acorns were second only to mescal as a staple food. In late July and August, large groups of gatherers sought out oak trees. Nayundiie's people gathered the acorns from Oak Springs on the west to Rock Creek on the east. This was work for women and girls, but sometimes boys like Felix would go along to climb up the trees and shake down the acorns. Usually the women used long poles to dislodge the nuts, but this could be risky work, since the bears also loved acorns.

Oak leaves were used to roll tobacco to make cigarettes. Felix and the other boys were not allowed to smoke until they became hunters. Unmarried girls might smoke, although it was considered scandalous. Almost all the grown men and women smoked, even though the Apaches did not cultivate tobacco. A wild species of tobacco grew on the north side of the east fork of the White River, but tobacco overall was rare and hard to find. This wild tobacco was milder than trade tobacco, and men often mixed in dried sumac and sage to make it smoke longer. Most tobacco was obtained in raids on the Mexicans or in trade with the Americans, and few trade items were as prized. Many men would trade a pony for just a small quantity.

Other important foods included piñon nuts, gathered in June; juniper berries, picked from October to December; sunflowers, harvested in the fall and ground into a fine meal that made both a pastry and a cereal; and the pods of mesquite trees, which ripened late in the summer. Mesquite pitch was given to the children to be chewed like gum, and it was also used to attach arrow points to the shafts. Gathering parties traveled down to the Salt River country in September and October to gather the mesquite pods.

This planting, gathering, hunting, and harvesting set the rhythm of life for the people of the White Mountains. Felix grew to young manhood in this world, became fluent in the language, embraced the culture with its many rituals and taboos, and became a member of his adoptive father's "Cottonwoods Joining" clan.

Felix looked forward to the celebrations that marked the annual harvests. He loved to dance, and as he grew older, he became a great favorite with the young girls, the red hair adding to his allure. A popular event was the wheel dance, where the girls got to choose their partners. They danced around a great bonfire and the drummers and singers, along with the single men willing to dance, formed on the west side. The single girls gathered in pairs in a wheel around the fire, and once the dance started, they would pick their male partners. The boys were required to dance when chosen by a tap on the shoulder, and there was a rush toward the popular boys and the good dancers. They faced the girls in the circle, dancing a few steps forward and a few steps backward as the human wheel revolved around the fire.

An Apache named Eva Tenney remembered Felix well, calling him by his later name. "I never miss any of those dances where Mickey was. I was the best dancer!" she recalled with a laugh. "We dance with the old people and we flirt with the good lookin' guys. Mickey was a good dancer."

"He looked like a white man," remembered another girl. "He was handsome."

No occasion was more important to the Western Apaches, nor gave a better opportunity for a truly grand social gathering, than did a girl's puberty ceremony. The Western Apaches called this four-day ceremony the sunrise dance, or the "getting her ready" dance, and it was a living validation of the importance of women within their matrilineal culture, as well as a reminder to all the people of White Painted Woman and the origins of the people. The physical transformation of the girl into White Painted Woman, which coincided with her menarche, was not only a personal journey for her, but for her community as well. During the ceremony the girl obtained the power of White Painted Woman and could bestow blessings for long life or good luck. She might even heal a wound with her touch.

The family had to obtain the services of a special singer, usually an older man with a good record of successful ceremonies. It was the singer who served as a sort of "master of ceremonies" and also supervised the erection of the sacred shelter where the songs were to be sung. Sometimes the singer was a shaman, and his services did not come cheaply. The family also had to obtain the services of a masked dancer shaman to organize the colorful dancers who represented the supernatural beings who lived in the mountains. The four-day ceremony was the social gathering of the year for the people, a time of spiritual rebirth but also of just plain good fun.

These shamans fascinated Felix. Among his most vivid memories was the fire dance, in which medicine men holding wands of eagle feathers jumped through fire untouched. "They would stagger about as if drunk," he recalled years later, "and scatter fire all over themselves without hurting themselves." On another occasion, a medicine man won over the people by stabbing himself. "Give me a knife," Felix remembered the shaman declaring. "See! I plunge it in my breast! Make me a cigarette." He smoked the cigarette and the smoke from it emerged out of his chest. "I saw it with my own eyes," Felix declared. "I saw the blood and the smoke come together." Felix absorbed this belief system and became one with it.

Dances and social gatherings were also a time for a variety of games, and among the Apaches, games were almost always accompanied by wagers. Some men had secret ceremonies to enhance their gambling skills, but they never spoke of such things.

Many of the games were meant to condition and train the boys. Felix and Black Rope were challenged to run to the top of a mountain with their mouths full of water. Upon their return they had to spit out all the water. Other times they might undertake a long race over broken country with a load on their backs. When they became adults, they would be expected to cover fifty to seventy-five miles on foot over the roughest terrain for several days at a time.

Horse races, footraces, wrestling matches, bow and arrow contests, and, most important, the hoop-and-pole game were all wagered upon. Many hours were spent playing hoop-and-pole, and great sums were bet on the outcome of these games. The Apaches, both men and women, loved to gamble, and the boys understood the serious nature of the contest. They were playing, yes, but they were also training to become fearsome warriors.

⊷══◎═⊷

TWO YEARS AFTER Felix had come to be a part of Nayundiie's family, the White Eyes came to the White Mountains. The people were near the falls of the Blue River when they heard that white men were camped at the springs two miles south of the Gila River. They decided to go and investigate, along with many other bands that had come down to the Gila to see as well.

All the boys were curious, and they went close to where the Apaches and White Eyes were talking. Black Rope had never seen white people before. "There were lots of them, all dressed the same," Black Rope marveled. "They wore blue pants, black shirts, and black hats. Later on we found out they were soldiers." Seeing a gaggle of boys, several soldiers came over with a big basket loaded down with beans, bread, and meat and gave it to them. This was taken back to camp and made into a tasty stew—the first American food Black Rope had ever had.

Black Rope did not report on how his new brother, Felix, reacted to these events. One thing is certain: Felix did not tell his story to the soldiers, nor did he ask for sanctuary. He had already become a White Mountain Apache.

Loaded down with beans and flour, Nayundiie's people returned north to their camp on Blue River in good spirits. From this time forward there was to be peace between many of the people of the White Mountains and the Americans.

Nayundiie usually lived with his boys among the "Cottonwoods Joining" clan, but sometimes he took them to be with his wife's family at Cedar Creek Crossing. But tragedy soon overtook his family. His oldest wife, the mother of Black Rope, died on one day and his younger wife died the next. The older boys, including Felix, stayed with him while his oldest daughter and Adahay took in the younger children.

"Boys," Nayundiie told his sons, "your mothers have died, and it is going to be a hard time for us now."

Once again, Felix was a motherless child.

7

THE HEAD OF
MANGAS COLORADAS

MANGAS COLORADAS WAS TIRED. SINCE 1846, THE old chief had been a friend to the Americans. He had reaffirmed that friendship by signing the 1852 treaty at Acoma promising to try to curb Chiricahua raids into Mexico. No one on either side viewed that as much more than a goodwill gesture, and the raids against the hated Mexicans of course continued, but Mangas had given the Americans diplomatic cover. He was ready to put aside the lashing by the miners at Pinos Altos and the betrayal of Cochise at Apache Pass if he could settle on the reservation that his new friend, the Indian agent Michael Steck, had promised him at Santa Lucia Springs. Mangas wished only to tend his cornfields and watch his grandchildren play; he was finished fighting.

Mangas was more determined than ever to make a new peace with the Americans. The wound he received during the battle for Apache Pass had led to a slow recovery; the incident had tempered his famed warrior spirit. Nearing seventy years of age, he had little stomach for more prolonged conflict. On September 19, 1862, he suddenly appeared at Acoma and sent a message to General Carleton expressing his strong desire for peace.

Peace with the Apaches was, of course, the furthest thing from the general's mind. "Mangas Coloradas sends me word he wants peace," Carleton wrote Colonel Joseph Rodman West on October 3, "but I have no faith in him." Carleton, in response to the peace overture, ordered West to attack Mangas's band.

"The campaign," declared the general, "must be a vigorous one and the punishment of that band of murderers and robbers must be thorough and sharp." All the males were to be killed, although Carleton again stipulated that women and children should be spared. He planned to settle the surviving Apaches at Bosque Redondo with the Mescaleros and Navajos he had already captured. Unlike Kit Carson, Colonel West warmly embraced his commander's orders.

It was mid-January before West, recently promoted to brigadier general, departed Mesilla with 250 men with plans to reoccupy the abandoned Fort McLane. He took with him young Merejildo Grijalva, a Sonoran captive who had lived for seven years with Cochise's band, as a scout and interpreter. Carleton urged General West to also employ the Confederate renegade Jack Swilling as a guide.

General West assured Carleton that Swilling was at the mines and available for service. A Georgia native, Swilling had served in the Mexican War as a teenager before migrating to Texas in 1857. He found work as a teamster with the Leach Wagon Road, a federal project connecting El Paso to Fort Yuma, and when that job ended, he had signed on with Butterfield's Overland Mail. Swilling, like James Tevis, left the stage line in the spring of 1860 to follow the gold rush to Pinos Altos and was soon washing gold out of the gulches and arroyos all along Bear Creek.

The mines near Pinos Altos, high atop a 7,365-foot peak, had been discovered by the Spanish in the late 1700s. Copper, of remarkably pure quality, was mined at Santa Rita del Cobre continuously after about 1800. The mines also became a popular rendezvous site for American fur trappers. In 1828, a young Kit Carson had briefly worked there. The notorious scalp hunter and mercenary James Kirker frequented the area as well, first trapping and later selling guns to the Apaches. For a time Kirker provided security for the mule trains heading south on the "Copper Road" to Janos and Chihuahua City. Despite Apache hostility, prospectors continued to explore the Mogollon Mountains in search of mineral wealth, and eventually Pinos Altos became their base of operations.

Swilling had been working the diggings and had also opened a saloon and gambling hall to mine the pockets of his fellow prospectors. As Apache stock depredations increased with the abandonment of nearby Fort McLane, Swilling had also helped organize the Arizona Guards as a local militia to protect Pinos Altos. They had been mustered into the Confederate army on August 8, 1861.

Swilling, who had ridden with Captain Hunter's Texans in the occupation of Tucson in late February 1862, participated in skirmishes with the advancing California Column. In early March the rebels captured Captain William McCleave and Swilling was ordered to escort him to Mesilla. McCleave was no ordinary prisoner, for he was an old comrade-in-arms and a great favorite of General Carleton. Along the way to Mesilla, Swilling formed a warm friendship with his Yankee prisoner. At one point on the trail, as they were shadowed by Apaches, he returned the captain's weapons to him and confessed to him that he "did not want the blood of white men on his hands."

By the time they reached Mesilla in April 1862, General Sibley's rebel army was in full retreat. The rebels released Captain McCleave, who soon reached Fort Thorn on the Rio Grande accompanied by his new friend Jack Swilling. McCleave, who had served in the dragoons with Carleton, easily secured Swilling employment as an express rider and scout for the general. Swilling, for some time disgusted by the inept leadership of rebel commanders Baylor and Sibley, now wisely switched sides.

Swilling discovered a remarkable band of adventurers encamped amid the ruins of the abandoned Fort McLane in January 1863 and promptly signed on with them. He joined forces with Joseph Reddeford Walker, who was commanding twenty men who had journeyed from California in hopes of striking a new El Dorado in the mountains of central Arizona.

Walker was a living legend all across the American frontier. Born in 1798 to an adventurous Tennessee clan—one brother died at the Alamo—Walker was among the first to pioneer the Santa Fe Trail in the early 1820s. Within a few years, he had explored the Rocky Mountains and beyond and was credited with the discovery of Yosemite. When the beaver trade played out, he joined his old comrade Kit Carson on Captain Frémont's second and third exploring expeditions to Mexican California. After spending several years in California he decided on a final quest in search of gold in the mountains of central Arizona—in the heart of Apacheria.

Swilling, his long hair tucked under a broad-brimmed sombrero, was as daring and reckless a spirit as any on the frontier and so fit in perfectly with Walker's band. He also was the sort who moved easily among the Apaches, for they could sense from his demeanor boldness worthy of respect.

Walker needed Swilling. They knew where they wanted to search for gold, but the problem was how to get there. The Apaches had dogged their journey since leaving the Rio Grande and now blocked them from entering Arizona.

Every pass through this rough, broken country was guarded by Apache warriors. They were like ghosts, sometimes appearing on distant ridgelines, but often as not marking their looming presence with signal smoke. In an attempt to pass over the well-marked trail at Stein's Peak, Walker's party made an uneasy camp in the shadow of the mountain. Several men went to investigate supposed signal fires at the base of the mountain. It was a signal all right, but not the type the men had expected. The smoke was simply a by-product of an Apache calling card. What Walker's men found there sickened them. The remains of three white men hung gruesomely by their ankles from a small piñon tree. Their heads dangled less than a foot above three small fires. The adventurers hastily retreated.

They attempted to find passage across the mountains again and again, only to encounter more Apache smoke. In their final attempt, they discovered yet another grim example of what awaited them if they proceeded. This time they came across eight bodies. "It was not the custom of the Apaches to scalp their victims," noted one of the stunned men, "but all of these were scalped except one, who had a luxurious suit of long black hair which may or may not have been the reason for their failure to scalp him. One of the bodies was in a sitting position, reclining a little backward against a bunch of cacti to which he had been bound and burned." Walker ordered the bodies hastily buried and led his men back to Pinos Altos.

◆─◎◎─◆

WHEN MANGAS COLORADAS returned to Pinos Altos after his failed peace mission to Acoma, he sought out Swilling. They held a council amid the ramshackle little community where some thirty families still precariously resided. Swilling greeted Mangas warmly, but he recognized the shotgun carried by the chief as belonging to a friend who had departed the Arizona Guards along with eight others to strike out for California. Swilling, carrying dispatches from Canby to Carleton, had found what was left of them at Apache Pass in July 1862. He seethed with anger, but controlled his emotions and disguised his true feelings. He offered Mangas blankets, beef rations, and other supplies if he would bring his people in. Mangas, delighted to finally receive a positive response to his peace overtures, promised to return within two weeks.

Mangas called his people in to council, meeting first with the Bedonkohes in the Peloncillo Mountains north of Stein's Peak, and then with the Chihennes. He assured the assembled warriors that the white men in the settlement were friendly and more reliable than those in Arizona. The warrior Geronimo spoke forcefully against this plan, for he did not trust the whites at Pinos Altos any more than he trusted the whites at Apache Pass. Mangas carried the day, soothing his men with talk of peace rather than the words of war. It was agreed that half of the Bedonkohes would travel the road set out by Mangas, while the other half would remain with Geronimo in Arizona until the peace was concluded. Geronimo insisted that most of the arms and ammunition go with Mangas in case of white treachery.

Mangas next met with other chiefs, Victorio and Juh, again pleading the cause of peace. They were also highly skeptical, but Mangas had faith in Swilling and, despite the recent betrayal of Cochise in the "cut the tent" episode, felt that the white men could now be trusted. The great chief was a formidable debater, and Victorio and Juh reluctantly agreed to his plan. Victorio insisted that he be allowed to accompany Mangas as a bodyguard.

Daniel Conner, a young Kentucky prospector who had joined the Walker party soon after it entered New Mexico, was with Swilling at the Pinos Altos parley. Swilling had convinced a dubious

Walker that if they could take Mangas prisoner, they might use him as a hostage to ensure safe passage across the mountains into Arizona. This plan was complicated by the sudden appearance of General West's advance guard of twenty soldiers under Captain Edmund Shirland. But, not surprisingly, Captain Shirland endorsed Swilling's plan, and a joint party of Walker's men and Shirland's soldiers departed Fort McLane for Pinos Altos before dawn on January 16, 1863. They hoisted a white flag, concealed the soldiers in the rudimentary log buildings of the village, and settled in to await Mangas.

Around noon the next day, Swilling suddenly let forth with a war whoop, signaling the appearance of Mangas. With young Conner by his side, along with a few of the other prospectors, Swilling slowly approached the chief. Swilling and Mangas began their treaty talk in broken Spanish. Conner, observing the talks, marveled at the chief's presence. "Mangas was a large athletic man considerably over six feet in height, with a large broad head covered with a tremendously heavy growth of long hair that reached to his waist," noted the Kentuckian. "His shoulders were broad and his chest full, and muscular. He stood erect and his step was proud and altogether he presented quite a model of physical manhood." Conner could not help but notice that "Swilling, though six feet tall, looked like a boy aside Mangas."

Swilling signaled his men as he laid his hand on the chief's shoulder. As the frontiersmen leveled their guns at the Apaches, Swilling told Mangas that they were taking him hostage to secure safe passage through Apache country. Mangas turned to Victorio and waved the bodyguard off, telling them to beware, for they "were not fooling with Mexicans now."

"Tell my people to look for me when they see me," he called back to Victorio as the Americans hustled him away. It wasn't until they entered the village and the soldiers emerged from the cabins that Mangas realized the full extent of his betrayal. Conner thought the chief dignified and stoic in the face of this stunning reversal of fortune.

Swilling hurried his prize south to Fort McLane. On January 18, General West arrived with the main column of troops from Mesilla and promptly demanded that the prisoner be turned over to him. When the diminutive West confronted the captive chief, Conner thought that he "looked like a pigmy" beside the old Apache. West unleashed a tirade at Mangas, who he declared had "murdered your last white victim, you old scoundrel," and ordered him confined in one of the adobe shacks.

As the sun retreated and a bitter cold set in, General West took the two soldiers of the evening guard aside for special instruction: "Men, that old murderer has got away from every soldier command and has left a trail of blood for 500 miles on the old stage line. I want him dead or alive to-morrow morning; do you understand? I want him dead." They understood.

The Walker party, even as they camped alongside the soldiers, always kept a sentry at night, and that night Daniel Conner drew the midnight watch. His sentry path took him near the place where Mangas slept beside the only campfire kept going all evening. Near midnight, as he approached the fire, Conner sensed that the two soldiers guarding Mangas were annoying the chief in some way, but each time he neared the fire, they stopped. He finally decided to hang back in the darkness to observe them. They stirred the fire, heating the points of their bayonets. When their blades became white hot they touched them to the feet and legs of Mangas. Finally the chief rose on one elbow, declaring in Spanish to the guards that he was no child to be played with. As he spoke they both raised their muskets and fired into him at point-blank range. Another sergeant rushed out of the darkness to discover the two guards standing over Mangas, smoking muskets in hand. The sergeant pushed past them and administered the coup de grâce with a pistol shot into the chief's head.

The camp was aroused, but the men, including Conner, were sent to their blankets with the report that the Apache chief had been killed while trying to escape. The sergeant hurried to General West's tent:

"Is he dead?" West asked.

"He is, sir," the sergeant replied.

"Very well, Sergeant, then let his guard go to sleep," the general ordered.

The general then returned to his own warm blankets, well satisfied with a good night's work.

The next morning, Conner watched with disgust as one of the California soldiers used a large Bowie knife to remove the scalp of Mangas. He casually wrapped the long hair around the severed skin and stuffed it into his pocket. The soldiers later rolled the chief's body into a blanket and dumped it into a nearby arroyo, throwing a little dirt and brush over it. This hasty burial would make their work less taxing when regimental assistant surgeon David B. Sturgeon arrived and ordered them to exhume the corpse so that he might acquire the head for scientific purposes. Sturgeon boiled the severed head of Mangas Coloradas in a large black kettle.

"It was the wonder of all who saw it," a California soldier breathlessly declared, "and was described by the surgeon as a marvel of size, symmetry, and closeness of bone texture." Dr. Sturgeon carefully packed the skull in his baggage, and in 1864, he gifted it to the famed phrenologist Professor Orson Squire Fowler. In his 1873 book, *Human Science or Phrenology,* Fowler would declare it "the shortest and broadest human skull I have ever seen," and pronounced the skull as larger even than that of Daniel Webster. For some time, he kept it on public display. In time the skull simply vanished—although it was rumored to have been sent to the Smithsonian.

On the same day as the murder of the great chief, General West ordered Captain McCleave and twenty cavalrymen back to Pinos Altos in search of the Apaches who had accompanied the Apache leader. Captain Shirland, with fifty more troopers, was ordered to scout into the mountains along the Mimbres River in search of Indians. McCleave's party reached Pinos Altos just as Mangas's people were coming in to inquire about him. Joined by the local miners, the soldiers attacked the unsuspecting Apaches. They killed eleven, including a son of Mangas, and wounded the chief's widow. On the morning of January 25, 1863, Shirland's men struck Victorio's people in the mountains above the Mimbres. The captain reported nine dead Apaches, but recorded no distinction of age or gender. He returned in triumph to Fort McLane with thirty-four head of recovered stock, including several army mules, and a collection of Apache scalps dangling from his troopers' saddles.

West, pleased with his campaign, led his soldiers back to Mesilla on January 25, 1863. In the long and tortured history of the bitter struggle between the United States government and the Indians for possession of the continent, few white men ever matched the stunning level of hypocrisy displayed by Brigadier General Joseph Rodman West in his official report of the death of Mangas Coloradas.

The chief had been killed, West reported to General Carleton, while attempting to escape. "I have thus dwelt at length upon this matter in order to show that even with a murderous Indian, whose life is clearly forfeited by all laws," he pontificated, "either human or divine, wherever found, the good faith of the U.S. Military authorities was in no way compromised."

Carleton readily accepted this thin tissue of deceit. He smugly reported to the War Department: "Mangas Coloradas, doubtless the worst Indian within our boundaries and one who has been the cause of more murders and torturing and of burning at the stake in this country than all together—has been killed." In a letter to a Kansas City friend, the general made clear the real reasoning behind the murder of Mangas. "Our troops have killed Mangus [sic] Colorado, his son, his brother, and some sixty of his braves," he wrote in April 1863, "and I am still prosecuting hostilities against the Gila Apaches, and propose to do so until people can live in that country, and explore and work the veins of precious metals which we know abound, with safety."

The killing of Mangas infuriated the Apaches. Cochise, already burning with anger after the "cut the tent" affair, now swore an oath to avenge the death of his father-in-law, mentor, and brother-in-arms.

Even more disturbing to Cochise and his people than the white man's perfidy was the cruel desecration of Mangas's body. This single act forever changed their behavior in their warfare against the White Eyes. "To an Apache the mutilation of the body is much worse than death, because the body must go through eternity in the mutilated condition," explained Juh's son Daklugie. "Little did White Eyes know what they were starting when they mutilated Mangas Coloradas. While there was little mutilation previously, it was nothing compared to what was to follow."

To Geronimo it was simply "the greatest of wrongs."

Not long after the death of Mangas, a Chiricahua war party ambushed an army patrol on the Jornada del Muerto near the San Diego Ford of the Rio Grande. The soldiers retreated with three wounded men, leaving two dead on the field, including their commander. The victorious Apaches cut off the lieutenant's head, carrying it off as a trophy—the first payment in blood atonement for the severed head of Mangas Coloradas.

8

THE CUSTOM OF
THE COUNTRY

I N JULY 1863, IN ONE OF HIS FIRST REPORTS BACK TO
General James Carleton after opening his campaign to subju-
gate the Navajos, Colonel Kit Carson requested permission to
distribute several captured women and children to his Ute allies. "It
is expected by the Utes, and has, I believe, been customary to allow
them to keep the women and children, and the property captured
by them, for their own use and benefit," Carson noted. "I ask it as
a favor that they be permitted to retain all that they may capture,"
he concluded. "I am satisfied that the future of the captives dis-
posed of in this manner would be much better than if sent even to
the Bosque Redondo. As a general thing the Utes dispose of their
captives to Mexican families, where they are fed and taken care of
and thus cease to require any further attention on the part of the
government."

For nearly two centuries this "custom of the country" had provided desperately needed Indian slaves to the impoverished and
labor-intensive economy of the Rio Grande settlements. Indian
slaves, in fact, had long been a form of trade currency in New Mexico. To the frontier colonel, for so long a resident of Hispanic New
Mexico, this seemed like a commonsense approach that solved the
dual problems of rewarding his Ute friends while also "detribal-
izing" the Indian captives. It also, of course, provided free labor
to work in the households and fields of prominent New Mexican
families.

Carleton's response shocked Carson. "All prisoners which are
captured by the troops or employees of your command will be

sent to Santa Fe," the general bluntly replied. "There will be no exceptions to this rule." The righteous New England Calvinist was as well aware of the "custom of the country." But he was equally aware of the fact that the federal government he served was fighting a great war to eradicate the evils of slavery from every corner of the republic. He ordered Carson to forward all Navajo captives to the Bosque Redondo.

But General Carleton would soon find this command a difficult one to enforce. Slavery had so long been a way of life in New Mexico that no one, including Carson, gave it much thought. Slavery in the Southwest was not dictated by race as it was in the South. There were few black slaves in the territory, and most of these people were the property of army officers. Most slaves were Indians who had been either purchased or captured in raids. They were invariably baptized into the Catholic Church and thus, in the minds of their owners, saved from eternal damnation by being enslaved. In the view of the New Mexicans, their enslavement was actually a spiritual benefit to the Indians.

HISTORICALLY, IT WAS the Spanish who brought institutional slavery to Apacheria. Native peoples, especially the Pueblos along the Rio Grande, had practiced some forms of slavery before the Spanish *entrada*. For the Apaches it was a common practice to capture women and children from other tribes and adopt them into the band, although some people were treated as slaves. The Apaches had no word for *slave* before the whites taught it to them. They called these captive people by a term that meant "they had to live with them." Those who were unwilling to join Apache society were killed. There was little slave traffic before the Spanish colonizers came in 1598, as there was no market or cultural imperative for it.

The Spanish had already developed three traditions of slavery by the time they encountered the Apaches. Slaves could be taken as a result of warfare against pagans or heretics. The prolonged war between the Spanish and the Moors also led to the *rescate*, or ransom, of Muslim captives as a means to save their souls by instruction in Catholicism by their new masters. This was applied in the New World to the purchase of Indian captives held by other Indians—which helped to create the expansive southwestern slave trade. Slavery was also justified as a proper punishment for rebels. Even though Spain never extended true dominion over the Apaches, the monarch still claimed them and their lands as his. Any resistance was thus rebellion, and legally punishable by enslavement.

Even though the Spanish king outlawed Indian slavery in 1542, it remained a common practice throughout Mexico, especially on the frontier. The *rescate* of Indian captives from other Indians became common, although slave-raiding parties still went out from the presidios. The Spanish soldiers, both regulars and militia, returned with scores of Apaches to work in the mines of northern Mexico, on the fortifications along the coast, and on local haciendas as field hands and domestic servants. In New Mexico, a friar characterized Indian slaves as the "gold and silver" of the land.

The Spanish imperial reorganization of 1772, with its centralization of military control over the Mexican provinces, initiated a new policy for the deportation of prisoners. From 1772 on, all Apache prisoners were to be forwarded to Mexico City for distribution throughout the empire. Under the guise of this legalistic reform, the imperial authorities stripped their frontier citizens of the lucrative traffic in Apache slaves as well as denying them vital prisoners for future captive exchanges. The Apaches were formally classified as prisoners of war and sentenced to a specific period of hard labor. This was often ten years on the Mexican coast, in Cuba, or other Spanish ports of the Caribbean basin. No Apache ever returned.

Between 1770 and 1810, Spanish soldiers conducted three thousand Apache prisoners from the northern frontier to Mexico City. The Apache women and children were destined for lives as domestic servants, and the Apache men were to work the fields or ports of Cuba. The deportations were finally halted after 1810 as Spain's New World empire crumbled in the face of independence movements.

The United States government also engaged in Indian deportation, but used a different set of terms and legalisms to justify it. Ironically, in several years' time, it would be the deportation of prisoners of war that marked the final chapter in the Apache Wars. The Americans did not, at least legally, enslave their Indian prisoners.

The federal government had called its glorified deportation policy "Indian Removal," and it had played a major role in American politics during the Jacksonian era. Back in May 1830, Congressman Davy Crockett had broken with then-president Andrew Jackson over the removal policy, denouncing it on the floor of the House of Representatives. Despite Crockett's opposition, the Indian Removal bill had passed Congress by a narrow margin and became the central tenet of American Indian policy for a generation.

Unlike Spanish policy, this American deportation action did not use the legalistic ruse of rebellion, for tribes who had always been friendly with the Americans were removed alongside those who had resisted the advance of the frontier. The United States government justified its action on the grounds of protecting the Indians from white settlers while allowing them time to become more "civilized." The fact that many of the Indians had already completely adapted to most norms of American culture did not save them from removal—for the root cause was always greed for Indian land. A wide variety of Indian tribes living east of the Mississippi River were removed by treaty to the so-called Indian Territory, which is present-day eastern Oklahoma.

It was this federal removal policy, along with the 1856 comments by the commissioner of Indian affairs on the need for future reservations, that informed General Carleton's construction of a plan for the tribes of the Southwest. His treatment of those tribes he deemed hostile to American settlement, as well as those tribes whose homeland had the potential for mineral wealth, was based on deportation, segregation, and civilization. Carleton wished to remove the tribes from their homelands, segregate them from the American settlements, and educate them in the agricultural arts so that they might lose their tribal identification and eventually be integrated into white society. After the Civil War ended in 1865, General Carleton's controversial experiment became the Indian policy of the federal government.

The Mescaleros had been the first victims of Carleton's policy. The general also hoped to deport the Jicarillas and eastern Chiricahuas to Bosque Redondo, the forty-square-mile plot of land along the Pecos River. It was not a desert; in fact Carleton had infuriated local cattlemen by confiscating their lush range for his Indian reservation. Even though the Mescaleros had visited the area in the past to trade with the Comanches, it was not a landscape suitable for a mountain people. The climate had been especially difficult for them to adjust to.

Captain John Cremony had been placed in command of the Mescalero exiles at the Bosque Redondo in 1863. When Cremony arrived he found nearly a foot of snow on the ground. "The Round Woods was only sixteen miles long and half a mile wide in the widest place," Cremony observed, "and for several miles afforded only a few scattered trees, which were by no means thick even in the densest portions."

It was obvious that locating enough timber to construct the necessary buildings and corrals as well as sufficient firewood to keep warm would be a major problem. The initial buildings of Fort Sumner would be of pathetic quality and none more so than the post hospital—"the place is only fit to keep pigs in," noted the post surgeon.

Cremony did not see himself as a jailkeeper, so he did whatever he could to make the Apaches as comfortable as possible in the inhospitable place. The Pecos River often flooded, and when it did not the water was brackish and alkaline. This not only made it difficult to farm but also led to chronic dysentery among both the troops and the Indians. This was good cattle country but a difficult place for large-scale farming. Yet Carleton expected the Apaches to eventually support themselves from their planted fields. They did the best they could with what they had, and Cremony admired them for it.

Indian superintendent for New Mexico Michael Steck shared Cremony's high opinion of the Mescaleros. He had always been fond of them and he did his best to help them, as did Mescalero agent Lorenzo Labadie, but both quickly found themselves in conflict with General Carleton. When Steck complained to his superiors in Washington about the pitiful living conditions for the Mescaleros at Bosque Redondo, he was bluntly informed that the nation was at war and that New Mexico was under martial law. He could cooperate with General Carleton or he could submit his resignation.

Labadie also clashed repeatedly with Carleton over allowing the Apaches to briefly return to the mountains to harvest mescal and to allow them to defend themselves against Comanche and Navajo raiding parties. Both Labadie and Captain Cremony eventually rode with Mescalero war parties in pursuit of Navajo raiders. As a result, Cremony was rebuked by his commander and Labadie was banished from the reservation.

The incredible success of Kit Carson's Navajo campaign, and the resultant arrival of eight thousand more prisoners at the Bosque Redondo in 1863 and 1864, doomed the reservation experiment quickly. Carleton had refused to believe Carson's repeated estimates of the potential for over eight thousand Navajo prisoners, and so he had to scramble to arrange even marginal rations for them. This was a population far beyond the capacity of the land to support or the government to ration.

Furthermore, the Mescaleros and the Navajos were, of course, traditional enemies with many old scores to settle, so this added fuel to the already highly combustible mix at Bosque Redondo. To make matters worse, the military authorities decided to turn over already tilled and irrigated Mescalero fields to the Navajos.

After disregarding the advice of both Carson and Steck regarding the folly of confining the Mescaleros and the Navajos on the same reservation, and on the inability of the Pecos River Valley to sustain so many people, Carleton appears to have had a change of heart, and he begged the federal government for additional assistance. The flinty general had suddenly become a grand humanitarian.

Unless increased aid was authorized by Congress, Carleton predicted that the Indian prisoners, both Navajo and Apache, would die by the thousands. "With other tribes whose lands we have acquired ever since the Pilgrims stepped on shore at Plymouth, this has been done too often," the general wrote on March 12, 1864. "For pity's sake, if not moved by any other consideration, let us as a great nation, for once treat the Indian as he deserves to be treated."

Congress, in response, appropriated $100,000 for additional food, clothing, and farming tools for the Indians at Bosque Redondo in June 1864. It was far too little and much too late. The supplies that eventually reached the reservation were barely serviceable. Broken and surplus goods had been unloaded from the eastern warehouses of war profiteers so that the Indians received moth-eaten clothing, flimsy bolts of cloth, and rusted or defective farming tools. Blankets, billed at $22 to the government, weighed a pound less than the standard-issue military blanket that cost $4.50. And so it went—as the Indians were defrauded, venal contractors made huge profits, and the Republican politicos in Washington looked the other way.

Captain Cremony, while never able to fully shake his ethnocentric bias against all Indians, came to develop an even deeper respect for the Mescaleros. They, in turn, appreciated his willingness to argue with his superiors on their behalf and his interest in their way of life. He rode with them on secret hunting parties and joined in their ceremonies. They confided in him and he made a serious attempt to understand their worldview.

"When will the white man ever become wise," Cremony asked, "and instead of treating the Indian with scornful indifference, give him credit for his intelligence, his quick and remarkable instincts, his powers of reflection and organization, and his inveterate opposition to all innovation?" Cremony had come to understand the simple truth that eluded the eastern humanitarians and Indian Bureau officials—that the Apaches had absolutely no interest in assimilating into American society as Christian farmers. To them it was but another form of slavery.

As the situation at Bosque Redondo deteriorated from bad to worse to nightmarish, Cremony was hard-pressed to make a case for the benefits of Apache assimilation. In a final debate Cremony found himself bested by Chief Cadete's Mescalero logic:

> *You say that because you learned from books, you can build all these big houses and talk with each other any distance, and do many wonderful things. Now, let me tell you what we think. You begin when you are little to work hard, and work until you are men in order to begin fresh work. You say that you work hard in order to learn to work well. After you get to be men, then you say, the labor of life commences; then you build the houses, and ships, and towns and everything. Then, after you have got them all, you die and leave them behind. Now, we call that slavery. You are slaves from the time you begin to talk until you die; but we are free as air. We never work, but the Mexicans and others work for us. Our wants are few and easily supplied. The river, the wood and plain yield all that we require, and we will not be slaves.*

Cremony and Chief Cadete enjoyed a smoke together while they thought about the chief's words. Not long after, late on November 3, 1865, Cadete quietly led his people away from the Bosque Redondo. Most headed back to their Sierra Blanca homeland, others scattered to the west into the Mogollon Mountains to join the Chiricahuas, some went out onto the Texas plains to join their occasional friends the Comanches, and still others went south to live with the Lipans. Cremony found the deserted camp on the morning of November 4 occupied only by nine sick Mescaleros who had been left behind. No soldiers were sent in pursuit, but from that day forward the Mescaleros were again at war with the Americans.

IN THE SPRING of 1863, news of a gold discovery in the mountains of central Arizona led General Carleton to designate all the land north of the Gila River as the District of Northern Arizona and to send three companies of California Volunteers to establish Fort Whipple near the new mines in December. On May 18, 1864, the fort was moved to Granite Creek, about a mile northeast of the new Arizona territorial capital of Prescott.

Carleton's ambitious policy to occupy all of Apacheria with new forts had also led to the establishment of Fort Bowie at Apache Pass on July 25, 1862. Fort Bowie eventually expanded to become one of the Southwest's premier posts, but at that point, the fort was little more than a scattering of tents around the vital spring with some protective stone breastworks. The Californians held the spring but could do little to protect the road from Cochise's warriors.

In February 1863, Charles Poston finally persuaded President Abraham Lincoln to separate Arizona from New Mexico along the 109th meridian to create a new territory. John Goodwin, a Republican lawyer, was appointed the first territorial governor of Arizona and Poston received the office of superintendent of Indian affairs. Poston reached Yuma just before Christmas to make a triumphal return to the land he had so recently been driven from.

Rumors of gold in Apache country had persisted for over a decade, but the Indians had managed to keep the miners out for years. In April 1863, two months after the murder of Mangas Coloradas, Joseph Walker and the remnants of his party departed the mountains of New Mexico for the newly created Arizona Territory. Walker's men, led by Jack Swilling, traveled through Apache Pass under cover of darkness to reach Tucson. Once there, they picked up a handful of new adventurers.

On May 10, 1863, the Walker party officially formed the "Pioneer Mining District" on the Hassayampa River a few miles below where the city of Prescott would soon be established. Walker and his men found a mountain of gold there, and by May 1864, more than a thousand people had crowded into the mile-high boomtown. Territorial secretary Richard C. McCormick suggested that the town be named for the American historian William H. Prescott—as his 1843 book, *The Conquest of Mexico,* was quite popular at the time.

Jack Swilling held a share of a claim that yielded $500,000 worth of nuggets off an acre of high-desert land. Swilling eventually sold this claim and went into the irrigation canal business in the Salt Valley. The result of this enterprise would eventually become the city of Phoenix, which replaced Prescott as the territorial capital in 1889. Millions of dollars in gold eventually were taken out of the mountains around Prescott at a time when gold was valued at twenty dollars an ounce. The gold strike proved critical to the opening of the territory to American settlement. But for the Yavapais and Apaches, it was catastrophic.

Swilling had made a small fortune from his claim on Antelope Mountain. The mountain was soon renamed Rich Hill, where gold nuggets littered the landscape and could be pried free with a butcher knife. Swilling sent two large nuggets to his benefactor Carleton.

"You must know that your discoveries and good luck have created quite an excitement," the general wrote back to Swilling. "I sincerely congratulate you on your fortune and believe no one better deserves it than yourself."

CARLETON FORWARDED Swilling's nuggets to Secretary of the Treasury Salmon P. Chase on September 20, 1863, with a special request. "These specimens were sent to me by Mr. Swilling, the discoverer of the new gold fields, near the San Francisco Mountains. If it is not improper, please give the largest piece of the gold to Mr. Lincoln. It will gratify him to know that Providence is blessing our country."

The general dearly hoped to win Chase and Lincoln over to his dream for Arizona. "If I can but have troops to whip away the Apaches, so that prospecting parties can explore the country and not be in fear all the time of being murdered," he pleaded, "you will, without the shadow of a doubt, find that our country has mines of the precious metals unsurpassed in richness, number and extent, by any in the world." But his hopes were dashed when the politicos in Washington made it clear that no soldiers could be spared for distant Arizona Territory.

IN JANUARY 1865, Arizona was transferred away from Carleton's command and into the Department of the Pacific, as most of the

California troops were mustered out of federal service to return home. In September of the following year, Carleton's many official sins, both real and imagined, finally caught up with him. He was removed from command and reduced to lieutenant colonel of the Fourth Cavalry in the postwar army reorganization.

The appalling conditions at Bosque Redondo, combined with Carleton's suppression of civil liberties in New Mexico, had embarrassed the government. A delegation led by General William T. Sherman investigated conditions at Bosque Redondo in the spring of 1867 and ordered the release of the Navajos. Despite an enormous expenditure on the reservation, hundreds of Navajos had died of disease and starvation by 1867. "I think we could better send them to the Fifth Avenue Hotel to board," Sherman grumbled as he reviewed the cost of Bosque Redondo. He negotiated a treaty that returned them to their Four Corners homeland in 1868.

As cruel as Kit Carson's campaign and the subsequent confinement at Bosque Redondo had been, it had actually saved the Navajos from the far harsher military operations that were to follow after 1865. The Navajos made their peace with the Americans and were thus spared what would soon be the fate of the Apaches.

Neither Carson nor Carleton survived long after the war. Carson, worn-out by his long years in the mountains and in government service, was promoted to brigadier general of volunteers in March 1865 and placed in command of Fort Garland, Colorado. General Sherman visited him there in 1866 to consult on the Navajo question. "His integrity is simply perfect," the general remarked to a fellow officer. "The red skins know it, and would trust Kit any day before they would us, or the President either." When Kit and his wife both died within weeks of each other in the spring of 1868, General Sherman took in their son William as a ward.

"Kit Carson was a good type of a class of men most useful in their day," commented the general on receiving the news of Carson's death, "but now as antiquated as Jason of the Golden Fleece, Ulysses of Troy, the Chevalier LaSalle of the Lakes, Daniel Boone of Kentucky, all belonging to the dead past." That "dead past," from Sherman's perspective, also included the Apaches.

Carleton did not live long after Carson. On January 7, 1873, he died in San Antonio of pneumonia in his fifty-eighth year. His passing was hardly noticed, but his reservation experiment at Bosque Redondo would have far-reaching consequences, not only in Apacheria, but throughout the entire American West.

9

CAMP GRANT

IN 1865, JUST AS THE CALIFORNIA TROOPS WERE DE-
parting Arizona, Johnny Ward moved his family out of Tucson. They did not return to the ranch on the Sonoita, for it
was still far too dangerous. Perhaps the memory of the abduction
four years before of Felix, who they both believed to be dead, was
too open a wound to allow Maria to go back. Ward and his remaining family moved down near Tubac, where he took to raising
hay and pigs on the abandoned Potrero ranch.

Ward was nearly sixty now, with a large family to care for. The
March 1866 territorial census listed his household as John and
Maria, along with Felix's half sister Teodora and four other children. They were among the 5,526 non-Indian inhabitants of the
still-besieged territory. Of all the early settlers on the Sonoita, only
the Wards and one other family remained.

The United States Army returned in the summer of 1865 to the
orphaned territory it had abandoned in 1861 and began to establish
a series of new military posts. Old Fort Breckinridge was reactivated
as Camp Grant, and a new post, Camp McDowell, was built on the
Verde River near its confluence with the Salt River. Thus began a
messy quilt of federal installations that were constructed and then
abandoned in response to the fluid Apache threat. By 1867, there
were eight troops (as cavalry companies were then called) of the
First and Eighth Cavalry, as well as twenty infantry companies in
Arizona. By 1869, reinforcements raised the total number of federal
soldiers to nearly two thousand men.

Commanding general William Tecumseh Sherman had little patience with the problem of Arizona, for the territory was busting his budget. "The cost of the military establishment in Arizona," he declared in 1869, "is out of all proportion to its value as part of the public domain." The enchantment of the desert Southwest was lost on the blunt general. "We had one war with Mexico to take Arizona," Sherman famously carped, "and we should have another to make her take it back."

Although the citizens of Arizona loudly complained over their perceived neglect by the military, they actually received a reasonable contingent of the troops available for frontier service. In the immediate aftermath of the Civil War, more than a million men were mustered out of the volunteer army. They were replaced by a standing army of 56,815 men commanded by General Ulysses S. Grant. Three-star lieutenant general William T. Sherman commanded the Division of the Missouri, which included most of the West, and in 1869 he took command of the army when Grant became president. His western command then went to Philip Sheridan. In the 1866 military reorganization, Congress, in recognition of the needs of westward expansion, increased the number of cavalry regiments from six to ten, and authorized the recruitment of one thousand Indian scouts if needed. Infantry regiments were increased from nineteen to forty-five.

Two of the new cavalry regiments, the Ninth and the Tenth, and two of the new infantry regiments, the Twenty-Fourth and the Twenty-Fifth, were composed of black enlisted men with white officers. These regiments came to be called "Buffalo Soldiers" by the Indians and the name stuck. These four black regiments consistently had the lowest desertion rates in the postwar army, despite receiving some of the worst assignments. The chaplain of the Tenth Cavalry astutely noted that his men "are possessed of the notion that the colored people of the whole country are more or less affected by their conduct in the Army." These soldiers understood that the eyes of the nation were on them and that many both inside and outside the army opposed the creation of the black regiments. They were determined to prove their critics wrong.

But Congress continued to constantly whittle away at this military establishment. By 1874, the army had been reduced to 25,000 enlisted men and 3,000 officers, half of its 1866 strength. Most of these troops were on Reconstruction duty in the South or were guarding the transcontinental railroad construction crews against the Great Plains tribes. This left few soldiers for duty in the Southwest.

From 1866 onward, tension between the military and the citizens they had been sent to protect ran high. It was apparent to many officers that hostilities were provoked by the citizens. Some felt that this resulted from the racism of the white population, while others sensed the profit motive at work. "Almost the only paying business the white inhabitants have in that Territory is supplying the troops," reported an army general in 1869. "Hostilities are therefore kept up with a view to protecting inhabitants, most of whom are supported by the hostilities." This cynical view of the Arizona population grew even more pronounced over the next twenty years.

ON APRIL 15, 1870, Arizona was established as a department within the Division of the Pacific, with a colonel named George Stoneman as commander. Colonel Stoneman, who had no taste for the Arizona desert, established his headquarters at Drum Barracks near Los Angeles on the breezy California coast. Stoneman, it would soon become apparent, would prove to be a careless and ineffective officer.

But the error of this appointment was also compounded by the decision to divide the territory of the Apaches between two distinct military commands. With Arizona now under the command of the Division of the Pacific, New Mexico and Texas, home to the Mescalero, Lipan, Jicarilla, Warm Springs, and Mimbres Apaches, were named part of the Division of the Missouri, which would be commanded by Lieutenant General Sheridan. This meant that communication, cooperation, or coordination against the Apaches, especially the Chiricahuas, would suffer greatly as a result of this absurd division of authority. The Americans remained obsessed with "lines on paper," but the Apaches moved about as freely as the wind.

Despite Stoneman's inaction, a remarkable young first lieutenant of the Third Cavalry, Howard Bass Cushing, became something of a legend throughout Apacheria for his determined campaigning. Cushing was one of four Wisconsin brothers who had achieved fame in the Civil War—one had died at Gettysburg, while another was a daring naval commando—but Howard had disgraced the family name in a drunken stupor soon after the war, and the episode had led to a court-martial and suspension for a year. Cushing wished to seek redemption on the frontier, and he quickly found it. He received the command of F Troop of the Third Cavalry on September 30, 1868, and proceeded to turn it into a crack unit. The lieutenant earned a reputation for boldness in patrols against Mescalero and Lipan Apaches in both New Mexico and Texas before being assigned to Camp Grant, Arizona, in March 1870.

"He was about five feet seven in height, spare, sinewy, active as a cat," noted Second Lieutenant John G. Bourke of Cushing, "slightly stoop-shouldered, sandy complexioned, keen gray or bluish-gray eyes, which looked you through when he spoke and gave a slight hint of the determination, coolness, and energy which had made his name famous all over the southwestern border."

Lieutenant Bourke had reached Camp Grant—which he described as "the most forlorn parody upon a military garrison in that most woe-begone of military departments, Arizona"—on March 10, 1870, and was assigned to Cushing's F Troop. Although an 1869 graduate of West Point, Bourke was hardly a typical shavetail. He had lied about his age to join the cavalry in 1862 when still only sixteen, won the Medal of Honor for his heroics at the Battle of Stones River, Tennessee, and then received an appointment to the US Military Academy at the end of the war. Few military officers could match Bourke's keen intellect and powers of observation. His wide-ranging interests led him to become a student of the land and its native peoples, as well as a master chronicler of the history he participated in.

Bourke had hardly settled into his new quarters before he was shocked by a local custom. Among the first Apaches he met at Camp Grant was a woman whose nose had been cut off by a jealous husband. "The woman was not at all bad looking," Bourke noted, "and there was not a man at the post who did not feel sorry for the unfortunate who, for some dereliction, real or imagined, had been so savagely disfigured."

James Tevis had witnessed a similar scene at the Apache Pass stage station a decade earlier. Cochise's brother-in-law had approached him in a quandary over what to do with his sister, who had committed adultery. The tribal leaders had given her the option of having her nose cut off or of being banished to labor in the mescal grounds. "She was a very good-looking squaw, about fifteen years of age," Tevis recalled. "I asked her which she preferred, to have her nose cut off, or to be banished from the tribe to the mescal grounds." She chose the latter and despite Tevis's offer of twenty horses for her, she was sent away. "It would ruin the morals of the tribe," a Chiricahua leader declared as he turned down Tevis's offer to save the girl. But this was a highly unusual incident and Tevis, in his time among the Apaches, did not see more than a handful of such mutilated women out of the hundreds he met.

Apaches, like all peoples, suffered from fits of jealousy and insecurity, sometimes with tragic consequences. A man was within his rights to kill both his wife and her paramour, although it was up to tribal leaders to cool his anger. Sometimes a shaman was consulted and love magic was used to regain a wife's affection. Since warriors were often gone for months at a time on raids into Mexico, a wife might easily feel neglected. Other domestic tensions could lead to problems. The birth of twins, for instance, was considered a sign of infidelity, and twins were always thought unlucky. Divorce was possible, although quite disruptive to the social order. "A man never whips his wife without reason," declared an Apache elder. "If he finds out she is unfaithful, he whips her, cuts her nose, or else kills her."

Although some Apache men were notorious "night crawlers," as the people called them, the blame for such affairs almost always fell on the woman. In this, the Apaches shared a common trait with

Victorian American society. This Apache response to adultery, as well as their overall treatment of women, was one of the excuses used by the Americans, and especially the liberal reformers in the East, for the subjugation of the tribe. Bourke later proudly proclaimed that among the first regulations "laid down for their guidance was that the women of the tribe must be treated just as kindly as the men." In time, though, these attempts to change the cultural relationship between Apache men and women would cause considerable trouble.

LIEUTENANT BOURKE, although he participated in several skirmishes alongside Cushing, was more often on duty at Camp Grant, where the threat of death from boredom was far greater than the chance of being killed by the Apaches. The main occupation of many officers was to drink themselves into oblivion, but not Bourke. He studied the nearby Indians, the plants, the animals, and waited patiently for the two-week-old California newspapers and the six-week-old New York papers. He decorated his quarters with Indian artifacts. A scout gave him an Apache scalp with ears attached, much like Kirker's men would have taken, and Bourke used it as a mat for his reading lamp. When a visiting friend saw his ghastly trophy and was sickened, Bourke realized just how brutalized he had become by his life at Camp Grant. He promptly buried the scalp.

In truth, this land was capable of desensitizing anyone. Vast expanses of desert broken by soaring mountain ranges, many of which seemed but a jumble of huge boulders cut by steep canyons, challenged the soldiers. The temperatures were often above a hundred degrees, while cooling rains were infrequent. When the rain came, usually during the summer monsoons, it poured down with a vengeance that caused dangerous flash floods. This was compounded by the wide variety of venomous snakes, spiders, scorpions, centipedes, and even a large poisonous lizard called the Gila monster. Little wonder that many army officers considered Arizona punishment duty.

Among the enlisted men, desertions were consistently at or above 30 percent. Most deserters carried off a good horse and a rifle, worth together from $150 to $300, and officers were certain that the local citizens encouraged these desertions by purchasing the horses and weapons for a third of their value. The army reward of a mere $20 certainly gave scant incentive to arrest a deserter. These soldiers were often Irish, German, or Italian immigrants fresh off the boat and looking for an easy passage to the goldfields, but they represented but a tiny percentage of the massive wave of European migration that brought more new immigrants into the eastern port cities every month than there were Apaches in all of Arizona and New Mexico.

Despite the heroics of Cushing, the army proved ineffective in dealing with the Apaches during the period from 1866 to 1870. There were countless scouting parties sent out in Arizona, resulting in 137 small-unit actions in which the army paid dearly—26 killed and 58 wounded. Military authorities claimed to have killed 649 Indians, but that seems an absurdly high number. In New Mexico, during the same period, the army engaged in 33 actions with Apaches and claimed to have killed 92. There was no doubt that the army, which had started the Apache War with Cochise in 1861, had by 1870 expanded the range of hostility across almost all of Arizona, from the Colorado River to the Mexican border.

The Apaches continued to strike at will and with amazing success. Travel remained dangerous, with stagecoaches and mail riders favored Apache targets. Charles Poston, who in 1864 was elected as Arizona's first territorial delegate to Congress, compiled a list of 425 Americans killed by Apaches from 1856 to 1862, and a partial list of 170 victims from 1865 to 1874.

But the 1868 election of Ulysses S. Grant as president boosted the sagging spirits of army officers and Arizona settlers alike. As commanding general, Grant had supported Generals Sherman and Sheridan in their campaigns against the plains tribes. Military leaders hoped that Grant would move to transfer complete control over Indian affairs out of the Department of the Interior and back to the War Department, where it had resided before 1849.

The Indian Bureau, as it existed then, was universally viewed with contempt by army officers; they felt it was hopelessly corrupt. To them it formed a central part of the so-called Indian Ring. This nebulous combination of crooked politicians, thieving bureaucrats, profiteering capitalists, and misguided humanitarians operated in the collective military mind as a grand conspiracy to defraud both the Indians and the government. Transferring control of Indian affairs back to the War Department would also provide employment for officers without commands in the rapidly shrinking postwar army. By 1869 it seemed certain that a transfer measure would pass both houses of Congress.

The first sign of trouble for the military came in Grant's inaugural address. "The proper treatment of the original occupants of this land—the Indians—is one deserving of careful study," Grant declared on March 4, 1869. "I will favor any course toward them which tends to their civilization and ultimate citizenship."

Then the president backed up his words with immediate action. He first met with humanitarian reformers, many of whom had been active in the abolitionist movement before the Civil War, then pushed Congress to establish a Board of Indian Commissioners. This board, authorized on April 10, 1869, was made up of religious leaders and noted reformers with a goal to extend Christianity to the Indians, oversee the fair disbursement of promised annuities, and establish new reservations throughout the West.

The old treaty system was to be abandoned. Indian agents and Indian superintendents were to be nominated by various church groups, and the "Peace Policy," as it was soon called, was to be administered by Indian Commissioner Ely S. Parker, a Seneca Indian who had been Grant's aide during the war. Under this new policy, the army could not enter or intervene on the reservation unless invited by the Indian agent, but all Indians off the reservation would be deemed as hostile and might be attacked. The Apaches, of course, had no reservations.

The people of the West were stunned by Grant's new Indian policy, especially when the first agents selected were Quakers. It seemed more than a bit absurd to many westerners to place individuals devoted to nonviolence in charge of warrior societies. General Phil Sheridan, who had outraged the humanitarians in 1869 by sarcastically stating that "the only good Indian is a dead Indian," quickly became the hero of the West. "Shall we Williampennize or Sheridanize the Indians?" asked a Nebraska newspaper in 1870. The answer came promptly from a Texas paper that editorialized: "Give us Phil Sheridan and send Philanthropy to the devil!" The pioneers in Arizona were in complete agreement with these sentiments.

Colonel Stoneman, in response to Grant's Peace Policy, curtailed campaigns and opened "feeding stations" at five military outposts where peaceful Apaches could come in for rations. One such station was at Camp Apache in the White Mountains, quite near the village of Felix Ward's Apache father, Nayundiie. Another was at Camp Grant on the San Pedro River. But Stoneman was vilified by the Tucson press for this policy. The citizens were certain that the women and children were being fed while the warriors continued to raid at will. In Pima County alone from July 1868 to July 1869, more than fifty Americans were slain, and in the following twelve months, forty-seven more were killed.

COCHISE CONTINUED TO be blamed for every depredation in southeastern Arizona and southwestern New Mexico. The chief had taken his people to Mexico after the Battle of Apache Pass in 1862, only returning in the summers to raid along the San Pedro and Santa Cruz. But the Mexicans had once again turned their attention to the Apaches, and in 1868 the Mexican government assigned a new garrison to Janos. No longer could Cochise and Juh sell their captured booty, livestock, and captives to the merchants of Janos in exchange for guns, ammunition, and liquor. The "den of thieves," as one American officer described Janos, had been shut down.

This renewed pressure from Mexican troops, which included a new scalp bounty, forced the Chiricahuas back to the Dragoon Mountains, which in turn made 1869 and 1870 particularly active years for Chiricahua raids in the Sonoita Valley.

In October 1869, Cochise's warriors took a mail coach in the Sulphur Springs Valley and killed the six occupants, including a prominent mine owner. That same month they captured a California-bound cattle herd, killed one of the Texas cowboys, and forced the survivors to flee to Fort Bowie.

Captain Reuben Bernard of the First Cavalry, who had been a dragoon sergeant with Bascom at Apache Pass in 1861, led several scouts out of Fort Bowie to track down Cochise. He and his troops then clashed with Cochise just to the north of the Mexican line and recovered the cattle as well as mail taken from the stagecoach. The Apaches left several dead men on the field.

Captain Bernard attempted to follow up this victory with a series of patrols, but on October 20, 1869, he was ambushed in Tex Canyon, a rocky, brush-covered piece of broken ground made to order for Cochise. Two soldiers were killed, a lieutenant and another trooper were badly wounded, and scout Merejildo Grijalva barely escaped capture. The Apaches knew Grijalva well. He was a former captive of theirs, and they often called out to him during skirmishes. "He would never be taken alive by them," noted a cavalry sergeant of Grijalva, "and he strictly adhered to the right rule observed by everyone in those days to always keep one bullet in reserve."

After that ambush, Bernard retired to Fort Bowie to lick his wounds and prepare for another scout into the Chiricahua Mountains. "When you go out hunting for Apaches, you have in your mind's eye what you are going to do," Grijalva remarked, "but you can never know what you may be led into or what you are going to find. It is a very uncertain business." Throughout the remainder of the year, Bernard and Grijalva were often in the saddle. Cochise was never cornered, but the troops disrupted any semblance of village life and forced him to keep his people on the move.

Lieutenant Cushing, determined to break Cochise's reign of terror on southeastern Arizona, departed Camp Grant on August 26, 1870, under orders to report to Governor Anson Safford in Tucson. After consulting with the governor, Cushing was given a free hand to operate along the San Pedro and throughout southeastern Arizona. The bold lieutenant kept his F Troop constantly in the field searching for Apache war parties, occasionally skirmishing with them. In February 1871, he struck two *rancherias* in the Santa Catalina and Pinal Mountains, driving the people into the snow while burning all their property and taking their stock. In the first two weeks of April, Cushing's company destroyed three more Apache *rancherias* north of the Gila, killing thirty Indians and burning vital food supplies. The Apaches came to recognize his face as the enemy.

On April 26, Cushing was ordered to take a select detail from his company and scout the Sonoita and Santa Cruz valleys in search of Cochise. Cushing headed south, accompanied by his English friend William Simpson, who went along as a civilian packer; Sergeant John Mott; and sixteen privates. He rested his horses at Camp Crittenden on April 29, then swung south of the Patagonia Mountains into Mexico. He reached Santa Cruz on May 1. Smoke signals had dogged his passage, so he knew that the Apaches were following. The hunter had become the hunted.

From the Mexican commander of the Santa Cruz garrison, Cushing learned that a large Apache *rancheria* was just across the border in the Huachuca Mountains. The American patrol departed Santa Cruz on May 2 to scout the Huachucas. Cushing did not find an Apache village, but there were plenty of signs of Indians around; as he moved north, he found the grass burned off ahead of him. The lieutenant decided to push on to the abandoned army installation Camp Wallen on the Babocomari River. The grass at the old military post was still burning when the troopers reached the Babocomari. The men were nervous, for it was obvious that the Apaches were near and in considerable numbers. Camp Crittenden was an easy march directly west through the Mustang Mountains, but Cushing was like a hound on a scent. His little command numbered under twenty, but numbers did not deter or impress Cushing. He decided to press on north to the next water source—Bear Springs in the Whetstone Mountains.

As it turned out, it was not Cochise who was trailing Cushing, for he was south in Sonora that month. It was Juh and Geronimo who were stalking the young officer. They already knew him well. Juh's son Daklugie remembered how his father had sworn to avenge the Apaches Cushing had attacked in the north.

Geronimo and Juh were something of an Apache odd couple. Geronimo, the Bedonkohe warrior, was thin, dour, and intense, while Juh, his Nednhi friend, was stout, jolly, and fun-loving. Juh (pronounced "Who" or "Whoa") was a giant among the Apaches; he stood at more than six feet in height. He stuttered badly; some said his stutter was the origin of his name. The two warriors had become inseparable friends as youths; they had then become relatives when Juh married Geronimo's beautiful cousin Ishton.

The other Chiricahua bands often looked down on Juh and his Nednhi people. To the other Chiricahuas, their southern cousins seemed entirely too devoted to raiding and warfare. They also often disagreed with one another's lifestyles. One Bedonkohe characterized the Nednhi as "outlaws recruited from other bands, and included in their membership a few Navajoes as well as Mexicans and whites who had been captured while children." Geronimo, although a Bedonkohe, obviously did not share these sentiments. He shared with Juh and the Nednhis a determination to fight. The two warriors rode together on countless raids against both the Mexicans and the Americans. And on this day, Juh and Geronimo were planning an elaborate ambush for the young lieutenant, but they were worried that Cushing would not take the bait.

They needn't have worried. Juh had laid a perfect ambush, with Geronimo in charge of the flanking warriors. Cushing rode right into the ambush and a sharp fight ensued. "The Indians were well handled by their chief, a thick, heavyset man, who never dismounted from a small brown horse during the fight," observed Sergeant Mott of Juh.

Cushing's friend Simpson had a new Henry repeater, with which he kept up a steady fire, pinning down the warriors. The Indians withdrew back to the rocks, but they left five dead on the field as the smoke cleared.

Juh and Geronimo then began to lay down a devastating fire from their hidden positions among the rocks, with Simpson, the best-armed man on the field, the first to fall. That was all Juh needed—he ordered his men forward. "It seemed as if every rock and bush became an Indian," declared Mott. Cushing was hit in the chest and then, as Mott attempted to pull him to safety, in the head. Two more troopers fell as the sergeant led a fighting retreat back to the Babocomari, leaving Cushing's body on the field. The soldiers rode all night, abandoning several pack mules on the way, and staggered into Camp Crittenden after midnight on May 6.

Messengers from Crittenden carried the word to Tucson that Cushing was dead. Within two days, three troops of cavalry were headed south, but Juh and Geronimo were long gone, secure in their favorite haunts deep in Mexico's Sierra Madre.

Lieutenant Bourke drew the sad duty of burying the mutilated bodies. The coyotes, crows, and buzzards had already feasted on the corpses. It was evident to Bourke that the Apaches had carried off several dead and wounded, but it was impossible to guess their loss. "The Apache was in no sense a coward," Bourke had to admit. "He knew his business, and played his cards to suit himself. He never lost a shot, and never lost a warrior in a fight where a brisk run across the nearest ridge would save his life."

Bourke buried the men in the little canyon where they fell. The bodies were later retrieved and carried to Camp Lowell for reburial. Cushing was, Bourke frankly stated, "the bravest man I ever saw."

"There is not a hostile tribe in Arizona and New Mexico that will not celebrate the killing of Cushing as a great triumph," declared the *New York Herald* on May 15, 1871. "He was a *beau sabreur*, an unrelenting fighter, and although the Indians have 'got him' at last, he sent before him a long procession of them to open his path to the 'undiscovered country.' "

10

MASSACRE

O N MAY 1, 1867, THE APACHES SWEPT OVER JOHNNY Ward's Potrero ranch. They came in broad daylight and took all his stock. He was wounded as the warriors seized his animals from the plow he was working in the field. Broken in body and spirit, he lingered throughout the long summer but died in October. The estate was valued at four hundred dollars by a probate court, and Maria, left with little, decided to return to Sonora with her children. She was ill by the time she crossed the border and soon died in Magdalena. Her children were farmed out to various families nearby. Maria died never knowing the fate of her lost boy.

Ward was among the most prominent victims of the Apaches but the list of dead mounted steadily throughout the next two years. Tucson had around three thousand residents by 1870, but outside the town limits there was no security for persons or property. Arizona pioneer John Spring noted that, between 1868 and 1871, "Cochise's band killed no less than thirty-four of my friends and acquaintances within a radius of 50 miles of Calabasas."

In August 1870, a mail coach was destroyed and its four occupants butchered on the road between Camp Goodwin and Tucson. The Indians also attacked the stage stations both to the east and the west of Tucson, and a large herd of cattle and work oxen was driven off from fields just outside of town. In raids around Camp McDowell, a wagon train was attacked, its captain killed, and twenty-five mules stolen, while the pay clerk and another soldier were killed not far from the post. On April 10, 1871, Apaches ran off most of the cattle herd at San Xavier, and a few days later another band of raiders killed four settlers on the San Pedro a few miles to the south of Camp Grant.

Throughout 1870 and 1871, the stock depredations and the attacks on wagon trains, stage lines, mail riders, and settlers were unrelenting. Colonel Stoneman, unmoved by either pleas or curses, embodied his name perfectly. He refused to change his stance and undertake offensive operations against the Apaches. But for the people in Tucson, it seemed time for a reckoning.

William Oury, now affectionately known as "Uncle Billy," formed a Committee of Public Safety made up of Tucson community leaders. The committee authorized the raising of a militia company, with Oury as captain, that included future mayor Sidney DeLong and Jesus Maria Elias, the leader of the large Hispanic community. Elias, in particular, had quite a score to settle, for two of his brothers had been killed at Tubac by the Apaches, while his brother Juan had been seriously wounded in a recent raid on their ranch outside Tucson. The Elias family had once run thousands of cattle on a vast ranch near Tubac, but the Apaches had decimated their herds, destroyed their crops, and burned their buildings. After the April 10, 1871, raid on their livestock near the mission San Xavier, Juan Elias had tracked the thieves almost to the gates of Camp Grant before recovering the animals. Nearly every citizen of Tucson had lost property, a friend, or a relative to the Apaches.

"Indian murders continue all round while Post-commanders are holding farcical peace talks and dispensing rations to the murderers," thundered an editorial in the *Tucson Citizen*. "Will the Department Commander longer permit the murderers to be fed by supplies furnished by the people's money?"

The committee sent a delegation, led by Oury and DeLong, to meet with Colonel Stoneman and apprise him of the depredations around Tucson. Stoneman, on an inspection tour of Arizona posts, was located by the delegation at the Gila River supply center of Florence. The two-hour meeting did not go well. Stoneman, once a soldier of great promise, felt himself banished to Arizona, where he now had to listen to the complaints of shopkeepers and ex-rebels. He informed them that he was committed to President Grant's Peace Policy, that moral suasion and rations would keep the peace, and that no more troops would be coming to Arizona. Furthermore, he told them that if the citizens kept up their incessant complaints, the troops now in the field would be withdrawn.

"We can expect nothing more from him than has been done," Uncle Billy reported back to the Tucson committee, "and if anything further is expected, we must depend upon our own efforts for its consummation."

CAMP GRANT WAS at that time commanded by First Lieutenant Royal E. Whitman of the Third Cavalry. Born in Turner, Maine, in 1833, Whitman had risen from the ranks during the Civil War to the colonelcy of the Thirtieth Maine Infantry. Through the patronage of General Oliver Otis Howard, a relative by marriage, he had secured a commission in the Third Cavalry in 1867. Whitman was a good officer, if a bit attached to the bottle, and a firm disciple of the Christian reformist zeal animating Grant's Peace Policy.

Not long after Whitman took command at Camp Grant, five Apache women, little more than skin and bones and with their scant clothing in tatters, approached Camp Grant waving a scrap of white cloth. The women were in search of a missing boy, who was indeed at Camp Grant but who had no interest in returning to the mountains. Although disappointed in the boy's decision, the women were delighted with the rations, blankets, and tobacco Whitman gave them during their brief visit. A week later, the women returned with word that their chief, Eskiminzin, wanted to meet with Whitman. The lieutenant promised safe passage for all who would come in for a talk.

Eskiminzin was forty-three, round-faced, short, and stocky. He brought with him his father-in-law, Santos; the Pinal leader Captain Chiquito; and two dozen armed warriors. The chief, who spoke with a pronounced stutter, declared that he wanted to make peace and to plant corn in Aravaipa Canyon along the stream he called "Little Running Water." Giving Cushing credit for his success, the chief said that his people were tired of hiding from the soldiers. He asked Whitman to issue rations to his people until they could plant and harvest their corn. The lieutenant urged Eskiminzin to take his people north to Camp Apache in the White Mountains and told him the soldiers there would feed the Aravaipa.

"That is not our country, neither are they our people. We are at peace with them, but never have mixed with them," Eskiminzin said of the White Mountain Apaches. "Our fathers and their fathers before them have lived in these mountains and have raised corn in this valley."

Whitman, torn between his duty as a soldier and his higher calling as a Christian, now exceeded his authority. The lieutenant told Eskiminzin to bring his people into Camp Grant and that they would be fed and protected by the soldiers while he awaited further orders from his department commander. "I had come to feel a strong personal interest in helping to show them the way to a higher civilization," Whitman declared.

As the Apaches departed, Whitman wrote Colonel Stoneman at Drum Barracks a full report on the meeting and on his plan to settle the Indians at Camp Grant. He asked Stoneman to approve his actions and send further instructions. The lieutenant realized that he was way out on a limb, for he had no authority to establish a reservation, so he anxiously awaited a response. Whitman knew that it would take at least five days for his message to reach California, and another five for Stoneman's response to reach him.

During the first week of March, Eskiminzin brought 150 people in, and within days that number doubled as Captain Chiquito and others came in. Whitman issued them all a pound of beef and a pound of corn per adult per day. He also put them to work gathering hay for the post and paid them with tickets they could exchange for goods at the sutler's store. Within two months, the women had brought in more than 150 tons of fodder.

By April there were five hundred Apaches at Camp Grant. Although he considered the Apaches as prisoners of war, Whitman did not disarm them, as he felt their weapons to be of poor quality. The naïve lieutenant, blindly dedicated to the president's Peace

Policy, somehow did not think to suspect the Indians of hiding their best weapons in mountain caches. Whitman also gave the men permission to go out on hunting parties as well as to guard the women when they went to gather mescal. He remained convinced that his careful inspection of the camps every three to five days guaranteed that no men could possibly have been absent on raids. Whitman, neither fool nor liar, was nevertheless a far too trusting soul. He also failed to understand that Eskiminzin could only answer for his own Aravaipa band. "I had come to feel respect for men who, ignorant and naked, were still ashamed to lie or steal," Whitman declared in defending his actions, "and for women who would work cheerfully like slaves to clothe themselves and their children, but untaught, held their virtue above price."

If Whitman was won over by Eskiminzin's professions of peace, he was hardly alone, for others at Camp Grant also trusted the words of the Aravaipa chief. Whitman's second in command, Lieutenant W. W. Robinson, was a reluctant convert. "I was strongly opposed to the peace policy with these Indians when they first came in," he later reported, "and was not convinced of their sincerity until I evidenced by watching their actions carefully."

THE SIMPLE TRUTH was that Eskiminzin was not lying about his desire for peace, but he was certainly promising Whitman more than he could possibly deliver in terms of his control over his warriors.

Many of the Apaches began to plant corn, but the ground was parched and the tools and seed Whitman had promised were slow in coming. Eskiminzin asked permission to take his people up Aravaipa Canyon about five miles to a place he called Big Sycamore Stands Alone. Here the waters of the stream still flowed freely. Whitman agreed to this, even though it made security more difficult. He had but fifty soldiers to guard his post and the Indians.

Six weeks after his original message to Stoneman, Lieutenant Whitman received a response from department headquarters. His message had been returned unopened because he had failed to properly write a brief synopsis on the outer envelope. He was reprimanded by a department clerk for this breach of regulations concerning official communications.

About the same time Whitman received his returned dispatch, Uncle Billy Oury and Jesus Elias met late one evening in a back room of Tucson's Congress Hall Saloon to plan their anti-Apache expedition. Oury's Tucson militia force numbered eighty-two men. "Americans all," Oury proudly described them to Don Jesus, "valiant and doughty knights resolved to do or die." There had been many nightly street meetings punctuated with fiery speeches by the Americans. The local press fanned the rhetorical flames with heated editorials denouncing Whitman and the Camp Grant experiment. Elias felt confident of enlisting forty or fifty Hispanics to the cause, but they would need even more men for an assault on the five hundred Apaches at the post. They decided to ride south the next morning to the Papago Village at Mission San Xavier del Bac to talk with Chief Francisco Galerita.

The Papago, or Tohono O'odham—the "Desert People," as they called themselves—farmed the floodplain of the Santa Cruz River. To the White Eyes they were a "peaceful," nonwarlike tribe, simply because they were semi-Christian agriculturalists who never contested the American invasion. Although they did not live by raiding, war was an important part of their life and culture, and like all tribal peoples, they celebrated the deeds of warriors. But the Papago did not seek material goods through warfare, although they became active participants in the borderlands slave trade. Instead they fought for spiritual power over their enemies. They dressed in the manner of the old Spanish presidial soldiers, and from youth they trained with their favored wooden war club and with bow and arrow. The Papago may not have been "warlike," but they were sturdy warriors. The Papago name for the Apaches was "enemy," and by 1871, they had fought a defensive war against them for more than two hundred years.

Francisco listened carefully to the words of his visitors. Oury and Elias hoped his people would join with them in an attack on their common enemy at Aravaipa Canyon and promised to provide guns. Francisco's people needed little encouragement to attack their traditional enemies. Francisco sent runners to Coyote Sitting's village at Pan Tak to recruit more warriors for the raid. He felt confident he might be able to field as many as one hundred men.

On Friday morning, April 28, 1871, a number of men, mostly Hispanic, began to slip quietly out of Tucson. They were headed for the Rillito, or little river, an oasis of green some eight miles to the east of town. By noon most had reached the rendezvous point. Francisco came up Pantano Wash from the south with ninety-two warriors, most on foot but two dozen mounted. Jesus and Juan Elias had recruited forty-six Hispanics, but Oury had been joined by only five Americans.

"Don Guillermo," Elias said to Oury with a smile, "your countrymen are grand on resoluting and speechifying, but when it comes to action, they show up exceedingly thin."

Uncle Billy could only nod in sad agreement, for the eighty bold souls who had signed up for the Tucson militia had dwindled down to six. "The valor of all these plumed knights seemed to have oozed out of their finger ends," he acknowledged.

A wagon soon pulled up to the group and the men hurried to unload its contents. Long boxes held Sharps carbines while others were loaded with ammunition. The weapons were compliments of Sam Hughes, Tucson merchant and Arizona adjutant general. At three o'clock Jesus Elias, who had been elected captain of the expedition, gave the order to march. One final act was to dispatch two men to Cañon del Oro to halt anyone attempting to travel the main road from Tucson to Camp Grant before dawn on April 30. The 146 men of the expedition—92 Papagos, 48 Hispanics, and 6 Americans—did not follow the main road but crossed over Reddington Pass between the Santa Catalinas and Rincons, and then went north up the San Pedro River to Camp Grant.

They traveled mostly at night, fearing army patrols or Apache hunting parties, and just before dawn on Sunday, April 30, they reached Eskiminzin's *rancheria* some five miles up Aravaipa Canyon from the army post. Elias and his Hispanics formed the southern edge of the silent line that advanced toward the village. Oury and the Americans moved in with Francisco and his Papagos from the north. The canyon walls were steep, rising high above the village, which limited escape routes. The Apaches, lulled into a false sense of security by Whitman's promises, had posted no guards save an old man and woman who played cards by a fire on the canyon rim. The card players never knew what hit them as the Papago warriors bashed in their skulls.

The slaughter commenced. The Papagos moved so quietly that most of the Apache victims died in their sleep from the blows of wooden war clubs. The barking of dogs and the cries of captive children awakened the village just as the sky began to brighten, but the canyon walls kept the village in darkness as the slaughter intensified. Soon the nightmarish scene was lit by the burning wickiups, casting bizarre shadows against the canyon walls. Some people scrambled up the rocks but were shot down by the Hispanics waiting in ambush.

Several Apaches, Eskiminzin among them, fled to the north, splashing across the shallow waters of Aravaipa Creek and up into the sheltering darkness of the canyon crevices. At the first sign of the attack, Eskiminzin awakened his family and led them to the creek. He carried his two-year-old daughter in his arms—but as he fled with her, he became separated from his two wives and five other children in the confusion. They all died under Papago war clubs. Eskiminzin escaped, but 125 of his people lay butchered behind him along the "Little Running Water."

The chief, who had played such a dangerous double game with Whitman by pledging to control his warriors when he knew he could not, and who had promised his people security that he knew he could not guarantee, had barely escaped with his life. He was one of only a handful of warriors in the camp that night—all the rest were out hunting, or preparing for a dance, or raiding to the south. Eskiminzin never told the truth of why the men had left the village defenseless that night, of why so many women and children had been abandoned to their eventual slaughter.

AFTER THE ATTACK, Elias and Oury led their band of raiders south, skirting Camp Grant and retracing their route along the San Pedro. They were slowed by the twenty-nine Apache children taken captive by Francisco's Papagos. Not a single raider had been injured. "By eight o'clock, our tired troops were resting and breakfasting on the San Pedro," Uncle Billy smugly declared, "a few miles above the post in full satisfaction of a work well done."

Lieutenant Whitman was having breakfast at about the same time when two riders galloped into the post. A sergeant handed Whitman a dispatch from Captain Thomas Dunn at Camp Lowell. Whitman read with alarm that a large number of citizens had departed Tucson and that Dunn believed them to be on their way to Camp Grant to attack the Apaches. The sergeant added that he had been waylaid on the road by armed men and held for several hours.

Whitman immediately ordered his two interpreters to ride to the *rancheria* up the canyon and tell Eskiminzin to bring all his people into the post. They returned with the news that they could find no one alive in the burned village. Whitman rushed to the canyon with the post doctor to discover a scene of horror.

"The work had been too thoroughly done," Whitman sadly reported. "The camp had been fired and the dead bodies of some twenty-one women and children were lying scattered over the ground; those who had been wounded in the first instance had their brains beaten out with stones." He was certain that "two of the best looking of the squaws" had been raped before being killed. He assigned burial parties and sent out search parties that found many more bodies. The total, according to Whitman, was 125 dead. All save eight of the dead were women and children. Two wounded women were found alive and were treated by the post surgeon.

Eskiminzin returned the following day, his baby daughter in his arms, to meet with Whitman. He did not blame the lieutenant, who was clearly devastated, but he did beg him to save the captured children. "Our little boys will grow up slaves, and our girls, as soon as they are large enough, will be diseased prostitutes, to get money for whoever owns them," he pleaded. "Our dead you cannot bring to life, but those that are living we gave to you, and we look to you, who can write and talk and have soldiers, to get them back."

Whitman sent a messenger to Camp Lowell with a brief report on the massacre and a request that Captain Dunn recover the children. "As they will undoubtedly be taken to Tucson," Whitman wrote, "and the government no longer recognizes private ownership of human beings, they should be turned over to your post." Dunn did nothing.

Whitman's detailed report of the massacre caused a sensation in the East. One newspaper described Arizona as a "sort of borderland between barbarism and civilization" but felt that, even for that benighted territory, this was an act of "unparalleled ferocity and malignity."

The shocked reformers in the East thought they had won a complete political victory with the implementation of the Peace Policy. The Indian rights activists had effectively used events like the 1864 Sand Creek Massacre in Colorado, the tragedy at Bosque Redondo, and the ghastly 1870 slaughter of Piegans in Montana by Sheridan's troopers to defeat the transfer bill, end the use of military officers as agents, and solidify national support for Christian reform efforts. They had felt confident that tragic events such as the Camp Grant massacre were a thing of the past.

The army attempted to show a united front in the face of stinging rebukes and petitions from the humanitarians. Sherman reminded Sheridan that there were "two classes of people, one demanding the utter extinction of the Indians, and the other full of love for their conversion to civilization and Christianity. Unfortunately, the army stands between and gets the cuff from both sides." Whatever the facts of Camp Grant, the generals were as one in their disdain for the actions of officers like Whitman who went outside the chain of command with their sensational reports.

President Grant, no doubt even more outraged that the massacre should occur at a post named in his honor, labeled Camp Grant as an act of "pure murder." He immediately ordered Vincent Colyer, the Quaker secretary of the Board of Indian Commissioners and a leading voice for Indian rights, to travel to Arizona and New

Mexico to investigate the massacre and explore the creation of new reservations for the various Apache tribes.

Grant bluntly informed Governor Safford, who was in sympathy with Oury and Elias, that if the Tucson conspirators were not brought to trial, he would place Arizona under martial law. Grant ordered US district attorney C. W. C. Rowell to Tucson to secure indictments against the massacre participants. At the same time, Colonel George Stoneman was dismissed as commander of the Department of Arizona effective June 4, 1871. His replacement would be Lieutenant Colonel George Crook of the Twenty-Third Infantry.

ESKIMINZIN, DESPITE his disgrace over his failure to protect the people, somehow managed to convince the survivors of his band, along with many Pinals, to return to Camp Grant. Whitman pledged protection, and more troops were soon transferred to Camp Grant to bolster security. An army patrol, coming south from Camp Apache the first week of June, encountered Eskiminzin and a small group of his people in Aravaipa Canyon and inexplicably opened fire. Before the soldiers realized their mistake, a warrior was killed.

"I have tried and my people have tried," Eskiminzin stuttered to Whitman. "But the peace you have promised to the Aravaipa has been broken, not once, but two times. Both times it was the Americans who broke the peace. The first one who breaks the peace is the one to blame." The chief stormed off with his people into the Pinal Mountains.

After departing Camp Grant, Eskiminzin rode to a nearby ranch owned by Charles McKinney, a thirty-five-year-old Irish immigrant. The little ranch was not far from Camp Grant on the San Pedro, and McKinney had long been a friend to Eskiminzin. He had often hired Aravaipa people to help harvest hay from his fields to sell to the soldiers at Camp Grant. The Irishman invited his old friend in to supper, and after dinner they sat together on the porch to smoke and talk of the troubling times. When the last smoke was put out, Eskiminzin rose, thanked his friend for his hospitality, pulled his revolver, and shot him dead at point-blank range. He then rode off into the mountains.

"I did it to teach my people that there must be no friendship between them and the white man," Eskiminzin sadly explained. "Anyone can kill an enemy, but it takes a strong man to kill a friend."

11

NANTAN LUPAN

LIEUTENANT COLONEL GEORGE CROOK WAS DOWN-
cast upon learning of his assignment to Arizona. He
found Indian fighting frustrating, despite his recent success as commander of the Department of the Columbia in the Pacific Northwest. "I was tired of Indian work," he complained, but
his protests were to no avail. President Grant had personally selected him for this mission, leapfrogging him over forty full colonels who outranked him. He would command in Arizona under his
brevet rank (an honorary rank bestowed for distinguished service)
of general. Secretary of War W. W. Belknap and General Sherman
both opposed Crook's assignment, but a piece of advice from General Sheridan to Grant proved crucial in Grant's decision making.

Crook and Sheridan, both from Ohio, had become close friends
at West Point years earlier and then served together in the Pacific
Northwest Indian wars. Over the course of the Civil War, both
men quickly won stars. When General Grant ordered Sheridan to
halt the Confederate invasion of the Shenandoah Valley in 1864,
he also assigned Crook to command one of the three corps of the
Army of the Shenandoah.

Future president Rutherford B. Hayes served under Crook
and worshipped his Civil War commander. "General Sheridan is
a whole-souled, brave man, and believes in Crook, his old class
and roommate at West Point," Hayes wrote home from the Shenandoah. "Intellectually he is not Crook's equal, so General Crook is
the brains of this army."

Crook emerged from the Civil War a major general of volunteers, but still only a captain in the regular army. Like his rival, the much younger George Custer, he received a promotion to lieutenant colonel in the army reorganization. Although often regarded as humble and unassuming, Crook was actually no less a slave to ambition than the flamboyant Custer; he was merely more subtle. "All that I require," Crook wrote the Division of the Pacific commander upon assuming his Arizona command, "are a few more horses and to be left alone."

Crook arrived in Tucson late in June 1871. His journey across the Arizona desert had been miserable. "Even at midnight, the heat was so intense that rest or sleep was impossible," Crook recalled. He traveled by military ambulance with only two companions— Andrew Peisen, a German immigrant who was Crook's "striker," or personal servant, and Archie McIntosh, a noted scout who had served him well in the Pacific Northwest. Captain Azor Nickerson, Crook's aide-de-camp, was left at Drum Barracks to handle administrative details.

The scout, McIntosh, was roaring drunk on the entire journey from Portland to Tucson. Born in 1834 to a Scottish fur trapper and his Chippewa bride, McIntosh had been sent back to Edinburgh, Scotland, to be educated. He returned to earn an enviable reputation as an interpreter and scout on the northwestern frontier. His brother Donald became an officer in the Seventh Cavalry and would die with Custer in the Battle of the Little Bighorn in 1876. Archie was even unhappier than Crook over the transfer to Arizona but, unlike his temperate boss, could at least drown his sorrow in whiskey.

Upon reaching Tucson, Crook met with Governor Anson Safford, Uncle Billy Oury, and other leading citizens. Their tales of woe won Crook over to the plight of the Arizona pioneers. Safford argued that the solution to the problem lay with the Hispanic population. They had been fighting the Apaches for generations, knew the country well, and could travel over it with but ten days' rations of dried beef and pinole on their backs. Crook, anxious to begin offensive operations, hired fifty Hispanic scouts and set the people of Tucson to work preparing dried beef and pinole to supply them.

Crook promptly ordered all the available officers in the southern district of Arizona to report to him. He interviewed each one carefully, learning all he could about the land, the climate, and the people, but also much about the officers. He rarely spoke but listened carefully. "This was the point of Crook's character which made the strongest impression upon every one coming in contact with him," recalled Lieutenant John Bourke, "his ability to learn all that his informant had to supply, without yielding in return the slightest suggestion of his own plans."

Bourke certainly impressed the taciturn general during his interview, for he was soon appointed to Crook's staff as aide-de-camp along with Lieutenant William Ross. Bourke would serve Crook ably for the next fifteen years as confidant, advisor, devoted friend, and clever press agent.

IN JUNE 1871, Crook sent a dispatch to his aide-de-camp, Captain Nickerson, to move department headquarters from Drum Barracks to Fort Whipple at Prescott. This pleased Safford, Oury, Elias, and other Arizona citizens. They were even more pleased by Crook's opinion of Lieutenant Whitman at Camp Grant, who, according to the general, "had deserted his colors and gone over to the 'Indian Ring' bag and baggage."

Crook's immediate plan was to march a large force to Fort Bowie. Crook was after Cochise, who he felt to be "the worst of all the Apaches," and his band of warriors.

On July 11, 1871, Crook led a grand military column, consisting of five troops of the Third Cavalry and fifty Hispanic scouts, out of Tucson toward Fort Bowie. Crook's purpose was to study the land, the climate, and the qualities of his officers and troops on the march to Fort Bowie and beyond. "We learned to know each other, we learned to know Crook, we learned to know the scouts and guides, and tell which of them were to be relied upon, and which were not worth their salt," Bourke later wrote.

When Crook reached Apache Pass, he discovered that Cochise's warriors had recently killed a mail rider near the post. Anxious to punish the murderers as well as avenge the death of Cushing, an incident all the soldiers mistakenly credited to Cochise, Crook led his column out of Fort Bowie under cover of darkness on July 17 and headed north. Scouts soon discovered the trail of some sixty warriors on the move with a large herd of stolen cattle. A troop of the Third Cavalry was sent in pursuit, but they bungled the attack and the warriors easily escaped. Frustrated, Crook now led his column northwest to Camp Grant and then on across the Gila River to Camp Apache.

North of the Gila, Crook encountered several Apache bands. Among them was Captain Chiquito, who had bolted from Camp Grant with his people back into the mountains after the massacre. Crook held his troops in close check to avoid any attack upon the Apaches while he opened negotiations. He told the chiefs that he wished to enroll the Apaches as scouts at Camp Apache, and that those who signed on would be fed, armed, and paid just like white soldiers.

He also had to convince his superiors in Washington that arming Apaches was good policy. "I have not only always found Indians used in this way of invaluable service to the troops," he wrote the adjutant general's office, "but that the treatment would go further to convince them of the benefit arising from their being friends, than all the blankets and promises government could heap upon them." Crook's reasoning went beyond the tactical value of the Apache scouts, for he had an ulterior motive as well. "It is not merely a question of catching them better with Indians," Crook declared, "but a broader and more enduring proposition—their disintegration."

On August 12, 1871, Crook rode into Camp Apache. He had with him his new military family—aides-de-camp John Bourke and William Ross, scout Archie McIntosh, striker Andrew Peisen, packmaster Tom Moore—and a small escort. Several Third Cavalry companies followed them in soon after. It would have been easy to mistake the bearded department commander, astride his mule, for a scout. Crook wore a cheap sack coat, civilian trousers, and a white cork helmet of the type used by the British in India.

Crook had come to the White Mountains to recruit Apache scouts. The Apaches would come to know him as Nantan Lupan.

Anxious to try out his new scouts, Crook ordered Captain Guy Henry to take three companies of the Third Cavalry, several of the Hispanic scouts, and a group of the new Apache recruits to scout westward toward Camp McDowell on the Verde River. They soon struck a *rancheria,* where they killed seven warriors and took eleven women as prisoners. Captain Henry reported back to Crook that his Apache scouts were "invaluable" but that the Hispanic scouts were too prone to kill noncombatants for bounty scalps. This confirmed Crook's suspicions and ended his experiment with the local Hispanics. Old hands like Merejildo Grijalva were kept on, but the other Hispanic scouts were dismissed.

Crook and his cavalry companies departed Camp Apache on August 15 for Camp Verde. His scout McIntosh led the way, although he was totally ignorant of the country. It proved to be a taxing march to the north up along the Mogollon Rim and then west to the Verde Valley. The trail, such as it was, proved difficult to follow and the little command was beset first by heat and thirst and then by a terrific thunderstorm. Even the unflappable Crook became a bit nervous as "trees were crashed to splinters not far from us." Water always came at a price of one sort or another in Apacheria.

As the party reached the western edge of the plateau they found themselves riding through an emerald forest of pine. The low humidity kept the underbrush sparse, so the forest was parklike and open. Crook, with but a handful of men, including Bourke, Ross, and packmaster Moore, leisurely rode ahead of the main column of troops. They conversed on the potential of the rich timberlands and the stunning beauty of all that surrounded them, when a sudden whizzing sound befuddled them all. The soldiers did not at first comprehend what was happening until the arrows thudded into nearby pine trees. They quickly got their bearings and, as Bourke put it, "every man had found his tree without waiting for any command."

A small band of Tonto Apaches had come within inches of kill-

The ruins of Johnny Ward's
ranch in the Sonoita Valley
(Arizona Historical Society).

Apache Pass as seen from the ruins
of Fort Bowie *(Author's collection).*

Cochise as depicted in Samuel Cozzens's *The Marvellous Country* in 1876 *(Author's collection)*.

Dos-teh-she, the wife of Cochise, daughter of Mangas Coloradas, and mother of Naiche *(Author's collection)*.

Mangas, the son of Mangas Coloradas *(Author's collection)*.

Geronimo was photographed at San Carlos in 1884 by A. Frank Randall *(Author's collection)*.

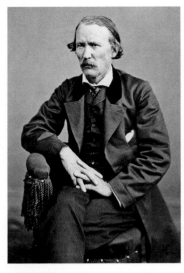

Kit Carson
(Author's collection).

General James Carleton
(Author's collection).

John Cremony
(Arizona Historical Society).

Jack Swilling and his adopted
Apache son Guillermo in
Prescott, 1875
(Robert McCubbin Collection).

Tom Jeffords *(Huntington Library)*.

General Howard greets Chief Santos at the Camp Grant peace parley. From Howard's *Famous Indian Chiefs (Author's collection)*.

General W. T. Sherman posed with his generals in 1865 at the end of the Civil War. O. O. Howard stands at the left, while Sherman sits in the center of the group, which includes (left to right) Generals Howard, Logan, Hazen, Davis, Slocum, Mower, and Blair *(Author's collection)*.

Eskiminzin *(Author's collection).*

Old one-eyed Miguel as he appeared on the trip east with General Howard *(Author's collection).*

John Clum with Diablo and Eskiminzin *(True West Archive).*

George Crook, Phil Sheridan, and John Nugen at West Point, 1853 *(U.S. Military Academy Archives).*

Crook and scouts at Camp Apache in 1874. In back stand Chief Patone, Diablo, Serveriano, Lt. Bernard Reilly, Captain George "Jake" Randall, Crook, Lt. William Rice, and Corydon Cooley, while kneeling right to left in front are Apache scouts Alchesay, Uclenny, Mose, and Mickey Free *(True West Archive)*.

General Crook on his mule, Apache, with scouts Dutchy and Alchesay *(True West Archive)*.

Captain John G. Bourke
(Author's collection).

Colonel Benjamin Grierson
(Author's collection).

Colonel Eugene Carr
(Author's collection).

General Nelson A. Miles
(Paul Hedren Collection).

Mickey Free in his prime *(Dan Harshberger, True West Archive).*

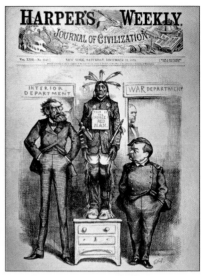

The rift between the War and Interior departments over Indian policy was captured by Thomas Nast in this 1878 cartoon cover for *Harper's Weekly* depicting Phil Sheridan and Interior Secretary Carl Schurz *(Author's collection).*

Al Sieber, on crutches, after being shot during the Apache Kid breakout from San Carlos *(True West Archive).*

The supposed fate of the captive boy Charlie McComas was depicted on the cover of the May 19, 1883, issue of *Frank Leslie's Illustrated Newspaper (Author's collection).*

ing the new department commander. Crook got off a quick shot that wounded one of the Apaches, but he and the other warriors quickly escaped before the rest of the troops arrived. The column pushed on to reach Camp Verde without further incident. The route they blazed became known as "Crook's Trail."

CROOK, PLEASED WITH his exploration of the country, as well as by the performance of both his troops and the Indian scouts, set to work on plans for the recruitment of more Apaches as scouts for a grand offensive to take place in the autumn. Lieutenant Ross, who as quartermaster was charged with enlisting non-Indians, hired on an impressive group of non-Apache scouts and packers. Archie McIntosh was on the military payroll, of course, along with Dan O'Leary, Merejildo Grijalva, and, most important, Al Sieber.

Born near Heidelberg, Germany, in 1844, Al Sieber had emigrated to America with his widowed mother and six siblings in 1849. His older brother had fought in the failed liberal revolution of 1848 in Germany and had determined that America would be the place to fulfill his democratic dreams. The family first settled alongside other German immigrants in Lancaster, Pennsylvania, but in 1856 moved west to Minneapolis, Minnesota. Young Albert found work as a teamster hauling logs to the booming lumber mills. He was not long in the mills, for Minnesota was the first state to tender troops in response to Lincoln's 1861 call for volunteers, and the strapping teenager soon joined the First Minnesota Volunteers.

By 1863, the five-foot-ten-inch, stockily built recruit was a seasoned veteran of Fair Oaks, Antietam, Fredericksburg, and Chancellorsville, although still a private. He later confessed to a friend that in those days he was "too full of the devil—played too many pranks" to ever win promotion. On July 2, 1863, the second day of the Battle of Gettysburg, Sieber fell when a shell fragment fractured his skull. As he collapsed, a bullet plowed up his right leg and came out at his knee. He was in a military hospital for five months before being mustered into the Invalid Corps in December. This unit of walking wounded served on picket and guard duty, and Sieber finished the war as a corporal at a prison camp in Elmira, New York. When mustered out of the army, he returned home to Minneapolis; but like so many other restless war veterans, he soon turned his face westward.

Sieber then traveled to California in 1866, and two years later he drove a herd of horses to Prescott. There he fell in with Dan O'Leary, one of the best scouts in the territory, and became the apt student of whatever this seasoned frontiersman was willing to teach him. That autumn, he found work as foreman on a ranch in the Williamson Valley, twenty miles northwest of Prescott. The exposed ranch was a favorite target of both Yavapais and Tonto Apaches, so young Sieber got quite a tutorial on Indian raiding practices. Eighteen men were killed on the trail between Prescott and the Williamson Valley in 1868 alone. Sieber went out on two "Apache hunts" with O'Leary and learned how to use his senses—to see, hear, and smell—and then to quickly analyze the evidence. He learned quickly that there was no room in this business for error.

Sieber lived among the Apaches for a time and studied them carefully. He learned and respected their culture, especially their mode of warfare. It was said that he could actually think like an Apache. He rose quickly after signing on as a packer at Camp Verde, for he was in many ways the indispensable man, and he quickly rose to be chief-of-scouts. "If there ever was a man who actually did not know physical fear," recalled an awestruck Lieutenant Britton Davis, "that man was Al Sieber."

Crook had his scouts, packers, and troops ready for a winter offensive when he received some disconcerting news in August 1871. "I discovered from the newspapers that a Mr. Vincent Colyer had been sent out by the 'Indian Ring' to interfere with my operations," Crook grumbled, "and that he was coming to Apache from New Mexico, and was going to make peace with the Apaches by the grace of God."

Colyer, cloaked in presidential authority, was coming to Apacheria to investigate the Camp Grant Massacre, as well as use a $70,000 congressional appropriation to establish fixed reservations for the various Apache bands. Colyer's humanitarian mission outraged the Arizona press, and threats against his life became so serious that Governor Safford provided him with protection. Crook ordered all of his officers to cooperate fully with Colyer, but despite the general's orders, Lieutenant Bourke privately referred to the peace commissioner as "that spawn of Hell, Vincent Colyer."

ESKIMINZIN, MEETING WITH Colyer at Camp Grant in September 1871, had quite a different opinion, expressing his astonishment that such a man "could not come of mortal parents, for no man so good as he was could be so born."

Vincent Colyer was certainly a good man, well-meaning, sincere, and deeply committed to bringing both Christ and civilization to the Apaches; but he was no match for the hard cases—both Indian and white—who made up the population of Arizona and New Mexico. Eskiminzin had him pegged just right—he was simply too perfect for this world.

Colyer had first arranged for a temporary reservation for the Chihennes at Canada Alamosa to the south of Ojo Caliente and northwest of the Rio Grande. Loco and Victorio had already settled their people there, and even small bands of Cochise's Chokonens had joined with them to draw government rations. This outraged the local citizens, who sent forth a petition to the New Mexico superintendent of Indian affairs in July 1871 that declared their intention to recover stolen stock from the Apaches and kill not only the Indians but all the "Indian agents, Indian traders, or Army officers" who got in their way.

Colyer fretted over security for these Apaches and decided to move their reservation north to the Tularosa Valley. But Loco and Victorio did not want to move. While they much preferred Ojo Caliente, they found Canada Alamosa, which had always been part of their homeland, more acceptable than Tularosa. Colyer also authorized the establishment of a permanent reservation for the Mescalero Apaches in their traditional homeland near Fort Stanton. Even though Colyer did not meet with the Mescalero people and was ignorant of the region involved, the reservation he proposed would eventually be established by Congress in May 1873.

On September 2, 1871, Colyer reached Camp Apache, where he quickly established a reservation for the White Mountain people. From Camp Apache, he wrote back to Washington of his delight upon learning of Crook "countermanding his order to enlist Apache Indians to fight Apaches." The starry-eyed Colyer praised Crook's "humanity and good sense" for "abandoning the practice of taking peaceable Indians from the corn-fields and compelling them to go on the war-path against their brethren."

Colyer next traveled to Camp Grant, where he surveyed the scene of tragedy and met with Eskiminzin and Captain Chiquito. No sooner had he arrived on September 13 than a large body of heavily armed citizens from Tucson approached Camp Grant. Lieutenant Whitman's cavalry detachment intercepted the sixty-man posse and turned them back. The Tucson newspaper ranted about this military effrontery, and Crook was highly displeased with this "unwarrantable" interference with the Tucson citizens. This was yet another black mark against Whitman in Crook's mind. Crook had also worked up quite a prejudice against Eskiminzin, who he referred to as "Old Skimmy," and who he was certain would make a fool of Colyer. Crook was wrong about Whitman, and perhaps even the wily Eskiminzin; it was clear that the Tucson posse was up to no good, and at the very least intended to awe Colyer and the Apaches with their show of force.

Colyer created a reservation at Camp Grant and named Lieutenant Whitman as agent. The reservation was a twenty-mile-by-twenty-mile square, bordered by the Gila River to the north and the Mount Graham foothills to the east. Aravaipa Canyon remained at its heart. Colyer also instructed Dr. R. A. Wilbur, the Papago agent, to investigate the fate of the captive Apache children taken from Camp Grant five months earlier. Wilbur reported that eight of the thirty children were in Tucson households but that he could not obtain their release. Of course Wilbur knew that the Papagos had taken most of the children and had already sold many into slavery in Mexico.

Soon Colyer traveled to Camp Verde, where he met with several Yavapai leaders and was deeply moved by their pitiful condition. He created a reservation for them in the Verde Valley and recommended that they be given guns and ammunition so they might sustain themselves by hunting. This was naturally considered an absurdity by the local citizens, as was the commissioner's characterization of the "roving Apaches of Arizona and New Mexico" as the most "intelligent, cheerful, and grateful tribe of Indians" in all the United States.

The president's envoy then moved on to Fort Whipple, where he was cordially welcomed by General Crook. Crook's good manners fooled Colyer into believing that the two men shared common goals, but in reality, the general was simply biding his time. After Colyer departed for San Francisco on October 7, Crook sent off a scathing letter to his friend Rutherford B. Hayes. "The fact is, there is too much money in this Indian business, for these people to die without a hard struggle," he wrote the future president on November 28, 1871, "and I am particularly anxious that the honest and good people of the country should understand what a gigantic fraud this Indian ring is."

Colyer, who made a living off his reform work, did seem blinded to frontier reality because of his Quaker beliefs; but there is no doubt that he was rigidly honest, certainly no tool of the nebulous Indian Ring that was such a bogeyman to Crook and other soldiers. Alas, Colyer's claim that he had solved the southwestern Indian problem was sadly not borne out by events that followed his departure. Crook's military had been reined in by Colyer, and within a few months, more than forty citizens had been killed by Apaches. One of these incidents, the Wickenburg stagecoach massacre, in early November, received wide publicity in the East because one of the seven victims was a celebrated young journalist. In the eyes of much of the eastern press, this tragic incident quickly discredited Colyer's portrayal of the Apaches as a peaceable tribe.

Eventually, it was Colyer's participation in the reformers' effort to oust Commissioner of Indian Affairs Ely S. Parker that led President Grant to abandon him. Parker, a full-blood Seneca who had served as Grant's aide-de-camp during the Civil War, came into conflict with the paternalistic racism of Colyer and the other leading reformers on the Board of Indian Commissioners soon after taking office in 1869. Hounded by charges of incompetence and financial misconduct, Parker finally resigned in disgust in June 1871. For his part, he saw a greater threat to the Indians in the religious zeal of the reformers than from his former army comrades. "Religious bigotry, intolerance and jealousies," he sadly commented, "robbed all the efforts made of their benevolent and humane character." Grant, who had been the best man at Parker's 1867 wedding—a controversial affair because he married a white woman—quickly soured on Colyer and soon forced his resignation. At this, Crook finally spoke his mind, expressing his delight to Hayes over the "decapitation" of "Vincent the Good."

COLYER, HOWEVER, HAD actually done Crook a great service by establishing reservations for the Apaches of Arizona and New Mexico, even if some of them were temporary and the boundaries vague. These reservations, at Apache, Grant, McDowell, Verde, Date Creek, Beale's Spring, and Tularosa, provided the military with a more clearly defined field of operation. The establishment of the reservations, seen by Colyer as a way to feed and protect the Apaches, was in reality the creation of expansive prison camps from which the Indians dared not depart. Any Apache who ventured off the reservation would be deemed a "hostile" and could be attacked by the army.

On November 9, 1871, General William T. Sherman, in response to the new reservation system, wrote the commander of the Division of the Pacific that "after general notice to Indians and whites of this policy, General Crook may feel assured that whatever measures of severity he may adopt to reduce those Apaches to a peaceful and subordinate condition, will be approved by the War Department and the President."

Crook promptly sent messages to all the Apache bands that they must report to their designated reservation by the middle of February 1872. Any Apaches who did not report in would be branded as "hostiles" and attacked by the troops. Crook at first directed his attention to the Yavapais drawing rations to the south of Fort Whipple at Date Creek. He had learned from scout Dan O'Leary that several Yavapais had been flashing around money taken in the Wickenburg stage massacre a few months earlier, and he was anxious to arrest the culprits. In March, Crook headed for Date Creek with two troops of cavalry, only to be recalled by a presidential order to suspend all offensive operations. Yet another peace commissioner was on his way to Arizona to negotiate with the Apaches.

12

THE CHRISTIAN
GENERAL

RIGADIER GENERAL OLIVER OTIS HOWARD, THE
famed "Christian general," was President Grant's new
envoy to the Apaches. Howard was not only cloaked in
presidential authority; he also outranked every military officer in
Arizona, including Crook. Grant wanted Howard to create more
secure and better-defined boundaries for Colyer's reservations,
which were now to be administered by agents selected by various
Christian denominations. He was also ordered to further investigate the Camp Grant affair, and to attempt to secure peace with
Cochise. This was a tall order, but Howard felt confident that he
could accomplish everything the president wished.

General Howard, born in Maine in 1830, was among the best-
known and most eccentric soldiers in an officers' corps studded with
famous generals and prima donnas. At West Point he had shocked
his classmates with his abolitionist views. Howard's obvious intel-
lectual gifts had secured him a position as instructor of mathemat-
ics at West Point in the years just before the Civil War. He had also
served as an informal chaplain at the academy, conducting prayer
meetings that diligently stuffed his students' minds with New Light
Christian theology as well as mathematical equations.

On June 7, 1861, Howard had resigned his regular army commission to accept an appointment as colonel of the Third Maine.
He had gone on to lose his right arm in the May 1862 Battle of Fair
Oaks, then he had almost lost his military reputation a year later
by his bungling at the Battle of Chancellorsville. He redeemed himself at Gettysburg and later that year was transferred west to join

General Sherman, where he ably commanded the Army of the Tennessee. His success secured Sherman's patronage, and Howard was rewarded at the end of the war with a promotion to brigadier general in the regular army. But even his friend Sherman occasionally bristled at the general's piety. "Well, that Christian soldier business is all right in its place," Sherman complained to Carl Schurz. "But he needn't put on airs when we are among ourselves."

In May 1865, President Andrew Johnson appointed Howard to head the Freedman's Bureau, charged with protecting the rights of the newly emancipated slaves in the South as well as securing their economic welfare. Howard also promoted black education and helped to establish the Washington, DC, university that still bears his name.

Upon Howard's arrival in Arizona, Crook was cordially contemptuous toward the new emissary. "I was very much amused at the General's opinion of himself," Crook snorted on Howard's arrival in Prescott. "He told me that he thought the Creator had placed him on earth to be the Moses to the Negro. Having accomplished that mission, he felt satisfied his next mission was with the Indian."

Crook's disdain turned out to be misplaced, for General Howard was no Colyer. Although he shared with Colyer a self-righteous religious paternalism, the general could also be a surprisingly level-headed pragmatist. His Civil War record, along with that ever-visible empty sleeve, gave him considerable credibility with the Arizona civilians as well. He was the perfect man for this difficult mission.

After the massacre at Camp Grant, a grand jury had been convened in Tucson in response to Grant's threat of the imposition of martial law to be followed by trial by court-martial of the murderers. On October 23, 1871, indictments for murder were returned against one hundred men, including William Oury, Sidney De-Long, the Elias brothers, and a long list of Hispanic and Papago defendants. The jury also indicted Eskiminzin for the murder of Charles McKinney, but he was never arrested or brought to trial. That night a mob of Tucson citizens burned US district attorney C. W. Rowell in effigy.

James McCaffry, a Maryland attorney who would later serve as the Arizona territorial attorney general, headed up the defense team with Granville Oury, Uncle Billy's brother, as his chief assistant. McCaffry also happened to be the Pima County district attorney. Judge John Titus, a Philadelphia attorney who had served as chief justice of the US district court in turbulent Utah Territory before accepting the same post in Arizona Territory in 1871, called the court to order on Tuesday morning, December 5, 1871.

Lieutenant Royal Whitman, fresh from his own inconclusive appearance before a military court-martial, was the prosecution's star witness. The defense, using that old legal gambit to blame the victim for the crime, put forward a parade of witnesses to testify to the guilt of the Apaches for recent depredations around Tucson. Oury, the ringleader, did not take the stand. Judge Titus remanded the case to the jury on December 11. It took nineteen minutes before a verdict of not guilty was returned. Many in the courtroom were puzzled as to what took the jury so long.

IN APRIL 1872, not that long after the verdict was handed down, General Howard, accompanied by an old friend, the Reverend Edward P. Smith, who later would serve as commissioner of Indian affairs from 1873 to 1875, met with Governor Anson Safford, who extended the hospitality of his home to the general. Even the local newspaper editor, John Wasson, who had been scathing in his repeated denunciations of Colyer and Whitman, treated Howard with courtesy both in person and in the pages of his *Arizona Citizen*. For his part, the general disguised his disgust with the Camp Grant verdict and attempted to keep up cordial relations with the city and state leaders.

After a visit of a few days, Howard's little group proceeded northeast to Camp Grant, arriving at the post on April 22, 1872. Howard's old friend Lieutenant Royal Whitman met him there. Whitman had been under arrest at Camp Crittenden since March on several of Crook's trumped-up charges. Howard, when he found out about this upon reaching Arizona, had ordered his immediate release. Whitman now urged Howard to place no trust in either Safford or Crook, for he claimed both approved of the Camp Grant Massacre.

Whitman arranged a council between Howard and the Apache leaders, including Eskiminzin and his father-in-law, Santos, for April 26. But when the soldiers climbed down from their military ambulance, the assembled Indians were startled by Howard's bizarre behavior. As Howard approached the seated chiefs, he suddenly fell to his knees in quite vocal prayer. "In two minutes there wasn't an Indian to be seen," recounted the shocked Whitman. "They scattered just like partridges when they see a hawk."

Whitman hurried after Eskiminzin. "What did he mean by bringing that man there, to make bad medicine against them," Eskiminzin asked Whitman.

The lieutenant laughed. "Why that doesn't mean anything," he told the chief. "He always does that when he begins any sort of undertaking—just as you spit on your hands when you go to draw your bow!"

The Apache chiefs returned to pledge peace as well as set forth their demands to Howard. Whitman should be restored to Camp Grant as their agent, Eskiminzin declared. Moreover, the Apache children taken captive must be returned, a formal peace needed to be concluded to prevent further Papago and Pima raids, and the reservation ought to be moved away from Camp Grant to where the water was better for their crops. Howard took note of their wishes and set May 20, 1872, as the date for all to gather for a second council.

Leaving Whitman at Camp Grant to make preparations for the grand council, Howard traveled west to Prescott to confer with Crook. He had briefly known Crook at West Point but had not seen much of him since. Howard considered Crook "a peculiar man" but respected his military record both in the Civil War and since. Regarding the Indians, they actually had much in common, and in the future the two would be allied as champions of Indian rights.

As Crook busied himself with preparations for the Camp Grant council, Howard traveled southwest to Camp Date Creek. Nearly a thousand Apache-Mohaves and Apache-Yumans, as the army incorrectly called the Yavapais, had come in for protection and to draw rations. Howard was anxious to secure Yavapai participation in the grand peace council, and he hoped that some of them would then travel with him to meet with President Grant in Washington.

After Howard's council with the Yavapais, he and Crook journeyed back to Tucson. There they met with Governor Safford, Jesus Elias, and lawyer McCaffry, who now represented several Hispanic families who held Aravaipa captives, to negotiate for the release of the children. Six children, four boys and two girls, were identified as being in Tucson households. McCaffry and Elias pleaded with Howard to leave the children with their "good Christian families" who loved them. Howard agreed that if the children were orphans he would allow them to remain in Tucson, but he demanded that McCaffry and Elias bring the six captives to the Camp Grant Council on May 20.

ON THE APPOINTED DAY all came together near the banks of the San Pedro, in one of the most remarkable gatherings ever held in the West. Governor Safford, along with McCaffry, Oury, Elias, and John Spring, who had left the army to open a school and acted now as a Spanish interpreter, along with several other prominent Tucson citizens, stood to one side with the six Apache children. Chief Francisco had brought twenty Papago warriors with him, while forty Pimas had followed Chief Antonio to Camp Grant. The O'odham people stood sullenly to the left, while the Apaches, led by Eskiminzin, Captain Chiquito, and Santos, gathered to the right, with several Tonto, Western Apache, and Yavapai leaders and warriors joining them.

General Howard, called Nantan Biganigode—or "His Arm Is Shortened"—by the Apaches, began the council on the afternoon of May 21. All the chiefs smoked with Howard, and then the general spoke.

"I am going to speak to you," he said. "We didn't any of us make this life. God made this life we are leading on this Earth." He pointed toward Safford, McCaffry, and Oury. "These white people have not been very good to the Indians."

Eskiminzin rose to speak but was so nervous he could not control his stuttering. He accused Elias of giving him threatening looks, which was likely true, then sat down to allow Santos to speak for the Aravaipa. Santos placed a stone before Howard and declared: "I don't know how to read or write. That stone is my paper. I want to make a peace that will last as long as that stone."

Crook, already angry over the cozy relationship between Howard and Whitman, viewed all this with a jaundiced eye. "The rascal had gone through this same operation so many times with other persons that he had it down pat," Crook fumed about the stone ceremony. "He hadn't promised anything, and didn't intend keeping this promise if he had."

Jesus Elias then spoke for the Tucson Hispanic community, warning the Apaches to obey their agent and the limits of their reservation or face extermination. Eskiminzin objected to this threat from one of the leaders of the massacre. "Have I not told Eskiminzin and Captain Chiquito that the Government has the power to destroy you all," Elias replied, "but that it does not want to do so; but wants to save you and have you live as other people live?" Elias declared himself satisfied with Eskiminzin's sincerity for peace.

Antonio now rose to speak for the Akimel O'odham (Pima), followed by Chief Francisco for the Tohono O'odham (Papago), and both pledged their people would keep the peace so long as the Apaches ceased their raids.

Howard then dealt with the most difficult question: the return of the captive children. He allowed Leopoldo Carillo to speak on behalf of the Tucson families who had "adopted" the children more than a year earlier. He presented the children as happy with their new lives in Tucson and implored the Apaches not to remove them from homes where they were loved. Howard supported this so long as the children were orphans.

Eskiminzin exploded in anger. He thought this had all been settled. Barely able to control his stutter, he admitted that the children were indeed orphans because many of the men standing across from him had murdered their parents. They still had living relatives who loved them and he demanded their immediate return.

Relatives of the children rushed forward to claim them and a tug-of-war erupted between the adoptive mothers and the Apaches. McCaffry rose and loudly denounced Howard as a liar. Several of the children, who had become attached to their new families, began to shriek and cling to their adoptive mothers. "I cannot stand this any longer!" Crook declared as he got up and stormed out.

McCaffry offered a bond to guarantee the return of the children if the courts or the president ruled it so. "Do you think we are dogs to sell our children?" Eskiminzin angrily retorted.

Howard, with events spinning out of control, called an end to the council until the following day. He sought out Crook's advice, for he was so angry at McCaffry that he planned to have him removed from office. Crook, seething over the children, unloaded on his superior. He was still furious over Howard's support for Whitman, which undermined his command, but also disgusted by the general's favoritism toward the Apaches over the citizens.

"General Howard, many of these people have lost their friends, relatives, and property by these Indians," he irately declared. "They carry their lives constantly in their hands, not knowing what moment is to be their last. Now, if, instead of affording relief, you not only fail to give it to them but outrage their feelings besides, you must not expect your position to shield you from hearing plain words. These people have suffered too much to have any false ideas of sentiment."

Crook took considerable satisfaction upon learning that his remarks had so disturbed Howard that he could not sleep until he found relief in prayer at three o'clock in the morning. Howard was a good man, doing the best he knew how to do, in an exceedingly difficult situation. The general had gone away from camp to sit alone and pray beneath the spectacular canopy of stars offered by the Arizona night sky. He found his answer.

The next morning Howard declared that the children would be turned over to the good Catholic wife of a sergeant at Camp Grant until President Grant could decide their fate. The six children were taken away as McCaffry and the Tucson citizens stormed out of the council. "A sort of a peace was patched up at this conference," commented John Spring, "but no one had any confidence in its permanency."

Howard also announced that Lieutenant Whitman would not remain as agent for the Aravaipa because of his precarious health. Crook, who would soon court-martial Whitman for a third time and force his resignation, had carried the day on this point. Howard promised Eskiminzin that he would move the Aravaipa agency from the unhealthy San Pedro, with its terrible memories, to the confluence of the San Carlos and Gila rivers adjacent to the Camp Apache reservation of the White Mountain people. While Eskiminzin hated to leave Aravaipa Canyon, he also realized that the water resources were not enough to support all the people who had gathered there. In the last several months, many people, among both the Apaches and the soldiers, had been sickened from malarial fevers common at Camp Grant, so it seemed a good time to move. Several months later, in February 1873, the Apaches, numbering nearly two thousand, crossed the mountains to settle at San Carlos.

Months later, President Grant eventually returned the six children to their Apache relatives. Several children were still held by Tucson families and many more were held by the Papagos. In time, as they grew older, the Papagos' captives were sold into slavery in Sonora for from fifty to one hundred dollars each. Old habits die hard.

Howard was well pleased with his work, and many years later remembered a climactic moment of joy that somehow no one else who was there witnessed. "The Indians of different tribes doubly embraced each other—Apache and Pima, Papago and Mojave— and even the Mexicans participated in the joy that became universal. I said to myself, 'Surely the Lord is with us.'"

Despite this profusion of brotherly love, Howard had a difficult time convincing the Indian leaders to accompany him back to Washington to meet with the "Great White Father." Eskiminzin refused to go, but Santos agreed, along with two Pimas and one

Papago, two Yavapai warriors, and three Western Apache chiefs—Eskeltesela, Old Pedro, and one-eyed Miguel.

The Indians traveled with Howard to the railhead in Pueblo, Colorado, and from there they went on to Washington. Dressed in brand-new suits, they met with President Grant in late June 1872 and were each given peace medals and fifty dollars. They soon also met with Vincent Colyer and members of the Dutch Reformed Church in New York City. President Grant had assigned that Christian denomination to have control over all the Apache agencies. While in New York, Howard arranged for Chief Miguel to be fitted with a glass eye, which caused considerable excitement when he returned to the White Mountains.

One of the most touching moments of the entire journey occurred in Washington when the Indians visited the College of Deaf Mutes. Miguel immediately established a rapport with the deaf boys and, with sign language, enthralled them with tales of the animals and forests far to the west where he lived. They responded with stories of their own, and for a brief moment common humanity overcame the yawning gulf of race and culture.

As General Howard's eyes welled with tears while he watched the Apaches and the deaf children, not far away, in the office of the secretary of war, orders were issued to General Crook in Arizona Territory. He was now free to begin military operations against all nonreservation Apaches. Nantan Lupan—the wolf—had been slipped from his chain.

13

MICKEY FREE

O N NOVEMBER 29, 1872, GENERAL GEORGE CROOK returned to Camp Apache; the word had already started to spread that he was looking to hire more Apache scouts. The long-delayed grand offensive was about to begin. Lieutenant Bourke was in charge of recruitment. "We lined up to be chosen," remembered Felix Ward's adopted brother John Rope. "These officers looked me over to see if I was all right. They felt my arms and legs and pounded my chest to see if I would cough. That's the way they did with all the scouts they picked."

The scouts that had enlisted before Crook took command in Arizona were often mixed-bloods or, like Merejildo Grijalva, captives raised by the Apaches. There was considerable prejudice against the use of Indian scouts in Arizona. The O'odham people, both Papago and Pima, despite their long history of warfare with the Apaches, frustrated the white soldiers with their elaborate death rituals after a battle. Yuma and Mohave scouts also proved problematic to their American officers. Lieutenant Thomas Cruse summed up their military service as simply "no good," and even the sympathetic Bourke characterized the Pimas as "a great fraud" as scouts. No one gave any thought to enlisting Apaches as scouts before the arrival of Crook.

On December 2, 1872, Bourke enrolled forty-seven Apache scouts, mostly Western White Mountain men. Bourke was particularly intrigued by a young red-haired Apache. He underestimated his age at eighteen, described his hair and eyes as black, his weight at 135 pounds, and his complexion as "copper." Of course, no mixed-blood scouts could be enrolled, so the red hair, single blue eye, and light complexion had to be fudged. Bourke named this unusual Apache recruit "Mickey Free."

Since the soldiers could not pronounce many of the scouts' Apache names, they simply gave them new names. "They struck everybody as being full of significance and perfectly appropriate at the time they were bestowed," recalled Lieutenant Bourke. In return, the Apaches called Bourke Nantan Hosh Dijoole, or Captain Cactus. The names stuck, and the Apache scouts became forever tagged as Peaches, Dutchy, Dandy-Jim, Cut-Mouth Mose, Buckshot, Daniel Webster, Slim Jim, and Mickey Free.

The one-eyed Felix, with his broad features, blunt nose, and wild mop of red hair, impressed the officers as both Irish and impish. Mickey Free was a colorful character in the popular 1840 novel *Charles O'Malley, The Irish Dragoon* by the author Charles Lever. The Irish author, who wrote under the pen name Harry Lorrequer, enjoyed considerable success with his military romances, and the O'Malley novel was his most popular work. The roguish Mickey Free was certainly his most famous character.

The name Mickey Free, combined with his unique, even exotic physical appearance, meant that the new army scout carried considerable baggage with him. Since he was illiterate, he could neither read about the literary character he was named for nor get the inside joke that the name insinuated to the army officers who met him. Because of his new name, he instantly became one of the best known of the Apache scouts and a character remembered by everyone he encountered. In time the true story of his origins spread, and soldier and civilian alike came to know Mickey Free as the boy whose abduction had started the war for Apacheria.

Over the past several years, Mickey Free had changed from a pioneer ranch boy into an Apache warrior. "Mickey Free was a warrior and they train him to be a warrior, and he went on Apache raids," remembered the great-granddaughter of Adahay. Mickey had spoken bluntly of his part in a raid against other Indians in which he had killed women and children. "They did that to our

Apache tribe, they kill a lotta Apache," she declared; "he was thinking about that and he was doing the same thing; and he is not an Apache? He sure thought he was Apache."

Mickey the warrior now began another chameleon-like transformation—this time into a white army scout. "This wandering half-breed, whose being caused the woeful events of a decade," commented Charles T. Connell, who briefly employed Mickey as an interpreter, "was an indolent creature." Connell believed that the scout's eye had been lost in combat with a bear: "He usually allowed his hair to fall over the affected eye, but his appearance with a defective eye, his ugly features and sneering countenance, gave him a decidedly repulsive appearance." As Connell's reaction to him made clear, Mickey Free would find the transformation back into the white world to be far more difficult than his transformation into an Apache.

CROOK HAD HARDLY been inactive before his return to Camp Apache. Hank Hewitt and John "Yank" Bartlett ran the finest mule train in the Southwest, and Crook kept them constantly employed lest someone else hire them. He had kept "Hank 'n' Yank's Pack Train," with its 145 superb mules, under contract while both Colyer and Howard negotiated with the Apaches. Crook had a fascination, bordering on an obsession, with mules. He overhauled the entire packtrain system and wisely invested resources in able packmasters such as Hank Hewitt, Tom Moore, and Tom Horn. He fired men who abused the animals and initiated a system that got rid of ill-fitting military pack cushions and replaced them with Mexican-inspired cushions stuffed with straw that evenly distributed the heavy packs on the mules. Several saddle blankets were layered on the mules to prevent sores, with the *aparejo* (pack-saddle) placed over them before the load was added.

"Every article used in these pack-trains had to be of the best materials," Bourke stated, "for the very excellent reason that while out on a scout, it was impossible to replace anything broken, and a column might be embarrassed by the failure of a train to arrive with ammunition or rations." Crook's packtrains became the army gold standard for generations to come.

The language of the packers quickly entered the army vocabulary. A skittish, inexperienced young mule had its tail shaved so as to be instantly recognizable to the packers. "Shavetail" soon became the name for every spit-and-polish, greenhorn lieutenant from the East. A bell-sharp mule was a sedate and well-trained animal, ready for the toughest job. That became the name for the seasoned old captain who had served many years on the frontier.

In December 1871, Crook's command had been reinforced by the Fifth Cavalry, replacing the Third Cavalry, in anticipation of the grand offensive. The regimental headquarters, under Major Eugene Carr, along with six companies, had departed their stations in Nebraska and Wyoming in November to travel to Fort McDowell. A second detachment of six companies of the Fifth reached Fort Yuma in January 1872 and was scattered to various Arizona posts.

Major Carr, with full Cossack beard and erect bearing, was a man who inspired confidence in all those around him. After his 1850 West Point graduation, he had served with the Mounted Rifles on the frontier from 1852 to 1860, suffering a serious arrow wound during an 1854 skirmish with Apaches in Texas. During the Civil War he received the Medal of Honor for his heroics and emerged from the war with brevets as major general in both the volunteer and regular service.

Crook declared that November 15, 1872, would be the official date to launch offensive operations. The cold was his ally, for it hampered movement by the Apache warriors, encumbered by their families, and prevented them from replenishing their food supplies. Crook counted on winter snow to provide his mobile strike forces and their packtrains with enough water. This was a risky gamble, but it would pay off for him.

The orders to the troops at every military post were the same: If the Apaches would surrender, they could; but if they chose to fight, they were to be relentlessly pursued and destroyed "in one good dose instead of in a number of petty engagements, but in either case were to be hunted down until the last one in hostility had been killed or captured." Women and children were to be captured, not killed, and all prisoners were to be well treated.

"When prisoners could be induced to enlist as scouts, they should be so enlisted," Crook ordered, "because the wilder the Apache was, the more he was likely to know of the wiles and stratagems of those still out in the mountains." No excuse was acceptable to Crook, and no sacrifice considered by him to be too great. The campaign was to be "short, sharp, and decisive."

On November 16, 1872, three cavalry columns departed Camp Hualapai, some thirty-six miles to the northwest of Fort Whipple. Each column was composed of a cavalry troop and thirty Hualapai or Mojave scouts. Sieber commanded the Hualapais, who were under orders to scour the Chino Valley and the headwaters of the Verde River all the way north to the San Francisco Mountains. Two similar columns left Camp Date Creek at the same time. Several newly enlisted Yavapai scouts guided the troops. The rest of the Yavapais were relocated to Camp Verde, then Camp Date Creek was closed as both reservation and military post.

The department commander's headquarters was to be in the field. Crook departed for Camp Apache on November 18 to recruit more Western Apaches as scouts and get another column into the field. They reached the camp on Friday, November 29, where they were greeted warmly by Captain George "Jake" Randall, the post commander and an officer in Crook's own Twenty-Third Infantry.

As Bourke busied himself recruiting Apache scouts, including Mickey Free, Crook conferred with Randall on offensive operations. Randall was to scout to the west along the Salt River to Fort McDowell. Corydon Cooley would command the Apache scouts. "I organized the troops there into commands composed of white troops and Indian scouts with a pack train for each, so they could act independently of each other," Crook reported. "While they were sufficiently large to prevent disaster, they were small enough to slip around out of sight of the hostiles."

Captain Randall, one of Crook's most trusted officers, was popular among the White Mountain people, who called him both

Nantan Jake and Nantan Black Moustache. Cooley, the commander of Mickey Free and the other Apache scouts, was an old frontier hand. Born in Virginia in 1836, he had journeyed to Santa Fe in 1856, where he had joined the New Mexico Volunteers and fought alongside Kit Carson at Valverde. He was at old Fort McLane when Mangas Coloradas was murdered, and then drifted into central Arizona with the first mining boom. Through fortunate marriages to two of Chief Pedro's daughters, Cora and Molly, he secured his place among the White Mountain people. Cora died in 1876 but Cooley's marriage to Molly lasted until his 1911 death.

Molly Cooley convinced Lieutenant Bourke that the key to solving the "Apache problem" lay with women. "Let the main work be done with the young women," Bourke urged his superiors, for "in all tribes the influence of the women, although silent, is most potent." Crook agreed.

Crook hurried onward to Camp Grant on Tuesday, December 3, so Bourke had to turn the duty of recruiting the rest of the White Mountain scouts over to Lieutenant Alexander Brodie of the First Cavalry. Brodie, a New Yorker who had graduated from West Point in 1870, later became one of Teddy Roosevelt's Rough Riders and then governor of Arizona Territory. Cooley and Brodie hurriedly completed the recruitment of the forty-seven Apache scouts for Captain Randall's expedition. Randall's small column scouted west along the Salt River, across the southern Tonto Basin, and all the way to Fort McDowell on the west bank of the Verde. Cooley and his scouts covered the point and the flanks of the column. This would be Mickey Free's first campaign as an American soldier.

A CHIEF NAMED Delshay, or Red Ant, and his band of two hundred Tonto Apaches formed Randall's main target. The chief was one of the most successful fighters in the mountains, so much so that he had disdained to talk peace with either Colyer or Howard. On the morning of December 10, 1872, one of Randall's detachments, with but eight soldiers and twenty scouts, struck Delshay's main encampment at Bad Rock Mountain. Mickey Free and the scouts did most of the fighting, killing fourteen Tontos in a two-hour battle before burning their *rancheria*. Delshay and most of his people managed to escape, but without their food stores and most of their mules.

Three days later, the scouts surprised another Tonto camp. They captured six women and a child and claimed to have killed eleven warriors. Randall led his triumphant column into Fort McDowell on December 16. Mickey and the White Mountain scouts had proven their worth. Even the Prescott *Arizona Weekly Miner* felt compelled to note that "the friendly Indians too deserve the thanks of all good Americans."

Lieutenant Bourke now became an even more devoted disciple of Crook's scout policy. "The longer we knew the Apache scouts," he declared, "the better we liked them. They were wilder and more suspicious than the Pimas and Maricopas, but far more reliable, and endowed with a greater amount of courage and daring."

Jake Randall had his men back in the field by the second week of January 1873. Lieutenant Brodie commanded forty-four men of the First Cavalry along with the Apache scouts. They scoured the country south of the White Mountains, crossed the Gila, and made camp on a mesa about two miles west of Mount Graham. This was to be the new location of Camp Grant. Crook was anxious to have the new camp fully operational to use as a base to, as he put it, "iron all the wrinkles out of Cochise's band." It was still a little tent city when Randall's command arrived, but within a few years it developed into one of the finest forts in the West. While at the new Camp Grant, Randall learned of a major engagement north of the Salt River that had occurred the previous December at a place ominously called Skeleton or Skull Cave.

A few weeks earlier, Captain William H. Brown had led two troops of the Fifth Cavalry and thirty newly enlisted Apache scouts under Archie McIntosh out on December 11. Crook had granted Bourke, anxious for action, permission to join Brown's command. Like Randall's column from Camp Apache, they hoped to find Delshay and his people. Brown instead discovered a Yavapai camp in the Salt River Canyon on December 28. The Yavapais sought shelter in a shallow cave, but were quickly cut down by murderous fire from Brown's men. Mothers covered their children with their bodies as bullets ricocheted off the cave walls. The soldiers heard screams and moans. Finally, the cave was silent.

Eighteen wounded women and children somehow survived the carnage. At least seventy-six Yavapais were killed. The slaughter at Skeleton Cave was just as horrific as what had happened at Camp Grant, and yet it was reported as a great military victory and accepted as such by the American public.

RANDALL DID NOT linger long at the new Camp Grant, departing on yet another scout of the Tonto Basin on February 15. A month of fruitless scouting followed before the column encountered a detachment of a troop of the Fifth Cavalry. They had just had a sharp fight with the Indians and had taken three women as prisoners. The women were now forced to reveal the site of their main village.

Randall took charge of the combined command and sent Mickey Free and the other scouts to locate the Yavapai *rancheria*. It was west of the Verde River atop an odd-shaped mountain called Turret Peak. Randall's troopers followed the scouts on foot, with gunnysacks wrapped over their boots to muffle the sound. It was tough going over sharp lava rock studded with cactus, and Mickey and the scouts had to physically pull several of the exhausted men up over the rocks. Through the darkness, they could make out Turret Peak looming above them. The *rancheria*, Mickey reported, was on the circular mesa that marked the top of the mountain.

Randall's men struck at dawn on March 27. The surprise was total. As Mickey and the scouts swept through the compact *rancheria*, the inhabitants fled toward the waiting soldiers and were shot down or captured. Some jumped off the cliff in an attempt to escape. A few managed to hide in the brush but many simply hurled themselves into eternity in a blind leap for freedom. All thirty-three warriors encountered were killed, while thirteen women and children were rounded up by the scouts.

Randall and his men reached Camp Verde on March 29 with

the prisoners. The Apache scouts had without a doubt earned their stripes in combat at Turret Peak. Lieutenant Brodie issued an order on April 2 that promoted Alchesay and two others to be sergeants, and Mickey Free and three others to be corporals. A war dance was held by the scouts to celebrate the victory and even a handful of the white officers joined in with Mickey and the scouts.

Smoke signals went up all across central Apacheria. Turret Peak, thought to be impregnable, had been the final straw. The people had been relentlessly pursued. It was impossible to make seasonal gathering journeys or even to hunt. The soldiers of Nantan Lupan were everywhere.

The Apaches straggled into Camp Verde as individuals, then as family groups, then finally as whole bands. Within weeks 1,200 people, both Yavapais and Tonto Apaches, had come in. On April 25, Randall's column, on its way back to Camp Apache, finally encountered Delshay's band at Canyon Creek above the Salt River. Randall wanted to fight but Delshay hoisted a white flag. The Tonto chief was the heart of native resistance in the Mogollon Rim country, but Randall brought his band into Camp Apache without a struggle.

Randall gave full credit to Mickey Free, Alchesay, and the other Apache scouts for the capture of this prize prisoner. "He said they used to have no difficulty in eluding the troops," Randall reported Delshay as saying upon his surrender, "but now the very rocks had gotten soft, they couldn't put their foot anywhere without leaving an impression by which we could follow." Delshay later complained that the White Mountain Apache scouts abused him, so Randall transferred him and his people to Camp Verde.

Crook was at Camp Verde in early April to personally accept the surrender of many of the Apache and Yavapai bands. A Yavapai chief came in with three hundred of his people on April 6. "The copper cartridge has done the business for us," he told Crook. "I am glad of the opportunity to surrender, but I do it not because I love you, but because I am afraid of General."

On April 9, 1873, Crook issued General Order 14, which officially ended the campaign. He congratulated his troops, who had "outwitted and beaten the wiliest of foes with slight loss, comparatively, to themselves, and finally closed an Indian war that has been waged since the days of Cortez."

Crook also recommended Alchesay, who had emerged as his favorite scout, for the Medal of Honor. In early June 1873, Captain Randall signed up twenty-six of his veteran scouts for another six months of service. Mickey Free reenlisted and was promoted to sergeant. His pay was now to be seventeen dollars a month.

ON OCTOBER 29, 1873, the telegraph line was completed between Fort Yuma and Prescott. The first message sent over that new line informed George Crook that he had been promoted two grades to brigadier general by President Grant. The appointment, soon confirmed by the Senate, caused considerable resentment in an army wedded to seniority. Two of Crook's ambitious young rivals, Nelson A. Miles and George Armstrong Custer, fumed with envy. In Arizona, however, Crook was the hero of the hour—"the Napoleon of successful Indian fighters," declared the *Prescott Miner.*

But the greatest of the Apache leaders, Cochise, still eluded the grasp of this frontier Napoleon.

14

TAGLITO

IS NAME WAS THOMAS JONATHAN JEFFORDS, BUT everyone called him "Captain" because he had been a Great Lakes ship pilot in his youth. Born in western New York in 1832, he grew to be a tall, spare man who sported a long red beard. Much of his early life remains a mystery, but he drifted west to Denver in 1858, and then south to Taos. He followed the Rio Grande to Mesilla, where he found work as a stage driver on the Butterfield route. When the Civil War broke out and the Butterfield line closed, he signed on as a dispatch rider for General Canby's Union forces. He was at the Battle of Valverde and later carried vital messages from Canby to Carleton's California Column in Tucson. Carleton liked the lanky redhead and kept Jeffords on as a scout and dispatch rider.

Once the war ended, Jeffords prospected for a while, but in October 1867, he joined with an old friend from the New Mexico Volunteers to form a stage line connecting Santa Fe to El Paso. They also carried passengers and mail west from Mesilla to Tucson and then on to Los Angeles. Jeffords's responsibility was the mail line between Santa Fe and Tucson. The mail was carried both on stages and on horseback, and the journey was always fraught with peril. The mail riders were well paid at $125 a month, but they rarely collected many paychecks. Jeffords claimed that he lost fourteen mail riders in a little over sixteen months. Unable to find men foolish enough to make the ride to Tucson, he decided to do the job himself. He delivered the mail but carried an Apache arrow scar on his body as a reward for his daring.

Jeffords, in true Yankee fashion, decided to solve this business issue by confronting the source of his problem: Cochise. "I made up my mind that I wanted to see him," said Jeffords of his first meeting with Cochise. "I had acquired a smattering knowledge of the Indian language," he modestly recalled, and "I went into his camp alone, fully armed."

Jeffords journeyed deep into the Dragoon Mountains in search of Cochise. He was promptly captured and taken before the great chief. There was something about this red-bearded man that impressed Cochise. A man so bold as to ride alone into the stronghold must carry powerful medicine. They would talk. Jeffords gave his guns to Cochise's wife for safekeeping, but announced that he would need them upon his departure. Bold talk, indeed, but Jeffords knew what he was doing.

"I found him to be a man of great natural ability, a splendid specimen of physical manhood, standing about six feet two, with an eye like an eagle," Jeffords recalled of their first meeting. "He respected me and I respected him. He was a man who scorned a liar, was always truthful in all things, his religion was truth and loyalty. My name with Cochise was Chickasaw, or Brother, and among his tribe I was known as Tyazalaton, which means 'Sandy Whiskers.'" Other Apaches called him Taglito, or "Red Whiskers."

At that first meeting, Jeffords asked that Cochise allow the mail riders to go about their business unmolested. He claimed that they posed no threat to the Apaches. The chief pondered this for a time and then agreed, and then Jeffords departed Cochise's stronghold in peace. One of the most remarkable friendships in frontier history had been formed.

GENERAL HOWARD, with his aide Lieutenant Joseph Sladen, returned to the Southwest late in the summer of 1872. President Grant had asked him to attempt to make peace with Cochise. Sladen had served on Howard's staff during the Civil War and later had assisted the general with the difficult administration of the Freedmen's Bureau. Howard reached Camp Apache on August 10 and sent out two messengers to Cochise. They failed to make contact. Howard decided to travel east across the mountains to the recently established Fort Tularosa in New Mexico in the hopes of meeting with some relatives of Cochise among the Chihennes.

The people at Camp Apache also told Howard that at Fort Tularosa he might find "a mysterious white man, known to the [Chihennes] who had visited Cochise frequently and was on friendly terms with him, and who could, if he chose, find Cochise." They called him Taglito. General Howard was naturally anxious to meet this man Taglito, but officers at Camp Apache sounded a stark warning.

Since that first meeting, Jeffords's friendship with Cochise had led people to be suspicious of both his motives and actions. "Jeffords had the reputation of having been in collusion with the Indians during our troubles," noted a lieutenant of the First Cavalry, "and of supplying them with ammunition." Major William R. Price of the Eighth Cavalry also claimed that he had witnesses willing to testify that Jeffords traded "powder, lead and caps for their stolen stock."

Many Arizona pioneers agreed with the army officers and none more so than German immigrant William Ohnesorgen, who operated a station house and toll bridge at the crossing of the San Pedro. "I knew Captain Jeffords," he told a local historian in 1929. "No good filthy fellow—filthy in his way of living—lived right among those damn things [Apaches]. Once in a while he would go down and haul one home with him—was a blood brother or something of Cochise." Some even whispered that Jeffords rode beside Cochise on raids into Mexico.

The soldiers at Camp Apache took Lieutenant Sladen aside to warn him of Jeffords's possible treachery. "We were warned that he was a suspicious character, and that we must be very wary in our dealings with him," Sladen jotted in his diary. "That his dealings with Cochise were suspected to be of a very unsavory character, and that he was believed to have furnished the latter with arms and ammunition with which to murder and plunder."

Howard and Sladen reached Fort Tularosa on Wednesday, September 4, 1872. Jeffords was not there, and while they awaited his return, they met with Victorio, Loco, Nana, Mangas, who was the son of Mangas Coloradas, and other Chihenne leaders. Howard found about three hundred Apaches there. The Tularosa reservation had been Vincent Colyer's idea, based solely on his perception that if the Chihennes were allowed to remain at Ojo Caliente, the heart of their country, or at nearby Canada Alamosa, they would come into conflict with Hispanic settlers. In compliance with Colyer's request, the army agreed to establish a small post in April 1872 to guard the new reservation, although its construction was never completed.

Howard learned that the Chihennes were highly discontented with their new reservation. The Tularosa Valley was beautiful, but it was not their home. They wished to return to Ojo Caliente, but if that was not possible, they would at least like to go back south seventy miles to Canada Alamosa. Victorio pointed out to Howard that even Cochise had briefly camped near Canada Alamosa and might yet come in to make peace there.

Howard was deeply impressed by the fifty-year-old Victorio. "He is really a fine-looking man. He was painted over the face and head," the general wrote his wife on September 8. "His hair is black but curls a little. I never saw this in a full-blooded Indian before. He is about five-foot-ten and well formed." The general agreed to travel with Victorio to Canada Alamosa to inspect its merits firsthand.

Jeffords returned to Fort Tularosa on September 7 and was informed that General Howard was looking for him. He was in no hurry to consent to a parley. "I was prejudiced against him on account of his well-known humanitarian ideas, and, to my mind, posing as a Christian soldier," Jeffords later confessed.

Soon enough, though, Howard learned that Jeffords had returned and immediately sought him out. "The first tent I entered, a tall, spare man, with reddish hair and whiskers of considerable length, rose to meet me," Howard remembered of their first encounter. "He was pleasant and affable, and I was in the outset prepossessed in his favor."

Howard and Jeffords exchanged pleasantries and then the general got down to business. He wanted Jeffords to take a message to Cochise and arrange for a parley.

Jeffords took a long puff on his cigar and said: "General Howard, Cochise won't come. The man that wants to talk to Cochise, must go where he is."

"Do you know where he is?" Howard asked.

"I can find him," Jeffords replied.

"Will you go to him, with a message from me?" the general asked.

Jeffords smiled, took a long, slow pull on the cigar, and replied: "General, I'll tell you what I'll do. I will take you to Cochise."

Howard did not hesitate to reply: "I will go with you, Mr. Jeffords."

The general had passed Jeffords's test. "Very well," he said, "it must be you and I alone. When will you start?"

Howard agreed to go at once. "I saw then that he was not only a brave man, and fearless as far as his person was concerned," Jeffords noted, "but was really in earnest about trying to stop the destructive war which Cochise was waging upon my countrymen."

Jeffords knew that he would need strong intermediaries if such a desperate expedition was to be successful. He immediately sought out Chie, who was the nephew of Cochise. After Lieutenant Bascom had hanged his father, Coyuntura, at Apache Pass, the boy Chie had been raised as a son by Cochise. Chie's sister was married to the Chihenne chief Ponce, whom Jeffords also hoped to enlist in the peace mission.

The little party, including Howard, Jeffords, Sladen, Chie, Victorio, and several of his warriors, left for Canada Alamosa on September 13, 1872. The general had exchanged his fine cavalry mount for a buckskin mule. This impressed Jeffords, amused the Apaches, and horrified Sladen. "The mule is an enduring animal, he will bear fatigue and cold, and heat and hunger and abuse," philosophized the lieutenant. "The greater the hardship, the more patient he becomes. But no man can trust a mule." The animal seemed an apt metaphor for the dangers of their mission.

They camped at Ojo Caliente the first night out and then pushed on through the imposing high-walled canyon that separated the hot springs from Canada Alamosa, which they reached early on September 16. Here Victorio pleaded with Howard to intercede on their behalf and have their reservation returned to the banks of the Alamosa River. "It is a fine country," Howard agreed, "just suited to the Indians." Nearby Hispanic settlements remained a problem, but he promised to press Victorio's case when he returned to Washington. He kept his word to Victorio, but the Indian Bureau refused to consent.

Victorio returned to Tularosa while Howard's party headed west in search of Ponce. "He and Chie will make us welcome to Cochise's stronghold," Jeffords assured Howard. Ponce was the son of a Chihenne chief by the same name who had been one of Cochise's closest friends before his 1854 murder in a drunken brawl with other Apaches. When Colyer had moved the reservation from Canada Alamosa to the Tularosa Valley, Ponce had refused to go. He and his followers lived and raided between the Rio Grande and the Dragoon Mountains. Ponce, according to Jeffords, was "a favorite friend of the old man."

Jeffords located Ponce's village on Cuchillo Negro Creek a dozen miles south of Canada Alamosa. Ponce, happy to see his old friend Taglito, said he would go if the general would give him a fine horse and agree to ration and protect his people at Canada Alamosa. This was all agreed to, but when Ponce joined the little party the next morning he was on foot. He had given the horse to his wife to console her during his absence. "On foot he went," noted Sladen, "and whether we travelled twenty miles up and down the rugged mountain sides, it was all the same to Ponce."

Howard also added a remarkable packmaster from Canada Alamosa named Zebina Nathaniel Streeter to his little party. "He was exceedingly bright, well-educated and intelligent, and at one time been a commissioned officer to the Mexican army," declared Sladen of their new companion. "But he was a great braggart and a wonderful liar."

Streeter's adventures did stretch credulity. Born in 1838, Streeter had grown up in Santa Barbara, California, where his widowed father had married into a prominent Hispanic family. The boy went to work as a vaquero on one of the large ranches owned by his stepmother's family. His family connections and vaquero skills won him a lieutenant's commission in Company B of the California "Native" Cavalry, but a drunken brawl resulted in a court-martial and dismissal from the service in October 1864. Streeter promptly reenlisted as a private and was soon on his way to Arizona under the command of Captain John Cremony.

By the time Streeter reached Tucson, the war was over, so he and his companions were assigned to Calabasas to protect the border from French troops fighting for Emperor Ferdinand Maximilian von Hapsburg. American officials were worried that the imperialist forces, once they had defeated the liberals under Benito Juárez, might attempt to overturn the Gadsden Purchase. Streeter, along with several other ex-soldiers, soon joined the forces of Juárez. His unit was called the "American Legion" and saw considerable combat. He emerged with the rank of colonel and Mexican citizenship as his reward, then was fortunate to escape with his life after joining in a conspiracy in June 1867 to save Maximilian from a firing squad. The plot was foiled and the American Legion disbanded. Streeter drifted north to find work at Fort Craig, New Mexico, where he met Jeffords, formed a lasting friendship, and assisted him in the melancholy movement of Victorio's people from Canada Alamosa to the Tularosa Valley.

Streeter became a great favorite with Howard and Sladen, especially around the evening campfire. "He would amuse us for hours with tales of his adventures and deeds," Sladen remembered.

With Ponce and Chie constantly scouting ahead, the little band traveled to Fort Bayard, which had been established in 1866 to protect the mines at nearby Pinos Altos. On September 24, they replenished their supplies and then pushed on to the two-year-old boomtown of Silver City, some ten miles to the west, to spend the night. The presence of Ponce and Chie with Howard's party created considerable excitement in the town. Rumors of a lynch mob soon reached the general, and the white men kept close watch over their two Apache companions throughout an uneasy night.

Since Howard's party was not heavily armed and had no military escort, they were relieved to depart Silver City early the next morning and head west to the headwaters of the Gila River. This was the homeland of Mangas Coloradas and the birthplace of Geronimo, but the white miners had now left their mark all across it.

They had not traveled far from Silver City when they found the road blocked by a party of six heavily armed miners in a surly mood and in search of Apache scalps. Howard placed himself between them and the Apaches.

"You will kill me first," the general exclaimed as he ordered them to disperse.

A tense moment followed before the men, with a curse for the "damnable peace policy," turned and rode away.

Ponce and Chie did not at first understand what had just happened but Jeffords, who had his own rifle at the ready, explained what Howard had said. Ponce and Chie laughed a short chuckling grunt and then moved out on the trail. They would never forget the courage of "Tatti Grande," as they called Howard, and they would one day share with Cochise the story of this white soldier who was willing to give his life to save an Apache.

A few days later Ponce, who was on the point, galloped back to Howard with the call "Apache! Apache!" Howard asked Jeffords how Ponce knew that the pony tracks he had found were Apache. Ponce laughed at this and answered: "Feet small, pony no shoes; Indian horse goes all around like Apache." Ponce had not only noticed the tracks did not go in a straight line like Americans did, but also that only the Chokonens of Cochise shod their horses with deerskin tied above the fetlocks.

On September 27, just north of Stein's Peak, they encountered the small *rancheria* of the Chokonen leader Nazee. The chief told Jeffords that Cochise was in the Dragoon Mountains but that Howard's party was far too large to be allowed to go there. If he wanted to meet with Cochise, Howard must go alone with Jeffords. Sladen insisted upon his right to share in the danger and Jeffords reluctantly agreed. The next morning Howard, Jeffords, Sladen, Ponce, and Chie headed west toward Dos Cabezas and into the

San Simon Valley. Their goal was the waterfall-fed spring at Indian Bread Rocks, some seven miles northeast of Apache Pass.

Ponce and Chie made smoke signals, and before long, two Apache boys arrived to guide them into Cochise's stronghold. The chief's scouts had been watching Howard's party for days. "We are in God's keeping," Howard said quietly to the uneasy Sladen.

On the last day of September 1872, they entered the west end of Cochise's stronghold, where they were welcomed by a band leader named Tygee. Cochise was not there but was expected to arrive the next day. They spent an anxious night in Tygee's *rancheria;* even Ponce and Chie seemed nervous to Sladen. The lieutenant was amazed at the natural fortification they had entered. The village sat in the center of a fifty-acre valley flanked on all sides by rocky bluffs some four hundred feet high. Through its center ran a crystal-clear stream, and narrow canyon entrances marked both ends of the stronghold.

At dawn Sladen awoke to Jeffords cooking bread in a frying pan, mixed with the last remnants of the knuckle bone of a ham. They still had some coffee, which brightened everyone's disposition, although Sladen wondered if this might not be his last meal.

Shouting was heard in the distance and they all looked up from their meal. In the distance the Apaches were gathering in a circle. "He is coming," Ponce said in Spanish, and then repeated it louder again and again.

The people seemed to pick up the chant: "He is coming!"

An Apache, armed with a lance and wildly painted with black and vermilion, galloped straight at them, pulling his pony to a sudden halt, followed by a mounted party of four. "It consisted of a fine looking Indian, who rode up with great dignity followed by a young man and two women," noted Sladen.

The man slowly dismounted and immediately embraced Jeffords. Taglito turned to Howard and said, "General, this is the man." Howard extended his hand and Cochise shook it as he carefully studied the general. *"Buenos días,"* he said.

Cochise then turned to Jeffords. "Will they do as they say they will?" he asked.

"Well, I don't know," Taglito replied. "I think they will, but I will see that they do not promise too much."

As Cochise talked with Jeffords, Sladen studied the chief. He was deeply impressed, as was everyone who met Cochise. "He was a remarkably fine looking man, fully six feet tall, as straight as an arrow, and well proportioned, the typical Indian face, rather long, high cheek bones, clear keen eye, and a Roman nose," he recorded later in his journal. "His cheeks were slightly painted with vermilion. A yellow silk handkerchief bound his hair, which was straight and black, with just a touch of silver."

The people who rode beside Cochise were his teenage son Naiche, his wife, and his sister. The forty-year-old sister fascinated Sladen, for he noticed that Cochise consulted with her on all important matters. He later learned that she was a woman warrior who had been widowed sometime before. He had met only one other such woman among the Apaches—Lozen, the sister of Victorio.

The group gathered themselves in a circle, surrounded by the people who pressed in to hear what was said. Through Jeffords, Cochise asked Howard why he had come to the land of the Chokonen.

"The president sent me to make peace between you and the white people," the general replied.

"No one wants peace more than I do," said Cochise.

Howard immediately suggested that Cochise bring his people to Canada Alamosa. They could live there and he would then bring down the Chihennes of Victorio and Loco to join with them.

"Why not give me Apache Pass?" Cochise responded. "Give me that and I will protect all the roads. I will see that nobody's property is taken by Indians."

Howard declared that he would prefer Cochise take his people to Canada Alamosa because the land was better for agriculture, and it would remove the Chiricahuas from the bitter recriminations of the people of Arizona. Still, he conceded that he had full power from the president to make peace and create a new reservation here in the Dragoon Mountains. Cochise said that he would need ten days to call in his warrior captains, who were out "making a living," as he delicately put it. He worried that army patrols might attack his warriors as they came in and insisted that Howard go to Fort Bowie to make certain all the soldiers were called back to their posts. Sladen and Jeffords could remain in the stronghold until the general returned. Howard objected to leaving Sladen as a glorified hostage but Cochise only laughed.

"Our young women will look after the young captain," he said with a smile. The Apache women clapped and laughed at this proposition. Howard said he would go and Chie agreed to guide him if Jeffords would give him his mule.

Cochise became somber as he concluded the council with a history of why he had gone to war. Although no one at the council knew his name, it all came back to Mickey Free.

"We were once a large people covering these mountains; we lived well; we were at peace," he said as he pointed across the horizon. "One day my best friend [Mangas] was seized by an officer of the white men and treacherously killed. The worst place of all is Apache Pass. There, five Indians, one my brother, were murdered. Their bodies were hung up and kept there till they were skeletons."

They had killed ten white men for every Apache killed, but they were tired of war and wanted peace. Cochise would place his faith in Howard to deliver that peace. Howard and Chie immediately set out for Fort Bowie. Sladen watched with mixed feelings as the general departed.

Cochise sensed his apprehension and told Jeffords to tell Sladen not to feel sad, for he was safe in the camp. "Tell the Captain that I will send off and get some *tiswin* and we will all get drunk and have a good time tonight," Cochise declared. Sladen, not initially charmed by this prospect, ended up developing a taste for *tiswin*. "It seemed a harmless beverage," he recalled, "and was a refreshing drink, sweet and pleasant to the taste, reminding me of the 'pop' of my childhood." Of course this fermented corn beverage had considerably more bite than soda pop.

As the days passed, Sladen came to better understand the humanity of the Apaches. He watched as they made fire with only a stick. "I wondered at the resources of these people who could command all the necessities of nature in a region so poorly supplied that a white man would have perished from want." He participated in their dances, admired the beauty and chastity of their women, developed a taste for mescal mixed with mesquite beans as well as horse meat, and delighted in the simple joys exhibited by their children. He formed a particular friendship with Naiche, the teenage son of Cochise, who attempted to teach him to speak Apache and shared his campsite at night.

Howard returned to the stronghold on October 4, bringing with him Streeter and three others with a wagon loaded down with corn, flour, sugar, coffee, as well as bolts of cloth for the ladies. They waited six more days for the return of all of Cochise's war captains. Cochise felt keenly disappointed that his eldest son, Taza, was still out on a raid in Sonora, but decided he could wait no longer to hold a grand council with General Howard.

The whites were excluded from the first part of the council. Howard fretted over this and wanted to edge closer to the great circle, but Jeffords held him back. "We will stay here," Jeffords told him. "They will let us know whether they want to make peace or not."

Howard paced back and forth as he listened to the muffled voices of the women as they slowly chanted, louder and louder. "Then all—men and women—sang with ever increasing volume of sound, and the women's voices rose higher and higher," he tensely observed. "It was a wild, weird performance." Then the call came for them to join the circle.

They gathered under the shade of an expansive oak, circle upon circle, with Howard, Jeffords, and Sladen alongside Cochise and his important war chiefs. Sladen was fascinated by one of these warriors, who sat next to Cochise and seemed to have considerable influence over him. "His sensual, cruel, crafty face, as well as his dissatisfied manner had prejudiced me against him from the first," Sladen freely admitted. This seemed to him a dangerous man.

Much of the conversation was only between the Apaches. "More than once I heard him use Jeffords's sobriquet 'Stag-li-to' meaning

Redbeard," Howard recalled of Cochise. "Our whole case was evidently being discussed." Howard realized that the success or failure of his mission, the very question of war or peace, depended upon the trust the Apaches placed in this man Taglito. He knew then that Jeffords was indispensable to peace in Apacheria now and in the future.

Sladen could not shake his apprehension over the Apache who interpreted Cochise's words from Apache into Spanish. The chief spoke Spanish quite well, so well, in fact, that he would sometimes correct the interpreter, and yet he clearly relied upon this man. Sladen's attention was drawn to the shirt worn by this Apache, for it was obviously of fine manufacture, with eyelets rather than buttons. No such shirt came out of a trader's store in Apacheria. He inched closer to get a better look at the shirt.

Howard agreed to Cochise's demand for a reservation in his own country, with an eastern boundary at the Arizona line and the southern boundary at the Mexican border, including most of the Chiricahua Mountains, as well as the valley to the west that included Sulphur Springs. No army troops or civilians were to be allowed on the reservation. The government would properly feed and clothe the Chiricahuas, and Taglito must be named their agent. Jeffords objected to this, but both Cochise and Howard were adamant that he must take the job or there would be no peace.

"Captain Jeffords," Howard said quietly but firmly, "I cannot make peace unless you consent to act as Indian agent."

Jeffords grumbled about his humiliation, as a lifelong Democrat, to take orders from Republicans, but agreed to take the job if his authority was absolute and all troops were kept off the reservation. Howard agreed to this and the treaty was made.

"Hereafter the white man and the Indian are to drink of the same water and eat of the same bread," Cochise declared as he closed the great council.

Sladen had inched ever closer to the scowling warrior who wore a white man's shirt, and just as the council concluded made a startling discovery. Written on the bottom of the shirt, as a laundry mark, was the name Cushing. Sladen shuddered, for before him sat the killer of Lieutenant Howard Bass Cushing.

As they walked away from the council circle, Sladen inquired if Jeffords knew the name of the warrior in the white shirt. Of course he knew, for it was the Bedonkohe Apache, Goyahkla—the warrior the Mexicans called Geronimo.

15

SAN CARLOS

GEORGE CROOK STEWED OVER GENERAL HOWARD'S treaty with Cochise. "I never could get to see the treaty stipulations, although I made official applications for them," Crook grumbled, "but the Indians understood that they could raid as much as they pleased in Mexico, provided they let us alone." Crook also blamed Howard for tensions at San Carlos and at Camp Verde. "The treaty stopped all operations against [Cochise] by me," he complained. "It had a bad effect on my Indians, as they thought I was afraid of Cochise, because I left him unmolested."

Crook soon had his hands full with those he so casually declared "my Indians." The new reservation created by Colyer and reaffirmed by Howard at San Carlos was an extension of the White Mountain Reservation headquartered at Camp Apache, and it soon turned into an administrative nightmare.

The interim agent was Dr. R. A. Wilbur, the former agent for the Tohono O'odham. He had practiced chicanery for so long that to him fraud was the normal way to conduct business. His constant cheating of the Indians and the government in ration issues was bad enough, but he also meddled in the volatile Apache politics at San Carlos in an attempt to secure the permanent agent's position for himself. When the new agent, Charles Larrabee, arrived in March 1873, he found the various tribal bands divided between those who supported Wilbur and those who opposed him. Larrabee soon learned that Wilbur had spread rumors among the Tonto headmen about him, and that the Apache leaders Chunz, Chan-deisi, and Cochinay planned to kill him.

Major William Brown arrived with Archie McIntosh and a detachment of the Fifth Cavalry to back up the new agent, but Larrabee sent them away. The Apaches naturally feared troops camped near them. McIntosh sensed trouble and urged Brown to stay, but the major did not wish to undercut civilian control at the agency. He did, however, leave Lieutenant Jacob Almy with a company of Fifth Cavalry troopers to provide some nominal security at San Carlos. This led Eskiminzin and Captain Chiquito to take their people away from the agency into the nearby mountains. They knew trouble was brewing. One Camp Grant Massacre was enough.

On May 27, ration day at the agency, more than a thousand Apaches gathered around Larrabee's crude storehouse. Most of the men were armed. Rumors had swirled for days that Larrabee was to be killed. Interpreter Merejildo Grijalva gathered a handful of troopers and went in search of the warrior Chan-deisi after he had loudly threatened the agent. Lieutenant Almy, hearing of this, rushed to the scene to join in the search and was soon lost to sight among the milling crowd. A shot was heard and Almy staggered toward Grijalva.

"Oh, my God!" the lieutenant cried as he clutched his bloody side. Another shot rang out and the lieutenant's skull exploded.

The soldiers opened fire but the Apaches scattered in every direction. The shaken Larrabee promptly resigned his position and turned San Carlos over to the army. The laurels won by Crook in his celebrated triumph over the Apaches were rapidly wilting away. Crook ordered Brown to take the field, and to accept no Indian surrender until the heads of Chunz, Cochinay, and Chan-deisi were delivered up. Crook meant exactly what he said—he wanted their heads for public display at San Carlos.

At Camp Verde, affairs were also spinning out of control. Delshay had remained troublesome since being forced to settle on the reservation, for he kept his friends and relatives among both the Tonto Apaches and the Yavapais in a constant state of agitation. Lieutenant Walter Schuyler, who was in charge at Verde, had worked wonders with Al Sieber at his side. Within weeks they had nearly sixty acres of land planted with melons and garden vegetables favored by the Indians, as well as many more acres prepared for corn and barley planting. A water wheel was constructed and a great irrigation ditch dug using "condemned" tools salvaged by Schuyler from nearby military posts. Even as this good work progressed, rumors swirled that the Indian Ring, headquartered in Tucson, had lobbied Congress to have all the Verde Indians moved to San Carlos. Furthermore, nearly all the federal contracts for San Carlos had of course been issued to Tucson merchants. This news flamed the smoldering discontent of Delshay and his followers.

Another issue that upset the Indians was Crook's order that all must be tagged. Each Indian was given a number that was stamped on a tag. These tags were in a variety of shapes to designate the various bands. Any Apache found off the reservation had to produce his tag as well as a written pass that corresponded to the tag number. Many of the warriors were naturally contemptuous of this dehumanizing system, and the tags quickly became a favored currency in games of chance.

The news from San Carlos was ominous, and it was clear to Schuyler at Camp Verde that he faced similar problems. He and Sieber were fighting a two-front war—one with the Apaches and the other with the federal Indian Bureau. Schuyler complained that the civilian agents were afraid of Delshay and attempted to constantly placate him. He worried that "the consequence may be trouble similar to that at San Carlos where Almy was killed." Sieber had advised Schuyler to always present a bold front to the Apaches, for "unless they fear a person, they despise him, and show in every way they can their contempt for his authority."

Schuyler fretted over Delshay and wrote Crook for permission to arrest him. Crook approved, but warned the young lieutenant not to "attempt to make the arrest unless you are sure of success, as failure will lead to bad consequences." Crook's anxiety was well placed, for Delshay was plotting to kill Schuyler at the first opportunity. In his view, this would give him notoriety once again with the young men, just like Chunz, Cochinay, and Chan-deisi had won by killing Almy at San Carlos.

Schuyler ordered Delshay and his people to come in to Camp

Verde from their nearby *rancheria* for a census count. He planned
to arrest Delshay, but the wily chief had a spy in Schuyler's camp
and so knew just what to expect. When Schuyler informed Delshay
that he was under arrest, the chief laughed as his warriors threw
aside their blankets to reveal their weapons. Sieber had wisely gathered his scouts as a rear guard, and they rushed forward to surround the lieutenant. It was a standoff. Delshay and his followers
bolted while Sieber restored order and hustled Schuyler back to his
quarters. The lieutenant was fortunate to be alive, although he now
faced the grim task of informing General Crook that more than
a thousand Indians, both Apaches and Yavapais, had just fled the
reservation.

"I have requested Maj. Randall to try and have Delche's [Del-
shay's] head," Crook wrote Lieutenant Schuyler. Crook's orders to
Randall were literal—once again, he actually wanted the Apache's
severed head delivered to him. The general sent out a list of Apaches
who were to be killed and what bounties would be paid upon the
delivery of their heads. Crook surmised that his own people would
turn on Delshay. "The more prompt these heads are brought in," he
told Schuyler, "the less liable other Indians, in the future, will be to
jeopardize their heads."

Once Crook's initial campaign had closed in April, he had ordered a consolidation of the White Mountain scouts. "These Indians will be selected from among the best of their several tribes,"
Crook instructed his officers, and "will constitute the police force
of the reservation." Sergeant Mickey Free had been among those
chosen to continue in service at Camp Apache. He was soon in the
saddle on a series of scouts in search of Apache fugitives.

In February 1874, Randall—along with Mickey and sixty
Apache scouts as well as several Fifth Cavalry troopers—marched
west along the Salt River. They then turned south to strike Eskiminzin's village in the mountains northwest of San Carlos. The battle
left all the village property and animals in Randall's possession,
along with thirty-four women and children. Chief Eskiminzin, realizing that his head was in jeopardy, soon came in from his mountain hideout to surrender to Randall.

Soon after, heads started being delivered in quick succession to the military authorities. In April, Randall ordered Mickey Free, along with fourteen White Mountain scouts, to bring in Pedro, a notorious warrior who had fled the reservation. Mickey left Camp Apache on April 26 and returned the next day to deliver Pedro's bloody head to Randall—"the captain with the big black mustache."

The warrior Cochinay, wanted for the murder of Lieutenant Almy at San Carlos, was bagged by Apache scouts within three miles of Tucson, and his head was delivered to San Carlos in May. His companion Chunz was run down in the Santa Catalina Mountains above Tucson by the scouts in July. His head and those of six compatriots were soon neatly arrayed on the parade ground of the military camp at San Carlos.

Delshay's days were numbered as well. Schuyler's Tonto scouts soon brought in a scalp with one ear attached and delivered it to Camp Verde. Sieber's scouts identified the scalp by a pearl shirt button dangling from the earlobe. These scout movements made it impossible for any of the Apache bands to remain off the reservation. Harassed, demoralized, and starving, they now returned to their agencies in ever greater numbers.

THE INDIAN BUREAU had considered closing San Carlos after Lieutenant Almy's assassination and the abrupt resignation of Indian agent Larrabee. During the previous eighteen months, there had been five different agents at San Carlos. A plan was developed to move all the Apaches north to the Camp Apache agency, but the agent there was barely able to deal with the White Mountain people already under his charge.

The commissioner of Indian affairs, Edward P. Smith, simply could not find anyone willing to serve at the San Carlos Agency. Then Smith remembered a bright young man he had met during his 1872 western journey with General Howard. John P. Clum had impressed Smith on several fronts. He was well educated, ambitious, obviously an adventurous spirit, and, most important, a member of the Dutch Reformed Church. That denomination had been assigned to select agents for Arizona Territory under President Grant's Peace Policy. Through his contacts with the church, Smith tracked down Clum and offered the twenty-two-year-old the dangerous job at San Carlos at the absurdly low pay of $1,500 a year.

Born near Claverack, New York, in 1851, Clum had grown up as a robust farm boy of exceptional intelligence and strong convictions. He attended Rutgers for a year studying divinity, and was a starter on that college's first football team, before joining the US Signal Corps as a meteorologist. Stationed at Santa Fe, he quickly developed an abiding love of the American West. Smith secured Clum's release from the Signal Corps, and the new Apache agent was soon on his way to Washington.

Once in Washington, Clum met with Commissioner Smith and General Howard and received a crash course on both the president's Peace Policy and the Apaches. The general briefed him fully on Arizona—the Camp Grant Massacre, the various Apache bands and leaders, as well as the local civilian and military personalities. He even gave him a letter of introduction to Eskiminzin. Clum also acquired copies of Vincent Colyer's reports to read on his journey back to the West. The trip took from April 25 until August 8, 1874, and cost, according to Clum's meticulous expense report, $365.50.

The fact that the stagecoach from the Colorado River to Tucson cost as much as his railroad fare from Washington to San Francisco, and that the dirt-floor lodging he acquired at Ohnesorgen's San Pedro Station, Arizona Territory, cost far more than his hotels in St. Louis, Omaha, San Francisco, or San Diego, certainly opened his eyes to just how far his pitiful salary was going to carry him. He also received very little encouragement from his Tucson stage driver.

"Better go back to the farm," the driver warned Clum upon learning of his final destination, "and save your money as well as your scalp."

"The Government is paying my traveling expenses, so I cannot lose any money by going to San Carlos," he quipped as he removed his hat to display his prematurely bald head, "and having no hair, I cannot very well lose my scalp."

Despite this bravado, the young Indian agent immediately purchased the newest Colt revolver and an ample supply of cartridges upon reaching Tucson. Clum was being characteristically pragmatic, but the pistol did not mean he had hardened in his opinion toward the Apaches. Howard had won Clum over to the Peace Policy, and his extensive reading of government reports on his long journey to San Carlos only reaffirmed the truth of the general's argument.

"These red men were simple and nomadic—yes—but they formed a nation, with laws, legends, and a history," he wrote. "Our noble white Government had bought the Apaches' land and their homes, but had not told the Apaches anything about the deal. And now, because the Apaches got sore about it, our Government was extending protection and guidance on the one hand, and cutting out their hearts with the other."

In his simple but direct way, Clum had come to understand the situation perfectly. The Apaches were caught in the middle of President Grant's so-called Peace Policy. Clum was now on a crusade, both personal and public, and he was just the man who might yet save the Apaches. He was highly principled yet studiously realistic, scrupulously honest, and brave beyond all reason. He was also brashly arrogant, rudely condescending, particularly disdainful of the military, and conceited beyond all reason.

"I determined that the Apaches would get a square deal," Clum declared upon reaching Arizona.

WHEN JOHN CLUM arrived at the San Carlos Agency late on a miserably hot August afternoon in 1874, despite all his preparations, he was horrified at his first view of his new post. "Of all the desolate, isolated human habitations!" he remarked in amazement.

He might well have thought himself transported back to medieval times, for the rotting heads of seven Apache warriors were arrayed on the parade ground of the adjacent military camp. Within a few days of his arrival at San Carlos, Clum was approached by six Apache warriors, led by Dis-a-lin. The Apache emptied a burlap bag from which tumbled the severed, scalped head of Delshay. It was indeed a rude introduction to his new position.

But one of Clum's first acts upon reaching San Carlos reflected his pragmatism. While he heartily disapproved of General Crook's severed head policy, which had forced the Apaches to betray their own leaders as well as break their cultural belief system, he nevertheless lobbied for the payment of the bounty on Delshay's head to Dis-a-lin, arguing that the warrior had delivered the entire head as opposed to the scalp delivered to Camp Verde. Dis-a-lin also brought in seventy-six members of Delshay's band as well as thirty-nine of his own people to San Carlos.

Crook was not disturbed by this contrasting claim. "When I visited the Verde reservation, they would convince me they had brought in his head," Crook declared with considerable amusement, "and when I went to San Carlos, they would convince me that they had brought in his head. Being satisfied that both parties were earnest in their beliefs, and the bringing of an extra head was not amiss, I paid both parties."

Crook's amusement displayed not only his callous nature but also a flaw in his Apache scout system that he studiously declined to recognize. The Tonto scouts had probably conducted an elaborate ruse to convince Crook and Sieber that the scalp with ears that they delivered belonged to Delshay. Many of them were bound to the charismatic chief by blood, and others had raided with him in the recent past. Dis-a-lin, on the other hand, was a rival to Delshay and essentially engaged in political assassination to bolster his position with tribal members while also currying favor with the white authorities. His gambit failed on both counts.

Within days of his arrival, Clum held a parley with the leading men of the seven hundred Pinal and Aravaipa people at San Carlos. A quick learner, he knew to have large baskets of Sonoran tobacco with a good supply of cigarette paper in the center of the conference circle. A novice at rolling cigarettes, Clum watched his Apache companions closely and joined in the big smoke with gusto. To the surprise and delight of the assembled chiefs, he informed them that he expected them to participate in the government of San Carlos. He intended to ban the soldiers from the reservation and allow an Indian police force to keep the peace. All offenders were to be tried by an Apache court and placed in the local guardhouse under the watchful eye of Apache guards. All weapons must be given up, but could be checked out of the storehouse for hunting. A strict prohibition on alcohol, both imported and home brewed, was to be in effect. Everyone was expected to work six days a week, and all would be paid in paper chits that could be redeemed at the agency store. His door, he declared, would always be open, and he wished them to speak freely of their concerns and complaints.

Within a few days, he had hired the first four members of his Apache police force: Eskinospas, the forceful and oversized leader of the police; Tauelclyee, the brother of Dis-a-lin; Goodah-Goodah, whom Clum called Goody-Goody; and a warrior Clum called Sneezer, plagued as he was by hay fever.

The first test of the police force came within a few weeks, when a *tulapai* operation was discovered in a canyon four miles west of the agency. Some twenty-five Apache men and women were busy with the laborious preparation of this potent brew, which in its original form was made from cooked mescal hearts. Only women actually concocted both *tulapai* and *tiswin*. As corn became more readily available to the Apaches through government rations, *tiswin* became the more popular beverage. By the 1870s the two names had become interchangeable for home brew and only old-timers would make the distinction. *Tulapai* was actually different from the less intoxicating *tiswin,* a mild corn beer called gray water by the Apaches. Many women gained considerable fame as *tiswin* brewmasters. Every woman had a different technique. Some added fermented mescal to the mix, others put in mesquite beans or oak root, and a few even added jimsonweed to give the *tiswin* some kick. Many Apaches swore by the healthful and nutritional benefits of *tulapai* and *tiswin*, which could also act as a powerful laxative. Clum did not buy into that argument for a minute. The surprised party was broken up and the ringleaders hauled before the tribal court, where they were sentenced to fifteen days at hard labor.

This episode cemented the bond between Clum and his new tribal police force. To mark the occasion, Eskinospas had a fine suit of buckskin made for Nantan Betunny-kahyeh (Boss with the High Forehead—pronounced "Be-toon-e-ki-ay"), which Clum proudly wore thereafter.

A far more serious test of police loyalty came some weeks after the *tulapai* raid. Des-a-lin had assumed increased importance at San Carlos, at least in his own mind, after his killing of Delshay. His arrogance and overbearing behavior quickly brought him into conflict with Clum. Des-a-lin beat both of his wives regularly, but he now increased the torture of the youngest wife by tying her to a tree and throwing knives at her for sport. When she reported this to Clum, the agent was not amused by such sideshow antics and publicly upbraided Des-a-lin. Des-a-lin brooded over this humiliation for a few days, acquired a pistol, and sought out the Indian agent. The Tonto chief found Clum in his office and attempted to shoot him but was instead shot dead by his own brother—the police officer Tauelclyee.

As the two men looked down at Des-a-lin's body, Tauelclyee absentmindedly stroked his smoking rifle and said: "I have killed my own chief and my own brother. But he was trying to kill you, and I am a policeman. It was my duty."

Clum warmly clasped his hand and assured the distraught man that what he had done was right, and that they would remain forever brothers and friends. From that day onward, Clum never doubted the loyalty of his Apache police officers. He had learned, as had Jeffords, Sieber, and Bourke before him, that to an Apache, honor was above all price.

Clum made three other important hires at San Carlos that contributed decisively to his initial success. First he signed Merejildo Grijalva to be his interpreter. Grijalva was a living encyclopedia of Apache lore, and Clum spent many a warm Arizona evening in deep conversation with the man he nicknamed Mary.

His second hire was Martin Sweeney, an ex–infantry sergeant

who became his clerk, confidant, and right-hand man. "Honest, industrious, good-natured, and fearless, he carried out my instructions almost before I issued them" was how Clum characterized the oversized, redheaded Irishman. Sweeney had been a prizefighter in New York before joining the army, and he was a tough but compassionate man who drilled the expanding Apache police force, oversaw construction projects, and generally kept order.

Clum also hired another former soldier, Clay Beauford, an ex-rebel from Virginia whose actual name was Welford Bridwell, to be chief of the expanded police force. The soft-spoken Virginian proved invaluable in a job that required considerable tact and nerves of steel. He had assumed the alias of Beauford in order to run away from home at age fourteen and enlist in the Confederate army, where he fought with George Pickett's division at Gettysburg and was wounded three times. After the surrender at Appomattox, unable to readjust to civilian life, he sought adventure in the West and in 1870 enlisted in the Fifth Cavalry. By the time the Fifth Cavalry was transferred to Arizona, he was first sergeant of Lieutenant Walter Schuyler's B Troop and soon won the Medal of Honor for gallantry against the Apaches in the "Red Rock Country" on November 26, 1872.

Beauford was so highly regarded that he often led expeditions of his own with the Apache scouts and in this way acquired a passable knowledge of their language. On one of these scouts, his detachment surprised the Aravaipa *rancheria* of Toga-de-chuz, a member of Captain Chiquito's band, and captured the Apache warrior and his family, including his twelve-year-old son, Has-kay-bay-nay-ntayl. Later, at San Carlos, Toga-de-chuz and Beauford became friends, and the warrior's boy also attached himself to the big Virginian. In due time, the boy became a sort of mascot to Beauford's Apache police force.

Beauford hired the youngster to do odd jobs on the reservation. In particular Has-kay-bay-nay-ntayl proved quite adept with horses, and as he got older he became one of the best wranglers in the territory. On ration day Beauford issued him a carbine and cartridges to shoot the agency beef in the issue corral. In this way the boy became an expert marksman, able to dispatch a steer with a single shot in the center of its forehead.

The Apache boy became the inseparable pal of young Joe Stevens, the son of local rancher and Indian trader George Stevens. The elder Stevens had come to Arizona in 1866 and had married a daughter of the White Mountain chief Eskeltesela. The boys often hunted together, and from his young half-Apache friend, as well as from Beauford, the boy learned English. "For years we hunted and journeyed over the mountains together," Joe Stevens recalled in 1898. "In all of these travels I scarcely heard him speak an unkind word of any person. He was gentle as a girl and as affectionate as it was possible for one to be."

In 1875, Beauford helped the boy find work in Globe, the new mining town just to the west of the reservation boundary. The teenager was bright, handsome, fluent in English, and eager to learn and to work. He found a steady job as a herder for a Globe butcher. Everyone liked the boy but no one could pronounce his Apache name, so he soon became known to all as Kid—or the Apache Kid.

In the end, John Clum's remarkable success at San Carlos proved to be his undoing. He was already a great favorite with Commissioner Edward Smith, and his efficiency and honesty even won over many critics in the Tucson civilian community, although most army officers remained skeptical. Smith decided to send a special commissioner to Arizona to investigate the possibility of consolidating even more Apaches under Clum's management. This "concentration policy" was already in place on the Great Plains, where the goal was to bring as many Indians together as possible on central reservations for economy of scale in both supply and administration. This would also open up Indian lands to white settlers. The anticipated arrival of the Southern Pacific Railroad in Arizona, although still some years off, made San Carlos an attractive location because of its proximity to the proposed rail line.

Special Indian Commissioner L. Edwin Dudley, a Civil War veteran who had previously worked with the Indians in New Mexico, first targeted the Tonto Apaches and the various bands of Yavapais at Camp Verde for removal to San Carlos. The Verde agency would be closed and the land opened up for white settlement.

Crook and his officers were outraged. "A ring of Federal officials, contractors, and others was formed in Tucson, which exerted great influence in the national capital," Bourke ranted, "and succeeded in securing peremptory orders that the Apaches should leave at once for the mouth of the sickly San Carlos, there to be herded with the other tribes." The military officers were helpless to intervene.

The cruel irony was that Crook's officers now had to assist the commissioner Dudley in the forced removal of the Indians. Rumors of such a move had circulated for months, but when Dudley announced it as fact, the Indians were stunned. Two of the largest Yavapai bands considered this their ancient homeland, and all the other bands—both Yavapai and Tonto—had made the best of their reservation confinement. They had done all that their agent and Lieutenant Schuyler had asked of them. Their irrigation ditches were completed and their tilled fields held the prospect of producing a surplus crop. They loudly protested the order but when told it came directly from the Great White Father—President Grant—they sullenly returned to their camps. All that night the women wailed.

Schuyler and Dr. William Corbusier begged the commissioner to at least move the Indians south on the wagon road around the mountains. Corbusier, an army surgeon, warned that unless the elderly and the children were carried in wagons, there might be many deaths on the trail. Dudley would not be moved, for he was determined to go by the shortest route directly over the mountains.

"They are Indians, let the beggars walk," Dudley declared as he dismissed the two officers.

Lieutenant George Eaton, with fifteen handpicked Fifth Cavalry troopers, was to provide the military escort for the 1,476 Yavapais and Tontos who were to walk the 180 miles to San Carlos. Commissioner Dudley would be in command. General Crook provided a packtrain of twenty-nine animals, while Dudley secured twenty-six additional mules from civilian sources. Since the mules and a small cattle herd could provide only a portion of the supplies required for the hard journey, Dudley sent a message to Clum to meet the caravan with rations from San Carlos.

In this forced exodus, called the "March of Tears" by the Yavapai, the services of Al Sieber and Mickey Free proved crucial. Sieber was to be the real trail boss, deferred to by both Dudley and Eaton. This journey marked the beginning of a remarkable partnership between the seasoned scout and the onetime captive boy.

MICKEY FREE HAD been hired on December 4, 1874, as an Indian interpreter at Camp Verde for $125 a month—quite a substantial increase over his $17-a-month scout wage—and added to the Fifth Cavalry quartermaster's payroll. He had guided General Crook and Lieutenant Bourke to the Hopi villages in October and "the young imp," as Bourke dubbed him, had won over both men. This paid rich dividends when they secured him this lucrative new position. Despite the fiction employed to enlist him as a White Mountain Apache scout, everyone now knew his story, his relationship to the Bascom affair, and his true racial heritage. Mickey, unlike the other Apache scouts, was free to come and go as he pleased like any other Arizona citizen.

It is possible that Mickey Free and Al Sieber had met before the former Apache scout sergeant assumed his new position with the Fifth Cavalry, but there is no record of it. The day after he was officially hired as an interpreter, Mickey greeted Sieber upon his return from a scout into the mountains. As Sieber rode in astride his favorite white jennet, followed by his twenty scouts and nine captive Apache women and children, the thirty-year-old chief-of-scouts cut quite a figure. The Indians all called him "Sibber," and the whites were already referring to all Apache scouts as "Sieber's Scouts" or "Sieber's Apaches." All were in awe of his unflinching courage, and it was said that he eventually bore twenty-nine arrow or bullet scars on his body.

Lieutenant Charles King remembered Sieber well from Camp Verde as a "powerful fellow, with a keen, intelligent face, and eyes

that were kindly to all his friends, but kindled at sight of foe."
Sieber's dress was always casual and never for show, but perfectly
suited to the time and place. "A broad-brimmed, battered slouch
hat was pulled well down over his brows; his flannel shirt and canvas trousers showed hard usage; his pistol belt hung loose and low
upon his hips and on each side a revolver swung," King vividly
recalled. "His rifle—Arizona fashion—was balanced athwart the
pommel of his saddle, and an old Navajo blanket was rolled at the
cantle. He wore Tonto leggings and moccasins, and a good sized
pair of Mexican spurs jingled at his heels."

Mickey, scrawny, disheveled, looking even younger than his
twenty-seven years, still dressed like a White Mountain Apache.
In time he would adopt considerable style as well, far more in fact
than Sieber ever sported. Some years later, when asked by Lieutenant Britton Davis about his enigmatic friend—who appeared to be
neither white nor Apache—Sieber simply replied with rough frontier affection that Mickey Free was "half Mexican, half Irish and
whole son of a bitch."

ON FEBRUARY 27, 1875, the sad column of exiled Indians departed Camp Verde for the two-week, 180-mile journey eastward
over the mountains and into exile at San Carlos. The Tontos, with
some of their Yavapai relatives and allies, took the lead. The main
body of Yavapais did not trust their backs to the Tontos and so
trailed behind. There were many ancient feuds as well as new scores
to settle. The march was almost immediately slowed by a brutal
snowstorm. The cavalry troopers often dismounted and walked
to allow the children as well as the aged and infirm to ride their
horses. The people had to carry all their possessions in baskets on
their backs, and one old man carried his infirm wife in a large basket that he had fashioned with holes in the bottom for her legs.
Before long the weakest of them began to fall alongside the trail.
Dudley allowed no halts for burials.

The packtrain rations gave out after the first week, while the
footsore cattle failed to keep up and wandered away. Dudley had

not thought to hire local cowboys from Prescott to herd them. "Even the moccasins wore out on the sharp rocks. Our clothing was torn to rags on the brush and cactus," remembered a young Yavapai girl of the ordeal. "With bleeding feet, weary in body and sick at heart, many wanted to die. Many did die."

On March 7, a deer was spotted on the ridge above the Yavapai camp and many shots were fired at it without success. As it scampered away opposite the soldiers' camp, Sieber took careful aim and felled it with a single shot. Before the pursuing Yavapais could reach the fallen animal, the Tontos carried it off to their camp. The next day Dr. Corbusier shot another deer and he and Lieutenant Eaton hung it up on a tree for the Yavapais, but again the Tontos rushed in and made off with the carcass. They brandished their weapons and warned off the starving Yavapais.

Corbusier was back in his tent when he heard the first shouts of "Kill the Tontos!" Armed Yavapai warriors, urged on by their screaming women, swept through the little group of army tents and rushed up toward the Tonto camps. Several shots rang out in quick succession.

Sieber and Mickey Free hurried forward after the Yavapais. Four Indians were already dead and a dozen more lay wounded on the ground before Mickey could part the contending factions. He waved his arms in the air and shouted as loudly as he could in Yavapai, then Tonto, and then again in Spanish for the men to back off. As Eaton and his troopers rushed up they found Mickey and Sieber in the midst of the milling mob. The two men had already pushed the crowd apart by the time the soldiers formed their line and sent everyone back to their camps.

Dr. Corbusier treated ten wounded men and the troopers buried four more. That night several Yavapai families melted back into the mountains to rejoin those who had remained hidden in the Verde Valley before the exodus began. Al Sieber and Mickey Free would later be sent to hunt down these people.

The swollen Salt River provided the final obstacle for the weary Indians. Even Dudley was moved by the difficulty at the ford. "The water was about waist deep to a tall man and the crossing was a pitiable sight, one which I could not witness without a feeling of pity, which brought tears to my eyes," the commissioner later wrote. "The crossing of the river reminded me of another exodus, and I wished that the waves might again be rolled back."

Dudley's crocodile tears won him no friends among the Indians. After a frigid night with no rations on the south side of the Salt River, the Yavapais had had enough. Corbusier was alarmed to see several warriors with their faces painted for war—faces black with noses stained red. He hurried to Dudley to warn him and found Mickey already there. A shot rang out and passed directly over the commissioner's head. Mickey rode over to the Yavapais to assure them that they had made their point and that the commissioner was going to ride to San Carlos to secure supplies. As the nervous Dudley hurried past them, the warriors brandished their weapons and cursed him in Yavapai, Spanish, and English. Mickey did not bother to translate.

Dudley, after only a few miles, was greatly relieved to meet John Clum with a cattle herd and several wagons loaded with supplies from San Carlos. They camped that night in Pinal Canyon, some thirty-five miles from San Carlos, and the dark mood of the Indians lightened somewhat as they feasted on Clum's cattle. Still, there was an ominous feel to the blustery night. As Clum surveyed the flickering Indian campfires all along the canyon, he was certain that the "occasional echoes sounded very much like Apache war talk."

Clum, who camped with the soldiers, now met Al Sieber and Mickey Free for the first time. They not only calmed his anxiety, but they also tutored him on the new residents of San Carlos. Clum eventually counted 1,361 Indians in Dudley's party. The arriving Yavapais and Tontos would more than double the Indian population on the reservation. Clum had played no part in the decision to remove the Verde Indians to San Carlos, and was more than a little nervous about how they would integrate with his Apaches. Many of the bands had fought one another in the past, and in this wild land, warriors tended to have long memories.

⋆⇒⦵⧤⋆

THE NEWCOMERS TO San Carlos set up their camps a few miles across the Gila River from the main agency. Clum's first problem was to disarm the Indians. He brought out his baskets of Sonoran tobacco and they all had a big smoke, but when he brought up the question of guns, both the Yavapais and Tontos refused to give up their weapons. Clum said he would withhold rations until all guns were turned over, and the Indians departed in a huff.

Eskiminzin, whom Clum had liberated from imprisonment at Camp Grant, went as the agent's emissary to explain to the new arrivals the rules at San Carlos. The old chief had some influence among the Tontos, but it was Sieber who came up with a solution. He secretly urged the Indians to turn over only their old and broken guns and to hide the rest. Seventy-five useless firearms, many of them quite antique, were delivered to Clum. The agent was perceptive enough to recognize the ruse but wise enough to declare victory and immediately issue the newcomers their beef rations. He called another council and asked the chiefs to nominate four men to join his police force. He explained how his labor system worked and the Yavapais, in particular, were soon hard at work on irrigation ditches. Within a few weeks it appeared that the Verde Indians had adapted quite well to San Carlos, and Agent Clum was able to report yet another triumph to Washington.

Sieber and Mickey Free recruited forty scouts from among the Tontos and reported back with them to Camp Verde on May 7. The following day, the scouts were on their way to Fort Whipple in response to rumors of Indian raiders near Prescott. The rumors proved unfounded, so Sieber took his scouts into Prescott—or Pine Woods, as the Tontos called it—to see the sights. They received a surprisingly warm reception from the residents, and in response Sieber decided to put on a grand war dance in the town plaza that Friday night. Mickey, who could never resist a dance, was in his element, and even Sieber joined in. "It was the first Apache frolic we ever attended," reported the editor of the *Arizona Miner* on May 21.

This was Sieber's last frolic for several weeks, for he and Mickey were soon back in the saddle in pursuit of Yavapai fugitives. In June alone they made three scouts out of Camp Verde. Ten Yavapai men were killed and thirteen women and children brought in as prisoners. During the first week of July, Sieber's scouts, with Mickey working as interpreter, went out on an expedition to the east fork of the Verde River that resulted in two sharp fights, thirty dead Yavapais, and fifteen prisoners.

One of the prisoners was a young boy, of perhaps five or six years old, whom Sieber pulled up onto the saddle behind him. As the white mule picked its way along the trail, the boy held on to Sieber's shirt. The scout suddenly felt a sharp pain in his side. The tyke had managed to sneak Sieber's knife out of its scabbard and was poking it into Sieber's side with all his might. As Sieber loudly cursed, a Tonto scout rode up alongside and whisked the boy off the mule and into the brush. Sieber was not seriously injured, but he had learned a valuable lesson. The incident had also given Mickey a very good laugh.

In the time between scouts, Mickey could be found at William Head's trading post at Camp Verde. His purchases reflected not only his new income but also an important change in his life. He upgraded his wardrobe with a broad-brimmed hat for $1.50 as well as a fine new pair of $12 boots. He also bought shirts, pants, suspenders, and underwear. He had decided to give up his old Apache outfit and put on some style. He also spent a considerable sum on cartridges. The lemon candy and tobacco and cigarette papers he bought reveal personal habits, while his purchases of numerous inexpensive shirts and multiple knives and spurs make it clear he was sharing his wealth with others, as was the Apache way.

The $14 he spent on calico and mantas, as well as $5 on a shawl and looking glass, meant that he had started to go courting. Sure enough, he soon married Ethlay, the sister-in-law of the White Mountain leader Baelka, in the Apache way. She bore him a son in 1876.

WHILE MICKEY FREE was busy pursuing a bride, and Al Sieber, who never displayed much interest in women, continued to pursue fugitive Yavapais, John Clum went in pursuit of naked ambition.

His success with the Verde newcomers had convinced the young agent of his own brilliance. He now began to measure his success by the number of Indians under his control. The more Indians under his able management, the better it was for them. That his growing reputation as their savior would flourish was just a bonus. Clum began to see his position at San Carlos as but a stepping-stone to a much higher government office.

The Camp Apache agency had long been in disarray, dominated by a protracted feud between the inept agent and the arrogant local military commander. Clum got along no better with the Camp Apache officers than did his counterpart there—when he first visited the post he was arrested for riding his horse too fast across the parade ground—but he used the situation to his advantage. He strenuously lobbied his friend and benefactor, Commissioner of Indian Affairs Smith, for permission to relocate the Western Apaches at Camp Apache down to San Carlos, some miles south. In June 1875, he received the order from Smith to proceed.

Eskiminzin once again stepped in to help. He and Clum convinced the White Mountain people to make the move. There would be no military cooperation this time, but the movement south was made without incident, although Chief Pedro's band refused to budge. The families of the White Mountain Apache scouts were also left at Camp Apache. As a sign of defiance to the military, Clum had all the agency buildings burned as he departed. This was an amazing display of government rivalry, as one federal official destroyed property to deny its use to other federal officials.

The scout John Rope noted that many of the people continued to plant their corn in their traditional fields near Camp Apache even though they drew their rations at San Carlos. Then they would drive their ration-issue cattle back to their *rancherias* near Camp Apache. This did not particularly bother Clum, for he was simply engaging in a numbers game. He now officially had 4,200 Indians at San Carlos.

General Crook, on the other hand, complained, but to no avail. "These Indians at Apache were a mountain Indian, and the heat and dust of San Carlos agency was quite equal at times to that of

Yuma, besides being malarious," he protested. "Their removal was one of those cruel things that greed has so often inflicted on the Indian."

Crook soon left Arizona, for General Sheridan wanted him on the northern plains for an anticipated war with the Sioux. He departed in March 1875 to be replaced by Colonel August V. Kautz, who proved to be an erratic and controversial commander.

Agent Clum now turned his attention to the one Apache band that had defied General Crook—the Chiricahuas of Cochise. In his dogged determination to relocate the Chiricahuas to San Carlos, Clum set in motion a series of increasingly tragic events that would cost thousands of lives. It also set him on a collision course with the man soon to be the most famous Indian in America—Geronimo.

16

GERONIMO

IT WAS LATE ON THE EVENING OF JUNE 7, 1874, WHEN Cochise and Tom Jeffords met for the final time. The great chief had been ill for months, his spirits bolstered by *tiswin* and warm memories of bygone days. He knew the end was near and had already called his leading men together to pledge their fidelity to his eldest son, Taza, to their white friend Taglito, and to the peace they had made with the Americans.

"Do you think you will ever see me alive again?" asked Cochise.

"No, I do not think I will," Jeffords said. "I think that by tomorrow night, you will be dead."

"Yes, I think so, too. Do you think we will ever meet again?"

Jeffords was taken aback for a moment. "I don't know. What is your opinion about it?"

"I have been thinking a good deal about it while I have been sick here, and I believe we will." Cochise pointed weakly toward the countless stars. "Good friends will meet again—up there."

The next morning, he was dead. A great wail went up from every voice in the east stronghold, then across the Dragoon Mountains, and soon throughout all of Apacheria. It kept up all day and all night.

Cochise's wife and sister prepared him for burial. They washed him, carefully combed his long hair, and placed a majestic feathered bonnet on his head. They painted his face for war, then wrapped his now-frail body in a splendid red woolen blanket.

That afternoon, a sad procession made its way deep up into the towering rocks of the stronghold. The two sons of Cochise, Taza and Naiche, led Cochise's horse upon which the body had been placed, followed by the chief's three wives, a shaman, and Jeffords. Cochise's faithful dog walked alongside the horse. Behind them, hundreds of Chokonen people followed. They carried many of their belongings with them to burn over the chief's grave. They took him high up amid the great rocks where a deep chasm existed. The horse was killed and rolled in, followed by his dog, then his weapons, and finally the body of Cochise was lowered by ropes into a final place of rest. A fire now consumed the clothing and property of the great chief, and then dark smoke rose above the stronghold along with their cries of lamentation. The greatest of the lords of Apacheria was no more.

OVER THE PAST several years, Jeffords and Cochise had worked diligently to keep the peace, despite the efforts of General Crook and many in Tucson to provoke a new war. Crook very much wished to make an object lesson of Cochise, which he convinced himself would curb the turbulent spirits among the other Apache bands. He also wanted the military glory, for despite his low-key demeanor, Crook was as addicted to self-promotion as many of his rivals.

The leading citizens of Tucson wanted the land of the Chiricahuas. Rumors of gold and silver in the Dragoon Mountains had swirled for years. Much like the Black Hills of Dakota, the mystery encouraged wild fantasies of mineral riches ripe for the picking. In fact, the Dragoons, unlike the Black Hills, held no mountain of gold. The excuse used most often by both Crook and the leaders of Arizona society to invade the Chiricahua Reservation was their sudden concern for the welfare of the citizens of Sonora.

The governor of Sonora sent Governor Anson Safford of Arizona a list of twenty different Chiricahua raids on his state between October 1872 and March 1873, and also lodged a formal complaint with the US State Department. Governor Safford, who in 1872 had traveled to the reservation and met with Cochise and Jeffords, dismissed the governor's claims as exaggerated and informed

American military authorities that "so far as the people of Arizona are concerned, I believe that Cochise has kept his word with us." Safford was also deeply impressed with Jeffords. "I do not believe any other man living could now manage them, wild as they are," he declared in 1872, "and I have strong hopes if the government will continue with him in charge, that peace may be maintained."

Special Commissioner L. Edwin Dudley agreed with Governor Safford. He had visited the Chiricahua Reservation just days before the death of Cochise. Dudley realized that many of the New Mexico Apaches from Tularosa had raided Sonora and then stopped in the Dragoons to draw rations from Jeffords. The number of Apaches at Tularosa had declined from more than 600 in January to fewer than 250 by December. They had moved to the Chiricahua Reservation, where Jeffords's more liberal administration suited them.

This was also true of Juh's Nednhi. Juh had always been more comfortable around Janos or deep in the Sierra Madre, but he still came into the new Chiricahua Reservation from time to time to trade, visit relatives, and draw rations. His best friend, the warrior Geronimo, was usually with him.

"Juh came and went as he wished, but he stayed sometimes for months on Cochise's reservation," remembered Juh's son Daklugie. "I often did see Red Beard. Every Apache child knew that he and the chief were great friends, though few could understand why Cochise would condescend to acknowledge a White Eye as brother. I could understand even less why my father, who hated white people worse even than I do, could like this man."

SPECIAL COMMISSIONER DUDLEY also recognized the almost mystic power Jeffords had with the Chiricahuas. Dudley had already secured the transfer of the Mimbres of Victorio and Loco from Tularosa to their beloved hot springs, but his ultimate goal was to eventually transfer both the Mescaleros and the Chiricahuas to Ojo Caliente as well. Dudley, like Clum, was measuring his personal success in the number of Indians under his control.

"I have seen no man who has so complete control over his Indians as Agent Jeffords, and I am sure that if they are removed, he would be the best man to make Agent at Hot Springs," Dudley reported to Indian Commissioner Edward Smith at the end of June 1874.

Jeffords was not adept at paperwork, but he had wisely hired Fred Hughes, an educated Englishman who had come to New Mexico with the California Volunteers, and General Howard's colorful packmaster, Zebina Streeter, as assistants. Hughes, in particular, kept meticulous records, which made clear how careful Jeffords was with his ration issues. The fact that the government cut the rations to save cost did not help, especially since the number of Apaches on the reservation steadily increased. Hughes reported 375 Chokonens, 250 Nednhis, 250 Bedonkohes, and 125 Chihennes on the Chiricahua Reservation at the time of Cochise's death.

Dudley also met with Taza, the heir apparent, and while pleased to find the son as committed to peace as his father was, he still worried that "he has not so much influence over the tribe."

Dudley's judgment proved correct, for no sooner had Cochise been buried than Taza's position as chief was challenged. A rebuke soon came from two turbulent warriors, Skinya and Pionsenay, who disputed Taza's right to leadership. Skinya, who was the father-in-law of Naiche, attempted to divide the two sons of Cochise. It all climaxed at a *tiswin* party that left two men dead, but in it Naiche stood steadfastly by his older brother.

Jeffords found himself in an increasingly untenable situation. While he still retained the loyalty of Taza and his Chokonens, he had a far more difficult time with the other bands who had settled on the reservation. Jeffords's liberal administration, which differed so markedly from the stern rules at San Carlos and Tularosa, actually encouraged the restless spirits among the various bands to settle at his agency. This was not productive of an orderly administration.

Not only had warriors brought their Chihenne families from Tularosa, but several other Western Apache bands had also come to the Chiricahua Reservation. The fluctuating number of Apaches rationed by Jeffords led to charges of corruption lodged against him by Clum and the Tucson press. They claimed that Jeffords had inflated his ration numbers to line his pockets. This was a lie, but still, it carried weight with many.

Jeffords also had to deal with Juh and Geronimo, who regularly raided into Mexico. Jeffords boldly confronted Geronimo and rescued a Mexican child from his camp. He also recovered stolen stock from both Geronimo and Juh. Jeffords and Juh were on reasonably friendly terms, and such matters might be easily settled with a wink and a smile, but dealing with Geronimo entailed a more protracted and dangerous negotiation. Both Geronimo and Juh realized that it was in their interest to cooperate with Jeffords, for his reservation offered them a convenient sanctuary, at least so long as they did not raid the Americans.

Hughes, who had accompanied Jeffords to Geronimo's camp to retrieve the captive boy, was not impressed by the notorious warrior. "I always looked upon him as one of the most worthless and cowardly fiends upon the reservation," Hughes recalled in 1886, and "on two different occasions I saw squaws thrash him soundly." Hughes became convinced that Geronimo's reputation was in some ways a myth manufactured by the army to bolster its budget and image. "I am inclined to the belief that the military have created Geronimo's chieftainship and kept him as much before the public," he grumbled.

The complaints from the governor of Sonora, the ill will of several highly placed military officers, the persistent agitation by John Clum that he could better manage the Chiricahuas at San Carlos, and the unrelenting charges in Arizona newspapers that Jeffords coddled the Apaches on his reservation all combined to convince Smith, the commissioner of Indian affairs, to send a special inspector to investigate.

The inspector got a cool reception from Jeffords when he reached the reservation late in November 1875. Jeffords was no government lackey, and he paid the visiting federal inspector all the respect he deserved—which was none. This was an unfortunate decision, of course, but Jeffords had never desired the job in the first place. He had wearied of risking his life on a daily basis only to find his name pilloried in the Tucson newspaper.

The inspector, who had visited with Clum before meeting with Jeffords, now filed a hatchet-job report insinuating incompetence if not outright fraud on the Chiricahua Reservation. His report was a complex web of lies and misrepresentations that urged the commissioner of Indian affairs to replace Jeffords with an Indian agent who would "gradually disarm them, break them of their *tiswin* drunks, introduce cattle and sheep herding among them, and if need be prepare for their removal to another Reservation." As it happened, the inspector knew just where the Chiricahuas should go. "I think the San Carlos Reservation will prove to be the best place suited to these Indians," he concluded.

The political vultures circled slowly over the Chiricahua Reservation. Then the warrior Pionsenay provided them with just the carrion they sought. Jeffords had always allowed *tiswin* on the reservation, but he had banned whiskey. On April 6, a rancher near Sulphur Springs sold whiskey to Pionsenay and another warrior for gold they had stolen in Sonora. The drunken warriors returned the next day to buy more whiskey, promptly shot the rancher and a cowboy, and took what they wanted. They then rejoined Skinya and a handful of warriors for a horse-stealing raid along the San Pedro River that left one settler dead and another wounded.

This gave John Wasson, the acerbic editor of the *Tucson Weekly Citizen,* whose torrent of invective against Lieutenant Royal Whitman had helped spark the Camp Grant Massacre, all the excuse he needed to turn on Jeffords. Wasson, an ally of Clum, was soon on his way to Washington to lobby for Chiricahua removal to San Carlos. Wasson was of course anxious to open the Chiricahua Reservation to white mining and cattle interests. Wasson's newspaper declared a full-scale outbreak to be under way and blamed Jeffords for selling whiskey and ammunition to the Apaches.

Now even Governor Safford turned on Jeffords and began to back Clum's concentration plan at San Carlos. Clum's personal ambitions worked in perfect harmony with the desire of Arizona leaders like Wasson and Safford to open up the Chiricahua Reservation to their white constituents. Jeffords was clearly in the way and had to be removed. Clum hurried to Tucson to meet with Safford the moment he heard of the killings to offer his services as commander of a force of two hundred San Carlos Apaches that would subdue the Chiricahuas.

"I disapproved of the management of the Indians by Agent Jeffords," Safford declared in a newspaper interview, even though his words directly contradicted his previous statements. "I thought the time had arrived to break up the reservation and put a stop to this disgraceful conduct."

A few days after Pionsenay's outbreak, several families left the Chiricahua Reservation for Ojo Caliente in New Mexico of their own accord. Colonel Edward Hatch, Ninth Cavalry, the able commander of the District of New Mexico, arrived at Ojo Caliente at about the same time as the fugitives from Jeffords's reservation. Victorio's people were already in a sullen mood because their beef rations were more than a month late and wanted the Chihennes to join them on the warpath. These fugitives from Jeffords's reservation, or "Arizona Indians," as Hatch labeled them, were actually mostly Victorio's own people who had now returned because of the troubles in Arizona. Several Chokonens had joined them and all were in a surly mood.

On April 21, 1876, Victorio faced down the war faction and gunfire erupted. Three of the Arizona Apaches were killed and several more wounded. They decamped the next morning and headed south for the mountains of Chihuahua. Among Victorio's band the only death was young Chie, the nephew of Cochise who had guided General Howard on his peace mission. Hatch, although pleased with the outcome of the gunfight, still worried about the increased dissatisfaction expressed to him by Victorio.

MEANWHILE, TOM JEFFORDS had been in the saddle much of the time since the Sulphur Springs murders. Accompanied by Taza and three Chokonen warriors, Jeffords had ridden to Sulphur Springs as soon as he learned of Pionsenay's breakout. Jeffords and the warriors were joined by Lieutenant Austin Henely with forty-four Sixth Cavalry troopers from Camp Bowie. Taza quickly picked up the trail of the renegades, and late in the evening of April 10, after marching more than eighty miles, he discovered Skinya's camp atop a high peak in the Dragoons. As the soldiers approached, the Apaches unleashed a volley of rifle fire and arrows. The two sides skirmished for two hours before Lieutenant Henely decided to withdraw. By morning Skinya and Pionsenay, along with their warriors, had slipped away into Sonora.

But Skinya soon returned, and on May 10, 1876, he requested a parley with Jeffords. The agent met the renegades some five miles from the agency, and although Skinya professed a desire to surrender, Pionsenay threatened to kill Jeffords. While Skinya covered his back, Jeffords hurriedly departed the council. Three weeks later Taza and Naiche met with Skinya's band. Rumors were swirling that all the Chiricahuas were to be removed to San Carlos, and Skinya wanted the two brothers to join him in a war against the White Eyes. An intense argument followed, guns were drawn, and Naiche killed his father-in-law, Skinya. Taza killed three others and wounded Pionsenay. Two of Taza's men were killed in the fight, and two more were wounded. Taza, in fear that Skinya's allies, who included Geronimo and Juh, might counterattack, sent a messenger to Jeffords requesting help.

Jeffords, with Lieutenant Henely and thirty troopers from Camp Bowie, rushed to Bonita Canyon to rescue the two sons of Cochise. They arrived near midnight to discover that Geronimo and the young Nednhi war leader Nolgee, with several Nednhi warriors, had come to help Skinya kill the brothers. A volley was fired over their heads, which calmed everyone down, and Jeffords boldly strode forward to talk with them. Jeffords somehow convinced Geronimo to travel to Fort Bowie for a parley with Colonel Kautz and Agent Clum. The next morning, June 5, 1876, Taza and Jeffords led 250 Apaches into Fort Bowie. Geronimo and Nolgee arrived later that afternoon.

⊷⊶◉⊷⊶

MEANWHILE, IN WASHINGTON, DC, with uncharacteristic speed and efficiency, as if it had all been plotted out well in advance, the cogs of the federal government had already ground out the orders necessary to remove the Chiricahuas to San Carlos. A few months before the Apaches converged on Fort Bowie for the parley, the machinations had begun. Governor Safford had sent a telegram on April 19, 1876, to John Wasson, who was in Washington to represent the interests of the Tucson business community—or the Indian Ring, as Crook labeled them—with the recommendation that the government close the Chiricahua Reservation and relocate the Indians to San Carlos.

Wasson knew just the man to handle this delicate mission—"the only man with the nerve, ability, and confidence to do it": John Clum. Wasson, working with the Arizona territorial representative to Congress, had money promptly appropriated by Congress to secure the Chiricahuas' removal.

On May 3, 1876, the commissioner of Indian affairs had ordered Clum to suspend Jeffords as agent, close the Chiricahua Reservation, and remove all the Apaches to San Carlos. Clum gladly accepted but requested troops just in case there was more resistance than his San Carlos police force could handle. On May 15, the secretary of war had issued orders to department commander Colonel Kautz to provide all necessary troops to support the removal. Colonel Kautz had replied that he would have columns in the field by June 2.

Thus the flagrant breach of the treaty General Howard had made with Cochise was officially secured. The dispossession of the Chiricahua Apaches of their homeland had begun.

Kautz had reached Tucson on May 31 to confer with Governor Safford. He had ordered most of the troops at his disposal to be stationed near the reservation, so seven companies of cavalry, 550 troops, and 100 Indian scouts took up positions. Al Sieber led the Indian scouts from Camp Verde with Mickey Free as interpreter. They eventually made camp west of the Chiricahua Mountains in case the Apaches attempted to break out. Clum also brought in fifty-four of his Apache police to Tucson, along with interpreter

Merejildo Grijalva. In order to bypass Jeffords, Governor Safford hired Jeffords's onetime assistant Fred Hughes to act as liaison with Taza.

It was nine in the morning on June 5, 1876, when Taza, Naiche, and Jeffords arrived at Apache Pass with 250 Chiricahuas. For Naiche it was a return to the place where as a child he had been held hostage and forced to witness the hanging of his uncle. An hour later, Colonel Kautz and Agent Clum, with five companies of the Sixth Cavalry behind them, rode in.

The San Carlos agent dismounted in the Camp Bowie parade ground and, before anyone spoke, handed Jeffords a telegram from the new Commissioner of Indian Affairs, John Quincy Smith, removing him as agent. This was the first notice Jeffords received of his dismissal, for despite the many rumors, he had been kept in the dark about the conspiracy to replace him and remove the Chiricahuas. Even Fred Hughes had not known that his friend was to be dismissed. In that moment, three years of Jeffords's tireless dedication to the cause of peace was over; he quietly withdrew into the shadows to watch the rest of the drama play out.

Taza, with no alternative left save war, reluctantly agreed to move his people to San Carlos. In an impassioned speech, translated by Grijalva, he declared that his actions were guided by the final wish of his father: to always live in peace with the Americans. He reminded Clum and Kautz that not only had he always kept the peace made by General Howard and his father, but he had also killed the Apaches responsible for the recent troubles. He pledged eternal friendship to the Americans. Hughes thought that both Clum and Kautz were deeply moved by Taza's speech, but it did not alter their determination to follow their orders. Clum did agree to allow the Chiricahuas to settle near old Camp Goodwin, away from the Western Apache camps, and to keep their arms for the time being.

Geronimo and Juh held a separate council with Clum and Kautz. Clum ignored Hughes's warning not to negotiate with Geronimo, so he agreed to give the Apaches four days to bring their people into Camp Bowie. After the warriors had left, an exasperated Hughes

took Kautz aside to warn him that Geronimo and Juh had no intention of going to San Carlos.

Kautz then ordered Sieber's Camp Verde detachment to pursue
the Nednhis and make sure they returned as promised. But Geronimo and Juh were in Sonora before Sieber and Free were in position to block their escape. They had quickly broken camp, taking
only what they needed, even killing their dogs lest their barking
give them away. Zebina Streeter, Jeffords's assistant, had gone with
them. Some said he went because he sympathized with their plight,
while others said he was in love with an Apache girl, but whatever
his reasons, he was soon branded a renegade with a price on his
head in both Sonora and Arizona. His defection only added to the
suspicion already attached to Jeffords.

On June 12, 1876, Clum departed Camp Bowie for San Carlos
with three hundred Chokonens led by Taza and twenty-two Bedonkohes under their leader Chiva. Three companies of cavalry
accompanied the Apaches, almost all of whom were women and children. Most of them rode in wagons. Clum had only forty-two Chiricahua men in his caravan, for the vast majority of the warriors had
fled east into New Mexico or south with Geronimo toward Sonora.
Clum used the small number of Chiricahuas as evidence of the fraud
involved in Jeffords's ration issues, rather than admitting that he had
only rounded up a third of the Apaches he had intended to bring in.

A week later, the *Tucson Weekly Citizen* applauded the end of
Jeffords's reservation, which it described as a "nursery for bad Indians." The *Citizen* pointed out that the former home of the Chiricahuas "is a rich domain of mountain and valley embracing some
of the best mineral and agriculture features of the Territory." The
editor was certain that this region of great potential wealth would
"soon be thrown open to settlers."

AFTER THE FAILED PARLEY, Geronimo and Juh, along with 208
of their people, camped near the southern foothills of the Chiricahua Mountains. While there, they sent several small raiding parties
out to gather provisions. The Apaches killed two prospectors near

Pinery Canyon, stole some horses and left two dead cowboys on the San Pedro, then made off with several horses near Santa Cruz. Sieber's Apache scouts did manage to overtake four of the raiders near the border and in a sharp skirmish killed two.

Geronimo and Juh then headed for favored haunts in Sonora. They had some hope of negotiating for a reservation there, but soon found that the Mexican state was in turmoil. They sent their new recruit Zebina Streeter to open talks, but it took the envoy some time to find someone to negotiate with. Geronimo became impatient and decided to go north to New Mexico, where his brother-in-law, Nana, and other friends and relatives lived on the Ojo Caliente Reservation. Juh took his people farther southwest to a favorite campsite along the Aros River in the Sierra Madre.

Geronimo and his people camped in the Florida Mountains in New Mexico's bootheel, where they joined up with a small band of Bedonkohes who had prospered by raids on ranches both to the north around Silver City and south across the line into Chihuahua. They sought safety along the international line, in the hopes that it would provide them with some security from attack.

COLONEL KAUTZ, WHILE not as aggressive with his troops or as politically astute as Crook, still did the best he could with his limited resources. Kautz recognized the value of the Apache scouts, so he had ordered the recruitment of a third company. He employed Apache scout companies at Camp Apache (A), Camp Verde (B), and Camp Bowie (C). All three companies were made up of Western Apaches, and the new Company C at Camp Bowie had been recruited from Pinals at San Carlos.

On January 4, 1877, Lieutenant John Anthony "Tony" Rucker, Sixth Cavalry, led seventeen of his troopers and thirty-four Apache scouts of the new Company C out of Camp Bowie to scout for Apaches east toward Stein's Peak. Rucker, the brother-in-law of General Sheridan, was a popular young officer renowned for both tenacity and courage. Near Stein's Peak, Rucker's scouts picked up a trail to the south and doggedly followed it to the northern Animas

Mountains. At dawn on January 9, Rucker and his men stormed an Apache *rancheria* of sixteen wickiups. Taken completely by surprise, the Apaches hastily abandoned their camp as the warriors fought a rearguard action while the women and children fled. Rucker counted ten dead Apaches in the camp. His men captured the entire pony herd, forty-six animals, and recovered a dozen rifles from the camp. The only prisoner was a young boy who turned out to be the nephew of Geronimo.

"We had nothing left; winter was beginning, and it was the coldest winter I ever knew," Geronimo later recalled of the attack. He decided to push on to Ojo Caliente, mix with Victorio's people, draw government rations, and enlist some young Chihenne warriors for a revenge raid.

At Ojo Caliente, Chief Loco was unhappy over the sudden appearance of Geronimo's people. Even Nana, Geronimo's brother-in-law, was worried. Victorio was wary as well, but the suffering of Geronimo's people moved him. He did not like Geronimo, but the laws of Chiricahua kinship and hospitality outweighed his personal feelings. "These people are not bothering us," he told Loco. Geronimo and his people could stay.

"Victorio had never approved of the ways of Geronimo," remembered his daughter Dilth-cleyhen. "His way of warfare cost the lives of too many of the younger, less experienced warriors. He fought for his own glory, not for the welfare of the Indeh."

Victorio's concerns proved prophetic. Geronimo, with a band of about fifty warriors, left Ojo Caliente late in January 1876 and traveled south to Mexico to enlist Juh in a great raid. They then swept north through the Sonoita, crossed over the mountains to the Santa Cruz Valley south of Tucson, and struck the Pima villages. Geronimo's men left nine dead in their wake and returned safely to Mexico with a large horse herd liberated from the Pimas and the Sonoita ranchers. Not a single warrior was killed.

GERONIMO AND HIS band then returned in triumph to Ojo Caliente with their share of the plunder. But a detachment from Camp

Bowie under Lieutenant Austin Henely had been trailing the raiders, and Henely's Apache scouts pointed out Geronimo as the leader of the raiding party. Henely, out of his military jurisdiction in New Mexico, took no action but reported back to Colonel Kautz his conclusion that the renegades were drawing rations on Victorio's reservation while raiding into Arizona.

Henely's report was forwarded up the chain of command to the War Department in Washington, and from there to the Interior Department. In 1877, Commissioner of Indian Affairs John Q. Smith reluctantly confessed that "the old reign of terror seemed to have returned to the southeastern portion of Arizona." On March 20, Smith telegraphed Agent John Clum at San Carlos to arrest Geronimo and remove him and his followers to San Carlos.

Beauford, who was already in the field with sixty San Carlos Apaches, received instructions from Clum to wait in Silver City, New Mexico. Unlike Lieutenant Henely, Agent Clum did not have to worry about invisible military department lines or territorial boundaries. Clum brought forty additional Apaches with him from San Carlos and met Beauford's force at Fort Bayard the second week of April. From the fort, he sent a message on April 15 to Commissioner Smith requesting permission to remove not just Geronimo and his followers but *all* the Apaches from Ojo Caliente to San Carlos. Smith, unable to even properly staff the troublesome agency, promptly agreed. Clum wired Colonel Kautz in Prescott to request military assistance and was rudely informed that, since Ojo Caliente resided in the Department of the Missouri, he needed to contact Colonel Hatch in Santa Fe for assistance. Clum then wired Hatch to request troops to assist with the removal. Hatch quickly ordered three companies of the Ninth Cavalry to rendezvous with Clum near the hot springs on April 21.

Clum, with an advance guard of twenty-two San Carlos police, arrived at Ojo Caliente on April 20. The agent was not there, but one of the agency employees gave Clum a message from Major James Wade that his troopers could not reach the agency before April 22. Clum realized that if he waited for the cavalry, his Apache police force would be discovered and Geronimo would certainly escape. He ordered Beauford to bring his sixty men into the agency under cover of darkness, where they were to conceal themselves in the commissary building just to the south of the main agency head-quarters. Clum and his men took up position in the adobe agency building. Both buildings fronted the west side of the parade ground. At the same time, he sent a message to Geronimo, who was camped about three miles away, with a request that he come in for a parley.

Clum had made a grand show of riding in with his escort of twenty-two San Carlos Apaches. He knew that their number would be quickly reported to Geronimo. He planned to use his relative lack of men to lull Geronimo into a false sense of superiority and lure him into the trap. Beauford's contingent of men were carefully concealed, while Clum and a handful of men waited for Geronimo on the porch of the agency office building. Each man had a loaded weapon and thirty rounds of ammunition. On a prearranged sig-nal, Beauford's men were to emerge from the commissary building and rush eastward to surround the parade ground. They were all prepared for a fight, but no one was to fire unless Clum or Beauford gave the order.

Now they waited in silence for what seemed an eternity as the sun rose over the mountains to the east. They all knew that they were outnumbered at least three to one.

The next morning was ration day, so Geronimo had planned to visit the agency anyway. A little after dawn, he came in with Ponce, Chatto, and fifty men, women, and children of his band. He anticipated no trouble, or at least none he could not handle. Geronimo, haughty as always, rode in ahead of the rest with a large party of painted and heavily armed warriors. Clum stepped for-ward from the adobe building, his hand casually resting on his hip above his .45. He told Geronimo he was under arrest. Geronimo looked Clum's twenty-two men up and down and scoffed:

"Nanten-betunny-kahyeh (Boss-with-the-high-forehead), you talk very brave but we are not going to San Carlos with you, and unless you are very careful, you and your Apache police will not go back to San Carlos either. Your bodies will stay here at Ojo Cali-ente to make food for the coyotes."

As Geronimo finished his threat, Clum touched his left hand to his sombrero. Doors sprang open and his eighty men rushed out of the commissary building and quickly surrounded Geronimo's men. Clum's hand moved to his revolver—a signal to the men behind him to point their rifles at Geronimo. Stepping forward, he seized Geronimo's rifle while one of the policemen leapt forward and stopped the warrior from grasping his knife. It was all over in a twinkling.

Clum had Geronimo clapped into chains, but not before his prisoner spat out his contempt:

"You are the false White-Eye who came to the Chiricahua Reservation a year ago and broke the peace treaty made by the Great Chief and Taglito and the one-arm general. Do not talk to me about breaking treaties—you and your sick brain!"

MAJOR WADE AND his Buffalo Soldiers arrived on April 22. The major was naturally pleased, and more than a little astonished, to find Geronimo and six other Apache leaders already in chains. One of these men was Ponce, who had so ably served General Howard as a guide, but who had since fallen under Geronimo's spell. Wade's men now scouted the area around the agency and brought in several more Apache families.

Clum met with Victorio and other Warm Springs leaders on April 24 and explained to them that their agency was to be closed and that they were to accompany him to San Carlos. Victorio was stunned, but he had no option save compliance. The thought of living at San Carlos seemed impossible, not only because it was so far from their homeland, but also because of the many blood feuds that existed between the different bands that had already been gathered there. There would be trouble for sure. To Victorio's people, Agent Clum became "Turkey Gobbler," because of the arrogant way he made demands and strutted about. Still, they had no choice but to obey. Clum's heavily armed San Carlos Apaches and Wade's three troops of the Ninth made resistance suicidal.

Victorio told his people to cache their weapons, for he knew that one day he would lead them back to Ojo Caliente. Several families, perhaps 150 people in all, took to the hills and hid from the soldiers. But the vast majority of the group gave in.

On April 30, a sad procession of 435 Warm Springs Apaches began the long, difficult walk to San Carlos. Geronimo and the other chained prisoners rode in a wagon under armed guard. The Buffalo Soldiers escorted them as far as the Arizona line. Clum refused to accept an escort of Colonel Kautz's troops once they crossed the territorial line, which added even more fuel to their fiery relationship. The caravan reached San Carlos on May 20, and Geronimo was locked safely in the agency guardhouse. Clum expected either civil or military authorities to take him into custody, but neither did. By this point Kautz hated Clum so intensely that he would rather see Geronimo go free than acknowledge the young agent's amazing coup. And that is exactly what came to pass.

Kautz, with great political calculation, sent a military officer to check on the number of Indians at San Carlos and to investigate the ration system. This naturally infuriated Clum, who demanded complete control over Apache affairs in Arizona, and a substantial increase in salary as well, under threat of immediate resignation. Commissioner Smith, weary of the infighting and controversy, promptly accepted Clum's resignation effective July 1, 1877.

Geronimo was kept shackled in the San Carlos guardhouse until July 1877, when an Indian Bureau inspector, acting as temporary agent since Clum's resignation, declared him "thoroughly subdued" and released him. From the moment he walked free out of the darkness of his cell into the blinding light and sweltering heat, Geronimo began to plot his revenge on the White Eyes.

17

LOZEN'S VISION

SAN CARLOS WAS A NIGHTMARE. NEARLY FIVE THOU-
sand people were now crammed into this barren wasteland.
Clum's departure from the reservation was catastrophic,
for despite his insufferable arrogance, he was honest and competent
as well as forceful and brave, and he commanded the respect of
many of the Apache band leaders.

The Indian Bureau had dispatched the inexperienced Henry
Hart from Ohio to take charge of the most difficult Indian reservation in the country. Hart arrived on August 21, 1877, to find
the Warm Springs people feuding with the Coyotero Apaches, and
all the bands restless over delayed and insufficient rations, as well
as an outbreak of malarial fevers and the dreaded smallpox. The
new agency administration drifted aimlessly, a sorry combination
of fear, incompetence, and eventual corruption.

The Chokonens were adrift as well. Clum had taken several of
the San Carlos band leaders, including Taza and Eskiminzin, on
an ill-fated junket to Washington in late July 1876. Taza had then
contracted pneumonia and died on September 26, 1876. They had
buried him in the Congressional Cemetery, with General Howard
and Indian Commissioner Smith in attendance.

Naiche continued to brood over his brother's death. Nothing
that Eskiminzin said about Taza's brief illness and grand funeral
could comfort him. He knew well how the White Eyes had dealt
with Mangas Coloradas, and he had witnessed the white soldiers
hang his uncle. He became convinced that Clum had used witchcraft to kill Taza. Naiche was not the strong leader Taza had been,

nor did he command the respect of the people. In his despair Naiche turned to a strong man with spiritual power for counsel and support. That man was Geronimo.

"Naiche was a good man in some ways, but you couldn't civilize him," recalled the son of one of Juh's warriors. "He liked his Indian dancing, and he liked his fighting, and he liked his drinking. . . . He was always influenced by Geronimo."

Tom Jeffords sensed trouble brewing. He arrived in San Carlos in August 1877 and visited with Naiche, Geronimo, and Victorio. Jeffords immediately realized that Victorio's Chihennes were deeply unhappy at San Carlos and warned army officers that an outbreak was inevitable. Colonel Kautz agreed. "So many antagonistic bands thrown together," he told his superiors, "will cause numbers to leave from fear of enemies among their own people."

Pionsenay, with sixteen followers, rode into San Carlos under cover of darkness on September 1, 1877. Zebina Streeter was with him. They had roamed free and raided at will in Mexico for almost a year and now were back with tales of their daring deeds, and rich plunder to display. An outbreak had already been planned, but the return of Pionsenay provided the spark.

Victorio now turned to his sister Lozen for counsel. She was always his most trusted advisor.

Lozen was a woman of both beauty and vision. All the Chiricahua people held her in awe because of her ability to foresee the future. She also had the power to heal the sick and injured. She had been courted by the boldest and strongest Chiricahua warriors, but had rejected them all. For a woman to not marry and bear children was considered a great problem within the tribe. But with Lozen it was different and the people understood. She could never marry.

She was noted, like her brother Victorio, for her wisdom and her courage, sometimes fighting alongside him in battle, but it was her spiritual power that set her apart from all others.

"Lozen is as my right hand," Victorio once said. "Strong as a man, braver than most, and cunning in strategy, Lozen is a shield to her people."

The Warm Springs people called her "Little Sister" as a term of reverence.

Geronimo called her "Woman Warrior."

Lozen chose service to the people above a traditional role as wife and mother and thus spurned the advances of all men. "She was magnificent on a horse," remembered her niece. "She could handle her rifle as well as any man, most of whom she could outrun on foot. She wielded her knife with utmost skill." She was a legendary horse thief and was renowned for her love and care of the animals that most Apaches considered expendable or as food.

"She put marriage from her mind and rode beside her brother as a warrior," the Warm Springs warrior Kaywaykla proudly declared. "She lives solely to aid him and her people. And she is sacred, even as White Painted Woman. She is respected above all living women."

LOZEN AND VICTORIO and almost all the Warm Springs people agreed that it was time to return to the sacred place at Ojo Caliente. Loco argued against the move, but he could sense that few of the people were with him. After dark on September 2, the Warm Springs people quietly departed in four distinct groups for New Mexico. Loco, Nana, Mangas, and Victorio led the 310 Apaches. Geronimo was conspicuously absent, for the Chihennes blamed him for all their troubles and especially the forced removal to San Carlos. They all crossed the Gila River, herding a large number of White Mountain Apache horses that they had appropriated. Victorio and a handful of warriors formed a rear guard, for they knew pursuit was inevitable.

Pionsenay provided some cover for Victorio's people by stealing six Coyotero horses and heading south toward Old Mexico with twenty-two followers. Apache police were quickly on his trail, but he escaped untouched across the border to reunite with Juh's Nednhis, who now numbered around three hundred. Within a year's time, Pionsenay and Juh's group would kill nearly a hundred Sonorans and make off with a rich treasure in captives, horses, and cattle.

In November, Pionsenay accompanied Juh on a visit to their old trading partners in the Chihuahua village of Janos. There they traded their plunder and sold their stolen Sonoran livestock. On their return to their *rancheria,* some eighteen miles southwest of Janos, they encountered forty Sonoran soldiers. In the sharp skirmish that followed, a single Apache warrior was left dead on the field. Pionsenay had been killed. The Mexican commander took the scalp of Pionsenay and carried it back as a trophy to Sonora.

Colonels Kautz and Hatch soon had several columns in the field in both Arizona and New Mexico. Beauford's Apache police caught up with a band of the Warm Springs fugitives and in two fights captured more than forty women and children and recovered forty-four horses. Beauford reported that the trail of the fugitives pointed northeast toward Ojo Caliente. Colonel Hatch now concentrated his troops in the vicinity of the hot springs and waited.

Although the soldiers and scouts all seemed to know where Victorio's people were going, somehow they could never find them. According to the Apaches, that was the result of Lozen's power. "Many times I have seen her stand and determine the location of the enemy," declared Kaywaykla. "With outstretched hands she would slowly turn as she sang a prayer:

> *Upon this earth*
> *On which we live*
> *Usen has Power.*
> *This Power is mine*
> *For locating the Enemy.*
> *I search for that Enemy.*
> *Which only Usen the Great*
> *Can show to me.*

"More often now, the warriors needed the seer's powers of discernment," remembered Dilth-cleyhen. "[Lozen] went with them whenever she could, being as close to her brother, despite their respect relationship, as he was to Loco or Nana." Lozen stayed by

Victorio's side both in camp and on the move. "Her importance increased with every success she predicted," according to Dilth-cleyhen. "She attended each war ceremony." As the people sat in the great circle before the fire in preparation for battle and heard the name of every great warrior called out, they always heard the name Lozen called the loudest.

LOZEN LED HER PEOPLE north around the troops gathered at Ojo Caliente and into the rough lava beds south of Fort Wingate, just below the Navajo Reservation. Colonel Edward Hatch, in anticipation of such a move, had sent two of his Navajo scouts to Wingate with orders to feed and care for any Apaches who were willing to come in. This warm welcome convinced Loco and Victorio to lead 187 Warm Springs Apaches into Wingate on October 8. Others still in the mountains soon followed.

Colonel Hatch was a good soldier and a compassionate man. He had risen from captain to brigadier general of volunteers during the Civil War to lead his Iowa cavalry brigade in Colonel Benjamin Grierson's famous 1863 raid through Mississippi. In 1866 he had been commissioned colonel of the Ninth Cavalry while his friend Grierson took command of the Tenth. Hatch was anxious to return Victorio's people to Ojo Caliente. He was convinced that this would encourage all the Mimbres holdouts, including those who had never gone to San Carlos, to settle on the reservation and bring an end to Apache raids in New Mexico. But the Department of the Interior wanted the Apaches returned to San Carlos or to be banished to the Indian Territory (present Oklahoma). General Sheridan, always delighted to frustrate Indian Bureau designs, ordered that the Apaches be sent to Ojo Caliente.

On November 10, 1877, Victorio's people, some 233 in number, arrived at Ojo Caliente, where they drew rations and waited for a decision from the Department of the Interior. General Sheridan and Colonel Hatch both urged that the Warm Springs people be left at Ojo Caliente. "As the motives which control the Indian Bureau in their objection to these Indians remaining at the Warm Springs reservation are unknown to me," Sheridan pointed out in exasperation, "it would be best to let them remain at the Warm Springs and I so recommend."

The motives of the Indian Bureau were indeed a mystery. It may have been simply that whatever the army recommended, no matter how sensible it was, the bureau would oppose. Commissioner of Indian Affairs Ezra Hayt, handpicked for the job by Secretary of the Interior Carl Schurz because of his liberal politics and humanitarian zeal, was actually involved in shady mining ventures with the equally corrupt Agent Hart at San Carlos. Hayt's simple solution to every crisis with the Indians—Cheyenne, Ute, Nez Perce, or Apache—was to ship them off to the Indian Territory. Schurz, who was honest to the core, supported Hayt because of his blind trust in the man and his almost pathological hatred of Sheridan and the military establishment. Whatever Sheridan recommended, Schurz was certain to oppose. Victorio and his people were unknowingly caught in the crossfire of petty political infighting in Washington.

General Sheridan was able to block removal of Victorio's people to the Indian Territory, but even the hero of the Shenandoah could not save them from San Carlos. Hayt pointed out that it had already been decided to sell off the public property at Ojo Caliente and for budgetary reasons an agency could not be continued there. Sheridan responded that the Apaches had been treated as prisoners of war for several months and thus fed by the army. If the Indian Bureau did not take charge of them, he proposed to turn them loose. It was his job to fight Indians, not feed them.

On August 31, 1878, the order went to Ojo Caliente to remove the Apaches back to San Carlos. Captain Frank Bennett of the Ninth Cavalry was assigned the miserable task of escort duty. When the captain informed the assembled Apaches of his orders on October 13, Victorio and Loco both reluctantly agreed to go. The next day, when they were supposed to assemble at the main agency, most of Victorio's people split into small bands and bolted for the mountains. Bennett sent troops in pursuit but the Apaches seemed to have vanished. The captain then delivered Loco and the remaining Apaches—twenty men, seventy-eight women, and seventy-five children—to San Carlos on November 25.

VICTORIO'S PEOPLE REUNITED in the mountains but soon split again, with old Nana leading sixty of the Apaches, mostly women and children, eastward to seek sanctuary on the Mescalero Reservation. Nana's first wife had been a Mescalero, and he still had many relatives and friends in the Sierra Blanca who might provide sanctuary to their Warm Springs cousins.

Lozen went with them, for she was usually the one placed in charge of the families. Young wives accompanied their warrior husbands on raids, for it was their task to build the campsites, cook the food, and nurse the wounded. The children were left in the care of the grandmothers, the widows, and the unmarried female relatives. Older warriors, grandfathers themselves, guarded these families.

Nana kept the people to the west of the Rio Grande in the Black Range as long as possible and traveled by night to avoid the American soldiers. It was difficult going. The weather turned cold and blustery, and the rain mixed often with snow or sleet. But Nana and Lozen kept the people moving, for it was too dangerous to stop to build fires and rest.

No one knew how old Nana was, but all agreed that he was certainly in his seventies at this point. Although quite tall, he was bent over with age and crippled by rheumatism. His left leg was lame, so the Warm Springs people called him Broken Foot, but never in his presence. It was against the custom of the people to ever call an Apache by name to his face, so Nana was called simply Nantan—the leader. He was a great warrior, although never a chief. Among the Chihennes he was renowned for his warm, affable nature—but toward the White Eyes he developed an unquenchable hatred that no amount of blood could ever satisfy.

The most dangerous portion of their journey was the fording of the Rio Grande and the crossing of the main road—the ancient Camino Real. The passage had to be made quickly to avoid detection. Nana, along with most of the warriors, had split away from the main party of women and children to search for food, so Lozen now led the people. Under cover of darkness they reached the bank of the river. The dark waters, swollen by recent rains, swirled and frothed. The ponies balked and even the warriors feared forcing them into the water. The women all began to sing as one the Prayer to the Great River. They sought to calm the raging waters by tapping their hands over their open mouths as they sang—so that their undulating song might soothe the river.

Lozen suddenly pushed forward astride her black horse, her rifle raised above her head. At the river's edge her horse reared and then plunged into the flood. She turned its head upstream and it swam to the far bank. One by one, the others followed. When one horse and rider was swept downstream, Lozen galloped along the bank and then again plunged into the torrent to guide the rider to safety.

When at last all the people had passed safely across, Lozen pointed eastward toward Salinas Peak in the nearby San Andres Mountains and ordered the people to go there. They were to wait at a favorite spring on the mountain for Nana and his warriors to rejoin them.

"Get the people mounted and start," she called out as she turned her horse back and again plunged into the river. "I go to join my brother!"

AMONG THE CASUALTIES of Victorio's outbreak was Colonel Kautz, who had been in a prolonged feud with Governor Safford even before the Apaches fled San Carlos. He was removed as department commander on March 7, 1878, and replaced with a colonel named Orlando B. Willcox. Willcox was scarcely more competent than Kautz but at least was wise enough to avoid political controversy.

Al Sieber, who had taken no part in the pursuit of Victorio, departed military service at the same time, although it had nothing to do with the removal of Kautz. He made his way to Globe, where an 1873 silver strike had created a boomtown only forty miles to the west of the San Carlos Agency headquarters. The silver played out in short order but rich copper mines made Globe prosperous. In time it became home to a wide array of miners—Americans, Englishmen, Italians, Mexicans—and many of them pushed into the reservation in search of silver. Sieber filed several claims but spent most of his time drinking, playing poker, and swapping tales in the local saloons.

Among those whom Sieber befriended in Globe was a grizzled prospector by the name of Ed Schieffelin who was determined to explore the country to the south along the San Pedro River. Schieffelin had prospected in California, Nevada, Idaho, and Oregon and knew his business, but Sieber warned him off. "That's Apache country," Al told Schieffelin. "You go out there and all you'll find will be your tombstone." Schieffelin ignored Sieber and in the spring of 1878 discovered a rich vein of silver in the Dragoon Mountain foothills east of the San Pedro. Within a decade silver valued at more than $30 million had been extracted from eleven mines near the boomtown that Schieffelin named Tombstone.

Mickey Free, who had rejoined Company B of the Apache scouts, was soon ordered to the mining camp of McMillenville, ten miles to the northeast of Globe, to protect the integrity of the San Carlos reservation from invasion by the miners.

The Apaches called Globe Besh-Ba-Gowah, or the metal village, and they watched in disbelief as the White Eyes dug furiously into the earth. As the miners pushed onto the reservation, it further intensified an already dangerous situation. Indian Agent Hart, as a front man for his silent partner Commissioner of Indian Affairs Hayt, had invested in several likely mining claims near McMillenville, and so it was only a matter of time before a twelve-mile strip of potentially rich mineral deposits was taken from the reservation and opened to the miners.

First Sergeant Mickey Free led his scouts east to nearby San Carlos in support of Captain Adna Chaffee, Sixth Cavalry, who had been sent by Willcox to replace the disgraced Agent Hart on July 6, 1879. The scandals surrounding Hart's corrupt administration had become so intolerable that the Indian Bureau had reluctantly agreed to the appointment of an army officer as temporary agent.

Chaffee, worried that Victorio might return to San Carlos to rescue the rest of his people, ordered all the Warm Springs and Chiricahua Apaches to congregate near the agency headquarters, and requested that the scouts come to San Carlos to reinforce Beauford's Indian police. Mickey was delighted with this new assignment, which re-united him with his wife and son. So a few months later, when the scouts were sent back to Fort McDowell, he decided not to reenlist. Captain Chaffee promptly hired him as an interpreter for San Car-los on December 7, 1879.

Al Sieber returned to government employment at about the same time. Colonel Willcox had suggested hiring Sieber in June, but it was the tough-as-nails Chaffee who managed to convince the scout to give up mining and poker and once again sign on with the army. Sieber could not help but admire Chaffee, who was in many ways his alter ego. Chaffee had risen from the ranks in the Civil War and had won further distinction in combat with the Comanches in Texas. He was a grim, no-nonsense, but practical officer, who would go on to fame in the Spanish-American War and the Boxer Rebellion before becoming President Theodore Roosevelt's army chief of staff in 1904. He was just the sort of man Sieber admired.

By the time Free and Sieber reunited at San Carlos, Geronimo was no longer there. The previous August, he had staged a *tiswin* party in the nearby mountains above Camp Thomas, where in a drunken stupor he had berated his young nephew. Suicide was rare among the Apaches, but the humiliated boy had killed himself shortly thereafter. Geronimo, mortified by his own behavior, took his three wives and other family members and fled San Carlos. He joined Juh in late August near Janos and within a month had at-tacked a Mexican wagon train near Casas Grandes, where his war-riors slaughtered all twenty-five men, women, and children.

SINCE HIS BREAKOUT from Ojo Caliente in October of the previ-ous year, Victorio and a small band of warriors had raided with impunity across western and southern New Mexico. Hard-pressed by troops, Victorio finally agreed to open talks with the Indian agent at the Mescalero Reservation. Nana, of course, was already there with sixty of the Warm Springs people. When the agent refused to issue rations to Victorio's people, all the Apaches bolted. On August 21, 1879, Victorio and Nana fled westward with all the Chihennes as well as several Mescalero recruits.

Victorio led them to Salinas Peak, the sacred mountain that was the highest point in the San Andres range. He knew that the bluecoats, both white and black, would be in search of his people. Lozen ascended the mountain as well, followed by young Kaywaykla and other Warm Springs Apaches. Kaywaykla remembered well the long calico skirt Lozen wore, with a long blouse over it. Her moccasins came up to her knees, and her knife was concealed in their fold. She stood alone with outstretched arms atop the peak and prayed to Usen. As she slowly turned, her hands began to tingle and her palms changed color. She knew from the intensity of the sensation just how close the bluecoats were, and from which direction they came. She turned to Victorio and pointed westward toward the Black Range.

Victorio and Lozen knew that they could not win a war against the White Eyes. Nor could they hope for sanctuary in Mexico, for Juh and Geronimo had stirred up the Mexicans against all Apaches. It was to be a war to the death—a last stand for the old ways—with no hope of victory, no hope for anything save honor, and the glory of a true warrior's death.

One of Victorio's first targets was symbolic: the army camp at Ojo Caliente. The Apaches swept in on September 4, 1879, killed all eight members of the horse guard, made off with sixty-eight horses and mules, and vanished back into the Black Range. A week later they struck again just to the south of the mining camp at Hillsboro. Troops from Fort Bayard followed Victorio's trail into a well-laid ambush near the headwaters of the Animas River. The command was saved from annihilation only by the abandonment of fifty-three of its mounts, considerable personal equipment, and a hospital wagon, which the Apaches hurried to round up. The soldiers estimated that they had faced at least a hundred Apaches. With each victory, Victorio's numbers seemed to increase, at least in the fevered imaginations of his opponents.

The number of men with Victorio fluctuated wildly during his war, but with the exception of the brief period in which he united with Juh and Geronimo, the warriors never numbered more than 120 at any one time. Several young Mescaleros and a few San Carlos Chiricahuas rallied to him, as did a handful of Texas Lipans and Comanches, but these recruits never exceeded forty warriors.

The American army marshaled an impressive force to hunt down Victorio. The entire Ninth Cavalry, nearly six hundred officers and enlisted men, were in New Mexico and they were reinforced by several companies of the Sixth Cavalry from Arizona and the Tenth Cavalry from Texas. Five companies of the Thirteenth Infantry were transferred to Fort Wingate in the summer of 1880 to bolster that garrison. Companies of Navajo scouts from Wingate as well as Apache scouts from Arizona were dispatched to New Mexico as well. In all the army put well over a thousand men in the field to take down Victorio's little band.

Among those called into the campaign was Lieutenant Charles Gatewood, with his Company A of the Apache scouts. Gatewood, a lanky Virginian who had graduated from West Point in 1877, was assigned to the Sixth Cavalry and ordered to Camp Apache to take command of the scout company on March 31, 1879. Gatewood proved a quick study. He wisely attached himself to the White Mountain scout leader Alchesay, who became his tutor and friend. Gatewood developed an affinity, even affection, for the Apache scouts and ranked them as far superior to other Indian scouts.

Gatewood's scout company was sent to New Mexico to reinforce Major Albert Morrow after the defeat of his troops on the Animas River. Victorio had left a trail of blood and wreckage across southern New Mexico and northern Chihuahua. Dozens of Americans and Mexicans had been killed and two wagon trains captured. The victims of one of the wagon train massacres were tortured and horribly mutilated, which meant that the Apaches had lost several prominent warriors in battle. Among the dead was young Kaywaykla's father. Not long afterward, his mother, Gouyen, married Kaytennae, one of Victorio's mightiest warriors.

Major Morrow, with a detachment of the Ninth as well as Gatewood's scouts, caught up with the raiders just south of the Mexican border on October 27. In the sharp skirmish that followed, Gatewood's men took the brunt of the fight with one scout killed and two others wounded. The Apaches escaped and then split up. They fouled the water holes behind them as they rode. Sometimes they would gut a coyote and submerge it, but more often they rode their ponies back and forth to collapse the banks and leave but a mudhole unfit to drink from.

When the bluecoats got too close, some of the old people were hidden among the rocks and left behind. New mothers with crying infants sometimes were left with the old ones. The people pushed on with no fires and little to eat save dried beef and mesquite beans. In desperation they killed their horses at the foot of a steep cliff and climbed up heights where no soldier dared to follow. Men used ropes to pull the women and children up from ledge to ledge. Lozen then led raiders out in search of more horses. "No man in the tribe was more skillful in stealing horses or stampeding a herd than she," bragged Kaywaykla.

Victorio led his people southeast toward Texas and eventually found refuge in the Candelaria Mountains, where a water hole on the northern slope provided a favored campsite. Just to the east was the main route between El Paso and Chihuahua City, a road that provided the Apaches with a steady stream of tempting targets.

Mexican militia from the nearby village of Carrizal discovered the location of the Apaches and boldly attacked. Victorio's warriors, who seemed to know that they were coming, ambushed the eighteen-man militia force, killed every soul, and then routed a column sent to rescue the initial band. More than thirty Mexicans fell.

Chihuahua governor Luis Terrazas, whose own ranch had suffered heavy stock losses to the Apaches, ordered two large columns into the field—one under the command of his cousin Colonel Joaquin Terrazas. Colonel Terrazas, a man of boundless energy and ambition, was fifty-one years of age. He was tall and slender, a chain-smoker and a veteran soldier who had fought for Juárez in the 1857 War of Reform and had then distinguished himself further against the French imperialists. In his youth he had been a scalp hunter, and in that bloody trade had acquired a reputation for cruel efficiency. He vowed to bring in the scalp of Victorio.

18

VICTORIO'S WAR

VICTORIO, AFTER HIS VICTORY OVER THE CARRIZAL militia, slipped back into New Mexico to trade at Tularosa and seek more recruits from the Mescalero Reservation. His people made camp in the San Andres Mountains, between the Jornada del Muerto and the Tularosa Valley. Intelligence concerning the location of Victorio's camp was soon conveyed to the US military.

Colonel Hatch came south from Santa Fe to take personal command of the American troops in the field. He called on his old comrade Grierson to bring five troops of the Tenth Cavalry, 280 men and scouts, up from Texas. At the same time a 155-man detachment of the Ninth would move west from Fort Stanton under Captain Henry Carroll. Hatch planned to come in from the west with a company of the Fifteenth Infantry as well as a company of Navajo scouts, three more troops of the Ninth under Morrow, a troop of the Sixth, and three Apache scout companies. An additional column from Ojo Caliente was to block any escape route to the north of the San Andres Mountains.

After crushing Victorio, Hatch planned to march on the Mescalero Reservation to disarm the Indians there and confiscate their horses in retaliation for their aid to their Warm Springs cousins. Hatch's plan must have looked splendid on paper, but it quickly began to unravel.

Captain Carroll's column from Fort Stanton marched west across the *malpais,* a lava-rock badland between the Sierra Blanca and the Rio Grande. Carroll was to rendezvous on April 7 with

Morrow in the San Andres near a spring in Hembrillo Canyon, but water, or the lack of it, quickly frustrated this plan. Carroll on April 4 camped at a spring in the malpais where the heavy mineral content of the water sickened half his men and most of his horses. Carroll divided his command and led his suffering troopers toward the spring in Hembrillo Canyon. He reached the canyon just before dark and blundered right into Victorio's main camp. Carroll had found water, all right, but Victorio controlled it.

Carroll had but seventy-one men with him when he rode into the steep-walled canyon. Victorio's ambush forced him to quickly dismount his force, with every fourth man designated to hold his horse and three others. Carroll now had but fifty men on his extended firing line. The thirst-crazed animals became unmanageable and several bolted for the spring, where they were captured by the Apaches. By nightfall the troopers were completely pinned down by the Indians. Fortunately for the soldiers, there was but a sliver of the crescent moon that night—and the darkness may well have saved them.

Meanwhile, Hatch was also facing a water crisis. A broken water pump at Aleman Well, a usually reliable source of water fifteen miles to the west of the San Andres, had brought his column to a halt. Hatch ordered the Sixth Cavalry troopers and Gatewood's scouts ahead to meet with Carroll on April 7, while he would follow with the main column once they secured water.

The detachment reached Hembrillo Canyon at dawn after a night march. They heard gunfire and advanced rapidly to discover Carroll and seven of his Buffalo Soldiers wounded, pinned down, and in desperate need of water. Two of the troopers later died of their wounds. Gatewood's scouts promptly launched a counterattack that drove Victorio's warriors from the spring. Victorio held his position in the hills throughout the day, while Nana and Lozen led the women and children south along the mountain chain to safety, and then the warriors slipped away at dusk.

Hatch, who was marching up from the south with three troops of the Ninth, hurried his men along the flats at the foot of the San Andres. From the mountains Victorio and Lozen watched the soldiers pass by below. The Apaches hurried out of the mountains, crossed the Rio Grande, and sought safety to the west in the Black Range.

Colonel Hatch claimed a victory over "three to four hundred" Apaches, an absurd exaggeration. Victorio had once again escaped, and Hatch had been fortunate merely to save Carroll's command and avoid yet another debacle. The frustrated colonel now turned his attention to the Mescaleros. Joined by Grierson's column from Texas, Hatch now marched on the Mescalero Reservation.

The Indian agent there protested this invasion as illegal, but Hatch claimed to have followed a "hot trail" directly from Hembrillo Canyon. One of the three Apache bodies found on the battlefield, the colonel insisted, had been positively identified as a Mescalero. The colonel planned to immediately disarm the Apaches and confiscate their ponies. But the Mescaleros, unlike the Apaches to the west, had adapted to the plains horse culture, and so the loss of their horses was particularly devastating.

Hatch and Grierson bungled the whole affair. The arrival of so many soldiers stampeded the Apaches. They took to the hills only to run headlong into the Tenth Cavalry. The troopers opened fire and killed fourteen Apaches. They herded the rest—men, women, and children—back to the agency. Two hundred ponies were confiscated and sent to Fort Stanton and the rest sold off to the local settlers. When the Indian agent protested this outrage to Washington, General Sherman replied that "undue sympathy for these savages amounts to aiding and abetting a common enemy."

Colonel Hatch returned to his Santa Fe headquarters to write a rather imaginative report on the "success" of his campaign. Meanwhile, Grierson went back to Texas, while Morrow led his Ninth Cavalry troopers into the Black Range in search of Victorio. While there, they completely broke down their jaded horses in futile patrols. The Sixth Cavalry and Gatewood's Apache scouts soon returned to Arizona. Hatch's grand campaign fizzled to a sorry close, while the Apache leader began to plan his next daring move.

--➤≡◉≡◈--

VICTORIO, IN HIS CAMP in the Black Range, brooded over the fate of Loco and the Chihenne families still held at San Carlos. He feared for their safety because of the bad blood with the White Mountain people, and he seethed with a desire to avenge the actions of the Apache scouts who had led the White Eyes against him. During the first week of May 1880, he and his son Washington led a raiding party of thirty-six warriors against San Carlos. They hoped to secure freedom for their families held there and capture horses, cattle, and ammunition, as well as to seek revenge against the White Mountain Apaches.

The raiders first struck the ranch of George Stevens on Eagle Creek and made off with all his horses and cattle, and then killed several White Mountain people, but they failed to liberate Loco and the Chihenne families because they had been moved under guard to the main agency.

A detachment of the Sixth Cavalry and several Apache scouts set out after Victorio's raiders but were ambushed at Ash Creek. A veteran sergeant was killed and an Apache scout wounded before the troopers retreated. Al Sieber, with Company C of the Apache scouts, was also in pursuit but his scouts lost the trail in the maze of New Mexico mountains. They returned empty-handed to Camp Thomas, just south of the Gila River. It was there that Colonel Eugene Carr's troops were being organized for another major offensive against Victorio.

When he returned, Sieber was surprised to find Tom Jeffords at Camp Thomas. Jeffords had joined the rush to the boomtown of Tombstone, where he had struck it rich and sold his claim for sixty thousand dollars. The former Indian agent was on an epic bender. He had ordered champagne and ice—it is difficult to discern which cost more—up from Tucson for a celebration of his newfound, and quickly dissipated, wealth. He invited Sieber to partake in a grand drunk exceptional even by Arizona standards.

Lieutenant Tom Cruse, a Kentuckian fresh out of West Point who had been with Gatewood at Hembrillo Canyon, arrived at Camp Thomas at the same time, en route to take command of Company A of the Apache scouts at Fort Apache. When Cruse entered the sutler's store, he found Jeffords's celebration at its peak and noticed that Sieber was "having the time of his life relaxing and more joyous every minute."

Cruse, a teetotaler, came near offending Jeffords by refusing all liquid refreshment, until rescued by Sieber, who purchased him a pound of candy and promised Jeffords to consume the lieutenant's share of the champagne. The evening proved a personal triumph for Cruse, who "was never more puffed up in my life when he [Sieber] told me that Gatewood and the packers had praised my actions in the Victorio fights—and that I would do."

Department commander Willcox had developed quite an admiration for Tom Jeffords, drunk or sober. Willcox had sent his aide-de-camp, Lieutenant Harry Haskell of the Twelfth Infantry, to confer with Jeffords on how to put together a peace mission similar to what General Howard had accomplished with Cochise. Willcox hoped Haskell and Jeffords could bring Geronimo and Juh back from Mexico.

Jeffords's sound advice led to a meeting between Haskell, Geronimo, and Juh across the international line on December 13, 1879. The Apaches were hard-pressed by Mexican troops, for all of northern Mexico had been aroused against them by Victorio's slaughter of the Carrizal militia. Haskell assured them that they could keep their weapons, that no one would be arrested, and that they could settle near Naiche's Chokonens at San Carlos. The Apaches discussed the peace proposal in a council among themselves and, after a heated debate, agreed to come in.

Jeffords met the returning Chiricahuas at Camp Rucker in the White River Canyon and enjoyed a warm reunion with both Geronimo and Juh. The Apaches, 103 in number—of which 21 were warriors—spent Christmas Day at Rucker and then pushed on to reach San Carlos on January 7.

Governor John Frémont, impressed by the key role played by Jeffords in bringing in Geronimo and Juh, promptly recommended him to be the new agent at San Carlos in place of Hart and to relieve Captain Chaffee from his emergency duty. Jeffords, the wily and rough frontiersman, must have reminded the governor of his old comrade Kit Carson. Colonel Willcox warmly endorsed the recommendation. Despite the obvious logic of this proposal, the Indian Bureau, as might be expected, appointed an inexperienced Marylander nominated by the Dutch Reformed Church. On June 1, 1880, Joseph Tiffany assumed his position over the 4,561 Apaches at San Carlos. He was portly, deeply religious, and totally unprepared for his new job. Tiffany would be the last agent appointed under Grant's Peace Policy, and his tenure quickly proved to be a lightning rod for controversy.

Victorio, following the battle at Hembrillo Canyon and the raid on San Carlos, had continued to elude all the troops sent against him. Colonel Hatch, with his Ninth Cavalry nearly on foot from stock losses, begged Sheridan for fresh troops. Southern New Mexico and eastern Arizona were in a state of near hysteria.

Colonel Willcox ordered Colonel Carr, who had left the Fifth to take command of the Sixth Cavalry in April 1879, to crush Victorio's band. "The fact that the old fellow has been able to do pretty much as he pleased in New Mexico," Willcox told Carr, "has been pretty much attributed to the color of his opponents in that country." Despite Willcox's racial aspersions on the Buffalo Soldiers, Carr's white troopers had no more luck in corralling Victorio than had the men of the Ninth.

Carr visited San Carlos in late June and early July 1880, with Tom Jeffords as his interpreter, to test the temper of Geronimo, Juh, and Naiche. All of Apacheria was alive with rumors that a grand breakout was planned. The Chiricahuas were restless and unhappy, and they opened up to Jeffords about their grievances: the rations were not what had been promised and they were not issued in a regular fashion; the people were not allowed to go into the mountains to gather their natural food supply of mescal and seasonal nuts and berries; they were treated little better than prisoners, confined to the Gila River subagency and closely watched, while the Western Apaches were allowed considerable freedom; they deeply distrusted Mickey Free, since he was a Western Apache, and wanted him removed as interpreter; and, finally and most important, the bad water along the river had led to many deaths from "the shaking sickness." Naiche reminded Jeffords that they had brought 325 Chiricahua Apaches to San Carlos in 1876. Four years later, more than one-third—125 men, women, and children—had already died from these terrible fevers.

Carr sat stunned as Jeffords translated Naiche's words. Ex–Indian agent Hart had never reported the deaths. It was soon discovered that Hart had also shortchanged the Indians on rations with rigged scales for beef, bought stolen Mexican cattle from outlaws and then sold the good cattle to the miners in Globe while he added the sickly culls to the agency herd, colluded with corrupt contractors, kept ghost employees on his payroll, inflated census counts to acquire extra rations to sell on the open market, and conspired with Commissioner Hayt to change the western reservation boundary to protect their secret mining claims. He had been physically expelled from the agency the previous July by Al Sieber on orders from Captain Chaffee.

The new agent, Tiffany, who had been on the job only a few days when Carr and Jeffords arrived, was sympathetic and apparently honest, but he could do little to accommodate the critical needs of the Chiricahuas, although he did agree to let them move from the Gila lowlands to the foothills near Mount Turnbull. He also decided to remove Mickey Free as interpreter in response to the council. Geronimo, in particular, feared and hated the one-eyed interpreter, but almost all the other Chiricahua leaders seemed to share in his distrust. They all still blamed Mickey for being the catalyst that started the war in the first place.

This marked the first time since 1872 that Mickey had not been employed by the government. He was, of course, far too valuable an asset to be unemployed for long. Charles T. Connell, who had been contracted to conduct a census on the reservation, hired him in February 1881 as his interpreter. The census proved difficult, as many of the White Mountain people remained scattered in the mountains near Fort Apache and were wary of being counted.

Mickey soon became uneasy. He heard many rumors of unrest and fretted over what his White Mountain friends told him. A medicine man called the Dreamer was preaching to the people that he would soon resurrect the old chiefs from the dead to lead a final war against the White Eyes. Mickey, growing alarmed, quit his job with Connell in March 1881 and rejoined Ethlay and his young son at San Carlos. They might well soon need his protection.

"Mickey Free was a wise Indian and thought that he could see trouble ahead," Connell grumbled, "and decided it [was] the best policy to return home to the subagency where his family dwelt." Once back at the agency Mickey was promptly again hired as a scout for the San Carlos Indian police at fifteen dollars a month, but he quickly found himself in conflict with Agent Tiffany when he stopped several men who were removing rations from the agency storehouse to sell in Globe. To his chagrin, he found himself arrested for halting the thieves and placed in the guardhouse for fifteen days by order of the Indian agent. Tiffany, who had employed the thieves, was simply following the common practice of siphoning off a percentage of the rations for sale in order to help balance his books, and Mickey had embarrassed him. On June 30, Tiffany removed Mickey from the police force. The agent quickly came to regret that decision.

19

TRES CASTILLOS

VICTORIO HAD RETREATED TO THE BLACK RANGE after the San Carlos raid. Although regular army troops in both New Mexico and Arizona could not find him, a detachment of sixty Apache scouts, led by an enigmatic Texan named Henry Parker, finally tracked him to the head of Palomas Creek. During the night of May 23, 1880, Parker placed his men on the steep cliffs that surrounded the camp and attacked at dawn. The battle continued all day until, under cover of darkness, Victorio led his people out of the canyon. Parker's Apache scouts had accomplished what a thousand troops had failed to do: inflict a telling defeat on Victorio. The scouts had killed at least thirty of Victorio's people—men, women, and children—and wounded the great chief himself. The fight on the headwaters of Palomas Creek proved to be the turning point of Victorio's War.

After this defeat, Victorio's people split into three groups and headed south to their favored sanctuary in Mexico's Candelaria Mountains. Kaytennae led one group, Nana the second, and Victorio the third. Kaytennae's band traveled south so close to Fort Cummings that they could hear the bugle calls, but the warrior knew that he had nothing to fear from the fort, for all the bluecoats were out in search of the Apaches. They crossed into Mexico west of the great river and reached the rendezvous site before Victorio.

Once all of Victorio's people had arrived in the Candelaria Mountains, the youngster Kaywaykla felt the unease of the adults around him. Almost all the people had arrived safely except for Lozen. She had backtracked to look for a missing woman even though the soldiers were close by. Everyone seemed worried that Lozen was not there to meet them. Nobody spoke her name, which Kaywaykla knew meant that they thought she was dead. They referred to her only as Victorio's sister or the Medicine Woman. Kaywaykla's grandmother sang Lozen's prayer over and over. The boy asked if the prayer song would have the same power. His grandmother shook her head no.

"It is the Power given her when we made her feast, the Power she had earned in her vigil on the Mountain," said the grandmother. "Nobody else can wield it."

Victorio's people now broke into ever smaller bands to avoid detection and kept constantly on the move. The women had to erect wickiups quickly and disguise them with tree branches and underbrush. They all covered their exposed faces, arms, and legs with dirt to help escape detection. Whenever possible they cached dried foods, water jugs, baskets, and even guns and knives in rock caverns and covered them with brush.

"Hide them deep," the grandmothers directed. "They'll be needed later—when we come back."

They carried their rations—usually dried venison, mesquite beans, and mescal—in buckskin bags suspended from their belts. Even children carried ration bags. "Don't eat this now," their mothers and grandmothers warned. "It is for an emergency." The time of "emergency" was upon them.

Some of the small bands of Victorio's Mescalero allies trailed south and then cut back east into Texas. They attacked several civilian parties, and when they neared Fort Quitman, the warriors jumped a wagon on the main road and killed the chief engineer for the Texas Pacific Railroad. This caused a sensation in West Texas, and a detachment of Texas Rangers was soon in the saddle in search of the Apaches.

A few Chihenne raiding parties still lingered in New Mexico in search of horses and cattle. Victorio's son, Washington, led a small band that struck ranches near Cooke's Canyon, where they killed five men and trailed their stolen stock toward the Mexican line. Parker's Apache scouts followed the raiders and, in a sharp clash on June 5, killed Washington and two of his warriors. This was another devastating blow to Victorio.

General Sherman, who had immediately recognized the importance of Parker's victory, pressured Hatch to follow up on Parker's battle and destroy Victorio's band. The general wanted the Apaches defeated as quickly as possible so that they would not impede investment in the Southern Pacific transcontinental line, which, Sherman reminded Hatch, was "so important to the whole country."

Hatch devised yet another massive expedition with converging columns, but there remained the pesky problem of the international border. Despite torturous negotiations between the US State Department and the regime of Porfirio Díaz, the Mexicans steadfastly refused to allow American troops across the border. Civilian and military leaders in both Chihuahua and Sonora favored such border crossings, especially when in hot pursuit of Apaches, but the rulers in Mexico City feared American intervention far more than Apache raiders.

Hatch's plan called for Colonel George P. Buell, with a mixed force of cavalry, infantry, and Pueblo scouts—nearly four hundred men—to cross the border in pursuit of Victorio's people. Colonel Carr was to move in from Arizona at the same time with six troops of the Sixth Cavalry and three companies of Apache scouts to rendezvous with Buell at Lake Guzman in northern Chihuahua. Hatch hoped that the Americans might coordinate their advance with the movements of Colonel Terrazas's command. Hatch also requested that Colonel Grierson's Tenth Cavalry again come north to guard the Rio Grande to prevent any more Mescaleros from joining Victorio. Grierson objected to leaving the Texas frontier unprotected and insisted that he use his troops to guard the water holes and prevent the Apaches from entering Texas.

Benjamin Grierson was a decidedly unconventional cavalryman. As a child his face had been scarred by a horse kick, and he remained deathly afraid of the animals for years. A music teacher before the Civil War, he had risen to be colonel of the Sixth Illinois Cavalry by 1862, and in April 1863, he had led his regiment and two others on a daring raid from LaGrange, Tennessee, to Baton

Rouge, Louisiana, that contributed to Grant's victory at Vicksburg that July. That raid, which Grant characterized as the most brilliant of the war, made Grierson a national hero.

In the army reorganization, Grierson had accepted command of the Tenth Cavalry. He had been a Lincoln Republican before the war and was, for his time and place, remarkably enlightened on racial issues. As colonel, he waged an unrelenting campaign against the distinctions between white and black soldiers and always demanded equal treatment for his men. "Colored troops will hold their place in the Army of the United States as long as the government lasts," he had assured his wife in 1867.

Grierson's regiment of black soldiers first saw service on the Great Plains in Sheridan's Cheyenne campaign. It was actually the Cheyenne and Comanche warriors who dubbed the troopers Buffalo Soldiers. Frances Roe, whose husband was an officer in the Third Infantry, made the first recorded reference to this nickname in an 1872 letter from Camp Supply in the Indian Territory. Her husband's regiment served alongside the Tenth Cavalry, and she wrote that "the Indians call them Buffalo Soldiers because their wooly heads are so much like the matted cushion that is between the horns of the buffalo." While she noted that her husband and other officers admitted that "negroes make good soldiers and fight like fiends," she felt the major advantage to serving alongside "colored troops—one can always have good servants."

Grierson, expecting the Apaches to head for the Rio Grande and cross into Texas, now moved his Buffalo Soldiers to several vital water holes to deny them to Victorio. He was determined not to use up his horses in fruitless pursuits, but rather wait for the Apaches to come to him. The Tenth Cavalry was to have the chance to prove its merit against the boldest of all the Apache leaders.

VICTORIO WAS, in fact, headed for Texas. Perhaps he and his warriors, in hopes of avoiding the troops on the Rio Grande, considered sweeping in an arc up through the Guadalupe Mountains just to the west of the Pecos River. But this was unfamiliar territory to the Warm Springs Apaches, although their Mescalero allies knew it well. Several Mescalero warriors had recently traveled south through the Guadalupes to raid in Texas and then join Victorio, and they now guided his people.

The Apaches, slowed by their large herd of cattle and horses, made straight for the Rio Grande. Victorio crossed his people over the river near Fort Quitman and made for Tinaja de las Palmas, the only water hole between the fort and Eagle Springs.

Colonel Grierson received word on July 29 that Victorio had crossed the river, and he immediately sent couriers off to Fort Quitman and Eagle Springs for help. Grierson then moved to Tinaja de las Palmas with seven men—a lieutenant, a sergeant, and five privates. The colonel's teenage son, on summer vacation from school, rode along. Late that night, soon after he took up position on a ridge 125 feet above the meager water hole, Grierson was reinforced by eleven men of G Troop. Grierson stroked his long beard as he positioned his men, who followed Apache tactics by rolling boulders into place to fortify the ridge, and waited for dawn.

The Apaches, who arrived late in the morning, spotted the soldiers along the ridge and attempted to skirt to the east to avoid a fight but instead ran right into more reinforcements coming from Eagle Springs. They retreated back toward Grierson. The fight lasted four hours, with one trooper killed and a lieutenant wounded, before Victorio fell back to the Rio Grande as more reinforcements from Fort Quitman galloped into view. Grierson knew that the Apaches would be back.

Victorio, who had left seven warriors dead on the field, was able to find momentary sanctuary west of the river to regroup. But on August 3, he crossed the river again and headed northeast in the direction of the Guadalupe Mountains. Grierson guessed that the Apaches, estimated to number between 125 and 150 warriors, would make for Rattlesnake Springs on the southwestern slope of the Sierra Diablo.

As Victorio advanced to the east, he did not know that he had already been dealt a crippling blow. Captain Thomas Lebo, with K Troop of the Tenth, had discovered Victorio's base camp on

August 4 in the Sierra Diablo. Lebo's men routed the handful of guards and captured twenty-five head of cattle as well as several pack mules loaded down with bread and dried beef.

Grierson ordered several patrols out to guard every available water hole and spring while he led four troops of the Tenth to Rattlesnake Springs. The troopers, riding mostly at night, made a remarkable sixty-five-mile march in twenty-one hours. Two troops of the Tenth were hidden along both sides of Rattlesnake Canyon to await Victorio while Grierson climbed up the rough, precipitous cliff, some two thousand feet above the canyon floor, to obtain a commanding view.

By noon on August 6, Grierson could see the distant dust cloud of the Apache advance. His men were ordered to hold their fire until the Apaches were at point-blank range in the canyon. Two hours later, the first of Victorio's scouts approached the canyon. The great chief did not have Lozen by his side, but he still sensed danger. As the Buffalo Soldiers carefully aimed their Springfield carbines, the Apaches suddenly halted. Victorio scattered his warriors into the rocks at the mouth of the canyon just as the soldiers fired a volley. The Apaches counted the rifles of the bluecoats and, desperate for water, decided to charge them. As Victorio's warriors galloped into the canyon, Grierson sent his two reserve troops of cavalry into the fray. A surprised Victorio called back his warriors, and for two more hours the two groups sniped at each other.

At four that afternoon, a dust cloud to the southeast heralded the arrival of Grierson's supply train from Fort Davis. In hopes of yet achieving victory, Victorio sent a war party after this new prize. The unguarded caravan seemed an easy target, but the infantry escort was actually hidden inside the wagons. As the Apaches rushed forward, the black infantrymen poured out of the wagons and quickly set up skirmish lines. The warriors were met with a withering fire. As Victorio attempted to regroup his warriors for another charge against the wagons, Grierson's cavalry galloped to the rescue. Exposed on the open plain and heavily outnumbered, the Apaches had no choice but to scatter back toward the Rio Grande.

Grierson's Pueblo Indian scouts trailed the Apaches back to the

Candelaria Mountains. The scouts reported the Apaches to be "in a very crippled and demoralized condition," and Grierson felt certain that "they are not now in condition to act in a body against any organized force." The colonel was right, for Victorio would never again cross back into the United States. The Buffalo Soldiers had scored a pivotal victory by forcing Victorio back into Mexico.

Two weeks later Colonel Buell crossed into Mexico with his combined force of infantry, cavalry, and Pueblo scouts, as well as a company of Texas Rangers. He hoped to rendezvous with Carr's column and then join with Mexican forces to encircle the Apaches.

MEXICAN COLONEL Joaquin Terrazas was proud, vain, and merciless. At over six feet, he towered above most of his soldiers. He kept four white horses with the command at all times so that he might always have a fresh mount as well as be easily identified on the battlefield. Terrazas's cousin, Chihuahua governor Luis Terrazas, was determined to destroy Victorio's band. Despite the stubborn position of the central government in Mexico City, the governor was willing to turn a blind eye to the massive American cross-border expedition. The governor needed Victorio dead and was more than happy to allow the Americans over the border if it would help solve his problems.

The colonel wished to help in this regard, but his problem was that he had no command. Terrazas, with customary energy, set about raising his little army. Terrazas left his cousin on August 25, 1880, and marched northeast in search of recruits. He had two soldiers, a servant, and a friend with him, along with the four white horses. The governor had promised him fifty regular soldiers and he recruited fifty more on his way north. The reward of two thousand pesos for Victorio as well as a substantial scalp bounty and the promise of Indian slaves helped with recruitment.

In Corralitos, he met with the famed Indian fighter Juan Mata Ortiz, who agreed to serve as second-in-command and brought with him 120 local recruits, some of them experienced Indian fighters. Like Terrazas, Mata Ortiz had hunted scalps in his youth and had battled the Apaches for decades. He was well loved by the people, who repeatedly elected him political chief of the Galeana district.

As Terrazas advanced north from Galeana and then turned east toward Carrizal, he enlisted even more men, such that by September 28, he had nearly 350 rather ragged volunteers under his command. He also recruited a company of Tarahumara Indian scouts and sent them out to search the Candelaria range and make contact with the American column.

Colonel Buell had reached Boca Grande Pass, to the north of Lake Guzman in Chihuahua, on September 24, where he had expected to rendezvous with Carr's Arizona column. But Carr's Apache scouts had reached Lake Guzman ahead of Buell and reported back that Victorio was not there, so Carr simply headed back to Arizona.

Victorio, pressed by Grierson to the east and Buell from the north, had led his people southeast, deeper into Mexico. Colonel Terrazas, although grateful for Buell's cooperation, could not allow such a large force of Americans to penetrate any deeper into his country. Buell's Apache scouts also worried the chain-smoking Mexican colonel. Almost all Mexican soldiers distrusted the Apache scouts and were incredulous that the Americans employed them. On October 9, Terrazas sent a message to Buell that any farther advance by the Americans into Mexico was objectionable.

Victorio, for his part, now had very few choices, and all were bad. He did not know that the Americans had withdrawn, but he did know that both the New Mexico and Texas borders were swarming with bluecoats. Grierson's Buffalo Soldiers blocked access to the Guadalupe Mountains and the Mescalero Reservation beyond, while Buell's troops prevented any movement up the Rio Grande and back into the Black Range.

Terrazas was confident. He knew from his scouts that the Apaches had fled southeast from the Candelarias, and that they were few in number, with women and children and a herd of cattle to slow them down. Not far to the south from his bivouac in the Pinos Mountains, there was a choice campsite at a small lake. Terrazas ordered his scouts to search the lake for Victorio's people.

They reported back that the Apaches had been there but had then headed south toward Tres Castillos (Three Castles) or Cerro Lagrimas (Hill of Tears). These rocky outcroppings rose above the expansive desert to the southwest, and each had small springs.

The Mexican officer sent ninety of his civilian militia back to their homes for fear they might slow his advance. Astride his white horse, he led his remaining 260 men south but soon divided his command. His second-in-command, Mata Ortiz, was sent south toward Cerro Lagrimas while Terrazas led his men westward onto the Llanos de los Castillos (Castle Plain). On October 13, Terrazas's scouts cut a fresh trail across the flat desert plain leading toward Tres Castillos.

THE APACHES HAD also divided into three groups. Victorio led the main band while Nana and Kaytennae led two smaller groups. Before the people split up, they held a night council. As the men gathered, Victorio noticed the boy Kaywaykla and called him over.

"Kaywaykla—His Enemies Lie Dead in Heaps," he said as he placed his hand upon the little boy's head. "Let this boy be called by that name henceforth—Kaywaykla. Someday you also may be a chief, but not unless you fulfill the meaning of your name. Do not forget."

Victorio then turned and strode to the council fire with old Nana hobbling at his side. The boy hurried behind them and squeezed himself in between the chief and Nana. He suddenly felt his arm tugged.

"Do not think that because your uncle has given you a warrior's name you can sit in the council," his mother, Gouyen, admonished Kaywaykla as she pulled him away.

The men in the fire circle all laughed. Victorio smiled, for the boy had brought a brief glimmer of joy to the circle. There had been no laughter for so long. "Let him stay," declared the chief. "Already every child in the tribe knows how desperate is our situation."

As his mother withdrew, Kaywaykla's grandmother sat behind Nana and glared at the boy. But Kaywaykla, right next to Victorio, was not about to budge despite his grandmother's disapproval. He watched as his uncle, Blanco, rolled tobacco in an oak leaf, lit it, and blew smoke in the four directions. Blanco was a great medicine man, but Kaywaykla wished that Lozen could be with them. She was sorely missed by all.

"What have you to suggest?" Victorio asked Nana.

"I have fought with three great chiefs of my people, Mangas Coloradas, Cochise, and Victorio," Nana replied. "The problems confronting you are more difficult than either of the others had to meet. Your wisdom has never failed us. Command and we obey."

Victorio ordered raiding parties out to secure desperately needed ammunition. Everyone sprang into action, and the families began to pack up what little they had. Victorio would remain with the families, then they would all rendezvous at Tres Castillos.

The three peaks, a jumble of boulders piled high one upon another, rose one hundred feet above the flat desert plain. At their base were immense mudflats that filled with water after the late-summer rains and briefly teemed with wildlife. Ducks paddled peacefully on the shallow lake while quail hurried about the tall grass where antelope grazed.

Terrazas pushed ahead of his troops with just eleven men, and they reached Tres Castillos midafternoon on October 14, 1880. He climbed the north peak, which was the highest and steepest of the three. As he searched the distant plain with his binoculars, he made out three distinct dust clouds some ten miles to the south of the lake. He had found Victorio. The colonel hurried back to rejoin Mata Ortiz and the main column. Terrazas then pressed his reunited force forward so that they reached Tres Castillos just after the Apaches.

Victorio led the main body, while Nana kept up the rear guard. Kaytennae, who had just completed a successful raid, followed behind with his men. The people were spread out for some distance. The Apaches were just beginning to build fires, water their horses, and set up camp by the shallow lake when the Mexican soldiers appeared. All was confusion as warriors rushed to their ponies and the women hurried the children away. Victorio led thirty men out to block the Mexican advance, and the Tarahumara scouts rode forth to meet them.

Mauricio Corredor led the Tarahumara scouts. He shouted a challenge to Victorio and the chief separated from his men and rode out onto the mudflat to meet the Tarahumara. As Victorio galloped forward, Corredor dismounted and brought down the great Apache chief with a single shot. As Victorio tumbled from his horse, his men rallied around him. They carried their wounded chief away, all the while firing at the Mexican scouts. Corredor pulled his men back as the main column arrived.

As the skirmish ended on the mudflats, Terrazas ordered Mata Ortiz and his detachment of cavalry to circle around to the north while he led his column to the south behind the Apaches. This movement was successful, but the dust cloud raised by the soldiers alerted the bands led by Nana and Kaytennae. As dusk approached they pulled back, uncertain of what to do next, for they could hear the distant gunfire. They were completely cut off from Victorio.

Victorio was carried by his warriors to the south mountain. Almost all of the Apache horses and pack mules had been captured by the Mexican cavalry. There was no way to escape. The Apache warriors dug in among the rocks and kept up a terrific fire until dark. The Mexicans took up positions on the middle mountain and all around the base of the south mountain. In the darkness, they did not dare to advance. The Apache signal fire cast an eerie glow over the three peaks. That night the Mexicans heard the Apaches above them sing their death song.

Victorio knew that their position was hopeless. The little ammunition they had when the Mexicans first attacked had all been expended. The great chief turned to a young Mescalero warrior who had fought well that day. "You are a man, but the end will be at sunrise," he said.

At dawn Terrazas sent his soldiers clamoring up the steep hillside. The fight quickly became hand-to-hand as the desperate Apaches leapt from behind boulders with spear and knife. Some fled in the confusion, the young Mescalero among them, and escaped to the west. Most were cut down by the Mexican snipers on the middle peak. Others were killed or captured by the cavalry once they were exposed on the desert flats.

Near the crest of the hill, Victorio's little band of warriors had thrown up stone breastworks. Here, with their ammunition gone, waited the last of Victorio's men. Two of his sons were there, along with Vicente, the brother-in-law of Geronimo; Turivo, the last son of Cuchillo Negro; as well as Tomaso Coloradas, the son of Mangas; and old Ponce, who had taken Howard to Cochise in 1872. One by one they were cut down as the determined Mexicans advanced.

Victorio and three warriors waited atop the hill. They stood as demigods of old—alone, bloodied, disdaining surrender, with nothing left to fight with but their knives. As the Mexican soldiers approached, the four Apaches plunged their knives into their own hearts. The last stand at Tres Castillos was over.

COLONEL JOAQUIN TERRAZAS—with his prisoners in chains behind him—marched his command into Chihuahua City in late October like a conquering Roman general. Apaches knew this place as the City of Mules. People crowded the streets and lined the rooftops to cheer the conqueror of Victorio. Church bells rang out and a band played a martial air.

Terrazas, astride his white horse, led the column followed by his staff. Their proud bearing could not disguise the weariness of both men and horses. Their clothing was tinged with blood and caked with dust. The men carried ten-foot-long poles with seventy-eight scalps attached. The crowd roared its approval at the passing scalps. One observer thought they looked much like the plumes carried by medieval knights, for Terrazas's men had taken the whole head of hair. One rider carried a solitary scalp, tinged with gray. This was the Tarahumara Indian scout Mauricio Corredor, who, like Terrazas, had been a scalp hunter in his youth. As the colonel's favorite scout, he had been assigned credit as the slayer of Victorio and was permitted to carry the most prized scalp.

Behind the front rank of soldiers with their grisly trophies came sixty-eight prisoners. All were women and children save a lone Comanche who had been protected by one of the scouts. Kaywaykla's grandmother was among the prisoners. She would be sold into slavery but would escape a year later, make an incredible journey north with another Apache woman, and rejoin her people. Two New Mexican boys, who had been rescued and who had identified Victorio's body for Terrazas, followed the column with the ten wounded soldiers. The Mexicans had lost but three men killed.

Corredor collected two thousand pesos for Victorio's scalp. The other scalps were worth $225 each, no matter the sex or age of the victim. Many of the captured women were taken to Guaymas, where a lively slave market still existed. Terrazas received an average price of $150 for his captives, but an attractive young woman could bring as much as $500. The captives earned Terrazas a total of $10,200. Governor Luis Terrazas took two of the captive children into his own household. When the American State Department inquired about the fate of the captives, it was informed by the Mexican ambassador that "following the custom adopted in such cases, [they] were distributed among various families of the State."

Governor Terrazas presented Corredor with a crimson jacket, a black doeskin vest and pants, and a white fur sombrero covered with spangles. A fine nickel-plated repeating rifle was the final reward for the man who had "killed" Victorio. "He is a peaceful Tarahumara Indian," noted a newspaper correspondent, "and bears his honors quietly."

AFTER THE DUST had settled and the soldiers had departed, Nana sent warriors out to attempt to locate survivors. Kaywaykla had been tending to his baby sister while his mother and grandmother gathered firewood when he heard the first shots. They all rushed for the sanctuary of the great boulders at the foot of the three towering peaks, and Kaywaykla lost sight of his grandmother and his baby sister in the confusion. The Mexican soldiers swept in between the Apaches and the protection of the rocks, firing at anything that moved. Kaywaykla and his mother scurried across the base of the mountain just as a full moon began to rise above the lake. They were soon joined by other stragglers, and they all headed west up a ravine, for they knew Nana must be nearby. Gouyen, who carried the weary Kaywaykla on her back, soon reached Nana's camp. The old warrior had but seventeen men with him but still sent a small band to track the Mexican column in case any captives might slip away. The warriors skirmished with some Mexican stragglers and rescued a captive girl, but the main column was long gone on the ninety-mile journey to the City of Mules.

Blanco and Suldeen, who were Kaywaykla's uncles, as well as Kaytennae, who was soon to marry Gouyen and become his stepfather, now arrived loaded down with plunder—which included desperately needed ammunition. They had left some of the captured cattle and sheep behind when they heard the gunfire and had seen Victorio's signal fire.

Kaytennae was devastated to realize what had happened in his absence. "Too late!" he muttered.

Nana, although not a chief, was a revered man of great wisdom, and it fell to him to comfort the people. "It is not too late so long as one Apache lives," he declared. "You have done well, my sons. You are tired and hungry. I will stand guard till you've had some rest."

The rescued captive told her story. Her mother had been shot right before her. The Mexicans had then taken her to a great bonfire and lashed her to a mesquite tree with her back to the flames. She had seen them bring in many more captives. The old men and women were taken aside and murdered by the Mexicans. A few boys, but no men, were among the captives. She knew nothing of Victorio's fate.

The next morning Nana sent Kaytennae and a handful of warriors back to Tres Castillos to search for survivors. They found none. The great fire the girl described had been a funeral pyre upon which the Mexicans had thrown the dead Apaches. At the summit of the south mountain, Kaytennae found the body of Victorio.

"We found the chief with his own knife in his heart. His ammunition belt was empty," Kaytennae told Nana. "Behind rocks we found three of his men who had died by their own knives, as had Victorio." They had buried them as best they could under piles of stones. All the other bodies had been burned by the Mexicans.

The cries of the people filled the night. All had lost husbands, wives, sons, daughters, brothers, and sisters.

Nana again talked to the people. They were not to mourn for Victorio. He had died free and unconquerable, as the greatest of all the Apache chiefs. Mangas Coloradas and Cochise would have envied his warrior death. Victorio would have thanked Usen for his death. It was now for the survivors to carry on—to continue the Apache race.

As winter approached, Nana led the pitiful remainder of Victorio's people back into New Mexico, where they made camp in the Florida Mountains. A sentinel reported to Nana that a lone rider was approaching their camp. The rider was a woman, but she carried a rifle. Nana, who instantly knew who the rider must be, mounted his horse and rode forth to meet her. It was Lozen.

She told Nana that during the flight into Mexico, she had stayed behind with a young Mescalero woman who was about to give birth. They concealed themselves as the Mescalero woman gave birth even as the bluecoats rode right past them. They wrapped the baby in a blanket and sought a good hiding place. Lozen stole a horse from the soldiers and then took the woman and her baby east to the Mescalero Reservation. While she was there among the Mescaleros, she heard of the great battle at Tres Castillos. She hurried to rejoin her people, but had a difficult time finding them, for Nana had done well in concealing their trail.

That night a feast was held. After all were fed, the singers and drummers took their place around the fire. Four times the people danced around the fire in a great circle. The names of all the warriors who had accomplished great deeds were called. The people cheered the warriors as they danced before the fire.

As the men took their places in the circle around the fire, Nana called out to them that there was yet one more warrior to be recognized.

"She whom we had mourned as dead has returned to her people," he declared. "Though she is a woman, there is no warrior more worthy than the sister of Victorio. Come, my daughter."

She stepped forward with her head bowed. As the people acclaimed her, she wept. She knew, as all the people knew, that if she had been with Victorio, he would have been warned of the approaching soldiers. She turned away from the fire but Nana called her back. He asked her to make medicine so that they might know if enemy soldiers were near.

She stepped back before the flickering fire and raised her cupped hands to the starlit sky with the palms up and sang:

> Over all in this world
> Usen has Power
> Sometimes He shares it
> With those of this earth.
> This Power He has given me
> For the benefit of my people.
> This Power is good.
> It is good, as He is good.
> This Power I may use
> For the good of my people.

"No enemy is near," she declared.

"For that we thank Usen," said Nana.

20

FORT APACHE

NANA AND LOZEN WERE AT A NEW STRONGHOLD IN the Sierra Madre when they first heard of the Dreamer. In the spring of 1881, Nock-ay-det-klinne, a leader of the Cibecue band of the Western Apaches, began to hold dances and to preach a new religion. This was the man the White Eyes called the Dreamer. He said that the people could dance back to life the great chiefs of the past—Mangas Coloradas, Cochise, and Victorio—and that this would lead to the restoration of their homeland. Nana was intrigued.

After Victorio's death at Tres Castillos, the surviving Chihennes and Mescaleros had lived by raiding the mining camps and isolated ranches around Silver City. They had quickly replenished their horse and cattle herds and had been joined by several more Mescalero and Warm Springs fugitives. Nana slipped back into Mexico, where they captured a large train of nineteen wagons just to the north of Galeana, killed all thirty of the Mexicans with it, and hurried west to the mountains of Sonora loaded down with booty. Nana then established a *rancheria* near Juh's old stronghold in the Sierra Madre to the west of Casas Grandes.

With his people well supplied and relatively safe, Nana decided to journey north to San Carlos to learn for himself the truth of this new religion. Kaytennae went with the old man. They traveled in secret to San Carlos, where they enjoyed the simple hospitality of Cochise's son Naiche. He agreed to go north with them to listen to Nock-ay-det-klinne and observe this new dance firsthand. His

camp was in the White Mountains about forty miles northwest of
Fort Apache.

The Dreamer's gatherings featured a liberal distribution of
tiswin before the dance commenced. People brought offerings to
this new prophet to support the dance, not unlike the pilgrims
to the backwoods camp meetings of frontier preachers. Men and
women danced in lines that faced a common center like the spokes
of a wheel. *Hoddentin,* the pollen of the tule plant used as a sacrifi-
cial powder, was sprinkled upon them as they moved to the rhyth-
mic beat of the drums.

Nana and Kaytennae, reluctant at first, finally joined in. It was
almost dawn when the Dreamer halted the dance. Accompanied
by a handful of followers, including Nana and Kaytennae, the
Dreamer walked up to the crest of a nearby hillside to confront the
dawn. He halted just below the crest and raised his arms in prayer
to Usen. Nana watched in awe as the ethereal forms of the great
lords of Apacheria—Mangas Coloradas, Cochise, and Victorio—
rose out of the ground above them all on the hilltop. They were
visible to their knees before they retreated back into the earth as
the sun rose.

"Nana said that he had seen this," remembered Juh's son Daklugie, "and the word of Nana was not to be questioned." Geronimo
and Juh met with Nana, Kaytennae, and Naiche back at San Carlos
and were told of what they had witnessed. Nana and Kaytennae
then left to rejoin their people in the Sierra Madre while Geronimo
and Juh traveled north to Cibecue Creek. Geronimo talked with
Nock-ay-det-klinne. The Dreamer, who was slight of frame and
frail, told him that he had died and had passed into the spirit land,
where he saw Indians he had known in life camped in a green valley with plenty of game and "was sorry when he was brought back
to consciousness."

Juh was caught up in the religious hysteria inspired by the
Dreamer, which with its mixture of Christian resurrection theology and nativist desire was a precursor of the Ghost Dance, which
would sweep up the Sioux eight years later with catastrophic results. But Geronimo remained skeptical. The Dreamer's dance

seemed so contrary to the basic belief system of the Chiricahua. But even the cynical Geronimo finally allowed himself to be seduced by the Dreamer's dogma. Geronimo later confessed to Juh's son Daklugie that "he had never understood why he and Juh could have been so easily influenced by that Medicine Man; but he had convinced them that the Apaches should leave revenge to Usen."

The message of peace became increasingly garbled as more and more Apaches—Chiricahua, Tonto, and Coyotero as well as Cibecue and White Mountain—flocked to the Dreamer's dances. Rumors soon reached both Fort Apache and San Carlos that the intent of the dance was to resurrect the great chiefs for a final war on the White Eyes.

At Fort Apache, Lieutenant Tom Cruse was among the few who took the rumors seriously. All of the Company A scouts under his command had asked for passes to allow them to attend the dances. They returned surly and began to mutter that the White Eyes would soon be gone from Apacheria. Even the head scout Alchesay had been swept up by the religious fervor. For a time, Nockay-det-klinne himself camped quite near the fort, and the incessant beating of the drums throughout the night kept everyone on edge.

In June 1881, Cruse decided to go and observe the dance himself. "As I looked at the swaying, engrossed figures, moving like automations to the thump of drums," wrote the young officer, "I was amazed at the fraternizing between tribes and elements which had always held for each other the most deadly aversion." Cruse reported his observation to Colonel Carr. The colonel expressed concern over the loyalty of the Apache scouts.

"I think my Scouts want to be loyal," Cruse replied, "but if it comes to a showdown, I don't see how they can side with us."

Carr took this under advisement but was unwilling to admit that he faced a crisis. He did order that the scouts' weapons be stored when they were not on duty. Carr had arrived at Fort Apache only at the end of May and was still uncertain of the issues and personalities at his new post. He had rightly perceived this temporary transfer as banishment from the relative comfort of Fort Lowell, engineered as a punishment as a result of an ongoing feud with Colonel Willcox.

Fort Apache, although greatly expanded in terms of both size and creature comforts since its 1870 establishment, remained one of the most isolated outposts of the republic in 1881. It rested on a high mountain plateau on the south bank of the White River, surrounded by mountains and lush stands of pine. It was forty miles north of San Carlos as the crow flies, but a considerably longer journey by horseback or wagon. The post, despite the change in its official designation from camp to fort in 1879, was still a ramshackle array of log buildings arranged around a large parade ground. At best Fort Apache was a three-company post—hardly an impressive command for a bird colonel and regimental commander.

None of this helped to improve the fifty-one-year-old colonel's increasingly sour disposition. Carr was anxious to avoid dealing with the Dreamer issue altogether, since he felt that the problem belonged to the Indian Bureau. The Apaches were on their reservation and had committed no hostile act against the whites. This was Agent Tiffany's problem, not his.

Mickey Free, after leaving Charles Connell's employment to return to San Carlos, had promptly been hired in early April as a scout by Albert Sterling, the new head of the Indian Police. Sterling had previously been chief-of-scouts at Fort Cummings, New Mexico, before accepting the San Carlos job in August 1880, after Clay Beauford resigned. Agent Tiffany now sent Sterling north with orders to bring Nock-ay-det-klinne to the agency headquarters for his own protection.

The Dreamer, after several delays, met with Tiffany in late July 1881 and assured the San Carlos agent of the benign nature of his dance. Tiffany remained worried that when the Dreamer failed to raise the dead, he might be killed by those who had given him presents. That would lead to more fighting between the White Mountain bands. The Indian Bureau's concentration of all the Apaches at San Carlos had only exacerbated these tensions.

Nock-ay-det-klinne's movement had come about as a result of

the long-standing feud between Chief Diablo's Cibecue Creek band of the Western Apaches and their White Mountain cousins. The year before, on August 30, 1880, the simmering feud had climaxed near Fort Apache in a brawl that left Diablo dead. Alchesay, who had killed the rival chief, was later wounded in retribution. Old Chief Pedro was also dangerously wounded, shot in both legs, and had to be rescued by Sterling's policemen. A warrior named Sanchez, who was deeply involved in this blood feud as well as openly contemptuous of the White Eyes, became chief of Diablo's band and was among the first to embrace the Dreamer's new religion.

The Dreamer had never intended to preach hostility toward the White Eyes, but rather to bring harmony to the divided Western Apaches and end the blood feud that followed the killing of Diablo. The five Western Apache bands—White Mountain, San Carlos, Cibecue, and Northern and Southern Tonto—might well share a common language and culture, but they had always remained quite distinct from one another in the pre-reservation years. John Clum had changed all that by bringing them all together onto one reservation, and now Tiffany had to deal with the potentially disastrous consequences.

Nock-ay-det-klinne seemed a potentially dangerous mystery to the Americans at both Fort Apache and San Carlos, but he had been well-known to the previous generation of soldiers and scouts. Mickey Free certainly knew who he was, as did Corydon Cooley and Al Sieber, but both Tiffany and Carr failed to consult with these old hands.

The experienced scouts would have told them that the Dreamer was the leader of one of the three Cibecue bands. His people lived on Canyon Creek and had always been friendly with the White Eyes. The soldiers at Camp Apache could not pronounce his name and so called him Bobby-del-klinne. He had served for a time as a scout in Crook's campaign against the Tontos. His reward for his friendship toward the White Eyes had been removal with his little band to San Carlos in 1875. Many of the Cibecue band eventually drifted back north, making camp to the northwest of Fort Apache. Early in May 1881, Nock-ay-det-klinne had obtained a pass from

Agent Tiffany to move his people to a summer camp on Cibecue Creek, some forty-five miles northwest of Fort Apache. It was there that he had begun his dance.

Events were rapidly spinning beyond the control of Nock-ay-det-klinne, Agent Tiffany, or Colonel Carr. The catalyst that set in motion a series of events leading to a great tragedy came not from San Carlos but rather from New Mexico.

THE DREAMER'S DANCE had inspired old Nana to plan a raid to avenge the death of Victorio. Many Apaches believed that Victorio's resurrection could not happen so long as the White Eyes remained, so Nana hoped that such a raid might speed the return of the great chief. Back in his Sierra Madre stronghold, Nana called for warriors to join him on a vengeance raid. Kaytennae was the first to step forward, followed by Mangas, the only surviving son of Mangas Coloradas, and the ambitious warrior Chatto. There were few warriors left for such a raid, and some men had to stay behind to protect the women and children. Nana had but fifteen men and, of course, Lozen.

Gouyen, Kaywaykla's mother, became jealous of the praise lavished on Lozen by Nana and Kaytennae. "I could do the same if I had anyone with whom to leave Kaywaykla," she told Kaytennae.

"Fortunately you do not," he replied. "I do not want you to risk your life in battle. I respect Lozen, but you are my wife."

On July 13, 1881, Nana's little band splashed across the Rio Grande not far from Fort Quitman, Texas. Along the El Paso–to–Chihuahua City road, they had already overtaken a stagecoach and then a small wagon train. Then they had killed four surveyors a few miles south of El Paso. Colonel Terrazas quickly had troops in pursuit, but the Apaches were long gone before the Mexican soldiers reached the Rio Grande.

Nana then led his war party north into New Mexico. He hoped to enlist warriors from the Mescalero Reservation, and within days he had twenty-five new recruits. The young men had heard of Nana's success in Mexico and were anxious to join him against the White Eyes. On July 17, they ambushed an army packtrain in Alamo Canyon, just south of the Mescalero Reservation, wounded the chief packer, and made off with three pack mules.

The pursuing troops followed a trail of dead and mutilated bodies into a little canyon on the northeastern slope of the San Andres. They immediately attacked on July 25, captured several mules as well as camp supplies, and claimed to have killed two Apaches, but no bodies were located. The commanding officer also noticed a woman fighting alongside the Apache warriors. The raiders slipped away to the west, left seven dead settlers along their trail, crossed the Rio Grande, and vanished into the San Mateo Mountains east of Ojo Caliente. There they ambushed a civilian posse from Chloride before cutting north toward Fort Wingate and the Navajo Reservation.

COLONEL EDWARD HATCH, in Santa Fe, was beset. His sigh of relief upon receipt of the news of Victorio's death had been premature. Hatch once again assumed personal command of all troops in the field, and within a matter of days had sixteen companies of the Ninth Cavalry and Fifteenth Infantry in the field. The recent completion of the future Atchison, Topeka & Santa Fe Railroad line from east to west across New Mexico, as well as south to Deming to connect with the Southern Pacific, gave Hatch a new level of mobility.

Hatch's troops were suddenly everywhere. Every fort—Cummings, Bayard, Selden, Stanton, Craig, and Wingate—sent forth patrols. Heavily armed bands of civilians combed the countryside. Not even the beloved Black Range could hide old Nana from the two companies of Apache scouts trailing him. Finding Nana's raiders was one thing—but vanquishing them was quite another.

Nana defeated the pursuing troops in two sharp engagements. First, on August 16, in a running fight along Cuchillo Negro Creek in the foothills of the Black Range, Nana's men killed two Buffalo Soldiers and captured several cavalry horses. The Apaches again

separated as they swept south toward the Mexican border, herding
their stolen stock and seven captives along the main road to the
Mimbres Valley. In the second engagement, seventeen Ninth Cavalry troopers and a civilian posse were ambushed in a narrow defile
called Gavilan Canyon. The lieutenant in command as well as the
leader of the posse and three troopers were killed. Gavilan Canyon proved to be the final engagement between the soldiers and the
Apaches. As reinforcements came in from both Texas and Arizona,
Nana's raiders slipped south past Fort Cummings, where Colonel
Hatch was now headquartered, across the railroad tracks to the
Florida Mountains, and then through the New Mexico bootheel
into Old Mexico.

Nana's raid had taken a little over six weeks. The old warrior
had paralyzed much of New Mexico with terror, kept more than
a thousand troops on the march, and killed at least fifty civilians
and soldiers while hardly losing a man. He had made off with seven
captives and crossed the international line loaded down with guns
and ammunition taken from the soldiers as well as more than two
hundred head of stolen horses, mules, and cattle.

The news of Nana's raid caused barely a ripple in the East,
where the nation was fixated by a death watch over President James
Garfield, who had been shot by a frustrated office seeker on July 2.
The gravely wounded Garfield lingered in agony throughout the
summer until September 19, 1881.

In Arizona, however, it was a different story. Nana's raid sent
shock waves throughout the territory. Colonel Willcox in Prescott
and Agent Tiffany at San Carlos both decided that a crisis was now
at hand. They determined that the Dreamer must be arrested or
killed. They did not much care which.

DURING THE LAST WEEK of August 1881, the telegraph operators
stationed across Arizona Territory were busy working their keys as
message after message about Nana's raid sped across the wires. In
response, Arizona Department commander Willcox sent orders to
Major James Biddle of the Sixth Cavalry, stationed at Fort Grant,

to hire a dependable scout at San Carlos and send him north to spy on the Dreamer and the Apaches gathered about him on the Cibecue. Major Biddle hired Mickey Free.

Mickey immediately headed north to Cibecue Creek. The August monsoon was in full force but despite the swollen streams, Mickey was soon at the Dreamer's camp, watching and keeping a low profile. He found a remarkable gathering of Indians—not just Western Apaches but also a scattering of Navajos, Yavapais, and Chiricahuas. Lozen was there as well, although Mickey did not know her, for she had come to San Carlos to visit relatives and then traveled north to see for herself this medicine man who said he would dance her brother back to life.

A detachment of Albert Sterling's San Carlos police, sent at the same time as Mickey to arrest Nock-ay-det-klinne, returned with a report that the Salt River was impassable and that they could not get through to Cibecue. The high waters of the Gila River also blocked Biddle's attempt to send two cavalry companies from Camp Thomas to reinforce the tiny garrison at Fort Apache. The usually shallow Gila was now a raging torrent, deeper than anyone could remember. Fort Apache was on its own.

Colonel Carr, at Fort Apache, contemplated his options. He had under his command two troops of his own Sixth Cavalry, about eighty men, and an understrength company of the Twelfth Infantry, as well as the twenty-five Apache scouts. The loyalty of the scouts was already in question, since thirteen were Cibecue men and the other twelve were from Pedro's White Mountain band. In all Carr had but 170 officers and men, including the scouts, and a handful of civilian employees. At least 600 Apaches were in the camps around the fort and forty miles to the northwest on Cibecue Creek.

On August 23, Sergeant Cut-Mouth Mose, a trusted scout so named because of a knife scar that disfigured his face, brought Chief Pedro, Alchesay, and Uclenay to see Carr. Pedro, who was still lame from his wounds from the fight a year before, assured Carr of his long-standing friendship with the Americans. Uclenay had just returned from Cibecue Creek and he testified to the peaceful intent of the Dreamer. "When he has a dance, he wants to have it without being disturbed; it is to bring the dead back and he don't want to be disturbed," declared Uclenay; "anything he does he gets on orders from the higher spirits."

Carr was also in communication with a "higher spirit": Colonel Willcox. The colonel had telegraphed Carr on August 15 to tell him that reinforcements were on the way and that he wanted the "Indian doctor" arrested as soon as possible. On the same day, Carr also received a telegram from Tiffany. "I believe the medicine man is working for his own personal benefit," the Indian agent declared. "I want him arrested or killed or both." Then the telegraph line went down.

The Fort Apache telegraph operator, Will Barnes, was sent with two troopers to repair the line. They discovered two places within ten miles of the post where the line had been cut by the Apaches, who often strung leather between the cut lines to make it more difficult to find the break. It was hoped that men from Camp Thomas would endeavor to repair any breaks farther to the south. But the high water kept repair crews from Thomas from reaching the downed line north of the Gila River, so Major Biddle called in his repair crews from Fort Grant. He assumed that Carr would send dispatches to him at Thomas by courier if there was any trouble.

Carr did not believe that the Dreamer posed a real threat, but he now had his orders from both Willcox and Tiffany. Carr had no choice but to arrest the Dreamer. On August 24, 1881, he met with his officers to discuss the situation. He made certain that each officer understood his displeasure with the order and especially the insinuation in it that Nock-ay-det-klinne should be killed. He also fretted over the loyalty of the Apache scouts.

Lieutenant Cruse argued that it would be better to have the scouts stay with the command than to leave them behind to possibly threaten the depleted garrison. Carr and his officers agreed with Cruse. The colonel then decided to make a final appeal to Nock-ay-det-klinne. He sent Sergeant Mose to Cibecue Creek with an order for the Dreamer to come to Fort Apache. The scout returned to the post to report that a big dance was scheduled for Friday night and that the medicine man might start for Fort Apache the day after.

Lieutenant John Bourke, on detached duty from General Crook's Omaha headquarters by order of General Sheridan to make an ethnographic study of the southwestern Indian tribes, reached Fort Apache on August 27. He had just visited with the Navajo, Zuni, and Hopi. Bourke was concerned even before he arrived at the post because he had found the Navajos indignant over their mistreatment by their Indian agent. They were in serious talks about joining with the Apaches against the White Eyes.

Carr, who knew Bourke well from the Great Sioux War, asked the lieutenant to visit with Chief Pedro. Carr confessed to Bourke that "things wore an ugly look" and implored the lieutenant to "give them a dose of Crook, they haven't forgotten him and the licking he gave them." The colonel gloomily concluded: "He is the only bulge we have on them now."

Carr's sixteen-year-old son, Clark, at the post on summer vacation from school, drove a wagon with Bourke and Lieutenant W. H. Carter to Pedro's camp. The Apaches were in the midst of a big *tiswin* party when Bourke arrived, and he felt they "were acting in a more bold and saucy manner than I have ever known." Both Pedro and Alchesay seemed particularly interested in Bourke's visit with the Navajo. It was clear that the Apaches expected help from the northern Indians. After the visit, an uneasy Bourke returned to Fort Apache to warn Carr "that these Indians were in for war."

THE NEXT MORNING, August 29, 1881, Carr assembled his troops on the parade ground at Fort Apache. The colonel of the Sixth made a grand show of his departure. Two troops of the Sixth Cavalry, five officers and seventy-nine troopers, along with twenty-three Apache scouts, interpreter Charles Hurrle, and several civilians including young Clark Carr, departed the fort at ten in the morning. Carr had so few officers that Captain Edmund Hentig, who had just received an assignment to recruiting duty in Philadelphia, insisted upon going with the column. His wife, who was quite ill, had left the post a few days before to seek medical care in Philadelphia after celebrating the captain's thirty-ninth birthday. The other officers were Lieutenants Cruse, W. H. Carter, and William Stanton as well as Assistant Surgeon George McCreery.

A week of torrential rain had given way to brilliant sunshine, which put all in a rather festive mood. Carr put on some style to impress Bourke, who joined him at the post flagstaff to watch the command pass in review. The two troops of cavalry were followed by thirty-five pack mules, who were led by chief packer Nat Nobles. The Apache scouts, each wearing the red flannel head band that signified their status, rode alongside the pack mules. Carr shook hands with Bourke and then trotted to the head of the column to lead his command forth from Fort Apache.

As the troopers vanished down the mesa to the river on the west, Bourke hurried to the small log cabin next to the adjutant's wood-framed office, where the telegraph office resided. Bourke gave Barnes, the telegraph operator, a long coded message to send to General Crook in Omaha and then departed for Fort Wingate. The telegraph had been restored the previous day, but as Barnes began to tap out Bourke's message, it went dead again. A two-man repair detail was promptly sent to investigate. They never returned.

Carr's column crossed the White River and followed the mountainous Verde Trail to the Apache camp on Cibecue Creek. They made good time the first day out and pitched camp some twenty-nine miles from the fort, on Carrizo Creek. Carr and Cruse met with the Apache scouts and issued each man twenty rounds of ammunition. Carr assured them that he meant no harm to Nock-ay-det-klinne or any other Apache, but that he had been ordered to arrest the medicine man. Sergeant Mose defended the Dreamer and requested permission to go to Cibecue to calm the people and assure them of Carr's peaceful intent. Carr agreed to this. He then pulled out his spyglass and passed it among the scouts. A comet streaked across the night sky above them and he wanted them all to look at it closely. This comet was not a sign from the Dreamer, he declared, but rather a sign of the white man's power.

Mose left for the Cibecue a little before dawn, and, soon after, Carr's column was in the saddle. They had not gone far when a courier from Fort Apache, John Colvig, handed a message to Captain Hentig. Major Melville A. Cochran, who had but sixty men to defend Fort Apache, sixteen of whom were in the post hospital, was worried. All the Apaches camped near the fort were gone, including the families of the scouts, and he had observed twenty-four well-armed warriors on Carr's trail to the Cibecue. He had also sent a rider to Camp Thomas to request that the promised reinforcements be hurried on. Carr read the dispatch, smiled, and remarked to Surgeon McCreery that he "thought they were getting a little alarmed up at Apache."

Cruse, riding in advance with his scouts, was about two miles from the village when Chief Sanchez, his face painted red, rode up on a white pony brandishing a Winchester.

"What do you want here, Nantan Eclatten?" he demanded of Cruse. The name meant "raw virgin lieutenant." Cruse fumed and ordered Sanchez away. The Apache rode on up the line of the column obviously counting the soldiers. More armed Apaches now appeared, bumping their ponies against the soldiers as the column advanced across the belly-deep water of Cibecue Creek.

Upon their arrival at the Dreamer's camp on August 30, 1881, the scout Sergeant Mose greeted Cruse and took him to the brush shelter where the Dreamer reclined on a Navajo blanket. Carr arrived soon after, and the medicine man rose to greet him. It was three o'clock.

Carr explained through interpreter Hurrle that he had come to take Nock-ay-det-klinne to Fort Apache for a talk, and that he would not be harmed so long as his people did not intervene. Sergeant Mose often repeated what Carr said, so that it became apparent that the scouts did not trust Hurrle to give a correct translation. Carr assigned Sergeant John McDonald and eight troopers to take charge of the medicine man. He told the Dreamer that if he attempted to escape, he would be killed. Nock-ay-det-klinne smiled and asked that his wife be able to accompany him, which Carr agreed to.

The colonel mounted his horse, and along with D Troop and the packtrain, he headed back toward a campsite he had selected a few miles from the village. As Carr and Hentig rode abreast at the head of the column, the colonel remarked to the captain that he "was rather ashamed to come out with all this force to arrest one poor little Indian." Hentig laughed in agreement.

The medicine man had nonchalantly returned to his wickiup to eat, and Cruse sent Sergeant Mose, the scout, and Sergeant McDonald to bring him along. This disturbed the Apaches who gathered around the Dreamer, and as the frail old man was brought to his horse, his wife danced ahead of him singing and tossing pollen to the wind.

"In spite of the brilliant sunlight," a nervous Cruse noted, "it was a weird and thrilling scene, almost like a nightmare."

Cruse and Lieutenant Stanton, who was commanding E Troop, led the party out of the village as more and more Apache warriors, painted and stripped for combat, appeared. Stanton quietly ordered his men to be ready.

"We nearly caught it back there," Cruse said to Stanton. "It looked like a fight."

"I thought so, too," he replied.

They soon reached Carr's camp, just a few hundred yards east of Cibecue Creek. The troopers were already preparing camp and the packers were unloading the mules. Cruse hurried ahead, crossed the creek, and reported to Carr.

"It looked pretty scaly for a while, as we came along," Cruse blurted out.

"What are you talking about?" Carr exclaimed. "You're always using words I don't understand. 'Scaly!' 'Scaly!' Now, what does that mean?"

Cruse said that it meant he and Stanton had seen several Apaches painted for war, to which the colonel, his temper on the rise, said he saw no hostile Apaches. Cruse pointed to the creek crossing where several armed Apaches were crossing into the army camp.

Just at that moment McDonald and Mose brought the Dreamer up to Carr. He ordered them to take the old man over to where the packers had unloaded their mules and guard him there among the baggage. He called down to Captain Hentig, who was near the creek, to stop the Indians from coming into the camp. Hentig called out to the Apaches to get away.

Cruse suddenly realized that his Indian scouts were arrayed on the edge of the mesa above the camp. He spotted Sanchez and several mounted warriors with them. One of the mounted warriors lifted his rifle in the air above his head and let loose a bloodcurdling war cry. Then, Lieutenant Cruse declared, "all hell broke loose!"

GRACIAS SEVERIANO GALLOPED into Fort Apache just after midnight that night with the startling news that Carr and most of his command had been killed earlier that day at Cibecue Creek. Severiano, a Mexican captive raised by the Apaches, was sometimes employed as an interpreter and was considered quite reliable. Major Cochran had already placed the fort on full alert. All surplus arms and ammunition, along with additional supplies of water and food, had been moved to the commissary storehouse. The women and children of the post, as well as some civilians who had come in, were placed there as well.

Cochran soon learned from the post trader that the Indians had also told him that Carr and all his men were dead. The major wrote a breathless dispatch to Camp Thomas: "General Carr's command reported all massacred at the Cibecue. Hurry up reinforcements, no time to lose, post threatened." A trooper volunteered to carry the message the seventy-three miles to Camp Thomas.

On August 31, 1881, Mickey Free was at Seven-Mile Canyon, some four miles from Fort Apache, on his way back to San Carlos, when he heard gunfire. The narrow canyon, where everyone on the trail stopped to water at a small spring, became a killing field right before his eyes. The two telegraph repairmen, along with another soldier returning to Fort Apache from ferry duty at the Black River crossing, were slaughtered, as were three Mormon settlers who blundered onto the scene soon after. The Apaches also got Cochran's dispatch rider. As the warriors stripped him, one of them smashed in his head with a rock, then did the same to each of the other victims they had captured.

The Apaches, whom Mickey recognized as members of Pedro's band, then hurried on in the direction of Fort Apache. Mickey galloped south to Fort Grant, where he reported to Lieutenant Harry Haskell, the staff officer who had brought in Juh and Geronimo, and told him what he had seen at both Cibecue just before the battle and at Seven-Mile Canyon. This confirmed a similar report Haskell had just received from Albert Sterling, the head of the Indian Police at San Carlos. Haskell promptly telegraphed Colonel Willcox in Prescott with the news that it appeared "beyond doubt that Carr and command were killed."

Newspapers from San Francisco to New York soon headlined "Mickey Free's Account of the Cibecue Massacre." It was a grand story—a combination of Custer's Last Stand and the Sepoy Mutiny—and the newspaper writers improved on Mickey's tale with sweeping embellishments and gripping details. The September 4, 1881, *New York Times* devoted three full columns to the story. Carr and his entire command had been massacred, read the breathless copy, and the Apache scouts had taken the lead in the slaughter.

Mickey did not wait around Fort Grant to read his press clippings but started back north immediately. He gathered up his family and his wife's White Mountain friends and hurried them to San Carlos. He knew that military retribution would come swiftly and was not likely to discriminate among the Apache bands.

MEANWHILE, AT Fort Apache, a nervous and increasingly agitated Major Cochran did the best he could to defend the post against an expected Apache onslaught. Several civilians had come into the fort in search of sanctuary the morning of August 31, the day after Carr's battle at Cibecue Creek, and Apaches could be seen on the nearby hillsides. The plaintive vision of Mrs. Carr, who might possibly have lost both her husband and her son, led Cochran to send twenty-three-year-old telegraph operator Barnes onto a high mesa to the north of the post to spy out the hoped-for return of Carr's column. This was dicey work.

Barnes passed through several abandoned Apache campsites on his way to the mesa. Everything was gone, even the dogs. Atop the mesa, Barnes scanned the horizon with his field glasses. All he saw were Apache smoke signals at several points to the west. He then spotted a handful of warriors moving up the mesa toward him and decided to fight rather than make a run for it. Then, far to the west, he made out first a dust cloud, and then cavalrymen—ten, thirty, forty men. It was Carr's column! The colonel was alive after all. Barnes signaled the good news by flag back to the post, then mounted his horse and galloped toward the troops as the Apaches fired several shots after him.

When Barnes reached the column he found Nobles, the chief packer, in the lead astride his great white horse, followed by his packtrain. The soldiers, several of whom were so badly wounded that they had to be held on to their horses, straggled behind. Barnes noticed the body of a trooper slung over the first pack animal in line, his lifeless hands dangling from beneath the blanket that covered him. At three that afternoon, September 1, 1881, what was left of Carr's column limped back into Fort Apache.

Carr had quite a bit of explaining to do, especially to his nemesis Willcox in Prescott. But Fort Apache was still entirely cut off from the outside world, so his official report could wait. That was just as well, for over the next several weeks and months, several contradictory accounts by the white participants at the Cibecue fight came to light. The Apache accounts were even more at odds with Carr's official report. Willcox would eventually decide to press for a court-martial for Carr. All accounts, however, agreed on one central point: the Apache scouts had mutinied.

IT HAD BEEN between three and four o'clock in the afternoon on August 30, 1881, that Carr's men began to lay out their camp along Cibecue Creek. The soldiers were busy caring for their horses, preparing fires, and bringing up water from the creek. Sergeant McDonald and Sergeant Mose, the scout, had placed their prisoner in a hollow square made by the packers as they unloaded their *aparejos*.

They were joined there by the Dreamer's wife. As several armed Apaches crossed the creek into the camp, Captain Hentig ordered them away. One was the scout Dandy Jim, who identified himself to the captain and was allowed to pass into camp. That was when Cruse noticed that the rest of the scouts had aligned themselves on the mesa some twenty yards above where he and Colonel Carr were standing, and that several mounted warriors had emerged from the brush to join them.

As a war cry sounded from where the scouts stood, Dandy Jim had turned and shot Captain Hentig in the back. The scouts then all fired as one into the camp. Lieutenant Carter, standing near them, had fired his pistol and then hit the dirt just as a volley was unleashed at him.

Carr, who had struck everyone as eerily calm, began to set up a perimeter. "Kill the medicine man!" he barked at McDonald. The sergeant turned and fired at Nock-ay-det-klinne but was wounded at the same instant and went down. Carter's orderly, who was nearby, turned and shot the Dreamer in the head. At that moment Nock-ay-det-klinne's teenage son galloped across the creek and into the camp in an attempt to rescue his father. The boy's mother wailed as he was blown off his pony. She picked up Hentig's pistol and was promptly shot down by a trooper. Amid this swirl of action, Sergeant Mose ran to Cruse's side to beg protection. He was the only Apache scout who remained loyal.

Lieutenant Stanton had quickly led his company in a counter-attack that drove the Apaches, including the scouts, back into the brush. He dismounted his men and set up a skirmish line along the creek. Dr. McCreery hurried to establish an aid station by the creek. With a large cottonwood tree for shelter, McCreery tended to the wounded under a galling fire.

Before the attack had started, the unsaddled horses and mules had been taken to the creek to be watered and then allowed to graze just south of the camp. A sergeant and three privates, assigned as herd guards, were surprised by a band of mounted Apaches led by Sanchez and Lozen. Two of the troopers were shot down and the animals stampeded. A few of Stanton's horses, left in the brush along the creek, were also captured by Lozen. Some of these still had extra ammunition on them, which the Apaches desperately needed.

Carr continued to walk up and down the line calmly issuing orders. A sergeant finally called out to him, "For God's sake, General, get under cover or you'll be killed sure." Carr calmly replied, "Oh, God damn these whelps, they can't hit me, God damn 'em."

Carr suddenly realized that he had not seen his young son since the gunfire had commenced. He called out for the boy, who calmly replied, "Here I am! What do you want?" Clark had been blazing away with his Winchester and having the time of his life. "I think that Clark was the only person in the whole command who got the slightest degree of enjoyment out of the whole fight," declared Cruse.

As darkness approached, the fire from the Apaches slackened and then ceased. Carr took stock of his situation: Captain Hentig and four troopers killed, another five wounded, with fifty of his horses and mules killed or run off. Three of his wounded were critical; all three of them would die the next day.

The dead were placed in a mass grave and a few words were read over them. All were in agreement that a night march back to Fort Apache was in order. Carr ordered the body of the Dreamer buried, but the troopers discovered that the old man was yet alive. One of the soldiers took an ax and crushed in Nock-ay-det-klinne's skull. The Apaches would later duplicate this act on every White Eye who fell into their hands.

THE TARDY REINFORCEMENTS Major Biddle had sent from Camp Thomas finally reached Fort Apache at three in the morning on September 3. They were surprised and elated to find Carr and most of his men still alive. The Apaches, upon spotting the fresh troops the previous afternoon, had scattered. The road to Camp Thomas still appeared too dangerous to send a message south, so John Colvig volunteered to carry dispatches north to Fort Wingate. It was the evening of September 4 before the news that Carr's command had not all been killed reached the outside world. By that time, the War Department had sent troops from California and New Mexico to Arizona to put down the Apache uprising.

"What I expect is action, results, not speculation," thundered General William Tecumseh Sherman to the commander of the Division of the Pacific. "All Apaches outside the reservation must be killed or captured, and if any of them take refuge on the reservation, that must not save the guilty parties who fired on General Carr's command."

21

BREAKOUT

THE KILLING OF THE DREAMER SENT SHOCK WAVES
throughout San Carlos. Soldiers now ringed the reservation and, despite the assurances of Agent Tiffany that
there was nothing to fear, Geronimo, Juh, and Naiche were rightly
paranoid. "Geronimo was like a wild animal," declared Chatto.
"Troops made him nervous."

At first the army hoped to enlist the Chiricahuas as scouts
against the White Mountain Apaches. The Chokonen chief Chihuahua had just returned to San Carlos after a stint as scout sergeant in New Mexico, and now Lieutenant Harry Haskell, at Camp
Thomas, tried to sign him up again and use him to entice other
Chiricahuas to become scouts. Haskell called in Tom Jeffords and
Archie McIntosh to meet with Chihuahua, Naiche, and Juh, but
the council proved fruitless. Naiche again pledged his friendship to
Jeffords, but he was not willing to fight either the White Mountain
or the Cibecue people.

Colonel Willcox, frustrated by Haskell's failure to enlist Chiricahua scouts and under intense pressure from Washington to kill
or arrest the Apaches who had fought Carr on the Cibecue, ordered
Major James Biddle to invade San Carlos with several troops of the
Sixth Cavalry and arrest George and Bonito, two White Mountain
leaders known to be at the subagency on the Gila River. On September 30, George and Bonito learned of this and fled to Naiche's
camp.

A council was called. Geronimo reminded the assembled warriors of the treachery of the White Eyes against Mangas Coloradas

at Fort McLane and Cochise at Apache Pass. Nor had Geronimo forgotten how Clum had placed chains on him at Ojo Caliente and then imprisoned him in the sweltering San Carlos guardhouse. It was, Geronimo argued, "more manly to die on the warpath than to be killed in prison."

Naiche, Chihuahua, and Chatto were reluctant to break out of San Carlos, but they could see that Geronimo had won over the people, so they agreed to go. Late on the night of September 30, 1881, Geronimo and Juh led 375 Chiricahuas south out of San Carlos. Bonito, with his small band of White Mountain people, joined them. George led his band out and headed back north into the White Mountains.

The Apaches, who broke into four groups under Juh, Naiche, Chatto, and Bonito, swept down the San Pedro Valley. Geronimo led a raiding party that captured two small freight trains and cleaned out a local rancher of his stock before rejoining Juh on the morning of October 2.

As target-of-opportunity raiders, they were delighted to spot an unguarded wagon train in the distance later that day. They struck the twelve-wagon freight train near the Cedar Springs station, some twenty miles to the north of Fort Grant, killed the wagon master and five teamsters, and made off with considerable loot and more than a hundred mules. Then they continued south along the eastern edge of the Sulphur Springs Valley.

As the Apaches moved openly along the stagecoach road, they soon came upon a four-man telegraph repair detail from Fort Grant. They killed the men and pulled down the lines. A cavalry detachment under Captain Reuben Bernard, trailing close behind the Apaches, soon discovered the still-warm bodies of the troopers. Then the soldiers suddenly came under fire from the nearby Pina-leno foothills. Captain Bernard set up skirmish lines and by late afternoon was fully engaged in a hot fight. The soldiers expended four thousand rounds of ammunition, lost a sergeant killed and three troopers wounded, and limped back to Fort Grant to refit.

On October 3, Geronimo and his raiders hit Henry Hooker's sprawling ranch and made off with 135 horses. Despite their large and ever-increasing herd of more than 500 animals, the main body of Chiricahuas made excellent time as they moved south down the flat valley floor. It began to rain that night as they went into camp at Point of Mountains.

Lightning turned the sky into a sheet of dancing flame, and as the rain increased, it covered the barren flats that the Apaches had crossed over, making a shallow lake that covered their trail. At sunup the next morning, the Apaches crossed the new railroad line about twenty miles southwest of Willcox and headed south toward the Dragoons, Cochise's old stronghold.

CAPTAIN BERNARD WAS again on their trail with two troops of the First Cavalry and two troops of the Sixth, as well as a small company of Apache scouts. The troopers and their horses were loaded onto boxcars and moved to Dragoon Summit, at the northern edge of the Dragoon Mountains. They soon united with two troops of the Ninth Cavalry from New Mexico.

Bernard and his men headed into a narrow canyon of the Dragoons, hoping to surprise the Chiricahuas in their camp—a difficult chore under the best of circumstances. The troops were not yet in position when their Apache scouts suddenly opened fire, alerting the Apache camp to their presence. Some officers believed that the scouts had purposefully warned their friends in the Indian camp. A running fight ensued as thirty warriors formed a rear guard to cover the escape of the women and children. The battle went on all day.

Bernard reported one Apache killed, although no body was located, as well as a young girl captured and forty animals recovered. The captive was dressed in such finery that it was thought she might be the daughter of a chief. Other soldiers said that an Indian woman was killed and a woman and two additional children captured.

While the Apaches had abandoned camp supplies and horses in their flight, and several of the warriors had been wounded, they still retained a huge herd and all their people save the woman and the captured children. Captain Bernard's scouts reported back to him that the Apaches were headed in the direction of Tombstone.

MAYOR JOHN CLUM of Tombstone received word of Geronimo's breakout from San Carlos on October 2. A breathless courier reported the Apaches not ten miles to the northeast. They had hit the nearby McLaury ranch and made off with fourteen horses. The messenger must have read Longfellow's poem on Paul Revere, for he kept shouting "Geronimo is coming!" as he galloped into Tombstone. The local mines sounded their alarm whistles. Women and children sought shelter as men grabbed their rifles and hurried to the mayor's office.

After John Clum had resigned as agent of the San Carlos Reservation in July 1876, he had moved to Tucson, bought the *Citizen,* and reinvented himself as a journalist. In 1880 he headed south to the new silver boomtown of Tombstone, founded a newspaper called the *Epitaph,* was soon elected mayor, and hired the Earp brothers to keep the peace.

By now, in 1881, Mayor John Clum and his handpicked lawmen, Wyatt and Virgil Earp, had their hands full with the so-called cowboys in Tombstone, who were led by Newman "Old Man" Clanton and Curly Bill Brocius. Cattle rustling and murder along the Arizona-Mexico border had reached epidemic proportions as Tombstone grew and provided a ready market for stolen beef. The Mexican government had already lodged several protests with the US State Department.

Despite his own problems in Tombstone, Clum had naturally followed the situation at San Carlos closely. He had little respect for the incompetent Tiffany and worried that the massive infusion of new troops into Arizona would stampede the Apaches. He was right, and now, despite his sympathy with all the Apaches save Geronimo, he determined on a course of action. He had no faith in the army, so he would lead the citizens of Tombstone out after Geronimo.

Clum's supply of good saddle horses was limited, so he carefully selected a posse of thirty-five men. It was a pretty tough crew, and included the chief of police Virgil Earp, along with his brothers Wyatt and Morgan, county sheriff Johnny Behan, and a colorful assortment of local hard cases. It took three hours to gather this group and supply them. While they waited, the mayor gave a grand speech.

"Remember, men, no quarter, no prisoners," declared Clum. "I delivered Geronimo to the army once, in irons. They turned him loose. If we get him this time, we will send him back to the army, nailed up in a long, narrow box, with a paper lily on his chest."

A good many of the citizens of the desert metropolis of five thousand souls turned out to cheer on the bold posse as it paraded down Allen Street and headed east toward Antelope Pass. No sooner had they reached the mountains than they were assaulted by a terrific downpour, accompanied by continuous thunder and lightning strikes that were all too close for comfort. Mother Nature appeared to be on the side of the Apaches. They passed a detachment of cavalry camped on the western edge of Sulphur Springs Valley: it was Captain Bernard and his men. Bernard told Clum that they had been on a hot trail, but confessed that it was simply too wet to continue on.

Clum's Tombstone bravados scoffed at this and rode on with soaked clothing, their boots rapidly filling with water. The mud slowed their horses to a tortured walk. Around midnight, they reached a ranch line cabin and decided to camp. They had been in the saddle for twelve hours. After two hours' rest they pushed on to the McLaury ranch, where they met up with the notorious Curly Bill Brocius and two of his cowboys. The Apache threat had driven even these tough gunmen to seek a safe haven. After breakfast the posse continued south, so that by noon they found themselves at the Mexican border.

Geronimo's trail was cold, they had no food, and they had no interest in invading Mexico. Clum gave the order to turn about and there was no voice of dissent. It was almost sundown when the tired citizens of Tombstone again reached Bernard's cavalry camp. The soldiers had not budged. They were happy to share their warm fires and army rations with Clum's posse, who now settled in for the night. The next morning Clum led his bedraggled band back to Tombstone. They had not fired a shot in anger, and the elusive Apaches were well on their way south of the border toward the Sierra Madre.

IT WAS MICKEY FREE who had carried the first news of the Chiricahua breakout to Agent Tiffany. He had continued his work as an army spy and had captured Dandy Jim, the accused killer of Captain Hentig, and another of the mutineers, Mucheco, on September 28, at the San Carlos subagency, where the men had foolishly attempted to draw rations. The following day he had delivered them to Captain Reuben Bernard at the main agency headquarters. Bernard clapped them in irons and sent them off to Camp Thomas for safekeeping.

Delivering up his former scout comrades to the army was rough duty for Mickey. The Chiricahuas already blamed him for all their misfortunes that resulted from his kidnapping, but now many of the White Mountain Apaches began to whisper that he was a traitor. The attempt to add George and Bonito to this prisoner tally led to the Chiricahua breakout the following day on September 30. As a result of the breakout, Mickey was again enlisted in the San Carlos Indian police force.

While public attention was focused on the futile army effort to capture Geronimo and the fugitive Chiricahuas, Mickey Free and his fellow Indian police officers moved to arrest the Apache scouts involved in the Cibecue mutiny. Within the first two weeks of October, they arrested five of the scouts, including Mickey's old comrades Sergeant Deadshot, Skippy, and Ashay, as well as the Dreamer's brother. The men had unwisely remained around San Carlos, perhaps hoping to blend in and avoid detection. The roundup continued as the police broke up several *tiswin* parties. At one of these in mid-October, several of Chief George's men were arrested. When a drunken Apache stabbed one of Mickey's comrades, the one-eyed scout went berserk and had to be restrained.

"Mickey Free wanted to kill the prisoners but was prevented by the Captain of Scouts," noted an eyewitness.

Mickey was then called to the main San Carlos headquarters to meet with Captain Adna Chaffee. The captain again hired Mickey as a special agent to return north and attempt to locate the remaining mutineers. It did not take Mickey long to learn that the ex-scouts were still in the vicinity of Fort Apache. They hid themselves in the mountains but came down to both Pedro's village and Corydon Cooley's ranch for supplies. Chaffee passed this intelligence on to Colonel Willcox. The department commander then ordered Colonel Carr at Fort Apache to send troops to Pedro's camp and Cooley's ranch to arrest or kill the Apache mutineers.

Carr was furious that Mickey Free had come north to the White Mountains as a spy without his knowledge. Carr's petulant response to headquarters that they should not "take for gospel everything Mickey Free, a notorious liar, says" contributed to Willcox's decision to court-martial the insubordinate colonel. Carr was, of course, still seething over Mickey's exaggerated report of his death at Cibecue.

A court-martial also awaited the two mutinous scouts brought in by Mickey Free, as well as two others who had surrendered to Agent Tiffany. The military court, which was convened at Fort Grant in November, sentenced Dandy Jim, Deadshot, and Skippy to death by hanging and sentenced Mucheco to life imprisonment at the military prison on Alcatraz Island in San Francisco Bay. President Chester Arthur approved the sentences and at noon, March 3, 1882, the three scouts were hanged at Fort Grant.

"I have always regretted the fate of Deadshot and Skippy. The former was the sage of the Indian company, the latter our clown and wag," Lieutenant Tom Cruse sadly noted. "Suicide was virtually unknown among the Apaches, but on the day that Deadshot was hanged at Grant, his squaw hanged herself to a tree on the San Carlos Agency."

The executions angered all the San Carlos Apaches and convinced the remaining fugitive scouts never to surrender. Tension on the reservation, already high after the hangings, increased as rumors swirled that Geronimo had sent messengers north from Mexico with word that he would soon return to San Carlos to rescue Loco's people.

AFTER THE BREAKOUT, Juh had led the San Carlos fugitives south toward his old stronghold in the Carcay Mountains near Janos. Along the way they crossed the trail of old Nana. Nana and the Warm Springs people were forewarned by Kaytennae that Juh's people were coming. Nana ordered Gouyen and the other women to prepare a feast, then he led Kaytennae and a small group of warriors to the entrance of their canyon sanctuary.

Juh and his advance guard reached the entrance to the narrow canyon just before dusk. Nana met him and they embraced. Juh told Nana that Geronimo was not far behind him and suggested that they ambush him.

"Geronimo likes to scare the Mexicans," Juh told Nana. "Let's play a joke on him."

The warriors hid in the canyon shadows among the rocks. Geronimo rode ahead of all the others right into the canyon.

"Welcome to my trap!" Nana called out.

"I knew all the time you were here," Geronimo barked. He was not amused, but jolly Juh had a good laugh.

"You did not," Nana replied as he embraced Geronimo. "And you the sly fox of the Apaches!"

Naiche led the others in soon after and there were warm greetings all around. The united bands now numbered nearly 450 people, with more than 100 warriors. After the feast the drummers and singers came forward and a dance circle was formed. Juh, despite his stutter, had a beautiful, deep voice and sang to the camp circle of the exploits of his people during their journey from San Carlos.

Juh now assumed leadership of the combined bands. He had always considered his Nednhi to be Mexican Indians and had considerable experience dealing with the Mexican authorities. He soon visited Janos with Nana to trade stolen American horses and mules for corn and ammunition. Juh also sent a Mexican captive turned Nednhi warrior as emissary to open talks with Colonel Joaquin Terrazas at Casas Grandes. Juh hoped to make peace once again in Chihuahua, and perhaps even secure some rations, while he continued to raid Sonora and Arizona.

Terrazas also had a plan. He hoped to lure the Apache leaders into a parley in town and kill them all.

On November 9, 1881, Juh and Geronimo met with Terrazas just east of Casas Grandes. The colonel invited them into town but they refused to go. Terrazas did provide rations and some cattle to the Apaches and patiently listened to Juh's request for a homeland in the Carcay Mountains. He promised to recommend this to his cousin the governor, but it was clear to Juh and Geronimo that Terrazas could not be trusted.

Juh and his warriors knew there would be much more fighting ahead, so they began to ponder a daring mission to San Carlos to liberate Loco and his people. This would add more than forty warriors to their force while reuniting many families. Nana favored this, of course, because Loco's people were the relatives of his Warm Springs band. And Geronimo was eager for those warrior recruits to help him fight the Mexicans.

Some suggested that Loco had perhaps become too comfortable with the rations of the White Eyes, and that the children at San Carlos would soon forget what it meant to be a Chiricahua Apache. The talking went on for days until finally, in exasperation, Gouyen shamed the warriors into action. "Here we are, hungry, and chased by the army," she declared, "while Loco is sitting on the reservation, fat and comfortable."

Geronimo then stepped forward to announce that he would lead a war party to rescue Loco's people from San Carlos. Who would go with him? Sixty-three warriors stepped forward, including Naiche, Chatto, Chihuahua, Mangas, and Kaytennae. Juh and Nana agreed to stay behind with thirty warriors to protect the families in the stronghold. Nana advised Geronimo to "take Lozen and no other women," for he would need her strong medicine on such a dangerous raid.

⊷⊜⊷

MICKEY FREE, BACK on the San Carlos police force, heard the rumors of Geronimo's return in the middle of February and reported
them to Tiffany. The Indian agent forwarded the news to Willcox,
who transferred two troops of cavalry to the Mexican border and
ordered out scout parties to search for the raiders. Mickey left the
police force and enlisted as a sergeant in a new scout company made
up of White Mountain Apaches along with a few Yavapais. They
went down to Camp Rucker near the Mexican line to keep watch.

Al Sieber was also in the saddle. He led a detachment of Apache
scouts into the Dragoons in late February in search of any sign of a
movement north from Mexico. John Y. F. "Bo" Blake of the Sixth
Cavalry commanded this expedition. A hopeless romantic of mer-
curial temperament, Blake had only recently graduated from West
Point and been assigned to Arizona. A fine officer with a promising
future, he so sympathized with the Apaches that he eventually resigned his commission and set out for Africa as a soldier of fortune.
In time he became famous as the dashing leader of the Irish Brigade
in the Boer War.

Sieber's scouts ranged east toward Stein's Peak on the border
between New Mexico and Arizona and there discovered a fresh
Apache trail coming from Mexico. Sieber sent a galloper to the
nearest telegraph station with the news that the Apaches were
headed toward San Carlos.

On April 19, 1882, Geronimo's raiders cut the telegraph line
near the subagency on the Gila River and, before dawn, descended
on Loco's San Carlos camp. Geronimo and Loco were old enemies.
Loco had blamed Geronimo for the forced removal of the Warm
Springs people to San Carlos. Now his protests were silenced by
Geronimo's rifle pointed at his heart. Geronimo would describe
this as a rescue, but to many of the Warm Springs people, it was
a kidnapping. Some of them later refused to identify themselves as
Chiricahuas.

Albert Sterling was awakened by the commotion in Loco's camp.
With one of his Apache police officers, he hurried to the scene.

They were promptly blown out of their saddles by the Apaches. An Apache warrior then rode through camp holding Sterling's boots.

"Take them all!" shouted Geronimo. "No one is to be left in the camp. Shoot down anyone who refuses to go with us!"

Tom Horn, a young government mule packer, had been living with Pedro's band of Apaches. They were camped just two miles north of Loco's village. The shots that killed Sterling woke Pedro's camp. Horn, along with several of his Coyotero friends, rushed up a nearby hill to see what was going on.

"Just as the sun came up, here they came. Great droves of horses and mules were strung out for about a mile and a half," Horn reported. "A small bunch of perhaps 20 warriors was in front, and behind was the main band of warriors."

Horn rode to Fort Thomas with news of the breakout. It took him about two hours, so it was midmorning before the telegraph lines began to click out the news. Al Sieber was then at the fort, and he recruited young Horn to join his pursuit of the Apache fugitives.

Tom Horn had reached Prescott, Arizona, early in 1881. The twenty-one-year-old had run away from his Missouri farm as a teenager to find work along the Santa Fe Trail. He was smart, tough, and remarkably good-natured, with a gift for storytelling. By the time he reached Prescott, he could speak Spanish fluently and soon picked up some Apache. Pedro's Apaches came to call Horn "Talking Boy." Horn thought it was because he spoke their language, but it was really because they admired his gift of gab.

In Prescott, the tall, lanky boy had fallen in with Sieber's old pals Long Jim Cook and Dan Ming, who had secured him a job with the army as a teamster and then as a "scrub," or apprentice, packer. A quick study, Horn was soon a master mule packer, a vital skill on the frontier. He found himself at Fort Apache soon after the Cibecue debacle as part of the military packtrains sent to reinforce the post. Sieber took an immediate liking to the gregarious youngster.

Sieber realized that lively times lay ahead. He wanted tough, talented young men like Horn whom he could trust and rely upon. He recruited another lad who was about the same age as Horn—

Has-kay-bay-nay-ntayl—Beauford's protégé, whom everyone had always simply called Kid. The boy was naturally delighted to leave his job in the Globe butcher shop for a new life of adventure. Sieber made the lad his personal assistant, much like an orderly in the army.

Horn called Kid "Sieber's pet Indian." Kid and the other scouts, who called Sieber "Sibi," were devoted to this white man who was so remarkably color-blind for his time and place.

On April 19, 1882, Sieber's scouts headed southeast in pursuit of the Apaches. The fugitives, who numbered more than four hundred people, of whom at least one hundred were warriors, had left a bloody trail. Eight miles east of San Carlos, at Dewey Flats, they captured three freight wagons loaded with several hundred gallons of whiskey. This delayed the warriors for a spell. While the warriors were distracted by their drinking spree, Loco sent his oldest wife and twenty-six of his relatives north to Fort Wingate and safety. The warriors drank all night.

This allowed Sieber's scouts to overtake the fugitives the next day, but when they attacked them at dawn, the troops managed only to scatter them. Sieber pursued the Apaches but quickly discovered that they had separated into a dozen small bands and scattered like quail into the Chiricahua Mountains. Others moved south down the San Simon Valley along the border between Arizona and New Mexico.

While Sieber and his men headed southeast after the fugitives, Mickey Free's detachment of scouts was on its way north through the Sulphur Springs Valley. Mickey, who had been promoted to first sergeant, had hoped to block the escape of the Apaches but missed them entirely. On April 24, the scout company reached the town of Willcox, some eighty miles east of Tucson, to refit before they headed back toward the Mexican border, which was another eighty miles to the south.

Sixth Cavalry trooper Anton Mazzanovich was in Willcox recuperating from Bernard's fight in the Dragoons. Mazzanovich, like so many frontier soldiers, was an immigrant. The Austrian had enlisted as a teenager in hopes of serving in the regimental band but

the only instrument he was taught to play was a Springfield carbine. He was excited to meet the famous Mickey Free.

"Mickey Free was a small man, a noted character and a famous
scout in those days. I had heard about him before but had not met
him until then," he recalled. "It appears that his father was an Irishman and his mother a Mexican woman." Mazzanovich "bucked
the tiger" with considerable pluck and won seventy-five dollars at a
Willcox faro table. "I placed $25 on the bar and told the proprietor
to treat every hombre in sight. The bar was quickly surrounded by
a motley crowd, which included cowpunchers, soldiers, Mexicans,
and the notorious Mickey Free. I could not bar him as he was only
an Indian by adoption. Then the bunch gave three cheers and a
cowboy yell, declaring that I was ace high."

On April 25, Mickey's scouts again headed south, this time in
concert with a troop of the Sixth Cavalry under Captain Daniel
Madden, a colorful British immigrant who had won his commission during the Civil War. Within a day they received news of an
Apache raid on Galeyville, a mining camp east of Tombstone that
was a notorious hideout for Curly Bill's rustlers. Initial reports
claimed the Apaches had wiped out the camp, but in reality the
raiders had killed just three men. Mickey's scouts followed their
trail eastward into New Mexico's bootheel. There the Apaches had
united with a much larger group in the Animas Mountains before
they all turned south into Old Mexico. American troops were ex-
plicitly forbidden to cross the international line, and so Madden
ordered his command to turn about and return to Arizona.

Lieutenant Colonel George Forsyth had by this time mobilized
five troops of his Fourth Cavalry along the Southern Pacific Railroad in southwestern New Mexico. He hoped to block the fugitives from crossing the rail line. "Sandy" Forsyth, one of the most
admired soldiers in the army, had served on General Sheridan's
staff during the Civil War and after until 1881, when he had been
rewarded with the Fourth Cavalry command. His 1868 stand at
Beecher's Island with fifty scouts against hundreds of Cheyennes
was legendary. He now commanded from a special train that
moved along the rail line.

Forsyth quickly sent out several patrols. One of them ran head-long into Geronimo northwest of Stein's Peak at a place where a great many had perished at the hands of the Apaches in the past: Doubtful Canyon. Four scouts were killed in the first volley as the rest of the little command hunkered down to await reinforcements. Forsyth personally led four troops of the Fourth in a wild ride to rescue the patrol. This raised a dust cloud that could be seen for miles.

Geronimo withdrew deeper into the convoluted labyrinth of rocky canyons and prepared another ambush at a place called Horseshoe Canyon. At the far end of the canyon was a muddy pool that provided the only water for miles. The thirsty troopers made right for the water, and as they dismounted to drink, the Apaches opened fire.

Forsyth's men, with two dead and another eight wounded, quickly regrouped and moved into the rocks against the enemy. The fighting lasted all afternoon, until the Apaches withdrew just before sunset. Geronimo had fought another successful rearguard action to screen the escape of the main body of Apache families. Forsyth, despite his four-to-one advantage in numbers, withdrew to the Gila River for water and to tend the wounded. By the time he returned to Horseshoe Canyon, the Apaches had vanished.

Meanwhile, Sieber's scouts had joined with two troops of the Sixth Cavalry under the command of Captains T. C. Tupper and William Rafferty at Galeyville in response to the April 24 Apache raid there. They had arrived ahead of Madden's detachment and had followed the raiders' trail down the San Simon Valley and then east to New Mexico. It was clear that the Apaches were headed for Mexico. Geronimo's raiders had left fifty civilians and seven soldiers dead in their wake, and had made off with a large herd of stolen horses, sheep, and cattle. By April 26, a week after the great escape from San Carlos, most of the Apaches had reunited in Mexico.

Sieber's scouts tracked the Galeyville raiders to the Animas Mountains and then south to the international line. It was obvi-ous to them that the raiders had joined with a much larger group.

Captain Tupper, with but 107 troopers and scouts in his command, conferred with Sieber and Rafferty as to their next course of action. His orders were clear that he was not to cross into Mexico. The Apaches knew that as well. Sieber felt confident that the Indians would let down their guard once they had arrived in Mexico. He knew a spring less than twenty miles across the line on the Janos Plain at Sierra Enmedio, or Middle Mountain, where the Apaches often camped.

Tupper sent Sieber and Horn, along with two of the Apache scouts, into Mexico to locate the Apaches. He would follow at a respectable distance. Under cover of darkness, at three in the morning on April 27, the captain led the rest of his little command across the border.

Sieber, along with Kid and Horn, easily located the Apache camp at Sierra Enmedio. The Apaches had built huge fires and were "making medicine," as Sieber put it. He crawled up among the rocks near the camp and, aided by the full moon, counted 115 warriors. The Apaches were camped in a flat, open basin near the spring. To the east a high ridge ran along the length of one side of the basin while two high hills rose above the Janos Plain on the other. The Apaches were in the second day of a four-day victory celebration. Geronimo and Loco felt so secure, they had not even put out sentries.

Sieber returned to Tupper's command to make certain that the troopers dismounted and did not smoke. He led them toward the camp from the west. The Indian scouts silently encircled the camp and placed themselves on the ridge between the Apache camp and the Sierra Enmedio to the east. Everyone had to be in place before dawn.

As the scouts moved into position above the sleeping camp, three Apache women suddenly came upon them. One of the scouts, a brother of the San Carlos policeman killed with Al Sterling, rose and shot one of the women. This revenge killing alerted the camp and caused all the scouts to open fire. In the dawn light it was impossible to pick targets, so the men fired at anything or anyone that moved. The cavalry was not yet in position when the scouts opened fire, but Tupper and Rafferty quickly wheeled them into line. Sieber had led the soldiers onto the plain opposite the ridge occupied by the scouts, and they now all heard the gunfire and saw the spits of flame from the scouts' rifles on the distant ridge.

Rafferty's fifty troopers galloped forward as one. The Apaches had quickly retreated to a rocky hill in the middle of the plain and from there began to fire into the advancing horsemen. In the dim light, most of their shots went high as the troopers rode past the rocks. One soldier was killed and two others wounded. Bo Blake led a detachment of twenty troopers right across the Apache line. Sieber expected him to be killed at any moment, but instead his men managed to sweep up the Apache pony herd and drove it out onto the Janos Plain.

Loco called out from the rocks for the Apache scouts to cease killing their own people. As he stepped forward from the rock outcropping, several of the scouts cursed him and unleashed a volley. The old chief fell with a leg wound.

Half a dozen warriors, led by Chatto, now flanked the scouts on the ridge and opened fire from the rear. This forced them onto the plain, where they were soon joined by the soldiers. As the Apaches concentrated their fire on the ridge, Loco, who was wounded and had already lost a son in the fight, gathered his people together and led them away from the rocky hill and to the nearby mountains. Geronimo and his warriors covered their escape.

Tupper held the field, and this time the troops really had scored a victory over the Apaches. A dozen warriors and five women were dead, and almost all the Apache camp property had been taken. Blake's capture of seventy-five horses and the killing of another fifteen ponies was a devastating loss to the Apaches. At this point, though, Tupper's command, with almost all their ammunition expended, had little choice but to withdraw. They reached their former campsite, nine miles to the north, at about eight that night, and began to cook the first meal they had eaten in twenty hours.

Amid great noise and a billowing dust cloud, Forsyth's column, now rested from their fight at Horseshoe Canyon, suddenly appeared. Forsyth was anxious to push on after the Indians, but

Tupper's men needed food and rest, and the colonel did not wish to go on without them. So the colonel, with his 450 men, also made camp for the night.

FAR TO THE southwest in his Carcay Mountain stronghold, Juh was worried. Two hundred fresh Mexican troops under Colonel Lorenzo Garcia were reported by his scouts to be at Janos. Colonel Garcia, who had both Mexican regulars and Sonoran militia in his force, was determined to clean out the Apaches. Juh and Nana decided to move their people back into the Sierra Madre for safety. At the same time, Juh sent several warriors north to find Geronimo and warn him of the Mexican troops. Garcia intercepted this group, killed most of them, and took two men prisoner. He tortured these men until they told him where they had planned to meet Geronimo. Then he executed them.

Colonel Garcia then prepared a careful ambush at Alisos Creek to the west of Janos, out on the flats a mile or so from the foothills of the Sierra Madre. The colonel hid his men along a shallow ravine on the south side of the creek. The soldiers waited patiently, and early in the morning of April 29, they were rewarded by the appearance of a long column of Apaches on the grassy plain that led to the creek.

Geronimo, still worried about the Americans, kept most of the warriors with him as a rear guard. The people traveled slowly, for they had few ponies and many wounded. They were strung out for almost a mile. In the lead rode an advance guard of fifteen warriors led by Naiche. Garcia kept his men in check, waiting for the main body of Apaches to reach the creek. Then he gave the order to open fire.

"Almost immediately Mexicans were right among us all, shooting down women and children right and left," remembered a young warrior. "People were falling and bleeding, and dying, on all sides of us. Whole families were slaughtered on the spot." The strong voice of Geronimo was heard above the chaos.

Geronimo's warriors, perhaps thirty in number, took up position in an arroyo and began to take a deadly toll on the Mexicans. Chihuahua was there, as was Geronimo's cousin Fun, and old Loco. Lozen was with them as well. A bag of cartridges had been dropped several yards from the arroyo and she suddenly rushed out, retrieved it, and returned amid a hail of gunfire. As other women hurriedly dug rifle pits, Lozen disbursed the cartridges to the warriors, reloaded her own weapon, and turned to fire at the Mexicans.

Garcia, determined to wipe out the warriors in the arroyo, ordered a captain to charge their position. Geronimo heard the Mexicans shouting orders and told his men to hold their fire until the Mexicans were close and then to kill the officers first. He heard the Mexican captain call out: "In those ditches is the red devil Geronimo and his hated band. This must be his last day!"

As the Mexicans charged, Geronimo rose from the arroyo and took careful aim at their captain and shot him dead. A war cry arose from the Apaches as they fired into the advancing Mexicans. Lozen was in the center of the battle, sending shot after shot into the now-faltering foe. The soldiers pulled back to the foothills, leaving half their number dead or wounded on the field.

Garcia gathered in his wounded and contemplated his next move. Late in the day he decided to burn the Apaches out by setting fire to the grass. Geronimo welcomed the smoke as a screen to cover their escape from the arroyo. He now proposed that they strangle the handful of infants with them so that their crying would not give them away as they made their escape. If the women did not agree to this, he said, he would leave them all.

Fun could not believe what Geronimo had just said and asked him to repeat himself. Three times before in battle, Geronimo had abandoned women and children to their fate. It was more important to him to save the fighting men. But Fun rejected such talk and threatened to shoot Geronimo if he dared to say such a thing again. Geronimo turned his back, climbed out of the arroyo, and vanished into the choking smoke.

Lozen and Fun helped the women and children to scramble out of their hiding places and, under cover of the smoke screen, they hurried toward the nearby hills. When the Mexican soldiers again charged the arroyo, they found it empty save for the dead.

By nightfall many of the families had reunited in the hills, where they sang songs of grief over those who had been lost. Seventy-eight Chiricahuas, almost all from Loco's band, had been killed. Only a dozen of the dead were warriors. Garcia had also captured thirty-three women, among them Loco's daughter. Many of the Chihenne survivors blamed Geronimo for this catastrophe. He was the one who had forced Loco's people at gunpoint to abandon the safety of San Carlos and then had led them into this ghastly massacre. "I am without friends," moaned Geronimo years later, "for my people have turned from me."

Colonel Forsyth's column of nearly six hundred men closely followed the trail of the Apache fugitives on April 30. They paused briefly at Tupper's battlefield, where they buried a fallen trooper and counted the Apache dead, and then pushed on. In the distance the soldiers could see smoke on the horizon. Forsyth made for the smoke and went into camp after dark on Alisos Creek. "I felt confident that we would overtake the hostiles the next day," Forsyth wrote, "and so did all my officers."

The next morning, however, the Americans were awakened by the sound of a Mexican bugle call. Colonel Garcia and an orderly now rode forth to meet with Forsyth. The colonel inquired if the Americans were aware that they were on Mexican soil. Forsyth, with Tom Horn as translator, replied that his troops were in pursuit of hostile Apaches. Garcia replied that he had already dealt with the Apaches and invited Forsyth to tour the battlefield.

The Americans were horrified by what they saw. "I counted twenty-one dead bodies—about half of them squaws, strewn along the creek bottom," noted Captain Rafferty. "Also, many dead Mexicans in full uniform unburied." Rafferty and Blake both reported "they never saw such shambles and ghastly scenes in their lives."

"The old bucks stood and fought for their families and there they died with them," said Sieber matter-of-factly. "Young bucks look out for themselves—old bucks fight for their families."

Sieber, Horn, and several officers joined a Mexican lieutenant for a walk over part of the expansive battlefield. "He showed us a washout pocket seven feet deep, filled with dead Apaches," noted a lieutenant, "and climbing down, fired his revolver into the breast of one still breathing."

Even more pitiful to the Americans were the pleas from the Apache prisoners. The women begged Kid and the other Apache scouts to ransom them from the Mexicans. Forsyth asked for the prisoners, claiming that they were American Indians, but Garcia would not release them. The Americans were in an untenable position and could not press the issue. Forsyth provided rations and medical assistance to Garcia's command and then, after an exchange of diplomatic notes, withdrew his command from Mexico.

Colonel Garcia, who had lost three officers and twenty enlisted men, with another sixteen wounded, gathered his prisoners and marched them east to Janos. Several months after the fight, Garcia was presented with a fine sword, inlaid with silver and gold, in recognition of his triumph. He also received the bounty for seventy-eight Apache scalps. The captured Apache children were given to the mayor and leading citizens of Bavispe. The women were transported to Guaymas, on the coast, to be sold as slaves. For the young women, it meant a life of prostitution or, at best, life as a mistress to a wealthy Mexican. For Colonel Garcia it meant a tidy profit of at least twenty thousand dollars.

Forsyth led his column back to American soil. He sent the Sixth Cavalry and Apache scouts back to Arizona while he returned to New Mexico to write his report. Sieber, at Fort McDowell, grumbled about Forsyth's mismanagement of the campaign. He felt that the majority of Loco's people had been killed, except for his young warriors, who were the real target of Geronimo's raid in the first place. "The young bucks will unite with Juh and there will be formed one of the strongest bands of Indians that has existed for years in this part of the country," he warned the editor of the *Prescott Weekly Courier*. "The time will come when we will have them to fight again."

Sieber's mood brightened when he heard the heartening news

that Colonel Willcox had been sacked. Sherman and Sheridan had finally had enough of his bungling. The debacle on the Cibecue and Geronimo's breakout were but two of many reasons that the high command had wearied of Willcox. The colonel's persecution of Carr, who was a particular favorite with Sheridan because of his fine combat record, was the final nail in Willcox's coffin. As of September 4, 1882, General George Crook was to take command. Nantan Lupan was once again on the hunt.

22

HELL'S FORTY ACRES

I HAVE KILLED MANY MEXICANS," GERONIMO DECLARED. "I do not know how many, for frequently I did not count them. Some of them were not worth counting."

After the slaughter on Alisos Creek, Geronimo was more determined than ever to seek vengeance on the hated Mexicans. But Loco did not want revenge. He cut his hair, as was the Apache custom when in mourning, but, unlike tribal practice, he never allowed it to grow long again. His search for peace had led his people into a ghastly massacre. He remained in mourning all the rest of his days. He was but a dead man walking when he reunited with Geronimo in the mountain foothills some five miles from Alisos Creek.

It took them nearly two weeks to reach Juh's mountain stronghold southwest of Casas Grandes. Several more of Loco's people perished during the trek. Juh's camp now held nearly six hundred Chiricahuas. The Apaches would have to conduct many raids to support so many people. Juh had a hundred warriors, and late in 1882, Geronimo led thirty of them on a grand raid into Sonora for plunder and revenge. Geronimo's new apprentice, Betzinez, joined him along with eighty others, which included several families. As Geronimo departed with his people, Juh led the rest of the Apaches even deeper into the Sierra Madre in search of a stronger sanctuary.

"They were like true creatures of the wild," declared Betzinez of Juh and Geronimo, "always sensing or anticipating danger."

Geronimo led his people south to the Sonoran town of Ures before he turned back north toward the Arizona border. They swooped down on freight and packtrains, isolated ranches, and solitary travelers. In early October 1882, Geronimo's band rejoined Juh in his new stronghold in a great canyon in the mountains north of the Aros River in Sonora. They returned weighted down with new guns, replenished ammunition, and a huge herd of stolen stock. They had left at least fifty Mexicans and a handful of Americans dead in their wake.

Geronimo was still not satisfied. He knew that Juan Mata Ortiz, who had been second-in-command at Tres Castillos, had a ranch near Galeana. He wanted that old man's head. In November 1882, Geronimo's band hit the Ortiz ranch, killed a vaquero, and made off with considerable stock. The wily Indian fighter was quickly on their trail with twenty-two men. When they reached the ominous Chocolate Canyon to the northwest of Galeana, Mata Ortiz offered his men a chance to withdraw, but they all agreed to follow him. The warriors of Geronimo, Nana, and Juh waited patiently as the Mexicans advanced deeper into the canyon before they sprang their trap. Mata Ortiz led what was left of his command to a little hill not far from the canyon where they dug in and made a stand.

It was over quickly. Only one man escaped: Geronimo had shouted to his warriors to let him go to tell the tale. Two warriors died in the ambush, but the price was worth it for Nana. These were some of the very Mexicans who had killed Victorio. The Apaches took their revenge on the last Mexican standing. It was old Mata Ortiz. They slowly roasted him alive.

The Chiricahuas divided once again, with Juh and some of the people returning to the stronghold while Geronimo and Chihuahua led another raid deep into Sonora. Loco and many of the Chihennes soon split from Juh to camp in the hills southeast of Casas Grandes.

Colonel Terrazas sent his soldiers after Juh's band. Before dawn on January 24, 1883, Mexican cavalry swept over Juh's camp some twenty miles west of the town of Guaynopa, surprising them and slaughtering men, women, and children. Among the dead was Ishton, Geronimo's beautiful cousin, who was Juh's favorite wife. Juh and Kaytennae, with a handful of warriors, led a counterattack back to the village in an attempt to rescue Apache prisoners;

but the Mexicans, numbering more than two hundred, were too strong, and the Apaches fled. Juh's crippled band made their way deeper into the Sierra Madre.

"It took a long time for my father to recover from that attack," remembered Daklugie. "In fact, I am not sure that he ever did."

Juh had lost his wife, his baby, and a son-in-law, and his daughter was crippled. Fourteen people were killed and thirty-three captured, among them two wives and two children of Geronimo, as well as the wife and two children of Chatto. There was considerable talk in the Apache camp that Juh had been drunk that night and had failed to properly set guards around the camp. Many of the people now departed Juh's camp and went north to join Geronimo.

Juh was now deserted by nearly all the people. Even his warmest friend, Geronimo, turned his back. He blamed him for the death of his beloved cousin and the capture of his wives and children. "Geronimo was never really a chief but he became one because of all the trouble," noted a Chokonen warrior.

Juh attempted to drown his sorrow in strong drink. After an epic bender in November 1883, he rode his pony off an embankment near Casas Grandes. He was found facedown in the Rio Aros by his son Daklugie. The old man was too heavy for the boy to pull out of the water. He died there, half-submerged, cradled in Daklugie's arms.

MICKEY FREE CONTINUED as a scout with the army until the end of September 1882. He was then rehired as a lieutenant of police at San Carlos at a salary of twenty dollars a month. He was anxious to return to San Carlos to be able to spend more time with Ethlay and their six-year-old son. At thirty-five years of age, he remained slim and youthful in appearance and cut quite a figure on the reservation.

Donald McIntosh, the son of Crook's scout Archie, remembered Mickey vividly from this time. "I was only fifteen years old then and I had never seen anything quite like Mickey Free," he recalled. "He had big cavalry boots on, the kind that came up high above the knee . . . and a big pistol belt around his waist and in it he carried two big dragoon pistols. He presented a fine figure in the prime of his life."

Tom Horn first encountered Mickey at San Carlos. "He now spoke both Mexican and Apache like a professor and was the wildest dare-devil in the world at this time," Horn recalled of the initial meeting. "He had long, fiery red hair and one blue eye, the other having been hooked out by a wounded deer when he was twelve years old. He had a small, red mustache, and a mug that looked like the original map of Ireland."

A unique bureaucratic problem arose when the new San Carlos Indian agent, Philip Wilcox, submitted his roster of policemen to the Indian Bureau in Washington. He truthfully listed the ethnic heritage of Mickey Free as "Irish and Mexican." This caused a brief dustup as the commissioner of Indian affairs reminded the fresh agent that such employees must be "an Indian and a member of the tribe, as required by the rules governing the U.S. Indian Police service."

"I have the honor to inform you that Mickey Free is of Irish and Mexican parentage, was born in Mexico, stolen by Indians when a child, adopted as a member of the tribe, a position he now holds in full fellowship," Wilcox replied. The Indian Bureau, for once, displayed some common sense and dropped the matter.

Affairs at San Carlos had remained lively after Loco's breakout. On July 6, 1882, Natiosh—one of the Cibecue ringleaders—had led sixty warriors on a raid against San Carlos. John Colvig, now called "Cibecue Charley" because of his service as a dispatch rider for Carr from Fort Apache, had replaced the slain Albert Sterling as chief of the San Carlos police. But Colvig was to meet the same fate as his predecessor when Natiosh's raiders shot him down along with three Indian policemen. Natiosh recruited a dozen warriors from Sanchez's band and hit the mining camp at McMillenville, then swept north into the Tonto Basin, loaded down with plunder and stolen stock.

Columns were soon in the field from several posts. Captain Adna Chaffee and I Troop of the Sixth Cavalry were out first from

McDowell, with Sieber, Horn, Kid, and eight Tonto scouts alongside him. They soon joined up with another detachment of twenty-six scouts under Lieutenant George Morgan from Whipple. Sieber took command of all the scouts. The combined command came upon a burned-out ranch house on the headwaters of Tonto Creek and discovered two mutilated bodies. After a hurried burial, the column headed north on the trail of the Apaches. The still-burning embers of the ranch cabin told Sieber that the raiders were not far ahead.

Major Andrew "Beans" Evans, an irascible old Third Cavalry Indian fighter, had replaced Carr in command of Fort Apache. Evans led two troops of his Third and two troops of the Sixth north on July 14. He and Lieutenant Tom Cruse, who had joined their group, discovered Chaffee's command north of the Salt River two days later.

Major Evans and Lieutenant Cruse met with Captain Chaffee and Sieber in a late-night war council. Evans told Chaffee that his White Mountain scouts had told him that Natiosh's band had too much of a lead to be overtaken. Sieber knew instantly that the scouts were protecting their kinsmen.

"I'm sure that the hostiles are just a little way ahead," Chaffee informed Evans. "Sieber thinks they expect close pursuit, and his idea is that they'll stop at General Springs to fight."

Evans agreed to let Chaffee and Sieber go ahead with I Troop and the scouts while he followed at a distance with the rest of the command. Sieber led Chaffee's "white horse" troop out of their camp at six thirty the next morning. Kid and the other scouts were dispatched to the right and left of the column. The country was so rugged that one wag commented that it "look[ed] as though during the Creation, it had been God's workshop, and the scraps had never been swept."

The Apaches made for General Springs exactly as Sieber had predicted. Sieber and Kid led several scouts along the rimrock above the floor of Chevelon Fork Canyon. They spied Natiosh's warriors hidden in the thick timber on the opposite rim of the canyon. Despite the heavy forest, the ground was parklike and free of underbrush, so concealment proved difficult.

Sieber warned Chaffee not to go into the canyon, so the captain deployed his men along the rim and a brisk firefight began on both sides of the canyon. Evans galloped up with the remaining three troops of cavalry and hurriedly conferred with Chaffee. "You found the Indians and they belong to you," he graciously told the captain.

Chaffee thanked the major and promptly ordered E Troop under Lieutenant Cruse and his own I Troop under Lieutenant Frank West to follow Sieber and his scouts to the right. They were to flank the Apaches and block their retreat to the north. Morgan's scouts, along with eighteen cavalry troopers, were to attempt the same flanking maneuver on the left side of the deep canyon. The rest of the troopers provided covering fire across the canyon from their position on the rimrock.

"Chaffee, in a fight, can beat any man swearing I ever heard," marveled the packer Tom Horn. "He swears by ear, and by note in a common way, and by everything else in a general way. He would swear when his men would miss a good shot, and he would swear when they made a good shot."

Sieber, with Kid, Horn, and a handful of scouts, made his way down to the floor of the canyon and then back up its steep walls north of the position of Natiosh's warriors. West and Cruse followed the scouts with their Sixth Cavalry troopers. The steep walls of the canyon made the late-afternoon shadows even darker, so the movement was not detected by the Apaches. Sieber's men emerged out of the canyon right behind the Apache pony herd. They quickly killed the guards and corralled the horses.

One of the Apache scouts now recognized his father and brother among Natiosh's band. He threw down his gun and ran toward them. Sieber called out to him to halt and then calmly took aim and shot him in the back of the head.

Morgan's flanking movement was successful, and as the Indians retreated to their ponies, they ran right into Sieber's force. The Apaches, surrounded and without their horses, made a brief but hopeless final stand. Lieutenant Morgan was terribly wounded in the last minutes of the battle, although Sieber promptly killed the Apache who had shot the young officer. As the Apaches broke and ran, Sieber took careful aim and dropped three in a row. Sixteen Apaches were found dead on the field, among them two of the scouts who had mutinied at Cibecue, as well as Natiosh. Two soldiers were killed and nine wounded. The Apache scouts lost one man—the one killed by Sieber.

A terrific hailstorm suddenly swept the rimrock. It added a punctuation point to the end of the battle. "It was over in twenty minutes, and the fight was over also," declared Horn of the storm. "All of us were so cold and wet, we could neither see nor shoot, and there was a regular torrent rushing in the bottom of the canyon." Lieutenant West noted that "Chaffee got so cold and wet, he had to stop swearing."

The remnants of Natiosh's band escaped during the storm. Most of the troops returned to their posts, although Major Evans, with Sieber and his scouts, continued to search for the Apache fugitives. Upon reaching Corydon Cooley's ranch, they learned that the Apaches had reported to him that over twenty Apaches had been killed and that the remainder had fled back to the reservation. The Battle of Big Dry Wash, as Major Evans officially named the fight, would prove to be the last major engagement between the army and the Apaches in Arizona.

THE BATTLE ALSO marked the end of Colonel Orlando Willcox's command in Arizona. The colonel thus departed on a high note, quite in contrast to his otherwise dismal performance as department commander. Despite his removal the colonel would be promoted four years later and allowed to retire as a brigadier general. Although the transfer of command from Willcox to George Crook was made in July, the general did not actually reach Prescott until September 4, 1882.

Crook, accompanied by Bourke and Sieber, was soon astride a trusty mule he called Apache and on his way to Fort Apache. There he met in council with Pedro, Alchesay, Cut-Mouth Moses, and some other White Mountain leaders. Crook called in Corydon Cooley and Gracias Severiano to interpret.

Bourke was struck by the sight of Old Pedro, whose hearing had failed him, using an ear trumpet at the council. "This use of an ear-trumpet by a so-called savage Apache struck me as very ludicrous," he commented. "The world does move."

Pedro had much to say. "When you were here, whenever you said a thing we knew it was true," he told Crook, "but we can't understand why you went away. Why did you leave us? Everything was all right while you were here."

The Apaches gave a litany of abuses, from the casual arrogance of the army officers to the unbridled corruption of the Indian agents. Every time they put in a crop of corn or saw their cattle herds increase, the Indian agents or the soldiers destroyed them. It was as if the White Eyes were determined to keep the Apaches forever dependent—which was exactly the truth.

"Our corn comes up finely, it looks well and grows fast for a time, but when it is knee-high it turns yellow and dies, and that's the way with the Agents," declared a White Mountain chief. "They do first rate when they first come, but they soon change and instead of helping us, they help themselves."

Lieutenant Bourke was infuriated. All the good work of Crook's previous command had been undone by the ignorance of army officers and the venality of Indian agents. He saw a grand conspiracy on the part of the government contractors and the local politicians to defraud both the Indians and the government. They were determined to keep the Apaches as wards of the state so that they could continue to profit by supplying both the reservation and the soldiers sent to guard it. War was good for business.

"The Tucson ring was determined that no Apache should be put to the embarrassment of working for his own living; once let the Apaches become self-supporting, and what would become of the boys," Bourke thundered. "Therefore, they must all be herded down on the malaria-reeking flats of the San Carlos, where the water is salt and the air poison, and one breathes a mixture of sand-blizzards and more flies than were supposed to be under the care of the great fly-god Beelzebub."

San Carlos was to be the next stop on Crook's tour, but before he departed Fort Apache, he called in every officer for an interview. Lieutenant Cruse and his comrades were shaking in their polished boots as they faced their new commander. They knew that he had been talking with the Apaches about the recent troubles.

"When one by one we were ushered into this tent, to face his statue-still face and utter silence, while Captain Bourke cross-examined like a prosecuting attorney, our uneasiness increased," recalled Cruse years later. "He was more Indian than the Indians," he said of Crook.

Cruse expected a court of inquiry, but he soon learned that Crook was only interested in getting at the truth of what had happened at Cibecue and at San Carlos. His goal was to recognize the legitimate grievances of the Indians and to return all the Apaches to their reservation.

On October 5, Crook issued a general order to make the new order of things clear to his soldiers: "Officers and soldiers serving in this department are reminded that one of the fundamental principles of the military character is justice to all—Indians as well as white men—and that a disregard of this principle is likely to bring about hostilities." He made it perfectly clear that troops were never to "become the instruments of oppression."

At San Carlos, Crook met with Indian leaders and again was regaled with tales of abuse. Fortunately, Agent Tiffany was gone and the new man, Philip P. Wilcox, a Colorado political hack, was anxious to cooperate with the general and spend as little time at San Carlos as possible. He quickly agreed to Crook's request that the White Mountain and Cibecue Apaches be allowed to return to their traditional villages around Fort Apache. A permanent garrison was to be established at San Carlos and Captain Emmet Crawford, Third Cavalry, and Lieutenant Charles Gatewood, Sixth Cavalry, were to take command of both Apache scouts and Indian police at San Carlos and Fort Apache. The number of Apache scouts was to be doubled to 250 men. Al Sieber was appointed chief-of-scouts, with Archie McIntosh and Sam Bowman as his assistants.

A test of the San Carlos stock scales that were used to weigh beef issued to the Indians uncovered that they were indeed rigged, so that each week Tiffany had paid the contractor for 1,500 pounds more beef than was actually delivered. Crook also learned that it was common practice to keep the cattle from water for several days before they were brought to San Carlos and then to water them in the Gila River just before they were weighed.

"In that hot, dry climate, they came on the scales looking like miniature Zeppelins," declared Lieutenant Britton Davis. "The Government was paying a pretty stiff price for half a barrel of Gila River water delivered with each beef. There was not enough fat on the animals to fry a jackrabbit."

Crook promptly fired the contractor and gave the beef contract to Henry Hooker, a local cattleman of impeccable integrity. He also wrote the Arizona federal district attorney to encourage him to indict Tiffany and the other "villains who fatten on the supplies intended for the use of Indians willing to lead peaceful and orderly lives."

Crook knew that the new agent would be attacked by the "Tucson ring." "These men are vampires who gorge themselves on the blood of their fellow creatures and still hang about the San Carlos Agency," he complained to the secretary of the interior.

Captain Bourke was pleased to reacquaint himself with many old friends at San Carlos, and most especially Mickey Free. "Mickey is today the most curious and interesting combination of good humor and sullenness, generosity, craft, and bloodthirsty cruelty to be found in America," Bourke noted in his diary. He was fascinated by the way Free projected cynicism about the Apache belief system and yet accepted the role of the shaman, or medicine man, and carefully followed warrior ritual when serving as a scout. Mickey even gave Bourke a small buckskin bag filled with *hoddentin,* the sacred pollen, to protect him.

Mickey lamented that the changing times had diminished the power of the medicine men. "The medicine men don't know so much now as they did when I was a boy, then truly they knew all things," he told the captain. A further sign to Bourke of Mickey's Apache acculturation was that the scout had taken a Tonto woman as a second wife. She had died after bearing Mickey another son, and her family, as was Apache custom, had taken in the baby. In this enigmatic man, so in limbo between two cultures, Bourke found an important informant for his ethnological work.

Bourke saw a different side of Mickey when the scout brought his young son to meet the captain. Bourke could not help but be moved by the pride the father displayed over the seven-year-old boy. He was not an Irishman, or a Mexican, or an Apache—not a warrior, a soldier, or a scout—he was simply a proud papa. Mickey Free had an entirely human side after all.

After having arrived back in San Carlos, Crook had decided to set up a secret service at the reservation to keep him informed on who was coming and going and who might be trusted. This was dangerous work. Mickey Free was to be the central agent in this spy operation, and the rest of the spy company consisted of seven trustworthy Apaches, two of whom were women. Two of the spies reported to Lieutenant Gatewood at Fort Apache, and the rest to Lieutenant Britton Davis forty miles to the south at San Carlos.

The Apaches called Davis "Fat Boy" because of his stocky build. The young lieutenant, fresh from West Point, was a particularly perceptive young officer. Crook found Davis, the son of the controversial Reconstruction governor of Texas, promising, so he assigned Davis the command of Apache scout companies B and C at San Carlos as well as giving him the position of assistant quartermaster. The quartermaster job allowed him greater flexibility in whom he hired and how he paid them.

Davis's introduction to San Carlos, which he dubbed "Hell's Forty Acres," was something of a rude awakening. He arrived alongside Captain Crawford of the Third, who was in overall command, and Lieutenant Gatewood of the Sixth, who was to be assigned to Fort Apache in a similar position as Davis held at San Carlos. They slept out in the open air on the ground their first night at San Carlos, and as Davis wrapped his blankets up the next morning, a ten-inch centipede fell out. He got no sympathy from Crawford, who claimed to have brushed a rattlesnake out of his bedding. As they were comparing notes, Gatewood walked up with a good-size tarantula that he had bedded down with. "All we lacked were a vinegarroon and a Gila monster to make our reptilian collection complete," Davis noted.

Mickey Free soon introduced the young officer to the pack rat as a delicacy. Davis watched in amazement as the scouts flushed a nest of rats, impaled them, and then dropped them without any preparation into a camp kettle full of boiling water. The boiled rats were then lifted out and stripped of hide and hair and gutted in one swift operation. Mickey brought Davis the nicely skinned hind legs of an especially juicy rat. The scouts all watched intently as Davis devoured this choice tidbit. He had passed a test and, in fact, confessed that he "found the morsel quite good, much like very tender chicken or frog legs."

Mickey was enlisted as first sergeant of scouts, although he actually served as both interpreter and liaison with the spies. Mickey's command of the Apache language was superb, but his English was limited and his Spanish quite tortured. An acquaintance pointed out that Mickey's Spanish "did not include any use of tenses, so that it was extremely difficult to tell whether he meant the present, future, or past."

Davis, who spoke Spanish fluently, worked closely with Mickey and came to utterly rely on him. "Mickey Free, five feet five, slim but muscular," Davis later wrote, "had lost the sight of one eye which gave him a sinister appearance. Captured by the Apache when a small child, his life had been spent among them and he had become to all intents and purposes an Apache; was married to an Apache, dressed as an Apache, and lived as the scouts lived."

Davis recognized that Mickey was distrusted by many of the Apaches, but he found the one-eyed scout to be indispensable. "The Indians suspect him of coloring things to suit the whites; Sieber's opinion of him could not be printed in polite words," Davis admitted. But he added: "He may have fooled me on occasion, but if he did, it was done so skillfully that I never found it out."

Among Mickey's spies was old Toga-de-chuz, the father of Kid. Mickey and Kid became friends during this time of change at San Carlos. Kid had performed with distinction during the Big Dry

Wash campaign and, despite his young age, had been promoted to scout sergeant. He began to court Nahthledeztelth, the teenage daughter of Chief Eskiminzin, the very same baby girl that the old chief had carried out of the Camp Grant massacre so many years before. Eskiminzin had established a little Apache settlement on the San Pedro south of the reservation where he had taken up farming.

Lieutenant Davis visited the settlement with his scouts and was deeply impressed. "They had adobe houses, fields under barbed wire fences, modern (for those days) farming implements, good teams, and cows," he noted with pleasure. These Apaches had adapted to the mode of life in Arizona, so that Davis felt their little community indistinguishable from any other Hispanic village in the territory. Davis dined with Eskiminzin, who was dressed in a store-bought suit and sporting a watch and chain in the vest. The chief's wife and lovely daughter, dressed in bright calicos, served the evening meal. "A very well-cooked and appetizing one as I remember it," wrote Davis.

To Davis the life of Eskiminzin seemed a testament to the hopes and aspirations of all the Apaches. For Kid it held a similar attraction, for he had now firmly cast his lot with the White Eyes and their way of life. His marriage to Eskiminzin's daughter would cement that commitment all the more.

"When first go San Pedro, white man pass by. Look back over shoulder; say 'There go ol' Skimmy,'" Eskiminzin said to Davis through Mickey. "Now white man pass by, raise hat, say 'Good Morning Mr. Skimmotzin.'" In Tucson, Eskiminzin did business with several stores and carried a line of credit worth several thousand dollars. Here, to Davis, was the living embodiment of all the humanitarian goals for the Indians and a dramatic realization of the dream of Apache assimilation into the white man's world.

23

SIERRA MADRE

ESKIMINZIN AND HIS ARAVAIPA FOLLOWERS HELD
out the promise of a bright future for the Apache people,
if only the White Eyes would accept them and work with
them. But to most of the residents of Arizona and New Mexico an
Apache was an Apache. The hopeful future that Eskiminzin represented for the Western Apaches was constantly in jeopardy because
of the actions of Geronimo and his Chiricahua followers.

"They are an incorrigible lot," General Crook said of the Chiricahuas to Secretary of the Interior Henry Teller. "Since it is believed they have killed not less than 1,000 persons in this country
and in Mexico, they are constantly trying to stir up mischief among
the Agency Indians, and so long as they can run back and forth
across the border, this Territory and New Mexico must look out
for trouble."

Crook, determined to undertake offensive operations to find and
attack the Chiricahuas, was blocked by steadfast Mexican opposition to any more cross-border incursion by US troops. A diplomatic
agreement had been reached that allowed "hot pursuit" of raiders
across the international line, and Crook now intended to interpret
it as liberally as possible.

Since the diplomats seemed incapable of reaching a broader
agreement, Crook decided to engage in some diplomacy of his own.
The general, accompanied by Bourke, traveled by rail to Chihuahua City to meet with Luis Terrazas and other Mexican officials,
where he received promises of cooperation if he were to pursue the
Apaches into Mexico.

"It is all very well," declared the mayor of Chihuahua City concerning the diplomats, "sitting at their ease in Washington and the city of Mexico to split straws over treaties, but those who live upon the borders of Sonora and Chihuahua, where nearly every family has lost a loved one, have other thoughts, and are determined that a few worthless savages must not be allowed to rob and murder any longer. The same feeling prevails in Arizona and New Mexico."

This sort of talk made the distant officials in Mexico City even more nervous, and they once again made clear their opposition to any invasion of Mexican soil by American troops. In response, General Sherman would officially warn Crook on April 28, 1883, "that no military movement must be made into, or within the Territory of Mexico, which is not authorized by the agreement." This may simply have been diplomatic cover by Sherman, for he was fully aware that preparations for an advance into Mexico had already been under way for weeks.

The rail station at Willcox—named for Crook's predecessor—was a beehive of activity. Every Southern Pacific train brought in more supplies for an extended campaign. Long Jim Cook's packtrain, with Tom Horn along as a packer, was also called down to Willcox. In March, Crook had ordered Sieber, McIntosh, and Mickey Free to join Captain Crawford and Lieutenant Gatewood at Willcox in anticipation of a movement across the border some eighty miles to the south, but he had still needed some overt act to use as an excuse to invade Mexico. In March, it was promptly delivered to him on a bloody platter.

Early that month, Chatto and Bonito had led a party of twenty-six warriors and novice boys north to Arizona. At the same time, Geronimo and Chihuahua, with a larger band of raiders, had invaded Sonora. The critical need for arms and ammunition was the main reason for both raiding parties. The Americans, of course, were far better supplied with the newest repeaters and more ammunition than the Mexicans.

Chatto, cunning and ambitious, saw the raid as an opportunity to enhance his position among the Chiricahuas. His name meant "flat nose," the result of a mule kick to the face when he was a youth. He was a Bedonkohe like Geronimo, but as a nephew of Mangas Coloradas, he had a more impressive bloodline among the Chiricahuas. He certainly saw himself in contention with Geronimo for leadership, but while famed as a bold warrior, he did not have the mystical power attributed to his older rival.

The raiders had swept across southeastern Arizona, killing a dozen prospectors and cowboys near Tombstone before turning northeast to move up the San Simon Valley with a large herd of captured horses and mules. They had lost one man, whose scalp with ears attached was soon making the rounds of the Tombstone saloons. As a result of this man's death, the Cibecue Apache warrior Tsoe grew disheartened and requested permission to return to visit with relatives at San Carlos. No one objected. Bonito gave him a horse, rifle, and supplies for the journey.

Mickey Free immediately learned of the return of Tsoe. Lieutenant Davis and his Indian scouts arrested the young warrior without incident on April 1. Davis telegraphed Crook the news that Tsoe, whom the soldiers dubbed "Peaches" because of his fair complexion, had left Chatto's raiders only days before not far from the New Mexico border. Crook ordered the captive sent south to the staging area at Willcox so that he could personally question him.

Chatto's raiders crossed into New Mexico and slaughtered a dozen more White Eyes before they turned south to escape back into Mexico through the Animas Mountains. As they passed the Burro Mountains on March 28, not far from the old stronghold of Mangas Coloradas, they came upon a family having a picnic under an expansive walnut tree in Thompson Canyon.

Judge Hamilton C. McComas, with his wife, Juniata, and six-year-old son, Charley, were on a journey from Silver City to Lordsburg when they stopped for a picnic lunch in the canyon at noon. The judge was a community leader in Silver City and well connected politically in the territory, while his beautiful wife was a member of a prominent New England family. By some horrible chance, fate placed them right along Chatto's escape route at just the wrong moment.

When McComas spied the onrushing Apaches, he grabbed his

Winchester to buy time while Juniata and Charley escaped in their buckboard. He went down with seven wounds as the warriors galloped after the wagon. A well-placed shot brought down one of the horses and a blow from a rifle stock knocked Juniata to the ground. Several more blows crushed her skull. Apaches never wasted bullets. As the warriors ransacked the wagon and stripped the two bodies, young Charley was pulled up onto Bonito's horse. Naiche's wife later took the blond-haired boy into her lodge and protected him. Her husband could not understand why the traumatized child would not speak. "We thought he had very little sense," Naiche concluded.

The murders sent shock waves across the Southwest and produced dire consequences for the Apaches not seen since the kidnapping of Mickey Free. Although Hispanic women and children had often been carried off by Apache raiders over the years, it was the slaughter of this prominent white couple—and the kidnapping of their blond, blue-eyed little boy—that electrified the nation. General Crook now had his excuse to invade Mexico in "hot pursuit" of the Chiricahuas. Little Charley McComas must be rescued!

On April 23, 1883, Crook set the troops and supplies he had gathered at Willcox in motion. A base camp was to be established at the San Bernardino Ranch, just north of the Mexican line. The old ranch had long been a landmark because of its springs and geographic position. The Spanish had used it as a military outpost and the Mexican army after them. In 1884 the celebrated Texas cattleman John Slaughter bought the ranch.

Crook intended to leave almost all his troops and supplies at San Bernardino while he personally led a "flying column," made up mostly of Apache scouts, into Mexico. Peaches had agreed to guide them to the Chiricahua stronghold in the Sierra Madre. The only regular army troops to go were the forty-two enlisted men of Captain Chaffee's I Troop, Sixth Cavalry. Crook's main force was made up of 193 Chiricahua, White Mountain, Tonto, and Yavapai scouts under Captain Crawford. Al Sieber was in overall command of the scouts, with Archie McIntosh, Gracias Severiano, and Sam Bowman as his assistants. Five well-equipped packtrains of 266 mules handled by 76 packers, including Jim Cook and Tom Horn, also went with the column. Each mule could carry nearly three hundred pounds, so the rations were far in excess of what the column required. Crook was taking supplies to the Chiricahuas. One of the mules was loaded with the cumbersome photographic equipment of Frank Randall, correspondent for the *New York Herald*. Crook was anxious to garner some favorable press while on this dangerous expedition. Crook's interpreter was Mickey Free.

A war dance was held by the Apache scouts the night before the advance into Mexico. They stripped to their breechcloths and moccasins and paraded around the fire, chanting, yelling out war cries, and firing their weapons in the air. It went on all night.

Some of the scouts were worried. "Chiricahuas could hide like coyotes and could smell danger a long way like wild animals," declared a San Carlos scout.

Crook laughed. Mickey translated as he told the scouts that they would catch the Chiricahuas within forty days. Mickey whispered to the general to tell the scouts that they might have all the captured property of the Chiricahuas. This statement led to bloodcurdling war cries of affirmation. A medicine man stepped forward to proclaim the certainty of their success, which also greatly increased the enthusiasm of the dancers.

On May 1, 1883, Crook, astride his mule and decked out in his canvas suit and pith helmet, led his column across the international line. The scouts moved ahead in small groups, with little semblance of order. Their rapid pace forced a cavalry horse to trot to keep up. They moved at a rate of about four miles an hour and could keep this up for at least fifteen miles without rest. Their raven locks were held in place by the scarlet cloth that marked them as army scouts—as did their Springfield carbines, 150 rounds of ammunition, and regulation canteens. They wore no uniforms, but dressed in long shirts of calico or plain cloth, girded by belts and reaching to their leggings. They invariably carried a knife, a medicine bag, and extra pairs of moccasins in their belt.

On May 5, they reached the Mexican village of Bacerac and marched down the dusty main street to make camp just outside.

The town had once prospered, but Chiricahua raiders had left the people impoverished. They greeted the Americans warmly and offered what little they had—chili, atole, and home-brewed mescal. Sieber, Horn, and several of the packers visited the village and purchased all the available liquor. They also helped themselves to ten choice Mexican cows and proceeded to have a grand barbecue to which they invited the locals, especially the senoritas. Several of the Apache scouts made their way to this party, but when White Mountain scout John Rope tried to join them, he was stopped by his adopted brother, Mickey Free.

"My grandson, don't go over where they are drinking," Mickey told Rope. "There is liable to be some trouble." Mickey used the important term of affection *my grandson* to underscore how serious he was. Mickey was protecting his younger brother from potential harm; he knew well that drinking always led to trouble for Apaches.

Bourke, who had left the fandango early, went to visit the scout camp. Most of the scouts busied themselves at monte. Almost every man was equally addicted to gambling and tobacco, and it was a wise officer who kept smokes handy to share. Mickey Free greeted his old friend and took him aside to point out to him how the scouts camped together based on clan affiliation. In a reflective mood, he shared with Bourke the contents of his medicine bag. He pulled the brass-headed tacks back to expose a collection of twigs and other natural objects that puzzled the captain. The bag, Mickey confessed, should only be opened in times of great stress. The twig was to be set upright on the ground, then Mickey had only to sing and dance around it to make him invulnerable to enemy bullets. This was powerful medicine.

Bourke soon received yet another lesson in Apache medicine when Randall, the newspaperman, rode into camp with a small owl he had somehow captured alive and tied to the pommel of his saddle. This halted the Apache scouts in their tracks. The owl was a powerful omen of evil and death, and they refused to proceed until it was set free. Crook liberated the bird and the advance toward the Sierra Madre continued, but several of the scouts remained unnerved.

Crook and his guide Peaches were depicted along with a group shot of the entire command as it was about to embark for the Sierra Madre in the June 2, 1883, *Frank Leslie's Illustrated Newspaper (Author's collection)*.

The war dance of Crook's Apache scouts as they prepared to search out Geronimo was captured by artist A. F. Harmer for the June 2, 1883, issue of *Harper's Weekly (Author's collection)*.

A. F. Harmer's sketch of Crook's packtrain in the Sierra Madre appeared in the August 4, 1883, *Harper's Weekly (Author's collection)*.

Nana comes into General Crook's Sierra Madre camp to surrender in this cover illustration from the July 7, 1883, *Harper's Weekly (Author's collection)*.

Arizona types by Frederic Remington appeared in the August 21, 1886, *Harper's Weekly (Author's collection)*.

Captain Crawford's body is finally returned to American soil, as depicted in the April 10, 1886, *Harper's Weekly (Author's collection)*.

White Mountain Apache scouts gathering for the hunt for Geronimo were depicted on the cover of *Frank Leslie's Illustrated Newspaper,* January 30, 1886 *(Author's collection).*

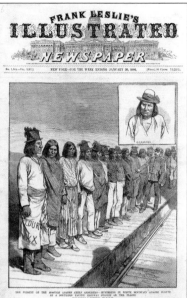

R. F. Zogbaum depicted General Sheridan in the West for the August 8, 1885, *Harper's Weekly (Author's collection).*

This remarkable photo of Crook's headquarters at Canyon de los Embudos in 1886 features the general in the center (pith helmet); with lanky Tom Horn in the front row to his left with the white shirt; and in the back far left, Tom Jeffords in a white shirt; and to the far right in a white hat, dark shirt, and suspenders is Al Sieber. John Bourke stands behind the general *(Arizona Historical Society).*

C. S. Fly captured the meeting of Geronimo and Crook at Canyon de los Embudos on March 25, 1886. Geronimo and Nana sit in the center across from Crook (in pith helmet) and John Bourke. Lt. Maus (in swept-back hat) sits between them *(True West Archive)*.

Geronimo and Naiche as prisoners at Fort Bowie before beginning the journey to Florida *(True West Archive)*.

Apache prisoners pose beside the prison train during a stop on the journey to Florida. In the front row are from left, Fun, Perico, Naiche, Geronimo, Chappo, and Garditha. Of the women in the back row center, the first on the left is Ha-o-zinne, wife of Naiche, and the woman next to her has been identified by some as Lozen, with Dahteste next to her *(True West Archive)*.

Mickey Free's arrest of the suspect scout was depicted by Frederic Remington to accompany his article "Massai's Crooked Trail in *Harper's New Monthly Magazine* *(Author's collection)*.

Mickey Free with his two wives Ethlay and Ochehey *(Marc Simmons, True West Archive)*.

C. S. Fly took this photograph during Crook's March 1886 meeting with Geronimo and identified the Apache scout in the center as Kid *(Author's collection)*.

The Apache prisoners at their 1889 trial in Globe. Front, left to right: Has-ten-tu-du-jay, Nah-deiz-az, Bach-e-on-al, Bi-the-ja-be-tish-to-ce-an, Hale. Back, left to right: El-cahn, Hos-cal-te, Sayes, Apache Kid, Bob McIntosh *(Arizona Historical Society)*.

The Apache Kid (rear right, wearing bandana) and other prisoners await trial *(Author's collection)*.

ONE OF THE KID'S BAND OF RENEGADES.

THE KID.

STOLEN WIVES OF THE KID.

TRAILING THE KID.

LIEUTENANT WILLIAMS AND HIS APACHE SCOUTS.

The hunt for the Apache Kid was featured in *Frank Leslie's Illustrated Newspaper.* The scout on the left in the bottom row group shot is Merijildo Grijalva *(Author's collection).*

Frederic Remington depicted two of the officers involved in the hunt for the Apache Kid—James Watson and Powhatan Clarke—in the March 22, 1890, *Harper's Weekly* *(Author's collection).*

Texas John Slaughter *(Author's collection).*

APACHE SLAUGHTER

In May, 1896, this Indian maiden was taken by ex-Sheriff John Slaughter during a skirmish with the Apache Indians near his ranch in Cochise county, just off of what is now BROADWAY OF AMERICA (US 80). She lived with the Slaughter family until she was seven years old when she died from burns received when her clothing accidentally caught fire.

Apache May Slaughter from an old postcard *(Author's collection).*

This W. A. Rogers cartoon from the September 23, 1886, issue of *Life* magazine lampooned the military establishment by suggesting that Geronimo should be employed as a West Point instructor *(Author's collection)*.

Geronimo (in black) rides alongside Comanche war leader Quanah Parker and other chiefs in Theodore Roosevelt's inaugural parade on March 4, 1905 *(True West Archive)*.

"Some of the scouts started to say their knees hurt them as an excuse to keep in the rear," remembered John Rope. "Some of them were always doing this way because they were afraid."

On May 7, guided by Peaches, the column left the river and turned east into the foothills of the Sierra Madre and began to climb. The mountains proved a tangle of canyons, thickly wooded, rocky, and steep. The well-beaten trail soon became little better than a goat path, although the nervous men saw signs of the Apaches everywhere. Carcasses of ponies and cattle were strewn along the trail or down in the canyons, where they had been butchered for food, and cast-off plunder littered the mountainsides.

Every time they crested a ridge, the soldiers and scouts discovered yet another higher one to be climbed. Even the sure-footed mules lost their step. Five were killed, one falling hundreds of feet over a precipice to its doom. The unfortunate animal was the one carrying Randall's cherished camera and glass plates with it. Just punishment, the scouts concluded, for his capture of the owl.

The scouts discovered a battle site, only a few weeks old, where Mexican troops had been defeated in an attempt to penetrate the stronghold. Colonel Lorenzo Garcia, who had slaughtered Loco's people on Alisos Creek, had led eighty federal troops and fifty militiamen into an Apache ambush on April 25. The scouts explored the rock fortifications erected by the Chiricahuas and found many Winchester casings. They also discovered where three Mexicans had been buried on the field under piles of rocks. The Mexican troops had gone no farther.

Crook pushed on, ever deeper into the endless canyons, passing countless animal bones. "Hundreds of dead animals were met at every turn," reported Randall; "in fact, death seemed to be reigning before our eyes."

At noon on May 9, they turned down a narrow, dark canyon that suddenly opened into a small grassy amphitheater through which a sparkling mountain brook flowed. This, Peaches informed Crook, was Juh's stronghold.

"The ashes of extinct fire, the straw of unused beds, the skeleton frame-work of dismantled huts, the play-grounds and dance-grounds, mescal-pits and acorn-meal mills were visible at every turn," noted Captain Bourke. Mickey Free brought in a black pony and a Winchester rifle that he found near the camp. The Chiricahuas had not been gone long. But where were they now?

On May 11, 1883, Crook called his officers and the scout leaders into a war council. The journey had been long and perilous, with the packtrain often holding back the column to under ten miles a day. Captain Crawford wanted to press ahead to do some reconnaissance with his scouts. Alchesay and the other scout leaders agreed. They were anxious for a fight and if the Chiricahuas refused to surrender, they were ready to kill them all. Through Mickey Free, Crook warned the scouts to spare all women and children as well as any man who surrendered. The scouts reluctantly agreed, but pointed out that men like Geronimo and Juh, who were "all the time raising trouble," should be killed no matter what.

Crawford, accompanied by Mickey Free, Sieber, Bowman, Severiano, McIntosh, and 143 of the scouts, would push ahead immediately. Crawford's plan was to keep a day ahead of the main column. Each man carried four days of rations, a canteen, a blanket, and a hundred rounds of ammunition.

"At that time I had never fought with the Chiricahuas and did not know how mean they were," recalled John Rope, "so I was always in the front."

On the morning of May 14, Sieber, in advance with Rope and a handful of scouts, discovered a Chiricahua village in a valley near the headwaters of the Bavispe River. He sent back word for Crawford to hurry the command forward. That evening Sieber and Crawford devised a plan to surround the village and attack at dawn. They hoped to compel the Apaches to surrender without a fight, since Crook wished to avoid hostilities. Alchesay and his White Mountain scouts were to advance toward the village while Crawford and Sieber led the remaining scouts around the flanks.

The village, which belonged to Chatto, Bonito, and Chihuahua, was quickly captured. The Apache warriors had only recently returned from a raid with a large herd of cattle. The women and children had busied themselves butchering the animals while most of the men had gone off on yet another raid. The people fled in panic, leaving everything behind. John Rope found only a baby alone and crying in the camp. As a result, there was little resistance, with only four Chiricahuas killed.

One of the dead, however, was an elderly woman who had walked toward the scouts to surrender. A San Carlos scout shot her down. This senseless act would have serious consequences, for the woman, who was the aunt of Chihuahua, was beloved in the camp.

The scouts burned thirty wickiups along with great quantities of baked mescal and other foods, rounded up forty-seven horses and mules, and captured five Chiricahuas—the baby, three children, and a young woman who proved to be the daughter of Bonito.

Geronimo was more than a hundred miles to the east on a kidnapping raid into Chihuahua. He had hoped to capture some Mexican women to trade for the people taken by the Mexicans in the attack on Juh's camp. On the road to Casas Grandes, the warriors had ambushed a wagon train and taken captive six women who were wives of soldiers at Casas Grandes. They tortured the men to death and took the women back to their camp. That evening, as the warriors sat eating, Geronimo suddenly dropped the chunk of cooked beef his novice Betzinez had prepared for him.

"Men, our people whom we left at our base camp are now in the hands of US troops!" he exclaimed. "What shall we do?"

The warriors all voted to head back to the stronghold. Everyone believed the power of Geronimo to see such things. They abandoned most of their captured cattle and hurried the Mexican captives along as best they could.

IN CROOK'S CAMP the Apache scouts occupied themselves in gambling over the plunder they had taken from the Chiricahua camp. They had made quite a haul of gold and silver watches, as well as a considerable amount of both American and Mexican currency. They also had brought in a photo album that the officers thought might have belonged to Judge McComas.

Crook spent the morning with Mickey Free and the captive

daughter of Bonito. She told the general that the camp had been that of her father and Chatto and that a small white boy named Charley had been there. She reported that the boy had run away with an elderly woman when the scouts attacked. She promised that, if released, she would bring back the boy and the rest of her father's people. She told Crook that her father, along with Loco and Chihuahua, was anxious to return to San Carlos. Geronimo and Chatto she was not so sure of.

Crook gave her food and tobacco and sent her, along with one of the captured boys, back to find Bonito. The next day Crook moved his camp five miles northeast to a valley where the water and grass were better. Pickets were posted on the surrounding hilltops and smoke signals sent up to let the Apaches know where they were.

That afternoon two women approached under a white flag. One was the sister of Chihuahua. She said that her brother would come in to talk if his white horse with a Mexican saddle was returned to him. One of the scouts was ordered to give up his prize and the woman left astride the horse. She said that her brother would come in the following day.

Mickey and several other scouts were busy gambling the next morning when Chihuahua, astride his white horse, galloped into the soldiers' camp. He carried a lance with the red cloth of a scout's headband tied to it and carried two pistols on his belt. He reined his horse in right in front of the oak tree where the scouts were gambling and demanded to know where Crook was. John Rope pointed toward the general's tent and Chihuahua galloped off, scattering soldiers and scouts alike as he rode through the camp. Mickey raced after him.

Chihuahua slipped off his horse before the general's tent. They shook hands as Mickey rushed up. As the winded Mickey interpreted, Crook declared that he had come to be a friend to the Chiricahuas and take them all back to live at San Carlos.

"If you want me for a friend, why did you kill that old woman, my aunt?" Chihuahua asked. "If I was trying to make friends with someone, I would not go and raid their camp and shoot their relatives. It seems to me that you are lying when you speak about being friends."

Crook had no good response except to repeat his peaceful intent, give Chihuahua some tobacco, and ask him to bring his people in. The haughty chief mounted his horse and galloped back out of the camp, once again scattering the soldiers and scouts.

The next day, nearly a hundred women and children arrived in Crook's camp. One of the women was the mother of the baby John Rope had found during the attack on Bonito's camp. She wailed and carried on about her baby. Mickey Free pulled her up short, telling her that she deserved "to have her guts eaten out by a coyote" for deserting her baby, but he gave her the child.

Mickey questioned the women closely about the McComas boy. They all repeated a similar story: the boy had run off into the brush when the scouts attacked and was fine. But no one seemed to know where he was. One of the women told Mickey that there was sure to be trouble when Geronimo returned from his raid into Chihuahua. "She said we had better all look out," John Rope recalled. The scouts gave up gambling and busied themselves building stone breastworks.

The next evening, Geronimo and his warriors appeared on the ridgetops above the camp. "The Chiricahuas were still fearful of treachery and hung like hawks or vultures to the protecting shadows of inaccessible pinnacles one thousand feet above our position," Bourke nervously observed.

The Chiricahua women waved empty flour bags as white flags and called out to the warriors to come into camp and not fight. Several of the scouts, including Chatto's brother-in-law, went up on the ridgeline to talk with the warriors. As a result, a few of the warriors came down to the camp to check on their families and talk with the scouts. They asked Mickey to tell Nantan Lupan that Geronimo would like to talk with him. Crook replied that Geronimo must come into the camp if he wanted to talk.

Crook was all bluff and bravado. He was in a completely untenable position in the heart of his enemy's country, with no hope of resupply or reinforcements. If attacked, he did not even have a viable escape route. To his advantage he had more than two hundred well-armed men and greatly outnumbered Geronimo's force, although the loyalty of his Apache scouts was still in question. Geronimo had superior knowledge of the terrain and his warriors were skilled, hardened fighters, but they lacked ammunition. The soldiers now held more than a hundred of their women and children hostage. Crook had also scored a stunning psychological victory by locating Juh's stronghold with his Apache scouts. It was a classic Mexican standoff.

24

TURKEY CREEK

GENERAL GEORGE CROOK WAS POSSESSED BY AN AB-
solute mania for hunting and fishing. He was apt to go
off at the most inexplicable moments to catch game,
which drove Captain Bourke and other staff officers crazy. Sure
enough, the morning after Geronimo and his warriors had appeared at the top of the ridgeline, Mickey Free, with John Rope and
several other scouts, watched in utter amazement as Crook, carrying his shotgun, wandered off alone to go bird hunting.

He vanished into a stand of tall yellow grass not far from the
main camp. The scouts, listening incredulously, heard the discharge
of his shotgun, and then all was quiet. Mickey grew increasingly
worried. When he ran over into the grass to find his general, he discovered that Crook had been taken prisoner by Geronimo and several warriors. They had taken his shotgun and even the dead birds.

Upon Mickey's arrival, the group opened up a parley and they
all squatted and talked for nearly two hours before Crook induced
Geronimo to come back to camp and join him for a late breakfast.

Bourke was amazed by Geronimo's Apache cavalcade, "as fine-
looking a lot of pirates as ever cut a throat or scuttled a ship."
As it turns out, Geronimo was not that much of a pirate, for he
did not kill Crook when he had the chance. In this, he displayed
a far greater sense of honor than Colonel West had shown in his
treatment of Mangas Coloradas. Geronimo was also simply being
shrewd. The old warrior recognized the sheer folly of killing Crook
and bringing on a fight with the Apache scouts and soldiers. He
did not have the warriors or the ammunition to prevail. Even as he

talked peace with Crook, Geronimo began to formulate another plan.

Crook had Mickey lie to Geronimo and tell him that two Mexican armies were on their way to the stronghold. The Chiricahuas must surrender to Nantan Lupan and return with him to San Carlos. Geronimo scoffed at this and declared that he did not even use guns to fight the Mexicans, but rather beat them to death with rocks.

Geronimo and his warriors departed, but even as they went back into the hills, more Chiricahua women and children were entering Crook's camp. They were later followed in by the five Mexican women, one with a baby clutched to her breast, who had been captured by Geronimo. He had simply abandoned them in the excitement of meeting with Crook, and they had followed the Chiricahua families into Crook's camp in search of food. They were naturally elated to discover themselves among the Americans, but they had a horrific tale to tell. They had been taken two weeks before by Geronimo, whose name they said struck terror into the hearts of the Mexican peasants who believed him to be the devil sent to punish them for their sins. In confirmation of Geronimo's boast, the women described how the men of their escort had all been tortured and then killed with stones.

Over the next two days Crook and Geronimo met repeatedly. Naiche and Chatto came in as well, as did Kaytennae with seventy-nine Warm Springs people. Crook offered everyone sanctuary at San Carlos and promised to protect them from retribution. He reminded them that if he took them all back to San Carlos, "the Americans and Mexicans will make a hard fight of it, for you have been murdering their people, stealing their stock, and burning their houses." The fact was, Crook asserted, "you are asking me to fight my own people in order to defend your wrongs."

Geronimo called a late-night council, not to discuss Crook's offer, but rather to plot a way to kill the Apache scouts. They would hold a victory dance and invite the White Mountain scouts to dance with the Chiricahua women. To make the invitation all the more enticing, the scouts would not be asked to pay their dance partners, as was the custom. When the scouts were all dancing, Geronimo and his warriors would slip up behind them and slit their throats.

Geronimo persuaded Chatto, Naiche, and Kaytennae with their warriors to join him in using the women to ensnare the scouts. The White Mountain scouts were quite excited by the invitation. They had been happily fraternizing with the Chiricahuas for several days, and it seemed as if past grievances were forgotten. Besides, many of the Chiricahua girls were very pretty.

At the last minute Sieber, who had a strange sixth sense about such things, forbade the scouts to leave camp. It was only later that he and Mickey learned the full extent of Geronimo's perfidy.

With their plan foiled, the chiefs led their people to Crook's camp for rations and for peace talks. On May 23, rations were issued to 220 Chiricahuas, with more people coming in by the hour. Crook ordered some of the stolen Mexican cattle butchered and encouraged the Chiricahua women in the baking of the mescal that they had gathered. With his rations almost gone, Crook had no choice but to head back to San Carlos with as many of the Chiricahuas as he could convince to join him. Loco brought his people in on May 24 and old Nana limped in soon after. Bourke thought that "Loco has by all odds the best face of all the Chiricahuas" but felt Nana's countenance to be marked by "cruelty and vindictiveness." Bourke confessed that all the Apache chiefs, including Geronimo, were "men of noticeable brain power, physically perfect and mentally acute—just the individuals to lead a forlorn hope in the face of every obstacle."

Geronimo met with Crook for a final time on May 28 and assured the general that he would catch up with the column as soon as he had located all of the scattered Chiricahuas. He did not want to leave anyone behind. He also promised to locate the lost McComas boy. Crook agreed to this arrangement, although he warned Geronimo that he could not prevent Mexican troops or American civilians from attacking the Chiricahuas who stayed behind.

On Sunday morning, June 10, 1883, Crook's colorful but weary caravan reached Arizona. Crook brought in 52 men and 273 women and children. Of the Apache leaders, only Loco, Nana, and

Bonito accompanied the column. Crook promptly sent forward a report on his triumphant capture of Geronimo and all the Apaches. He cited several of his men for special commendation, including Captain Crawford, Al Sieber, and Mickey Free.

Even Bourke, ever the general's devoted press agent, felt that they might well have been tricked by Geronimo. "Present appearances point to a plan to work off all surplus women and children and decrepit men upon this command, leaving the Apache incorrigibles free to continue depredations upon Mexico," he confessed to his diary.

Among the Apache scouts, the gossip was that Geronimo had stayed in Mexico to kill Mexicans and steal stock. "Some of the Chiricahuas asked for permission to gather a lot of horses from the Mexicans before they left Mexico. General Crook gave them permission," declared John Rope. "They did not like the little San Carlos ponies and wanted to get some good horses before going back."

Crook had failed to rescue Charley McComas or to disarm and bring in most of the leading Apache warriors, but he had redeemed Loco's people and delivered them safely to San Carlos. He also knew that he had a powerful trump card in the Chiricahua families he had brought back. The warriors would undoubtedly eventually return to their families.

The Arizona press was initially ecstatic over Crook's campaign, and the *New-York Tribune* declared the campaign "a brilliant success," but the laurel wreaths wilted quickly. Even as Al Sieber led his painted scouts and their Chiricahua "prisoners" into San Carlos on June 23, Agent Wilcox was enlisting the support of his friend the secretary of the interior to allow him to refuse to accept the Chiricahuas. Wilcox did not want the responsibility, and the other San Carlos Indians did not welcome the Chiricahuas back. Crook was soon on a train headed to Washington for a July 7 summit meeting with Secretary of the Interior Henry Teller, Secretary of War Robert Lincoln, and Commissioner of Indian Affairs Hiram Price. Crook left the meeting with full control over the Chiricahuas at San Carlos. Wilcox would manage the other San Carlos bands. Captain Crawford was now to have command of both the Apache scouts and the San Carlos police, with Gatewood and Davis as his assistants. Crook had achieved one of his goals: the partial reinstatement of military control at San Carlos.

The adulation heaped on Crook quickly turned to scorn as weeks turned to months without the promised appearance of Geronimo and his warriors. The story of Crook's careless bird-hunting sortie and subsequent capture by Geronimo leaked out, despite the best efforts of Crook and Bourke to suppress it, and the newspapers began to ask just who had surrendered to whom.

The fact that the armed warriors had been left in Mexico and that they had been promised no retaliation for past offenses rankled most of the people of Arizona and New Mexico. "To attempt to punish one or a dozen of the tribe for deeds of which all were equally guilty, would be a gross act of tyranny," Crook lectured the public. "Vengeance is just as much to be deprecated as a silly sentimentalism." Such sentiments won Crook few friends in the Southwest.

The initial story of Crook's capture was leaked to the press after the general's meeting with Teller and Lincoln. Since the Indian Bureau opposed the return of the Chiricahuas to San Carlos, it likely originated with Teller or his Indian commissioner. The story was widely circulated, as was Captain Bourke's ringing denunciation of it.

Secretary Teller was asked directly by a *Philadelphia Press* reporter, "Did Crook capture the Apaches, or did the Apaches capture Crook?" Teller replied evasively that "he did not know." Lincoln declared the story to be "utterly without foundation."

Crook also faced criticism from the family of Charley McComas. "Since General Crook's campaign, nothing has been done to obtain the boy," complained the boy's uncle, a prominent Kansas politician, in an August letter to the secretary of state: "It seems to me that if the boy was a British subject, that government would get him if it cost about half the island to do it."

Crook ordered Mickey Free to again question the Chiricahuas about the McComas boy, and as a result a white boy captive was discovered with the Warm Springs people. But after he proved not to be Charley, Al Sieber felt more and more certain that the boy was dead. The repeated questions about Charley McComas led Mickey to discover a dozen other Hispanic captives among the Chiricahuas.

Crook, who had no children, obviously did not understand the grief of the McComas family and their determination to rescue their lost child. Crook only added to their distress when he responded that in his dealings with the Apaches "I was careful to impress on them the fact that we cared very little for the boy, but showed them the great advantage it would be to them to have him returned to his people."

This callous statement was a true reflection of Crook's position: he actually cared "very little" about the child except as an excuse to have launched his expedition into the Sierra Madre. The grieving family received no closure. The boy had indeed been killed soon after the scouts had attacked the camp of Bonito and Chihuahua. When Chihuahua's aunt was killed by a scout, her son was so outraged that in his grief he immediately sought out the little captive Charley McComas and smashed in his skull with a stone. The Apaches quite naturally continued to cover up the boy's murder for another sixty years, while tales persisted into the 1930s that the child had grown to manhood as a white Apache roaming the Sierra Madre.

The mounting criticism led Crook to order Britton Davis and Mickey Free to the border in September with a detachment of ten Apache scouts to try to learn where Geronimo was. Three Chiricahuas went with them as potential envoys.

Just before he headed south with Davis, Mickey enjoyed a remarkable reunion with his half brother Santiago Ward. Santiago had been born after Mickey's kidnapping and had never seen his brother but thought "he looked very much like his sister, fair with grayish eyes." Santiago had been raised in Mexico but had come north with his sister and now worked as a soap maker in a Tucson meat market. A friend had told him that his long-lost brother was a famous scout at San Carlos. Santiago was naturally perplexed as to why his brother was called Mickey Free.

Santiago told Mickey about the death of his parents and attempted to get him to visit with his remaining family, but the scout refused. "He never would do it," Santiago noted, "always made some excuse." Mickey Free had long ago shaken off the last vestige of Felix Ward.

Mickey secured Santiago a job at San Carlos as a packer, and they traveled together with the soldiers and scouts down to the San Bernardino Ranch to search for Geronimo. The first sign of the return of the Apaches came in late October when Naiche, Chihuahua, and Geronimo's teenage son Chappo brought seventy-nine people north across the border. Kaytennae, Chihuahua's brother Ulzanna, and Lozen with eight warriors crossed the border with a large herd of stolen Mexican horses several days later.

"Geronimo assured me he would come," Naiche told Mickey, "and told his son who came along with me to come back and let him know where we were going to be settled and how we were getting along." Mickey also received confirmation of the rumored death of Juh. This left Geronimo and Chatto, with ninety Chiricahuas, as the final holdouts.

By December the pressure on Crook had increased exponentially, and in response he asked Chappo and Chihuahua to return to Mexico and contact Geronimo. These envoys carried Crook's guarantee of fair treatment and no reprisals if Geronimo would return to San Carlos. At the same time Crawford sent orders to the border to request that Lieutenant Davis escort the Apaches to San Carlos and make sure no civilian interfered with them.

Chatto, with fifteen warriors and a fine herd of Mexican horses, reached San Bernardino on February 7, 1884. The Bedonkohe warrior was in a jolly mood and decided to slaughter a pony and have a feast in honor of Lieutenant Davis. He told Mickey to call Davis over to watch the preparation of the feast, but the lieutenant would utterly fail this test of manhood.

"I had witnessed the struggles of the beautiful creature as he roped it and cut its throat," Davis remarked. "I had no heart for the feast and lost caste with him by my squeamishness."

Mickey shared Chatto's taste for pony and gladly ate the lieutenant's portion. In time Chatto shared quarters with Mickey and joined him as a scout. "We have had different fires," he declared, "but now we and the white men have but one fire and will not fight any more."

Davis came to rely on Chatto almost as much as he did Mickey and secured him the rank of first sergeant. The lieutenant felt Chatto to be "one of the finest men, red or white, I have ever known." Many of the Chiricahuas, however, felt Chatto to be a traitor just like Mickey Free.

Kaywaykla spat out their names: "Mickey Free! That miserable little coyote was trusted, and old and honest scouts disregarded. Chatto! Turncoat and traitor!"

Daklugie echoed this sentiment when he labeled Chatto as "the arch traitor—a sort of Benedict Arnold to us."

GERONIMO MET Lieutenant Davis on February 26, 1884, in the Animas Valley of New Mexico. Chappo and Chihuahua were with him, along with eight warriors and twenty-two women and children. The warriors drove nearly a hundred Mexican horses and an even larger herd of cattle. This stock would slow the march to San Carlos considerably as the cavalcade made its way around the southern point of the Chiricahua Mountains and moved north up the Sulphur Springs Valley. Davis attempted to prod Geronimo with a warning that the Mexican owners of the herd might soon appear.

"Mexicans! My squaws can whip all the Mexicans in Chihuahua," he exclaimed. "We don't fight Mexicans with cartridges," he noted with contempt. "Cartridges cost too much. We keep them to fight your white soldiers. We fight Mexicans with rocks."

Geronimo and his people were finally settled on the Gila River, in the same spot from which he had kidnapped Loco, in March 1884. To Geronimo's dismay, though, Captain Crawford promptly seized Geronimo's stolen cattle herd, sold the animals at auction, and sent the proceeds to the State Department to be used to compensate Mexican claims. It was hoped that this act of goodwill might lead the Mexican government to respond to the repeated entreaties to return the captured Chiricahua families to San Carlos.

But that was not to be the case. The sale outraged Geronimo, who viewed the cattle as the just spoils of war, and he never forgave either Crook or Crawford.

CROOK VISITED San Carlos in May to meet with the Chiricahua leaders before all 520 people were to be marched north to their new home on Turkey Creek, seventeen miles southwest of Fort Apache. All the Chiricahua chiefs were pleased with this move into the mountains except for Geronimo. He did not care to live in White Mountain Apache country, where so many of the army scouts had come from. He wanted the Chiricahuas to live as one people, isolated from the other Apache bands, and suggested Eagle Creek as a good site with plenty of game and mescal plants. Since Eagle Creek was beyond the reservation boundary, his plea was dismissed by Crook.

Crook assigned Davis to be in command at Turkey Creek, which the lieutenant described as "a beauty spot and a game paradise," with Mickey Free and Sam Bowman to assist him. Gatewood, at nearby Fort Apache, who was in charge of the White Mountain people, fretted over the concentration of the Chiricahuas at Turkey Creek. He warned Crook that they should be scattered over the reservation or they would bolt within a year. The general ignored the soft-spoken Virginian.

Tom Horn was hired at San Carlos to help with the agency cattle herd, although he often worked as an assistant to chief-of-scouts Al Sieber. On occasion Sieber, with Horn, Kid, and Mickey Free, visited the ranches in Pleasant Valley and along the Verde River, as well as south toward Tombstone. "We were treated by the settlers to everything they had to give us, and we lived fat and enjoyed the trip," Horn remembered. Sieber was a great favorite with the settlers, and Horn, Kid, and Mickey were celebrated as "Sieber's boys."

At a San Simon ranch, these boys were lavishly entertained. Horn struck up a conversation with a particularly winsome blonde ranch belle who was enthralled to meet a real live Indian scout.

"All the cowboys say that your man Micky is one of the greatest scouts alive and one of the bravest men, but I am sure he looks like a villain," she breathlessly purred.

Horn was a true friend to his red-haired companion. "I told her that Mickey was a gentleman and a scholar, and that I also considered him a judge of beauty, as he had told me that the white lady with blue eyes and blonde hair was the prettiest woman he had ever seen," Horn related. "Next day I noticed she had Mickey in her house feeding him sweet cakes and giving him lemonade to drink!"

When Mickey was not eating sweet cakes, he might be found on detached duty with General Crook. In early October 1884, Crook requested that Mickey join him as interpreter on a visit to Fort Apache and San Carlos. Mickey and Peaches, along with a packtrain, met the general near the northwest corner of the reservation. Crook, as usual, was taking his time and hunting all along his journey from Prescott. This gave Captain Bourke considerable time to question Mickey about Apache cultural and spiritual beliefs. Bourke watched in amazement as Mickey made fire in twenty seconds by rubbing sticks together. Bourke then brewed some tea and produced a can of preserves for their afternoon snack.

"Mickey Free told me that Apaches after death go to *Chindin Kungua* (House of Ghosts) but may also become Animals, especially Snakes, Coyotes, Owls, and Bears," Bourke wrote in his diary. This naturally explained the Apache fear and avoidance of these animals. Mickey remained cynical.

"But Captain, that's only what they say," he told Bourke. "I don't believe they go anywhere. I think they just fly around in the trees like birds." Yet Mickey still believed in the power of the shamans. Bourke treasured the small buckskin sack filled with *hoddentin* that Mickey gave to him.

Crook was pleased with what he saw when he finally reached Fort Apache. The general met with Sanchez, who was now chief despite his prominent role in the Cibecue fight. Old Pedro had become both deaf and lame and so had turned his chieftainship over to the thirty-four-year-old Alchesay, who had already been anointed as Crook's favorite scout and was now both the White Mountain chief and a Medal of Honor recipient. Lieutenant Davis brought in several Chiricahuas from Turkey Creek to meet with Crook and was pleased to report that their freshly planted fields were prospering. Crook informed his superiors in Washington that the best-tilled farms at Turkey Creek were those of Chatto and Geronimo, "who last year were our worst enemies."

It was not Geronimo—who Lieutenant Davis had discovered was distrusted by many Chiricahuas and feared by others because of his mystical powers—but rather Kaytennae who was suspected of sowing more unrest than corn at Turkey Creek. Davis learned that the Warm Springs warrior was plotting to kill him and then bolt the reservation. This plot was uncovered by Davis's Apache spies, who had reported it directly to him because they distrusted Mickey Free. They told Davis that Mickey "might betray them to some of their friends." Mickey, although hotheaded at times, had proven his loyalty countless times, but the Apaches still distrusted him as the "coyote" who first started the great war with the White Eyes. This was a dangerous game for all involved.

Davis arrested Kaytennae and sent him to Crawford at San Carlos. Crawford then decided to make an example of him to all the Apaches, promptly placing him in irons and lodging him in the guardhouse. On June 27, 1884, Kaytennae was tried on charges of inciting a rebellion before a jury of twelve Western Apache chiefs, with Eskiminzin as jury foreman and Crawford as judge. It took Eskiminzin's jury less than an hour to convict him. Crawford sentenced Kaytennae to three years' hard labor at the military prison at Alcatraz.

Crook was shocked by the harsh sentence and attempted to convince Crawford to soften it. But the captain was adamant, so Crook had little choice but to back him. By August, Kaytennae was on a train bound for San Francisco. Crook, who was far more interested in converting Kaytennae than in punishing him, wrote to Division of the Pacific headquarters in San Francisco to encourage lenient treatment for the Apache.

Kaywaykla blamed his stepfather's imprisonment on Mickey Free and Chatto, and other Warm Springs Apaches agreed with him. Chatto indeed saw Kaytennae as a rival for leadership, but so did Geronimo. Lieutenant Davis discovered that Geronimo was anxious to have Kaytennae out of the way. Geronimo's "only redeeming traits were courage and determination," Davis declared. "His word, no matter how earnestly pledged, was worthless."

Geronimo now blamed Mickey Free for every bad tale told about him. In time he became convinced that Mickey was going to assassinate him, or at least he would use that as an excuse for his later actions.

TISWIN CONTINUED TO be the greatest problem on the reservation. General Crook had expressly forbidden *tiswin* brewing and wife beating, and these two issues soon preoccupied Davis, Gatewood, and Crawford.

Al Sieber, assigned to San Carlos as chief-of-scouts, spent much of his time at the sutler's store drinking and swapping yarns with the old boys. Sieber had a great thirst, which was often exacerbated by, as Tom Horn put it, "the rheumatism, and some of his old wounds." But when Sieber was sober, he was often out breaking up Apache *tiswin* parties, home-brew binges that often resulted in acts of violence. Such a killing, even if during a *tiswin* party, then called for retribution. The question was not so much about alcohol as it was an effort to keep the peace.

Sieber enforced Crook's *tiswin* rule with a brutal vigor. Tom Horn joined Sieber on one of these "*tiswin* raids" and even the rough frontiersman was shocked by what happened. Sieber and Horn surprised an old Apache called Centipede in the act of preparing a potent pot of home brew. Centipede, as tough as Sieber, called the scout a "meddlesome old squaw" and went for his rifle. Before the Apache could grab his gun, Sieber had him by the hair, and to Horn's surprise "made one swipe at him with his knife which nearly cut his head off." Sieber then stuffed the dead Apache into the large *tiswin* brew pot. He ordered the Apache women who were helping the brewmaster to tell everyone what had happened and "that they had better leave off making that stuff."

When, years later, Tom Horn became one of the most notorious gunmen on the frontier, men puzzled over how such a celebrated scout could have become a killer for hire. Jim King, who knew Horn in Arizona, recognized that the young scout had received his tutelage as a killer as one of "Sieber's boys." Horn, "by custom and habit, had the idea baked into his very soul," King contended, "that there was nothing wrong in killing renegade thieves." Horn's tutors, declared King, "were savage Apache warriors."

Lieutenant Davis faced an even greater problem with *tiswin* at Turkey Creek, but he refused to resort to Sieber's brutal tactics. The carefully tilled cornfields that Davis and Crook were so proud of were becoming the very source of trouble and discontent. Corn, which was not issued as a ration by the government to the Apaches, was the essential ingredient of *tiswin*. The cornfields promoted the expansion of *tiswin* across the reservation. Mickey and Chatto kept the improvised guardhouse well stocked with hungover Apaches after *tiswin* parties.

The *tiswin* drunks were actually but a symptom of the growing discontent among Geronimo and several other Chiricahua leaders. The Chiricahuas despised and distrusted Mickey Free and had little respect for young Lieutenant Davis. With the exception of Geronimo they trusted Captain Crawford, but the captain had tired of his incessant conflict with the San Carlos agent and the petty efforts by the Indian Bureau to undercut military rule at San Carlos. In early March 1885, General Crook reluctantly agreed to allow Crawford to leave his reservation duties and rejoin his regiment in Texas.

When the Chiricahuas learned that Captain Crawford was no longer in command at San Carlos, it fueled their fear that Crook would also depart and that the hated Indian Bureau would regain control. All the promises made by Crook in the Sierra Madre would be swept aside. Geronimo feared that he would soon be arrested and put on a train bound for Alcatraz. Their unease soon reached a fever pitch.

On May 15, 1885, Lieutenant Davis awoke to a commotion

outside his tent. He emerged into the dawn light to find all the Chiricahua leaders waiting for him. Geronimo, Naiche, and Chihuahua were still so drunk from a *tiswin* party the night before that they could barely stand. Loco, Nana, and Bonito were hungover but upright. Two dozen warriors, some of them armed, milled around behind their leaders. Davis was relieved to be greeted by Mickey Free and to see Chatto and several armed scouts standing nearby.

Everyone squatted on the ground as Loco began to speak in defense of the simple joys of *tiswin* and of the natural right of men to beat their wives. Chihuahua staggered to his feet and interrupted. "What I have to say can be said in a few words. Then Loco can take all the rest of the day to talk if he wishes to," he declared. Mickey interpreted as Chihuahua railed against the hypocrisy of the *tiswin* prohibition when white soldiers drank all the time. "They were not children to be taught how to live with their women and what they should eat or drink," he lectured Davis. "The treatment of their wives was their own business. They were not ill-treated when they behaved." He pointed out that the Chiricahuas had been keeping the peace and harmed no one.

As Davis replied with a lecture of his own on the evils of *tiswin* and wife beating, old Nana spit out an angry sentence or two and then limped away. Davis asked Mickey what Nana had said, but the interpreter dodged the question. When Davis demanded to know, Mickey responded that Nana had said "Tell the Nantan Enchan (stout chief) that he can't advise me how to treat my women. He is only a boy. I killed men before he was born."

Geronimo and the others all grunted in approval. "We all drank *tiswin* last night," Chihuahua added. "What are you going to do about it?! Are you going to put us all in jail?"

Lieutenant Davis was cowed. He had Mickey tell the Chiricahuas that he would telegraph Nantan Lupan for directions on just what to do. The Apaches departed in an ugly mood. Davis sent a telegraph message to Captain Francis Pierce, his superior at San Carlos, to be forwarded to General Crook, requesting instructions on how to proceed.

Captain Francis Pierce of the First Infantry had been assigned to replace Captain Crawford. Pierce, a steady and capable officer, had been a colonel of New York volunteers during the Civil War, but he had no experience with Apaches. Pierce, perplexed by the telegram, sought Al Sieber's advice. The chief-of-scouts had been up all night gambling and drinking with his pals. When Pierce woke him up, he gave a bleary-eyed once-over to the message and replied: "It's nothing but a *tiswin* drunk. Don't pay any attention to it. Davis will handle it." He rolled back into his blankets and Pierce pigeonholed the message. Crook never received the telegram.

Davis anxiously awaited a reply. One day, two days, and then three passed with no response. On Sunday afternoon, Davis was umpiring a baseball game between the two post nines at Fort Apache. In the midst of the game Mickey Free galloped onto the field. Dismounting from his lathered pony, he told Davis that the Chiricahuas had broken out, but he did not know how many.

The telegraph line between Fort Apache and San Carlos had been cut. Unable to contact Crook, Captain Allen Smith put two troops of the Fourth Cavalry, about eighty men, in the saddle and headed for Turkey Creek. Gatewood joined him with eleven of his White Mountain scouts.

Davis and Mickey returned to Turkey Creek to muster the scouts and attempt to learn just how many Chiricahuas had bolted. Davis kept additional cartridges in his large wall tent, and these now had to be issued to his scouts. The scouts were allowed only five cartridges at a time, as ammunition was currency on the reservation and was often gambled away. Davis noticed that three of his thirty scouts, including Sergeant Perico, who was Geronimo's half brother, were absent. He worried about the loyalty of the others and so had Chatto, Dutchy, and Mickey keep an eye on the assembly as he gathered up ammunition.

It was already dark by the time the Fort Apache column reached Turkey Creek. They joined with Lieutenant Davis's scouts and all immediately set off in pursuit of the Apaches. Forty-two of the 118 Chiricahua men and teenage boys had left the reservation, along with 92 women and children. They were under the leadership of Naiche, Chihuahua, Nana, Mangas, and Geronimo. Loco and

Bonito had been threatened with death by Geronimo unless they joined him but had refused to lead their people out. More than four hundred Chiricahuas remained on the reservation.

"Geronimo is reported to have said that Mickey Free and I were responsible for his leaving the Reservation," Davis later noted. "If he made such a statement, it was simply a lie to 'save his face.' Mickey had nothing whatever to do with it, and the causes of the outbreak were matters entirely beyond my control."

The column followed the Apaches throughout the evening of May 17, their way illuminated by the eerie glow of forest fires set by the fugitives. The Apaches kept ahead of the troops but were forced to abandon twenty of their footsore ponies and considerable camp equipment. On May 18, the command camped on Eagle Creek, more than seventy miles south of Turkey Creek.

"The rest of your trip will be a funeral march, burying dead bodies," Lieutenant James Parker bitterly remarked. Davis agreed. He decided to return to Fort Apache with his scouts to refit and obtain orders from General Crook. It was going to be a long campaign.

25

DEVIL'S BACKBONE

THE FUGITIVES MOVED RAPIDLY AND KILLED EVERY-one they met along the way. The troopers of the Fourth Cavalry followed and stopped time after time to bury the dead. This was done quickly by stacking stones atop the bodies. "We became very expert in the business," noted Lieutenant Parker.

The Apaches split into two groups, with one led by Geronimo and Mangas and the other by Naiche and Chihuahua. While camped on the San Francisco River, a tributary of the Gila, near the border with New Mexico, Chihuahua was visited by one of the scout deserters. He told Chihuahua that Lieutenant Davis, Mickey Free, and Chatto were on their trail. This greatly surprised the chief, since he had only left the reservation because Geronimo had told him that he had ordered those very men killed and that they must all flee together before the soldiers retaliated.

Chihuahua, enraged to discover that he had been deceived, mounted his pony and went in search of Geronimo's camp. He was joined by his brother Ulzanna; the two intended to shoot Geronimo on sight. This might satisfy Nantan Lupan and secure their families safe passage back to San Carlos. Word reached Geronimo of Chihuahua's wrath and so he, along with Mangas and Naiche, broke camp and fled to the east. Chiricahua unity, fragile to begin with, was now hopelessly shattered.

Geronimo sought sanctuary in the Mogollon Mountains of New Mexico, but after skirmishing with troops at Devil's Canyon, he scurried over the mountains to the east fork of the Gila River and the Black Range. The Apaches discovered that their old haunts were now dotted with mining camps and ranches. Geronimo looked on these settlers as a farmer might view a lush field of wheat ready for the harvest.

The warriors swept down on the isolated ranches. Three miles north of Silver City, they struck a lumber camp and slaughtered the Marques family—a father, mother, and three young children. They also hit the Phillips ranch, not far from Fort Bayard, where they killed the rancher and his wife along with two children less than six years of age. The oldest child, a girl, they hanged on a meat hook in the barn. A posse from Silver City found her alive, although she died soon after. An outraged New Mexico press now condemned Crook and his policy of appeasement and demanded the utter extermination of the Chiricahuas.

At Guadalupe Canyon, in southwestern New Mexico, Captain Henry Lawton of the Fourth Cavalry had left his packtrain under the watch of a sergeant and seven troopers while he and army surgeon Leonard Wood scouted after the Apaches. While they were gone, at noon on June 8, Chihuahua, with a dozen warriors, attacked the soldiers' camp, killed the sergeant and two troopers, and captured the wagons, loaded with forty days' worth of army rations and several thousand rounds of ammunition. The warriors carried their booty south across the nearby Mexican border. They were soon joined on the Bavispe River in Sonora by Naiche and his band. Geronimo and Mangas led their people across the international line near Lake Palomas.

Crook ordered troops out from every Arizona post and soon had twenty troops of cavalry and more than one hundred Indian scouts in the field. They failed to catch the fugitives, but Crook took some slight solace in the fact that the Apaches had been driven south of the international line. The general placed troops all along the border to prevent the Chiricahuas from crossing back. Yet another campaign into Mexico would be necessary.

Crook ordered Lieutenant Davis and Mickey Free to organize their scouts and press after the fugitives. "Get into communication with the hostiles if possible," he told Davis, and then "send in your scouts among them to disintegrate them if you can."

Davis and Mickey departed Fort Apache on May 29 with twenty-two Chiricahua scouts under Chatto, thirty-two White Mountain and two San Carlos Apaches, as well as a packtrain. One of the San Carlos scouts was undoubtedly Sieber's protégé, Kid. A series of fruitless pursuits led Davis's scouts to Fort Bowie on June 5, where the lieutenant received new orders from Crook that instructed him to lead his scouts to Skeleton Canyon and rendezvous there with Captain Emmet Crawford.

Crook was desperate, and so he recalled Crawford back from Texas and sent him to the Mexican line with A Troop of the Sixth Cavalry and Al Sieber for his chief-of-scouts. Crook, who had complete faith in Crawford, left it up to the captain to decide if he wished to take the cavalrymen into Mexico or just rely on the Apache scouts.

Davis was also delighted to have Crawford back. The young lieutenant felt that the tall, handsome forty-two-year-old captain "would have been an ideal knight of King Arthur's Court." There was a melancholy air to Crawford that puzzled Davis. "Something had saddened his early life, and I never knew him to laugh aloud," noted Davis. "His expressed wish was that he might die in the act of saving the lives of others."

Crawford led his column south on June 11. He took a single Sixth Cavalry troop with him, under Captain Henry Kendall and Lieutenant Robert Hanna, along with the 130 Apache scouts under Davis. Sieber acted as chief-of-scouts and Mickey Free as interpreter. The packtrains of Long Jim Cook and Henry Daly, fifty pack mules to each, supported Crawford's column. Tom Horn was assigned as a scout and Spanish interpreter, useful for helping Mickey work through the rough edges of his tortured Spanish.

Mickey interpreted Chatto's reassurances to Crawford that he knew exactly where Geronimo would rendezvous with Chihuahua in Mexico. The captain decided to follow Chatto's lead and not bother to follow any trails left by the Apache fugitives. Chatto, who had so recently been on raids in this country, was anxious to avoid all Mexican towns.

Lieutenant Hanna also found Mickey particularly fascinating. "The Apache rejoiced in the name of 'Mickey Free,'" the Sixth

Cavalry officer later wrote. "Mickey certainly had a Milesian cast of countenance, although in every other respect he seemed a thorough Indian."

Crook ordered a second column into Mexico under Captain Wirt Davis, a Virginian who had risen from the ranks in the Fourth Cavalry during the Civil War. Captain Davis had two troops of the Fourth and 102 Apache scouts led by Lieutenant Matthias Day of the Ninth Cavalry. The scouts were mostly White Mountain and San Carlos, and all wore white headbands rather than the red headbands of Crawford's scouts. This column departed Fort Bowie on July 7 and headed toward the Sierra Madre.

Crawford, who had followed the Bavispe River south, decided to unleash Chatto and send him into the Sierra Madre without Sieber or Mickey. Chatto took thirty scouts out under cover of darkness on June 22, 1885. They quickly discovered the trail of a dozen Chiricahua raiders and followed it into the mountains. Heavy rain soon washed away the tracks but Chatto knew just where the returning raiders would camp and led his men directly to the site. They reached the camp just after dawn on June 23, almost stumbling upon it in the driving rainstorm. Chatto's men immediately opened fire on the Chiricahua camp, and while the men escaped over the ridges to safety, the scouts captured fifteen women and children and much of the booty the warriors had taken from the army supply camp at Guadalupe Canyon. Chatto quickly realized that the camp he had taken was Chihuahua's. Among the captives were all of the chief's family as well as the wife and two children of his brother Ulzanna.

Chatto released one of the women and sent her to deliver a message to Chihuahua. The chief could secure the release of his family by killing Geronimo. Chihuahua certainly blamed Geronimo for many of his troubles, but the only Chiricahua he now wanted to kill was the traitor Chatto. Chihuahua and Ulzanna were already plotting their revenge.

◈

CRAWFORD SENT THE prisoners back to Fort Bowie under escort of Lieutenant Hanna with ten troopers, ten scouts, and Daly's packtrain mules. Crook, delighted with Crawford's strike, decided to hold the captives in close confinement at Fort Bowie in the hope of luring Chihuahua back into Arizona.

On August 7, Captain Wirt Davis's column discovered Geronimo's new camp at Bugatseka. Lieutenant Day's scouts began to encircle the encampment but a braying mule sounded the alarm. As Geronimo attempted to rally his warriors, several of the scouts recognized him. He scooped up his baby boy and ran for the brush; fifty rifles blazed away as he dodged and ducked. The scouts thought they had hit him, for he dropped the child, then vanished into a thicket. Day's scouts captured fifteen women and children, among them the wives of both Geronimo and Mangas, as well as five of Geronimo's children. Geronimo's daughter was one of three prisoners who had been wounded.

Lieutenant Day returned with his prisoners to his packtrain, where he was delighted by the unexpected arrival of Crawford's command. Crawford immediately had the two wives of Geronimo, two of Day's prisoners, brought to his tent. Mickey and Chatto peppered the frightened women with questions. They admitted that Naiche was somewhere on the western slope of the Sierra Madre, but they truthfully reported that they knew nothing of Chihuahua's band or of the plans of Geronimo. Crawford momentarily lost control, pulled his pistol, and threatened to shoot the women if they did not tell him where to find Geronimo. Mickey pleaded that they did not know anything more, so Crawford put down his gun and dismissed them all.

Crawford pressed on to the east after Geronimo, while Wirt Davis and Lieutenant Day's scouts scoured the western slopes of the mountains for any signs of Naiche and Chihuahua. The latter had been raiding across Sonora with his handful of warriors and had even crossed into Arizona in search of his family before troops drove him back across the international line. Chihuahua then united with Naiche in the Azul Mountains, where they briefly conducted several bloody raids before splitting up in late August. Wirt Davis was soon hot on Chihuahua's trail.

Geronimo, with Nana and forty people, mostly men and boys but also a few women—including Lozen—had headed farther southeast in Mexico after Day's attack on their village. Mangas had split off from them with a small party and never rejoined them. He may well have blamed Geronimo for the capture of his wife.

Crawford decided to cut his scouts loose again. He ordered Davis, Sieber, and Mickey to pursue Geronimo's fugitives with Chatto and forty-one scouts. Three packers with seven of the best mules were sent with Davis, but the lieutenant and his men were expected to mostly live off the land.

Sieber detailed Tom Horn to command the Apache scouts who remained with Crawford. Horn's able management was not lost on the captain, especially when two of the scouts got into a quarrel and the remaining scouts grabbed their weapons and took up sides. Horn and Crawford waded into the middle of this tense confrontation, quieted the two sides, and disarmed the belligerents. From that moment on, Crawford began to view Horn as a younger version of Sieber.

Davis departed on August 13 under a heavy rain. Some of the scouts believed that Geronimo had brought the rain, which continued for five days. The men pushed on over mountains that soared well over eight thousand feet, determined to put an end to Geronimo's bloody career. In doing so, the Chiricahua scouts thought they might yet save their people from the wrath of the White Eyes.

As the road grew longer, food quickly became an issue. Davis sent a messenger back to Crawford to hurry forward some pack mules with rations. At the same time, he liberated several Mexican cows from their owners to feed his men, which not surprisingly meant that Mexican troops were soon on his trail.

Once he received Davis's message, Crawford dispatched Lieutenant Charles Elliott with eight scouts, two packers, and six mules with three days' rations. They made rapid progress and were soon camped in the foothills just a few miles behind Davis. Suddenly their camp was raked by a volley from Mexican militia.

While two of his Apache scouts slipped away to find Davis, Lieutenant Elliott boldly advanced with a white flag. Several Mexicans came forward with smiles on their faces and their hands extended in friendship. Elliott and one of his Spanish-speaking packers shook hands and began to explain their mission when the Mexicans leveled and cocked their rifles. They accused Elliott of stealing their cattle and threatened him with instant death if he did not order his Apaches to surrender. As the scouts came forward and dropped their weapons, they were quickly surrounded by fifty Mexicans. The militiamen, who reeked of mescal, herded the Apaches together and tied their hands behind their backs. They were taken to nearby San Buenaventura, paraded through the village streets as a mob yelled curses at them, and then locked in a squalid building that passed for a jail.

Davis and Sieber, having been notified by the two scouts who had slipped away that Elliot and his men had run into trouble, reached Elliott's old camp just before dark. They were greatly relieved to find no dead bodies, and a clear trail leading toward San Buenaventura. But they did have a difficult time holding their angry scouts in check, for they were all anxious to clean out the Mexicans. Davis instructed Sieber to keep a tight watch on the scouts while he went alone to San Buenaventura to meet with the Mexican authorities and secure the release of Elliott and his scouts.

Davis started at once for San Buenaventura despite a violent thunderstorm that turned the night pitch-black. When he was six miles from town, four Mexican soldiers suddenly appeared out of the darkness to confront the soaked lieutenant. He attempted to explain to the men who he was, when a sudden flash of lightning illuminated the scene and appeared to leave the Mexicans terror-stricken. Confused, Davis turned to look behind him, when another flash revealed Chatto and ten Apaches stripped for action and armed to the teeth.

Chatto told Davis that he did not trust the Mexicans and so had slipped away from Sieber to either protect or avenge the stout lieutenant. Davis could not help but smile. He sent two of the scouts back to bring up Sieber, Mickey, and the rest of the scouts, then proceeded with the Mexican soldiers to San Buenaventura, followed by Chatto and the scouts. Once in town, Davis met with the local commander, explained his mission, and paid for the slaughtered cows, which secured the release of Elliott and his men. The apologetic Mexican commander ordered a feast prepared for everyone.

It was noon the following day before Davis could depart the village and resume the pursuit. Geronimo had gained half a day on them while they feasted. Three days later, from the crest of a string of hills, they spotted Geronimo's band—little more than dots on a vast plain—twenty miles distant and headed north toward New Mexico. With no hope of overtaking Geronimo, Davis led his starving, footsore command northeast toward El Paso. They had crossed from west to east over the Sierra Madre and made their way across the Chihuahuan desert under the most exacting of conditions. They finally staggered into Fort Bliss, Texas, on September 5, 1885, after a five-hundred-mile march of twenty-four days. Davis immediately wired Crook that Geronimo was headed back into New Mexico.

Geronimo had but five warriors and five women with him when he crossed the international line just to the east of Palomas Lake that September. General Crook assumed the Apaches would attempt to reach either the Mescalero Reservation or the Navajo Reservation, so an offer of one hundred dollars was posted at each place for the head of any Chiricahua. But Geronimo had no interest in those places, for he was intent on rescuing the captured families that were held at Fort Apache.

By the third week of September, Geronimo had made his way to the White River near Fort Apache, only to learn that the families captured in Mexico were not at Fort Apache. But his young Mescalero wife and her son, whom he had sent to the Mescalero Reservation in May to recruit warriors, were in the Chiricahua camp near the fort. She had been betrayed by the Mescaleros, who wanted nothing to do with Geronimo, and sent under guard to Fort Apache.

Under cover of darkness, Geronimo snuck into the village and made off with his wife and child and a choice selection of White Mountain ponies. By October 10, he was safely in Mexico after easily eluding the White Mountain scouts and bluecoats sent after him. While Crook had sent his columns into Mexico after Geronimo, the wily warrior had returned to snatch his wife and child from under the shadow of Fort Apache. Crook was humiliated.

To ADD TO the general's woes, Lieutenant Davis suddenly resigned from the army. The gruesome march across Chihuahua had been the final straw for Davis. In El Paso, a chance encounter with an old family friend opened up the opportunity for a lucrative position as a ranch manager in Mexico. Nothing Crook said could dissuade the young officer from submitting his resignation.

Sieber and Mickey Free were ordered to report to Captain Francis Pierce at San Carlos. Pierce had been appointed as the sole Indian agent, which finally ended the problem of dual authority with the Indian Bureau. Mickey hurried back to Fort Apache that September for a reunion with Ethlay and their nine-year-old boy.

Captain Crawford now recruited a new detachment of Indian scouts for yet another mission into the Sierra Madre after Geronimo. But at Fort Apache, both Mickey and Chatto declined to sign up for this new enlistment. They shared with Britton Davis a disinclination to return to the Sierra Madre. Mickey was soon on his way to Crook's headquarters at Fort Whipple on detached duty. Sieber also needed a rest, and so his place as Crawford's chief-of-scouts was taken by Tom Horn.

While Mickey Free was traveling to Fort Whipple in late October 1885, Chihuahua and his brother Ulzanna were crossing back into New Mexico. While Chihuahua raided southwestern New Mexico, Ulzanna and a dozen warriors headed for Fort Apache in search of their captured relatives. Ulzanna also dearly hoped to kill Mickey Free and Chatto. The Chiricahuas swept across the White Mountain camps near Fort Apache and left twenty-one dead in their wake, with the loss of only one warrior.

Mickey was frantic when word reached Fort Whipple of Ulzanna's raid. Crook's adjutant wired Fort Apache to inquire of the status of Ethlay and the boy. They were safe. General Crook promptly signed an order that transferred Mickey back to the quartermaster department at Fort Apache.

By the second week of December, Ulzanna had reunited with his brother Chihuahua in New Mexico and within a few days they were back in Mexico. Ulzanna's raiders had covered more than a thousand miles, killed thirty-eight people, and captured nearly three hundred horses and mules. Crook's vaunted line of defense had proven to be a sieve.

It was Ulzanna's bold raid that brought General Sheridan west. The general had just penned a vigorous defense of Crook's Arizona operations and had assured the citizens of the Southwest, and his own superiors in Washington, that "General Crook is the best man we have to deal with these hostile Indians." The election of the Democrat Grover Cleveland as president the previous year, 1884, and his appointment of William Endicott as secretary of war had brought to an abrupt end the cozy relationship the army high command had enjoyed with every Republican administration since Lincoln. The political pressure on army commander Sheridan now came from both the East and the West.

Sheridan had decided to attach New Mexico to Crook's Department of Arizona to better coordinate troop movements, so he traveled to Fort Bowie to meet with Crook on November 29, 1885. Sheridan found Crawford at Fort Bowie with nearly one hundred Apache scouts ready to press south into the Sierra Madre.

Sheridan and Secretary of War Endicott had discussed the removal of all the Chiricahuas from Arizona to either Florida or the Indian Territory, so he now presented that option to Crook and Crawford. Captain Crawford was horrified. Many of his scouts were Chiricahuas, and he had absolute confidence in them. He did not see how he could possibly ask them to campaign in Mexico if their own families were to be banished from their homeland.

Sheridan, unwilling to undercut one of his finest officers on the eve of a campaign, relented. The Chiricahuas could stay in Arizona for now.

Crook was adamant alongside Crawford that removal would be catastrophic for the Apaches. He pointed to Kaytennae, who he claimed was a perfectly reformed Indian after but two years at Alcatraz. Send the other Chiricahua leaders to prison for a year or two, he pleaded with Sheridan, but allow the people to remain in their homeland.

Sheridan agreed to give Crook one more chance, but he was far from happy with the whole situation. He was doubly frustrated that Crook's reliance on Apache scouts, which he disapproved of, had aborted a discussion of the removal of the Chiricahuas to the east. Sheridan opposed the use of any Indians as soldiers. He was convinced that it was bad policy to use inexpensive noncitizens as soldiers when the army was being constantly reduced in size. His position contradicted the repeated use of native auxiliaries in the armed forces of both the European powers and the American military since colonial days, but reflected his determination to protect his budget. Of course, the irony was that more than a third of Sheridan's soldiers, like the general himself, were foreign-born immigrants to the United States.

CAPTAIN EMMET CRAWFORD crossed into Sonora at Agua Prieta on December 11, 1885, for what he hoped would be the final manhunt for Geronimo. This time he would approach Geronimo's mountain stronghold from the west. Before his departure, the moody captain told a friend that a premonition haunted him that he would never return from Mexico. Crawford had Tom Horn with him as chief-of-scouts, as well as Lieutenants Marion Maus, First Infantry, and William Shipp, Tenth Cavalry, in command of the Indian scout companies. Old Concepcion, a former Mexican captive of the Apaches, joined the command as interpreter in place of Mickey Free.

It quickly became apparent that Crawford's command had as

much to fear from their supposed Mexican allies as from the hostile Apaches. The scouts unfortunately contributed to this tense situation. At Guasabas, in Sonora, a group of scouts and packers got roaring drunk, hurrahed the town, and made unwelcome advances to the local ladies. Most of the men returned to Crawford's camp, but a handful of the scouts, led by Kid, remained and pretty much had the town treed. They ran off the local constable who attempted to arrest them, but were soon confronted by Major Emilio Kosterlitzky and six of his *rurales* who had ridden in from Bavispe to confront the troublemakers.

A tense showdown followed. When the Apaches made a fight of it, Kosterlitzky wounded one of them, which caused the rest to bolt. He also captured one Apache—Kid.

Major Kosterlitzky thought it might be a good idea to execute his prisoner as an example to the other *mansos,* or tame Apaches, as the Mexicans called the scouts. Without Sieber's firm hand, the scouts had left a trail of dead and roasted Mexican cattle all the way from the Arizona line. Most of the locals were fed up with the Americans and their Indian scouts.

Kosterlitzky was a remarkable man but had a past shrouded in mystery. He had been born in Moscow in 1853 to a Russian father and a German mother, and was raised in Germany before entering military school in Russia. He became an officer in the Russian navy but for some unexplained reason deserted his post in 1872 while at port in Venezuela. Within a year, he was in Sonora, where he enlisted in the Mexican army and rose rapidly in rank to become a favorite of the dictator Porfirio Díaz. In time he became something of a warlord over Sonora, respected on both sides of the international line for his courage, integrity, and Old World sense of gallantry. He spoke Russian, German, French, Spanish, and English and was renowned as much for his disarming charm as for an iron will that made his *rurales* the terror of both the bandits and the Apaches in Sonora.

The Russian officer contemplated the fate of his young Apache prisoner. The village alcalde, with an eye toward the money the American soldiers brought into Sonora, pleaded for Kid's life. He feared that an execution would anger Captain Crawford. Koster-litzky relented, and Kid was fined twenty dollars for disturbing the peace and sent back to Crawford's camp. Neither the Russian officer nor the young Apache scout could imagine how dramatically their lives would intersect again soon.

CRAWFORD'S COLUMN, with the chastised Kid in tow, moved steadily south along the Bavispe River. Chief-of-scouts Horn left Crawford's column on Christmas day, leading the way on foot with ten of the scouts. It did not take them long to strike a trail. The Apaches had been busy raiding in Sonora, and several small parties of warriors were meeting up deep in the Sierra Madre. Horn was a bit nervous, for he was several days ahead of the main column, but he had total confidence in Crawford. "He looked good to me," Horn remarked, and "had a regular wolf snap to his jaw."

Along the Aros River just west of the Chihuahua line, there lies a tortured jumble of canyons and towering peaks that the Mexicans called Espinosa del Diablo—the Devil's Backbone. It was here that Horn discovered the Apaches. Butchered cattle and mules marked the recently trod trail of the warriors. His scouts were soon close enough to smell the smoke from the smoldering Apache mescal pits.

The Chihuahua bands of Geronimo, Naiche, Nana, and Chihuahua had just reunited for the first time since May 1885. Only Mangas remained aloof in Chihuahua, for he refused to rejoin Geronimo.

Crawford hurried to catch up with Horn. He crossed a landscape of high, jagged ridges and precipitous canyons that impressed one officer as a landscape only some infernal power could have created. A large jaguar momentarily crossed their path and snarled out his cry of defiance before bounding away. This was indeed the devil's land. Crawford's scouts told him that they had detected a trail made by Naiche, for the Chokonen chief favored buckskin covers on the feet of his ponies just as his father Cochise had done.

Crawford decided to leave behind several men who had played out. He donned moccasins for the twelve-hour march to join up with Horn and his scouts and managed to meet up with them just before dawn on January 10, 1886. The enemy camp was just below.

Crawford determined on an immediate attack. He kept several Apache scouts with him to the north while Horn and Lieutenants Maus and Shipp led detachments to surround the sleeping village. As the scouts moved into position, the mules in the Apache camp began to bray.

A handful of warriors came out to check on the mules, and Shipp's White Mountain scouts, unable to resist such tempting targets, opened fire. They had many scores to settle with the Chiricahuas after Ulzanna's raid on Fort Apache. But it was too dark to pick out targets, and the firing quickly became indiscriminate. Horn tried to rally his scouts and reestablish order but had no luck. He could hear Geronimo calling for the women and children to head south for the Aros River. Horn rushed toward the sound of Geronimo's voice, for Crawford had given him a direct order to kill the Apache leader, but he had to halt his pursuit when his scouts lagged back in the captured camp. The White Mountain scouts proved timid, nor were the Chiricahua scouts anxious to pursue their relatives any farther. The fugitives quickly vanished into the timber and brush that bordered the nearby Aros River south of their camp. By dawn, the fight was over.

The combined Apache bands, who numbered about eighty people, twenty-four of whom were warriors or large boys, left no dead or wounded in the village, but had abandoned everything. As Crawford's men moved through the village, they found camp supplies and considerable Mexican plunder, and also rounded up thirty horses and mules. The Apaches would be hard-pressed to survive in the high mountains without any of their supplies.

THE EXHAUSTED COMMAND made camp around the captured *rancheria*. Many of the scouts camped on the ridgeline above while feasting on captured roasted mescal. That afternoon, the warrior Lozen came into the camp to parley with Crawford. Geronimo, Naiche, and Chihuahua were willing to talk with Crawford about a return to San Carlos, she told him. The captain gave Lozen some food and sent her back to Geronimo with the message that he would meet him the next day on a plateau about a mile from the *rancheria.*

A cold mist hung about Crawford's camp the next morning. Several of the scouts rose before dawn, built up the campfires, and began to make coffee. Then, from the rocks above the camp, gunshots rang out. The scouts scattered and took cover behind boulders. Crawford was up at once. Along with Maus, Shipp, and Horn, he rushed to the main camp to see what the gunfire was about.

Horn called out in Spanish that they were Americans and to cease fire. As the gunfire subsided, Crawford, accompanied by Maus and Horn, left the cover of the rocks and boldly approached the unknown foe. All three men were unarmed. Ten heavily armed Mexicans emerged from the foggy mist to meet them.

In the lead was Major Mauricio Corredor, the trophy rifle he had been presented as a reward for slaying Victorio cradled in his arms. The tall officer and four companions brushed past Horn and made straight for Crawford and Maus while the other Mexicans moved to the flanks of the American party. The lieutenant, who was fluent in Spanish, explained who they were and why they were there. Corredor appeared nervous as he surveyed the situation. Behind Maus and Crawford, the distinct click of shells being loaded into Springfield rifles could be heard.

The Apache scouts began to banter with the Mexicans and their Tarahumara Indian scouts.

"You are going to meet up with men today!" shouted a Chiricahua scout.

"We killed Victorio and we can kill every one of you," responded a Tarahumara.

Crawford turned to Maus: "For God's sake, don't let them fire!"

As Maus turned to confront the scouts, Corredor and his men backed away. "*No tiros, no tiros,*" the major exclaimed.

Crawford instinctively climbed atop a nearby boulder and waved a white silk handkerchief for all to see. He was wearing his uniform with captain's bars and a brown campaign hat. A single shot rang out. Maus thought that it seemed to echo over and over and over. He turned to see Crawford take a shot to the head and fall from the boulder. His brains oozed out over his face and down the great rock.

Horn wheeled toward his captain only to be confronted by Corredor. The tall Mexican officer smiled as he fired at the American scout at point-blank range. Horn went down with a bullet to his arm. Within seconds, Corredor was shot through the heart. Scout Dutchy, who was Crawford's orderly, killed the man who had shot his captain. The Apache scouts killed or wounded all ten of the Mexicans who had advanced with Corredor. Victorio's death had been avenged at last.

From a high bluff on the other side of the Aros River, Geronimo stood with Naiche, Nana, and Chihuahua. They watched in amazement for more than an hour as the Apache scouts and the Mexican militia, who numbered about 150, blazed away at one aother. It was clear that the scouts had the upper hand. Geronimo was not a man given to mirth—but he laughed, and laughed, and laughed.

AFTER NEARLY two hours, the gunfire ceased. Maus, now in command, was in a desperate situation. He was outnumbered by hostile Mexicans to his front, and he had hostile Apaches to his rear. He had five wounded men, little ammunition, and no idea just where his unprotected packtrain was.

Horn, whose wound was not serious, boldly approached the Mexicans in response to their call for a parley. Maus tried to call him back. As Horn advanced into their ranks, a distraught old Mexican confronted him. He brandished Corredor's splendid trophy rifle. "Our captain is killed," he raged. "Here is his gun and I'd like to kill a Gringo with the same gun."

Horn was in a sour mood as well. He loudly dismissed the Mexican claim that they had mistaken the American force for Geronimo's renegades. Horn asked pointedly if they were so blind that "they did not know an American from a broncho at twenty-five yards?"

Lieutenant Maus joined Horn. He found the Mexicans downcast and apologetic and so agreed to send the American doctor to attend to their wounded as soon as he arrived. Dr. T. B. Davis came up with the packtrain later that afternoon. He promptly attended to Crawford, who was unconscious but somehow still alive, but he told Maus that the captain's wound was fatal. He then went to the Mexican camp and did the best he could for their wounded men. Maus also sent Horn over with five of the captured Apache ponies for the Mexicans to transport their wounded on.

The following day, Maus, accompanied by the interpreter Old Concepcion, returned to the Mexican encampment. It was raining, so they called the lieutenant over into a rocky overhang that formed a shallow cave. As he entered, he found fifty rifles pointed at him. The Mexicans demanded all the American mules and rations and threatened to kill Maus if he did not accede to their demands. Any lingering doubt Maus had that the Mexican attack was not deliberate quickly vanished.

In the American camp, the scouts could see what was going on. They began to strip for battle and call out to the Mexicans to come and fight them. They declared that Geronimo had sent word that he and his warriors would join the scouts in cleaning out the Mexicans.

This had quite an impact on Mexican bravado. They released Maus under his word to control his scouts and to send them six more mules to carry off their wounded. Maus immediately organized a retreat out of the mountains. A litter was constructed for Crawford and the most seriously wounded scout was placed on a mule. Several scouts were left as a rear guard, but the Mexicans were also clearly withdrawing in the opposite direction. The column made only three miles that first day, but Maus was delighted to place any distance he possibly could between himself and the Mexicans. Henry Daly's packtrain soon joined them with much-needed supplies. They made camp that night breathing a sigh of relief.

⋅◦⟐◦⋅

THAT NIGHT LOZEN and Dahteste came to the American camp. The two women told Maus that Geronimo wished to meet with him but that the officer must come unarmed. On January 15, 1886, Maus, accompanied by Horn, Old Concepcion, and a handful of scouts, met with Naiche, Nana, Chihuahua, and Geronimo. The Apaches were all heavily armed.

As they sat in a circle, Geronimo asked, "Why did you come down here?"

"I came here to capture or destroy you and your band," the nervous lieutenant replied.

This blunt honesty both amused and pleased Geronimo. He extended his hand to Maus and they shook. Now they could get down to business. Geronimo once again related his tale of woe, of how Mickey Free had conspired to kill him, which forced his flight from Turkey Creek. He was, of course, innocent of all the crimes charged against him, he insisted. He would be happy to meet with Nantan Lupan in a month or so near the American border to discuss his return to San Carlos. He would send up smoke signals when he was ready to talk.

Geronimo agreed to send in several people to act as hostages for his good faith. This was the same gambit he had used on Crook almost three years earlier, in 1883. Old crippled Nana led in nine people the next morning. Numbered among them were Geronimo's pregnant young Mescalero wife, one of the warrior's daughters, who was quite ill, and the wife of Naiche with her child. Once again, the wily warrior was unloading those who might slow him down. Geronimo pressed his friends among the Chiricahua scouts to secure ammunition for him from the packtrain.

On January 17, the severely wounded Crawford suddenly opened his eyes. As Maus pressed his hand, the captain tried to speak but could not. Maus assured him that all was well and that Geronimo had agreed to come in. Crawford shook his head in assent and died the next morning. They carried him on a mule to Nacori, where they wrapped him in canvas before burial in the local cemetery. There was no lumber for a coffin.

On February 1, 1886, Maus led his battered command back across the border. Nana and the other hostages were taken to Fort Bowie. General Crook, devastated by the loss of Crawford, may well have blamed Maus, for he inexplicably declined to meet with the young officer when he reached Fort Bowie. In typical fashion, the general went quail hunting for several days while Maus cooled his heels before finally giving up on Crook and returning to the border to watch for smoke signals. The exhausted lieutenant then settled in at John Slaughter's San Bernardino Ranch to await Geronimo.

Crook had secured Kaytennae's release from Alcatraz in the hope he could help convince Geronimo to surrender, so he ordered the young warrior to the border as well. Crook wished to offer Geronimo and the other Chiricahua leaders a period of two years' imprisonment in the east before they might return to San Carlos. The citizens of Arizona and New Mexico, of course, demanded only a hangman's noose for Geronimo.

General Sheridan wanted to turn Geronimo over to the local authorities. "If he cannot be dealt with summarily," Sheridan grumbled, "the Dry Tortugas would be a good reservation for him." Sheridan badly needed results. He made it perfectly clear to Crook that no terms of surrender could be offered to Geronimo that included a promise of a return to Arizona. His defense of Crook to President Cleveland, as well as to the angry citizens of Arizona and New Mexico, had worn pretty thin. Everyone, from the president of the United States on down, now demanded Geronimo in chains or dead.

26

THE WIND AND
THE DARKNESS

GERONIMO'S SMOKE SIGNALS WERE SPOTTED ON March 14, 1886. Lieutenant Maus arranged for the Apaches to meet with General Crook at Cañon de los Embudos (Canyon of the Funnels), some eighteen miles inside Chihuahua, directly south in Mexico of where New Mexico and Arizona met. Maus was anxious to get the Apaches into American territory, for he did not trust the Mexicans, but Geronimo refused. The large herd of stolen Mexican cattle with Geronimo did little to ease the lieutenant's anxiety.

General Crook, accompanied by his aides John Bourke and Cyrus Roberts, did not reach Cañon de los Embudos until just before noon on March 25. Then, in a bizarre repetition of his Sierra Madre misadventure, Crook once again went out hunting. Along with Captain Roberts, he had managed to down an antelope, when Geronimo and Naiche, with a handful of warriors, suddenly appeared. They greeted the pair of hunters and escorted them to Lieutenant Maus's nearby encampment.

Crook immediately made for the packers' camp on the right bank of the Rio Embudos, where lunch was being prepared. Henry Daly sidled over and gave Crook an earful. The general was three days late and the Apaches, both Geronimo's people and the scouts, had occupied their time in nightly drunks, alcohol provided courtesy of a whiskey peddler from Tombstone. Daly reported that Geronimo's people were hungover and surly.

Tombstone photographer C. S. Fly, whom the general had invited to come along to record the event for posterity, was also with them. Kaytennae, Nana, Alchesay, and Dos-teh-seh, the widow of Cochise and mother of Naiche, came in as well with the packtrain. Mickey Free was conspicuously absent, for his presence would only have infuriated Geronimo.

Geronimo and Naiche soon made their way to the packers' camp. The Apache camp was about six hundred yards away from the military camp, with a deep ravine separating the two. The area had abundant forage for the horses and mules, while a clear stream worked its way through the Canyon of the Funnels. The canyon got its name from the many conical rock formations produced by an ancient lava flow.

Crook selected a shaded glade under a large sycamore and seated himself on a little ledge at the base of a knoll. This placed him above the Apaches. Geronimo sat cross-legged on the ground across from Crook, with Nana seated next to him. Everyone else began to gather around them.

"Come down and hear the old man give Geronimo hell," Bourke called out to Daly as he hurried to join Crook. The captain counted twenty-four well-armed warriors gathered near the conference site. He was surprised by how well dressed and equipped all of them were, considering Crawford's destruction of their camp. The hunting in Mexico had obviously been good.

Just as everyone began to settle in, Chihuahua and Ulzanna made a noisy arrival. They galloped through the packers' camp and dismounted at the glade. Crook warmly greeted Chihuahua and then everyone posed for Fly's camera. The careful photographer even moved several of the Apaches.

Beads of sweat formed on Geronimo's face as he fidgeted with a small leather medicine bag. He began, of course, with his standard rant against Mickey Free. "I want to talk first of the causes that led me to leave the reservation," he declared. "I don't know what harm I did to those three men, Chatto, Mickey Free, and Lieutenant Davis. I was living peaceably and satisfied when people began to speak bad of me." Mickey had told him that he was to be arrested and hanged. They had all conspired against him, so he had no choice but to break out. In a pointed reference to Crook's sending out Mickey and other scouts to bring in heads, he remarked that "sometimes a man does something and men are sent out to bring in his head. I do not want such things to happen to us."

While Geronimo spoke, General Crook looked down at the ground. His refusal to make eye contact finally got to Geronimo. "What is the matter that you don't speak to me?" he exclaimed. "I wish you would look and smile at me. The Sun, the Darkness, the Winds, are all listening to what we now say."

"I have heard what you have said," Crook finally responded. "You promised me in the Sierra Madre that that peace should last, but you have lied about it."

"If you think I am not telling the truth, then I don't think you came down here in good faith," Geronimo retorted. "I want no more of this."

The armed warriors murmured and grunted in agreement. Crook's officers grew uneasy, for the council brought to mind the 1873 Modoc peace conference where General Edward Canby had been assassinated by the Indian leader Captain Jack. That murder had secured Crook his brigadier general's star. Naiche waved his hand and silenced the warriors. The soldiers breathed a sigh of relief.

"You must make up your own mind whether you will stay out on the warpath or surrender unconditionally," Crook stated. "If you stay out, I'll keep after you and kill the last one, even if it takes fifty years."

The council broke up on this grim note, but Crook was hardly finished. That night he sent Kaytennae and Alchesay to Geronimo's camp with the promise that if they would all surrender, they would face only two years of exile in the East before a return to San Carlos. This was, of course, in direct contradiction of his clear instructions from Sheridan. The two warriors worked wonders on several of the Apache headmen, although Geronimo remained aloof.

Chihuahua and Naiche visited with Crook the next morning. The two were prepared to surrender unconditionally but told Crook that Geronimo would never agree to that. The general again offered them all two years' exile in the East and then a return to San Carlos, but only if they could bring in Geronimo. He also promised that their families, held as prisoners at Fort Bowie, would accompany them. This was an important inducement to both men.

As Crook talked with Chihuahua and Naiche, Tom Horn went to find Geronimo and found the old warrior stewing. Geronimo was jealous of the attention Crook had paid to Chihuahua and angry that many of the Chiricahuas were willing to give up so easily. Horn could see that there was a clear break between the two Apache leaders.

At noon on March 27, 1886, Chihuahua, Naiche, and Geronimo came into Crook's camp to surrender.

"I surrender myself to you, because I believe in you and you do not deceive us," Chihuahua said as he offered his hand to the general.

"*En-juh,*" Crook replied as he shook his hand. It meant both "It is good" and "It is over."

"When I was free, I gave orders, but now I surrender to you. I throw myself at your feet," declared Naiche.

Geronimo now stepped forward. He had painted his face black with pounded galena. "Now I give myself up to you. Do with me what you please," he said as he shook Crook's hand. "Once I moved about like the wind. Now I surrender to you, and that is all."

CROOK IMMEDIATELY dispatched riders to Fort Bowie with the details of the terms offered. He must have felt considerable anxiety over the expected reaction from Washington. "I had to act at once," he told Sheridan.

The mood among the soldiers was somewhat celebratory, but Henry Daly was worried. As the packer mingled with the Chiricahuas, he could sense that both Naiche and Geronimo were deeply offended by Crook's deference to Chihuahua. That evening it was obvious that all the Chiricahuas, save Chihuahua's band, had acquired more whiskey. A great commotion arose from their camp after darkness fell, and several shots were fired in the direction of the packers' camp. Daly hurried over to Crook's camp and warned Bourke and Maus to expect trouble.

The next morning, as Crook ate his breakfast, Kaytennae and Alchesay visited to tell him that the Chiricahuas were restless. Naiche had gotten so drunk the night before that he had accidentally wounded his wife in a shooting spree and was now passed out. They asked permission to take some warriors back to the Chiricahua camp to clean out the whiskey shop. But Crook told them not to worry.

By seven that morning he and his staff were on their way back to Fort Bowie. He left Lieutenant Maus to deal with the drunken Apaches. Someone had set fire to the grass near the camp, and as the smoke mixed with swirling sand, it tinted the sky a blood red. Crook and his staff reached Fort Bowie in a blinding sandstorm late in the afternoon of March 29.

HENRY DALY'S INTUITION had been correct. He had expected trouble from the moment Crook departed. The perceptive Irishman was incredulous that a general officer would leave the security of so dangerous a character as Geronimo in the hands of a first lieutenant of infantry, the youthful chief-of-scouts Horn, and eighty Apache scouts.

Maus and Horn managed to gather up their prisoners for what turned out to be an abbreviated march north toward San Carlos the first day. Daly had to provide Geronimo with some "hair of the dog" mescal to keep him in the saddle. The packmaster warned Maus that he was sure that the Apaches were about to bolt. That night Daly slept clutching his Winchester.

Sure enough, around three in the morning, Daly was awakened by the tinkle from the bell horse: someone was stealing stock. Daly ran over to awaken Maus. They hurried over to the camp to find all of Geronimo's people gone. The ruckus stirred the remainder of the Apaches, and Chihuahua and Kaytennae soon joined Maus and Daly. Kaytennae agreed to ride out along Geronimo's trail while the soldiers and Apache scouts prepared their pursuit. Chihuahua confessed to Daly that Geronimo "would never return of his own accord."

Maus instructed Horn to make a careful selection of trustworthy scouts for the pursuit. The remaining twenty scouts would accompany the troop escort to take Chihuahua's people the rest of the way to Fort Bowie. That band consisted of fifteen men and forty-seven women and children. Among the warriors were Chihuahua, Ulzanna, and Nana, but Maus well knew that the only warrior name that mattered to the press and to Washington was that of Geronimo.

Maus followed the warriors down to Fronteras. Geronimo, along with Naiche and Lozen, had led eighteen warriors, fourteen women, and seven children back toward the Sierra Madre. They had broken into several small groups and raided along the Magdalena River with bloody success. At this point the scouts lost their trail, so Maus reluctantly turned around and returned to Fort Bowie to face the wrath of General Crook.

CROOK, MEANWHILE, had reached Fort Bowie on the afternoon of March 29, 1886, to find the Arizona territorial governor and a delegation of leading citizens on hand to greet the hero of the hour. The "hero" soon received a telegram from Sheridan instructing him that President Cleveland did not approve the surrender terms to the Apaches. Only unconditional surrender was acceptable to the White House.

Crook objected. The Apaches would certainly bolt if faced with any new terms, he warned Sheridan. The commanding general responded that Crook was to offer the Apaches their lives and nothing else. If they refused, then Crook was to use his troops to destroy them once and for all.

Sheridan had protected his friend as long as he could, but the game was finally up. To President Cleveland and Secretary of War Endicott, it seemed as if a handful of Indian outlaws were holding the government of the United States hostage. Crook might view this as warfare, but the authorities in Washington had long ago ceased to do so. Geronimo and his followers were little better than frontier desperadoes and needed to be dealt with summarily.

Crook had played a dangerous game, and now his calculated duplicity toward both his superiors in Washington and the Apaches reaped a whirlwind. He was convinced that he alone understood the Apaches. He dismissed the outrage of westerners who suffered at the hands of Apache raiders. And he now lectured his military and political superiors on how only he knew what was best for the Indians. His paternalistic vision for the Chiricahuas at least would have allowed them to remain as subjugated people in their homeland. Ultimately, however, his unbridled arrogance alienated both his Washington superiors and Geronimo's Apaches.

On March 30, the same day that Crook received Sheridan's telegram with the order to accept only unconditional surrender or to destroy Geronimo's band, a messenger galloped into Fort Bowie. He handed the general a dispatch with the news that Geronimo had bolted.

The receipt of this unwelcome news, needless to say, infuriated Sheridan. "I feel ashamed of the whole business," he at first wrote Crook, before calming himself and crossing out the line. He continued that Geronimo's escape "has occasioned great disappointment. It seems strange that Geronimo and party could have escaped without the knowledge of the scouts."

Crook responded with a ringing defense of the loyalty of the Apache scouts, but Sheridan was finished with that debate. He tersely reminded Crook that he had forty-six companies of infantry and forty troops of cavalry at his disposal and that he must start to make good use of them to defend the frontier.

"I believe that the plan upon which I have conducted operations is the one most likely to prove successful in the end," Crook replied on April 1, 1886. "It may be, however, that I am too much wedded to my own views in this matter, and as I have spent nearly eight years of the hardest work of my life in this department, respectfully request that I may now be relieved from its command."

On April 2, Crook received a telegram from Sheridan that reassigned him to command the Department of the Platte. Brigadier General Nelson A. Miles would take Crook's place in Arizona.

Crook still had the melancholy duty of sending Chihuahua and his people off to their Florida exile. He did not inform them that President Cleveland had overruled the terms of surrender and that they were never to return to Arizona. The Chiricahuas departed Fort Bowie before noon on April 7.

The Apache cavalcade numbered seventy-six souls—fifteen men, twenty-nine women, and thirty-three children—and included old Nana and the fierce Ulzanna as well as Chihuahua. Tension mounted at the Bowie Station when it came time to disarm the warriors. This had never happened before, but Chihuahua calmed the people, the men gave up their weapons, and everyone boarded the train. Crook thoughtfully gave the captain in charge of the guard detail $125 to buy coffee and treats for the Apaches during the long train trip to Fort Marion, Florida.

On April 11, 1886, General Miles reached Fort Bowie to take command of the Department of Arizona. The fort's six-pounder boomed forth a welcome as Crook grimly shook the hand of his bitter rival and escorted him to his quarters. The next day Crook left for Prescott to pack up and depart for Omaha.

MICKEY FREE WAS now living at Fort Apache with Ethlay and their nine-year-old son at Canyon Day, which was not far from Turkey Creek. Crook had personally reassigned him to the quartermaster's department at Fort Apache the previous December in response to Ulzanna's raid, and he had remained there ever since. Unfortunately, around the time Crook was leaving Arizona, tragedy began to stalk Mickey.

Many of Ethlay's relatives also lived at Canyon Day, and clan friction was starting to build between the western and eastern White Mountain residents of the village. These tensions boiled over at a *tiswin* party in the summer of 1886. The men, all members of the rival clan of Mickey's wife, got more and more belligerent the more they drank. Mickey, who was unaware of the *tiswin* revelers, sent his son and his young nephew off to water the family horse. The boys, inseparable friends, jumped on the horse bareback and raced along the ridgeline toward the creek. They passed at some distance from the *tiswin* revelers.

The drunken Apaches saw the boys, members of the rival clan, silhouetted against the sky on the nearby ridge. Taunts and dares followed. A warrior aimed his rifle. In his drunken stupor, he could barely steady it, but he managed to fire a single shot. Both boys tumbled off the horse.

Ancient custom and Apache law dictated the right of Mickey to seek out the men responsible for his son's death and kill them. A clan blood feud would surely have followed. Mickey also knew that the law of the White Eyes prevented him from taking vengeance. Now he wrestled with exactly who he was—Apache or white soldier. He decided not to seek revenge. He indeed belonged to the white world.

AFTER THE TRAGEDY, Mickey packed up Ethlay and all their goods and moved over to the east fork of the White River.

"Mickey got mad. When you're his age and fought all your life and walk from one end of the world to the other end on foot, you get mad but you don't want to fight no more," said Ethlay's niece. He vented his anger on his wife's family, for he blamed their clan feud for the death of his son.

"I've been good to you people," he told them as he departed. "I help you in every way, and I am the only one with cattle and I feed you, and here my son is killed on account of those nasty mouths."

Mickey retreated into his grief but wasn't allowed to grieve for long. He was soon called back into government service by the new department commander, Brigadier General Nelson A. Miles.

"A BRAVE PEACOCK" is how Theodore Roosevelt characterized Nelson Miles. The forty-seven-year-old general was indeed vain and pompous, but he was also ruthlessly efficient and happily unburdened with the self-righteous moralism that had hamstrung Crook. His outstanding Civil War record won him colonel's eagles in the postwar army despite his lack of a West Point education, and a series of successful campaigns against the Cheyenne, Sioux, and Nez Perce had secured him a brigadier's star in 1880. Miles was a man who got things done.

Major Anson Mills, who knew both Crook and Miles well, had no doubt that Miles was the better man. "Miles wasn't so good a soldier as Crook, but he was possessed of more generosity, governed by warmer impulses, perhaps actuated by a shrewder worldly wisdom," Mills confessed to Captain Bourke. "Miles made friends who swore by him, Crook never made any."

Sheridan, Crook's one powerful friend in the army, had given up on him. Sheridan and Miles had never been close, although they shared a mutual respect, and the commanding general expected Miles to carefully adhere to his instructions. Sheridan impressed on Miles "the necessity of making active and prominent use of the Regular troops of your command."

At first Miles followed Sheridan's directives closely. He occupied key water holes and mountain passes with troops, established an extensive heliograph system to allow rapid communication, and organized flying columns of cavalry to pursue Apache raiders. The department had been reinforced by all twelve companies of the Tenth Cavalry a few months before. Colonel Benjamin Grierson had established his headquarters at Fort Whipple in May 1885, while the troops were scattered at Forts Grant, Thomas, Apache, and Verde.

Miles's main strike force consisted of a select group of Fourth Cavalry and Eighth Infantry soldiers, two packtrains under packmaster Henry Daly, along with thirty Apache scouts, with Tom Horn again as chief-of-scouts, all under the command of Captain Henry Lawton. Captain Lawton was a hard-drinking Civil War veteran who had risen from the ranks to come out of the war with a commission and a Medal of Honor. On the frontier, he had made a reputation for energy and efficiency in campaigns against the Texas Comanches and Montana Cheyennes.

Miles also assigned Dr. Leonard Wood, an athletic Harvard man and exceptional contract surgeon who had been on the frontier for less than a year, to assist Lawton. Wood, blessed with a winning personality and active mind, impressed everyone who met him. Although a medical officer, he was anxious for active service as a line officer. Miles gave the twenty-six-year-old officer just that chance.

Miles also made a rather surprising addition to Lawton's command when he hired a special scout for the expedition. "Late in the afternoon, old man Streeter, known as the White Apache on account of his long experience with the Apaches and supposed knowledge of and friendship with them, came into camp with orders to report for duty with us," Wood jotted in his diary on June 13. Miles was either unaware, or simply did not care, that Arizona had put a price on Zebina Streeter's head three years before as a renegade fighting alongside the Apaches. Miles believed he had put together a crack unit that would capture America's most infamous Indian warrior and finally put an end to this seemingly endless war.

EVEN AS MILES set his troops in motion, Geronimo hardly remained idle. It was if he was taunting the new military commander. On April 27, Geronimo led a raid into Arizona to plunder ranches along the Santa Cruz River. The Apaches casually rode into the village of Calabasas and collected every horse they could find. Then they calmly departed and rode west to the isolated ranch of a frontiersman named Anson Peck, some eight miles northwest of Nogales.

Peck and a companion had ridden out early that morning in search of stray cattle, leaving behind his pregnant wife, Petra, who had a babe in arms, and her niece Trinidad Verdin. Petra was standing in the ranch house doorway with her baby when the Apaches approached. A young warrior shot her down instantly, then picked up the crying infant and bashed its brains out against the wall. Trinidad ran and crawled under the bed, only to be pulled out by her ankles. The warrior was about to kill her when Geronimo strode in and stayed his hand. He picked the sobbing girl up and put her on a horse behind Chappo.

Then the Apaches set fire to the ranch house and took off, riding west. They had gone but two miles when they encountered Peck and his companion roping cattle. The two men were unarmed. Peck's friend was shot down, but again, before Peck was killed, Geronimo appeared and ordered his warriors to release the frightened man. The warriors had stripped Peck down to his red long johns, which caused Geronimo to laugh. He called Peck "Mangas Coloradas," but the shaken rancher did not get the joke. Those red pants had inexplicably saved Peck's life.

Geronimo then rode back into Sonora, leaving fourteen dead Arizonans in his wake. Captain Thomas Lebo, a veteran of the Victorio campaign, was soon in hot pursuit with his troop of the Tenth Cavalry. Captain Lebo rode into an ambush south of Nogales and lost one man killed and another wounded. The wounded Buffalo Soldier was pulled to safety by Lieutenant Powhatan Clarke under a galling fire from the Apaches. Young Clarke, who was a great favorite with the regiment, received the Medal of Honor for his valor that day. Lebo thought he had faced eighty warriors and was certain his men had killed at least two. The Apaches, who numbered but sixteen, escaped under cover of darkness with no casualties. General Miles was furious. He posted a two-thousand-dollar reward for Geronimo, dead or alive.

Naiche now decided to split off from Geronimo and head to Fort Apache with eight men and nineteen women and children. They cut a bloody swath as they moved north, killing thirteen people. "It was war," Naiche explained years later. "Anybody who saw us would kill us, and we did the same thing."

Under cover of darkness on May 25, Naiche and seven warriors visited the Chiricahua camp near Fort Apache only to discover that many of their family members had already been sent east with Chihuahua's people. Dos-teh-seh was there, and she pleaded with her son to surrender to the new soldier chief. But Naiche could not bring himself to trust the soldiers and soon departed. With troops on his trail, he killed three cowboys and captured forty horses before he crossed back into Sonora.

Mickey Free had learned of Naiche's visit to the camp near Fort Apache and reported the details to General Miles. The general promptly contacted Tom Jeffords, the former Indian agent, to request that he use his influence on Naiche to induce him to surrender. Jeffords took the trail, but he could not overtake the Apaches. On June 9 Naiche reunited with Geronimo near the summit of the Azul Mountains.

CAPTAIN LAWTON LED his column out of Fort Huachuca on May 5, 1886. The post band struck up "The Girl I Left Behind Me" as Tom Horn led out his twenty White Mountain and San Carlos Apache scouts to take the advance. Lawton's command logged more than five hundred fruitless miles without firing a single shot. He had to send back several of his men and scouts and secure fresh replacements, but he never faltered from his pursuit. On June 12 he discovered Geronimo's camp in the Azul Mountains. But the Apaches, who numbered but forty souls, had split into three groups and scattered.

A week later Lawton encountered thirty Mexican militiamen near a watering hole called El Gusano. The Mexicans had just had a hard fight with Geronimo and were licking their wounds. They told the American their story.

Just after noon on June 17, they had surprised Geronimo's band, which consisted of only six Apaches and the captive girl, Trinidad Verdin, and routed them. Geronimo had ordered his people to flee, then he pulled Trinidad up onto his horse and galloped up the rocky hillside. His young wife had been wounded by the first Mexican volley. She had turned to empty her pistol into the advancing soldiers, so they shot her down and rode over her in pursuit of Geronimo, whose horse stumbled in the rocks. He and Trinidad tumbled off and as he rose, he was wounded. The little girl was so bruised from the fall that she could hardly move. The Mexicans rushed toward her but Geronimo took careful aim and shot three soldiers, each of whom was hit directly in the head. The Mexicans fled back to the abandoned Apache camp, where Trinidad eventually joined them. Geronimo once again vanished.

The Mexicans first suspected Lawton's scouts of belonging to Geronimo's band, but the captain and Dr. Wood strode forward and calmed them. The Americans noticed three dead soldiers as well as the body of a scalped Apache woman. Surgeon Wood helped to bury the woman and took a string of beads from around her neck. Lawton recovered Trinidad from the Mexicans and retired back with her to Agua Fria to await fresh troops. Streeter was sent north with reports for Miles and a request for new orders.

General Miles, accompanied by Tom Jeffords, traveled to Fort Apache not long after Naiche's visit to meet with the Chiricahuas and test their temper. On the last day of June, Miles met with several leading Apaches, with Mickey Free translating. The spit-and-polish general was disgusted by Mickey's disheveled appearance, not knowing that the famous scout was still in mourning over his son.

Miles was prejudiced against all Apaches, but especially against the four hundred Chiricahuas at Fort Apache. He was disturbed to learn that the Indians, despite technically being prisoners of war, were still quite well armed. Miles found the young men "insolent, violent, and restless." He characterized the Chiricahuas as the most "troublesome, desperate, disreputable band of human beings I had never seen before and hope never to see again."

Before he arrived at Fort Apache, Miles had already decided to remove the Chiricahuas to the Indian Territory, and the visit only bolstered that decision. Even while plotting the removal, Miles decided to enlist a couple of warriors for a desperate mission. The two warriors he recruited, Kayitah and Martine, who had relatives out with Geronimo, agreed to go to Mexico to attempt to open negotiations. They both had ridden with Geronimo and knew him well. Miles also recalled Lieutenant Charles Gatewood from Fort Wingate to accompany the two scouts and attempt to open up new surrender talks with Geronimo. Gatewood in turn enlisted George Wrattan, a former trader at San Carlos who was reasonably fluent in Apache, to join his little command.

By July 21, Gatewood and his companions were near Slaughter's San Bernardino ranch, where they rendezvoused with Lieutenant James Parker's troop of the Fourth Cavalry. Gatewood's chronic rheumatism was acting up, for it was the rainy season, so Parker waited for him to recover. This delayed them several days, but within the week, they were all on their way south to find Lawton.

GENERAL MILES WAS determined to remove all the Chiricahuas from Arizona to the Indian Territory, but he received a surprisingly cool reception from General Sheridan to his plan. Sheridan remembered all too well the problems that had followed the transfer of Victorio's people to San Carlos. To make matters worse, Miles wanted to settle the Apaches next to the reservation of their ancient enemies, the Comanches.

President Cleveland, as well as his cabinet secretaries for war and the interior, was not inclined to be as negative. Such an action would curry favor with the people of New Mexico and Arizona, free up scarce water resources, and allow the Apache reservation to be downsized. In 1883 the Arizona territorial legislature had petitioned to have all the reservations terminated, and in 1885 the legislature had specifically requested the abolishment of the San Carlos and White Mountain reserves. It goes without saying that the settlers had a vote and the Indians did not. To the politicians, it was as simple as that.

Miles selected ten men and three women for an Apache delegation to visit Washington. They were to meet with the president and discuss removal to the Indian Territory. The decision on removal, of course, had already been made. Chatto and the Chokonen leader Noche headed the Chiricahua delegation, while Loco and Kaytennae led the Warm Springs people. Mickey Free accompanied them as the Apache-to-Spanish interpreter, with Sam Bowman as the Spanish-to-English half of the team. Two additional interpreters were added by Captain Joseph Dorst of Miles's staff, who escorted the party.

It was late on Saturday, July 17, after an eight-day train trip, when the delegation finally reached Washington. They were lodged in the creaking Beveridge Hotel a few blocks from the White House. Captain John Bourke, upon learning that the Apaches had arrived, hurried to greet them. He was mortified by the poor accommodations, for it was obvious that the government had no interest in impressing them.

Bourke was stunned by the appearance of his old friend Mickey Free. His long red hair was filthy and uncombed, his clothing tattered and dirty, which Bourke read as a sign "of deep grief over the recent killing of his little boy, not 10 years old." It appeared that a lifetime of violence and pain had finally claimed Mickey Free.

The good captain attempted to get everyone out of their dingy quarters to treat them to the pleasures of Washington. He escorted them to Harris's Bijou Theatre on Ninth Street to see a Mexican band and an opera singer. After the show he took them to soda fountains, which they liked very much, and to an ice cream parlor, which they disliked, because the cold burned their mouths.

After a week in the capital, the Indian delegation met with Secretary of the Interior L. Q. C. Lamar. The former lieutenant colonel of the Confederate army lectured the Apaches on the benefits of removal from Arizona to the East. Loco, as spokesman for the group, told Lamar that they were happy in their homeland. The secretary simply smiled and shook everyone's hand.

A reporter for the *Washington Star* noted that "the half-breed who interpreted into Spanish wore a soiled calico shirt and a pair of blue overalls and as he had only one eye, his appearance was not prepossessing." The unadorned Wild West would remain a puzzle to the sophisticated East.

The next day, the entire delegation met with Secretary of War Endicott. Chatto told the secretary that the Chiricahuas were happy at Fort Apache and wished to remain there. He also asked Endicott if his family had been rescued from Mexican captivity. Endicott told Mickey to assure Chatto that everything possible was being done to restore his family to him. Chatto, of course, would never see them again.

At noon on July 27, Captains Dorst and Bourke escorted the Apache delegation to the White House. Endicott had carefully instructed the Apaches to not speak to President Cleveland unless spoken to, and to not bother him with any speeches. The corpulent president met the Indians in the library and shook the hand of each Apache. Cleveland told Mickey to remind the Apaches that their statements to Lamar and Endicott had been written down and did not need to be restated.

"And tell them," he said to Bourke, who then translated to Spanish for Mickey, "that I will give the matter very careful attention."

President Cleveland gave Chatto a silver peace medal. The once-flourishing peace medal business was obviously in serious decline: the medal bore the likeness of former president Chester Arthur. The rest of the delegation received impressive certificates, which were only of slightly less value than the worthless peace medal. Then the president shook everyone's hand once again and departed.

Three days later, Captain Bourke was summoned to the White House for a meeting with the president, Endicott, Lamar, and Captain Dorst. The president was anxious to send all the Chiricahuas to Florida and wondered what Bourke and Dorst thought should be done with the Apache delegation. Dorst, speaking for Miles, was enthusiastic about the plan. He suggested that the delegation be held at Fort Leavenworth until they could join the rest of the Apaches at Fort Marion in Florida.

Bourke was horrified. He pointed out that these people had all been at peace since 1883, and that Chatto and many others had given valuable service as army scouts against Geronimo. General Crook had promised them that they could remain in their homeland. But even as he spoke, Bourke realized that the fix was in.

As Cleveland ignorantly prattled on, Bourke became fixated on the president's bulk. "I could not help remarking what an enormous *neck* he had and how very small a *head*," he wrote in his diary that night. "He impressed me as being self-opinionated, stubborn, and not too tenacious of the truth, a man of great sinuosity of morals, narrow in his views, fond of flattery and lacking the breadth of thought which extended travel and study alone can give."

The Apaches remained in Washington for another week while the administration set its new removal plan in motion. Sheridan was instructed to ask Miles if sending all the Chiricahuas to Florida met with his approval. It did, of course, and the reluctant Sheridan had to surrender to the inevitable.

Captain Dorst led the delegation, now quite impatient to return to Fort Apache, to the Indian school at Carlisle, Pennsylvania, where Loco was reunited with his son. Dorst held them there for five days while he awaited orders from Miles, but when none arrived, they proceeded to Fort Leavenworth. Mickey Free pressed Dorst for an explanation about just what was going on, as it was clear to him that something was amiss. Dorst was still in the dark as to the plans of Cleveland and Miles, but soon enough, they all got their answer.

Miles informed Dorst that the president had decided to remove all the Chiricahuas, including the Warm Springs people, from Arizona to Florida. This operation was already under way under the direction of Lieutenant Colonel James Wade at Fort Apache. Miles had objected to the Florida location, even suggesting Fort Union in New Mexico as an alternative, but he had been overruled by President Cleveland. The general now ordered Dorst to inform the members of the delegation that they were suddenly prisoners of war and were to be sent to Fort Marion, Florida, to join their families. Mickey Free accompanied the party as interpreter.

As Mickey translated, Dorst told the Apaches that this was being done for their own safety. To make this rank betrayal legal, the captain presented the Apache leaders with a document promising their people land, livestock, farm tools, and cash payments for life to the chiefs. Stunned but with no alternative, Chatto, Loco, and the others made their marks on the documents, signing away their freedom and their homes. They were soon all on their way to Florida. Chatto still wore his peace medal.

--==◦◦==--

GERONIMO WAS AN OUTCAST. His followers had been imprisoned in the East, while the Warm Springs people at San Carlos and Alchesay's people at Fort Apache hated him for the misery he had brought upon them. Even Mangas, still at large with a handful of followers, refused to join with him against their common foe.

Geronimo had but thirty-four people left, many of them women and children, while one quarter of the entire US Army now pursued him. Furthermore, Emilio Kosterlitzky's Sonoran *rurales* combed the western slopes of the Sierra Madre in search of him, while Colonel Joaquin Terrazas's militia guarded every water hole and river crossing in Chihuahua. Never in American history had so many sought to kill so few.

General Miles kept in as close contact as possible with Lawton and Gatewood. Lawton's command was totally broken down by their fruitless pursuit of Geronimo, but they kept on the trail despite daunting terrain and blistering heat. Miles repeatedly reminded Lawton that any means the captain might use to kill Geronimo would be approved. Failure was clearly not an option. Gatewood had joined Lawton but was in ill health and a sour mood.

Dr. Leonard Wood had received his wish to be a line officer. He and Tom Horn went out often on extended scouts but found no Apaches. Wood did not hold out much hope for Gatewood's success. "Gatewood stated that he has no faith in this plan and is disgusted with it," Wood noted in his journal, "and wants to go home. He is not in especially good health."

Lawton was just as unhappy with the mission as Gatewood. The lieutenant's assignment to bring in Geronimo was a clear sign that General Miles had given up on Lawton's campaign and was willing to return to Crook's flawed policy of negotiation. The glory of bagging the most famous Indian warrior of all time was slipping from Lawton's grasp.

Lawton was disgusted by the arrival of Gatewood and his two Apache emissaries but knew that he had no choice but to support their mission. Lawton wanted to fight the Apaches, not negotiate with them. "But if I find Geronimo I will attack him," he told Lieutenant Parker. "I refuse to have anything to do with this plan to treat with him."

On August 24, Geronimo sent Lozen and Dahteste into Fronteras to barter hides and jerky for food and mescal and to see if the Mexicans were open to peace talks. This was dangerous work and the women were fortunate to escape with their lives, not to mention the coffee, sugar, and mescal they brought back loaded on three mules. Gatewood's two scouts picked up the women's trail and followed it south. The bold scouts, Kayitah and Martine, entered the warriors' camp above the Bavispe River in the Teras Mountains and convinced Geronimo to meet with Gatewood. The next morning Geronimo and Naiche greeted Gatewood, whom they both knew well, in a shady glen alongside the Bavispe.

Gatewood had come alone as Geronimo had requested, with George Wrattan along as interpreter. Geronimo remarked on how ill his old friend looked and embraced him. Geronimo called the lieutenant by his Apache name of Bay-chen-daysen, which meant Long Nose. As other Apaches drifted in and stood nearby, Gatewood stated the terms offered by Miles.

"Surrender, and you will be sent to join the rest of your people in Florida, there to await the decision of the President of the United States as to your final disposition," the lieutenant bluntly stated. "Accept these terms, or fight it out to the bitter end."

Geronimo was stunned. He again repeated his story of how he had been driven to flee the reservation by Mickey Free, and how all he wanted was to now return to Turkey Creek and live in peace. This is what Nantan Lupan had promised. But Gatewood did not budge. He simply restated the terms offered by Miles, at which point Geronimo withdrew to consult with his warriors.

After some time, Geronimo returned. "Take us to the reservation or fight," he declared. Bay-chen-daysen then told him that they no longer had a reservation, for General Miles had sent all the Chiricahua people to Florida as prisoners of war. Geronimo did not believe this was even possible. He stared at Gatewood intently as if attempting to read his mind. Martine and Kayitah confirmed Gatewood's story. The warriors again talked among themselves.

"We want your advice," Geronimo finally stated. "Consider yourself one of us and not a white man. Remember all that has been said today, and as an Apache, what would you advise us to do? Should we surrender, or should we fight it out?"

"I would trust General Miles and take him at his word," Gatewood replied.

Geronimo told Gatewood that they would come to him in the morning with their answer.

The warriors went back to their camp atop the mountain to smoke, talk, and make medicine. That night was dark, with ominous clouds covering the moon and stars. The eighteen warriors talked all night. Finally Perico rose to speak.

"I am going to surrender," he said. "My wife and children have been captured. I love them and want to be with them." Fun rose to agree with Perico. Others rose as well.

"You have been great fighters in battle," Geronimo said as he scanned the faces of his warriors reflected in the firelight. "If you are going to surrender, there is no use [in] my going without you. I will give up with you."

ON THE MORNING of August 26, Geronimo and five warriors appeared at Gatewood's camp as promised. Lawton joined Gatewood that morning, so he and Geronimo smoked and agreed that the Apaches could retain their arms until a formal surrender ceremony with General Miles at Skeleton Canyon, some sixty miles southeast of Fort Bowie on American soil.

Messengers were sent north to inform General Miles of the surrender, while the column, with Gatewood and Geronimo's band apart from Lawton's soldiers and scouts, slowly advanced toward the American line. They had not gone far when a Mexican force from Fronteras, 180 strong, confronted them to demand that the Apaches be turned over. Lawton refused and a tense situation followed before the Mexican officer eventually backed down.

Geronimo was anxious for a final crack at the Mexicans and faced down the Mexican commander with his hand on the butt of his pistol before Lawton jumped between them. Lieutenant Wood was with Geronimo in this case. He was "hoping that there would be a fight and thereby have a chance to even up with the Mexicans for poor Crawford's death." Both Wood and Geronimo were frustrated by Lawton's diplomacy.

On September 2, 1886, Lawton's column reached the narrow entrance to Skeleton Canyon on the western slope of the Peloncillo Mountains, where troops awaited them. Geronimo was naturally nervous and camped away from the soldiers. He was not worried for himself, he later explained to the interpreter George Wrattan, but for his warriors.

"They are not going to kill me," Geronimo told Wrattan. "I have the promise of Usen, but my warriors are not so protected."

It was late the next day before Miles arrived. The general was nervous as well, for he did not want a repeat of the Crook fiasco at Cañon de los Embudos.

Geronimo rode down from his isolated camp to meet Miles. He came alone and unarmed. As the two men faced each other in stiff formality, the interpreter introduced the general and said to Geronimo, "General Miles is your friend."

"I never saw him, but I have been in need of friends," Geronimo replied. "Why has he not been with me?"

When this was interpreted, the general and his officers broke into laughter. All the tension evaporated as their good humor echoed through Skeleton Canyon. Miles was somewhat charmed by the bold warrior who stood before him.

"He was one of the brightest, most resolute, determined looking men that I have ever encountered," said the general of Geronimo. "He had the clearest, sharpest dark eye I think I have ever seen, unless it was that of General Sherman when he was at the prime of life."

Geronimo again told the tale of how Mickey Free had plotted to kill him, which left him no choice but to break out. To his great pleasure, Miles nodded in agreement to this story. "This statement is confirmed by others and not disproved by [Mickey Free]'s face," Miles later told Secretary of the Interior Lamar.

Geronimo, who felt that he had finally met a general who understood him, asked if he and his people might not now return to Turkey Creek. Miles told him no, for the Chiricahuas were all gone from the White Mountains to Florida. Geronimo must now surrender with only the promise that his life would be spared. He and his people would be sent to Florida to join their relatives.

"This is the fourth time I have surrendered," he said to Miles.

"And I think it is the last time," the general replied.

ON SEPTEMBER 5, Miles started for Fort Bowie by wagon with Geronimo, Naiche, and three other warriors. Lawton followed with the rest of the prisoners. Geronimo and Naiche barely had time to try on their new cavalry boots at Fort Bowie before they were hurried to the railway station with their people.

General Miles, like Crook before him, now placed his personal sense of honor above the demands of the Washington politicians. He was determined to get Geronimo and Naiche on a train to Florida before President Cleveland could order them turned over to Arizona civil authorities.

The train would depart Bowie Station at 2:55 the afternoon of September 8, 1886. Lawton was placed in charge of the prisoners, with Wrattan as his interpreter. Among the prisoners were the army scouts Kayitah and Martine, who had led Gatewood to Geronimo. In addition to the fifteen Chiricahua men, nine women, including Lozen, and two children, there was an additional prisoner of war. The day before, Chappo's wife had borne Geronimo a grandson. Chappo carried the infant onto the train as the Fourth Cavalry band played "Auld Lang Syne."

The train rattled on to El Paso and then San Antonio, where an order from President Cleveland briefly halted it. The president still hoped to turn Geronimo over to the Arizona courts, but he finally relented and let the train move onward, to New Orleans and finally to Florida. Geronimo arrived at Fort Pickens, across the bay from Pensacola, on the morning of October 25. Others went to Fort Marion, near St. Augustine. It was the beginning of twenty-seven years as prisoners of war for the Chiricahua people.

LIEUTENANT COLONEL WADE had his orders. August 29 was ration day at Fort Apache, and Wade had sent word that there would also be a roll call. The people were puzzled, but they had no leaders who might talk with Wade to see what was going on. They did not know it then, but their chiefs had been kidnapped after meeting with the president of the United States and were now being held as prisoners of war.

As the Apaches gathered for the roll call, they were suddenly surrounded by cavalry. The men, including the army scouts, were disarmed and placed in barracks under close confinement. The women and children were told to gather their belongings in order to travel to the East to be reunited with their chiefs and meet the president. It was all over quickly.

On September 4, the people—383 in number—were loaded onto wagons for the eighty-mile journey north to the railway station at Holbrook. There were not enough wagons, so many people rode ponies or walked. They brought all their horses and cattle with them. After an eight-day journey, they reached Holbrook, where they were loaded onto twelve cars of the Atlantic & Pacific Railroad. They were informed that their livestock would be sold and the proceeds sent to them. Many of their belongings would not fit into the two baggage cars and so they were left piled at the depot for the locals to claim as souvenirs. There was nothing the Apaches could do in protest, for armed soldiers were everywhere.

The train pulled out on September 13, 1886, and headed east. The Apache dogs had followed along with their masters to Holbrook, but none were allowed on the train. The pups began to bark and yelp and howl as the train rumbled away. The Holbrook citizens watched in astonishment as hundreds of the loyal animals ran barking after the train. They soon vanished beyond the desert horizon. Some of the dogs ran more than twenty miles before they collapsed and died in the searing desert heat.

27

APACHE KID

FTER THE REMOVAL OF THE CHIRICAHUA PEOPLE, it was all *tiswin* drunks and blood feuds at San Carlos. Al Sieber, with Mickey Free, Kid, and a handful of Apache scouts, did their best to keep a lid on the simmering pot that was the reservation. Even with Geronimo imprisoned far to the east, the troubles of the Apache people were hardly over.

Tom Horn had departed army service soon after the Chiricahua removal. He had led Apache and Pima scouts for Lieutenant Carter Johnson in a futile search for Mangas and his small band throughout September 1886, but quickly tired of this work and resigned in the final week of that month. Horn soon discovered more lucrative opportunities for a man with his talent with a gun.

Mangas, with a dwindling band of three warriors and eight women and children, moved slowly north from Chihuahua toward Fort Apache. They did not raid and carefully evaded the troops and scouts sent to find them. Mangas hoped to simply melt invisibly into the Apache camps on Turkey Creek, but on October 18, 1886, they encountered a troop of the Tenth Cavalry. The Buffalo Soldiers rounded up all the people, disarmed them, took everything from them, and then escorted them to Fort Apache. Mangas was soon imprisoned with his old rival Geronimo at Fort Pickens.

One Apache managed to escape from the prison train. Massai, a Warm Springs warrior, was renowned among his people for his restless spirit and independent ways. After Geronimo had forced Loco's people to break out, Massai had trailed them into Mexico to retrieve his wife. He had gone out with Geronimo in 1885 but soon tired of the warpath and returned alone to rejoin his family at Fort Apache. For a time, he served as a scout for Lieutenant Maus. When Wade's soldiers arrested all the Warm Springs warriors for transport to Florida, Massai attempted to rally the men but failed. Their spirits were broken.

Somewhere near St. Louis, Massai slipped from the train and vanished into the black night. Darkness was his ally, for he moved at night and hid by day, stole to live, and followed the rail line and the stars back to Fort Apache. Once there, he preyed upon both White Eye and Apache like a lobo wolf. Every door, both white and Apache, was closed to him and every hand was turned against him.

Mickey Free had bid farewell to his friend Chatto at the ancient Spanish fort at St. Augustine in early October and made his way by rail back to Holbrook, then by wagon to Fort Apache and Ethlay. He had been gone more than three months, had seen the great cities of the East, had met the fat President Cleveland, and had finally come to fully understand the bottomless depths of the white man's perfidy.

With his service as special agent and interpreter over, he rejoined the Apache scouts. The thirty-eight-year-old was made first sergeant of Company E of the scouts, a twenty-man force that was assigned to keep order on the White Mountain Reservation.

Mickey was soon sent out on Massai's trail. But the elusive ex-scout was wily and had no trouble evading the scout patrols sent after him. The manhunt turned from weeks to months and then to years as Massai struck near Fort Apache and then at San Carlos. He took food, horses, guns, and women, then simply vanished into the mountains.

Lieutenant Carter Johnson, Tenth Cavalry, who commanded Mickey's scout company, related a tale of Massai's shadow raids. An Indian woman was found dead under a walnut tree not far from Fort Apache where she and her daughter, Natastale, had been gathering nuts. The daughter was missing. Johnson's Apache scouts followed pony tracks from the dead woman to a *tiswin* debauch in the nearby hills. The pony, which belonged to one of Johnson's scouts, had then been set loose, and the scouts followed some familiar moccasin tracks straight back into the camp. But the scout they seized protested his innocence so vehemently that Johnson had second thoughts as he lodged the culprit in the guardhouse.

"I sent my first sergeant, the famous Mickey Free, with a picked party of trailers, back to the walnut tree," Johnson recalled. Mickey quickly discovered the tracks of a different horse and pony by the tree and followed them north to Alchesay's camp. Soon enough, he came upon the carcass of the butchered pony next to the trail. Mickey feared that the murderer belonged to Alchesay's people, for the dead woman's band had an ancient blood feud with them.

Mickey cleared the arrested scout, who was released, but now an even greater problem confronted Johnson. The lieutenant sent for Alchesay, who denied that any of his people were involved and pledged to join with Mickey in tracking down the murderer. They promptly set out and soon picked up the trail to the east of Alchesay's village. It twisted and turned for more than forty miles into the mountains.

Mickey discovered a camp where the mare had been butchered for steaks and jerked meat. He could tell that the girl was alive, for it was clear that she had been tied to a tree to sleep. Mickey also found a cast-off fire stick in the camp, so he and Alchesay knew that the killer must be Massai. The *bronco* Apache must have long since run out of matches. Massai's trail then vanished into the towering White Mountains, where he had forced the girl to tread only on stones in order to leave no tracks.

They returned to Fort Apache with only the fire stick to show for their trouble, but at least Mickey had proven the innocence of the accused scout as well as that of Alchesay's people. There would be no blood feud retribution. The fire stick puzzled Johnson, and there were few others in the Apache camp who still knew how to use it. Mickey quickly displayed how it worked and lit his cigarette by the fire.

Several months after the fire stick incident, the girl, Natastale, returned to Fort Apache astride a fine horse loaded down with plunder. She told Johnson how Massai had killed her mother and carried her off to cook and work in his camp. He stole horses for them to ride and in time they reached the Sierra Madre. He often brooded over whether to kill her, but she made herself useful and his heart softened, so he returned her to the White Mountains. He admonished her to tell the white soldier chief "that she was a pretty good girl, better than the San Carlos woman, and that he would come again and get another."

In time, Massai traveled east to the country of the Mescaleros, where he kidnapped a young woman he spied bathing. He had broken a strong cultural taboo as he watched her bathe, dress, and braid her hair. He did not take the girl by force but instead asked her to be his bride.

The woman, Zanagoliche, agreed to the marriage, for Massai was a mighty warrior whose deeds were told and retold in hushed tones around every campfire from San Carlos to Mescalero. They were married in the Apache way, and she bore him six children despite their fugitive life.

At long last, in 1906, the gray-haired warrior would be ambushed for the last time. Some New Mexico cowboys whose stock he had stolen attacked and killed him, then they burned his body in a great bonfire and took off his head to claim any reward. After they rode off, Zanagoliche buried his charred remains. She found his belt buckle in the ashes and on her deathbed gave it to her daughter Alberta Begay.

"Your father was not a murderer. He killed only to protect us," she told Alberta. "Be sure to keep this buckle that belonged to your father." The talisman of the *bronco* warrior Massai was thus saved to be passed down on the Mescalero Reservation for generations.

AL SIEBER AND KID had gone out on Massai's twisted trail more than once, but he eluded them just as he had evaded Mickey Free. Kid, despite his youth, had long since emerged as a great favorite with Sieber. But Sieber was not alone in his admiration of Kid's talents. The young Apache scout had proven his worth under fire at Big Dry Wash and in Mexico. Even his brush with death at the hands of Emilio Kosterlitzky had enhanced his reputation for daring among his comrades. He had emerged as a natural leader among the scouts long before his promotion to first sergeant.

One army officer told a *Los Angeles Times* correspondent of how Kid once pointed out to him a band of riders some fifteen miles distant out on the plain. The officer's field glasses could detect but specks in a cloud of dust, but Kid noted the number of white riders, the number of Indian scout riders, and the number of pack mules. It was easy for him, as he could tell the ethnicity of the riders by how they rode their horses. When they later met up with the party, the officer learned that Kid's numbers had been perfectly correct.

KID CUT QUITE a figure—square-jawed with high cheekbones and piercing eyes—and he made an impression on all who met him. His natural intelligence as well as his fluency in both English and Apache complemented his handsome features. He dressed in a mishmash of white and Apache clothing, favoring high-top cavalry boots, a black sombrero, and a flowing silk bandana.

When the handsome young scout decided to court old Eskiminzin's beautiful daughter, he didn't have much trouble winning her over. A bride price was fixed and he carried her off to his lodge. The daughter, named Nahthledeztelth, was so radiant in both spirit and appearance that even after she bore Kid a daughter, the soldiers at San Carlos, who could not pronounce her name, still simply called her "Beauty."

It was not long after the birth of Kid's daughter that a massive earthquake rolled under San Carlos and the surrounding mountains. In Sonora fifty people died on May 3, 1887. The Apaches saw this natural disaster as the darkest of omens. Drums began to beat across the reservation as the shamans sent incantations to Usen for deliverance. Repeated aftershocks kept everyone on edge even if they did not believe in omens.

Up in the hills above San Carlos, a grand *tiswin* gathering was planned to accompany more pleas to Usen. Kid's father, Toga-de-chuz, was among the celebrants. As often occurred during a *tiswin* debauch, Toga-de-chuz exchanged some words with another old warrior, a man named Gon-zizzie, the brother of Rip. Rip, years earlier, had courted the woman who would marry Toga-de-chuz and eventually give birth to Kid. Rip never got over this rejection, and it had led to a decades-long family feud. For some reason, Gon-zizzie decided to settle matters that night.

Sieber got wind of the *tiswin* party and sent Kid and several scouts to break it up. They reached the scene to find Toga-de-chuz sprawled dead in front of the black *tiswin* kettle with a bullet in his back. Not far away, one of the scouts found the body of Gon-zizzie. Toga-de-chuz's friends had taken revenge and then dispersed.

Kid stood stock-still, looking down on his father's body. Kid knew that it was old Rip who had set this all in motion, and that Gon-zizzie had been but his tool. Apache custom gave him the right to exact vengeance, but the law of the White Eyes forbade it. He now faced the exact same dilemma his friend Mickey Free had confronted only a few months before. It was a long ride back to San Carlos.

Two weeks later Sieber and the San Carlos agent, Captain Francis Pierce, had to travel north to Fort Apache for a few days. Sieber placed the still-grieving Kid in charge of all the scouts and the guardhouse at San Carlos, perhaps hoping to bolster the boy's spirits with the important assignment. The old scout had warned Kid against seeking vengeance: it was a new day, he told him, and the old ways were over.

Sieber had not been gone long when Kid came to a decision. The local band chief, Gonshayee, kept the pot stirring and continued to egg Kid on. With four scout companions, Kid rode up to Rip's village on the Aravaipa. The old man had been warned and attempted to flee, but Kid blocked his passage and shot Rip right through the heart.

Sieber and Pierce, upon hearing the news, hurried straight back to San Carlos. Sieber immediately sent Gonshayee into the mountains to convince Kid to come in. It was late afternoon on June 1 when Kid led his four companions into San Carlos and made directly for Sieber's tent.

"Frank, that looks like old times," remarked Ed Arhelger, the agency blacksmith, to Frank Porter as they watched the line of heavily armed scouts ride in. "I believe we're going to have some fun here tonight."

A large crowd of Apaches, many of whom were armed, followed the riders toward Sieber's tent. Captain Pierce hurried over to join Sieber, who stood directly in front of his tent. Agency interpreter Antonio Diaz also joined Sieber.

"Hello, Kid," Sieber said coldly as the scouts dismounted. He ordered them to surrender their weapons and pointed toward a table in front of the tent. Kid was the first to step forward. He handed his carbine and gun belt to Pierce, then turned and instructed his companions to place their guns on the table as well.

Diaz, who had no love for Kid, asked the scout where he had been. "We have been off and have killed a man on the Aravaipa," Kid replied. "It is no matter of yours nor of the agent."

"Calaboose," Pierce exclaimed as he pointed to the nearby guardhouse. As Kid turned toward the jail, Diaz grinned broadly and made a sign for island—he meant to taunt Kid that Alcatraz would be his next home.

Pierce noticed murmuring and movement among the crowd and then the glint of sunlight on gunmetal. He no sooner called out a warning to Sieber than gunfire erupted. A Yaqui named Miguel fired the first shot, which was followed by a score more.

Kid made a move for his gun on the table, but Sieber grabbed it first and shoved the scout back on his heels. Kid bolted away as Sieber swept all the guns off the table just as the other scouts reached for them. Sieber quickly retreated into his tent to retrieve his own rifle and then rushed back out. A fusillade of bullets greeted him. The scout Curley, long a rival of Kid for position in the scouts, took aim and fired at Sieber. The .45-70 slug shattered Sieber's left ankle and sent him tumbling. His fall likely saved his life as more bullets continued to pepper his tent. In the confusion, Kid and his companions fled, some on horseback but most on foot. They were quickly joined in their flight by a dozen other San Carlos Apaches.

Arhelger had certainly been right: it was just like old times. Troops galloped off in pursuit as Captain Pierce knelt beside Sieber, who writhed in pain in a pool of blood and bone fragments. Pierce sent a rider after Dr. T. B. Davis, who had just departed that morning for Globe.

Tom Horn rode into San Carlos at about two that next morning. The Kid's band, a total of seventeen men, had stolen Horn's favorite horse from his mining claim eleven miles south at Deer Creek. He found the agency in an uproar, even at that late hour. The earthquake, the incantations of the shamans, and now Kid's outbreak led even old hands to think a new war was imminent.

Horn, for his part, had been keeping busy since Geronimo's surrender. For a while he had ranched in Pleasant Valley, where he became embroiled in a vicious range war between two families. Horn had been deputized by Sheriff Glenn Reynolds of Gila County in an effort to keep the peace. Horn had then retired to his Deer Creek mine, but still carried a badge as a deputy for Reynolds.

Sieber told Horn what had happened between grimaces as the doctor worked on his leg. The leg was, as Horn delicately put it, "shattered all to pieces." Dr. Davis wanted to amputate, but Sieber refused to consider it. He had kept his right leg after a horrible wound at Gettysburg, and he was not about to give up the left one now.

THE APACHES MADE for Mount Turnbull, then turned south along the San Pedro. They killed a man north of Benson and stole some horses. Kid hoped to avoid any killing, but his companion Gonshayee was hot for blood and shot the White Eye down. A few days later, they killed another rancher near Crittenden. This time the Yaqui, Miguel, was the shooter.

On June 13, 1887, while Kid and his warriors were on the run, General Nelson Miles departed Los Angeles for San Carlos. He downplayed the outbreak to the press but soon discovered that a thousand Apaches had departed for the mountains above San Carlos to dance. The shamans were making big medicine.

Lieutenant Carter Johnson, with a detachment of Apache scouts led by Mickey Free, was hot on Kid's trail. They soon located the fugitives in the Rincon Mountains to the east of Tucson. On June 11, Johnson surprised the Apaches high in the Rincons, scattered the warriors, and captured all their ponies and baggage, including Horn's horse. Kid led his men in a desperate slide down a precipitous rocky slope toward the San Pedro River. Mickey told Lieutenant Johnson that he thought the Apaches were headed back to San Carlos.

On June 18, Gonshayee came in and surrendered. Miles questioned the man closely, and when he gave good information, he set him at liberty. The general sent Gonshayee, as well as Kid's mother and Beauty, to talk the outlaw into surrendering. Kid agreed to come in on June 25 if Miles would recall the troops. Miles agreed to this and Kid kept his word as well.

On June 25, 1887, Kid and six others returned with Gonshayee and surrendered to Captain Pierce. They were placed in the San Carlos guardhouse. That same day, General Miles ordered a court-martial convened to try Kid and the four other Apache scouts. The fate of Gonshayee, who had quietly engineered much of the trouble, and the other San Carlos renegades would be decided in a civilian court.

The general elected to do so with a great deal of forethought. He knew he could exert control over a court-martial, while a civilian court was certain to hang the scouts. He felt considerable sympathy for Kid, but could only go so far to protect the former scout. He appointed Major Anson Mills, Tenth Cavalry, with whom he enjoyed a warm relationship, as head of the court. The trial convened on June 28, 1887, with First Lieutenant John Baldwin, Ninth Infantry, as defense counsel. Baldwin had been pulled from other cases by Miles because of his excellent reputation, but the appointment gave him only a few days to prepare his case. The charge was mutiny and desertion. The penalty on conviction was death.

Second Lieutenant Laurence Tyson served as judge advocate, or prosecutor, and his star witnesses were Captain Pierce, Sieber, and interpreter Antonio Diaz. All three testified that Kid had not fired a weapon, but Sieber pointedly remarked that Kid had attempted to retrieve his carbine. Sieber was certain that Kid had given a signal to his companions to grab their guns and bolt while Gonshayee's warriors covered them. Then Sieber's testimony was cut short by the pain from his wound, which made it impossible for him to continue.

As his final witness before the court, Baldwin called Kid to testify. Kid spoke in Apache and Bob McIntosh, the half-blood son of Archie, translated for the court. Kid claimed that he had never considered or attempted mutiny, but he did admit that he had "left here without permission from Sieber or the Captain." He had "drank a whole lot of *tiswin*" and then "as soon as I got up to Rip's camp, I saw Rip and shot him." He had been absent for only five days and had come in voluntarily in response to Sieber's order. Kid concluded his testimony with a poignant statement reflective of the cultural crosscurrents that so bedeviled him:

> *I am First Sergeant Kid, San Carlos, Arizona Territory. God sent bad spirit in my heart, I think. You all know all the people can't get along very well in the world. There are some good people and some bad people amongst them all. I am not afraid to tell all these things because I have not done very much harm. I killed only one man whose name is Rip because he killed my father. I am not educated like you and therefore can't say very much. If I had made any arrangement before I came in, I would not have given up arms at Mr. Sieber's tent. That is all I have to say.*

Baldwin's closing argument pointed to the cultural divide between Kid the soldier and Kid the Apache. He reiterated to the court that Kid had engaged in no overt act of mutiny and that the young scout "fears no punishment that right and justice will decree."

The eight members of the court deliberated for only a few hours. Major Mills announced the verdict: Kid was guilty of mutiny and desertion. The sentence of the court was death by firing squad. The four other scouts received the same sentence.

On July 29, 1887, General Miles concluded his review of the court-martial proceedings and ordered Major Mills to reconvene the court and review the verdict. Mills got the message from Miles, but not quite clearly enough. A week later, the court submitted a revised verdict of life imprisonment at hard labor. Miles, frustrated by the court, used his power as department commander to mitigate the sentence to ten years' confinement in the military prison on Alcatraz Island.

"The Rock" had been designated as a military prison in 1868. The former Fort Alcatraz, which still served as a lighthouse, was home to an eighty-eight-man garrison of the First Artillery, and contained officers' quarters, barracks, powder magazines, stables, housing for the officers' Chinese servants, and even a bowling alley. It had 185 eight-by-twelve-foot cells in four brick-and-wood prison buildings. There was no wall around these buildings, and convicts were allowed to move about the island during the day so long as they avoided the army barracks and battery emplacements. Escape was considered impossible.

Kid and his companions reached the damp, fog-shrouded island in March 1888. Their lives would become a constant routine of reveille at five, assembly for a head count, breakfast, work details, followed by a noon meal, more work, and then supper at five. Each night they drifted off to sleep to the clang of the fog bell.

In Washington, the judge advocate general reviewed the court-martial file of Kid. He was particularly impressed by the arguments presented by General Miles against the court's sentence. He concluded that the trial had not been fair, that the Apaches did not understand the nature of the charges against them, and that it was clear from the testimony that none of the scouts had fired a shot during the melee. He recommended that Secretary of War Endicott remit the sentences. It took six months for Endicott to review the case and reach a conclusion. On October 20, 1888, orders were sent to General Oliver O. Howard, commander of the Division of the Pacific, to release Kid and his four fellow scouts.

The freed Apaches traveled by train to Casa Grande, and then by stagecoach to San Carlos. Their return caused considerable consternation among the citizens of Arizona. "The Indians arrived home on stage, and after crossing the Gila at San Carlos, the Tenth

Cavalry Band met them at the river and serenaded them into the camp," grumbled blacksmith Arhelger, "which caused a great deal of ill-feeling among the people at San Carlos."

AL SIEBER, FOR ONE, was certainly not finished with the Apache Kid. His wound had not healed, nor had his deep sense of betrayal. Dr. Davis had been able to save Sieber's leg, although there had been so much bone loss that it was now significantly shorter than the other leg. Sieber was still on crutches when Kid and his companions returned as free men to San Carlos. Since military law had failed him, Sieber turned to the civil authorities in Globe.

Gila County sheriff Glenn Reynolds was a remarkable specimen of the pioneer stock that settled the American Southwest. A Texan by birth, he had become a cattleman and lawman by choice, elected sheriff of Thockmorton County, Texas, before leading a drive of two thousand head of prime Texas beef to Fort Bowie in 1885. Upon his departure, the grateful citizens of Albany, Texas, bestowed a fine gold watch—engraved with his name and images of sheep and cattle—upon him. He eventually settled in the mining boomtown of Globe, where the thirty-six-year-old was elected Gila County sheriff in 1888. Globe was more than a bit rough around the edges, so Reynolds had employed a familiar face as his top gun. Tom Horn and his partner Jerry Ryan were Reynolds's deputies.

Sieber found Sheriff Reynolds and other Gila County authorities more than happy to oblige his request that Kid be arrested for attempted murder and tried in territorial court. Reynolds wrote General Miles in October 1889 to request military assistance for the arrest of Kid and several other Apaches on territorial warrants. Miles, despite his sympathy for Kid, instructed the new San Carlos agent, Captain John Bullis, and chief-of-scouts Sieber to assist the sheriff. Sieber had at first hoped to arrest Kid and charge him in federal court for the two murders that occurred during the outbreak, but a recent ruling by the United States Supreme Court had frustrated that plan.

Arizona was still in an uproar over an April 1889 Supreme Court decision that freed several Apaches convicted in federal courts and held in federal prisons. Among those released were Gonshayee, who had been convicted of murder during Kid's outbreak; Nahdeizaz, who had killed an army lieutenant during a land dispute; and Captain Jack, whom Kid had once arrested. The Indian Rights Association had filed cases on behalf of the imprisoned Indians.

The Supreme Court had ruled that Gonshayee, Nahdeizaz, and nine other Apache Indians had been wrongfully tried in federal court and overturned their convictions on the grounds that the court had no jurisdiction over them. This did not, however, save the Indians from retrial in territorial court. Gonshayee and Nahdeizaz were promptly arrested, retried, convicted, and sentenced to hang.

The end result of the Indian Rights Association case was that the two men exchanged long terms in a federal penitentiary for a short walk to the gallows. But Gonshayee and two other convicted Apaches refused to go out this way. They killed each other in a suicide pact before they could be hanged.

In the wake of this Supreme Court decision, a territorial warrant for Kid's arrest for the attempted murder of Al Sieber was issued on October 14, 1889. The well-meaning effort of the Indian Rights Association now placed Kid in jeopardy. Sieber's dogged persistence had finally paid off.

At this time, Kid and Beauty were living at the mouth of a small canyon six miles south of San Carlos. Reynolds knew that Kid would recognize him, so he sent his deputy, Jerry Ryan, instead to make the arrest. Ryan rode toward the Kid's home, followed at a safe distance by Reynolds. By chance he encountered Kid on the road to San Carlos, and as he approached, he offered him a smoke. Ryan handed him his tobacco pouch and some paper, and as Kid rolled a smoke, the deputy pulled his pistol and arrested him.

The trial began on the morning of October 29, 1889, in the Gila County courthouse in Globe. The problem of double jeopardy was neatly sidestepped, since the charge was for a different offense. In the court-martial, Kid had been tried for mutiny. Now he was being charged with attempted murder. Sieber was to be the chief witness. Sieber had joked with Sheriff Reynolds that he would be punctual for the trial, since he was coming to the courthouse to apply for citizenship papers. Perjury would be one of Sieber's first acts as a brand-new citizen of the United States of America.

Judge Joseph H. Kibbey, a recent judicial appointee of President Benjamin Harrison, and who would later serve as territorial governor, presided. Kid had two court-appointed lawyers, while old Merejildo Grijalva served as court interpreter. The man who as a child had been the prisoner of Cochise was now to be an eyewitness to the final chapter in the long struggle for Apacheria.

Sieber was the star witness. He testified that Kid had shot him, even though he knew his protégé had not so much as even touched a weapon during the melee. Antonio Diaz and Frank Porter both lied and backed up Sieber's testimony as well. They were followed on the stand by the scout Curley, who also identified Kid as the shooter. Blacksmith Ed Arhelger fidgeted in his chair as he heard these lies. He had witnessed Curley fire the shot that wounded Sieber, but both prosecution and defense neglected to call him to testify. He well knew why. The fix was in.

Kid was called to the stand. He testified that Curley had shot Sieber out of jealousy. Curley had been Kid's rival for the hand of Beauty and his bitterness over her rejection of him had been compounded by Sieber's favoritism toward Kid as a scout. Kid reiterated that he could never shoot at Sieber. Beauty then took the stand. She testified to Curley's jealousy and to the good character of her husband.

The prosecutor recalled Sieber to the stand. The old scout limped up and testified that Kid's story about Curley's jealousy was a clever fantasy constructed to cover his own crimes. Brief closing arguments followed, then the judge sent the jury out to deliberate.

It did not take long. Kid was found guilty as charged. Three of his scout companions—Hale, Sayes, and Bacheonal—were convicted as his accessories.

"All were promptly found guilty," noted Arhelger, "which I

think was wrong, but the sentiment was such that a good Indian was a dead Indian."

The next morning, Judge Kibbey sentenced Kid and his three companions to seven years in the Yuma Territorial Prison. The prison was a notorious hellhole even by frontier standards; this was a death sentence. Sieber's revenge was complete.

28

THE LAST FREE APACHE

SHERIFF GLENN REYNOLDS CHECKED THE TIME ON his elaborate pocket watch as his deputies loaded the prisoners onto Eugene Middleton's stage. It was five o'clock on a cold, miserable Friday morning. A mix of rain and snow spit down on them. Sieber had offered Reynolds some Apache scouts as escort for his journey with Kid and the other prisoners to Yuma, but the sheriff had declined. "I don't need your scouts," he told Al. "I can take those Indians alone with a corn-cob and a lightening-bug."

Deputy Jerry Ryan herded the nine handcuffed prisoners, eight Apaches and a Hispanic named Jesus Avott, toward the stage. He was aided by William "Hunkydory" Holmes, a local character famed for his bad poetry and jovial good nature. His nickname was derived from one of his poems. Reynolds had hired Holmes to replace Tom Horn, who had gone off to Phoenix for a territorial roping contest. Deputy Ryan would hold down the office in Globe.

Reynolds mounted his horse and gave Middleton the sign to move out. Middleton was nervous about his cargo, but Reynolds had brought along plenty of firepower. He carried a double-barreled shotgun as well as his .45, Holmes carried a pistol and a Winchester, and Middleton carried his own pistol as well.

The stage reached the Riverside Stage Station, some forty miles south of Globe, before dark. The rain had increased steadily and Middleton was happy to get across the Gila River before it became swollen with runoff. The prisoners got a hearty meal of Irish stew and rice pudding before Reynolds chained them together for the night. Middleton, who knew Kid, shared a smoke with him. The

Apaches would sleep sitting up on a long bench with their backs to the wall. Avott, who had been convicted of embezzlement, was allowed to sleep separately. Reynolds and Holmes took turns at watch during the night.

The train for Yuma was scheduled to depart Casa Grande at four in the afternoon, so Middleton was anxious to get an early start. He did not fancy spending another night with the Apache prisoners. They were all up by four that morning and, after a hurried breakfast, were back on the road.

The rain was heavy and the thermometer dropping rapidly, so Reynolds left his horse at Riverside and climbed inside the stage with Holmes and the Apaches. Avott was placed in the boot at the rear of the stage. The gray, cold dawn gave way to some spotty sunlight by the time the stage reached Kelvin Grade. But this steep, sandy wash, which climbed up to a saguaro-covered ridgeline, was too much for the stage to maneuver with its load, so Reynolds and Holmes hustled the Apaches and Avott off the stage. Kid and another Apache named Hoscalte were left handcuffed inside. It was cold and so Reynolds buttoned his heavy overcoat over his pistol belt as he led off with Avott behind the stage. Holmes brought up the rear with the six Apaches chained in pairs ahead of him.

The stagecoach lurched ahead up the grade and out of sight over the ridge. Just at that moment, two of the prisoners, Sayes and Elcahn, jumped the sheriff, grappling for his shotgun. Holmes had hardly reacted when another two of the Apaches, Bacheonal and Hale, turned on him and knocked him to the ground. Bacheonal seized Holmes's rifle and turned to run to where his companions were still struggling with Reynolds. He shot the sheriff dead, then turned to finish off Holmes, only to discover that the deputy was already dead. The fright had given him a heart attack.

The terrified Avott ran after the stage. As Middleton pulled the team up and turned, he saw Avott scamper into the brush beside the road. Just then Bacheonal fired and the driver, hit in the neck, tumbled off the stage. Middleton lay on the cold ground in a warm pool of his own blood, but somehow the man remained conscious.

The Apaches had taken the keys from Reynolds and now freed Kid and Hoscalte. They then gathered over Middleton, and Elcahn picked up a stone to smash in the driver's skull. Then Middleton heard Kid talking in angry tones and sensed that he had stopped Elcahn. The Apache dropped the stone and bent down and took Middleton's coat and gun. Middleton's act of kindness with the smoke had been repaid. The Apaches hurried away to loot the bodies of Reynolds and Holmes. They took the coat, weapons, and fancy watch off the sheriff and stripped Holmes as well. It had begun to snow as they left, and their trail was quickly covered with a blanket of white.

Avott hid in the brush until he was certain the Apaches were gone. He returned to the stage to find only a congealed puddle of blood where Middleton had fallen. He cut a horse free from the team and galloped off to nearby Florence to sound the alarm. In the months to come, he would receive a pardon for his crimes as a result.

Middleton staggered back on the road to Riverside, where some horrified passengers on the stage to Globe saw him emerge ghostlike out of the snowstorm. The stage driver mounted Reynolds's horse and galloped back to Globe to get help while his passengers nursed Middleton, whose wound was serious but not fatal.

A telegram from Florence soon reached San Carlos and was rushed to Sieber, who was still confined to his sickbed.

"I was afraid of that," the chief-of-scouts grumbled, "and that was why I offered a scout escort to Casa Grande." He quickly had a detail of twenty scouts in the field.

Mickey Free was soon back in the saddle with his scout detachment out of Fort Apache. A cavalry troop hurried to Kelvin Grade, where they were joined by a civilian posse from Florence. Some cowboys had discovered the bodies and had guarded them from wolves until help arrived.

Tom Horn learned of the killings while still in Phoenix. He was crestfallen. "Had I not gone to the fair, I would have been with Reynolds, and I could have understood what they [Apaches] said, and it would never have happened," he lamented. "I won the prize roping at the fair, but it was at a very heavy cost."

On November 5, 1889, a report came in that Kid and Bacheonal had been seen only a few miles from San Carlos. Sieber sent out scouts but they lost the trail. It was assumed that the Apaches were attempting to contact their families, so Sieber sent scouts to spy on Eskiminzin's farm. He felt certain that Kid would come to get Beauty.

On November 5, the territorial governor posted a $500 reward for Kid and his accomplices, which was followed a few days later by an additional offer of $50 a head for any of the eight by Gila County. Sheriff Jerry Ryan also offered an additional reward for the return of Reynolds's gold watch. In time, the territory of Arizona increased the reward for Kid to $5,000—dead or alive.

ON MARCH 2, 1890, Apache warriors killed a freight-wagon driver on the road between San Carlos and Fort Thomas. Within the hour, Lieutenant Powhatan Clarke was in the saddle with his troop of Buffalo Soldiers. It was not long before they came upon a smoldering freight wagon and found the freighter's body. Clarke led his troop on down the river toward San Carlos, stopping to inspect dark and abandoned Indian camps along the way. The abandoned camps, he felt, were an ominous sign.

At dawn the command headed northwest on a trail that the scouts declared to have been made by five warriors. These Apaches had two of the freighter's big draft horses with them, and the scouts thought they might be Kid's men. The trail led some fifty miles into the Sierra Ancha, where the scouts' horses found it difficult to travel. Clarke and several scouts pressed on over the rocks on foot while the troopers remained on the canyon floor.

Suddenly several shots echoed across the canyon. The scouts, stripped for battle down to breechcloths with their hair tied back, waved for the troops to hurry forward. Before the soldiers could reach them, they had overwhelmed the foe. Hale, one of Kid's companions, was dead while another Apache was mortally wounded. Two warriors and a boy were captured.

The death of Hale confirmed Sieber's belief that Kid had not fled to Mexico but remained in the vicinity of San Carlos. This increased Sieber's suspicion that Beauty, who lived on her father's farm on the San Pedro just off the reservation, must be in contact with her husband. Sieber was also certain old Eskiminzin had to be sneaking supplies to Kid.

Sieber kept his spies in the field and liberally distributed bribes among the San Carlos people in hopes of turning someone against Kid. He finally found his man in a former scout named Josh, who was in trouble with the law for murder. Josh agreed to lead the soldiers to where the renegades had recently camped in the southeast corner of the reservation.

In early May, Sheriff Jerry Ryan and a civilian posse joined with the San Carlos troops and scouts for the pursuit. They surprised the Apaches at Ash Flat. In a running fight, they killed four of the fugitives. Josh cut off Bacheonal's head to take back to San Carlos, wanting to be certain that he would get the reward. Sheriff Ryan distributed two hundred dollars in reward money among the scouts in payment for the dead fugitives, and Josh received his pardon.

Sieber kept up the pressure on the family members of the remaining fugitives. This led Hoscalte to come in and surrender in October. Along with Elcahn and Sayes, Hoscalte had sought shelter at the village of his father-in-law in the summer of 1890, only to be turned away. Sayes had flown into a rage and killed Hoscalte's relative. Hoscalte, devastated by the death he had brought upon his family, turned himself in at San Carlos. He reported that the other two former scouts were still at the village on Mescal Creek. The troops and scouts Sieber sent after them caught them napping. Elcahn was killed, and the wounded Sayes was clapped back in chains to face trial for Reynolds's murder. He was sentenced to life imprisonment at Yuma, where Hoscalte joined him to complete his seven-year sentence. Both men contracted tuberculosis at Yuma and would die within a day of each other in March 1894.

Kid, the last survivor from the stagecoach escape, now headed for Mexico. On his way south, he killed two of John Slaughter's cowboys some twenty miles southeast of the San Bernardino Ranch.

"The Kid is the only one of the eight convicts who has not come to grief," gloated the Globe *Arizona Silver Belt* on October 11. The Apache outlaw was now "a legal target for those who can cock a gun and draw a bead through the sights of a Winchester."

IN MAY 1890, Emilio Kosterlitzky and a small detachment of his *rurales* were on the trail of a band of smugglers. Suddenly they came upon the dead bodies of the fugitive smugglers. The Apache trail leading away from the scene was fresh, and Kosterlitzky set on it at once. The next day, the *rurales* found themselves on an immense flat that led to a rock-strewn outcropping. It was perfect for an ambush. The Russian had a hunting dog and set him on the trail to sniff out the boulders ahead. The *rurales* charged after the sound of the barking dog and were met with a volley from the rocks.

The *rurales* managed to withstand the onslaught and drive the hidden Apaches from the hill, but not before two of Kosterlitzky's men had fallen. To the Russian's fury, several of the Apaches managed to escape. Kosterlitzky and his *rurales* found three dead warriors left behind. Kosterlitzky inspected the bodies. From one he retrieved a pistol and an ornate gold watch. The watch was engraved with images of sheep and cattle as well as the name Glenn Reynolds. The pistol had the name Reynolds etched in the grip. Kosterlitzky forwarded the items to Mexico City along with a description of the gray-haired Apache he had taken them from. The Apache Kid had escaped yet again.

AL SIEBER, UPON hearing this news, was determined that Kid would find no succor at San Carlos. He convinced Captain Bullis to arrest Eskiminzin and all the Apaches on his farm on the San Pedro—which included Kid's mother; his wife, Beauty; and her daughter—and send them east. In May 1891, Eskiminzin was arrested without charges and held in the San Carlos guardhouse until a roundup of some forty of his relatives and followers was completed. They were sent to Fort Wingate for several months and then removed to the Mount Vernon Barracks, Alabama, to join the other Chiricahua prisoners of war.

But soon enough, Sieber was himself banished from San Carlos as well. He had never gotten along particularly well with Captain Bullis, who had replaced Pierce at San Carlos. Bullis had made a name for himself as the commander of a unique band of mixed-blood Seminole Indian–African American scouts on the Rio Grande, and felt himself to be quite an expert on Indian scouts. This led him into immediate conflict with Sieber. There was clearly not enough room at San Carlos for two scout experts.

Bullis, who was not above exploiting his position for his own financial advantage, was notorious for having made a fortune in Texas by dispossessing Hispanic ranchers of their land. Many Arizona locals who hated Eskiminzin and coveted his rich farm were now quite happy with Bullis; the arrest of Eskiminzin allowed the locals to seize his land and cattle. At San Carlos, Bullis had Apaches arrested on trumped-up charges and then forced them to work on road construction gangs. Sieber, who objected to this forced labor, threatened to expose the haughty captain and told Bullis in colorful terms just what he thought of him. The captain promptly fired Sieber and gave him three days to depart the reservation.

Bullis bragged to his superiors that he had dismissed Sieber, whom he described as "a drunkard, vulgar, profane and brutal in his treatment of the Indians." The captain's triumph was brief, for he was soon thereafter investigated on corruption charges. Although he was somehow exonerated, he was still removed as agent a few months later.

MICKEY FREE ALSO left government service soon after Sieber was dismissed. When his enlistment ended on July 16, 1893, the first sergeant of scouts decided that twenty years as scout, policeman, and interpreter were enough. At forty-six, he retired to raise cattle and farm his land along the East Fork of the White River.

Mickey's family had expanded with the adoption of Ethlay's

nephew into the household. The boy took the name Horace Free. A much younger second wife, Ochehey, who was Ethlay's niece, also joined the household. She bore Mickey a son, whom they named Johnnie, in 1894, and a daughter, Fannie, two years later. But tragedy continued to stalk Mickey's family when, in 1899, a fever carried off both Ochehey and their son.

Some people said that Mickey could not quit the life of a scout. The year he left government service happened to coincide with the dramatic increase in the reward on Kid's head to five thousand dollars. Soon enough, to be sure, Mickey went out on a long final mission to capture Kid. Mickey decided to trail Kid into New Mexico, and then he continued south to the Sierra Madre. There he realized that his prey had doubled back into Arizona, so he followed him there as well.

In the end, Mickey's eight-month quest ended not far from where it had begun—in Aravaipa Canyon. Mickey claimed to have discovered the decomposed body of Kid in a cave there, surrounded by his rifle, knife, pistol, and army belt as well as several Mexican gold coins. Mickey took what was left of Kid's scalp back to San Carlos. No one accepted the scalp as evidence, and there was considerable feeling that perhaps Mickey was simply providing cover for his friend, giving the Apache Kid a chance to disappear into history without looking back.

Tom Horn also joined the manhunt. In recent years, Horn had been making quite a reputation for himself as a "range detective," or hired gunman, for Wyoming cattlemen, but his deadly success had forced his employers to send him back to Arizona in 1895 until affairs cooled off. Horn was soon hired by the Seventh Cavalry commander at Fort Grant to lead troops and scouts into Mexico after Kid. After four months and several forlorn scouts across the border, Horn gave up his quest for the bounty on Kid's head to return to Wyoming and his more lucrative career as a hired killer.

Many others continued to come forward to claim the reward for

Kid's head. In February 1894, an old frontiersman named Wallapai Clark killed an Apache woman and wounded the man with her as they attempted to steal horses from his claim in the Santa Catalinas. Clark sent for help, then he and a posse followed a trail of blood deep into the mountains. They never found the Apache warrior, whom Clark was certain he had mortally wounded, but the dead Apache was identified as a young woman recently kidnapped by Kid. This tale certainly tied in with Mickey Free's discovery of the dead Apache in Aravaipa Canyon.

FOR A DEAD MAN, Kid made surprisingly regular visits to his old haunts. After the deportation of Beauty, he took particular pleasure in raiding San Carlos and stealing women to keep his camp. Unlike Massai, Kid did not kill the women he stole, but sent them back to the reservation when he tired of them. Then the abductions stopped, and across San Carlos all agreed that Kid had fallen in love with his latest captive and taken her as a bride.

Kid's anger seemed equally as fixated on his own people as on the whites. Every death of an Apache or of a miner or cowboy was attributed to Kid, and for every real crime, ten more were reported by an increasingly hysterical territorial press.

The story quickly became national, with several stories printed in the *New York Times*. The *San Francisco Examiner* for April 29, 1894, labeled Kid as an Apache Ishmael who had "written his name in letters of blood throughout the land." The *Examiner* had to admit that "there is a certain romance in the matter, too, notwithstanding the hideous brutality of the man."

The press reports built pressure on both the army and the law to bring in Kid. Special military detachments, one led by Powhatan Clarke, were assigned to track down the outlaw. Bounty hunters, sheriffs' posses, bands of cowboys—all scoured the countryside; but while Kid was often sighted, he was never taken. Usually he rode alone, occasionally with Massai, and sometimes with a small band of *bronco* Apaches. Many young men wanted to ride with him, but Kid knew his chances were best as a lone wolf.

⤚⊸⊘⊶⤙

TEXAS JOHN SLAUGHTER had no interest in the bounty on Kid's head, but he was sick and tired of his cowboys being ambushed and his stock being stolen. His San Bernardino Ranch, situated right on the international border, had become a favorite target for Kid.

Slaughter, although born in Louisiana in 1841, had been raised in Texas, where he had won his nickname as a Texas Ranger. He was a successful rancher in both Texas and New Mexico before moving with his young bride, Viola Howell, to southern Arizona in 1880. He purchased the San Bernardino Ranch in 1884. Two years later he was elected sheriff of Cochise County and took up head-quarters in Tombstone, where he administered his own brand of gun-smoke justice. Short in stature but enormous in reputation, he stuttered much like the Apache leaders Juh and Eskiminzin. Men tended not to comment on his stutter.

Slaughter had had enough of Kid by May 1896. One of his best friends had been killed by Kid in Guadalupe Canyon, then a local farmer named Merrill and his daughter had been murdered near Solomonville, and finally a man named Alfred Hand had been killed and his cabin ransacked on Cave Creek not far from Slaughter's own ranch.

Slaughter, with several of his vaqueros, decided to set out in pursuit of the Apache raiders. They were joined by a Seventh Cavalry patrol commanded by Lieutenant Nathan Averill, fresh from West Point and eager for action. They trailed the Indians some fifty miles into Mexico and discovered their *rancheria* in the foothills of the Sierra Madre.

Slaughter's vaqueros charged the camp at dawn on May 7, 1896. They went in on foot with Averill and his troopers, guided by Slaughter's foreman, Jeff Fisher, who attacked from the opposite direction. The camp was hidden and fortified with rock emplacements so that only one Apache warrior fell as the people retreated. Slaughter saw a woman running back into a wickiup and attempted to capture her, but she eluded him.

Slaughter entered the wickiup to discover a baby girl. She whimpered softly as he picked her up and wrapped her in a brown shawl that lay nearby. The shawl, he later learned, had belonged to the murdered Merrill girl. The old man's heart melted as he cradled the baby in his arms. His reverie ended as the Apaches, who had retreated to a ridge above their camp, opened fire on the soldiers.

A lively exchange of fire followed, but the death of another warrior convinced the Apaches to pull away. Averill burned the camp but Kid had managed to escape yet again.

"We found a little girl, about two years old, and everything else they had in the world, four or five wickies full," the lieutenant later reported. "If it had not been for Mr. Slaughter and his man Fisher, we would never have been able to do anything."

When they reached his San Bernardino Ranch, Slaughter galloped in with the baby in his arms. He and his wife were childless. "Here, Vi," he exclaimed. "Here is a little Apache for you!"

Lieutenant Averill's Apache scouts spoke in hushed tones as they told Slaughter that the baby was the daughter of the Apache Kid. In time the scouts became quite attached to the baby girl and made her a tiny pair of ornate moccasins.

Slaughter and his wife named the little girl Apache May and called her Patchey for short. She became a surrogate daughter to the local cowboys, but her affection was reserved for the man she called Don Juan: Slaughter. "The little thing adored him from the very first and used to follow him about the place holding the top of his boot to steady her wavering baby feet," recalled one ranch hand. "When he rode away on his horse, she would wait with Indian patience, perhaps for hours, watching the gate for his return."

The first week of June 1896, Slaughter and his wife took the baby into Tombstone to be photographed at C. S. Fly's studio. It created a sensation. "As soon as it became known that the papoose was in town, a steady stream of people visited Fly's Gallery to catch a glimpse of the young captive," reported the *Tombstone Epitaph*. "The papoose is a chubby girl about two or three years of age, with a good head of coarse, black hair, large beautiful eyes, and for her size is strong and healthy, complexion that color which distinguishes an Apache."

Other Arizona newspapers were not as enamored of Apache May as was the *Epitaph*. One paper editorialized that the child should be taken by the heels and have her brains dashed out, as "human life will never be absolutely safe in Arizona till the last Apache is dead."

In February 1900, when both Slaughter and his wife were away for the day, the little six-year-old began to play a bit too close to a fire. Her dress quickly became engulfed in flames. Ranch foreman Jeff Fisher gathered her up in a blanket and put out the flames, but it was too late. Horribly burned, she lingered through the night and died the next morning in Slaughter's arms. Fisher made a tiny coffin, soaked in his own tears, and they buried her not far from the ranch house. The little girl's death broke old Slaughter, and he never recovered.

A fellow rancher later commented on the briefly intertwined lives of the Apache Kid's daughter and the old frontiersman: "I reckon that this little Apache waif, all alone among a hostile people, looked upon John as the only living God. And I reckon that all the love and sympathy and tenderness in John's being went out to that Apache kid."

THE FATE OF the Apache Kid remains a mystery. Many, including his old friend Mickey Free, said he was dead. Tom Horn and Jimmy Stevens both claimed that Kid had died in the mountains from consumption, a story that had been brought to San Carlos by an Indian woman. Sieber continued to search repeatedly for Kid, but without success. He remained convinced that he was still alive.

In 1899, Major Emilio Kosterlitzky reported that the Kid and his woman were high in the Sierra Madre, living among the Tarahumara Indians. There they had found peace at last. The Apache Kid, the last free Apache, had simply vanished into those fog-shrouded mountains—into the mists of legend.

EPILOGUE

At Fort Pickens, in Pensacola Bay, Geronimo became quite a tourist attraction. "You can go over to Santa Rosa Island, see Fort Pickens and Geronimo and gather beautiful shells and marine curiosities on the beach," bragged the *Pensacola Commercial*. The seventeen prisoners at Fort Pickens often staged dances for the tourists and sold handicrafts to them. George Wrattan, who had gone to the Sierra Madre with Gatewood and was now an interpreter for the prisoners, taught Geronimo how to print his name, and the old warrior began to sell his autograph for ten cents and his photograph for two dollars.

At Fort Marion, across the state near St. Augustine, where the rest of the Chiricahuas were being kept, there were no tourists. There it was only misery. The ancient masonry fortification, although about the same size as Fort Pickens, had 489 men, women, and children crowded into it. The army did the best it could to care for these prisoners of war, but the sanitary conditions were appalling.

Captain John Bourke, once again, would ride to the rescue. In 1887, Bourke contacted Herbert Welsh, the influential leader of the Indian Rights Association, with a report on the conditions at Fort Marion. Welsh accompanied Bourke on a visit to St. Augustine in March 1887. There, they met with Chatto, Kaytennae, Chihuahua, Dutchy, Martine, Kayitah, and old Nana. From each the men received a tale of woe and betrayal. Welsh listened carefully to their stories and wrote a heart-wrenching report that highlighted the stark betrayal of these scouts who had so loyally served the army.

Bourke asked Welsh to hide his role in the report, but it was obvious to everyone in the army that the warmhearted captain was the source of all this damning information. General Sheridan and General Miles were furious. Bourke might enjoy the admiration of Francis Parkman, John Wesley Powell, Herbert Welsh, and other leading intellectuals of the day, but his army career was ruined. The self-centered Crook had long since abandoned his loyal staff officer. Bourke was soon transferred to command a troop of the Third Cavalry on the Mexican border. He died on June 8, 1896, at age forty-nine, broken down by his years of frontier service, still holding the rank of captain that he had received in 1882.

But Bourke's crusade did save the Chiricahua and Warm Springs people at Fort Marion. Welsh's report forced the Cleveland administration's hand, and General Sheridan was ordered to find a more healthful location in which to hold the Apache prisoners. Sheridan decided on Mount Vernon Barracks, amid the Pine Barrens some thirty miles from Mobile, Alabama. On April 18, 1887, Sheridan ordered that the Fort Marion prisoners be sent to Alabama.

Thirty of the women and children, the families of Geronimo and his warriors, were kept in Florida at Fort Pickens. Sheridan was determined to keep Geronimo in Florida, but at least allowed the wives and children to now join their men.

At the same time as the transfer to Alabama, Sheridan ordered the Apache children to be sent to the Indian school at Carlisle, Pennsylvania. Sixty-two children went north to Captain Richard Pratt's famous school, where their hair was cut, their clothes exchanged for uniforms, and their customs and language forbidden. Kaywaykla, Daklugie, Chappo, and Betzinez were among those who were sent there, and although they learned much, they were miserable. Some, but not all, were fortunate to escape the coughing sickness—tuberculosis—that claimed many of the children. Geronimo's son Chappo did not survive it.

General Sheridan suffered a fatal heart attack on August 5, 1888. Sheridan's former best friend turned bitter enemy had only words of scorn for his West Point roommate.

"The adulations heaped on him by a grateful nation for his supposed genius turned his head," George Crook wrote in his diary, "which added to his natural disposition, caused him to bloat his little carcass with debauchery and dissipation which carried him off prematurely."

Crook, now a major general in command of Sheridan's old Division of the Missouri, continued to lobby for the Chiricahuas, and most especially for his scouts. Joined by General Oliver Otis Howard, Herbert Welsh, and the influential senator Henry Dawes, Crook urged removal of the Apaches to Fort Sill, in the Indian Territory (present Oklahoma). General Miles, who had originally suggested just such a reservation, now vigorously opposed the move. This led to a renewal in the newspapers of the old feud between Crook and Miles.

The debate ended on March 21, 1890, when Crook was struck down by a heart attack at his Chicago home. Geronimo was just as unkind to the dead general as Crook had been to Sheridan. "I think that General Crook's death was sent by the Almighty as a punishment for the many evil deeds he committed," grumbled the unrepentant warrior.

ON MAY 13, 1888, a year after the rest of the Apaches had been moved to Mount Vernon Barracks, Geronimo and the other forty-five Fort Pickens prisoners arrived there. No one came forward to greet Geronimo. Captain Walter Reed, the post doctor who was later to win fame for the conquest of yellow fever, watched as Geronimo walked slowly into the Apache camp.

"While he gazed intently," Reed recalled, "a woman emerged from a distant tent to advance slowly and with bowed head. Hesitantly she advanced and then hurried to the chief, threw her arms around his neck, and wept as if her heart would break. During this trying ordeal, not a muscle of the old warrior's face relaxed, nor did he show any outward sign of recognition that his only daughter was twining her arms around him."

The city fathers of Mobile, Alabama, were elated to have such a celebrity at Mount Vernon. "The placing of the Indians at Mt.

Vernon will add greatly to the attractiveness of that place as a Sunday school picnic resort," proclaimed the *Mobile Register*.

But not every visitor was smitten with Geronimo. One observed that the famous Apache was "about as mild mannered a man as ever scuttled a ship or cut a throat and for that matter butchered defenseless women and children."

Dr. Reed did his best for the people imprisoned at Mount Vernon. He urged the military commander to increase rations to what a regular soldier received per day. Although he accomplished this, there was little he could do to combat the chronic lung diseases: tuberculosis, which the Apaches called "coughing sickness," and malarial fever, or the "shaking sickness."

Lozen was among the first to contract the coughing sickness, and she rapidly wasted away. They buried her in an unmarked grave alongside the almost fifty other men, women, and children who perished at Mount Vernon Barracks.

Her friend Dahteste mourned for Lozen all the rest of her days. As an old woman, she told the great oral historian of the Apaches, Eve Ball: "I could hardly believe my good fortune in being permitted to know this courageous woman."

The army had put the Apaches to work building cabins and laying out roads. A school was built so that the children could be educated at Mount Vernon and not have to be sent away to Carlisle, which was a great boost to the morale of the people. Many ended up adjusting quite well to their new home, including Geronimo, but one holdout refused to be reconstructed.

Old Nana encouraged the people to believe that it was only a matter of time until they would be returned to their homeland. One day a lady philanthropist visited Mount Vernon Barracks to write a report on the conditions there. Nana told her that the people did not want to stay there but wished instead to go back to their homeland. The lady had brought a small globe with her and handed it to Nana. She told him that people were coming from all over the globe to America, that the country was becoming crowded. The Apaches could no longer roam over the vast territory that once was their land.

Nana stared at the globe, shaken to the core. He told the visitor to give it to a younger man, for he was too old to learn. Kaytennae reached down and took the globe from his shaking hands. After that visit, Nana slipped into a deep depression from which he never recovered. He now understood that he and his people would never go home.

JOHN CLUM, WHO was in Alabama on business for his new employer the postal service, visited the Apache prisoners in 1894. He was surprised to find Eskiminzin among the Chiricahua and Warm Springs prisoners. Clum asked Eskiminzin why he was a prisoner, to which the old chief simply replied, "Great lies—you know." At this, Clum sent off letters to the commissioner of Indian affairs as well as Welsh at the Indian Rights Association. No official in the army or the Indian Bureau could explain the cause of Eskiminzin's imprisonment beyond "as a military precaution."

The authorities quietly returned the chief and his people, including Beauty and her daughter, back to San Carlos in November 1894. The old chief, content to be back in his homeland, died a year later. His grandchild, the daughter of Beauty and Kid, eventually married a white San Carlos Indian trader but died quite young. Beauty vanished from the historical record.

In October 1894, the Apache prisoners were transferred from Alabama to Fort Sill, Oklahoma Territory. The military wished to close Mount Vernon Barracks, as an economical measure. Among those who made the journey by train was Nana, with a little over a year to live, and Dos-teh-seh, the mother of Naiche and widow of Cochise. The people of Oklahoma, still close to their frontier past, did not view the new arrivals as a potential tourist attraction. One local paper editorialized, "Here we go to see the king of murderers and prince of fiery destruction now made glorious by the sentimental adulation of insane freaks and misguided philanthropists. The old devil Geronimo should have been hung fifteen years ago." Despite that warm welcome, the Apache prisoners adapted well to their new homes, took up farming, and prospered.

Geronimo remained quite the celebrity, hawking his autograph at fairs and expositions around the country and even riding in President Theodore Roosevelt's 1905 inaugural parade. He asked Roosevelt to allow him to return to Arizona: "I pray you to cut the ropes and make me free. Let me die in my own country, an old man who has been punished enough and is free." The president refused.

Woodworth Clum, son of Geronimo's first captor, was beside the president as Geronimo passed the reviewing stand. "Why did you select Geronimo to march in your parade, Mr. President?" Clum asked. "He is the greatest single-handed murderer in American history."

"I wanted to give the people a good show," TR replied.

IT HAD INDEED all been a grand show. For Geronimo, it ended one cold night outside Lawton, Oklahoma, when he fell from his horse in a drunken stupor. He lay half-submerged in a creek all night, then contracted pneumonia and died on February 17, 1909. They buried him in the graveyard at Cache Creek, near Fort Sill.

The death of Geronimo liberated the Chiricahuas from their status as prisoners of war. In 1913, the government offered the Apaches the choice of staying in Oklahoma and taking allotments of land, or of relocating to the Mescalero Reservation in the White Mountains of New Mexico. Some chose to stay, and they became the ancestors of today's Fort Sill Apaches. But most chose to go back to New Mexico. They settled on a separate reserve at Whitetail, although they soon intermarried with their Mescalero cousins.

Naiche, who had emerged from Geronimo's shadow to be a fine leader of his people, moved to Whitetail with his mother, wife, and six children. He died in 1921.

Chihuahua had died at Fort Sill in 1901, but his widow, his son, and his three grandchildren went on to New Mexico.

Loco and Mangas both died at Fort Sill, but their descendants relocated to the Mescalero Reservation. Martine and Kayitah, the bold scouts who had talked Geronimo into meeting Gatewood, both went to Whitetail. So did Betzinez, who wrote an invaluable memoir of his life before his death in 1960. Kaywaykla also went to Mescalero, where in his last years he dictated his story of the Warm Springs people to the masterful oral historian Eve Ball.

Kaytennae, Kaywaykla's stepfather and the successor to Nana as chief of the Warm Springs Apaches, lived to see his people returned to New Mexico. He died in 1918.

Chatto, shunned by many of his people, also went to the Mescalero Reservation in 1913. He had lost a son to disease at Carlisle, while four more of his children had died at Fort Sill. He lived to be eighty, only to die in a car crash on an icy reservation road in 1934.

John Clum worked in a variety of government positions after he left Tombstone in 1882. He went to Alaska with his old pal Wyatt Earp during the 1898 gold rush, but no adventure ever equaled his time as agent to the Apaches. He settled in Los Angeles and wrote a series of self-serving but valuable articles on his Arizona days. His son, Woodworth, crafted a romantic memoir titled *Apache Agent* in 1936, which became something of a bestseller. Clum died from a heart attack in Los Angeles on May 2, 1932.

Tom Jeffords, Taglito, became a hermit. He retreated from the world with his hounds to a ranch he called Owl's Head, about thirty-five miles north of Tucson. Robert Forbes, who interviewed him in 1913, described him as a "tall, somewhat slender man of about 165 pounds, with a sparse, reddish beard." He never married, and lived alone until his death in February 1914. Despised by most Arizonans in his own time, although beloved by the Chiricahuas, he was made famous to a later generation by *Blood Brother,* a splendid 1947 novel by Elliott Arnold that inspired the film and television series *Broken Arrow.*

General Nelson Miles served as the last commanding officer of the United States Army before the general staff system was inaugurated. Marion Maus was on his staff and rose to brigadier general before his 1909 death. Charles Gatewood also served briefly as a staff officer, but he lost the confidence of Miles just as he had alienated Crook. He then rejoined his regiment in Wyoming, where he was terribly injured in an accident and forced to retire as a lieutenant. He died in 1896.

Gatewood's reputation became a pawn in the feud between Crook and Miles, and many believed that he was denied his rightful credit for bringing in Geronimo. His success, however, was the direct result of the hard campaign waged by Lawton and Wood, who were both amply rewarded with honors. Lawton went on to serve in the Spanish-American War and died as a major general in combat east of Manila in the Philippines in December 1899. Leonard Wood eventually served as governor general of that conquered island in a distinguished military career that saw him command the Rough Riders in Cuba and eventually become army chief of staff from 1910 to 1914. He was favored to receive the Republican nomination for president in 1920 but was passed over by the party bosses in favor of the more pliable Warren G. Harding. He died in April 1927.

Lieutenant General Miles feuded with President Theodore Roosevelt over the imperialist misadventure in the Philippines, where both Lawton and Wood had so ably served. Miles thought it a great mistake. He was forced to retire on August 3, 1903, without a word of praise from the president or the secretary of war. It was a humiliating end to a distinguished military career. The old soldier died on May 16, 1925. Miles, who loved the circus, had taken his grandchildren to a performance of the Barnum and Bailey circus in Washington. The band struck up "The Star-Spangled Banner" and he rose and saluted. As the anthem ended, he slumped back in his seat—dead from a heart attack.

Mickey Free had at first prospered on the Fort Apache Reservation, but the death of Ethlay in 1900 left him broken and alone. He moved into a one-room sod-and-stone hut along the East Fork of the White River, priding himself on a little vegetable garden that he carefully tended.

"The next time I saw Mickey Free," remembered Archie's son Donald McIntosh, "how the mighty had fallen. He was no longer the swashbuckling big shot in blue uniform and big boots. He was a dried up, bent, little old man, rather a pathetic figure."

Mickey Free was but a final remnant of a bygone era, for he had outlived nearly all his contemporaries. The exact date of Mickey Free's death is unknown. It was sometime in the spring of 1914, just before the whole world was convulsed by a great war. He was buried, Apache-style, in a canyon not far from his home. As was the custom, his little house was burned. The white world took no note of his passing.

Tom Horn had become a range detective for the Pinkertons, but then decided to freelance as a hired gun to the big ranchers in Colorado and Wyoming. He was hanged for murder in Cheyenne, Wyoming, on November 20, 1903. He died game, just as he had lived.

On February 19, 1907, while Al Sieber was directing an Apache work crew building a road to the Tonto Dam under construction near Globe, a great boulder came loose. Sieber was too crippled to escape the landslide, and the old scout was crushed to death. Arizona old-timers whispered that the Apaches had pushed the boulder down on Sieber. There were still many old scores to settle.

After 1900, stories of the Apache Kid began to fade from the newspapers. There were still infrequent Kid sightings, by both Apaches and whites, but most people assumed he was dead. The reward was never paid.

In 1907, there was a flurry of interest in a newspaper report from Chicago that a posse of New Mexico cowboys had killed Kid, cut off his head, and sent it to Yale University for the Skull and Bones Society. The folks in Arizona were amused by this. On May 25, 1907, the *Tucson Daily Citizen* responded that at least eighteen Arizona heroes had claimed to have killed the Apache Kid.

"In certain of our fairest homes, the soap holders and tobacco boxes are made of what is solemnly averred to be the skull of this bad Indian. If the Skull and Bones Society would like a stack of skulls of the Apache Kid, it can get them here at wholesale rates."

At San Carlos, Kid's name was spoken in hushed tones, as he still had relatives there. A famed ethnologist named Grenville Goodwin had traveled to the Sierra Madre in 1931 in hopes of solving the mystery of Kid and of a rumored lost tribe of Apaches descended from him. "Many of those I talk to here speak darkly of the Apache Kid," noted Neil Goodwin, his son. "I even hear of the lingering fear among his living relatives that they might suffer repercussions for the crimes he committed.

"As frightened as people on the reservation were of the Kid, there is an undercurrent of admiration in the stories of my father and others have recorded about him," wrote Neil. "The Kid was a dark folk hero, a celebrated outlaw. He was at large in Mexico, living off the land, raiding when he felt like it. It was the old Apache way."

HELGE INGSTAD, the famed explorer best known for discovering a site in Newfoundland that had proven the Vikings had beaten Columbus to the New World, also went in search of the lost Apaches of the Sierra Madre in 1936. He lived for a time with Mormons who had fled to Mexico from Utah to escape the persecution of polygamists, and from them he heard many stories of the Apache Kid. A family in the isolated Cave Valley claimed to have killed Kid in 1899, and most of the Mormons in the settlement agreed that this was true.

Ingstad's Mormon friends led him to a Mexican family in Chihuahua who lived near the Mormon settlement of Garcia. There he met Lupe, the daughter of the Apache Kid. Ingstad was enthralled. "She is around forty, large and strongly built," he wrote. "Her hair is pitch black and swept back, her face finely featured with skin taut over protruding cheekbones. She looks tough and aggressive, but at the same time intelligent."

Lupe, married to a Mexican man and fluent in Spanish, said she had been captured in 1910 and raised by a childless Mexican couple in Nacori Chico. When she grew older, she went back into the mountains in search of her people but could not find them. Her Apache father and mother were dead, so she returned to her Mexican foster parents. It had been a long time ago, but she still remembered her father well.

"My father was a scout for the American soldiers at San Carlos, but was arrested and then killed two men," she told Ingstad. "After that he fled into the Sierra Madre. He was a great warrior."

Ingstad had not found the lost tribe of Apaches that he sought. But he had found the lost child of the Apache Kid and solved the mystery of the fate of the last of the great lords of Apacheria.

ACKNOWLEDGMENTS

WHILE WRITING IS indeed a solitary craft, an author nevertheless entails many obligations, and this is especially true of nonfiction writers. It is a particular pleasure to acknowledge those who have helped me in the creation of this book. I'm sure there are others who I may have overlooked, and I hope they will forgive my oversight.

James Donovan is not only a splendid agent but also a first-rate editor. He is equally famed for his bluntness as well as for his insights into the book business. He sometimes reminds me of a character out of a forties' film noir, a film interest that we share along with the Alamo, Custer, and Broadway musicals. Like the hard-boiled hero of one of those films, he, of course, has a deeply concealed sentimental streak. He carefully worked over the many drafts of my initial book proposal and then edited early chapter drafts. He was assisted in this by his ace associate Melissa Shultz. My debt to them is incalculable.

My patient and talented editor at Crown, Kevin Doughten, proved wise beyond his years and was an absolute pleasure to work with. His advice was invaluable, and his editorial hand firm but light. He is a master at bringing authors—even old ones—gently around. He worked diligently to make this the best book possible. Any faults with this book are a result of my failure to follow his sound advice.

It is not difficult to understand why Molly Stern, publisher at Crown, has such an enviable reputation in the book world. I cannot thank her enough for her faith in this project and its author. Also at Crown I wish to thank Claire Potter, Jesse Aylen, Stephanie Knapp, Rachel Rokicki, Rebecca Welbourn, Sarah Pekdemir, Claire Posner, and Sarah Grimm. My first editor at Crown, Sean Desmond, was a great champion for the project and an outstanding editor. He moved on to become editorial director at Twelve, a division of Hachette. Also, thanks are due Miriam Chotiner-Gardner, who left Crown before this book was in press but helped greatly with earlier manuscript drafts.

At the Arizona Historical Society, I wish to thank director Anne Woosley and her wonderful staff, and especially those invaluable librarians Laura Hoff, Caitlin Lampman, and Lizet Zepeda. I owe a special debt to my old friend Bruce Dinges, the AHS director of publications and editor of the Journal of Arizona History. He assisted me in innumerable ways even after—quite literally—being run over by a truck.

The University of New Mexico supported this book with a generous research grant that allowed me to hire an ace research assistant, Candolin Cook. Ms. Cook, who is working on her doctorate under my direction, provided me with a mass of wonderful research materials, far more in fact than I could use. Her assistance was invaluable. In the department of history, I am ever so grateful to Melissa Bokovoy, Charles Steen, Durwood Ball,Virginia Scharff, Sam Truett, Linda Hall, and Margaret Connell-Szasz.

Yolanda Martinez, the UNM history department office manager, has been my confidant, advisor, and dear friend for thirty years, and never proved more so than during the writing of this book. Barbara Wafer and Dana Ellison went far above and beyond the call of duty in their generous assistance at several crisis points during the production of this manuscript. Thanks are also due to Hazel Mendoza-Jayme, Xayo Meunphalangchai, and Amanda Baca.

Robert M. Utley, Larry Ball, and Ed Sweeney were extremely generous with research materials from their own work on the Apache Wars. They also provided invaluable advice. Utley, who has been my mentor in western history since 1976, was, as usual, a fount of wisdom. Shelly Dudley kindly shared her research in the Schuyler Papers at the Huntington Library, while Victoria Smith provided essential research on Mickey Free and other Arizona captives. It was Professor Smith who discovered the intriguing document on Free signed by Howard Cushing.

David Zucker, Bob Boze Bell, and Stephen Harrigan all critiqued an earlier draft of the manuscript at a critical point and gave suggestions for revision that provided a major breakthrough. I simply cannot thank them enough. Bell first sparked my interest in Mickey Free when we attempted a graphic novel (he is a marvelous artist) and screenplay on him. That project was aborted, but we hope it may yet come to fruition.

Thanks are also due Hampton Sides, Jason Strykowski, Thom Ross, Rusty York, Jerry Thompson, T. J. Stiles, John Lacy, Marvin Kaiser, John Langellier, Kirk Ellis, Jeff Guinn, Marshall Trimble, Jay Van Orden, Michael Blake, Roger Nichols, Christopher Cleveland, Robert Carriker, Greg Lalire, Carol Markstrom, Allan Radbourne, Jim Dunham, Doug McChristian, Jerome Greene, Paul Fees, Paul Hedren, Charles Rankin, Eli Paul, Brian Dippie, Donald Fork, Tim Gravensteter, Doug Hocking, Dan Aranda, Robert Watt, Bud Shapard, Jim Turner, Johnny Boggs, Byron Price, Mike Koury, Daniel Martinez, Meghan Saar, Daniel Harsberger, Stuart Rosebrook, Carole Compton Glenn, Robert Ray, Andrew Fenady, Forrest Fenn, and Robert McCubbin.

My children—Laura, Caitlin, Lorena, Chelsea, and Paul Andy— were constant sources of encouragement. They have all sat through many a tale of the Apache Wars, and they proved wonderful sounding boards. They all gave sage advice. Chelsea and Lorena also provided crucial computer assistance and opened up to me the grand mysteries of the Internet.

Tracy Lee—my beautiful and multitalented wife—placed her stamp on every page of this book, and not only because she typed most of it. She cajoled, threatened, and inspired me to "Go Ahead!" as Davy Crockett would say, despite my own self-doubts and frustrations. This book could never have been completed without her; but then again, I simply cannot function without her. She is my rock.

Often while writing this story of the "motherless child" Mickey Free, my thoughts drifted back to the unknown German woman who gave me the gift of life and then gave me up. She, of course, never could have known that I would find a home in the land of her nation's enemy, where every door was opened, every hand extended in help, and every dream possible. I so very much hope that she found peace.

NOTES

1. APACHERIA

3   "had a red head": Charles D. Poston, *Building a State in Apache Land*, 96–97; Allan Radbourne, *Mickey Free*, 2–4; Thomas E. Sheridan, *Arizona: A History*, 63. Also see John Ward File and Mickey Free File, Arizona Historical Society (AHS).

4   defend the indefensible: Louis Bernard Schmidt, "Manifest Opportunity and the Gadsden Purchase," *Arizona and the West* (Autumn 1961): 253. For the impact of Apache and Comanche raids on northern Mexico, see Brian DeLay, *War of a Thousand Deserts*, 297–340; Joseph F. Park, "The Apaches in Mexican-American Relations, 1848–1861: A Footnote to the Gadsden Treaty," *Arizona and the West* 3 (Summer 1961): 129–46. The standard work on the treaty remains the 1923 study by Paul N. Garber, *The Gadsden Purchase*. Also see Rachel St. John, *Line in the Sand: A History of the U.S.-Mexico Border*, for a more modern interpretation.

4   impossible to enforce: William H. Goetzmann, *Army Exploration in the American West*, 194–97; Schmidt, "Manifest Opportunity," 245–64. Useful pictorial representations of the various border proposals are in Henry P. Walker and Don Bufkin, *Historical Atlas of Arizona*, 18–22; and Warren A. Beck and Ynez D. Haase, *Historical Atlas of New Mexico*, 26–29.

4   heart of Apacheria: Sheridan, *Arizona*, 65–66, 119–26; Marshall Trimble, *Arizona*, 121–23, 130–38; Thomas Edwin Farish, *History of Arizona*, 1:183–98.

5   "perfect state of nature": Poston, *Apache Land*, 72–74; Frank C. Lockwood, *Arizona Characters*, 31–34; A. W. Gressinger, *Charles D. Poston: Sunland Seer*, 26–27.

6   new market for cattle and crops: Constance Wynn Altshuler, *Starting with Defiance: Nineteenth Century Arizona Military Posts*, 47–48; Poston, *Apache Land*, 82.

6   "carry off all the females": Bernard L. Fontana and Cameron Green-

leaf, "Johnny Ward's Ranch: A Study in Historic Archaeology," *Kiva* 28 (October–December 1962): 1–37; Sheridan, *Arizona*, 63.

6   **took his stepfather's name:** Radbourne, *Mickey Free*, 2–8; Victoria A. O. Smith, "White Eyes, Red Heart, Blue Coat: The Life and Times of Mickey Free," 36–40; Mickey Free File and John Ward File, AHS.

7   **"farmers in the neighborhood":** *Tubac Weekly Arizonian*, March 3, 1859; Fontana and Greenleaf, "Johnny Ward's Ranch," 1–37; Radbourne, *Mickey Free*, 4–8. Also see Elizabeth R. Brownell, *They Lived in Tubac.*

8   **"dolphin and shark":** Percy Gatling Hamlin, ed., *The Making of a Soldier: Letters of General R. S. Ewell*, 82.

10   **and perhaps less:** For overviews of the complex history of the Apache people, see Alfonso Ortiz, ed., *Handbook of North American Indians*, vol. 10, *Southwest*, 368–488; James L. Haley, *Apaches: A History and Culture Portrait;* Donald Worcester, *The Apaches: Eagles of the Southwest;* Keith H. Basso and Morris E. Opler, ed., *Apachean Culture History and Ethnology;* Morris E. Opler, *An Apache Life-Way;* Grenville Goodwin, *The Social Organization of the Western Apache;* Frank C. Lockwood, *The Apache Indians;* and Richard J. Perry, *Western Apache Heritage: People of the Mountain Corridor.* There are many additional anthropological and historical studies of various Apache bands that will be cited throughout this book.

10   **mountains of western and southern New Mexico:** Coronado's men made no contact with any Apaches in what was to become Arizona, but did identify a group in eastern New Mexico as Querechos in 1540. They may have been Jicarillas, Mescaleros, or Lipans. See Perry, *Western Apache Heritage*, 1–17, 49–53, 110–54; Haley, *Apaches*, 24–42; Worcester, *The Apaches*, 3–23; Edward H. Spicer, *Cycles of Conquest*, 229–32.

11   **beyond the Gila River:** Sheridan, *Arizona*, 33–50. Also see Kieran McCarty, *Desert Documentary: The Spanish Years, 1767–1821;* David Weber, *Barbaros: Spaniards and Their Savages in the Age of Enlightenment;* and Max L. Moorhead, *The Apache Frontier: Jacob Ugarte and Spanish-Indian Relations in Northern New Spain, 1769–1791.*

11   **war of extermination:** C. L. Sonnichsen, *Tucson: The Life and Times of an American City*, 7–14. Also see Max L. Moorhead, *The Presidio: Bastion of the Spanish Borderlands.*

12   **taken captive by the Apaches:** Lockwood, *Apache Indians*, 8–29; Sheridan, *Arizona*, 44; Opler, *Apache Life-Way*, 316–53; Haley, *Apaches*, 116–21; John C. Cremony, *Life Among the Apaches*, 142–43, 266–67; Keith H. Basso, ed., *Western Apache Raiding and Warfare*, 223–98.

13   **spirits of the dead:** Haley, *Apaches*, 120; Cremony, *Life Among the Apaches*, 257–61; Eve Ball, Nora Henn, and Lynda Sanchez, *Indeh*, 4, 11–12.

13   **"dispersed and movable *rancherias*":** Jack S. Williams and Robert L.

Hoover, *Arms of the Apacheria*, 9–19, 22–27, 44–59; Marshall Trimble, *Arizona*, 49–53. Also see William B. Griffen, *Apaches at War and Peace*, 1–18.

14 **laid waste to the land:** Sheridan, *Arizona*, 48–50; Sonnichsen, *Tucson*, 17–31.

15 **or east to El Paso:** Two excellent studies of Janos are Griffen, *Apaches at War and Peace*, and Lance R. Blyth, *Chiricahua and Janos: Communities of Violence in the Southwestern Borderlands, 1680–1880*.

15 **a new name—Geronimo:** S. M. Barrett, ed., *Geronimo's Story of His Life*, 43–46; Angie Debo, *Geronimo: The Man, His Time, His Place*, 13, 37–38; Edwin R. Sweeney, "I Had Lost All: Geronimo and the Carrasco Massacre of 1851," *Journal of Arizona History* 27 (Spring 1986): 35–52; Robert M. Utley, *Geronimo*, 18–19, 21–22; Sherry Robinson, *Apache Voices: Their Stories of Survival as Told to Eve Ball*, 57; Ball, *Indeh*, 61, 87.

16 **custom of lifting hair:** Rex W. Strickland, "The Birth and Death of a Legend: The Johnson Massacre of 1837," *Arizona and the West* 18 (Autumn 1976): 257–86; Ralph Adam Smith, *Borderlander: The Life of James Kirker, 1793–1852*, 70; Dan Thrapp, *Encyclopedia of Frontier Biography*, 2:731–32; William A. Griffen, *Utmost Good Faith: Patterns of Apache-Mexican Hostilities in Northern Chihuahua Border Warfare, 1821–1848*, 50–53.

16 **new name Mangas Coloradas:** Edwin R. Sweeney, *Mangas Coloradas: Chief of the Chiricahua Apaches*, 70–79; Ball, *Indeh*, 22; Eve Ball, *In the Days of Victorio: Recollections of a Warm Springs Apache*, 46; Ruth McDonald Boyer and Narcissus Duffy Graydon, *Apache Mothers and Daughters: Four Generations of a Family*, 25–27; Opler, *Life-Way*, 335.

2. RED SLEEVES

18 **just such a leader:** Sweeney, *Mangas Coloradas*, 3–67. This is an exceptional biography of the Apache leader.

19 **perfect reign of terror:** Ball, *Days of Victorio*, 46; Smith, *Borderlander*, 171; Griffen, *Utmost Good Faith*, 43–67; Lockwood, *Apache Indians*, 30–40; Worcester, *Apaches*, 36–49; DeLay, *War of a Thousand Deserts*, 297–99.

20 **formidable band of cutthroats:** James Kirker's amazing career is recounted in William Cochran McGaw, *Savage Scene: The Life and Times of James Kirker, Frontier King*, as well as in the more scholarly book by Ralph Adam Smith, *Borderlander*. Also see James Hobbs, *Wild Life in the Far West: Personal Adventures of a Border Mountain Man*, 67–169; Trimble, *Arizona*, 141; *Santa Fe Republican*, May 20, 1847; David J. Weber, *The Taos Trappers*, 221–25.

21 **"Indian hunters in pay of the state":** Sweeney, *Mangas Coloradas*, 135–36; McGaw, *Savage Scene*, 140, 151–53.

22   **dark omen of calamity:** Angie Debo, *Geronimo: The Man, His Time, His Place*, 7–9; Jason Betzinez, *I Fought with Geronimo*, 14–16.

22   **recalled an Apache warrior:** Betzinez, *Geronimo*, 4–6; Ball, *Indeh*, 246–52; Sweeney, *Mangas Coloradas*, 146–47.

23   **common cause against Mexico:** Harvey Lewis Carter, ed., *"Dear Old Kit": The Historical Christopher Carson—With a New Edition of the Carson Memoirs*, 111–12. Carter's book is the most useful of the many editions of Kit Carson's autobiography. Also see Edwin L. Sabin, *Kit Carson Days, 1809–1868: Adventures in the Path of Empire*, 2:511–12; Sweeney, *Mangas Coloradas*, 140–43.

23   **the conquered territory:** Hampton Sides, *Blood and Thunder: An Epic of the American West*, 128–33; Winston Groom, *Kearney's March: The Epic Creation of the American West, 1846–1847*, 139–49; Otis E. Young, *The West of Philip St. George Cooke, 1809–1895*, 193–223; Jeffrey V. Pearson, "Philip St. George Cooke," in Paul Andrew Hutton and Durwood Ball, eds., *Soldiers West: Biographies of the Military Frontier*, 93–121; John Taylor Hughes, *Doniphan's Expedition*, 104–7.

24   **deep irony in the warrior's statement:** Ross Calvin, ed., *Lieutenant Emory Reports: A Reprint of Lieutenant W. H. Emory's Notes on a Military Reconnaissance*, 97–102; Betzinez, *Geronimo*, 13; Sweeney, *Mangas Coloradas*, 143–45; Hughes, *Doniphan's Expedition*, 108–11. Also see Goetzmann, *Army Exploration in the American West*, 127–44.

25   **Apache vengeance was complete:** Betzinez, *Geronimo*, 6–9; Sweeney, *Mangas Coloradas*, 147–49.

25   **agreed to nothing else:** William H. Goetzmann, *Exploration and Empire: The Explorer and the Scientist in the Winning of the American West*, 261–64; Goetzmann, *Army Exploration*, 167–208; Dan L. Thrapp, *Encyclopedia of Frontier Biography*, 1:68–69. Also see John Russell Bartlett, *Personal Narrative of Explorations and Incidents in Texas, New Mexico, California, Sonora, and Chihuahua*, 1:300–27; Sweeney, *Mangas Coloradas*, 232–33; Ruth McDonald Boyer and Narcissus Duffy Gayton, *Apache Mothers and Daughters*, 43–44.

26   **"being his own master":** Cremony, *Life Among the Apaches*, 21, 47–48; Sweeney, *Mangas Coloradas*, 229–30; Thrapp, *Encyclopedia of Frontier Biography*, 1:342–43.

26   **greater recompense for their loss:** Bartlett, *Personal Narrative*, 1:303–17, 398–405; Goetzmann, *Army Exploration*, 179–80; Cremony, *Life Among the Apaches*, 52–66; Sweeney, *Mangas Coloradas*, 235–37. A rich literature has developed around the issue of captivity, much of which began with the seminal work by James F. Brooks, *Captives and Cousins: Slavery, Kinship, and Community in the Southwest Borderlands*.

27   **so many events to come:** Cremony, *Life Among the Apaches*, 66–72; Sweeney, *Mangas Coloradas*, 237–40; Bartlett, *Personal Narrative*, 1:331–39, 351–54.

28   **into the early summer months:** Jerry D. Thompson, "With the Third

Infantry in New Mexico, 1851–1853: The Lost Diary of Private Sylvester W. Matson," *Journal of Arizona History* 31 (Winter 1990): 361–72; Sweeney, *Mangas Coloradas*, 240, 244–47.

29   **despite the treaty forbidding it:** Sweeney, *Mangas Coloradas*, 251–60; Durwood Ball, *Army Regulars on the Western Frontier*, 20–23, 66–67; Robert M. Utley, *Frontiersmen in Blue*, 89–90; Clinton E. Brooks and Frank D. Reeve, eds., *Forts and Forays: James A. Bennett—a Dragoon in New Mexico, 1850–1856*, 38–39. A copy of the treaty is in the Michael Steck Papers, University of New Mexico Library.

29   **to write them in blood:** Goetzmann, *Army Exploration*, 186–97; Schmidt, "Manifest Opportunity," 245–64; Sheridan, *Arizona*, 65–66, 119–26.

30   **near Fort Thorn:** Thrapp, *Encyclopedia of Frontier Biography*, 3:1361–62; Sweeney, *Mangas Coloradas*, 331–32, 512.

31   **"keep faith with them":** Poston, *Apache Land*, 64–67; Lockwood, *Apache Indians*, 92–94; Sweeney, *Mangas Coloradas*, 333–34.

31   **popular Indian agent:** Frank McNitt, *Navajo Wars: Military Campaigns, Slave Raids, and Reprisals*, 98–99, 224–46, 267–97; Ruth M. Underhill, *The Navajos*, 103–5; Sweeney, *Mangas Coloradas*, 343–47. The civilian and military accounts refer to these Apache bands by various generic names, such as Coyoteros, but they were referring to Western Apaches of eastern White Mountain bands.

32   **frustrated American soldiers:** Robert M. Utley, *Frontiersmen in Blue: The United States Army and the Indian, 1848–1865*, 155–59; Hamlin, ed., *Making of a Soldier*, 82–83; Thrapp, *Encyclopedia of Frontier Biography*, 1:136; Frank D. Reeve, ed., "Puritan and Apache: A Diary of Lt. H.M. Lazelle," *New Mexico Historical Review* 23 (October 1948): 82–114; Lockwood, *Apache Indians*, 96–99; William S. Kiser, *Dragoons in Apacheland*, 213–17; Sweeney, *Mangas Coloradas*, 353–54.

33   **would change everything:** John Van Deusen DuBois, *Campaigns in the West, 1856–1861*, 22; Donald C. Pfanz, *Richard S. Ewell: A Soldier's Life*, 93–94; Kiser, *Dragoons in Apacheland*, 220–31; DuBois, *Campaigns in the West*, 28–30; Steck to Bonneville, September 3, 1857, Steck Papers, University of New Mexico Library.

3. THE LOST BOY

36   **he would be a warrior:** Radbourne, *Mickey Free*, 14–15, 237; Basso, ed., *Western Apache Raiding*, 256–57, 264–75, 284–98; Opler, *Apache Life-Way*, 137–38, 332–36; Haley, *Apaches*, 63–75; Paul R. Nickens and Kathleen M. Nickens, "Victor of Old San Carlos," *Journal of Arizona History* 56 (Autumn 2015): 277–322; Smith, "White Eyes, Red Heart, Blue Coat," 47–60.

37   **pleaded with Ward to recover the lost boy:** Radbourne, *Mickey Free*, 9; Victoria Smith, *Captive Arizona*, 57–58; Smith, "White Eyes, Red Heart, Blue Coat," 40–41; John Ward File, AHS.

38   **Johnny Ward arrived:** Benjamin Sacks, "New Evidence on the Bascom Affair," *Arizona and the West* 4 (Autumn 1962): 261–78; Constance Altshuler, ed., *Latest from Arizona*, 165–66, 174–76; Radbourne, *Mickey Free*, 10–11; *St. Louis Republican*, February 11, 1861; Edwin Sweeney, *Cochise*, 142–48. Few events in Apache history have been written about quite as much as the so-called Bascom Affair. The best version is in the Cochise biography by the ever reliable Edwin Sweeney. Also see Robert M. Utley, "The Bascom Affair: A Reconstruction," *Arizona and the West* 3 (Spring 1961): 59–68; Charles K. Mills, "Incident at Apache Pass," *Journal of America's Military Past* 27 (Spring/Summer 2000): 76–88; Lockwood, *Apache Indians*, 100–109; Haley, *Apaches*, 224–30; Dan L. Thrapp, *Conquest of Apacheria*, 15–18; Paul I. Wellman, *Death in the Desert*, 59–60; David L. Roberts, *Once They Moved Like the Wind*, 21–29; Ralph Hedrick Ogle, *Federal Control of the Western Apaches, 1848–1886*, 43–45; Farish, *Arizona*, 2:30–35; Lockwood, *Arizona Characters*, 62–66; Peter Aleshire, *Cochise: The Life and Times of the Great Apache Chief*, 119–35; and Terry Mort, *The Wrath of Cochise*.

39   **mighty Chokonen chief:** Robert M. Utley, *A Clash of Cultures: Fort Bowie and the Chiricahua Apaches*, 12–13; Oscar Osburn Winther, *The Transportation Frontier*, 48–51; Robert N. Mullin, *Stagecoach Pioneers of the Southwest*, 32–34; Waterman L. Ormsby, *The Butterfield Overland Mail*, 80–87; Oscar Osburn Winther, "The Southern Overland Mail and Stagecoach Line, 1857–1861," *New Mexico Historical Review* 32 (April 1957): 81–106.

41   **were not so optimistic:** Sweeney, *Cochise*, 3–98; Edwin Sweeney, "Cochise and the Prelude to the Bascom Affair," *New Mexico Historical Review* 64 (October 1989): 432–42; Merejildo Grijalva quoted in Fred Hughes Collection, AHS; James Tevis, *Arizona in the '50's*, 94–100, 123–24, 149; Farish, *Arizona*, 2:30; A. M. Gustafson, ed., *John Spring's Arizona*, 52; Ball, *Indeh*, 22–23; Samuel Woodworth Cozzens, *The Marvelous Country*, 85–86; *Tucson Weekly Arizonian*, July 14, 1859.

42   **the following day:** Heitman, *Historical Register*, 1:197; Thrapp, *Encyclopedia of Frontier Biography*, 1:70; Utley, "The Bascom Affair," 59–62; Altshuler, ed., *Latest from Arizona*, 165–66, 169–70.

44   **"cut the tent":** Sergeant Daniel Robinson left a detailed and gripping account of this incident in "The Affair at Apache Pass," *Sports Afield* 7 (August 1896): 79–84, but a more detailed and superbly annotated version is in Douglas C. McChristian and Larry L. Ludwig, "Eyewitness to the Bascom Affair: An Account by Sergeant Daniel Robinson, Seventh Infantry," *Journal of Arizona History* 42 (Autumn 2001): 277–300. Bascom's official report is conveniently reprinted in Sacks, "New Evidence," 264–66. The originals are in Register of Letters Received, Department of New Mexico, 1854–1865, microfilm roll 14, M1120, National Archives. Also see the eyewitness report by Hubert Oberly, "Why Apaches Made War," in an undated 1886 newspaper interview

in the J. D. Irwin Papers, MS376, AHS. Captain J. D. Irwin's account is in "The Fight at Apache Pass," *Infantry Journal* 32 (April 1928): 1–8, while Cochise left his version in an interview with W. F. Arny published in the *Santa Fe New Mexican*, November 1, 1870. Also see Sweeney, *Cochise*, 148–52; Ball, *Days of Victorio*, 47; Barrett, ed., *Geronimo's Story*, 113–18; Ball, *Indeh*, 22–26; and Don Russell, *One Hundred and Three Fights and Scrimmages: The Story of General Reuben F. Bernard*, 14–27.

45   **war to the death:** Cremony, *Life Among the Apaches*, 47–48; Ball, *Days of Victorio*, 46–47; Ball, *Indeh*, 10; J. P. Dunn, *Massacres of the Mountains*, 326; Wellman, *Death in the Desert*, 55–57; Dan L. Thrapp, *Victorio and the Mimbres Apaches*, 67–74; Farish, *Arizona*, 2:124–26; Boyer and Gayton, *Apache Mothers and Daughters*, 32–33; Woodworth Clum, *Apache Agent: The Story of John P. Clum*, 29–33; Thompson, ed., "With the Third Infantry," 392. All white accounts of this dramatic incident seem to flow from John Cremony. Clum's account is highly sensationalized. Private Sylvester Matson's diary, edited by Thompson, identifies a son of Ponce as the Apache who was whipped. The story was passed down in Apache oral tradition as collected by Eve Ball and Ruth Boyer. Edwin Sweeney, the author of the definitive biography of Mangas Coloradas, discounts the story. Sweeney, *Mangas Coloradas*, 399–406.

46   **vanished beyond the hill:** McChristian and Ludwig, eds., "Eyewitness to the Bascom Affair," 287–90; Sweeney, *Cochise*, 152–53. Douglas C. McChristian, *Fort Bowie: Combat Post of the Southwest, 1858–1894*, 14–35, contains a careful reconstruction of the Bascom Affair with thoughtful commentary of the conflicting eyewitness accounts. Stage driver A. B. Culver left an account that was published in the *Arizonian*, February 9, 1861, a copy of which is in the James Wallace File, Hayden Collection, AHS. Also see Barrett, ed., *Geronimo's Story*, 116–17; Altshuler, ed., *Latest from Arizona*, 174–78; Sweeney, *Cochise*, 153–56; and William A. Bell, *New Tracks in North America*, 279–80, which contains an account from William Oury on the fate of Wallace.

49   **died on the spot:** This harrowing stagecoach ride was related by William Buckley in an interview in the *Alta California*, February 19, 1861, which is in the William F. Buckley File, Hayden Collection, AHS; and William Oury's account in the *Tucson Arizona Star*, June 28, 1877, in the William S. Oury File, Hayden Collection, AHS. Douglas McChristian disputes this dramatic tale in *Fort Bowie*, 29–30, 288, but Sweeney accepts the story in *Cochise*, 156–58.

49   **both Texas and Arizona:** For William S. Oury, see Frank C. Lockwood, *Life in Old Tucson, 1854–1864: As Remembered by the Little Maid Atanacia Santa Cruz*, 92–102; Farish, *Arizona*, 2:269–70; Thrapp, *Encyclopedia of Frontier Biography*, 2:1095–96; and Cornelius C. Smith Jr., *William Sanders Oury: History-Maker of the Southwest*.

50 **preparation for battle:** Oury File, AHS; Smith, *Oury*, 121–29; Irwin Papers, MS 376, AHS; Jerry D. Thompson, *Desert Tiger: Paddy Graydon*, 20; Sweeney, *Cochise*, 158, 161; Sacks, "New Evidence," 265; Donald C. Pfanz, ed., *The Letters of Richard Ewell*, 140.

51 **His plan had failed:** McChristian and Ludwig, eds., "Eyewitness to the Bascom Affair," 290–91; Sweeney, *Cochise*, 159–61; Barrett, ed., *Geronimo's Story*, 117–18; Betzinez, *Geronimo*, 40–42.

52 **after the Friday battle:** Irwin Papers, MS. 376, AHS; Sacks, "New Evidence," 264–65; Thompson, *Desert Tiger*, 20–21; Heitman, *Historical Register*, 1:564.

54 **"only good Indians are dead ones":** Oury File, AHS; McChristian, *Fort Bowie*, 33–34; Sweeney, *Cochise*, 162–63; Oberly, "Why the Apaches Made War," MS. 276, Irwin Papers, AHS; *Santa Fe New Mexican*, November 1, 1870; McChristian and Ludwig, ed., "Eyewitness to the Bascom Affair," 292–93; Altshuler, ed., *Latest from Arizona*, 177–78.

54 **"adorn that profession":** Poston, *Apache Land*, 99; Sweeney, *Cochise*, 163–65; McChristian, *Fort Bowie*, 34–35; Utley, *Clash of Cultures*, 21–23.

4. APACHE PASS

57 **"'on a peach tree'":** Radbourne, *Mickey Free*, 14–16; Perry, *Western Apache Heritage*, 7–8, 155–56; Goodwin, *Social Organization of the Western Apache*, 1–62; Ian W. Record, *Big Sycamore Stands Alone: The Western Apaches, Aravaipa, and the Struggle for Place*, 43–54.

57 **"war to the Chiricahua":** Ball, *Days of Victorio*, 155; Sweeney, *Grijalva*, 7–8.

58 **the Apache Kid:** Phyllis de la Garza, *The Apache Kid*, 1–2; Dan Williamson, "The Apache Kid," 14–15; Earle R. Forrest and Edwin B. Hill, *Lone War Trail of the Apache Kid*, 31–35; William Sparks, *The Apache Kid*, 10–11.

60 **back to Cooke's Canyon:** Sweeney, *Cochise*, 175–78; Thompson, *Desert Tiger*, 22–24; Altshuler, ed., *Latest from Arizona*, 182–99; *Tucson Star*, July 20, 1879; Sweeney, *Mangas Coloradas*, 408–16; Thrapp, *Conquest*, 18–19; Winther, *Transportation Frontier*, 50–53; Tevis, *Arizona in the '50's*, 229–30; Poston, *Apache Land*, 100–101; Farish, *Arizona*, 2:59–60. *Arizona Daily Star*, July 27, 1879, contains William Oury's account of the fight.

61 **thrown back the advance of the American frontier:** Altshuler, ed., *Latest from Arizona*, 202; Poston, *Apache Land*, 101–5; Virginia Roberts, *With Their Own Blood*, 97–102; Raphael Pumpelly, *Across America and Asia*, 36–67.

62 **not a moment too soon:** For the remarkable story of the Grundy Ake Wagon Train, see Virginia Roberts, "Jack Pennington in Early Arizona," 326–29; James B. O'Neil, *They Die but Once*, 38–46; Roberts, *With*

Their Own Blood, 101–18; Sweeney, *Cochise*, 177–78, 183–85; *Tucson Weekly Arizonian*, August 10, 1861; William F. Scott, address to Society of Arizona Pioneers, July 6, 1894, William F. Scott File, AHS; Albert R. Bates, *Jack Swilling*, 20–23.

63 **hands of these White Eyes:** William F. Scott address, July 6, 1894, Scott File, AHS; Allen, "Pinos Altos," 302–5; Bates, *Jack Swilling*, 23–25; Sweeney, *Cochise*, 186–88; Roberts, *With Their Own Blood*, 118–21; Sweeney, *Mangas Coloradas*, 423–26; L. Boyd Finch, *Confederate Pathway to the Pacific*, 92–93.

64 **over to the rebel cause:** George Wythe Baylor, *John Robert Baylor: Confederate Governor of Arizona*, 1–17; Jerry D. Thompson, ed., *Into the Far, Wild Country: True Tales of the Southwest by George Wythe Baylor*, 181–207; Max L. Heyman Jr., *Prudent Soldier: A Biography of Major General E. R. S. Canby, 1817–1873*, 137–65; Heitman, *Historical Register*, 1:722; Walter Earl Pittman, *New Mexico and the Civil War*, 11–19; Sweeney, *Cochise*, 194–95; Finch, *Confederate Pathway to the Pacific*, 70–78, 106–22; Andrew E. Masich, *The Civil War in Arizona: The Story of the California Volunteers, 1861–1865*, 10–12; Sonnichsen, *Tucson*, 59–63; *War of the Rebellion: A Compilation of Official Records of the Union and Confederate Armies* [O.R.], 4:791–94.

65 **four days later:** Aurora Hunt, *The Army of the Pacific, 1860–1866*, 19–51; Utley, *Frontiersmen in Blue*, 211–20; Aurora Hunt, *Major General James Henry Carleton, 1814–1873: Frontier Dragoon*, 187–213; Adam Kane, "James H. Carleton," in Hutton and Ball, eds., *Soldiers West*, 122–48; Masich, *Civil War in Arizona*, 9–36, 186–88; Finch, *Confederate Pathway*, 125–54; Thrapp, *Encyclopedia of Frontier Biography*, 3:1525; Baylor, *Into the Far, Wild Country*, 192–94; Baylor, *John Robert Baylor*, 11–17.

67 **at Apache Pass:** Lockwood, *Life in Old Tucson*, 103–27; Masich, *Civil War in Arizona*, 45–52; Sweeney, *Cochise*, 196–98; *War of Rebellion*, series 50, Part 1:120–31; Sweeney, *Mangas Coloradas*, 430–31; Utley, *Geronimo*, 47–48; Cremony, *Life Among the Apaches*, 155–58.

69 **all the difference that day:** For the Battle of Apache Pass, see Sweeney, *Cochise*, 199–201; McChristian, *Fort Bowie*, 48–63; Utley, *Clash of Cultures*, 25–27. Also see Lockwood, *Apache Indians*, 135–41; Wellman, *Death in the Desert*, 74–80; Haley, *Apaches*, 231–35. For participant accounts, see Allan Radbourne, ed., "The Battle for Apache Pass: Reports of the California Volunteers," *English Westerners Brand Book* 34 (Spring 2001): 1–32; Cremony, *Life Among the Apaches*, 155–67; Richard H. Orton, *Records of California Men in the War of the Rebellion*, 46–60, 354; Albert J. Fountain, "Battle of Apache Pass," in Joseph Miller, ed., *Arizona Cavalcade*, 30–35; Neil B. Carmony, ed., *The Civil War in Apacheland: Sergeant George Hand's Diary*, 64–65, 92, 111–12; Henry P. Walker, ed., "Soldier in the California Column: The Diary of

John W. Teal," *Arizona and the West* 13 (Spring 1971): 33–82. For an overview of the Civil War campaigns in the Southwest, see Utley, *Frontiersmen in Blue*, 231–60.

70 **met no resistance:** Walker, ed., "Soldier in the California Column," 40–41.

70 **a very different form:** Ball, *Indeh*, 20; Cremony, *Life Among the Apaches*, 159–60; Ball, *Days of Victorio*, 47; Blyth, *Chiricahua and Janos*, 174–75; Sweeney, *Mangas Coloradas*, 438–40.

5. KIT CARSON'S WAY

71 **thought of the Jicarillas:** Hunt, *Carleton*, 241–43; Paul Andrew Hutton, "Kit Carson's Ride," *Wild West* 19 (April 2007): 28–37; Veronica E. Valarde Tiller, *The Jicarilla Apache Tribe: A History*, 4–6. Also see Delores A. Gunnerson, *The Jicarilla Apaches: A Study in Survival*, for the Spanish period as well as B. Sunday Eiselt, *Becoming White Clay: A History of Archaeology of Jicarilla Apache Enclavement*.

72 **greater national hero:** Paul Hutton, "Why Is This Man Forgotten?" *True West* 53 (March 2006): 24–32. The literature on Carson is vast, but the best modern biography is Hampton Sides, *Blood and Thunder: An Epic of the American West*. Carson's autobiography is an invaluable source, and the best version is the annotated edition by Harvey Lewis Carter, ed., *"Dear Old Kit": The Historical Christopher Carson*.

72 **"courage or daring":** William T. Sherman, *Memoirs of General William T. Sherman, Written by Himself*, I:46.

73 **a population of around five hundred:** Tiller, *Jicarilla Apache,* 12–30.

73 **to do his job:** Annie Heloise Abel, ed., *The Official Correspondence of James S. Calhoun*, 20, 42, 69; Hutton, "Kit Carson's Ride," 31–32; Ball, *Army Regulars on the Western Frontier*, 20–22.

74 **reckoning was coming:** Sabin, *Kit Carson Days*, II:634–39, 651; Tom Dunlay, *Kit Carson and the Indians*, 157.

74 **killed Lobo Blanco:** Ball, *Army Regulars*, 21–22; Abel, ed., *Calhoun Correspondence*, 517–41; Tiller, *Jicarilla Apache*, 40–42; Theodore F. Rodenbough, comp., *From Everglade to Canyon with the Second United States Cavalry*, 176–78, 485–86; Sabin, *Kit Carson Days*, II:622; Clinton E. Brooks and Frank D. Reeve, eds., *Forts and Forays: A Dragoon in New Mexico*, 48.

75 **let the survivors go:** Tiller, *Jicarilla Apache*, 37; Dunlay, *Kit Carson and the Indians*, 162–63. For the Embudo Mountain battle, see Homer K. Davidson, *Black Jack Davidson: A Cavalry Commander on the Western Frontier*, 69–72; Brooks and Reeve, eds., *Forts and Forays*, 54.

75 **vast territory:** Tiller, *Jicarilla Apache*, 47–48.

76 **chief-of-scouts:** Sabin, *Kit Carson Days*, II:661–62; Pearson, "Philip St. George Cooke," in Hutton and Ball, eds., *Soldiers West*, 93–121; Albert G. Brackett, *History of the United States Cavalry*, 34–52, 134–36;

Dunlay, *Kit Carson and the Indians*, 164–65; Alfred Barnaby Thomas, *The Jicarilla Apache Indians: A History, 1598–1888*, 9. For Cooke's campaign, see Otis Young, *The West of Philip St. George Cooke, 1809–1895*, 255–60; Cooke's narrative in Rodenbough, comp., *From Everglade to Canyon*, 178–80; and Carson's account in Carter, ed., *"Dear Old Kit,"* 135–38.

76 **simply as hostiles:** Sides, *Blood and Thunder*, 319; Carter, ed., *"Dear Old Kit,"* 142; Sabin, *Kit Carson Days*, II, 665; Dunlay, *Kit Carson and the Indians*, 168. For the campaign, see Hunt, *Carleton*, 137–41.

77 **United States government:** Dunlay, *Kit Carson and the Indians*, 171–85; David Meriwether, *My Life in the Mountains and on the Plains*, 231–32; Thelma S. Guild and Harvey L. Carter, *Kit Carson*, 212–13. For the treaty, see Tiller, *Jicarilla Apache*, 51–55; and Thomas, *Jicarilla Apache*, part 3, 14–15.

78 **proud of his regiment:** Max L. Heyman Jr., *Prudent Soldier: A Biography of Major General E. R. S. Canby*, 141–47; Sides, *Blood and Thunder*, 275–82; Ball, *Army Regulars*, 189–203; Sabin, *Kit Carson Days*, II:674–85; Jacqueline Dorgan Meketa, ed., *Legacy of Honor: The Life of Rafael Chacon, a Nineteenth-Century New Mexican*, 121–45. Also see Roy C. Colton, *The Civil War in the Western Territories*, 7; Alvin M. Josephy Jr., *The Civil War in the American West*, 34–37.

78 **stood in his way:** John P. Wilson, *When the Texans Come: Missing Records from the Civil War in the Southwest, 1861–1862*, 1–4, 17–51; Flint Whitlock, *Distant Bugles, Distant Drums*, 22–23; Josephy, *Civil War in the American West*, 31–60. For Fort Craig, see Charles Carroll and Lynne Sebastian, eds., *Fort Craig: The United States Fort on the Camino Real*; Jerry D. Thompson, ed., *New Mexico Territory During the Civil War: Wallen and Evans Inspection Reports, 1862–1863*, 97–110; and Edward Eckert and Nicholas J. Amato, eds., *Ten Years in the Saddle*, 123.

80 **157 wounded:** Thompson, *Desert Tiger*, 24–37; Ovando J. Hollister, *History of the First Regiment of Colorado Volunteers*, 155–56; Alonso Ferdinand Ickis, *Bloody Trails Along the Rio Grande*, 74; George H. Pettis, "The Confederate Invasion of New Mexico and Arizona," *Battles and Leaders of the Civil War*, II:105; Don E. Alberts, ed., *Rebels on the Rio Grande: The Civil War Journal of A. B. Peticolas*, 45, 119; Sides, *Blood and Thunder*, 287–88; Meketa, ed., *Chacon*, 163–86; Josephy, *Civil War in the American West*, 166–67. All US mounted forces were consolidated into a single Cavalry Corps by a congressional act of August 3, 1861. Thus the First Dragoons (organized 1833), the second Dragoons (organized 1836), the Regiment of Mounted Riflemen (organized 1846), the First and Second Cavalry (organized 1855), and the Third Cavalry (organized 1861) became the First through the Sixth Regiments of Cavalry based on the date of their organization. This caused considerable lamentation on the part of the old dragoons, for they now had to exchange their uniforms with orange facings for the yellow facings of the new cav-

alry regiments. The troops were, however, permitted to wear out their old uniforms, so at Valverde all the dragoons, now in the Second Cavalry, fought wearing the orange (a not inconsequential fact, since so many of them were from northern Ireland). Rodenbough, comp., *From Everglade to Canyon*, 237–241; Randy Steffen, *Horse Soldiers*, II:34–94; John Langellier, *U.S. Dragoons*, 36–42; Gregory J. Urwin, *The United States Cavalry*, 112–13. For the Battle of Valverde, also see Josephy, *War on the Frontier*, 24–25; Heyman, *Prudent Soldier*, 165–70; Wilson, *When the Texans Came*, 242–56; Sabin, *Kit Carson Days*, II:674–93, 843–46; and John Taylor, *Bloody Valverde: A Civil War Battle on the Rio Grande*.

80   **replaced by Brigadier General Carleton:** Heyman, *Prudent Soldier*, 181–87, 349–84; Josephy, *Civil War in the American West*, 67–92; Walter Earl Pittman, *New Mexico and the Civil War*, 52–109; Wilson, *When the Texans Came*, 258–74; and Hollister, *History of the First Regiment*, 71–184.

80   **"instructions about them":** William A. Keleher, *Turmoil in New Mexico*, 286–87; Sabin, *Kit Carson Days*, II:701.

82   **now sent Carson:** C. L. Sonnichsen, *The Mescalero Apaches*, 13–64; Morris E. Opler, "Mescalero Apache," in Alfonso Ortiz, ed., *Handbook of North American Indians: The Southwest*, 419–39.

83   **history of Apacheria:** Thompson, *Desert Tiger*, 49–53; Howard Bryan, *Wildest of the Wild West*, 50–52; Lawrence Kelly, *Navajo Roundup*, 12–15, 34.

83   **"Gallinas Massacre":** The Gallinas Massacre is highly controversial. Graydon's account is in his letter of October 23, 1862, and Morrison's report is October 24, 1862, Letters Received, Department of New Mexico, RG 393, National Archives. Also see Sonnichsen, *Mescalero Apaches*, 111–12; Kelly, *Navajo Roundup*, 12–14; Sabin, *Kit Carson Days*, II:704; and Dale F. Giese, ed., *My Life with the Army in the West: Memories of James E. Farmer*, 49–50.

83   **left both men dead:** *Santa Fe Gazette*, November 15, 1862; *New York Times*, December 9, 1862; *San Francisco Daily Alta California*, February 14, 1863; B. C. Hernandez, "The Tragic Death of Doctor J. M. Whitlock in 1868 at Fort Stanton, New Mexico," *New Mexico Historical Review* 16 (January 1941): 104–6; Meketa, ed., *Chacon*, 269–73; Giese, ed., *My Life with the Army*, 49–51; Keleher, *Turmoil in New Mexico*, 289–91, 485; and Thompson, *Desert Tiger*, 56–63, which is the most reliable account of Paddy Graydon's death.

84   **Mescalero leaders to Santa Fe:** Sonnichsen, *Mescalero Apaches*, 113; Dunlay, *Kit Carson and the Indians*, 244–45.

84   **warriors into productive farmers:** Sabin, *Kit Carson Days*, II:705; Dunlay, *Kit Carson and the Indians*, 246–47.

85   **campaign against the Navajos:** Guild and Carter, *Kit Carson*, 229–30; Sides, *Blood and Thunder*, 334–36.

85   **more generals to come:** Keleher, *Turmoil in New Mexico*, 291–92.

6. PEOPLE OF THE WHITE MOUNTAINS

86   **lost boy now had a family:** Basso, ed., *Western Apache Raiding*, 135; Radbourne, *Mickey Free*, 15–17; Smith, "White Eyes, Red Heart, Blue Coat," 60–62.

86   **together by blood:** Robert N. Bellah, *Apache Kinship Systems*, 82–107. The standard work on this topic remains Grenville Goodwin, *The Social Organization of the Western Apache*.

87   **got enough to eat for once:** Radbourne, *Mickey Free*, 16–18; Winfred Buskirk, *The Western Apache: Living with the Land Before 1950*, 117.

88   **"even kill him":** Goodwin, *Social Organization*, 475–76; Bellah, *Apache Kinship*, 86; Basso, ed., *Western Apache Raiding*, 97; Opler, *Apache Life-Way*, 50.

89   **cure the sick:** Buskirk, *Western Apache*, 126–27; Opler, *Apache Life-Way*, 224–27, 288–93; John G. Bourke, *The Medicine Men of the Apache*, 30; Ball, *In the Days of Victorio*, 55–56.

89   **powers of a great warrior:** Buskirk, *Western Apache*, 159–60; Opler, *Apache Life-Way*, 50–54, 65–76.

91   **"Cottonwoods Joining" clan:** Opler, *Apache Life-Way*, 441–42; Buskirk, *Western Apache*, 161–99; Basso, ed., *Western Apache Raiding*, 93–96;

92   **"He was handsome":** Radbourne, *Mickey Free*, 144.

93   **just plain good fun:** Carol A. Markstrom, *Empowerment of North American Indian Girls*, 192–301; Opler, *Apache Life-Way*, 82–134.

93   **became one with it:** Radbourne, *Mickey Free*, 182.

93   **become fearsome warriors:** Haley, *Apaches*, 159–67; Opler, *Apache Life-Way*, 443–56.

94   **people of the White Mountains and the Americans:** Basso, ed., *Western Apache Raiding*, 98–100.

94   **motherless child:** Smith, "White Eyes, Red Heart, Blue Coat," 60–62; Radbourne, *Mickey Free*, 17–21. Also see Goodwin, *Social Organization*, 664; and Opler, *Apache Life-Way*, 55–56.

7. THE HEAD OF MANGAS COLORADAS

96   **embraced his commander's orders:** Sweeney, *Mangas Coloradas*, 444–47; *War of the Rebellion*, series I, vol. 50, pt. 2, 147–48; Thrapp, *Victorio and the Mimbres Apaches*, 82.

97   **now wisely switched sides:** Sweeney, *Merejildo Grijalva*, 15; Sweeney, *Mangas Coloradas*, 447. For Pinos Altos, see R. S. Allen, "Pinos Altos, New Mexico," *New Mexico Historical Review* 23 (October 1948): 302–32; and David J. Weber, *The Mexican Frontier*, 142–43. For Swilling, see Farish, *Arizona*, 2:251–57; and Bates, *Jack Swilling*, 23–28.

98   **worthy of respect:** Al Bates, "Jack Swilling and the Walker Exploratory Party," *Territorial Times* 1 (May 2008): 13–17. For Walker's career, see Daniel Ellis Conner, *Joseph Reddeford Walker and the Arizona Adven-*

ture, edited by Donald J. Berthrong and Odessa Davenport, xiv–xx; and Bill Gilbert, *Westering Man: The Life of Joseph Walker.*

98   **back to Pinos Altos:** Conner, *Walker,* 27–28, 30–31.

99   **within two weeks:** William Fours File, Hayden Collection, AHS; Sweeney, *Mangas,* 446; Bates, *Swilling,* 30; Masich, *Civil War Arizona,* 246–48.

99   **accompany Mangas as bodyguard:** Barrett, ed., *Geronimo's Story,* 119; Ball, *Days of Victorio,* 47–48; Sweeney, *Mangas,* 448; Ball, *Indeh,* 19.

100   **reversal of fortune:** Conner, *Walker,* 34–42, is a remarkable eyewitness account of the events. A slightly different version, also by Conner, is in Thomas Farish's invaluable *History of Arizona,* 2:143–53. Also see James McClintock, *Arizona,* 1:177.

101   **one of the adobe shacks:** Sweeney, *Mangas,* 454; Conner, *Walker,* 37. Fort McLane had been established in December 1860 just south of present-day Hurley, New Mexico, to guard the mines at nearby Pinos Altos from the Apaches. It was initially named for Secretary of War John Floyd, but when he resigned to join the Confederacy it was renamed in honor of Captain George McLane, who had recently been slain by the Navajos. The post was abandoned upon the outbreak of the Civil War and the troops withdrawn. Today nothing remains to mark the location of the fort or the place where Mangas Coloradas was murdered. Daniel C. B. Rathbun and David V. Alexander, *New Mexico Frontier Military Place Names,* 116–18.

102   **a good night's work:** Frank Lockwood, *Pioneer Days,* 159; Conner, *Walker,* 38–39. Clark Stocking of the California Volunteers left this eyewitness account of West's perfidy. Stocking's details vary somewhat from Conner's version of events. See McClintock, *Arizona,* I:178; Clark B. Stocking File, and William Fours File, Hayden Collection, AHS; Sweeney, *Mangas Coloradas,* 457–58; and Thrapp, *Conquest,* 22–23. Also see Lee Myers, "The Enigma of Mangas Coloradas' Death," *New Mexico Historical Review* 41 (October 1966): 287–304; and Darlis Miller, *California Column,* 17.

102   **sent to the Smithsonian:** Conner, *Walker,* 40–41; Myers, "Enigma," 290–91; Farish, *Arizona,* 2:145. Also see Orson S. Fowler, *Human Sciences or Phrenology,* 195.

103   **"we know abound, with safety":** Neil Carmony, ed., *The Civil War in Apacheland,* 101; Sweeney, *Mangas Coloradas,* 460–62; West to Cutler, January 28, 1863, M619, R195, RG94, National Archives; Keleher, *Turmoil,* 293.

104   **head of Mangas Coloradas:** Sweeney, *Cochise,* 205; Ball, *Indeh,* 20; Ball, *Days of Victorio,* 48; Barrett, ed., *Geronimo's Story,* 119; Carmony, ed., *Civil War in Apacheland,* 126–27; Utley, *Frontiersmen in Blue,* 253.

8. THE CUSTOM OF THE COUNTRY

105 **"part of the government":** Carson to Carleton, July 24, 1863, in Kelly, *Navajo Roundup*, 30–31.

106 **difficult one to enforce:** Carleton to Carson, August 18, 1863, in Kelly, *Navajo Roundup*, 31–32.

106 **benefit to the Indians:** Peonage was not legally abolished in New Mexico until 1867, and it persisted for another generation after that. New Mexico's federal attorney described peonage as "a species of slavery as abject and oppressive as any found upon the American continent." W. W. H. Davis, *El Gringo: New Mexico and Her People* (New York: Harper, 1857), 231–32. The standard work on this complicated topic is Brooks, *Captives & Cousins*. Also see Juliana Barr, *Peace Came in the Form of a Woman: Indians and Spaniards in the Texas Borderlands;* L. R. Bailey, *Indian Slave Trade in the Southwest;* Carl Coke Rister, *Border Captives: The Traffic in Prisoners by Southern Plains Indians, 1835–1875;* Clifford J. Walker, *Gone the Way of the Earth: Indian Slave Trade in the Old Southwest;* and several of the essays in Catherine M. Cameron, ed., *Invisible Citizens: Captives and Their Consequences.*

107 **crumbled in the face of independence movements:** Paul T. Conrad, "Indian Slavery by the Spanish," in Lynn Dumenil, ed., *The Oxford Encyclopedia of American Social History;* Mark Santiago, *The Jar of Severed Hands: Spanish Deportation of Apache Prisoners of War, 1770–1810.* Also see Paul T. Conrad, "Captive Fates: Displaced American Indians in the Southwest Borderlands, Mexico, and Cuba, 1500–1800" (Ph.D. diss., University of Texas at Austin, 2011); Matthew Babcock, "Turning Apaches into Spaniards: North America's Forgotten Indian Reservations" (Ph.D. diss., Southern Methodist University, 2008); and Boyer and Gayton, *Apache Mothers and Daughters,* 26–27.

108 **eastern Oklahoma:** For the evolution of Indian Removal and Jacksonian Indian Policy, see Francis Paul Prucha, *The Great Father: The United States Government and the American Indians,* 2 vols., I:179–314. Also see Paul Andrew Hutton, "Mr. Crockett Goes to Washington," *American History* 35 (April 2000): 26–27.

109 **noted the post surgeon:** Cremony, *Among the Apaches,* 200; Haley, *Apaches,* 242; Sonnichsen, *Mescalero Apaches,* 113–15. Also see Robert Trennert, *Alternative to Extinction: Federal Indian Policy and the Beginnings of the Reservation System, 1846–51,* for the origins of the reservation concept.

109 **admired them for it:** Cremony, *Among the Apaches,* 242–44.

110 **banished from the reservation:** Sonnichsen, *Mescalero Apaches,* 118–30.

111 **looked the other way:** Kelly, *Navajo Roundup,* 128; Sonnichsen, *Mescalero Apaches,* 131–33.

112 **"we will not be slaves":** Cremony, *Among the Apaches,* 187; John C. Cremony, "The Apache Race," *Overland Monthly* 1 (September 1868): 207.

113 **so recently been driven from:** McChristian, *Fort Bowie*, 64–104; Alt-shuler, *Starting with Defiance*, 15–18, 63–67; Utley, *Frontiersmen in Blue*, 254–55; Poston, *Apache Land*, 110–26; Trimble, *Arizona*, 314–16; Farish, *History of Arizona*, 3:47–70.

114 **it was catastrophic:** Lockwood, *Pioneer Days*, 198; Farish, *History of Arizona*, I:353–55; Conner, *Walker*, 43–133; Gilbert, *Westering Man*, 267–77; Bates, *Jack Swilling*, 38–42; Robert L. Spude, "Who Were the First Hassayampers?" *Territorial Times* 2 (May 2009): 1–7; Trimble, *Arizona*, 220–22; Farish, *History of Arizona*, 2:211–15.

114 **for distant Arizona territory:** Farish, *History of Arizona*, 3:14–17, 21–23; Hunt, *Carleton*, 273–96. Jack Swilling continued to buccaneer his way through Arizona history. He was instrumental in laying out Phoenix in 1868 and ensured its prosperity with his Salt River irrigation company. He returned to the mountains, where he prospered with mining claims. His addiction to morphine led many to consider him a dangerous character, while his business dealings made him many enemies. In 1878 he was unfairly charged with a stagecoach holdup near Wickenburg and died in the Yuma jail while awaiting trial. Bates, *Jack Swilling*, 42–88. Not long after Prescott was founded, Joseph Walker departed. He found no comfort in the mining boomtown he had help to found. "We have opened the area to civilization," he told Conner, "and now it is up to civilization to do the rest." Walker, almost totally blind, died in Contra Costa County, California, on November 13, 1872. Gilbert, *Westering Man*, 273; Conner, *Arizona Adventure*, 200.

115 **Four Corners homeland in 1868:** Utley, *Frontiersmen in Blue*, 257–59; Masich, *Civil War in Arizona*, 283–84; Kane, "General Carleton," in Hutton and Ball, eds., *Soldiers West*, 141–43; Sherman quote in House Exec. Docs., 39th Congress, 2nd Session, no. 23, p. 15; Gerald Thompson, *Army and the Navajo*, 140–65; Kelly, *Navajo Roundup*, 159–70. Also see Lynn R. Bailey, *Bosque Redondo: The Navajo Internment at Fort Sumner, New Mexico, 1863–1868*.

115 **also included the Apaches:** Edward S. Ellis, *The Life of Kit Carson*, 248–59, which prints letters from Generals Sherman and Rusling. Also see Hutton, "Why Is This Man Forgotten?" 24–32; and Sides, *Blood and Thunder*, 380–95.

9. CAMP GRANT

117 **one other family remained:** Radbourne, *Mickey Free*, 12–13; "Reminiscences of Santiago Ward," 85–86.

118 **"make her take it back":** Lockwood, *Apache Indians*, 161–62; Sheridan, *Arizona*, 71; Robert M. Utley, *Frontier Regulars*, 170–72.

119 **for duty in the Southwest:** Utley, *Frontier Regulars*, 10–43; William H. Leckie and Shirley A. Leckie, *The Buffalo Soldiers: A Narrative of the Black Cavalry in the West*, 3–18; Arlen L. Fowler, *The Black Infantry*

in the West, 1869–1891, 3–15, 114–44; Elizabeth D. Leonard, *Men of Color to Arms! Black Soldiers, Indian Wars, and the Quest for Equality,* 1–75. *Army and Navy Journal,* January 27, 1877, contains the chaplain's quote. For the origin of the name "Buffalo Soldier," see Francis M. A. Roe, *Army Letters from an Officer's Wife,* 65; and Frank N. Schubert, ed., *Voices of the Buffalo Soldier,* 47–49.

119   the next twenty years: *Annual Report of the Secretary of War* (1869), 124.

120   as freely as the wind: Paul Andrew Hutton, *Phil Sheridan and His Army,* 28–30, 115–17; Utley, *Frontier Regulars,* 192–93; Warner, *Generals in Blue,* 481–82.

120   "all over the southwestern border": John G. Bourke, *On the Border with Crook,* 1–5; Kenneth A. Randall, *Only the Echoes: The Life of Howard Bass Cushing,* 5–40. Also see Theron Haight, *Three Wisconsin Cushings.*

120   he participated in: Bourke, *On the Border with Crook,* 1–5, 29–30; Joseph C. Porter, *Paper Medicine Man: John Gregory Bourke and His American West,* 1–8; Charles M. Robinson III, ed., *The Diaries of John Gregory Bourke,* 1:1–24. Captain Bourke's voluminous diaries have been partially edited by the late Charles Robinson and published by the University of North Texas Press. The originals are at West Point.

122   cause considerable trouble: Bourke, *On the Border,* 17; Tevis, *Arizona in the '50's,* 152–53. Also see Opler, *Apache Life-Way,* 406–12; Goodwin, *Social Organization of the Western Apache,* 284–373.

122   buried the scalp: Bourke Diary, 95:65; Porter, *Paper Medicine Man,* 10–11.

123   from 1865 to 1874: Lockwood, *Apache Indians,* 176–78; Utley, *Frontier Regulars,* 18–25, 171–73; Roberts, *Once They Moved Like the Wind,* 54–56.

124   had no reservations: *Army and Navy Journal,* February 26, 1876; Hutton, *Phil Sheridan and His Army,* 98, 180–82, 197–98; Robert Winston Mardock, *The Reformers and the American Indian,* 42–46, 139–41, 159–67; Utley, *Frontier Regulars,* 188–92; Prucha, *Great Father,* 1:501.

125   agreement with these sentiments: *Columbus (Texas) Platte Journal,* June 29, 1870; *Chicago Tribune,* April 25, 1870; Hutton, *Phil Sheridan,* 180.

125   forty-seven more were killed: Lockwood, *Apache Indians,* 174–76; Ogle, *Western Apaches,* 76–79; Karl Jacoby, *Shadows at Dawn: A Borderlands Massacre and the Violence of History,* 124–28.

126   to flee to Fort Bowie: Sweeney, *Cochise,* 253, 266, 313.

126   forced him to keep his people on the move: Gustafson, ed., *John Spring's Arizona,* 124–27; Sweeney, *Cochise,* 272–75; Russell, *One Hundred and Three Fights,* 63–80; Sweeney, *Grijalva,* 26.

129   Camp Crittenden after midnight on May 6: For Cushing's last fight, see Thrapp, *Conquest,* 70–78; Ball, *Indeh,* 26–27; and Thrapp, *Juh,* 10–11.

129   "to the 'undiscovered country'": *New York Herald,* May 15, 1871.

10. MASSACRE

130 **the fate of her lost boy:** Mrs. George Kitt, "Reminiscences of Santiago Ward, March 12, 1934," and "Miscellaneous Probate Cases of Pima County, 1864 to 1889—John Ward," John Ward File, Hayden Collection, AHS; Radbourne, *Mickey Free*, 13–14, 122; Smith, *Captive Arizona*, 70.

131 **time for a reckoning:** Lockwood, *Apache Indians*, 175–76; A. M. Gustafson, ed., *John Spring's Arizona*, 191–92; Sonnichsen, *Tucson*, 75–81; Roberts, *With Their Own Blood*, 156.

131 **"by the people's money":** Tucson *Arizona Citizen*, March 25, 1871; Lockwood, *Life in Old Tucson*, 92–102; Ian W. Record, *Big Sycamore Stands Alone: The Western Apaches, Aravaipa, and the Struggle for Place*, 198–206. William Oury's account "The So-called Camp Grant Massacre" was published in the *Tucson Weekly Arizona Star* and is in the William Sanders Oury File, Hayden Collection, AHS. Also see the Jesus Maria Elias File, Hayden Collection, AHS, and the Atanacia Hughes manuscript, AHS.

132 **"efforts for its consummation":** Lockwood, *Apache Indians*, 179–82; Warner, *Generals in Blue*, 481–82; Roberts, *With Their Own Blood*, 170–74; Sonnichsen, *Tucson*, 79–83. There are several studies of the Camp Grant Massacre. Two excellent recent books published in 2008 are by the historian Karl Jacoby, *Shadows at Dawn*, and by the ethnologist Ian W. Record, *Big Sycamore Stands Alone*. Two useful articles are George P. Hammond, "The Camp Grant Massacre: A Chapter in Apache History," *Proceedings of the Pacific Coast Branch of the American Historical Association* (1929): 1–16; and James R. Hastings, "The Tragedy at Camp Grant in 1871," *Arizona and the West* 1 (Summer 1959): 146–60. Two additional works of value are Don Schellie, *Vast Domain of Blood: The Story of the Camp Grant Massacre;* and Chip Colwell-Chanthaphonh, *Massacre at Camp Grant: Forgetting and Remembering Apache History*. Also see the chapters in Thrapp, *Conquest*, 79–94; Haley, *Apaches*, 254–63; and Wellman, *Death in the Desert*, 90–99.

133 **Whitman declared:** This is based on Whitman's report, reprinted in Hammond, "The Camp Grant Massacre," 7–10, and an additional report by Whitman on May 17, 1871, to Colonel J. G. C. Lee reprinted in Appendix A of Vincent Colyer, *Peace with the Apaches of New Mexico and Arizona: Report of Vincent Colyer, Member of Board of Indian Commissioners*, 31–33. For Whitman, see Heitman, *Historical Register*, 1:1030; Thrapp, *Encyclopedia of Frontier Biography*, 3:1560–61; and Thrapp, *Conquest*, 79–81. For Eskiminzin, see Clum, "Es-kin-in-zin," 1–27; Record, *Big Sycamore Stands Alone*, 184–89; Colwell-Chanthaphonh, *Massacre at Camp Grant*, 19–25; Thrapp, *Encyclopedia of Frontier Biography*, 1:467–68; and Leo W. Banks, *Double Cross: Treachery in the Apache Wars*, 43–52.

134 **"watching their actions carefully":** Colyer, *Peace with the Apaches*, 36–38; Hammond, "Camp Grant Massacre," 9; Thrapp, *Conquest*, 82–84; Jacoby, *Shadows at Dawn*, 130–32.

135 **concerning official communications:** Bourke, *On the Border*, 103–4; Hastings, "Tragedy at Camp Grant," 149–50. Hastings speculates that the inept General Stoneman did read the message but returned it as unopened to dodge responsibility if anything went wrong.

136 **one hundred men:** Bernard L. Fontana, "Pima and Papago: Introduction," and "History of the Papago," in Ortiz, ed., *Handbook of North American Indians: Southwest*, 502–23; Jacoby, *Shadows at Dawn*, 13–46, 136–40; Thrapp, *Conquest*, 87–89.

136 **nod in sad agreement:** Roberts, *With Their Own Blood*, 171–74; Record, *Big Sycamore Stands Alone*, 212; Schellie, *Vast Domain of Blood*, 110–26.

138 **"a work well done":** The details of the massacre are reconstructed from William S. Oury, "The Camp Grant Massacre," unpublished manuscript, 1885, AHS; William Bailey, "The Camp Grant Massacre," unpublished manuscript, AHS; Atanacia Hughes, manuscript, AHS; Charles Wood, "Camp Grant Massacre," unpublished manuscript, Charles Morgan Wood Collection, AHS; William Oury File, Sam Hughes File, Sidney R. DeLong File, and Juan Elias File, all in the Hayden Collection, AHS; Oury in the *Tucson Arizona Star*, July 3, 1879; Whitman in Colyer, *Peace with the Apaches*, 31–38; memoir of Andrew H. Cargill, "The Camp Grant Massacre," *Arizona Historical Review* 7 (July 1936): 73–79; Smith, *Oury*, 186–203; Colwell-Chanthaphonh, *Massacre at Camp Grant*, 58–70; Record, *Big Sycamore Stands Alone*, 216–45, 265–70; Schellie, *Vast Domain of Blood*, 123–67; Jacoby, *Shadows at Dawn*, 38–46, 84–93, 124–40, 220–29. Valuable testimony from the trial of the massacre participants is recorded in the *Alta California*, February 3–4, 1872. The memoirs of both Oury and Cargill are conveniently reprinted in Cozzens, ed., *Struggle for Apacheria*, 57–67.

139 **Dunn did nothing:** Colyer, *Peace with the Apaches*, 32–33; Hammond, "Camp Grant Massacre," 15–16; Hastings, "Tragedy at Camp Grant," 152–54; Cargill, "Camp Grant Massacre," 77–79; Haley, *Apaches*, 261; Schellie, *Vast Domain of Blood*, 160.

139 **"unparalleled ferocity and malignity":** (Boston) *Every Saturday*, August 19, 1871.

139 **their sensational reports:** Sherman to Sheridan, March 5, 7, 1870, Box 91, Sheridan Papers.

140 **Crook of the Twenty-Third Infantry:** Schellie, *Vast Domain of Blood*, 199–203; Schmitt, ed., *Crook Autobiography*, 159–63; Robinson, *General Crook*, 104–7.

140 **into the Pinal Mountains:** Record, *Big Sycamore Stands Alone*, 264.

141 **"takes a strong man to kill a friend":** Scout Sam Bowman told this story to Britton Davis, but there were several other versions of the same tale.

Eskiminzin even confessed to the killing to Vincent Colyer and was later indicted by a Tucson grand jury for McKinney's murder but was never tried. Britton Davis, *The Truth About Geronimo*, 61; Schellie, *Vast Domain of Blood*, 189; Banks, *Double Cross*, 47–52.

11. NANTAN LUPAN

142 **in Grant's decision making:** Martin F. Schmitt, ed., *General George Crook: His Autobiography*, 159–60; Hutton, *Phil Sheridan and His Army*, 126. For Crook's career, see Paul Magid, *George Crook: From the Redwoods to Appomattox;* Paul Magid, *The Gray Fox;* and Charles Robinson, *General Crook and the Western Frontier.*

143 **"to be left alone":** James T. King, "George Crook: Indian Fighter and Humanitarian," *Arizona and the West* 9 (Winter 1967): 339; C. R. Williams, ed., *Diary and Letters of Rutherford Birchard Hayes*, 5:514; Philip H. Sheridan, *Personal Memoirs*, 2:33–42; Hutton, *Phil Sheridan and His Army*, 123–29. Also see Jerome A. Greene, "George Crook," in Hutton and Ball, eds., *Soldiers West*, 246–72.

144 **clever press agent:** Schmitt, ed., *Crook Autobiography*, 162–63; Porter, *Paper Medicine Man*, 12–13.

144 **"bag and baggage":** Schmitt, ed., *Crook Autobiography*, 170.

145 **the Gila River to Camp Apache:** Bourke, *On the Border*, 136–37; Schmitt, ed., *Crook Autobiography*, 176; Sweeney, *Cochise*, 318–19; Magid, *Gray Fox*, 68–74; McChristian, *Fort Bowie*, 132.

145 **"their disintegration":** Dunlay, *Wolves for the Blue Soldiers*, 89; Robinson, *General Crook*, 111.

146 **Hispanic scouts were dismissed:** Thrapp, *Conquest*, 100; Robinson, *General Crook*, 112.

147 **known as "Crook's Trail":** Schmitt, ed., *Crook Autobiography*, 166; Bourke, *On the Border*, 147. Also see Johnny D. Boggs, "The Legendary Crook's Trail," *True West* 62 (October 2015): 40–45.

148 **"that man was Al Sieber":** Britton Davis, *The Truth About Geronimo*, 35–36. For Al Sieber's career, see Dan L. Thrapp, *Al Sieber, Chief of Scouts*, 3–90.

149 **"that spawn of Hell, Vincent Colyer":** Schmitt, ed., *Crook Autobiography*, 167; Robinson, *General Crook*, 113.

150 **established by Congress in May 1873:** Colyer, *Peace with the Apaches*, 54–56; Sonnichsen, *Mescalero Apaches*, 155–57; Thrapp, *Victorio*, 138–40; Schmitt, ed., *Crook Autobiography*, 168.

151 **"gigantic fraud this Indian ring is":** George Crook to R. B. Hayes, November 28, 187, Crook Collection, Rutherford B. Hayes Papers, Hayes Presidential Center, Fremont, Ohio; Jacoby, *Shadows at Dawn*, 229; Schellie, *Vast Domain of Blood*, 180.

152 **"Vincent the Good":** Kvasnicka and Viola, eds., *Commissioners of Indian Affairs*, 127–30; Thrapp, *Conquest*, 105.

152 "War Department and the President": Colyer, *Peace with the Apaches*, 55.
153 to negotiate with the Apaches: Thrapp, *Conquest*, 106–7; Magid, *Gray Fox*, 87–91.

12. THE CHRISTIAN GENERAL

155 "next mission was with the Indian": Schmitt, ed., *Crook Autobiography*. O. O. Howard was also a prolific author. He wrote a two-volume memoir as well as *My Life and Experiences Among Our Hostile Indians* and *Famous Indian Chiefs I Have Known*. A fine biography is John A. Carpenter, *Sword and Olive Branch*. Also see Scott L. Stabler, "Oliver Otis Howard," in Hutton and Ball, eds., *Soldiers West*, 201–25.

156 what took the jury so long: The trial is covered in Record, *Big Sycamore Stands Alone*, 268–70; Schellie, *Vast Domain of Blood*, 213–47; Farish, *Arizona*, 8:161–69; and Jacoby, *Shadows at Dawn*, 183–88.

158 to the Camp Grant Council on May 20: Thrapp, *Conquest*, 109–11; Schmitt, ed., *Crook Autobiography*, 170–71; Braatz, *Surviving Conquest*, 127–28.

160 "any false ideas of sentiment": Schmitt, ed., *Crook Autobiography*, 172–73; Magid, *Gray Fox*, 94–99.

161 "surely the Lord is with us": Howard, *My Life and Experiences*, 157; A. M. Gustafson, ed., *John Spring's Arizona*, 251–53; Howard, *Famous Indian Chiefs*, 85; Jacoby, *Shadows at Dawn*, 250–52; Record, *Big Sycamore Stands Alone*, 170–79.

162 yawning gulf of race and culture: Howard, *Famous Indian Chiefs*, 98–111.

162 slipped from his chain: Magid, *Gray Fox*, 101–3; Robinson, *General Crook*, 125; Schmitt, ed., *Crook Autobiography*, 173–74.

13. MICKEY FREE

163 "with all the scouts they picked": Greenville Goodwin, "Experiences of an Indian Scout: Excerpts from the Life of John Rope," *Arizona Historical Review* 7 (January 1936): 43.

164 started the war for Apacheria: Allan Radbourne, "The Naming of Mickey Free," *Journal of Arizona History* 17 (Autumn 1976): 341–46: Smith, "White Eyes, Red Heat, Blue Coat," 58; Mickey Free File, AHS. A clothing requisition for "Mickey Free, F-1" signed by Lt. Howard Cushing at Fort Whipple and dated February 24, 1870, suggests that Felix Ward may have received his new name before Crook's campaign. Mickey Free, Apache Scout File, CM, MSM-204/OV2, Hayden Arizona Collection, Arizona State University.

165 his transformation into an Apache: Radbourne, *Mickey Free*, 20; Charles Connell, "Mickey Free," *Arizona Citizen*, April 10, 1921, Connell File, AHS.

166 who had served many years on the frontier: Bourke, *On the Border*, 176–78; Thrapp, *Conquest*, 106.

166 both the volunteer and regular service: For Eugene Carr's career, see James T. King, *War Eagle*.

167 "short, sharp, and decisive": Bourke, *On the Border*, 182; Thrapp, *Conquest*, 119–24.

167 closed as both reservation and military post: Altshuler, *Starting with Defiance*, 25–26. Also see Braatz, *Surviving Conquest*, 134–35.

167 "out of sight of the hostiles": Schmitt, ed., *Crook Autobiography*, 175.

168 Crook agreed: Bourke, *On the Border*, 179–80. For Clayton Cooley, see Thrapp, *Encyclopedia of Frontier Biography*, 1:315–16.

169 "greater amount of courage and daring": (Prescott) *Arizona Weekly Miner*, December 27, 1872; Bourke, *On the Border*, 203; Radbourne, *Mickey Free*, 25–27; Thrapp, *Conquest*, 124.

170 accepted as such by the American public: For the Salt River Canyon massacre, see Robinson, *General Crook*, 132–34; Bourke, *On the Border*, 185–88; Thrapp, *Conquest*, 127–30. Also see Gregory McNamee, *The Only One Living to Tell: The Autobiography of a Yavapai Indian;* and Mike Burns, *All of My People Were Killed: The Memoir of Mike Burns (Hoomothya), a Captive Indian.*

171 the white officers joined in with Mickey and the scouts: Radbourne, *Mickey Free*, 27–28; Thrapp, *Conquest*, 135–37.

172 now to be seventeen dollars a month: Schmitt, ed., *Crook Autobiography*, 179; Braatz, *Surviving Conquest*, 139–40; Robinson, *General Crook*, 136; Radbourne, *Mickey Free*, 31.

172 frontier Napoleon: Thrapp, *Conquest*, 143. Also see Magid, *Gray Fox*, 87–126.

14. TAGLITO

174 "alone, fully armed": Farish, *Arizona*, 2:228–29; Lockwood, *Arizona Characters*, 66–68; Robert Forbes, "Letter to the Editor," *Journal of Arizona History* 7 (Summer 1966): 87–88. There is no biography of Tom Jeffords, but the story of his friendship with Cochise has been told in the bestselling novel by Elliott Arnold, *Blood Brother* (New York: Duell, Sloan & Pearce, 1947), which in turn was the basis for the 1950 film *Broken Arrow,* starring James Stewart and Jeff Chandler, and the 1956–58 ABC television series with Michael Ansara and John Lupton. Arnold's novel, and especially Delmer Daves's popular film, contributed greatly to a dramatic change in the negative presentation of Indians in American popular culture. Jeffords's daring ride into Cochise's stronghold and his enduring friendship with the great chief seem overly dramatic to some authors. Thomas Sheridan, in his highly regarded history of Arizona, discounts the story as "a moral fable simplified for western novels and Hollywood movies," but presents no evidence to support his reasoning. Edwin Sweeney,

the biographer of Cochise and the leading modern authority on the Apache Wars, suggests that Jeffords actually first made contact with Cochise in 1870 while he was prospecting, and not earlier when he worked for the overland mail. He notes that several mail riders were killed after Jeffords's alleged 1867 meeting with Cochise. See Sweeney, *Cochise*, 292–96, and Sheridan, *Arizona*, 97–98. Arizona territorial governor A. P. K. Safford met with Jeffords and Cochise in November 1872 and gave a detailed account of the conference in a letter to the *Tucson Arizona Citizen*, December 7, 1872, in which he praises Jeffords highly and gives a brief account of the Indian agent's career. Safford seems to suggest that Jeffords had first met Cochise only three years before, but he also confirms the chagrin Jeffords felt over the deaths of his twenty-one mail riders. These deaths determined Jeffords on his plan to meet with Cochise and make peace. "This act inspired Cochise," Safford related, "with a profound respect for his courage and sincerity." Safford was certain that it was this friendship between Cochise and Jeffords that was responsible for the peace. Daklugie, the son of Juh, said that Jeffords was captured and taken as a prisoner, which certainly makes more sense than Jeffords riding unmolested into the Cochise stronghold. Ball, *Indeh*, 27–28. Jeffords, who was not a man given to hyperbole or boasting, gave his version of the meeting directly to Thomas Farish and Robert Forbes. Lockwood believed the story and so do I. Jeffords had no reason not to tell the truth. Sometimes the romantic story of the past actually is true. Also see C. L. Sonnichsen, "Who Was Tom Jeffords?" *Journal of Arizona History* 23 (Winter 1982): 381–406; Harry G. Cramer III, "Tom Jeffords—Indian Agent," *Journal of Arizona History* 29 (Summer 1988): 117–130; and Lockwood, *Apache Indians*, 110–24. Jeffords material can also be found in the Tom Jeffords File, Hayden Collection, AHS; and S. W. Grant, "Captain Jeffords," interview with Mrs. George F. Kitt, November 5, 1926, Jeffords Biographical File, AHS.

174 Taglito, or "Red Whiskers": Farish, *Arizona*, 2:229–30; Robert Forbes, May 30, 1966, letter to the editor, *Journal of Arizona History* 7 (Summer 1966): 87–88; Sweeney, *Cochise*, 291–96.

175 "with which to murder and plunder": Edwin R. Sweeney, ed., *Making Peace with Cochise: The 1872 Journal of Captain Alton Sladen*, 3–24, 30; Heitman, *Historical Register*, 1:890; Howard, *My Life and Experiences*, 186–87; Sweeney, *Cochise*, 315–16, 449. Also see the William Ohnesorgen manuscript, Jeffords File, AHS; and Charles Henry Veil, *The Memoirs of Charles Henry Veil*, 139.

176 inspect its merits firsthand: Howard quoted in Sweeney, ed., *Making Peace*, 135; Thrapp, *Victorio*, 139–40, 151.

176 Jeffords later confessed: Jeffords quoted in Farish, *Arizona*, 2:231.

177 "waging upon my countrymen": Howard, *My Life and Experiences*, 187–89; Sweeney, ed., *Making Peace*, 33; Jeffords quoted in Farish, *Arizona*, 2:231.

177   the dangers of their mission: Sweeney, ed., *Making Peace*, 37, 136; Howard, *Famous Indian Chiefs*, 112–19.

178   refused to consent: Thrapp, *Victorio*, 150–53, 168.

178   "all the same to Ponce": Howard, *My Life and Experiences*, 188–91; Sweeney, ed., *Making Peace*, 43.

179   Sladen remembered: Sweeney, ed., *Making Peace*, 40, 87; Lynn R. Bailey, *White Apache: The Life and Times of Zebina Nathaniel Streeter*, 1–61; Thrapp, *Encyclopedia of Frontier Biography*, 3:1378.

180   to save an Apache: Howard, *My Life and Experiences*, 191–92; Howard, *Famous Indians*, 121–22; Sweeney, ed., *Making Peace*, 47–49.

181   "we are in God's keeping": Howard, *My Life and Experiences*, 193; Sweeney, ed., *Making Peace*, 51–56.

182   "promise too much": Farish, *Arizona*, 2:232–33. Also see Lockwood, *Arizona Characters*, 70–74; and Sweeney, *Cochise*, 340–66.

182   his sister: Sweeney, ed., *Making Peace*, 63–64.

183   mixed feelings as the general departed: Howard, *My Life and Experiences*, 205–10.

184   shared his campsite at night: Sweeney, ed., *Making Peace*, 70–82.

184   to join the circle: Farish, *Arizona*, 2:234; Howard, *My Life and Experiences*, 212–19.

185   he closed the great council: Sweeney, ed., *Making Peace*, 89–91; Howard, *My Life and Experiences*, 220–22; Farish, *Arizona*, 2:234–35.

186   the killer of Lieutenant Howard Bass Cushing: Sweeney, ed., *Making Peace*, 91–93, 158–60; Barrett, ed., *Geronimo's Story*, 128–29; Utley, *Geronimo*, 63–64. Jeffords left an account of the council that is in the John Rockfellow File, Arizona Historical Society.

15. SAN CARLOS

187   an administrative nightmare: Schmitt, ed., *Crook Autobiography*, 177. Crook sent Major William Brown and Lieutenant John Bourke to meet with Cochise. The chief promised not to molest the Americans but refused to halt raids into Mexico. Bourke Diary, 1:125–27, 180–83; Bourke, *On the Border*, 235–36. Bourke's diary of the meeting is reprinted as "A Conference with Cochise" in Cozzens, ed., *Struggle for Apacheria*, 152–54.

188   for public display at San Carlos: Thrapp, *Conquest*, 144–45; Price, *Fifth Cavalry*, 519–23.

189   discontent of Delshay and his followers: Bourke, *On the Border*, 215–16; Thrapp, *Sieber*, 114–25; Price, *Fifth Cavalry*, 533–34.

189   games of chance: Bourke, *On the Border*, 219. The tag system was not abandoned until 1913. See Haley, *Apaches*, 358.

189   "contempt for his authority": Schuyler to Schuyler, July 6, 1873, Schuyler Papers, Huntington Library; Thrapp, *Sieber*, 119.

190   had just fled the reservation: Crook to Schuyler, September 15, 1873, Schuyler Papers, Huntington Library; Thrapp, *Sieber*, 121–24; *Prescott*

Arizona Miner, September 27 and October 4, 1873. Also see Carl P. Johnson, "A War Chief of the Tontos," *Overland Monthly* 28 (November 1896): 528–32; and for the Indian perspective, Timothy Braatz, *Surviving Conquest*, 141–43.

190 "jeopardize their heads": Crook to Schuyler, June 23, 1874, Schuyler Papers, Huntington Library; Robinson, *General Crook*, 139; Thrapp, *Conquest*, 125–37, 160.

191 in ever greater numbers: Paul Andrew Hutton, "The Severed Heads Campaign," *True West* 62 (March 2015): 28–33; Radbourne, *Mickey Free*, 32–40; Price, *Fifth Cavalry*, 150–53, 658–62, 704; Thrapp, *Conquest*, 156–61; Crook to Schuyler, June 23, 1874, Schuyler Papers, Huntington Library; Robert Wooster, ed., *Soldier, Surgeon, Scholar*, 84; Paul L. Hedren, "Captain Charles King at Sunset Pass," *Journal of Arizona History* 17 (Autumn 1976): 253–64; Schmitt, ed., *Crook Autobiography*, 181–82.

193 "lose my scalp": Abstract of disbursements, vouchers, 1–71, and Edward P. Smith to John Clum, February 24, 1874, manuscript 284, Box 1, John P. Clum Papers, Special Collections, University of Arizona Library; Woodworth Clum, *Apache Agent*, 102–30; Gary Ledoux, *Nantan: The Life and Times of John P. Clum*, 1:119–30; Thrapp, *Conquest*, 161–65.

193 upon reaching Arizona: Clum, *Apache Agent*, 124–25.

194 "I paid both parties": Schmitt, ed., *Crook Autobiography*, 181–82; Thrapp, *Conquest*, 161–68; Clum, *Apache Agent*, 130–33.

195 concerns and complaints: Neil B. Carmony, ed., *Apache Days and Tombstone Nights: John Clum's Autobiography*, 102–4; Clum, *Apache Agent*, 134.

196 honor was above all price: Opler, *Apache Life-Way*, 368–70; Bud Shapard, *Loco: Apache Peacemaker*, 15–16, 212–13; Boyer and Gayton, *Apache Mothers and Daughters*, 38–39; Lockwood, *Apache Indians*, 213–14; John P. Clum, "The San Carlos Apache Police," *Arizona Historical Review* 3 (October 1930): 21–43; Clum, *Apache Agent*, 136–39, 166–69; Clum, "Es-kin-in-zin," 1–4.

197 generally kept order: Sweeney, *Grijalva*, 45–60; Clum, *Apache Agent*, 139–42; Ledoux, *Nantan*, 1:254.

198 as Kid—or the Apache Kid: H. E. Dunlap, "Clay Beauford–Welford C. Bridwell: Soldier Under Two Flags; Captain of Apache Police; Arizona Legislator," *Arizona Historical Review* 3 (October 1930): 44–66; William Sparks, *The Apache Kid, A Bear Fight and Other True Stories of the Old West*, 10–11; "Apache Kid's Boy Partner," *Omaha Daily Bee*, August 22, 1898.

199 opened up for white settlement: Prucha, *The Great Father*, 1:316–18, 562–81; Bourke, *On the Border*, 235; Wooster, ed., *Soldier, Surgeon, Scholar*, 72–83, 187; Braatz, *Surviving Conquest*, 124–37.

199 helpless to intervene: Bourke, *On the Border*, 216–17.

199 dismissed the two officers: Wooster, ed., *Soldier, Surgeon, Scholar*, 90; Braatz, *Surviving Conquest*, 173.

200 onetime captive boy: Thrapp, *Sieber*, 159–62; Radbourne, *Mickey Free*, 46–49; Braatz, *Surviving Conquest*, 174–77.

200 scars on his body: Radbourne, *Mickey Free*, 46–47; Lockwood, *More Arizona Characters*, 17–40; Thrapp, *Sieber*, 152–55, 176.

201 "jingled at his heels": Charles King, *Sunset Pass*, 7.

201 "whole son of a bitch": Davis, *Geronimo*, 36–37; Thrapp, *Sieber*, 262.

202 "Many did die": Braatz, *Surviving Conquest*, 174; Wooster, ed., *Soldier, Surgeon, Scholar*, 90.

202 hunt down these people: Thrapp, *Sieber*, 163–66; Radbourne, *Mickey Free*, 48; George O. Eaton, "Stopping an Apache Battle," *Journal of the U.S. Cavalry Association* 12 (July 1908): 12–18.

203 "might again be rolled back": L. Edwin Dudley, "The Apache-Yumas and Apache-Mojaves," *American Antiquarian* 8 (September 1886): 276–84; Thrapp, *Sieber*, 166–67.

203 tended to have long memories: Clum, *Apache Agent*, 149–50; Clum, "San Carlos Police," 41–42; Braatz, *Surviving Conquest*, 176–77; Wooster, ed., *Soldier, Surgeon, Scholar*, 92–93; Magid, *Gray Fox*, 127–32.

204 another triumph to Washington: Thrapp, *Sieber*, 167–69; Radbourne, *Mickey Free*, 48–49; Clum, *Apache Agent*, 151–54.

205 She bore him a son in 1876: *Prescott Arizona Miner*, May 21, 1875; Lockwood, *More Arizona Characters*, 22; Radbourne, *Mickey Free*, 50–54; Thrapp, *Sieber*, 180–82.

206 Indians at San Carlos: Clum, "Es-kin-in-zin," 5–6; Clum, *Apache Agent*, 155–61; Basso, ed., *Western Apache Raiding*, 101–2; Lockwood, *Apache Indians*, 211–13; Ogle, *Western Apaches*, 126–32.

207 an erratic and controversial commander: Schmitt, ed., *Crook Autobiography*, 184; Bourke, *On the Border*, 239–40; Robinson, *General Crook*, 159–61; Warner, *Generals in Blue*, 257–58.

16. GERONIMO

209 was no more: *Tucson Arizona Daily Star*, January 31, 1886; Farish, *Arizona*, 2:236–37; Lockwood, *Arizona Characters*, 80–81; Sweeney, ed., *Cochise, Firsthand Accounts*, 277–90.

210 "may be maintained": A. P. K. Safford, "Something about Cochise," in Cozzens, ed., *Struggle for Apacheria*, 124–31; Thrapp, *Conquest*, 168–69; Ogle, *Western Apaches*, 107, 166–68.

210 "could like this man": Ball, *Indeh*, 27–31; *Tucson Arizona Daily Star*, January 27, 1886.

211 end of June 1874: Thrapp, *Victorio*, 165–68.

211 "influence over the tribe": Sonnichsen, "Who Was Tom Jeffords?" 393–95; Thrapp, *Victorio*, 167. For Fred Hughes, see Cozzens, ed., *Struggle for Apacheria*, 132–37, and for Zebina Streeter, see Thrapp, *Encyclopedia of Frontier Biography*, 3:1, 378–79, and Lynn R. Bailey, *White Apache: The Life and Times of Zebina Nathaniel Streeter*. Also see

Mardith K. Schuetz, *Archaeology of Tom Jeffords' Chiricahua Indian Agency*, 1–67.

212   **weight with many:** Edwin R. Sweeney, *From Cochise to Geronimo: The Chiricahua Apaches, 1874–1886*, 21–39; C. L. Sonnichsen, "Tom Jeffords and the Editors," *Journal of Arizona History* 29 (Summer 1988): 117–30; Harry G. Cramer, "Tom Jeffords—Indian Agent," *Journal of Arizona History* 17 (Autumn 1976): 265–300.

212   **he grumbled:** *Tucson Arizona Daily Star*, January 27 and 31, 1886.

213   **he concluded:** Sweeney, *From Cochise to Geronimo*, 44.

214   **"this disgraceful conduct":** *Tucson Weekly Citizen*, May 20, 1876; Cramer, "Tom Jeffords," 290; Sonnichsen, "Jeffords and the Editors," 121–22; Sweeney, *From Cochise to Geronimo*, 47–53.

214   **expressed to him by Victorio:** Thrapp, *Victorio*, 176; Sweeney, *From Cochise to Geronimo*, 50–51.

215   **arrived later that afternoon:** Farish, *Arizona*, 2:237–39; McChristian, *Fort Bowie*, 162–63; Utley, *Geronimo*, 79–80.

216   **homeland had begun:** Sweeney, *From Cochise to Geronimo*, 51–58; Cramer, "Tom Jeffords," 294–96.

218   **already attached to Jeffords:** Clum, *Apache Agent*, 172–80; Sweeney, *From Cochise to Geronimo*, 58–59; Thrapp, *Conquest*, 170–71; Lockwood, *Apache Indians*, 214–18; John P. Clum, "Geronimo," *New Mexico Historical Review* 3 (January 1928): 13–26; Bailey, *White Apache*, 82–86. Jeffords's account is in Silver City *Herald*, July 22, 1876.

218   **"thrown open to settlers":** *Tucson Weekly Citizen*, June 24, 1876; Clum, *Apache Agent*, 180–84; Sweeney, *From Cochise to Geronimo*, 59–63.

219   **security from attack:** Radbourne, *Mickey Free*, 53–54; Bailey, *White Apache*, 85–88; Utley, *Geronimo*, 86–87.

219   **recruited from Pinals at San Carlos:** Sweeney, *From Cochise to Geronimo*, 69–76. Also see Andrew Wallace, "General August V. Kautz in Arizona, 1874–1878," *Arizoniana* 4 (Winter 1963): 54–65.

220   **for a revenge raid:** Heitman, *Historical Register*, 1:849; McChristian, *Fort Bowie*, 164–67; Sweeney, *From Cochise to Geronimo*, 76–78; Barrett, ed., *Geronimo's Story*, 124–28.

220   **"the welfare of the Indeh":** Opler, *Apache Life-Way*, 462–63; Boyer and Gayton, *Apache Mothers and Daughters*, 67; Shapard, *Loco*, 92–93.

221   **while raiding into Arizona:** Utley, *Geronimo*, 87; Sweeney, *From Cochise to Geronimo*, 78–81.

221   **near the hot springs on April 21:** Clum, "Geronimo," 24–28; Debo, *Geronimo*, 103–5; Thrapp, *Victorio*, 186–87.

223   **"you and your sick brain":** This dramatic incident is recounted in Clum, "Geronimo," 29–34; Clum, *Apache Agent*, 204–28; Barrett, ed., *Geronimo's Story*, 131–33; Debo, *Geronimo*, 106–7; Utley, *Geronimo*, 90–91. Also see Sweeney, *From Cochise to Geronimo*, 81–85; Roberts, *Once They Moved Like the Wind*, 162–69; Lockwood, *Apache Indians*, 218–

24; Thrapp, *Conquest*, 171–75; Haley, *Apaches*, 313–17. Clum kept Geronimo's rifle as a trophy of his grand adventure. It was passed down to his son Henry Woodworth Clum (the author of *Apache Agent*), who used it as a lampstand. The family eventually donated the Geronimo rifle to the Arizona Historical Society in Tucson. Ledoux, *Clum*, 1:226.

223 **made resistance suicidal:** Thrapp, *Victorio*, 181–91; Boyer and Gayton, *Apache Mothers and Daughters*, 67–68, 95–99; Ball, *Indeh*, 39; Debo, *Geronimo*, 110.

224 **exactly what came to pass:** Clum, "Geronimo," 36–40; Shapard, *Loco*, 97–104; Sweeney, *From Cochise to Geronimo*, 86–87; Ledoux, *Clum*, 1:229–40; and John P. Clum, "Victorio: Chief of the Warm Springs Apaches, *Arizona Historical Review* 2 (January 1930): 74–90.

224 **plot his revenge on the White Eyes:** Clum, *Apache Agent*, 249–62; Carmony, ed., *Apache Days and Tombstone Nights*, 13–47; Utley, *Geronimo*, 92–94.

17. LOZEN'S VISION

225 **eventual corruption:** Thrapp, *Victorio*, 192–95; Sweeney, *From Cochise to Geronimo*, 92–94.

226 **"influenced by Geronimo":** Morris E. Opler, "A Chiricahua Apache's Account of the Geronimo Campaign of 1886," *New Mexico Historical Review* 13 (October 1938): 369; John P. Clum, "Apaches as Thespians in 1876," *New Mexico Historical Review* 6 (January 1931): 87–90; Sweeney, *From Cochise to Geronimo*, 67–69; Ball, *Days of Victorio*, 50–52; Clum, *Apache Agent*, 198–201.

226 **"among their own people":** Thrapp, *Victorio*, 193–94; Sweeney, *From Cochise to Geronimo*, 92–93.

227 **"respected above all living women":** Ball, *Days of Victorio*, 14–15; Boyer and Gayton, *Apache Mothers and Daughters*, 54–55; Robinson, *Apache Voices*, 3–15; Stockel, *Women of the Apache Nation*, 29–51; Ball, *Indeh*, 103–4; Buchanan, *Apache Women Warriors*, 27–38; Goodwin, *Social Organization of the Western Apache*, 224–25, 537–38. Also see Susan Hazen Hammond, "Lozen," *Arizona Highways* 72 (February 1996): 10–13; H. Henrietta Stockel, *Chiricahua Apache Women and Children: Safekeepers of the Heritage*, 65–75; and Peter Aleshire, *Lozen*.

227 **pursuit was inevitable:** Shapard, *Loco*, 104–5; Bailey, *White Apache*, 85–95.

228 **trophy to Sonora:** Sweeney, *From Cochise to Geronimo*, 104–5; Shapard, *Loco*, 105.

228 **hot springs and waited:** Thrapp, *Victorio*, 198–99.

229 **the name Lozen called the loudest:** Ball, *Days of Victorio*, 15; Thrapp, *Victorio*, 374; Buchanan, *Apache Women Warriors*, 33–34; Boyer and Gayton, *Apache Mothers and Daughters*, 54–55.

229 returned to San Carlos: Thrapp, *Victorio*, 201–4, 360; Barnes, *Arizona Place Names*, 230–31; Warner, *Generals in Blue*, 215–16; Leckie, *Buffalo Soldiers*, 7–8; Heitman, *Historical Register*, 1:510.

231 to San Carlos on November 25: Sheridan to Sherman, November 12–26, 1878, Box 20, Sheridan Papers; Hutton, *Phil Sheridan and His Army*, 339–40; "Synopsis of General Sheridan's Supplemental Report," Box 89, Sheridan Papers; Thrapp, *Victorio*, 205–8.

231 blood could ever satisfy: Shapard, *Loco*, 110, 121–25; *Tucson Arizona Star*, March 29, 1880; Thrapp, *Victorio*, 211; Betzinez, *Geronimo*, 50–51; Ball, *Days of Victorio*, 8; Thrapp, *Encyclopedia of Frontier Biography*, 2:1038–39.

232 "I go to join my brother": Ball, *Days of Victorio*, 9–10; Roberts, *Once They Moved Like the Wind*, 177–78.

232 avoid political controversy: Warner, *Generals in Blue*, 558–59; Thrapp, *Encyclopedia of Frontier Biography*, 3:1566; Scott, ed., *Forgotten Valor*, 1–8.

233 named Tombstone: *Prescott Miner*, August 22, 1879; Thrapp, *Sieber*, 191–92, 209–10; Trimble, *Arizona*, 223–24; Walter Noble Burns, *Tombstone*, 1–3. Also see Charles F. Bennett File, Arizona Historical Society.

234 sort of man Sieber admired: Works Projects Administration, *Arizona: A State Guide*, 195–96; Radbourne, *Mickey Free*, 62. For Chaffee's spectacular career, see William Harding Carter, *The Life of Lieutenant General Chaffee*. A brief profile is in Thrapp, *Encyclopedia of Frontier Biography*, 1:246–47.

234 all twenty-five men, women, and children: Utley, *Geronimo*, 96–99.

235 toward the Black Range: Thrapp, *Victorio*, 218–20; Chamberlain, *Victorio*, 160–63; Sonnichsen, *Mescalero Apaches*, 179–81; Ball, *Days of Victorio*, 11, 64–66; Robinson, *Apache Voices*, 6.

236 never exceeded forty warriors: Thrapp, *Victorio*, 218–40; Chamberlain, *Victorio*, 171–72; Ball, *Days of Victorio*, 73.

236 superior to other Indian scouts: Thrapp, *Conquest*, 261; Billington, *New Mexico's Buffalo Soldiers*, 90; Louis Kraft, ed., *Gatewood Memoir*, xv–xxxvii; Thrapp, *Encyclopedia of Frontier Biography*, 2:543–44.

237 one of Victorio's mightiest warriors: Ball, *Days of Victorio*, 106.

237 bragged Kaywaykla: Thrapp, *Victorio*, 248–49; Ball, *Days of Victorio*, 73–76; Robinson, *Apache Voices*, 4–8.

238 the scalp of Victorio: Thrapp, *Victorio*, 254–55, 373.

18. VICTORIO'S WAR

239 quickly began to unravel: Hatch to Pope, February 25, 1880, File 6058–1879, Adjutant General Office, RG 94, National Archives. This file contains extensive correspondence on the campaign. Also see *Annual Report of the Secretary of War* (1880), 1:88; Thrapp, *Conquest*, 193–95; Leckie,

Buffalo Soldiers, 211, 216–22; Sweeney, *From Cochise*, 150; and Thrapp, *Victorio*, 261–62.

241 **west in the Black Range:** The best account of the Battle of Hembrillo Canyon is Karl W. Laumbach, *Hembrillo: An Apache Battlefield of the Victorio War*, an archaeological report prepared for the White Sands Missile Range as Research Report 00–06 in 2001. More easily accessible accounts are in Thomas Cruse, *Apache Days*, 67–77; Thrapp, *Victorio*, 261–71; Watt, *Apache Tactics*, 49–52; Utley, *Frontier Regulars*, 360–61; Leckie, *Buffalo Soldiers*, 216–22; and Ball, *Days of Victorio*, 83–87. The 1932 interview with Nash-Kin is in the Grenville Goodwin Papers, Arizona State Museum.

241 **"aiding and abetting a common enemy":** Thrapp, *Victorio*, 272–73; Leckie, *Buffalo Soldiers*, 222–24; Sonnichsen, *Mescalero Apaches*, 193–99, 235–37.

242 **offensive against Victorio:** Ross Santee, *Apache Land*, 178–81; Sweeney, *From Cochise*, 153–55.

243 **"that I would do":** Thomas Cruse to Frank Lockwood, January 6, 1934, Lockwood file, AHS; Lockwood, *More Arizona Characters*, 25–26; Thrapp, *Sieber*, 218.

244 **a lightning rod for controversy:** Utley, *Geronimo*, 102–3; Mary Lee Spence, ed., *Arizona Diary of Lily Frémont*, 143, 163; Sweeney, *From Cochise*, 143–60. Also see Allan Radbourne, "The Juh-Geronimo Surrender of 1879," *English Westerner's Brand Book* 21 (1983): 1–18; and John Bret Harte, "The Strange Case of Joseph C. Tiffany," *Journal of Arizona History* 16 (Winter 1975): 383–86.

244 **men of the Ninth:** Sweeney, *From Cochise*, 155.

245 **orders from Captain Chaffee:** Cruse, *Apache Days*, 38–41; Carter, *Chaffee*, 86–89; Sweeney, *From Cochise*, 133.

246 **regret that decision:** Connell biography of Mickey Free in *Tucson Citizen*, April 10, 1921, in Mickey Free File, AHS; Radbourne, *Mickey Free*, 71–74; Sweeney, *From Cochise*, 163.

19. TRES CASTILLOS

247 **turning point of Victorio's War:** Thrapp, *Victorio*, 277–81; Thrapp, *Conquest*, 200; Stockel, *Women of the Apache Nation*, 29; Chamberlain, *Victorio*, 189–90; Cruse, *Apache Days*, 83–84.

248 **time of "emergency" was upon them:** Ball, *Days of Victorio*, 86–87; Boyer and Gayton, *Apache Mothers and Daughters*, 94–95.

249 **devastating blow to Victorio:** Sheridan, *Record of Engagements*, 95; Thrapp, *Victorio*, 282–371; Richard Selcer, "A Premonition of Death," *Wild West* 27 (August 2014): 60–66; Sweeney, *From Cochise*, 165.

249 **more than Apache raiders:** Sherman to Sheridan, May 28, 1880, Sheridan Papers; Bruce J. Dinges, "The Victorio Campaign of 1880: Coop-

eration and Conflict on the United States–Mexico Border," *New Mexico Historical Review* 62 (January 1987): 81–94.

249 **Apaches from entering Texas:** *Annual Report of the Secretary of War* (1880), 158–63; Leckie, *Buffalo Soldiers*, 227; Heitman, *Historical Register*, 1:260; Martin L. Crimmins, "Colonel Buell's Expedition into Mexico in 1880," *New Mexico Historical Review* 10 (April 1935): 133–42.

250 **assured his wife in 1867:** Benjamin Grierson to Alice Grierson, November 18, 1871, Benjamin Grierson Papers, Illinois State Historical Society; Sherman to Hancock, January 24, 1867, Benjamin Grierson Papers, Newberry Library; Grierson to Alice Grierson, December 21, 1868, Grierson Papers, Newberry Library; Warner, *Generals in Blue*, 189–90; Hutton, *Phil Sheridan and His Army*, 227–28; Leckie, *Buffalo Soldiers*, 14–15. For Grierson's full biography, see William and Shirley Leckie, *Unlikely Warriors: General Benjamin Grierson and His Family*. Also see Anson Mills, *My Story*, 182.

250 **"always have good servants":** Frances M. A. Roe, *Army Letters from an Officer's Wife*, 65; Schubert, *Voices of the Buffalo Soldier*, 47–49; Leckie, *Buffalo Soldiers*, 26–27; *Army and Navy Journal*, November 8, 1873.

251 **the Apaches would be back:** Leckie, *Unlikely Warriors*, 261–64; Thrapp, *Victorio*, 285–89; Leckie, *Buffalo Soldiers*, 228.

253 **back into Mexico:** Leckie, *Buffalo Soldiers*, 229–30; Schubert, *Voices of the Buffalo Soldier*, 107; Utley, *Frontier Regulars*, 363–64; Thrapp, *Victorio*, 289–90.

254 **contact with the American column:** Thrapp, *Victorio*, 293–97.

254 **into Mexico was objectionable:** King, *War Eagle*, 193–94; Dinges, "The Victorio Campaign of 1880," 92–93.

255 **leading toward Tres Castillos:** Thrapp, *Victorio*, 300–301.

256 **rendezvous at Tres Castillos:** Ball, *Days of Victorio*, 88–90; Robinson, *Apache Voices*, 17–26.

257 **the main column arrived:** Thrapp, *Victorio*, 302; Robinson, *Apache Voices*, 21–22.

258 **The last stand at Tres Castillos was over:** Sweeney, *From Cochise*, 165; Ball, *Indeh*, 83; Thrapp, *Victorio*, 303–7; Chamberlain, *Victorio*, 204–7.

259 **"bears his honors quietly":** Sweeney, *From Cochise*, 165–66; Blyth, *Chiricahua and Janos*, 187–96; Shapard, *Loco*, 123, 183–84; Robinson, *Apache Voices*, 29–32; Ball, *Indeh*, 83; Thrapp, *Victorio*, 311, 375.

261 **to continue the Apache race:** Ball, *Days of Victorio*, 94–102; Ball, *Indeh*, 83.

262 **"For that we thank Usen":** Ball, *Days of Victorio*, 115–20, 126–28; Thrapp, *Victorio*, 309–10.

20. FORT APACHE

263 **new dance firsthand:** Ball, *Days of Victorio*, 109; Thrapp, ed., *Dateline Fort Bowie*, 157; Stephen H. Lekson, *Nana's Raid*, 7.

265 **"leave revenge to Usen":** Debo, *Geronimo*, 128–29; Ball, *Indeh*, 53–54; Bourke, *Medicine Men*, 30; Barrett, ed., *Geronimo's Story*, 208.

265 **"they can side with us":** Cruse, *Apache Days*, 95–96, 100; Thrapp, *Conquest*, 219–20; W. H. Carter, *From Yorktown*, 209.

266 **Tiffany's problem, not his:** King, *War Eagle*, 196–97; Summerhayes, *Vanished Arizona*, 88; Altshuler, *It Started with Defiance*, 10.

266 **exacerbated these tensions:** Betzinez, *Geronimo*, 56; Radbourne, *Mickey Free*, 75; Charles Collins, *Apache Nightmare*, 16; Thrapp, *Encyclopedia of Frontier Biography*, 3:1365–66.

267 **potentially disastrous consequences:** Goodwin, *Social Organization of the Western Apache*, 1–62; Perry, *Western Apache*, 3–14; Keith H. Basso, "Western Apache," in Ortiz, ed., *Handbook of North American Indians: Southwest*, 462–88.

268 **he had begun his dance:** Lori Davisson, "New Light on the Cibecue Fight: Untangling Apache Identities," *Journal of Arizona History* 20 (Winter 1979): 441–42; Collins, *Apache Nightmare*, 14–17; Thrapp, *Sierra Madre*, 3–5; Lockwood, *Apache Indians*, 235–36. Also see Bourke, *Medicine Men of the Apache*, and Dr. L. Y. Loring's report reprinted in Cozzens, ed., *Struggle for Apacheria*, 182–202.

268 **"you are my wife":** Ball, *Days of Victorio*, 119–20.

270 **horses, mules, and cattle:** The best account of the raid is Stephen H. Lekson, *Nana's Raid: Apache Warfare in New Mexico, 1881*. Also see Sheridan, *Record of Engagements*, 99–100; Ball, *Indeh*, 47–49, 83; Thrapp, *Conquest*, 211–16; Arthur Bibo and A. E. Roland, "The Ballad of Placida Romero: History of an Apache Raid, a Captured Woman, and a Song," *New Mexico Historical Review* 86 (Summer 2011): 279–324; Thrapp, ed., *Dateline Fort Bowie*, 158–59; Beyer and Keydel, *Deeds of Valor*, 2:277–81; Schubert, *Voices of the Buffalo Soldier*, 100–6; Leckie, *Buffalo Soldiers*, 236–37; Schubert, *Black Valor*, 79–84.

271 **Fort Apache was on its own:** Radbourne, *Mickey Free*, 74–75; John Bret Harte, "San Carlos Reservation," 616–19.

272 **if there was any trouble:** Sweeney, *From Cochise*, 177–78; King, *War Eagle*, 199; Will Barnes, *Apaches and Longhorns*, 52–57.

272 **for Fort Apache the day after:** Cruse, *Apache Days*, 99–101.

273 **"these Indians were in for war":** Bourke Diary, 45:2069–70; Porter, *Paper Medicine Man*, 144–45; Barnes, *Apaches and Longhorns*, 53–54; Collins, *Apache Nightmare*, 30–31.

274 **They never returned:** Barnes, *Apaches and Longhorns*, 54–55; Cruse, *Apache Days*, 102–4; Carter, *From Yorktown*, 212–13.

275 **"alarmed up at Apache":** King, *War Eagle*, 207; Collins, *Apache Nightmare*, 39–42.

276 **"I thought so too"**: Cruse, *Apache Days*, 105–8; Carter, *From Yorktown*, 213–14; Collins, *Apache Nightmare*, 48.

277 **"all hell broke loose"**: Carter, *From Yorktown*, 214–15; Cruse, *Apache Days*, 110–12.

277 **to Camp Thomas**: Barnes, *Apaches and Longhorns*, 55–57; Collins, *Apache Nightmare*, 70–71.

278 **"Carr and command were killed"**: Radbourne, *Mickey Free*, 75–76; *Arizona Weekly Star*, September 8 and October 1, 1881.

278 **among the Apache bands**: *New York Times*, September 4, 1881; Radbourne, *Mickey Free*, 78–80.

279 **the Apache scouts had mutinied**: Barnes, *Apaches and Longhorns*, 58–62; Carter, *From Yorktown*, 220.

281 **who fell into their hands**: Apache accounts of Cibecue are in Bourke Diary, 60:21–43, which are conveniently reprinted in "The Apache Story of the Cibecue," in Cozzens, ed., *Struggle for Apacheria*, 295–310. The best secondary account is in Collins, *Apache Nightmare*, 45–69. Also see Cruse, *Apache Days*, 113–19; Carter, *From Yorktown*, 215–20; Barnes, *Apaches and Longhorns*, 62–65; Mazzanovich, *Trailing Geronimo*, 124–25; Ball, *Indeh*, 54–55; and the account by Mike Burns in Farish, *Arizona*, 3:335–39.

282 **"who fired on General Carr's command"**: Barnes, *Apaches and Longhorns*, 65–70; King, *War Eagle*, 213–15; Collins, *Apache Nightmare*, 74–94, 101–5; Utley, *Frontier Regulars*, 373. John Clum, then editing the *Tombstone Epitaph*, was horrified by the blunders made by Agent Tiffany and the military in dealing with the Cibecue crisis. His account of events is in John P. Clum, "Apache Misrule: A Bungling Agent Sets the Military Arm in Motion," *New Mexico Historical Review* 5 (April 1930): 138–239. A second part, dealing with the later breakout by Geronimo and Juh, was published in the July 1930 issue of the *NMHR*.

21. BREAKOUT

283 **"Troops made him nervous"**: Chatto quoted in Utley, *Geronimo*, 110.

284 **"than to be killed in prison"**: Barrett, ed., *Geronimo's Story*, 133–34; Debo, *Geronimo*, 130–32; Clum, "Apache Misrule, Concluded," 221–39; Sweeney, *From Cochise*, 179–80.

284 **back to Fort Grant to refit**: Mazzanovich, *Trailing Geronimo*, 160–76; Russell, *One Hundred and Three Fights*, 157–61; Utley, *Geronimo*, 110–11. Major George Sanford was in command of the troops but illness had led him to turn command over to Reuben Bernard.

286 **direction of Tombstone**: Mazzanovich, *Trailing Geronimo*, 181–86; Russell, *One Hundred and Three Fights*, 163–65; Sweeney, *From Cochise*, 185–90.

287 **"paper lily on his chest"**: Clum, *Apache Agent*, 265–67; Clum, *Apache Days and Tombstone Nights*, 48–50.

288   **toward the Sierra Madre:** Mazzanovich, *Trailing Geronimo*, 189–90; Clum, *Apache Days and Tombstone Nights*, 50–53; Ledoux, *Nantan*, 1:358–59.

288   **Indian police force:** Radbourne, *Mickey Free*, 78–79; Collins, *Apache Nightmare*, 151.

289   **noted an eyewitness:** *Globe Arizona Silver Belt*, October 22, 1881.

289   **"a tree on the San Carlos Agency":** Cruse, *Apache Days*, 139; King, *War Eagle*, 220–24; Radbourne, *Mickey Free*, 81–82; Collins, *Apache Nightmare*, 194–204; Mazzanovich, *Trailing Geronimo*, 205–14.

290   **journey from San Carlos:** Ball, *Days of Victorio*, 123–26; Debo, *Geronimo*, 135.

291   **Terrazas could not be trusted:** Sweeney, *From Cochise*, 192–93.

291   **on such a dangerous raid:** Debo, *Geronimo*, 137–39; Shapard, *Loco*, 144–45; Sweeney, *From Cochise*, 196, 206; Ball, *Days of Victorio*, 136–39.

292   **Mexican line to keep watch:** Radbourne, *Mickey Free*, 83–85; Smith, *Captive Arizona*, 117–19.

292   **in the Boer War:** Thrapp, *Sieber*, 223–24; Heitman, *Historical Register*, 1:223; Thrapp, *Encyclopedia of Frontier Biography*, 1:125–26. Also see J. Y. F. Blake, *A West Pointer with the Boers*, and Toby Giese, *The Saga of John Fillmore Blake*. The young officer was the great-grandfather of *Dances with Wolves* author Michael Blake.

293   **"Shoot down anyone who refuses to go":** Betzinez, *Geronimo*, 56–57; Shapard, *Loco*, 152–54; Rope narrative in Basso, ed., *Western Apache Raiding*, 145–46; Grenville Goodwin, "Experiences of an Indian Scout, Part Two," *Arizona Historical Review* 7 (April 1936): 44–47. Also see Santee, *Apache Land*, 167–71; Debo, *Geronimo*, 140–42; Clum, *Apache Agent*, 272–77; and Thrapp, *Conquest*, 236–38.

293   **pursuit of the Apache fugitives:** Horn, *Life of Horn*, 44–47. *Coyotero* was a generic term used by both soldiers and civilians in reference to the various Western Apache bands.

293   **liking to the gregarious youngster:** Larry D. Ball, *Tom Horn*, 3–46.

294   **color-blind for his time and place:** Sparks, *Apache Kid*, 10; de la Garza, *Apache Kid*, 7–8, 15–17; Santee, *Apache Land*, 93–94.

294   **back toward the Mexican border:** Shapard, *Loco*, 157–58; Thrapp, *Conquest*, 237; McClintock, *Arizona*, 1:236–37; Sweeney, *From Cochise*, 214–15; Betzinez, *Geronimo*, 60–62.

295   **"that I was ace high":** Mazzanovich, *Trailing Geronimo*, 195, 203.

295   **turn about and return to Arizona:** Radbourne, *Mickey Free*, 88–90; Heitman, *Historical Register*, 1:683.

295   **moved along the rail line:** For Forsyth's colorful career, see Hutton, *Phil Sheridan and His Army*, 45–48, 166–69; Heitman, *Historical Register*, 1:430; Thrapp, *Encyclopedia of Frontier Biography*, 2:509. Forsyth wrote two books: a memoir titled *Thrilling Days in Army Life*, in 1900, and *The Story of the Soldier*, published that same year. For his full biography, see David Dixon, *Hero of Beecher Island*.

296 the Apaches had vanished: Betzinez, *Geronimo*, 62–65; Forsyth, *Thrilling Days*, 79–120; Utley, *Geronimo*, 116–17; Shapard, *Loco*, 159–63; Dixon, *Hero of Beecher Island*, 149–55. Al Sieber criticized Forsyth's actions in an interview in the *Prescott Weekly Courier*, May 27, 1882.

299 made camp for the night: Horn, *Life of Horn*, 80–81; William A. Rafferty left his account in the *Arizona Daily Star*, May 17, 1882, which is conveniently reprinted as "Rafferty's Trail" in Cozzens, ed., *Struggle for Apacheria*, 286–89. Also see Horn, *Life of Horn*, 80–81; Betzinez, *Geronimo*, 68–70; Shapard, *Loco*, 164–75; Carter, *From Yorktown*, 229–32; Thrapp, *Sieber*, 229–35; Al Sieber in *Prescott Weekly Courier*, May 27, 1882.

299 plain that led to the creek: Sweeney, *From Cochise*, 223.

299 Geronimo was heard above the chaos: Betzinez, *Geronimo*, 70–72.

300 "this must be his last day": Barrett, ed., *Geronimo's Story*, 107–8; Sweeney, *From Cochise*, 225; Ball, *Days of Victorio*, 142–45.

301 "for my people have turned from me": Debo, *Geronimo*, 151–52, 432; Ball, *Days of Victorio*, 144; Sweeney, *From Cochise*, 226–27; Robinson, *Apache Voices*, 35–44; Shapard, *Loco*, 176–86.

301 "old bucks fight for their families": Forsyth, *Thrilling Days*, 114–15; Shapard, *Loco*, 174; Thrapp, *Sieber*, 239–40; Horn, *Life of Horn*, 90–92.

302 withdrew his command from Mexico: Dixon, *Hero of Beecher Island*, 160–61; Forsyth, *Thrilling Days*, 118–21; Shapard, *Loco*, 178–79; Thrapp, *Sieber*, 240–43.

302 a tidy profit of at least twenty-thousand dollars: Shapard, *Loco*, 182–86.

302 "we will have them to fight again": Sieber in *Prescott Weekly Courier*, May 27, 1882, and Rafferty in *Arizona Daily Star*, May 17, 1882. Both interviews are reprinted in Cozzens, ed., *Struggle for Apacheria*, 286–94.

22. HELL'S FORTY ACRES

304 "Some of them were not worth counting": Barrett, ed., *Geronimo's Story*, 110.

304 "always sensing or anticipating danger": Betzinez, *Geronimo*, 76–77, 81; Shapard, *Loco*, 188.

305 They slowly roasted him alive: Debo, *Geronimo*, 158–63; Sweeney, *From Cochise*, 239–53; Bailey, *White Apache*, 106; Betzinez, *Geronimo*, 93–96, 143.

306 cradled in Daklugie's arms: Ball, *Indeh*, 70–77; Thrapp, *Juh*, 39; Betzinez, *Geronimo*, 122; Ball, *Days of Victorio*, 146–48; Shapard, *Loco*, 190; Sweeney, *From Cochise*, 289.

307 "prime of his life": Radbourne, *Mickey Free*, 97–98, 200.

307 dropped the matter: Horn, *Life of Horn*, 32. The Mickey Free File, Hayden Collection, Arizona Historical Society contains copies of the rosters and correspondence.

308 "stop at General Springs to fight": Carter, *Life of Chaffee*, 93–94; Cruse, *Apache Days*, 158–61; Thrapp, *Sieber*, 244–46; George H. Morgan,

"Fight at the Big Dry Wash," in Carroll, ed., *Papers of the Order of Indian Wars*, 249–54.

308 "had never been swept": *Arizona Star*, April 13, 1883; Carter, *From Yorktown*, 244–35.

309 "made a good shot": Horn, *Life of Horn*, 108–9; Morgan, "Fight at the Big Dry Wash," 253; Thrapp, *Sieber*, 249–53; Cruse, *Apache Days*, 161–63; Carter, *From Yorktown*, 233–37. Also see Will C. Barnes, "The Apaches' Last Stand in Arizona: The Battle of Big Dry Wash," *Arizona Historical Review* 3 (January 1931): 36–59.

310 between the army and the Apaches in Arizona: Cruse, *Apache Days*, 167–72; Thrapp, *Sieber*, 253–57; Carter, *Life of Chaffee*, 95–98; Morgan, "Fight at the Big Dry Wash," 253–54; Horn, *Life of Horn*, 110. Also see Ball, *Tom Horn*, 28–30.

311 "the great fly-god Beelzebub": Bourke, *On the Border*, 434–38; Thrapp, *Apacheria*, 261; *Tucson Star*, November 5, 1882.

312 return all the Apaches to their reservation: Cruse, *Apache Days*, 179–80.

312 "become the instruments of oppression": General Order No. 43, October 5, 1882, Department of Arizona, George Crook, Annual Report, 1883.

312 as his assistants: Sweeney, *From Cochise*, 282.

313 complained to the secretary of the interior: Davis, *Geronimo*, 41–43; Bourke, *On the Border*, 445; Robinson, *General Crook*, 257.

314 an entirely human side after all: Bourke Diary, 74:79 and 75:3–7; Radbourne, *Mickey Free*, 142–43, 182; Porter, *Paper Medicine Man*, 180.

315 "very tender chicken or frog legs": Davis, *Geronimo*, 30–31, 36–39, 65; Robinson, *General Crook*, 258–59.

315 "the present, future, or past": Robert Hanna, "With Crawford in Mexico," in Cozzens, ed., *Struggle for Apacheria*, 511.

315 "I never found it out": Davis, *Geronimo*, 36–37.

316 into the white man's world: De la Garza, *Apache Kid*, 16; Davis, *Geronimo*, 62–63; Clum, "Es-kin-in-zin," 21–22.

23. SIERRA MADRE

317 "must look out for trouble": George Crook to Henry Teller, March 16, 1883, Crook Collection, Hayes Presidential Center, Ohio.

318 "in Arizona and New Mexico": Thrapp, *Conquest*, 274–76; Robinson, *Crook*, 261–62; Thrapp, *Sierra Madre*, 172; *New York Herald*, May 22, 1883.

318 on a bloody platter: Sherman to Crook, April 28, 1883, Crook Collection, Hayes Presidential Center; Thrapp, *Conquest*, 276.

319 personally question him: Betzinez, *Geronimo*, 102, 107–8; Sweeney, *From Cochise*, 290–94; Lockwood, *Apache Indians*, 264–66; Bourke, *Apache Campaign*, 14–17.

320 "Little Charley McComas must be rescued": Sweeney, *From Cochise*, 295; Marc Simmons, *Massacre*, 100–49; Thrapp, *Conquest*, 270–71.

320 **Slaughter bought the ranch:** Barnes, *Arizona Place Names*, 380; Erwin, *John Horton Slaughter*, 138–44.

321 **was Mickey Free:** Bourke, *Apache Campaign*, 12–17; Thrapp, *Sierra Madre Adventure*, 128–29; Robinson, *Crook*, 262–63.

321 **enthusiasm of the dancers:** John Rope and Grenville Goodwin, "Experiences of an Indian Scout, Part Two," *Arizona Historical Review* 7 (April 1936): 55–56; Rope narrative in Basso, ed. *Western Apache Raiding*, 154; Sweeney, *From Cochise*, 305; Bourke, *Apache Campaign*, 17–18; Radbourne, *Mickey Free*, 106.

322 **This was powerful medicine:** Bourke Diary, 66:70–72, 78–81, and 74:79; Bourke, *Apache Campaign*, 25–26, 49–56; Goodwin and Rope, "Experiences of an Indian Scout, Part Two," 57.

323 **"they were afraid":** Rope narrative in Basso, ed., *Western Apache Raiding*, 159; Bourke, *Apache Campaign*, 58.

323 **"death seemed to be reigning before our eyes":** Randall quoted in *Albuquerque Daily Democrat*, June 21, 1883, which reprints an undated story from the *El Paso Times;* Bourke, *Apache Campaign*, 59–64; Bourke Diary, 67:24, 27, 32. Several excerpts from Bourke's diaries, vols. 66 and 68, are conveniently reprinted in Cozzens, ed., *Struggle for Apacheria*, 346–85.

324 **where were they now:** Bourke, *Apache Campaign*, 66; Bourke Diary, 67:33–34. Rumors abounded in the eastern press that Crook and his men had all been killed. See *Chicago Times*, May 24, 1883; *New-York Tribune*, May 10, 1883; *Boston Globe*, May 27, 1883.

324 **"so I was always in the front":** Goodwin and Rope, "Experiences of an Indian Scout, Part Two," 63; Bourke, *Apache Campaign*, 68–69; Bourke Diary, 67:30–32.

325 **the daughter of Bonito:** Thrapp, *Sierra Madre*, 143–46; Goodwin and Rope, "Experiences of an Indian Scout, Part Two," 63–64; Betzinez, *Geronimo*, 118–20; Ball, *Indeh*, 51; Sweeney, *From Cochise*, 306–7; Simmons, *Massacre*, 180–82.

325 **along as best they could:** Betzinez, *Geronimo*, 113–15.

327 **scattering the soldiers and scouts:** Goodwin and Rope, "Experiences of an Indian Scout, Part Two," 64–65; Bourke Diary, 67:56–60; Bourke, *Apache Campaign*, 81–82; Thrapp, *Sierra Madre*, 148–52.

327 **gave her the child:** John Rope narrative in Basso, ed., *Western Apache Raiding*, 164.

328 **classic Mexican standoff:** Goodwin and Rope, "Experiences of an Indian Scout, Part Two," 65–66; Thrapp, *Sierra Madre*, 154–55; Bourke, *Apache Campaign*, 85.

24. TURKEY CREEK

329 **for a late breakfast:** Goodwin and Rope, "Experiences of an Indian Scout, Part Two," 67; Ball, *Indeh*, 154; Thrapp, *Sierra Madre*, 155–58; Thrapp, *Conquest*, 295–302. Dan Thrapp discounted the story of

Crook's capture, but conceded that it might be true but if so was a clever ploy on Crook's part to open negotiations with Geronimo. He presents no evidence for this conclusion. Crook and Bourke are strangely silent in their writings concerning the incident, although Bourke later vigorously denied to the press that it occurred. Thrapp's interpretive influence is obvious in Angie Debo's statement that this was "the most supremely courageous act of his [Crook's] adventurous career." Peter Aleshire, Allan Radbourne, and Charles Robinson all follow Thrapp and Debo on this question. Robert Utley and Edwin Sweeney ignore the incident in their books. David Roberts, on the other hand, reached the only logical conclusion in his superb *Once They Moved Like the Wind*, 235–36, which is that Crook went bird hunting and was grabbed by the Apaches. Bourke's silence on the incident actually speaks volumes. If Crook had engaged in a gambit to open negotiations, Bourke would have trumpeted it to the world. The simple fact is that Apache scout John Rope, who witnessed the incident, had it right. Crook, as he had done countless times before, recklessly went hunting. (On the very day that Custer's Seventh Cavalry was being slaughtered only a few miles to the northeast, Crook was bear hunting in the Big Horn Mountains.) It all worked out for the best, however, at least momentarily. Also see Debo, *Geronimo*, 183; Aleshire, *Fox and the Whirlwind*, 251; Radbourne, *Mickey Free*, 116; and Robinson, *General Crook*, 265.

330 **killed with stones:** Bourke, *Apache Campaign*, 85, 93–96.

331 **extent of Geronimo's perfidy:** Betzinez, *Geronimo*, 118–20; Debo, *Geronimo*, 189–90; Thrapp, *Conquest*, 290; Thrapp, *Sieber*, 282–83; Goodwin and Rope, "Experiences of an Indian Scout, Part Two," 68–69; Rope narrative in Basso, ed., *Western Apache Raiding*, 169, 308; Thrapp, *Sierra Madre*, 161–62.

332 **Captain Crawford, Al Sieber, and Mickey Free:** Bourke, *Apache Campaign*, 99–110; Shapard, *Loco*, 199–200; Thrapp, *Sierra Madre*, 163–66. Crook gives his version of events in his Annual Report for 1883.

332 **"good horses before going back":** Bourke Diary, 68:20; Davis, *Geronimo*, 69; Goodwin and Rope, "Experiences of an Indian Scout, Part Two," 69.

332 **did not welcome the Chiricahuas back:** *Tucson Star*, June 20, 1883; Thrapp, *Conquest*, 295.

333 **few friends in the Southwest:** Crook, Annual Report, 1883; Robinson, *General Crook*, 266–67.

333 **"utterly without foundation":** Thrapp, *Conquest*, 296–97; *Philadelphia Press*, July 17 and July 18, 1883; Bourke Diary, 72:99–102.

334 **roaming the Sierra Madre:** Sweeney, *From Cochise*, 325–26; Simmons, *Massacre*, 188–206.

335 **as the final holdouts:** Santiago Ward as told to Mrs. George F. Kitt, March 12, 1934, Mickey Free File, Arizona Historical Society; Radbourne, *Mickey Free*, 123.

336 **"a sort of Benedict Arnold to us":** Davis, *Geronimo*, 80–81; Radbourne,

Mickey Free, 126; Ball, *Days of Victorio*, 163; Ball, *Indeh*, 83–84; Sweeney, *From Cochise*, 380.

336 **"we fight Mexicans with rocks"**: Davis, *Geronimo*, 87. Also see Utley, *Geronimo*, 147–48; Debo, *Geronimo*, 199.

337 **never forgave either Crook or Crawford**: Crook, Annual Report, 1884; Thrapp, *Sierra Madre*, 176; Barrett, ed., *Geronimo's Story*, 135–36.

337 **ignored the soft-spoken Virginian**: Sweeney, *From Cochise*, 364; Davis, *Geronimo*, 112.

338 **"giving him lemonade to drink"**: Horn, *Life of Tom Horn*, 125–26, 185–86.

338 **that Mickey gave to him**: Bourke Diary, 74:75, 79–80; Radbourne, *Mickey Free*, 138–43.

339 **"who last year were our worst enemies"**: Crook, Annual Report, 1884.

339 **a dangerous game for all involved**: Davis, *Geronimo*, 39, 112–30.

339 **lenient treatment for the Apache**: Sweeney, *From Cochise*, 372–75; Crook to Crawford, July 11, 1884, Crook Collection, Hayes Presidential Center; the records of the trial are in "Trial of Kaetennae," RG 393, National Archives.

340 **excuse for his later actions**: Davis, *Geronimo*, 142–43; Ball, *Days of Victorio*, 156–57; Radbourne, *Mickey Free*, 135–37.

341 **"savage Apache warriors"**: Thrapp, *Sieber*, 290–92; Crawford to Crook, March 28, 1884, and April 6, 1884, Crook Collection, Hayes Presidential Center; Larry Ball, "The Two Tom Horns," *Journal of the Wild West History Association* 5 (August 2012): 15–16; Horn, *Life of Horn*, 28–29. For more on the *tiswin* problem, see Utley, *Geronimo*, 11; Shapard, *Loco*, 212–23; Sweeney, *From Cochise*, 21; Buskirk, *Western Apache*, 216–19.

343 **Crook never received the telegram**: Davis, *Geronimo*, 35–36, 141–48; Radbourne, *Mickey Free*, 152–53; Thrapp, *Sieber*, 293–96.

344 **"matters entirely beyond my control"**: Radbourne, *Mickey Free*, 153–55; Davis, *Geronimo*, 149–50; Utley, *Geronimo*, 157–58; Sweeney, *From Cochise*, 405–7.

344 **going to be a long campaign**: James Parker, *Old Army*, 153–54.

25. DEVIL'S BACKBONE

345 **noted Lieutenant Parker**: Parker, *Old Army*, 155–56.

345 **hopelessly shattered**: Sweeney, *From Cochise*, 410; Utley, *Geronimo*, 161–62.

346 **near Lake Palomas**: Thrapp, *Conquest*, 319–20; Sweeney, *From Cochise*, 425–28.

346 **"disintegrate them if you can"**: Radbourne, *Mickey Free*, 155–56; Utley, *Geronimo*, 162–63.

347 **"saving the lives of others"**: Davis, *Geronimo*, 31–32.

348 **"he seemed a thorough Indian"**: Hanna, "With Crawford in Mexico,"

in Cozzens, ed., *Struggle for Apacheria*, 511–12; Cruse, *Apache Days*, 219–21.

348 **headed toward the Sierra Madre:** Faulk, *Geronimo Campaign*, 75–77; Thrapp, *Conquest*, 328.

348 **plotting their revenge:** Davis, *Geronimo*, 166–69; Hanna, "With Crawford in Mexico," in Cozzens, ed., *Struggle for Apacheria*, 514–15; Sweeney, *From Cochise*, 434–35; Thrapp, *Conquest*, 330–32.

349 **dismissed them all:** Davis, *Geronimo*, 174–78; Barrett, ed., *Geronimo's Own Story*, 136–37; Debo, *Geronimo*, 244–45.

350 **younger version of Sieber:** Sweeney, *From Cochise*, 446–48; Utley, *Geronimo*, 166–67.

352 **a feast prepared for everyone:** Charles P. Elliott, "The Geronimo Campaign of 1885–1886," in Cozzens, ed., *Struggle for Apacheria*, 436–39; Sweeney, *From Cochise*, 454–58; Radbourne, *Mickey Free*, 162–63; Henry W. Daly, "The Geronimo Campaign," in Cozzens, ed., *Struggle for Apacheria*, 454–55; Davis, *Geronimo*, 176–89.

352 **headed back into New Mexico:** Thrapp, *Sieber*, 309–12; Davis, *Geronimo*, 189–94.

353 **Crook was humiliated:** Barrett, ed., *Geronimo's Story*, 140–41; Utley, *Geronimo*, 172–74; Sweeney, *From Cochise*, 461–64; Daniel Aranda, "Santiago McKinn, Indian Captive," *Real West* 24 (June 1981): 41–43.

354 **had proven to be a sieve:** Davis, *Geronimo*, 194–95; Radbourne, *Mickey Free*, 169; Thrapp, *Conquest*, 334–39.

355 **immigrants to the United States:** *Annual Report of the Secretary of War* (1885), 1:62; Hutton, *Phil Sheridan and His Army*, 364–66; Schmitt, ed., *Crook Autobiography*, 251–59; *Annual Report of the Secretary of War* (1886), 1:7, 71. Also see Dunlay, *Wolves for the Blue Soldiers*, 66, 178; Eve Ball, "The Apache Scouts: A Chiricahua Appraisal," *Arizona and the West* 7 (Winter 1965): 515–28.

357 **intersect again soon:** Hooker, *Child of the Fighting Tenth*, 183–86; William E. Shipp, "Captain Crawford's Last Expedition," in Cozzens, ed., *Struggle for Apacheria*, 516–23; Sparks, *Apache Kid*, 11–12; Cornelius Smith, *Kosterlitzky*, 90–91.

357 **"had a regular wolf snap to his jaw":** Horn, *Life of Horn*, 202; Utley, *Geronimo*, 177–78; Ball, *Tom Horn*, 54–57.

357 **Cochise had done:** Shipp, "Captain Crawford's Last Expedition," 522–25; Horn, *Life of Horn*, 203–7; Sweeney, *From Cochise*, 494–97. Lieutenant Shipp later died in the famous July 1898 charge up San Juan Hill in Cuba.

357 **on a plateau about a mile from the *rancheria*:** Maus narrative in Miles, *Recollections*, 450–71. Also see Horn, *Life of Horn*, 208–17; Shipp, "Captain Crawford's Last Expedition," 524–25; Ball, *Days of Victorio*, 182; Robinson, *Apache Voices*, 12; and Stockel, *Women of the Apache Nation*, 49.

360 **Victorio's death had been avenged at last:** Miles, *Recollections*, 457–60; Horn, *Life of Horn*, 218–21; Shipp, "Captain Crawford's Last Expedition," 526–28; Thrapp, ed., *Dateline Fort Bowie*, 182; Morris E. Opler, "A Chiricahua Apache's Account of the Geronimo Campaign of 1886," *New Mexico Historical Review* 13 (October 1938): 373–75; Sweeney, *From Cochise*, 502–3.

362 **There was no lumber for a coffin:** Maus interview in *San Francisco Chronicle*, July 11, 1886; Robinson, *Apache Voices*, 12; Debo, *Geronimo*, 250–52; Miles, *Recollections*, 461–65; Horn, *Life of Horn*, 222–29; Shipp, "Captain Crawford's Last Expedition," 529–31; Daly, "Geronimo Campaign," 464–65; Ball, *Tom Horn*, 57–71; Sweeney, *From Cochise*, 507. Also see Shelly Bowen Hatfield, "The Death of Emmet Crawford: Who Was to Blame?" *Journal of Arizona History* 29 (Summer 1988): 131–48; and Jerome A. Greene, "The Crawford Affair: International Implications of the Geronimo Campaign," *Journal of the West* 11 (January 1972): 143–53.

363 **Geronimo in chains or dead:** Hutton, *Phil Sheridan and His Army*, 243–44, 256, 341–42; *Army and Navy Register*, September 18, 1886; *Annual Report of the Secretary of War* (1886), 1:72–74; Schmitt, ed., *Crook Autobiography*, 265–76, 289–301.

26. THE WIND AND THE DARKNESS

365 **hunting in Mexico had obviously been good:** Bourke Diary, 80:134 and 81:115–46; Jay Van Orden, *Geronimo's Surrender: The 1886 C. S. Fly Photographs*, 1–7, 27; Daly, "The Geronimo Campaign," in Cozzens, ed., *Struggle for Apacheria*, 466–67; Thrapp, ed., *Dateline Fort Bowie*, 20; Utley, *Geronimo*, 187; Bourke, *On the Border*, 472–74.

366 **"even if it takes fifty years":** Bourke, *On the Border*, 474–76; Debo, *Geronimo*, 257–59; Sweeney, *From Cochise*, 520–23.

367 **"I surrender to you, and that is all":** Bourke, *On the Border*, 476–79; Horn, *Life of Horn*, 235; Thrapp, ed., *Dateline Fort Bowie*, 28–32; Sweeney, *From Cochise*, 523; Debo, *Geronimo*, 260–63; Thrapp, *Conquest*, 345; Van Orden, *Geronimo's Surrender*, 5.

368 **late in the afternoon of March 29:** Daly, "The Geronimo Campaign," 472–73; Bourke, *On the Border*, 480–81; Schmitt, ed., *Crook Autobiography*, 261.

369 **"would never return of his own accord":** Daly, "The Geronimo Campaign," 474–76; Horn, *Life of Horn*, 236–37.

371 **Miles would take Crook's place in Arizona:** Sheridan to Crook, March 31, 1886, Box 36, Sheridan Papers; *Annual Report of the Secretary of War* (1886), 1:147–55; Bourke, *On the Border*, 465–83; Schmitt, ed., *Crook Autobiography*, 260–63; Hutton, *Phil Sheridan and His Army*, 366–67.

371 **pack up and depart for Omaha:** Charles Roberts Diary, Arizona Historical Society; Schmitt, ed., *Crook Autobiography*, 266; Robinson, *General Crook*, 283–85; Bourke, *On the Border*, 477; Sweeney, *From Cochise*, 532; Thrapp, ed., *Dateline Fort Bowie*, 36–37, 57–58, 66–67.

372 **"on account of those nasty mouths":** Radbourne, *Mickey Free*, 172–75. General Crook had lost confidence in Charles Gatewood and had banished him to Fort Wingate. He was replaced by Lieutenant James Lockett. See Kraft, ed., *Gatewood Memoir*, 104–5.

373 **Miles was a man who got things done:** For Nelson Miles, see Robert Wooster, *Nelson Miles and the Twilight of the Old Army;* Jerome A. Greene, *Yellowstone Command: Colonel Nelson A. Miles and the Great Sioux War, 1876–1877;* Peter R. DeMontravel, *A Hero to His Fighting Men: Nelson A. Miles, 1839–1925;* and Virginia Weisel Johnson, *The Unregimented General: A Biography of Nelson A. Miles.* The general wrote two memoirs: *Personal Recollections* in 1896 and *Serving the Republic* in 1911.

373 **"Crook never made any":** Porter, *Paper Medicine Man*, 251.

373 **Forts Grant, Thomas, Apache, and Verde:** Hutton, *Phil Sheridan and His Army*, 139, 367; Johnson, *The Unregimented General*, 89; Leckie, *Buffalo Soldiers*, 246–51; Wooster, *Nelson A. Miles*, 144–49.

374 **an end to this seemingly endless war:** Leonard Wood, *Chasing Geronimo*, 51; Bailey, *White Apache*, 125–29; Daly, "The Geronimo Campaign," 479; Faulk, *Geronimo Campaign*, 105–6; Miles, *Serving the Republic*, 224. Zebina Streeter would eventually be killed at the Mexican town of Nacozari in an 1889 gunfight over a woman he was courting. For Wood's career, see Herman Hagedorn, *Leonard Wood: A Biography;* Jack C. Lane, *Armed Progressive: General Leonard Wood;* and Jack McCallum, *Leonard Wood.*

375 **reward for Geronimo, dead or alive:** For the attack on Peck's ranch, see Kieran McCarty and C. L. Sonnichsen, "Trini Verdin and the Truth of History," *Journal of Arizona History* 14 (Summer 1973): 149–64. Also see Bigelow, *Bloody Trail of Geronimo*, 183–84; Sweeney, *From Cochise*, 537–38; Wood, *Chasing Geronimo*, 28; Miles, *Recollections*, 489–90; Beyer, ed., *Deeds of Valor*, 2:294–98; Davis, *Geronimo*, 219; Schubert, *Voices of the Buffalo Soldiers*, 139–40; Leckie, *Buffalo Soldiers*, 249–50.

376 **near the summit of the Azul Mountains:** Sweeney, *From Cochise*, 543–48.

377 **with reports for Miles and a request for new orders:** Daly, "The Geronimo Campaign," 480; Wood, *Chasing Geronimo*, 55–56; McCarty and Sonnichsen, "Trini Verdin," 154–64; Bailey, *White Apache*, 129.

378 **their way south to find Lawton:** Miles, *Recollections*, 496–97; Radbourne, *Mickey Free*, 176–77; Wood, *Chasing Geronimo*, 87–88; Parker, *Old Army*, 174–77; Utley, *Geronimo*, 200; Kraft, *Gatewood and Geronimo*, 133–43.

379 had finally claimed Mickey Free: Bourke Diary, 82:76–83; Porter, *Paper Medicine Man*, 211–14; Radbourne, *Mickey Free*, 177–80.

379 a puzzle to the sophisticated East: *Washington Star*, July 19, 1886; Bourke Diary, 82:80–84; Radbourne, *Mickey Free*, 181–84.

380 once again and departed: Porter, *Paper Medicine Man*, 215; Shapard, *Loco*, 221–24.

381 "study alone can give": Bourke Diary, 82:109–10.

381 Chatto still wore his peace medal: Radbourne, *Mickey Free*, 185–88; Shapard, *Loco*, 225–26.

382 "He is not in especially good health": Wood, *Chasing Geronimo*, 88–89.

383 alongside the Bavispe: Parker, *Old Army*, 174–79; Robinson, *Apache Voices*, 12–13; Utley, *Geronimo*, 205–10.

384 "I will give up with you": Wood, *Chasing Geronimo*, 104; Kraft, *Gatewood and Geronimo*, 161–72. Also see Charles B. Gatewood, "The Surrender of Geronimo," in Carroll, ed., *Papers of the Order of Indian Wars*, 106–13.

385 "my warriors are not so protected": Wood, *Chasing Geronimo*, 105; Ball, *Indeh*, 131; Utley, *Geronimo*, 213–17.

387 years as prisoners of war for the Chiricahua people: Barrett, ed., *Geronimo's Story*, 172; Miles, *Recollections*, 519–28; Sweeney, *From Cochise*, 571–75; Debo, *Geronimo*, 290–98.

387 collapsed and died in the searing desert heat: Shapard, *Loco*, 226–27.

27. APACHE KID

389 every hand was turned against him: Ball, *Indeh*, 115–19, 134–36; Thrapp, *Conquest*, 365–66; Betzinez, *Geronimo*, 143–45; Sparks, *Apache Kid*, 28–31; Ball, *Victorio*, 195; Robinson, *Apache Voices*, 87–100. For Tom Horn, see Horn, *Life of Horn*, 248–50; Ball, *Tom Horn*, 96–98. The story of Massai was later celebrated in a novel by Paul I. Wellman, *Broncho Apache* (Garden City, NY: Doubleday, 1936), which inspired the 1954 motion picture *Apache* starring Burt Lancaster as Massai and John McIntyre as Al Sieber.

391 on the Mescalero Reservation for generations: Frederic Remington, "Massai's Crooked Trail," *Crooked Trails*, 79–91; Radbourne, *Mickey Free*, 191–92; Robinson, *Apache Voices*, 97–100; Ball, *Indeh*, 248–61; Miles, *Recollections*, 529.

392 simply called her "Beauty": *Los Angeles Times*, November 11, 1894; Thrapp, *Conquest*, 323–24; Hayes, *Apache Vengeance*, 19–20; Thrapp, *Sieber*, 322; Williamson, "Apache Kid," 30–31; Sparks, *Apache Kid*, 13–14.

392 did not believe in omens: De la Garza, *Apache Kid*, 27. Also see E. Fay Bennett, "An Afternoon of Terror: The Sonoran Earthquake of May 3, 1887," *Arizona and the West* 19 (Summer 1977): 107–20.

393 shot Rip right through the heart: Thrapp, *Sieber*, 320–25; McKanna,

Court-Martial, 15–16, 53–55; Hill, *Lone War Trail*, 37–40; de la Garza, *Apache Kid*, 29.

395 **departed that morning for Globe:** Arhelger File, AHS; Williamson, "Apache Kid," 14–15, 30–31; McKanna, *Court-Martial*, 82–118; Thrapp, *Sieber*, 325–27; Sparks, *Apache Kid*, 16–17.

395 **not about to give up the left one now:** Horn, *Life of Horn*, 249–53; Ball, *Tom Horn*, 112–15; Nunis, *Tom Horn*, 47–50; de la Garza, *Apache Kid*, 31–34, 37, 41; Monaghan, *Tom Horn*, 110–13.

396 **The penalty on conviction was death:** Miles, *Recollections*, 536; Radbourne, *Mickey Free*, 193; McKanna, *Court-Martial*, 59, 62–63; Williamson, "Apache Kid," 13–14.

398 **military prison on Alcatraz Island:** The court-martial is covered in great detail in McKanna, *Court-Martial*, 64–118; de la Garza, *Apache Kid*, 41–54; Thrapp, *Sieber*, 329–33. The 148-page transcript is in Judge Advocate General, Records Received 4475, RG 153, National Archives.

399 **"ill-feeling among the people at San Carlos":** Arhelger File, AHS; McKanna, *Court-Martial*, 119–44; de la Garza, *Apache Kid*, 55–65.

400 **before they could be hanged:** Sparks, *Apache Kid*, 17–18; McKanna, *White Justice*, 82–123, 139–40; Hayes, *Apache Vengeance*, 31–36, 124–30. Also see *Flagstaff Arizona Champion*, June 18, 1887.

402 **Sieber's revenge was complete:** Arhelger File, AHS; Hayes, *Apache Vengeance*, 49–50; Thrapp, *Sieber*, 335–37; de la Garza, *Apache Kid*, 80–85; McKanna, *Court-Martial*, 140–42. A reaffirmation of Arhelger's comment can be found in the statistics of Arizona territorial murder and manslaughter convictions: more than 80 percent convictions for Apaches and fewer than 45 percent convictions for whites. Far more whites also had murder charges dropped to manslaughter. If the Apache was charged with killing a white man, the conviction rate was 100 percent. Apache-on-Apache violence accounts for the rare acquittals. McKanna, *White Justice*, 35, 167–83.

28. THE LAST FREE APACHE

405 **had a detail of twenty scouts in the field:** Williamson, "Apache Kid," 14–15, 30–31; Hayes, *Apache Vengeance*, 69–112; Sparks, *Apache Kid*, 22–26; Hill, *Lone War Trail*, 45–51; de la Garza, *Apache Kid*, 85–99, 115–32. Also see Paul Andrew Hutton, "Legend of the Apache Kid," *Wild West* 27 (December 2014): 30–39.

405 **"a very heavy cost":** Horn, *Life of Horn*, 255–56; Ball, *Tom Horn*, 115–17; Radbourne, *Mickey Free*, 201–2; de la Garza, *Apache Kid*, 97–98.

406 **Two warriors and a boy were captured:** Powhatan Clarke, "A Hot Trail," *Cosmopolitan* 17 (October 1894): 706–16; James W. Watson, "Scouting in Arizona, 1890," in Cozzens, ed., *Struggle for Apacheria*, 642–48; de la Garza, *Apache Kid*, 104–5; Thrapp, *Sieber*, 342–44.

408 **"the sights of a Winchester":** *Globe Arizona Silver Belt*, October 11,

1890; Williamson, "Apache Kid," 31; Hayes, *Apache Vengeance*, 137–48; de la Garza, *Apache Kid*, 109. Statistics on prisoners show that 37 percent of the Indian prisoners in Yuma Territorial Prison died. McKanna, *White Justice*, 174–76.

408 **Apache Kid had escaped yet again:** Sparks, *Apache Kid*, 42–45; Hayes, *Apache Vengeance*, 159–64, 171–75.

409 **as agent a few months later:** Thrapp, *Sieber*, 363–73; Lockwood, *More Arizona Characters*, 30–31; Clum, "Es-kin-in-zin," 14–27; Thrapp, *Encyclopedia of Frontier Biography*, 1:189–90. Also see Edward S. Wallace, "General John Lapham Bullis: Thunderbolt of the Texas Frontier," *Southwestern Historical Quarterly* 55 (July 1951).

410 **without looking back:** Radbourne, *Mickey Free*, 207–10; Griffith, *Mickey Free*, 180–89.

411 **the dead Apache in Aravaipa Canyon:** Hill, *Lone War Trail*, 77–82, 100–102; Sparks, *Apache Kid*, 41–42. Also see J. Frank Dobie, *Apache Gold*.

411 **chances were best as a lone wolf:** "An Indian Ishmael," *St. Louis Republic*, May 12, 1894, reprinting the *San Francisco Examiner* story. Also see *New York Times*, August 13, 1893; *Washington Post*, December 24, 1893; *Philadelphia Press*, December 27, 1895; and *Omaha Daily Bee*, August 22, 1898, for detailed feature stories on the Apache Kid. The Apache Kid File, Arizona Historical Society, has many newspaper clippings, although several are not dated.

412 **tended not to comment on his stutter:** Erwin, *John Horton Slaughter*, 222–23; de la Garza, *Apache Kid*, 167–68.

413 **"watching the gate for his return":** Smith, *Captive Arizona*, 171–78; Erwin, *John Horton Slaughter*, 301–4. The Mathilde Hampe Papers, Arizona Historical Society, are a treasure trove of John Slaughter/Apache May materials. Also see Burns, *Tombstone*, 342–59.

414 **"till the last Apache is dead":** *Tombstone Epitaph*, June 3, 1896; Smith, *Captive Arizona*, 176.

414 **"tenderness in John's being went out to that Apache kid":** Edwin Williams Narrative, clipping, Apache May File, Arizona Historical Society; Erwin, *John Horton Slaughter*, 308–11; Smith, *Captive Arizona*, 180–82.

EPILOGUE

416 **Geronimo's son Chappo did not survive it:** Porter, *Paper Medicine Man*, 223–39; Utley, *Geronimo*, 240–49; Ball, *Indeh*, 140–59; Betzinez, *Geronimo*, 149–59. Also see Herbert Welsh, *The Apache Prisoners in Fort Marion, St. Augustine, Florida;* H. Henrietta Stockel, *Shame and Endurance: The Untold Story of the Chiricahua Apache Prisoners of War;* and Paul Andrew Hutton, "Was Geronimo a Terrorist?" *True West* 58 (August 2011): 24–31.

417 grumbled the unrepentant warrior: Hutton, *Phil Sheridan and His Army*, 125; Barret, ed., *Geronimo's Story*, 139–40.

418 "permitted to know this courageous woman": Ball, *Indeh*, 153–54; Robinson, *Apache Voices*, 12–14; Walter Reed, "Geronimo and His Warriors in Captivity," *Illustrated American* 3 (August 16, 1890): 231–35, which is also conveniently reprinted in the invaluable sourcebook by Cozzens, *Struggle for Apacheria*, 627; Utley, *Geronimo*, 235–37.

419 he and his people would never go home: Ball, *Indeh*, 157.

419 Beauty vanished from the historical record: John P. Clum, "Es-kin-in-zin," *New Mexico Historical Review* 5 (January 1929): 1–27; Dan R. Williamson, "The Apache Kid," *Arizona Highways* 15 (May 1939): 14–15, 30–31.

420 "I wanted to give the people a good show," TR replied: Clum, *Apache Agent*, 291–92; Sharon S. Magee, "The Selling of Geronimo," *Arizona Highways* 71 (August 1995): 12–19; Hutton, "Was Geronimo a Terrorist?," 26–27.

421 car crash on an icy reservation road in 1934: Utley, *Geronimo*, 262, 270–73; William Hafford, "Chato the Betrayed," *Arizona Highways* 69 (February 1993): 14–17.

421 heart attack in Los Angeles on May 2, 1932: Clum, *Apache Agent*, vii–xv; Ledoux, *Nantan*, 2:81–273.

421 inspired the film and television series *Broken Arrow*: Box 5, Forbes Collection, AHS; Farish, *Arizona*, 2:228–40; Sonnichsen, "Who Was Tom Jeffords?" 381–406.

422 dead from a heart attack: Wooster, *Nelson A. Miles*, 252–64; Kraft, *Gatewood and Geronimo*, 208–18; Lane, ed., *Chasing Geronimo*, 113–18.

423 The white world took no note of his passing: Radbourne, *Mickey Free*, 196–217; Thrapp, *Sieber*, 374–401; Ball, *Tom Horn*, 408–34.

423 "can get them at wholesale rates": *Tucson Daily Citizen*, May 25, 1907.

424 "It was the old Apache way": Grenville Goodwin and Neil Goodwin, *The Apache Diaries: The Father-Son Journey*, 114–21. Also see Morris E. Opler, ed., *Grenville Goodwin Among the Western Apache: Letters from the Field*, 47–49, 55–56.

424 last of the great lords of Apacheria: Helge Ingstad, *The Apache Indians: In Search of the Missing Tribe*, 171–77; Goodwin, *Apache Diaries*, 109–13.

BIBLIOGRAPHY

MANUSCRIPT COLLECTIONS

Apache Kid Ephemera File. Arizona Historical Society, Tucson.

Apache May File, Arizona Historical Society, Tucson.

Baldwin, Frank, Papers. Huntington Library, San Marino, California.

Ball, Eve, Papers. Harold B. Lee Library, Brigham Young University, Provo, Utah.

Bourke, John G., Diaries. United States Military Academy Archives, West Point, New York.

Clum, John P. Special Collections, University of Tucson Library, Tucson.

Connell, Charles, File. Arizona Historical Society, Tucson.

Crook, George, Papers. Hayes Library, Rutherford B. Hayes Presidential Center, Fremont, Ohio.

Erwin, Allen A., Papers. Arizona Historical Society, Tucson.

Forbes, Robert H., Collection. Arizona Historical Society, Tucson.

Free, Mickey, File. Hayden Collection, Arizona Historical Society, Tucson.

Freeman, Merrill P., Papers. Arizona Historical Society, Tucson.

Gatewood, Charles, Papers. Arizona Historical Society, Tucson.

Goodwin, Grenville, Papers. Arizona State Museum, Tucson.

Grierson, Benjamin H., Papers. Ayer Manuscripts, Newberry Library, Chicago.

Hampe, Mathilde, Papers. Arizona Historical Society, Tucson.

Hayes, Rutherford B., Papers. Hayes Library, Rutherford B. Hayes Presidential Center, Fremont, Ohio.

Kirkland, William H., Manuscripts. Allen Collection, Arizona Historical Society, Tucson.

Lawton, Henry, Papers. Manuscript Division, Library of Congress, Washington, DC.

Official Register of the Officers and Cadets of the US Military Academy, West Point, New York. United States Military Academy Archives, West Point.

Page, John, File. Hayden Collection, Arizona Historical Society, Tucson.

Pennington, Elias, File. Hayden Collection, Arizona Historical Society, Tucson.

Records of United States Army Continental Commands, RG 393, Military Division of the Missouri, 1866–91. National Archives, Washington, DC.

Roberts, Charles D., Diary. Arizona Historical Society, Tucson.

Schuyler, Walter, Papers. Huntington Library, San Marino, California.

Scott, Hugh L., Papers. Library of Congress, Washington, DC.

Sheridan, Michael V., File. Chicago Historical Society.

Sheridan, Philip H., Collection. Chicago Historical Society.

Sheridan, Philip H., Papers. Manuscript Division, Library of Congress, Washington DC.

Sherman, William Tecumseh, Family Papers. University of Notre Dame Archives. Memorial Library, Notre Dame, Indiana.

Sherman, William Tecumseh, Papers. Manuscript Division, Library of Congress, Washington, DC.

Steck, Michael, Papers. University of New Mexico Library, Albuquerque.

US Board of Indian Commissioners, *Second Annual Report, 1870* (Washington, DC, 1871).

US Bureau of Indian Affairs. Annual Reports, 1849–87.

US Congress. Senate Ex. Doc. 117, 49th Cong., 2d sess.

US Congress. Senate Ex. Doc. 35, 51st Cong., 1st sess.

US National Archives and Records Administration. RG 75, OIA Treaty File; OIA NM LR.

US National Archives and Records Administration. RG 77, TE, OCE LR.

US National Archives and Records Administration. Microfilm. RG 94, LR OAG, 1871–80, M666: Roll 24, 2465 AGO 1871, Correspondence Relating to Vincent Colyer; Roll 123, 3383 AGO 1873, Correspondence Relating to Howard's Mission to Cochise; Roll 194, 1504 AGO 1875, Correspondence Relating to ouster of James E. Roberts as agent at Fort Apache and removal of Apaches to San Carlos by Clum; Roll 265, 2576 AGO 1875, Correspondence relating to removal of Chiricahuas to San Carlos; Roll 326, 1927 AGO 1877, Correspondence relating to arrest and removal of Geronimo's band from Ojo Caliente to San Carlos; Roll 366, 5705 AGO 1877, Correspondence relating to operations against Warm Springs Indians who fled San Carlos, 1877–79; Rolls 526–28, 6058 AGO 1879, Papers relating to operations against Victorio, 1879–81, NARA.

US National Archives and Records Administration. Microfilm. RG 94, LR OAG, 1881–89, M689: Roll 44, 4746 AGO 1881, Correspondence concerning efforts to capture Chiricahuas terrorizing border region of District of NM, July–December 1881; Rolls 96–97, 1749 AGO 1882, Papers relating to the outbreaks in NM and AZ by Chiricahuas who escaped from San Carlos; Rolls 173–202, Papers relating to Chiricahua uprising under Geronimo et al.; Roll 536, 3264 AGO 1887, Reports of Miles and others concerning operations in AZ against Apaches.

US National Archives and Records Administration. RG 98, DNM LR.

US National Archives and Records Administration. RG 108, Hq. Army LR.

US War Department. Annual Reports of the Secretary of War, 1866–87.

Wood, Leonard, Papers. Manuscript Division, Library of Congress, Washington, DC.

DISSERTATIONS

Babcock, Matthew. "Turning Apaches into Spaniards: North America's Forgotten Indian Reservations." Ph.D. diss., Southern Methodist University, 2008.

Bret Harte, John. "The San Carlos Indian Reservation, 1872–1886: An Administrative History." Ph.D. diss., University of Arizona, 1972.

Burkhardt, William. "White Mountain Apache Cult Movements: A Study in Ethnohistory." Ph.D. diss., University of Arizona, 1976.

Conrad, Paul T. "Captive Fates: Displaced American Indians in the Southwest Borderlands, Mexico, and Cuba, 1500–1800." Ph.D. diss., University of Texas at Austin, 2011.

Mason, Joyce Evelyn. "The Use of Indian Scouts in the Apache Wars, 1870–1886." Ph.D. diss., Indiana University, 1970.

Record, Ian Wilson. "Aravaipa: Apache Peoplehood and the Legacy of Particular Geography and Historical Experience." Ph.D. diss., University of Arizona, 2004.

Rockwell, Susan L. "The Autobiography of Mike Burns, Yavapai Apache." Ph.D. diss., Arizona State University, 2001.

Smith, Victoria A. O. "White Eyes, Red Heart, Blue Coat: The Life and Times of Mickey Free." Ph.D. diss., Arizona State University, 2002.

ARTICLES

Allen, R. S. "Pinos Altos, New Mexico." *New Mexico Historical Review* 23 (October 1948): 302–32.

Anderson, Douglas F. "Protestantism, Progress, and Prosperity: John P. Clum and 'Civilizing' the U.S. Southwest, 1871–1886." *Western Historical Quarterly* 33 (Autumn 2002): 315–35.

Anderson, Hattie M. "Mining and Indian Fighting in Arizona and New Mexico, 1858–1861: Memoirs of Hank Smith." *Panhandle-Plains Historical Review* 1 (1920): 67–115.

Aranda, Daniel D. "Josanie: Apache Warrior." *True West* 23 (May 1976): 38–39.

———. "Santiago McKinn, Indian Captive." *Real West* 24 (June 1981): 41–43.

Ball, Eve. "The Apache Scouts: A Chiricahua Appraisal." *Arizona and the West* 7 (Winter 1965): 315–28.

———. "Juh's Stronghold in Mexico." *Journal of Arizona History* 15 (Spring 1971): 73–84.

Ball, Larry D. "Tom Horn and the Talking Boy Controversy." *Journal of Arizona History* 45 (Winter 2004): 333–56.

———. "The Two Tom Horns." *Wild West History Association Journal* 5 (August 2012): 10–20.

———. "William Edwardy: Frontier Journalist and Adventurer." *Journal of Arizona History* 56 (Autumn 2015): 245–76.

Barnes, Will C. "In the Apache Country." *Overland Monthly* 9 (February 1887): 172–80.

Basso, Keith H. "Western Apache." In William C. Sturtevant, ed., *Handbook of North American Indians: Southwest*, vol. 10 (Washington, DC: Smithsonian Institution, 1983), 462–88.

Bell, Bob Boze. "Cave Creek Ambush." *True West* 58 (December 2011): 52–53.

———. "Cut the Tent, Unleash the War: Cochise vs. Lt. Bascom." *True West* 58 (January 2011): 48–51.

———. "Tragic Fight on the Devil's Backbone." *True West* 58 (August 2011): 58–61.

Bell, Bob Boze, and Paul Andrew Hutton. "Mickey Free." *True West* 55 (December 2008): 39–58.

Billington, Monroe. "Black Soldiers at Fort Selden, New Mexico, 1866–1891." *New Mexico Historical Review* 62 (January 1987): 65–80.

Bourke, John G. "Apache Mythology." *Journal of American Folklore* 3 (July–September 1890): 209–12.

———. "General Crook in the Indian Country." *Century Magazine* 41 (March 1891): 643–60

Bret Harte, John. "Conflict at San Carlos: The Military-Civilian Struggle for Control, 1882–85." *Arizona and the West* 15 (Spring 1973): 27–44.

———. "The Strange Case of Joseph P. Tiffany: Indian Agent in Disgrace." *Journal of Arizona History* 16 (Winter 1975): 383–404.

Cargill, Andrew H. "The Camp Grant Massacre." *Arizona Historical Review* 7 (July 1936): 73–79.

Clum, John P. "Apache Misrule." *New Mexico Historical Review* 5 (April 1930): 138–239.

———. "The Apaches." *New Mexico Historical Review* 4 (April 1929): 107–27.

———. "Es-kin-in-zin." *New Mexico Historical Review* 4 (January 1929): 1–27.

———. "Geronimo." *New Mexico Historical Review* 3 (January 1928): 1–40; (April 1928): 121–44; (July 1928): 217–64.

———. "The San Carlos Apache Police." *New Mexico Historical Review* 4 (July 1929): 203–19.

Coppersmith, Clifford P. "Indians in the Army: Professional Advocacy and the Regularization of Indian Military Service, 1889–1897." *Military History of the West* 26 (Fall 1996): 159–85.

Cramer, Harry G. "Tom Jeffords—Indian Agent." *Journal of Arizona History* 17 (Autumn 1976): 265–300.

Cremony, John C. "The Apache Race." *Overland Monthly* 1 (September 1868): 201–9.

Crook, George. "The Apache Problem." *Journal of the Military Service Institution of the United States* 7 (September 1886): 257–69.

Daly, Henry W. "The Geronimo Campaign Concluded." *Journal of the U.S. Cavalry Association* 19 (October 1908): 247–62.

———. "Scouts Good and Bad." *American Legion Monthly* 5 (August 1928): 24–25, 66–70.

Davis, Britton. "The Difficulties of Indian Warfare." *Army and Navy Journal* 33 (October 24, 1885): 242–44.

Davisson, Lori. "Fifty Years at Fort Apache." *Journal of Arizona History* 17 (Autumn 1976): 301–20.

———. "New Light on the Cibecue Fight: Untangling Apache Identities." *Journal of Arizona History* 20 (Winter 1979): 423–44.

Dinges, Bruce J. "The Victorio Campaign of 1880: Cooperation and Conflict on the United States–Mexico Border." *New Mexico Historical Review* 62 (January 1987): 81–104.

Elliott, Charles P. "The Geronimo Campaign of 1885–1886." *Journal of the U.S. Cavalry Association* 21 (September 1910): 211–36.

Ellis, Richard N. "The Humanitarian Soldiers." *Journal of Arizona History* 10 (Summer 1969): 53–66.

Feaver, Eric. "Indian Soldiers, 1891–96: An Experiment on the Closing Frontier." *Prologue: Journal of the National Archives* 7 (Summer 1975): 109–18.

Fontana, Bernard L., and J. Cameron Greenleaf. "Johnny Ward's Ranch: A Study in Historic Archaeology." *Kiva* 28 (October–December 1962): 1–115.

Gale, Jack C. "An Ambush for Natchez." *True West* 27 (July–August 1980): 32–37.

———. "Lebo in Pursuit." *Journal of Arizona History* 21 (Spring 1980): 13–24.

Goodwin, Grenville. "Experiences of an Indian Scout: Excerpts from the Life of John Rope, an 'Old Timer' of the White Mountain Apaches." *Arizona Historical Review* 7 (January 1936): 31–68; (April 1936): 31–73.

Greene, Jerome A. "The Crawford Affair: International Implications of the Geronimo Campaign." *Journal of the West* 11 (January 1972): 143–53.

Griffen, William B. "The Chiricahua Apache Population Resident at the Janos Presidio, 1792–1858." *Journal of the Southwest* 33 (Summer 1991): 151–99.

———. "The Compás: A Chiricahua Apache Family of the Late 18th and Early 19th Century." *American Indian Quarterly* 7 (Spring 1983): 21–49.

———. "Apache Indians and the Northern Mexican Peace Establishments." In *Southwestern Culture History: Collected Papers in Honor of Albert Schroeder*, ed. Charles H. Lange, *Papers of the Archaeological Society of New Mexico* 10 (1985): 183–95.

Hanna, Robert. "With Crawford into Mexico." *Overland Monthly* 8 (July 1886): 78–83.

Hastings, James R. "The Tragedy at Camp Grant in 1871." *Arizona and the West* 1 (Summer 1959): 146–60.

Hatfield, Shelly Bowen. "The Death of Emmet Crawford: Who Was to Blame?" *Journal of Arizona History* 29 (Summer 1988): 131–48.

Hedren, Paul L. "Captain Charles King at Sunset Pass." *Journal of Arizona History* 17 (Autumn 1976): 253–64.

Hutton, Paul Andrew. "Camels Go West." *Wild West* 20 (December 2007): 40–47.

———. "The Gift of Cochise." *True West* 58 (December 2011): 50–51.

———. "Legend of the Apache Kid." *Wild West* 27 (December 2014): 30–39.

———. "Phil Sheridan's Pyrrhic Victory: The Piegan Massacre, Army Politics, and the Transfer Debate." *Montana, the Magazine of Western History* 32 (Spring 1982): 32–43.

———. "The Severed Heads Campaign." *True West* 62 (March 2015): 28–33.

———. "Was Geronimo a Terrorist? SEAL Team 6, Bin Laden and the Irony of History." *True West* 58 (August 2011): 22–31.

Judd, Ira. "The Apache Kid." *Arizona Highways* 29 (September 1955): 32–35.

Kane, Adam. "Army Politics and Indian Wars: Charles B. Gatewood and the Geronimo Campaign of 1886." *Military History of the West* 26 (Fall 1996): 109–28.

Kitt, Mrs. G. F., ed. "Reminiscences of Santiago Ward." *Arizona Historical Review* 6 (October 1935): 85–86.

Kraft, Louis. "Geronimo's Gunfighter Attitude." *Wild West* 28 (October 2015): 28–37.

Langellier, John. "Honorable Warriors: Indian Scouts in Arizona and New Mexico Territories." *True West* 59 (July 2012): 24–33.

———. "There Will Be War: Cochise and the Bascom Affair." *True West* 58 (January 2011): 52–57.

Lyon, Juana Fraser. "Archie McIntosh, the Scottish Indian Scout." *Journal of Arizona History* 7 (Autumn 1966): 103–22.

Marion, Jeanie. "'As Long as the Stone Lasts': General O. O. Howard's 1872 Peace Conference." *Journal of Arizona History* 35 (Summer 1994): 109–40.

Markstrom, Carol A., and Doug Hocking. "Certain Death in Doubtful Canyon." *Wild West* 28 (October 2015): 38–45.

———. "Massacre at Dawn in Arizona Territory." *Wild West* 26 (October 2013): 34–39.

McCarthy, Kiernan, and C. L. Sonnichsen. "Trina Verdin and the Truth of History." *Journal of Arizona History* 14 (Summer 1973): 149–64.

McChristian, Douglas C., and Larry L. Ludwig. "Eyewitness to the Bascom Affair: An Account by Sergeant Daniel Robinson, Seventh Infantry." *Journal of Arizona History* 42 (Autumn 2001): 277–300.

Mehren, Lawrence L., ed. "Scouting for Mescaleros: The Price Campaign of 1873." *Arizona and the West* 10 (Summer 1968): 171–90.

Miles, Nelson A. "On the Trail of Geronimo." *Cosmopolitan* 51 (June 1911): 249–62.

Murphy, Lawrence R. "Cantonment Burgwin, New Mexico, 1852–1860." *Arizona and the West* 15 (Spring 1973): 5–26.

Myers, Lee. "The Enigma of Mangas Coloradas' Death." *New Mexico Historical Review* 41 (January 1966): 287–304.

Nickens, Paul R., and Kathleen N. Nickens. "Victor of Old San Carlos." *Journal of Arizona History* 56 (Autumn 2015): 277–322.

Nickerson, Azor H. "An Apache Raid." *Harper's Weekly* 41 (July 10, 1897): 693–94.

Opler, Morris E. "A Chiricahua's Account of the Geronimo Campaign of 1886 [Samuel E. Kenoi]." *New Mexico Historical Review* 13 (October 1938): 337–86.

———. "The Identity of the Apache Mansos." *American Anthropologist* 44 (October–December 1942): 725.

———. "Some Implications of Culture Theory for Anthropology and Psychology." *American Journal of Orthopsychiatry* 18 (October 1948): 617.

———. "An Interpretation of Ambivalence of Two American Indian Tribes." *Journal of Social Psychology* 7 (1936): 32–116.

Opler, Morris E., and Harry Hoijer. "The Raid and War-Path Language of the Chiricahua Apache." *American Anthropologist* 42 (October–December 1942): 617–35.

Park, Joseph F. "The Apaches in Mexican-American Relations." *Arizona and the West* 3 (Summer 1961): 129–46.

Pettit, James S. "Apache Campaign Notes—1886." *Journal of the Military Service Institution of the United States* 7 (September 1886): 331–38.

Radbourne, Allan. "The Battle for Apache Pass: Reports of the California Volunteers." *English Westerners' Brand Book* 34 (2001).

———. "Dutchy: Indian Scout and Apache Raider." *True West* 45 (November and December 1998): 38–45.

———. "Geronimo's Contraband Cattle." *Missionaries, Indians and Soldiers: Studies in Cultural Interaction* (1996): 1–24.

———. "Geronimo's Last Raid into Arizona." *True West* 41 (March 1994): 22–29.

———. "The Juh-Geronimo Surrender of 1879." *English Westerners' Brand Book* 21 (1983): 1–18.

———. "The Naming of Mickey Free." *Journal of Arizona History* 17 (Autumn 1976): 341–46.

Reed, Bill. "Fort McDowell—The Most Unhappy Post." *Journal of Arizona History* 17 (Autumn 1976): 321–40.

Reed, Walter. "Geronimo and His Warriors in Captivity." *Illustrated American* 3 (August 16, 1890): 231–35.

Reeve, Frank D., ed. "Puritan and Apache: A Diary." *New Mexico Historical Review* 23 (October 1948): 269–302; 24 (January 1949): 12–53.

Roberts, Virginia Culin. "Jack Pennington in Early Arizona," *Arizona and the West* 23 (Winter 1981): 317–34.

Robinson, D. "The Affair at Apache Pass." *Sports Afield* 17 (August 1896): 79–84.

Rolak, Bruno. "General Miles's Mirrors: The Heliograph in the Geronimo Campaign of 1886." *Journal of Arizona History* 16 (Summer 1975): 145–60.

Sacks, Benjamin H., ed. "New Evidence on the Bascom Affair." *Arizona and the West* 4 (Autumn 1962): 261–78.

———. "The Origins of Fort Buchanan." *Arizona and the West* 7 (Autumn 1965): 207–26.

Salzman, M. "Geronimo, the Napoleon of the Indians." *Journal of Arizona History* 8 (Winter 1967): 215–47.

Sanchez, Lynda. "Red Hot Chili Weapon: How a Chili Bomb Rescued Captive Apaches in the Sierra Madres," *True West* 60 (March 2013): 30–33.

Schmidt, Louis Bernard. "Manifest Opportunity and the Gadsden Purchase." *Arizona and the West* 3 (Autumn 1961): 245–64.

Schwatka, Frederick. "Among the Apaches." *Century* 34 (May 1887): 41–52.

Selcer, Richard. "A Premonition of Death: General James Byrne." *Wild West* 27 (August 2014): 60–65.

Shipp, William E. "Captain Crawford's Last Expedition." *Journal of the United States Cavalry Association* 5 (December 1892): 343–61.

Smith, Ralph A. "Apache Plunder Trails Southward, 1831–1840." *New Mexico Historical Review* 87 (January 1962): 20–42.

———. "The Scalp Hunt in Chihuahua—1849." *New Mexico Historical Review* 40 (April 1965): 116–40.

Sonnichsen, C. L. "Who Was Tom Jeffords?" *Journal of Arizona History* 23 (Winter 1982): 381–406.

Stevens, Robert C. "The Apache Menace in Sonora, 1831–1849." *Arizona and the West* 6 (Autumn 1964): 211–22.

Stockel, H. Henrietta. "Geronimo: Facts, Anecdotes, and Hearsay." *Journal of the West* 47 (Spring 2008): 3–11.

Stout, Joe A., Jr. "Soldiering and Suffering in the Geronimo Campaign: Reminiscences of Lawrence R. Jerome." *Journal of the West* 11 (January 1972): 206–24.

Sweeney, Edwin R. "Chihuahua of the Chiricahuas." *Wild West* 13 (August 2000): 25–28, 67.

———. "Cochise and the Prelude to the Bascom Affair." *New Mexico Historical Review* 64 (October 1989): 427–46.

———. "Geronimo and Chatto: Alternative Apache Ways." *Wild West* 20 (August 2007): 30–39.

———. "Geronimo: Apache Shaman." *Wild West* 25 (February 2013): 28–34.

———. "I Had Lost All: Geronimo and the Carrasco Massacre of 1851." *Journal of Arizona History* 27 (Spring 1986): 35–52.

Tate, Michael L. "Soldiers of the Line: Apache Companies in the U.S. Army, 1891–1897." *Arizona and the West* 16 (Winter 1974): 343–64.

Thompson, Jerry D. "Brave Christian Soldiers: The New Mexico Territorial Militia in the Civil War." *New Mexico Historical Review* 89 (Summer 2014): 263–320.

———. "The Vulture over the Carrion: Captain James 'Paddy' Graydon and the Civil War in the Territory of New Mexico." *Journal of Arizona History* 24 (Winter 1983): 381–404.

———. "With the Third Infantry in New Mexico, 1851–1853: The Lost Diary of Private Sylvester W. Matson," *Journal of Arizona History* 31 (Winter 1990): 349–404.

Utley, Robert M. "The Bascom Affair: A Reconstruction," *Arizona and the West* 3 (Spring 1961): 59–68.

———. "Honor in Defeat," *True West* 60 (February 2013): 32–37.

———. "Victorio's War." *MHQ: The Quarterly Journal of Military History* 21 (Autumn 2008): 20–29.

Valputic, Marian E., and Harold H. Longfellow, eds. "The Fight at Chiricahua Pass in 1869: As Described by L. L. Dorr, M.D." *Arizona and the West* 13 (Winter 1971): 369–78.

Walker, Henry P., ed. "Colonel Bonneville's Report: The Department of New Mexico in 1859." *Arizona and the West* 22 (Autumn 1980): 343–62.

———. "Soldier in the California Column: The Diary of John W. Teal." *Arizona and the West* 13 (Spring 1971): 33–82.

Watt, Robert N. " 'Horses Worn to Mere Shadows': The Ninth Cavalry's Campaign against the Apaches in New Mexico Territory, 1879–1881." *New Mexico Historical Review* 86 (Spring 2011): 197–22.

———. "A Reevaluation of Colonel Benjamin H. Grierson's Trans-Pecos Campaign Against Victorio, July–August 1880." *Southwestern Historical Quarterly* 118 (January 2015): 241–61.

Wharfield, H. B. "Apache Kid and the Record." *Journal of Arizona History* 6 (Spring 1965): 37–46.

Williamson, Dan R. "The Apache Kid: Red Renegade of the West." *Arizona Highways* 15 (May 1939): 14–15, 30–31.

Wrattan, Albert E. "George Wrattan, Friend of the Apaches." *Journal of Arizona History* 27 (Spring 1986): 91–124.

Wright, Erik. "Mickey Free: Apache Captive and Free Man." *Wild West* 26 (August 2013): 60–64.

Wright, Harry R. "In the Days of Geronimo." *Pearson's Magazine* 26 (February 1905): 196–200.

MEMOIRS

Arny, W. F. M. *Indian Agent in New Mexico: The Journal of Special Agent W. F. M. Arny, 1870*. Ed. Lawrence R. Murphy. Santa Fe, NM: Stagecoach Press, 1967.

Averell, William Woods. *Ten Years in the Saddle: The Memoir of William Woods Averell*. Eds. Edward K. Eckert and Nicholas J. Amato. San Rafael, CA: Presidio Press, 1978.

Ball, Eve. *In the Days of Victorio: Recollections of a Warm Springs Apache*. Tucson: University of Arizona Press, 1970.

Barnes, Will C. *Apaches and Longhorns: Reminiscences of Will C. Barnes*. Ed. Frank C. Lockwood. Los Angeles: Ward Ritchie Press, 1941.

Barrett, S. M., ed. *Geronimo's Story of His Life*. New York: Duffield, 1906.

Bell, William A. *New Tracks in North America*. London: Chapman & Hall, 1870.

Bennett, James A. *Forts and Forays: A Dragoon in New Mexico, 1850–1856*. Eds. Clinton E. Brooks and Frank D. Reeve. Albuquerque: University of New Mexico Press, 1948.

Betzinez, Jason, with Wilbur Sturtevant Nye. *I Fought with Geronimo*. Harrisburg, PA: Stackpole, 1959.

Bigelow, John, Jr. *On the Bloody Trail of Geronimo*. Ed. Arthur Woodward. Los Angeles: Westernlore Press, 1958.

Blake, J. Y. F. *A West Pointer with the Boers*. Boston: Angel Guardian Press, 1903.

Bourke, John G. *An Apache Campaign in the Sierra Madre: An Account of the Expedition in Pursuit of Hostile Chiricahua Apaches in the Spring of 1883*. New York: Charles Scribner's Sons, 1958.

———. *The Diaries of John Gregory Bourke*. Vol. 1, *November 20, 1872–July 28, 1876*. Ed. Charles M. Robinson III. Denton: University of North Texas Press, 2003.

———. *The Diaries of John Gregory Bourke*. Vol. 5, *May 23, 1881–August 26, 1881*. Ed. Charles M. Robinson III. Denton: University of North Texas Press, 2013.

———. *On the Border with Crook*. New York: Charles Scribner's Sons, 1891.

Browne, J. Ross. *A Tour Through Arizona 1864 or Adventures in the Apache Country*. Tucson: Arizona Silhouettes, 1951.

———. *J. Ross Browne: His Letters, Journals and Writings*. Ed. Lina Fergusson Browne. Albuquerque: University of New Mexico Press, 1969.

Burns, Mike. *All of My People Were Killed: The Memoir of Mike Burns (Hoomothya), a Captive Indian*. Prescott, AZ: Sharlot Hall Museum, 2010.

———. *The Only One Living to Tell: The Autobiography of a Yavapai Indian*. Ed. Gregory McNamee. Tucson: University of Arizona Press, 2012.

Calhoun, James S. *The Official Correspondence of James S. Calhoun*. Ed. Annie Heloise Abel. Washington, DC: US Government Printing Office, 1915.

Carroll, John M., ed. *The Papers of the Order of the Indian Wars*. Fort Collins, CO: Old Army Press, 1975.

Carter, Harvey Lewis, ed. *"Dear Old Kit": The Historical Christopher Carson*. Norman: University of Oklahoma Press, 1968.

Chacon, Rafael. *Legacy of Honor: The Life of Rafael Chacon, a Nineteenth-Century New Mexican*. Ed. Jacqueline Dorgan Meketa. Albuquerque: University of New Mexico Press, 1986.

Clum, John. *Apache Days and Tombstone Nights: John Clum's Autobiography, 1877–1887*. Ed. Neil B. Carmony. Silver City, NM: High-Lonesome Books, 1997.

Colyer, Vincent. *Peace with the Apaches of New Mexico and Arizona: Report of Vincent Colyer, Member of Board of Indian Commissioners. 1871.* Washington, DC: US Government Printing Office, 1872.

———. *Report of Western Trip, Board of Indian Commissioners: First Annual Report, 1869.* Washington, DC, 1870, 54–55.

Conner, Daniel Ellis. *Joseph Reddeford Walker and the Arizona Adventure.* Eds. Donald J. Berthrong and Odessa Davenport. Norman: University of Oklahoma Press, 1956.

Corbusier, Fanny Dunbar. *Fanny Dunbar Corbusier: Recollections of Her Army Life, 1869–1908.* Ed. Patricia Y. Stallard. Norman: University of Oklahoma Press, 2003.

Corbusier, William Henry. *Soldier, Surgeon, Scholar: The Memoirs of William Henry Corbusier, 1844–1930.* Ed. Robert Wooster. Norman: University of Oklahoma Press, 2003.

Cozzens, Peter, ed. *Eyewitness to the Indian Wars, 1865–1890: The Army and the Indian.* Mechanicsburg, PA: Stackpole Books, 2005.

———, ed. *Eyewitness to the Indian Wars, 1865–1890: The Struggle for Apacheria.* Mechanicsburg, PA: Stackpole Books, 2001.

Cozzens, Samuel Woodworth. *The Marvelous Country, or Three Years in Arizona and New Mexico.* New York: Lee & Shepard, 1876.

Cremony, John C. *Life Among the Apaches.* San Francisco: A. Roman, 1868.

Crook, George. *Crook's Resume of Operations Against Apache Indians, 1882–1886.* Ed. Barry C. Johnson. London: Johnson-Taunton Military Press, 1971.

———. *General George Crook: His Autobiography.* Ed. Martin F. Schmitt. Norman: University of Oklahoma Press, 1946.

Cruse, Thomas. *Apache Days and After.* Caldwell, ID: Caxton, 1941.

Davis, Britton. *The Truth About Geronimo.* Ed. M. M. Quaife. New Haven, CT: Yale University Press, 1929.

Farmer, James E. *My Life with the Army in the West.* Ed. Dale F. Giese. Santa Fe, NM: Stagecoach Press, 1967.

Forsyth, George A. *Thrilling Days in Army Life.* New York: Harper & Brothers, 1902.

Frazer, Robert W. *Mansfield on the Condition of the Western Forts, 1853–54.* Norman: University of Oklahoma Press, 1963.

Gatewood, Charles. *Lt. Charles Gatewood and His Apache Wars Memoir.* Ed. Louis Kraft. Lincoln: University of Nebraska Press, 2005.

Gustafson, A. M., ed. *John Spring's Arizona.* Tucson: University of Arizona Press, 1966.

Hall, J. *Sonora: Travels and Adventures in Sonora.* Chicago: J. M. W. Jones, 1881.

Hamlin, Percy Gatling, ed. *The Making of a Soldier: Letters of General R. S. Ewell.* Richmond, VA: Whittet & Shepperson, 1935.

Hand, George. *The Civil War in Apacheland: Sergeant George Hand's Diary:*

California, Arizona, West Texas, New Mexico, 1861–64. Ed. Neil B. Carmony. Silver City, NM: High-Lonesome Books, 1996.

Hein, O. L. *Memories of Long Ago by an Old Army Officer*. New York: G. P. Putnam's Sons, 1925.

Hobbs, James. *Wild Life in the Far West; Personal Adventures of a Border Mountain Man*. Hartford, CT: Wiley, Waterman & Eaton, 1872.

Hooker, Forrestine C. *Child of the Fighting Tenth: On the Frontier with the Buffalo Soldiers*. Ed. Steve Wilson. New York: Oxford University Press, 2003.

Horn, Tom. *The Life of Tom Horn: Government Scout and Interpreter*. New York: Jingle Bob/Crown Publishers, 1977.

Howard, O. O. *Famous Indian Chiefs I Have Known*. New York: Century, 1912.

———. *My Life and Experiences Among Our Hostile Indians*. Hartford, CT: A. T. Worthington, 1907.

Humfreville, J. Lee. *Twenty Years Among Our Hostile Indians*. New York: Hunter, 1903.

Leupp, Francis E. *Notes of a Summer Tour Among the Indians of the Southwest*. Philadelphia: Indian Rights Association, 1897.

Lockwood, Frank C. *Life in Old Tucson, 1854–1864: As Remembered by the Little Maid Atanacia Santa Cruz*. Los Angeles: Ward Ritchie Press, 1943.

Lummis, Charles F. *General Crook and the Apache Wars*. Ed. Turbese Lummis Fiske. Flagstaff, AZ: Northland Press, 1966.

Mazzanovich, Anton. *Trailing Geronimo*. Hollywood, CA: A. Mazzanovich, 1931.

Meriwether, David. *My Life in the Mountains and on the Plains*. Ed. Robert A. Griffen. Norman: University of Oklahoma Press, 1965.

Miles, Nelson A. *Personal Recollections and Observations of General Nelson A. Miles*. Chicago: Werner, 1896.

———. *Serving the Republic: Memoirs of the Civil and Military Life of Nelson A. Miles*. New York: Harper & Brothers, 1911.

Parker, James. *The Old Army: Memories, 1872–1918*. Philadelphia: Dorrance, 1929.

Pfanz, Donald C., ed. *The Letters of Richard S. Ewell*. Knoxville: University of Tennessee Press, 2012.

Poston, Charles D. *Building a State in Apache Land*. Tempe, AZ: Aztec Press, 1963.

Price, George F. *Across the Continent with the Fifth Cavalry*. New York: Antiquarian Press, 1959.

Pumpelly, Raphael. *Across America and Asia: Notes of a Five Years' Journey Around the World and of Residence in Arizona, Japan and China*. New York: Leypold & Holt, 1870.

Scott, Hugh L. *Some Memories of a Soldier*. New York: Century, 1928.

Sladen, Joseph A. *Making Peace with Cochise: The 1872 Journal of Captain*

Joseph Alton Sladen. Ed. Edwin R. Sweeney. Norman: University of Oklahoma Press, 1997.

Sparks, William. *The Apache Kid, a Bear Fight, and Other True Stories of the Old West*. Los Angeles: Skelton, 1926.

Splete, Allen P., and Marilyn D. Splete, eds. *Frederic Remington: Selected Letters*. New York: Abbeville Press, 1988.

Summerhayes, Martha. *Vanished Arizona: Recollections of the Army Life of a New England Woman*. Salem, MA: Salem Press, 1911.

Sweeney, Edwin R., ed. *Cochise: Firsthand Accounts of the Chiricahua Apache Chief*. Norman: University of Oklahoma Press, 2014.

Tevis, James H. *Arizona in the '50's*. Albuquerque: University of New Mexico Press, 1954.

Thompson, Jerry D., ed. *New Mexico Territory During the Civil War: Wallen and Evans Inspection Reports, 1862–1863*. Albuquerque: University of New Mexico Press, 2008.

Utley, Robert M., ed. *An Army Doctor on the Western Frontier: Journals and Letters of John Vance Lauderdale, 1864–1890*. Albuquerque: University of New Mexico Press, 2014.

Veil, Charles Henry. *The Memoirs of Charles Henry Veil: A Soldier's Recollections of the Civil War and the Arizona Territory*. Ed. Herman J. Viola. New York: Orion Books, 1993.

Walters, Lorenzo. *Tombstone's Yesterday*. Tucson, AZ: Acme, 1928.

Welsh, Herbert. *The Apache Prisoners in Fort Marion, St. Augustine, Florida*. Philadelphia: Indian Rights Association, 1887.

Wharfield, H. B. *With Scouts and Cavalry at Fort Apache*. Tucson: Arizona Pioneers' Historical Society, 1965.

Wood, Leonard. *Chasing Geronimo: The Journal of Leonard Wood, May–September 1886*. Ed. Jack C. Lane. Albuquerque: University of New Mexico Press, 1970.

BOOKS

Adams, Alexander B. *Geronimo: A Biography*. New York: Putnam, 1971.

Adjutant General's Office. *Chronological List of Actions, etc., with Indians from January 15, 1837, to January, 1891*. Fort Collins, CO: Old Army Press, 1979.

Aleshire, Peter. *Cochise: The Life and Times of the Great Apache Chief*. New York: John Wiley, 2001.

———. *The Fox and the Whirlwind: General George Crook and Geronimo*. New York: John Wiley, 2000.

———. *Warrior Woman: The Story of Lozen, Apache Warrior and Shaman*. New York: St. Martin's Press, 2001.

Alexander, David V. *Arizona Frontier Military Place Names, 1846–1912*. Las Cruces, NM: Yucca Tree Press, 1998.

Altshuler, Constance Wynn. *Cavalry Yellow and Infantry Blue: Army Officers in Arizona Between 1851 and 1886.* Tucson: Arizona Historical Society, 1991.

———. *Chains of Command: Arizona and the Army, 1856–1875.* Tucson: Arizona Historical Society, 1981.

———, ed. *Latest from Arizona! The Hesperian Letters, 1859–1861.* Tucson: Arizona Pioneers' Historical Society, 1969.

———. *Starting with Defiance: Nineteenth Century Arizona Military Posts.* Tucson: Arizona Historical Society, 1983.

Bailey, Lynn R. *Bosque Redondo: The Navajo Internment at Fort Sumner, New Mexico, 1863–1868.* Tucson, AZ: Westernlore Press, 1998.

———. *Indian Slave Trade in the Southwest.* Los Angeles: Westernlore Press, 1966.

———. *White Apache: The Life and Times of Zebina Nathaniel Streeter.* Tucson, AZ: Westernlore Press, 2010.

Ball, Durwood. *Army Regulars on the Western Frontier, 1848–1861.* Norman: University of Oklahoma Press, 2001.

Ball, Eve, with Nora Henn and Lynda Sanchez. *Indeh: An Apache Odyssey.* Provo, UT: Brigham Young University Press, 1980.

Ball, Larry D. *Tom Horn in Life and Legend.* Norman: University of Oklahoma Press, 2014.

Banks, Leo W. *Double Cross: Treachery in the Apache Wars.* Phoenix: Arizona Highways Books, 2001.

Barnes, Will C. *Arizona Place Names.* Revised and enlarged by Byrd H. Granger. Tucson: University of Arizona Press, 1979.

Barr, Juliana. *Peace Came in the Form of a Woman: Indians and Spaniards in the Texas Borderlands.* Chapel Hill: University of North Carolina Press, 2007.

Barrick, Nona, and Mary Taylor. *The Mesilla Guard, 1851–61.* El Paso: Texas Western Press, 1976.

Basso, Keith H. *The Cibecue Apache.* New York: Holt, Rinehart & Winston, 1970.

———, ed. *Western Apache Raiding and Warfare, from the Notes of Grenville Goodwin.* Tucson: University of Arizona Press, 1971.

———. *Western Apache Witchcraft.* Tucson: University of Arizona Press, 1969.

Basso, Keith H., and Morris E. Opler, eds. *Apachean Culture History and Ethnology.* Tucson: University of Arizona Press, 1971.

Bates, Albert R. *Jack Swilling: Arizona's Most Lied About Pioneer.* Tucson, AZ: Wheatmark, 2008.

Baylor, George Wythe. *John Robert Baylor: Confederate Governor of Arizona.* Ed. Odie B. Faulk. Tucson: Arizona Pioneers' Historical Society, 1966.

Bender, Averam B. *A Study of Jicarilla Apache Indians, 1846–1887.* New York: Garland, 1974.

Billington, Monroe Lee. *New Mexico's Buffalo Soldiers, 1866–1900.* Niwot: University Press of Colorado, 1991.

Blyth, Lance R. *Chiricahua and Janos: Communities of Violence in the Southwestern Borderlands, 1680–1880.* Lincoln: University of Nebraska Press, 2012.

Boyer, Ruth McDonald, and Narcissus Duffy Gayton. *Apache Mothers and Daughters: Four Generations of a Family.* Norman: University of Oklahoma Press, 1992.

Braatz, Timothy. *Surviving Conquest: A History of the Yavapai Peoples.* Lincoln: University of Nebraska Press, 2003.

Brackett, Albert G. *History of the United States Cavalry.* New York: Harper & Brothers, 1865.

Brandes, Ray. *Frontier Military Posts of Arizona.* Globe, AZ: Dale Stuart King, 1960.

Brooks, James F. *Captives and Cousins: Slavery, Kinship, and Community in the Southwest Borderlands.* Chapel Hill: University of North Carolina Press, 2002.

Brown, Dee. *Bury My Heart at Wounded Knee: An Indian History of the American West.* New York: Holt, Rinehart & Winston, 1970.

Brownell, Elizabeth R. *They Lived in Tubac.* Tucson, AZ: Westernlore Press, 1986.

Buchanan, Kimberly Moore. *Apache Women Warriors.* El Paso: Texas Western Press, 1986.

Burns, Walter Noble. *Tombstone: An Iliad of the Southwest.* New York: Grosset & Dunlap, 1929.

Buskirk, Winfred. *The Western Apache: Living with the Land Before 1950.* Norman: University of Oklahoma Press, 1986.

Cameron, Catherine M., ed. *Invisible Citizens: Captives and Their Consequences.* Salt Lake City: University of Utah Press, 2008.

Carpenter, John A. *Sword and Olive Branch: Oliver Otis Howard.* Pittsburgh: University of Pittsburgh Press, 1964.

Carroll, Charles and Lynne Sebastian, eds. *Fort Craig: The United States Fort on the Camino Real.* Socorro, NM: Bureau of Land Management, 2000.

Carter, William H. *From Yorktown to Santiago with the Sixth U.S. Cavalry.* Austin, TX: State House Press, 1989.

———. *The Life of Lieutenant General Chaffee.* Chicago: University of Chicago Press, 1917.

Chamberlain, Kathleen P. *Victorio: Apache Warrior and Chief.* Norman: University of Oklahoma Press, 2007.

Clements, William M. *Imagining Geronimo: An Apache Icon in Popular Culture.* Albuquerque: University of New Mexico Press, 2013.

Clum, Woodworth. *Apache Agent: The Story of John P. Clum.* Boston: Houghton Mifflin, 1936.

Coffman, Edward. *The Old Army: A Portrait of the American Army in Peacetime, 1784–1898.* New York: Oxford University Press, 1986.

Cole, D. C. *The Chiricahua Apache 1846–1876: From War to Reservation.* Albuquerque: University of New Mexico Press, 1988.

Collins, Charles. *Apache Nightmare: The Battle at Cibecue Creek*. Norman: University of Oklahoma Press, 1999.

————. *The Great Escape: The Apache Outbreak of 1881*. Tucson, AZ: Westernlore Press, 1994.

Davidson, Homer K. *Black Jack Davidson: A Cavalry Commander on the Western Frontier*. Glendale, CA: Arthur H. Clark, 1974.

Dawson, Joseph G. *Doniphan's Epic March: The 1st Missouri Volunteers in the Mexican War*. Lawrence: University Press of Kansas, 1999.

Debo, Angie. *Geronimo: The Man, His Time, His Place*. Norman: University of Oklahoma Press, 1976.

De la Garza, Phyllis. *The Apache Kid*. Tucson, AZ: Westernlore Press, 1995.

DeLay, Brian. *War of a Thousand Deserts: Indian Raids and the U.S.-Mexican War*. New Haven, CT: Yale University Press, 2008.

Deming, Therese O. *Cosel: With Geronimo on His Last Raid, the Story of an Indian Boy*. Philadelphia: F. A. Davis, 1938.

DeMontravel, Peter R. *A Hero to His Fighting Men: Nelson A. Miles, 1839–1925*. Kent, OH: Kent State University Press, 1998.

Dinges, Bruce J., ed. *Arizona 100: A Centennial Gathering of Essential Books on the Grand Canyon State*. Tucson: Arizona Historical Society, 2012.

Dixon, David. *Hero of Beecher Island: The Life and Military Career of George A. Forsyth*. Lincoln: University of Nebraska Press, 1994.

Dobyns, Henry F. *The Apache People*. Phoenix: Indian Tribal Series, 1971.

Duffield, H. M. *Deeds of Valor*. 2 vols. Detroit: Perrien-Keydel, 1906.

Dunlay, Thomas W. *Kit Carson and the Indians*. Lincoln: University of Nebraska Press, 2000.

————. *Wolves for the Blue Soldiers: Indian Scouts and Auxiliaries with the United States Army, 1860–90*. Lincoln: University of Nebraska Press, 1982.

Dunn, J. P. *Massacres of the Mountains: A History of the Indian Wars of the Far West, 1815–1875*. New York: Harper & Brothers, 1886.

Eiselt, B. Sunday. *Becoming White Clay: A History and Archaeology of Jicarilla Apache Enclavement*. Salt Lake City: University of Utah Press, 2012.

Ellis, Edward. *The Life of Kit Carson*. New York: Grossett & Dunlap, 1889.

Ellis, Richard N. *General Pope and U.S. Indian Policy*. Albuquerque: University of New Mexico Press, 1970.

Erwin, Allen A. *The Southwest of John Horton Slaughter*. Glendale, CA: Arthur H. Clark Company, 1965.

Farish, Thomas Edwin. *History of Arizona*. 8 vols. San Francisco: Filmer Brothers, 1915.

Faulk, Odie B. *Crimson Desert: Indian Wars of the American Southwest*. New York: Oxford University Press, 1974.

————. *Destiny Road: The Gila Trail and the Opening of the Southwest*. New York: Oxford University Press, 1973.

————. *The Geronimo Campaign*. New York: Oxford University Press, 1969.

Finch, L. Boyd. *Confederate Pathway to the Pacific: Major Sherod Hunter and Arizona Territory C.S.A.* Tucson: Arizona Historical Society, 1996.

Forrest, Earle R., and Edwin B. Hill. *Lone War Trail of Apache Kid.* Pasadena, CA: Trail's End, 1947.

Forsyth, George A. *The Story of the Soldier.* New York: D. Appleton, 1900.

Frazer, Robert W. *Forts of the West: Military Forts and Presidios and Posts Commonly Called Forts West of the Mississippi River to 1898.* Norman: University of Oklahoma Press, 1977.

Fritz, Henry E. *The Movement for Indian Assimilation, 1860–1890.* Philadelphia: University of Pennsylvania Press, 1963.

Gardner, Mark L. *Geronimo: A Biography.* Tucson, AZ: Western National Parks Association, 2006.

Giese, Toby. *The Saga of John Fillmore Blake: The Last Missouri Rogue.* Independence, MO: Herald House, 1994.

Goodwin, Grenville. *The Social Organization of the Western Apache.* Tucson: University of Arizona Press, 1969.

Goodwin, Grenville, and Neil Goodwin. *The Apache Diaries: A Father-Son Journey.* Lincoln: University of Nebraska Press, 2000.

Gregg, Robert D. *The Influence of Border Troubles on Relations Between the United States and Mexico, 1876–1910.* New York: Da Capo Press, 1970.

Gressinger, A. W. *Charles D. Poston: Sunland Seer.* Globe, AZ: Dale Stuart King, 1961.

Griffen, William B. *Apaches at War and Peace: The Janos Presidio, 1750–1858.* Norman: University of Oklahoma Press, 1998.

———. *Utmost Good Faith: Patterns of Apache-Mexican Hostilities in Northern Chihuahua Border Warfare, 1821–1848.* Albuquerque: University of New Mexico Press, 1988.

Griffith, A. Kenny. *Mickey Free—Manhunter.* Caldwell, ID: Caxton Press, 1969.

Groom, Winston. *Kearny's March: The Epic Creation of the American West, 1846–1847.* New York: Knopf, 2011.

Guild, Thelma S., and Harvey L. Carter. *Kit Carson: A Pattern for Heroes.* Lincoln: University of Nebraska Press, 1984.

Gunnerson, Dolores A. *The Jicarilla Apaches: A Study in Survival.* DeKalb: Northern Illinois University Press, 1974.

Gwynne, S. C. *Empire of the Summer Moon.* New York: Scribner, 2010.

Hagedorn, Herman. *Leonard Wood: A Biography.* 2 vols. New York: Harcourt, Brace, 1920.

Haley, James L. *Apaches: A History and Culture Portrait.* Norman: University of Oklahoma Press, 1981.

Hamalainen, Pekka. *The Comanche Empire.* New Haven, CT: Yale University Press, 2008.

Harrison, Mike, John Williams, and Sigrid Khera. *Oral History of the Yavapai.* Ed. Carolina C. Butler. Gilbert, AZ: Acacia, 2012.

Hayes, Jess G. *Apache Vengeance: True Story of the Apache Kid.* Albuquerque: University of New Mexico Press, 1954.

Heard, J. Norman. *White into Red: A Study of the Assimilation of White Persons Captured by Indians.* Metuchen, NJ: Scarecrow Press, 1973.

Heitman, Francis B. *Historical Register and Dictionary of the United States Army, 1789–1903.* 2 vols. Washington, DC: US Government Printing Office, 1903.

Hunt, Aurora. *Major General James Henry Carleton, 1814–1873: Western Frontier Dragoon.* Glendale, CA: Arthur H. Clark, 1958.

Hutton, Paul Andrew. *Phil Sheridan and His Army.* Lincoln: University of Nebraska Press, 1985.

———, ed. *Western Heritage: A Selection of Wrangler Award-Winning Articles.* Norman: University of Oklahoma Press, 2011.

Hutton, Paul Andrew, and Durwood Ball, eds. *Soldiers West: Biographies from the Military Frontier.* Norman: University of Oklahoma Press, 2009.

Ingstad, Helge. *The Apache Indians: In Search of the Missing Tribe.* Lincoln: University of Nebraska Press, 2004.

Jacoby, Karl. *Shadows at Dawn: A Borderlands Massacre and the Violence of History.* New York: Penguin Press, 2008.

John, Elizabeth A. H., ed. *Views from the Apache Frontier: Report on the Northern Provinces of New Spain by Jose Cortes.* Norman: University of Oklahoma Press, 1989.

Johnson, Eric S., comp. *No Greater Calling: A Chronological Record of Sacrifice and Heroism During the Western Indian Wars, 1865–1898.* Arglen, PA: Schiffer, 2012.

Johnson, Virginia Weisel. *The Unregimented General: A Biography of Nelson A. Miles.* Cambridge, MA: Houghton Mifflin Company, 1962.

Josephy, Alvin M., Jr. *The Civil War in the American West.* New York: Knopf, 1991.

Kappler, Charles J., comp. *Indian Affairs: Laws and Treaties.* 7 vols. Washington, DC: US Government Printing Office, 1902–3.

Keleher, William A. *Turmoil in New Mexico, 1846–1868.* Santa Fe, NM: Rydal Press, 1952.

Kelly, Lawrence C. *Navajo Roundup: Selected Correspondence of Kit Carson's Expedition Against the Navajo, 1863–1865.* Boulder, CO: Pruett, 1970.

Kenner, Charles L. *A History of New Mexican–Plains Indian Relations.* Norman: University of Oklahoma Press, 1969.

Kessell, John L. *Spain in the Southwest: A Narrative History of Colonial New Mexico, Arizona, Texas, and California.* Norman: University of Oklahoma Press, 2002.

King, James T. *War Eagle: A Life of General Eugene A. Carr.* Lincoln: University of Nebraska Press, 1963.

Kiser, William S. *Dragoons in Apacheland: Conquest and Resistance in Southern New Mexico, 1846–1861.* Norman: University of Oklahoma Press, 2012.

Knight, Oliver. *Life and Manners in the Frontier Army.* Norman: University of Oklahoma Press, 1978.

Kraft, Louis. *Gatewood and Geronimo*. Albuquerque: University of New Mexico Press, 2000.

Kuhn, Berndt. *Chronicles of War: Apache and Yavapai Resistance in the Southwestern United States and Northern Mexico, 1821–1937*. Tucson: Arizona Historical Society, 2014.

Kvasnicka, Robert M., and Herman J. Viola, eds. *The Commissioners of Indian Affairs, 1824–1977*. Lincoln: University of Nebraska Press, 1979.

Lahti, Janne. *Cultural Construction of Empire: The U.S. Army in Arizona and New Mexico*. Lincoln: University of Nebraska Press, 2012.

Lamar, Howard. *The Far Southwest, 1846–1912: A Territorial History*. New Haven, CT: Yale University Press, 1966.

Lane, Jack C. *Armed Progressive: General Leonard Wood*. San Rafael, CA: Presidio Press, 1978.

Langellier, John P. *Southern Arizona Military Outposts*. Charleston, SC: Arcadia, 2011.

Lawrence, Deborah, and Jon Lawrence. *Violent Encounters: Interviews on Western Massacres*. Norman: University of Oklahoma Press, 2011.

Leckie, William H., and Shirley A. Leckie. *The Buffalo Soldiers: A Narrative of the Black Cavalry in the West*. Norman: University of Oklahoma Press, 2003.

———. *Unlikely Warriors: General Benjamin Grierson and His Family*. Norman: University of Oklahoma Press, 1984.

Leckson, Stephen H. *Nana's Raid: Apache Warfare in New Mexico, 1881*. El Paso: Texas Western Press, 1987.

Ledoux, Gary. *Nantan: The Life and Times of John P. Clum*. Vol. 1, *Claverack to Tombstone, 1851–1882*. Bloomington, IN: Trafford, 2007.

———. *Nantan: The Life and Times of John P. Clum*. Vol. 2, *Tombstone to Los Angeles, 1882–1932*. Bloomington, IN: Trafford, 2008.

Leonard, Elizabeth D. *Men of Color to Arms! Black Soldiers, Indian Wars, and the Quest for Equality*. New York: Norton, 2010.

Lister, Florence C., and Robert H. Lister. *Chihuahua: Storehouse of Storms*. Albuquerque: University of New Mexico Press, 1966.

Lockwood, Frank C. *The Apache Indians*. New York: Macmillan, 1938.

———. *Arizona Characters*. Los Angeles: Times-Mirror Press, 1928.

———. *More Arizona Characters: University of Arizona Bulletin 6*. Tucson: University of Arizona Press, 1942.

———. *Pioneer Days in Arizona: From the Spanish Occupation to Statehood*. New York: Macmillan, 1932.

Magid, Paul. *George Crook: From the Redwoods to Appomattox*. Norman: University of Oklahoma Press, 2011.

———. *The Gray Fox: George Crook and the Indian Wars*. Norman: University of Oklahoma Press, 2015.

McCallum, Jack. *Leonard Wood*. New York: New York University Press, 2006.

McCarty, Kieran, ed. *Desert Documentary: The Spanish Years, 1767–1821.* Tucson: Arizona Historical Society, 1976.

———, ed. *A Frontier Documentary: Sonora and Tucson, 1821–1848.* Tucson: University of Arizona Press, 1997.

McChristian, Douglas C. *Fort Bowie, Arizona: Combat Post of the Southwest, 1858–1894.* Norman: University of Oklahoma Press, 2005.

———, ed. *Frontier Army Trooper: The Letters of Private Eddie Matthews, 1869–1874.* Albuquerque: University of New Mexico Press, 2013.

McClintock, James A. *Arizona.* 3 vols. Chicago: S. J. Clarke, 1916.

McGaw, William Cochran. *Savage Scene: The Life and Times of James Kirker.* New York: Hastings House, 1972.

McGinty, Brian. *The Oatman Massacre: A Tale of Desert Captivity and Survival.* Norman: University of Oklahoma Press, 2005.

McKanna, Clare V., Jr. *Court-Martial of Apache Kid: Renegade of Renegades.* Lubbock: Texas Tech University Press, 2009.

———. *White Justice in Arizona: Apache Murder Trials in the Nineteenth Century.* Lubbock: Texas Tech University Press, 2005.

Mifflin, Margot. *The Blue Tattoo: The Life of Olive Oatman.* Lincoln: University of Nebraska Press, 2009.

Miller, Darlis. *The California Column in New Mexico.* Albuquerque: University of New Mexico Press, 1982.

———. *Captain Jack Crawford: Buckskin Poet, Scout, and Showman.* Albuquerque: University of New Mexico Press, 1993.

Monaghan, Jay. *Last of the Bad Men: The Legend of Tom Horn.* Indianapolis: Bobbs-Merrill, 1946.

Moorhead, Max L. *The Apache Frontier: Jacobo Ugarte and Spanish-Indian Relations in Northern New Spain, 1769–1791.* Norman: University of Oklahoma Press, 1968.

———. *The Presidio: Bastion of the Spanish Borderlands.* Norman: University of Oklahoma Press, 1975.

Mort, Terry. *The Wrath of Cochise.* New York: Pegasus Books, 2013.

Moulton, Candy. *The Writer's Guide to Everyday Life in the Wild West.* Cincinnati: Writer's Digest Books, 1999.

Murphy, Lawrence R. *Frontier Crusader: William F. M. Arny.* Tucson: University of Arizona Press, 1972.

Nickens, Paul, and Kathleen Nickens. *Old San Carlos.* Charleston, SC: Arcadia, 2008.

Nunis, Doyce B. *The Life of Tom Horn Revisited.* Los Angeles: Los Angeles Corral of the Westerners, 1992.

Nye, W. S. *Carbine and Lance: The Story of Old Fort Sill.* Norman: University of Oklahoma Press, 1937.

Ogle, Ralph Hedrick. *Federal Control of the Western Apaches, 1848–1886.* Albuquerque: University of New Mexico Press, 1970.

O'Neil, James B. *They Die but Once: The Story of a Tejano.* New York: Knight, 1935.

Opler, Morris E. *An Apache Life-Way: The Economic, Social, and Religious Institutions of the Chiricahua Apache Indians.* Chicago: University of Chicago Press, 1965.

———. *Apache Odyssey: A Journey between Two Worlds.* New York: Holt, Rinehart, & Winston, 1969.

———, ed. *Grenville Goodwin Among the Western Apache: Letters from the Field.* Tucson: University of Arizona Press, 1973.

———. *Myths and Tales of the Chiricahua Apache Indians.* New York: American Folk-Lore Society, 1942.

———. *Myths and Tales of the Jicarilla Apache Indians.* New York: American Folk-Lore Society, 1938.

Perry, Richard J. *Western Apache Heritage: People of the Mountain Corridor.* Austin: University of Texas Press, 1991.

Pfanz, Donald C. *Richard S. Ewell: A Soldier's Life.* Chapel Hill: University of North Carolina Press, 1998.

Pierce, Michael D. *The Most Promising Young Officer: A Life of Ranald Slidell Mackenzie.* Norman: University of Oklahoma Press, 1993.

Porter, Joseph C. *Paper Medicine Man: John Gregory Bourke and His American West.* Norman: University of Oklahoma Press, 1986.

Prucha, Francis Paul. *American Indian Policy in Crisis: Christian Reformers and the Indian, 1865–1900.* Norman: University of Oklahoma Press, 1976.

———. *The Great Father: The United States Government and the American Indians.* 2 vols. Lincoln: University of Nebraska Press, 1984.

Radbourne, Allan. *Mickey Free: Apache Captive, Interpreter, and Indian Scout.* Tucson: Arizona Historical Society, 2005.

Randall, Kenneth A. *Only the Echoes: The Life of Howard Bass Cushing.* Las Cruces, NM: Yucca Tree Press, 1995.

Rathbun, Daniel C. B., and David V. Alexander. *New Mexico Frontier Military Place Names.* Las Cruces, NM: Yucca Tree Press, 2003.

Record, Ian W. *Big Sycamore Stands Alone: The Western Apaches, Aravaipa, and the Struggle for Place.* Norman: University of Oklahoma Press, 2008.

Remington, Frederic. *Crooked Trails.* New York: Harper & Brothers, 1923.

Rister, Carl Coke. *Border Captives: The Traffic in Prisoners by Southern Plains Indians, 1835–1875.* Norman: University of Oklahoma Press, 1940.

———. *The Southwestern Frontier: 1865–1881.* Cleveland: Arthur H. Clark, 1928.

Roberts, David. *A Newer World: Kit Carson, John C. Frémont, and the Claiming of the American West.* New York: Simon & Schuster, 2000.

———. *Once They Moved Like the Wind: Cochise, Geronimo, and the Apache Wars.* New York: Simon & Schuster, 1993.

Roberts, Virginia Culin. *With Their Own Blood: A Saga of Southwestern Pioneers.* Fort Worth: Texas Christian University Press, 1992.

Robinson, Charles M., III. *General Crook and the Western Frontier.* Norman: University of Oklahoma Press, 2001.

Robinson, Sherry. *Apache Voices: Their Stories of Survival as Told to Eve Ball.* Albuquerque: University of New Mexico Press, 2000.

———. *I Fought a Good Fight: A History of the Lipan Apaches.* Denton: University of North Texas Press, 2013.

Russell, Don. *Campaigning with King: Charles King, Chronicler of the Old Army.* Ed. Paul L. Hedren. Lincoln: University of Nebraska Press, 1991.

———. *One Hundred and Three Fights and Scrimmages: The Story of General Reuben F. Bernard.* Washington, DC: US Cavalry Association, 1936.

Santee, Ross. *Apache Land.* New York: Charles Scribner's Sons, 1947.

Santiago, Mark. *The Jar of Severed Hands: Spanish Deportation of Apache Prisoners of War, 1770–1810.* Norman: University of Oklahoma Press, 2011.

Schellie, Don. *Vast Domain of Blood: The Story of the Camp Grant Massacre.* Los Angeles: Westernlore Press, 1968.

Schroeder, Albert H. *Apache Indians.* Vol. 4, *A Study of the Apache Indians.* New York: Garland, 1974.

Schubert, Frank N. *Black Valor: Buffalo Soldiers and the Medal of Honor, 1870–1898.* Lanham, MD: Rowman & Littlefield, 1997.

———. *Voices of the Buffalo Soldier: Records, Reports, and Recollections of Military Life and Service in the West.* Albuquerque: University of New Mexico Press, 2003.

Schuetz, Mardith K. *Archaeology of Tom Jeffords' Chiricahua Indian Agency.* Las Cruces, NM: COAS, 1986.

Shapard, Bud. *Chief Loco: Apache Peacemaker.* Norman: University of Oklahoma Press, 2010.

Sheridan, Thomas E. *Arizona: A History.* Rev. ed. Tucson: University of Arizona Press, 2012.

Sides, Hampton. *Blood and Thunder: An Epic of the American West.* New York: Doubleday, 2006.

Simmons, Marc. *Massacre on the Lordsburg Road: A Tragedy of the Apache Wars.* College Station: Texas A&M University Press, 1997.

Skinner, Woodward R. (Woody). *The Apache Rock Crumbles: The Captivity of Geronimo's People.* Pensacola, FL: Skinner, 1987.

Smith, Cornelius C., Jr. *Emilio Kosterlitzky: Eagle of Sonora.* Glendale, CA: Arthur H. Clark, 1970.

———. *William Sanders Oury.* Tucson: University of Arizona Press, 1967.

Smith, Ralph Adam. *Borderlander: The Life of James Kirker, 1793–1852.* Norman: University of Oklahoma Press, 1999.

Smith, Victoria. *Captive Arizona, 1851–1900.* Lincoln: University of Nebraska Press, 2009.

Sonnichsen, C. L., ed. *Geronimo and the End of the Apache Wars.* Lincoln: University of Nebraska Press, 1990.

———. *The Mescalero Apaches.* Norman: University of Oklahoma Press, 1973.

———. *Tucson: The Life and Times of an American City.* Norman: University of Oklahoma Press, 1982.

Stockel, H. Henrietta. *Chiricahua Apache Women and Children: Safekeepers of the Heritage.* College Station: Texas A&M University Press, 2000.

———. *Shame and Endurance: The Untold Story of the Chiricahua Apache Prisoners of War.* Tucson: University of Arizona Press, 2004.

———. *Women of the Apache Nation: Voices of Truth.* Reno: University of Nevada Press, 1991.

Stout, Joseph A. *Apache Lightning: The Last Great Battles of the Ojo Calientes.* New York: Oxford University Press, 1974.

———. *Schemers and Dreamers: Filibustering in Mexico, 1848–1921.* Fort Worth: Texas Christian University Press, 2002.

Sturtevant, William C., and Alfonso Ortiz, eds. *Handbook of North American Indians: Southwest.* Vol. 10. Washington, DC: Smithsonian Institution, 1983.

Sweeney, Edwin R. *Cochise: Chiricahua Apache Chief.* Norman: University of Oklahoma Press, 1991.

———. *From Cochise to Geronimo: The Chiricahua Apaches, 1874–86.* Norman: University of Oklahoma Press, 2010.

———. *Mangas Coloradas: Chief of the Chiricahua Apaches.* Norman: University of Oklahoma Press, 1998.

———. *Merejildo Grijalva: Apache Captive, Army Scout.* El Paso: Texas Western Press, 1992.

Tate, Michael L. *The Frontier Army in the Settlement of the West.* Norman: University of Oklahoma Press, 1999.

Taylor, John. *Bloody Valverde: A Civil War Battle on the Rio Grande, February 21, 1862.* Albuquerque: University of New Mexico Press, 1995.

Thomas, Alfred Barnaby. *The Jicarilla Apache Indians: A History, 1598–1888.* New York: Garland, 1974.

Thompson, Jerry D. *Desert Tiger: Captain Paddy Graydon and the Civil War in the Far Southwest.* El Paso: Texas Western Press, 1992.

Thrapp, Dan L. *Al Sieber, Chief of Scouts.* Norman: University of Oklahoma Press, 1964.

———. *The Conquest of Apacheria.* Norman: University of Oklahoma Press, 1967.

———, ed. *Dateline Fort Bowie: Charles Fletcher Lummis Reports on an Apache War.* Norman: University of Oklahoma Press, 1979.

———, ed. *Dictionary of Frontier Biography.* 3 vols. Glendale, CA: Arthur H. Clark, 1988.

———. *General Crook and the Sierra Madre Adventure.* Norman: University of Oklahoma Press, 1974.

———. *Juh, an Incredible Indian.* El Paso: Texas Western Press, 1973.

———. *Victorio and the Mimbres Apaches.* Norman: University of Oklahoma Press, 1974.

Tiller, Veronica E. Velarde. *Culture and Customs of the Apache Indians.* Santa Barbara, CA: Greenwood, 2011.

――――. *The Jicarilla Apache Tribe: A History.* Albuquerque: BowArrow, 2000.

Trennert, Robert A. *Alternative to Extinction: Federal Indian Policy and the Beginnings of the Reservation System, 1846–51.* Philadelphia: Temple University Press, 1975.

Trimble, Marshall. *Arizona: A Panoramic History of a Frontier State.* Garden City, NY: Doubleday, 1977.

Truett, Samuel, and Elliott Young, eds. *Continental Crossroads: Remapping U.S.-Mexico Borderlands History.* Durham, NC: Duke University Press, 2004.

Turchenske, John Anthony, Jr. *The Chiricahua Apache Prisoners of War, Fort Sill, 1894–1914.* Niwot: University Press of Colorado, 1997.

Turner, Jim. *Arizona: A Celebration of the Grand Canyon State.* Layton, UT: Gibbs Smith, 2011.

Utley, Robert M. *A Clash of Cultures: Fort Bowie and the Chiricahua Apaches.* Washington, DC: National Park Service, 1977.

――――. *Frontier Regulars: The United States Army and the Indian, 1866–1890.* New York: Macmillan, 1973.

――――. *Frontiersmen in Blue: The United States Army and the Indian, 1846–1865.* New York: Macmillan, 1967.

――――. *Geronimo.* New Haven, CT: Yale University Press, 2012.

――――. *The Indian Frontier of the American West, 1846–1890.* Albuquerque: University of New Mexico Press, 1984.

Walker, Clifford J. *Gone the Way of the Earth: Indian Slave Trade in the Old Southwest.* Barstow, CA: Mojave River Valley Museum Association, 2009.

Watson, Samuel J. *Peacekeepers and Conquerors: The Army Officer Corps on the American Frontier, 1821–1846.* Lawrence: University Press of Kansas, 2013.

Watt, Robert N. *Apache Tactics, 1830–86.* London: Osprey, 2012.

Weber, David J. *The Mexican Frontier, 1821–1846: The American Southwest Under Mexico.* Albuquerque: University of New Mexico Press, 1982.

――――, ed. *New Spain's Far Northern Frontier: Essays on Spain in the American West, 1540–1821.* Albuquerque: University of New Mexico Press, 1979.

――――. *The Taos Trappers: The Fur Trade in the Far Southwest, 1540–1846.* Norman: University of New Mexico Press, 1971.

Welsh, Herbert. *The Apache Prisoners in Fort Marion, St. Augustine, Florida.* Philadelphia: Indian Rights Association, 1887.

Whitlock, Flint. *Distant Bugles, Distant Drums: The Union Response to the Confederate Invasion of New Mexico.* Boulder: University Press of Colorado, 2006.

Williams, Jack S., and Robert L. Hoover. *Arms of the Apacheria: A Comparison of Apachean and Spanish Fighting Techniques in the Later Eighteenth Century.* Greeley: Museum of Anthropology, University of Northern Colorado, 1983.

Winther, Oscar Osburn. *The Transportation Frontier: Trans-Mississippi West, 1865–1890*. New York: Holt, Rinehart & Winston, 1964.

Wooster, Robert. *The American Military Frontiers: The United States Army in the West, 1783–1900*. Albuquerque: University of New Mexico Press, 2009.

———. *The Military and United States Indian Policy 1865–1903*. New Haven, CT: Yale University Press, 1988.

———. *Nelson A. Miles and the Twilight of the Frontier Army*. Lincoln: University of Nebraska Press, 1995.

Worcester, Donald E. *The Apaches: Eagles of the Southwest*. Norman: University of Oklahoma Press, 1979.

INDEX